RUSSELL H. HARDIMAN, EDITOR

at the
HEART of
LITURGY

An Essential Guide for Celebrating the Paschal Mystery

YEARS A, B, C

TWENTY-THIRD PUBLICATIONS
Mystic, CT 06355

North American Edition 1999

At the Heart of Liturgy is a revised and expanded edition of *The Years of the Year: The Paschal Mystery Celebrated in Christian Worship*, published by Pastoral Liturgy Publications, Freemantle, Western Australia. The essays in this book were first published in the Western Australian journal, *Pastoral Liturgy*.

Twenty-Third Publications
185 Willow Street
P.O. Box 180
Mystic, CT 06355
(860) 536-2611
(800) 321-0411

©1999 by Russell H. Hardiman. All rights reserved. No part of this publication may be reproduced in any manner without prior written permission of the publisher. Write to Permissions Editor.

ISBN:0-89622-977-7
Library of Congress Card Catalog Number 99-70803
Printed in the U.S.A.

DEDICATION

For the Most Rev. Sir Launcelot John Goody

Titular Bishop of Abydos, 1951-1954
Bishop of Bunbury, 1954-1968
Archbishop of Perth, 1968-1983

Mentor, patron and benefactor, bishop and family friend

In colour schemes we don't agree,
Tho' all else to us is harmony,
For what to you as blue can be,
To me is streaky white

What made you hint my lack of taste,
When green in blue bathroom I placed,
And finding fault good time to waste,
If you could not improve it

Tho' legal youth may near its end,
And your sweetness, to those around, you lend,
You're still a lass, so don't pretend,
Your elders yet to teach!

Poem, dated 23.3.36, presented by Dr LJ Goody, parish priest of Boulder, to the editor's mother, Miss Agatha Russell, who had criticized the color scheme in his renovated Presbytery.

Acknowledgments

The chapters of this book originally appeared in the Journal *Pastoral Liturgy*, 2/10 Pennlake Drive, Spearwood, Western Australia 6153.

The Season of Advent Jayne N. Ahearn. vol 26 (1) Advent/Christmas 1995; *The Readings of Advent* Russell Hardiman. vol 26 (1) Advent/Christmas 1995; *Plan of the Lectionary Cycle of Readings for Advent* vole 26 (1) Advent/Christmas 1995; *The Advent Wreath* Russell Hardiman vol 19 (1) Advent/Christmas 1988; *The Season of Christmastide* Russell Hardiman vol. 29 (1) Advent Christmas 1998; *The Readings of Christmastide* Russell Hardiman vol 29 (1) Advent/Christmas 1998 *Paschal Mystery in the Christmas Season* vol 26 (1) Advent/Christmas 1995; *Unwrapping the Season of Christmas and Christmas Wrapping* Russell Hardiman vol 19 (1) Advent/Christmas 1988; *Christmas Trimmings* Russell Hardiman vol 19 (1) Advent/Christmas 1988; *The Season of Lent.* Jayne N. Ahearn.vol 23 (2) Lent 1993; *Restoring Unity to the 90 Days: Lent as Preparation for Easter* Jayne N. Ahearn vol 22 (2) Lent 1992; *The Scrutinies: Not for RCIA Only* Jayne N. Ahearn. vol 22 (2) Lent 1992; *Holy Week and the Paschal Triduum* Jayne N. Ahearn. vol 23 (2) Lent 1993; *Rite for Receiving the Holy Oils* Jayne Ahearn vol 23 (2) Lent/Holy Week 1993; *The Season of Easter* Jayne N. Ahearn. vol 23 (3) Easter 1993; *Passover and The Easter Season* Russell Hardiman. vol 19 (2) Lent 1989; ; *Restoring the Unity to the 90 Days: Easter as Reflection of Lent* Jayne N. Ahearn vol 22 (3) Easter 1992; *On Sunday* Jayne N. Ahearn vol 23 (4) Ordinary Time 1993; *Sundays in Ordinary Time* Jayne N. Ahearn. vol 23 (4) Ordinary Time 1993; *Reading the Gospel of Matthew.* Jerome Neyrey SJ.vol 26 (1) Advent/Christmas 1995 and vol 26 (4/5) Ordinary Time 1996; *The Year of Grace with Matthew: Matthew in the Lectionary* Paddy Meagher, SJ, vol 29 4/5) Ordinary Time1999; *The Location is Everything: The Craft of Mark's Gospel* Jerome Neyrey SJ. vol 24 (3; 4; 5) Ordinary Time 1994; *The Gospel of Mark.* Paddy Meagher SJ vol 27 (1; 4/5) Ordinary Time 1997; *Reading the Gospel of Luke* Jerome Neyrey vol 24 (4;5) Ordinary Time 1995; *The Lukan Narrative of Jesus* Paddy Meagher, SJ, vol 28 (4/5) Ordinary Time 1998. *The Paschal Mystery in the Eucharistic Prayer* Russell Hardiman vol 27 (4/5) Ordinary Time 1997; *The Penitential Rite* Jayne N. Ahearn vol 22 (2) Lent 1992; *Rite of Blessing and Sprinkling Holy Water.* Jayne N. Ahearn. vol 22 (3) Easter 1992; *The Structure of the Lectionary* Russell Hardiman vol 27 (1) Advent/Christmas 1996; *Ongoing Formation for Lectors* Jayne N. Ahearn.vol 23 (3) Easter 1993; *The Prayer of the Faithful.* Jayne N. Ahearn.vol 23 (1) Advent 1993; *Singing the Liturgy: What are the priorities ?* Jayne N. Ahearn. vol 22 (4/5) Ordinary Time 1992; *Language and Liturgy: Why be Inclusive ?* Jayne N. Ahearn vol 23 (3) Easter 1993; *The Funeral: Meaning, Value and Function* Gerry Smith. vol 20 (2) Lent 1990; *A Funeral Service at the Crematorium* Russell Hardiman. vol 23 (2) Lent 1993; *Ceremony for the Interment of Ashes* Russell Hardiman. vol 20 (2) Lent/Holy Week 1989; *Popular Devotions of the Christian People* Russell Hardiman vol 27 (1) Advent/Christmas 1996; *The Paschal Mystery in the Christmas Crib* Russell Hardiman vol 27 (1) Advent/Christmas 1996; *Cross or Crucifix: The Tradition Continues.* Russell Hardiman vol 27 (2/3) Lent-Easter 1997; *The Stations of the Cross through the Centuries* Russell Hardiman vol 27 (2/3) Lent/Eastertide 1997.

Contents

FOREWORD   Most Rev. B. J. Hickey
Episcopal Chairman of the
National Liturgical
Commission   ix

CONTRIBUTORS   x

INTRODUCTION   Russell Hardiman
Editor   3

THE PASCHAL MYSTERY IN THE LITURGICAL SEASONS

ADVENT

The Season of Advent	Jayne Newton Ahearn	11
The Readings of Advent	Russell Hardiman	19
The Advent Wreath	Russell Hardiman	25

CHRISTMAS

The Season of Christmas	Russell Hardiman	28
The Readings of Christmas	Russell Hardiman	36
The Paschal Mystery in the Christmas Season	Russell Hardiman	52
Unwrapping the Season of Christmas and Christmas Wrapping	Russell Hardiman	54

LENT

The Season of Lent	Jayne Newton Ahearn	57
Restoring Unity to the 90 Days: Lent as Preparation for Easter	Jayne Newton Ahearn	62
The Scrutinies: Not for RCIA only	Jayne Newton Ahearn	69

TRIDUUM

Holy Week and the Paschal Triduum	Jayne Newton Ahearn	74
Rite for Receiving the Holy Oils	Jayne Newton Ahearn	79

EASTER

The Season of Easter	Jayne Newton Ahearn	80
Passover and The Easter Season	Russell Hardiman	87
Restoring Unity to the 90 Days: Easter as Reflection of Lent	Jayne Newton Ahearn	90

THE PASCHAL MYSTERY IN ORDINARY TIME

SUNDAY

On Sunday	Jayne Newton Ahearn	97
Sundays in Ordinary Time	Jayne Newton Ahearn	100

YEAR A

Reading the Gospel of Matthew: From womb to tomb with the Messiah	Jerome Neyrey, SJ	104
Matthew's Gospel in the Lectionary	Paddy Meagher, SJ	131

YEAR B

The Location is Everything: The Craft of Mark's Gospel	Jerome Neyrey, SJ	183
The Gospel of Mark	Paddy Meagher, SJ	201

YEAR C

Luke: Jesus Teaches "The Way" on His Way to Jerusalem	Jerome Neyrey, SJ	235

The Structure of the Lukan Narrative of Jesus	Paddy Meagher, SJ	255
The Gospel of Luke in Year C	Paddy Meagher, SJ	260

THE PASCHAL MYSTERY IN THE ORDER OF MASS

EUCHARISTIC PRAYER

The Paschal Mystery in the Eucharistic Prayer	Russell Hardiman	303

GATHERING RITES

Rite of Blessing and Sprinkling of Holy Water	Jayne Newton Ahearn	310
The Penitential Rite	Jayne Newton Ahearn	313

LITURGY OF THE WORD

The Word and the Lectionary	Russell Hardiman	316
Ongoing Formation for Lectors	Jayne Newton Ahearn	320

PRAYER OF THE FAITHFUL

The Prayer of the Faithful: What for and How to…	Jayne Newton Ahearn	324

MUSIC

Singing the Liturgy: What are the Priorities?	Jayne Newton Ahearn	328

LANGUAGE

Language and Liturgy: Why be Inclusive?	Jayne Newton Ahearn	331

THE PASCHAL MYSTERY IN BEREAVEMENT

FUNERALS

The Funeral: Meaning, Value and Function	Gerry Smith	337

CREMATIONS

A Funeral Service at the Crematorium	Russell Hardiman	342
Ceremony of Internment of Ashes	Russell Hardiman	345

THE PASCHAL MYSTERY AND POPULAR DEVOTIONS

Popular Devotions of the Christian People	Russell Hardiman	349
The Paschal Mystery in the Christmas Crib	Russell Hardiman	352
Cross or Crucifix: The Tradition Continues	Russell Hardiman	356
The Stations of the Cross Through the Centuries	Russell Hardiman	362
The Rosary Through the Ages	Russell Hardiman	369

St Mary's Cathedral,
Victoria Square, Perth,
Western Australia 6000
Tel (09) 325 9177
Fax (09) 221 1716

Foreword

It is in the Sacred Liturgy of the Church that the people of God grow into a deeper union with Christ as they celebrate in word and sacrament the great paschal mystery of the death and resurrection of Jesus, our Saviour.

The publication of this book of essays taken from the many issues of *"Pastoral Liturgy"* since 1970 marks an important phase in the implementation of the liturgical renewal called for by the Second Vatican Council.

My predecessor Archbishop Lancelot Goody established the W.A. Liturgy Commission to promote good liturgy throughout the W.A. Province. *"Pastoral Liturgy"* was its publishing arm.

We celebrate in this collection of essays the richness of the Church's liturgical life. This volume brings together scholarly yet very readable articles on almost all aspects of the liturgy. It recalls the role of *"Pastoral Liturgy"* in helping priests and liturgy teams to prepare for each Sunday and major Feastday by supplying them with commentaries, prayers, themes, and suggestions for a better understanding of the Readings and a reverent and heartfelt celebration of the Eucharist.

Its scope extends beyond the Eucharist to other sacraments as well, to ensure that they became true community celebrations of Jesus' saving action among his people.

"Pastoral Liturgy" has been used as a teaching resource, a model for liturgical practice and seasonal planning. It has also been drawn on for personal spiritual reading and has been a comfort to the elderly and others unable to attend Mass.

In its scope it will be a fruitful resource for liturgy groups who will be glad to find in a single volume a wealth of eminently practical and profound liturgical riches.

I am pleased to note that this volume contains a long and scholarly article on the Eucharistic Prayer. Many liturgical writers give little attention to the Eucharistic Prayer, which is a pity, because it is the prayer that draws everything to a focal point. It is in the Eucharistic Prayer that the people of God are able to become one with Christ in the great Sacrifice of Praise.

The lack of attention given to the Eucharisitic Prayer is, I believe, central to the complaints of more traditional people that much of our traditional theological understanding of the Mass has been neglected.

This volume helps recover the Church's full understanding of the liturgy and leads to a deeper and more meaningful participation in the divine mysteries. It is, in the words of the Decree on the Sacred Liturgy *"an exercise of the priestly office of Jesus Christ"*. Through it, *"public worship is performed by the mystical body of Jesus Christ, that is, by the Head and his members"*. (*Sacrosanctum Concilium No. 7*).

Fr Russell Hardiman and his helpers are to be congratulated on the publication of this valuable volume of essays.

+B. J. Hickey

Most Rev Barry J Hickey
Archbishop of Perth
Chairman of the National Liturgical Commission

CONTRIBUTORS

Jayne Newton Ahearn, a native of Sheboygin, Wisconsin, lectured at the University of Hawaii in Genetics for over twenty years. Jayne became a Catholic through the Rite of Christian Initiation of Adults and proceeded to work in liturgy at the parish level. She completed a Masters in Liturgical Studies at the University of Notre Dame, Indiana. Her experience has included campus ministry, parish liturgist, director of a diocesan liturgy office as well as being a contributor as writer and associate editor of *Pastoral Liturgy*.

Russell Hugh Hardiman, a priest of the Bunbury Diocese in Western Australia, was the first Australian graduate with a doctorate in liturgy from Sant'Anselmo, in 1970. He is currently senior lecturer in Liturgy, University of Notre Dame Australia. Besides twenty-five years of full-time parish ministry he has been lecturing in liturgy in Western Australia for eighteen years and has been publishing editor of *Pastoral Liturgy* since 1970.

Patrick (Paddy) Meagher, SJ, though Australian born, is a member of Hazaribag Province of the Jesuits in India. He has been Professor of New Testament at Vidyajyoti College of Theology, New Delhi and for three years has been a Visiting Lecturer, University of Notre Dame, Australia. He was a doctoral graduate of the Biblical Institute in Rome in 1984.

Jerome Neyrey, SJ, is a Jesuit of the New Orleans Province. After doctoral studies at Yale University he is now professor of New Testament, University of Notre Dame du Lac, Indiana. He was a visiting lecturer at the University of Notre Dame Australia in 1995. He was program chair of the Catholic Biblical Association in 1996.

Gerard Smith is director of Grief Management Educational Services in Perth, Western Australia. After many years working with funeral directors he saw the need for grief education and now runs his own company in this sphere and provides a consultancy service to funeral directors as well as running parish based courses and groups on grief management.

At the Heart of Liturgy

Introduction
Russell Hardiman

It is fashionable, to the extent of being normal these days, for a book to have both a title and a subtitle, with the title being a snappy, marketable, attractively catching phrase while the subtitle is an explanation of the content or the thrust of the argument.

When books are a collection of papers from a conference, or a collection of essays from a variety of authors from a common source, such as a journal, or when the volume is collection of essays in the form of a "Festschrift" in honor of a colleague, mentor, or famous figure—these are the occasions when the title becomes like an umbrella whose ribs help tie together a number of disparate sources.

Such is the nature of this collection of essays, all of which have originally appeared in the journal *Pastoral Liturgy*, founded in 1970, which makes it Australia's oldest continuously published liturgical magazine.

THE TITLE

The genesis of the work goes back many years and comes from personal experience at many levels in celebrating the liturgical cycle of the seasons of the church's year. The title expresses the goal of liturgical celebration: the experience of the divine presence in the human, the transcendent in the language and practice of ritual. At the functional level this presumes an awareness of the theological principles that underpin the structures, patterns, forms, and symbols of our tradition.

There are theological and historical insights that should underpin a profound pastoral sensibility as to how to bring alive the patterns of worship of our Judeo-Christian tradition. Many of the essays in this work link the historical origins and the pastoral potential for liturgical celebration today.

Vatican II's central goal in the renewal of the liturgy was to affirm that in the liturgy was the summit of the church's activity, at the same time that it was the source of the church's power (*SC* no. 10).

One of the major reforms of Vatican II has been the restructuring of the liturgical year with clear emphasis being given to the major feasts of Easter and Christmas, with their times of preparation in Lent and Advent as well as the times of intensification in Eastertide and Christmastide. The priority of the "temporal cycle" is emphasized by the thrust of the Sundays through the year called "Ordinary Time," not in the sense that is ordinary time as if insignificant compared to special times, but in the sequence of numbering in order.

Before Vatican II there had developed a proliferation of feasts in the "Sanctoral Cycle" to the extent that very frequently, it seemed that the greatest priority was given to days of the Our Lord or Our Lady, the saints (especially of Europe) and the devotional emphases given to certain octaves or titles of devotion. Even today that pattern is still deeply embedded in the devotional life of many faithful parishioners, who see May as the month of Our Lady, June as the month of the Sacred Heart, October as the month of the Rosary, November as the month of the Holy Souls, and so on. The heart of the liturgy has been restored to the center rather than expressed at the periphery.

The renewed emphasis in the integrity of the key feasts and seasons of the liturgical year has been complemented by the structure of the lectionary. Vatican II mandated that a richer fare from the table of God's word should be opened up to God's faithful by a restructured cycle of readings over several years (*SC* no. 51). This mandate saw fruit in 1969 with the publication of the "Ordo of Readings for Mass," which was re-expressed in a second edition in 1981 from Rome's Congregation for Divine Worship. The principal feature of the *Roman Lectionary* is the development of the three-year cycle, in which the permanent qualities of the sequence of feasts and seasons are celebrated in different sets of readings over the three years, with the original names of Year A, B, and C.

THE PASCHAL MYSTERY: MORE THAN A SUBTITLE

The significant phrase in the subtitle of this book is "the heart"of the work, just as the paschal mystery is the very heart of Christian worship. The recapturing of the theology of the paschal mystery has been a major element of the theology of the liturgy in the documents of Vatican II and the reform afterwards.

There is no other theme for the Eucharist than the celebration of the paschal mystery of Jesus Christ. Some years back, in the first flush of enthusiasm after Vatican II, there was a great interest in theme Masses. The presumption was that the ideal was to select a theme, then build the preparation for the liturgy around the various elements of participation to develop that theme.

Fortunately, there is not so much keenness for themes these days. Maybe it is an expression of the fact that people have run out of positive psychic energy to compose their own Masses; more hopefully perhaps it is an indication of how deeply appreciated is the biblical mentality today and hence an ability to handle the assigned readings of the day; more likely still, it could be the awareness of the inherent power and potential in God's Word and to the primary Christian response in emptying ourselves to take on Christ, rather than simply presuming to reduce God's Word to a self-service counter at which we select our favorite texts and share them with others.

In short, maybe the fruits of the renewal in biblical studies and the biblical movement are starting to show themselves at the grass-roots in schools, parishes, and communities, just as the fruits of the liturgical movement are also now able to be perceived in issues like communion from the cup, levels of liturgical ministry, and worship in the language of the people, which are prominent results of Vatican II renewal.

Theme Masses, one example of the tension between theory and practice, are a good reminder of the importance of placing the paschal mystery in its rightful place.

A similar example of the dichotomy is seen every Holy Week, where in some Latin cultures there are the bizarre scenes, so loved by the television news directors, of dramatic crucifixions, of spectacular processions, of gory reproductions of Christ's sufferings.

This trend toward sensational expression obscures the hope of new life in the resurrection with tear-jerker reproductions of Christ's suffering and is an example of what may happen, in the words of Henri Oster "... when one deserts the centre for the periphery ...." He is worth quoting more fully:

> Too often, Easter is considered but one feast among others. It is agreed, of course, that Easter is "traditionally" the most important feast, but Christmas is much dearer to their heart. In some Christian countries, the solemnity of the Pasch can in no way measure up to the pomp of Corpus Christi. Such as these would put the feast of the Most Holy Trinity on equal rank with Easter because of its doctrinal depth, or that of the Sacred Heart for its religious richness.
>
> There can be no doubt about for anyone that this development is deeply regrettable, for when one deserts the center for the periphery, he chances the loss of all. When the life-giving function of the heart is taken away, the body dies. Happily for Christianity and for us, however, the paschal mystery stands at the center of Christianity and can never be entirely taken away, even if pastors and faithful should one day lose sight of it completely. (*The Paschal Mystery in Parish Life*. New York: Herder & Herder, 1967, pp. 12-13)

This emphasis on the ongoing process of promoting a fuller understanding of the paschal mystery becomes the motif that links together what otherwise could appear as a series of separate articles from disparate authors. It is the unifying element that covers the whole range of articles dealing with the liturgical years and its seasons; with the primacy of the Easter Triduum itself; with the series of articles on the eucharistic prayer and on other parts of the Mass; with the overflow into the celebration of Christian funerals, even in the relatively infrequent practice of cremation with the subsequent internment of ashes; with the more broadly based experience of popular devotions. A glance through the table of contents would confirm the overview of how many articles are drawn together under one heading.

One common denominator among all these quite

various aspects of our Christian tradition is the common sacramental principle that in our human celebration and ritual expression we encounter the divine. To celebrate the paschal mystery is not to refer to it only at Easter but to see the element of passing over from death to life as the paradigmatic example for us to follow in our humanity to share Christ's divinity.

This is not a radically new element in the prayer tradition of our church. It is not some new buzzword that becomes the flavor of the month. In fact, it is frequently the motif of the presidential prayers at Mass, especially in the opening prayers or collects, or in the prayers over the gifts, or the prayers after communion. Thus the collect for the First Sunday of Lent invites us to pray:

> Father,
> through our observance of Lent,
> help us to understand the meaning
> of Your Son's death and resurrection,
> and teach us to reflect it in our lives.

The formal invitation to the prayer, included in the ICEL translation, is that this Lent will help us to reproduce in our lives the self-sacrificing love of Christ, itself a powerful summary of the purpose of our celebrating the paschal mystery in Lent, as the intensification time for modeling the pattern all Christian life, for if we learn to imitate Christ in our understanding of his dying and rising then we are motivated to reflect it in our living.

The sentiment of this oration is not only expressed in the stark, sober, sparse tones of the prayers of the early centuries, illustrating what Edmund Bishop (in spite of his name, the English lay pioneer of the liturgical movement in the nineteenth century), was to call "the genius of the Roman Rite." Even in medieval times, when there arose an enormous surge of interest in promoting the devotions that could link people with the historic life of Jesus and his mission in the Holy Land, there was the goal of facilitating for the baptized layperson a level of prayer, suited for their way of life even without being able to read, so that they could pray and celebrate with the clergy, whether in the cathedral or monastic traditions.

The concluding prayer for the rosary expresses these insights into the celebration of the paschal mystery in the phrases that have been memorized for centuries by ordinary folk.

> O God, whose only begotten Son
> by his life, death and resurrection
> has purchased for us the rewards of eternal life,
> grant, we beseech you,
> that in meditating upon these mysteries of the most holy
> Rosary of the Blessed Virgin Mary,
> we may both imitate what they contain,
> and obtain what they promise
> through the same Christ Our Lord.

In the years since Vatican II the growth in appreciation of the profound basis of the paschal mystery as the heart of liturgy has been given a huge boost by its treatment in the *Catechism of the Catholic Church* (Vatican City, 1994). For all the mixed views that have been expressed about the Catechism most commentators agree that two of its strongest elements are the introductory chapter on the liturgy (no. 1066-1209) and the introductory sections dealing with prayer (no. 2550-2758). At any event, the unique contribution of the Catechism, in its special synthesis of the teaching of the church after Vatican II, is particularly fully expressed in the paragraphs that develop its thesis: The Celebration of the Christian Mystery (no. 1066f.). This is a profoundly Trinitarian theology of the liturgy, with special segments that show how the liturgy is the work of the Holy Trinity:

• The Father—Source and Goal of the Liturgy (no. 1077f.)

• Christ's Work in the Liturgy (no. 1084f.)

• The Holy Spirit in Church in the Liturgy (no. 1091f.)

Its strength is in the powerful insight that the Holy Spirit is the church's living memory (no. 1099). Hence the Spirit and the church work together to manifest God's work of salvation in the liturgy, primarily through the proclamation of the Word of God and through the work of *anamnesis*, of making remembrance of the marvelous works of God in times of old that continue now in our day.

Breaking open the Word is to build a bridge that transports that loving concern of God in the many and marvelous ways of the prophets to these last times when he speaks through his Son (Heb 1:1). The all-encompassing theological vision of time is the source of how those saving events are actualized and make their fruits present for us now.

In the liturgy of the Church, it is principally his own Paschal mystery that Christ signifies and makes present. During his earthly life Jesus announced his Paschal mystery by his teaching and anticipated it by his actions. When his Hour comes, he lives out the unique event of history which does not pass away: Jesus dies, is buried, rises from the dead, and is seated at the right hand of the Father "once and for all." His Paschal mystery is a real event that occurred in our history, but it is unique: all other historical events happen once, and then pass away, swallowed up in the past. The Paschal mystery of Christ, by contrast, because by his death he destroyed death, and all that Christ is—all that he did and suffered for all men—participates in the divine eternity, and so transcends all times while being made present in them all. The event of the Cross and Resurrection abides and draws everything toward life. (CCC no. 1085)

Christian liturgy not only recalls the events that saved us but actualizes them, makes them present. The Paschal mystery of Christ is celebrated, not repeated. It is the celebrations that are repeated, and in each celebration there is an outpouring of the Holy Spirit that makes the unique mystery present. (CCC no. 1104)

The essays in this collection portray a variety of the facets inherent in this great mystery. The chapters by Jayne Ahearn give a development of the notion of "pasch" and how it was understood and celebrated in the life of the church, and are particularly to be recommended. Nearly all the essays dealing with the biblical readings and the theology of proclamation, along with the notes on the structure of the lectionary, are designed to underline the primacy of this theology of paschal mystery.

The essays dealing with popular devotions may, at first, appear to have little to do with contemporary spirituality or theology, but in fact the opposite is true. At a deeper level, the devotions have their function and rightful place in the tradition of the church precisely because they help to put a human face on the complex mystery, they bring into daily life the inspiring presence of the Jesus who is human, like us in all things but sin.

The Trinitarian theology of the liturgy is exemplified in the traditional pattern and structure of the eucharistic prayer, the heart of the Christian Eucharist. After centuries of sole use of the Roman Canon in the Western tradition we now have a variety of ten eucharistic prayers, along with a collection of nearly one hundred prefaces. It is possible to miss the wood for the trees, by not understanding the unity in the variety of these texts.

The major essay on the eucharistic prayer explores the traditional structure of this prayer, as outlined in the *General Instruction of the Roman Missal* and the Catechism and as illustrated in the newest of prayers, the so-called Swiss Prayer.

The paschal mystery of Christ's death and resurrection is celebrated not just at every Easter, or just at every Eucharist. It is also celebrated at every funeral. Hence, the section on funerals and cremations is very much in keeping with the thrust of this book. The vision of faith enables us to celebrate funerals with comfort of hope in eternal life. Hence, to share the funeral liturgies of cremation and interment of ashes, which I prepared for my own parents, is a personal tribute and pastoral offering to others.

This offering is made with the sense of encouragement to celebrate funerals well and to learn from them the Christian hope of life beyond life. This pattern is marvelously expressed by Mark Searle, who also showed how to live it as he prepared to face his own terminal illness and death.

> If ... we were to learn from the celebration of the paschal mystery to surrender our lives totally to God in Christ, the death of the Christian would be but the further and final rehearsal of a pattern learned in life and practiced over and over again in a lifetime of liturgical participation… for those who have learned from the prayers and rituals of the Christian liturgy how to let go of all that we cling to to save ourselves from the void, the final surrender of death will be a familiar and joyous sacrifice. (*Assembly* vol 5 (5) 1979)

Further perusal of the table of contents may reinforce the overview that enables so many disparate articles to be seen as coherently linked together, yet with an integrity of their own.

DEDICATION

Finally, a word about the motive behind dedicating this work to a father-figure of liturgy in Western Australia, who also, as bishop and personal mentor, had a strong influence on my life.

In July 1962 my family was called to my father's hospital bed because the staff did not think he would live beyond the day. (He lived another 19 years!) That same day I had been told that Bishop Goody of Bunbury had secured a place at the Propaganda Fide College and that I was going to Rome for my seminary theology studies. I arrived in Rome the week before Vatican II started, a period of lifting the horizons that has never finished. For a country lad from Albany it was heady stuff to be in the Piazza at St. Peter's to see the procession of Council Fathers in their marvelous parade in a panoply of splendor. It was an experience of the international church to witness this historic event; and even more so, to live in an international context at the Urban College *De Propaganda Fide* where our graduation class saw sixty-nine priests ordained from twenty-seven countries after our journey of four years matched the council's journey of four years; it was a mind-expanding experience to have our ex-students of the College, now Council Fathers as Bishops, celebrate the Community Mass in the Chapel and to be exposed to the multitude of rites in the Catholic Church from places like India, Egypt, Lebanon, Syria, Iraq that were so different from the Latin rite I had been led to believe was universal; it was stimulating to be taken on a heritage tour by my Bishop, then Launcelot Goody of Bunbury, to visit the monastery at Fafa, where St. Benedict built his second foundation after Subiaco, or the place where St. Francis painted the first crib in the monastery at Greccio. In short, it was the beginning experience of a perspective I like to think has been ongoing, continually being reshaped.

After ordination and pastoral work in my home parish I was scheduled to return to Rome to start postgraduate studies in canon law. Around that time, as the first liturgical changes after Vatican II were being implemented, my parish priest, the Vicar General, suggested to Bishop Goody that, seeing how liturgy was the area changing the most, maybe it would be more fruitful for the diocese to have someone study liturgy. Bishop Goody concurred, so my life changed from the prospects of canon law to liturgy.

The next three years at the Pontifical Liturgical Institute of Sant'Anselmo were something of a revolution. Sant'Anselmo was the second university in the world (after the Institute Catholique in Paris) to offer graduate and doctoral programs in liturgical studies. Most of my professors were actually *periti* or expert advisors at the Vatican Council and many were now participants in post-conciliar commissions preparing the detail of the reformed rites mandated by Vatican II.

It was a stimulating experience to learn to appreciate the historical perspective that undergirds the factors that shaped the development of worship patterns and how they came to be regulated formally by the instructions printed in red, the "rubrics." For one trained in rubrics as an MC it was a revolution to see the theological and pastoral insights that directed the reform initiated by Vatican II, compared to the ruthless obedience demanded by the rubrical mentality of pre Vatican II times. It was a humbling revelation to be exposed to the scholarship of the great liturgists, such as Joseph Jungmann SJ, who spent his whole life proving the inadequacy of the rubrics, yet never bent a rubric in his life. It was a mind-expanding exposure to the fullest tradition of our church, a tradition that is fifteen hundred years older than the fixed, uniform, inflexible Roman Rite implemented after the Council of Trent. It was a time of enthusiasm and hope for the future with great expectations of the impact the new liturgy of Vatican II would make in parishes.

When I returned to Western Australia in 1970, the first person in Australasia to graduate with a doctorate in liturgy, my mentor from Bunbury Diocese was now Archbishop Goody of Perth. Sometime in the course of that year he proposed to the suffragan bishops in Western Australia to form the Liturgy Commission of Western Australia to serve all dioceses in WA, along the same lines as the Catholic Education Commission of WA had been established for all dioceses, a structure unique in Australia.

As a member of this newly established liturgy commission, I floated the proposal to publish a pastoral magazine to help priests in parishes to adjust to the New Rite of Mass, the *Novus Ordo Missae* released in 1969, and especially to facilitate the adaptation of the new lectionary, then brand new. The original model for this service was an Italian journal *Liturgia della Parola*, which provided educational articles on the liturgy in general along with a neat service providing worship aids in the form of separate cards/pages for commentators and priest/celebrants with all the spoken parts on respective pages.

This was the impetus for the publication of *Pastoral*

Liturgy in October 1970. Though circulating originally in the dioceses of Western Australia, it now goes to every diocese in Australia and to some twenty countries overseas. Its subscribers now come from all mainstream Christian churches with a strong liturgical tradition, an ecumenical dimension that I presume to say would appeal to Archbishop Goody.

Little did the parish priest of Boulder, the young Dr. Goody in the 1930s, realize that, when he made a bet with another priest as to which of the Russell girls would marry first, my mother (who had taught him to play bridge) would make him the winner of that bet. His poem to my mother in response to her criticism of his color scheme is a microcosm of his private life when most only knew him as the public figure of a bishop. Now I can continue that family connection through three generations, both in private and in public, and dedicate this book to him, as a tribute to the one who labored so much in the implementation of Vatican II in Western Australia.

ACKNOWLEDGMENTS

Quite obviously this book would not have reached this stage without the collaboration of many people. Some may have recognized their part, others may not.

First, I have to thank the loyal subscribers to *Pastoral Liturgy*. Without their faithfulness in continuing to renew their subscriptions and their spontaneous words of encouragement and gratitude, which have refreshed me on many an occasion when I doubted the efforts were worthwhile, the magazine would certainly never have been able to be kept going. Likewise, the work of the subscription managers has enabled the network to be maintained. For some fifteen years my parents loyally kept the books, and in recent years, Margaret Bevan of Waroona has kept the subscribers happy most of the time.

I gratefully acknowledge my colleague as associate editor, Jayne Ahearn, with her many articles and worship notes over the years. It has not always been easy collaborating from one side of the world to the other, but in itself that is a powerful symbol of the unifying capacity of the church's patterns of worship. Of recent years I have been able to draw on the generosity and talents of colleagues, who have lectured in the College of Theology at the University of Notre Dame Australia. The commentaries for the full cycle of readings for Years A, B, C by Jerome Neyrey, SJ, have been warmly received by our readers, one of whom remarked that in all his priestly ministry he had never come across a homily aid that helped as much as Jerry's articles did. Paddy Meagher, SJ, has prepared the homily reflections for the Years of Matthew, Mark, and Luke, and I know he enjoys an equally warm response. Gerry Smith's work as a bereavement counselor has prepared him to appreciate the function of the funeral as more than to dispose of the body: it is to give the grieving family and other mourners a ritual opportunity to express their farewell, while commending the deceased to God, as their faith leads them. His article shows how the Order of Christian Funerals well expresses the important place of funerals.

The project of the volume has been a long time in its gestation, but it would never have been born without the patience and skill of the technical editor, Peta Wellstead.

This collection of liturgical essays is both a tribute to the formation process we have entered into since Vatican II as well as the encouragement in the need to keep on keeping on. Truly we can look back in thanksgiving and go forward in faith.

THE PASCHAL MYSTERY
in the Liturgical Seasons

The Season of Advent

Jayne Newton Ahearn

DESCRIPTION

Advent has a twofold character; as a season to prepare for Christmas when Christ's first coming to us is remembered; as a season when that remembrance directs the mind and heart to await Christ's second coming at the end of time. Advent is thus a period for devout and joyful expectation (*General Norms for the Liturgical Year and the Calendar* no. 39, *Ceremonial of Bishops* no. 235).

Advent begins with evening prayer 1 of the Sunday falling on or closest to 30 November and ends before evening prayer 1 of Christmas. The Sundays of this season are named the First, Second, Third, and Fourth Sundays of Advent. The weekdays from 17 December to 24 December inclusive serve to prepare more directly for the Lord's birth (*GNLYC* nos. 40-42).

HISTORICAL ORIGINS

The origins of Advent are not primarily western; yet Advent is much more highly developed in the West. The season has mixed origins, and there are various opinions of how it arose. Before the time of Justinian there was a mobile feast of Mary on the Sunday before Christmas celebrating the conception of Jesus. This feast was retained in both East and West. On the preceding Sunday the conception of John the Baptizer was celebrated. Called the Weeks of Annunciations in the Syriac tradition, this period expanded into Advent in all the Eastern traditions.

The focus of the incarnation cycle in the East was the Epiphany of Jesus as the Christ at his baptism in the Jordan. Thus initiation was celebrated at Christmas time and so Advent was a time of preparation for baptism. This preparation period was of varying lengths of time ranging from an unspecified period in the Coptic tradition, to forty days in the Byzantine tradition, fifty days in the Armenian tradition, and ten weeks in the Ethiopian tradition, and included fasting.

Rome had no tradition of baptism at Christmas, for the Western focus of Christmas had shifted to the manger scene at Bethlehem. The period of preparation, which fell at the end of the year, had instead an eschatological orientation. The pagan feast of *adventus* celebrated the coming of a god to its temple to be with the people, or the coming of a god as emperor. This concept was carried into the observance of Advent as the Christian faithful waited with joyful expectation for the return of Christ as king and judge at the end of time.

The celebration of Advent in the West makes its appearance at the end of the fifth century in Spain and in Gaul as a five- to six-week preparation period. This spread to northern Italy in the sixth century. When Advent was adopted in Rome at the time of Gregory the Great, its duration was reduced to four weeks.

THEOLOGY

Advent comes at the end of the civil year and at the beginning of the liturgical year. As such, the season elicits contemplation of the past, of the present, and of the future. The season evolved in the northern hemisphere where the natural signs of the end of the year are days with ever-decreasing hours of light, falling temperatures and snow, and dormancy or death of trees, shrubs, and flowers so that the world of color becomes black, grey, and white. It is a depressing and frightening time for many. It could be the end of the world. It is naturally a time to long for the return of light, warmth, living things, beginning anew, a time to await a rescuer, a savior.

Advent is about the coming of Jesus: the coming of Jesus as the human babe of Bethlehem, the coming of Jesus as the king and judge at the end of time, the coming of Jesus into our lives *now*. Advent is preparation for the remembering (*anamnesis*) of the incarnation. Advent is also preparation for the *parousia*, the fulfillment of God's kingdom. And, as St. Bernard wrote, the coming of Christ into our personal lives allows us to pass from the first coming to the third coming.

Thus, during Advent we look forward to the coming of the kingdom, and we seek ways to be more authentic signs of the kingdom already present, thereby hastening the day of fulfillment. Indeed, the earliest focus of Advent was eschatological, a vigil in preparation for the coming of the Bridegroom (see Matthew 25). In a twelfth-century homily Peter of Bluoius summarized the western theology of Advent in terms of the bridesmaids' vigil in Matthew 25 and the triumphant entry into Jerusalem in John 12. Jesus comes to us at midnight; of this we are certain, but *when* we are uncertain.

In the East, this vigil that is Advent has a strong Marian focus. Mary is the model of the church, and of the Christian. Mary was the first disciple and therefore the model for all disciples. We become more fully a sacrament of the kingdom by conforming to the pattern of Mary's life.

In the middle ages, probably under the influence of Irish monks, the eschatological focus was superseded by a penitential focus. Fear of final judgment associated with the second coming led to the need for repentance. This began in Gaul and spread through the western church. Liturgical renewal after Vatican II restored Advent as a season of preparation for the threefold coming of Christ: past, present, and future.

The prayer that Jesus taught us is the prayer of Advent. We call upon God as our Father, whose name we honor, and we ask that God's kingdom will come on earth and be fulfilled among us *now*. As we conclude this prayer at Mass the presider says that "we wait in joyful hope for the coming of our Savior, Jesus Christ." When we gather to make Eucharist, the church is most fully made visible as the sign that the kingdom has already begun. St. Paul wrote to the Corinthians that "we proclaim the Lord's death until he comes" (1 Cor 11:26). Our words of remembrance summarize the meaning of Advent; Christ (was born) has died; Christ is risen; Christ will come again.

ADVENT AND THE LECTIONARY

The readings for the Sundays of Advent of each liturgical year cycle are explored elsewhere in this volume. The general focus of each Advent Sunday is similar from year to year. But, as each gospel writer presents the story of the Jesus event from a different viewpoint, so Advent in each liturgical year takes on a different aspect. The gospel for Christ the King, which concludes one liturgical year and directly precedes Advent, sets us in the direction for the coming year.

On Christ the King of Year C, the gospel is of Jesus on the cross forgiving the repentant thief. Making fun of Jesus, the people and soldiers say, "if you are the Messiah" and "if you are the king of the Jews." And over Jesus' head is the inscription: "This is the King of the Jews." In Year A, the year of Matthew, the gospel writer presents Jesus as the fulfillment of prophetic promise in continuity with the Judaic tradition. To that end the formula: "to fulfill what the Lord had said through the prophet" is heard repeatedly, followed by a quote from Hebrew Scripture. Jesus preaches about the kingdom or reign of God. Matthew is the gospel that speaks of the church, the new Israel, the community of believing disciples who are on mission to be a sign of the kingdom of God and of the reconciliation with God that the kingdom brings for all of humanity.

The second reading for Christ the King, Year C, from Colossians, speaks of us as having been rescued from the power of darkness and made worthy to share with the saints in light. The readings of Year A in Advent and beyond draw heavily upon the image of darkness being overcome by light.

The gospel of Christ the King, Year A, is the scene of the final judgment. Jesus separates those who are blessed by God to enter the eternal kingdom from those who are not. The criterion Jesus uses is whether we have recognized his presence in one another and especially in those among us who are most in need. We know that Jesus identifies with humankind, in our hunger and thirst, in our loneliness and vulnerability, in our pain and our fear. As we enter Year B, the year of Mark's gospel, we long for and encounter God among us; God in flesh. Mark will tell us the good news about Jesus of Nazareth who was human like us and yet remained faithful to God so that all of us are saved by his self-offering. "Show us your face and we shall be saved." The Jesus of Mark is one among us whom we do not know; he repeatedly tells his disciples, "Don't tell anyone." Early in his ministry, Jesus appears powerful, healing the sick and casting out demons; then gradually seems to relinquish power. Jesus is engaged in a battle with "the strong man" (Satan, the evil one); a battle that is won not by force but by love and faithfulness. The Jesus of Mark is the suffering servant who embraces the cross and makes of it the sign and means of victory over sin and death.

The prelude to Year C is Christ the King, Year B. The gospel is from John's passion narrative when Jesus, on his journey to the cross, is before Pilate. Jesus inquires of Pilate why he asks the question, "Are you the King of the Jews?" Pilate replies that he is not a Jew and therefore just trying to understand the situation. Jesus tells Pilate that he has come to testify to Truth and everyone who belongs to the truth will listen to his voice. We know from the rest of the exchange between them that Pilate is more than curious about Jesus, that Pilate does come to an understanding of who Jesus is while most of Israel does not. The first and second readings that day are joyful in their vision and promise of the everlasting kingdom of those saved by the blood of Christ, peoples of all nations and languages.

Luke's gospel, the gospel of Year C, was addressed primarily to Gentile Christians to trace their beginnings from the Hebrew experience to the early church. It is the good news of universal salvation. All (Jews and Gentiles, women and men) are reconciled to God and to one another in Christ. There is great joy and rejoicing; Zechariah, Mary, and the angels burst into song at the wonders God does. Celebration of reconciliation occurs and is recognized around the dinner table. Salvation for all means justice for those who are poor or marginalized, and peace for those who are sick or lost in sin. All this is accomplished through the work of the Holy Spirit. Luke's gospel is framed as a journey, a metaphor with which we have become more familiar through the rites of Christian initiation.

In Advent each year we watch, we prepare, we joyfully anticipate the return of Jesus as king, the coming of Jesus into our lives each day, and the remembrance of the incarnation of Jesus. In Year A we celebrate Jesus, messiah and king, fulfillment of prophetic promise of a savior who will be the glorious light that overcomes the darkness of sin and death. In Year B we celebrate Jesus, the Word made flesh, God among us as stranger, as poor and vulnerable, who teaches us the way of the cross. And in Year C we celebrate Jesus, the savior born of the Holy Spirit to bring peace and justice to any who seek the way of truth.

WORSHIP ENVIRONMENT

Advent is the season to simplify. Clear out everything superfluous from the sanctuary, from the nave, and especially from the church entryway where tables and bulletin boards can be quite cluttered.

The environment for Advent is determined by:
a) the readings of the entire Advent/Christmas season;
b) the challenges that the Advent readings pose to the community and the responses the community will make in preparation for the coming of the kingdom. It is then the task of the environment team to put this into visual expression.

Advent is our most countercultural season. While the secular world puts out the Christmas decorations by Halloween (October 31st), the church does not begin to celebrate Christmas until the evening of December 24th. The Advent environment should lead into the environment for Christmas. Advent is about preparing, so decide where the manger scene will be, where the Christmas tree will be, and then clear that space.

Advent is a season of darkness with the promise of light, a season of tension and uncertainty with the promise of peace, a season of longing with the promise of fulfillment. Advent is about expectation and being surprised by the unexpected. The colors of the season are shades of deep blue (Sarum blue), purple, and grey. On the third Sunday, Gaudete or "Rejoice" Sunday, shades of rose (not hot pink!) may come into the scheme.

Candles, especially the candles of the Advent wreath, should be a prominent part of the Advent environment. Within the wreath, instead of placing all four candles on the First Sunday, set only the one candle to be lighted and add a candle each week. At Christmas, the blue or purple candles of the Advent wreath are replaced with white candles, and the Christ candle is added in the center.

MUSIC

Responsorial Psalm. The seasonal psalms for Advent are Psalm 24/25 and Psalm 84/85. Selection of one for use throughout the season is framed by the Scriptures in relationship to the needs and situation of the particular parish.

Psalm 25

Lift Up My Soul	Tim Manion
To You, O God, I Lift Up My Soul	Bob Hurd
To You, O Lord	Marty Haugen
To You, O Lord	Scott Soper
To You, O Lord	Robert J. Thompson/Joseph Gelineau
To You, O Lord	Christopher Willcock

Psalm 85

A Voice In the Wilderness	Chris Robinson
Come, O Lord, and Set Us Free	Balhoff, Daigle, Ducote
Let Us See Your Kindness	Marty Haugen
Lord, Let Us See Your Kindness	Noel Ancell
Lord, Let Us See Your Kindness	Christopher Willcock
Lord, Make Us Turn To You	Marty Haugen
Show Us Your Kindness	Bob Hurd

The psalm setting by Marty Haugen, *Lord, Make Us Turn To You*, is particularly appropriate for the B cycle of Advent. Haugen has provided three sets of three verses, which are the texts of the psalms proper to the First, Second, and Third Sundays of Advent. For the Fourth Sunday, repeat verses 7, 8, and 9 taken from the Magnificat and appropriate for the readings of the day.

Gospel Acclamation. During Advent, "Alleluia" may be combined with "Maranatha, Come, Lord." *Advent Gospel Acclamation* by David Haas combines a very strong yet simple alleluia sung by the assembly with a verse for each Sunday sung by the cantor that ends with all singing "Lord Jesus, come!" In her wonderful collection *God Beyond All Names*, Bernadette Farrell has composed *Litany of the Word* as a dialogue between cantor and assembly with "Alleluia" and "Maranatha" alternating as the response. To invocations such as "Word of justice, Word of mercy, Come to dwell here, Live within us," the assembly responds "Alleluia" and "Maranatha." *Litany of the Word* would serve well for the gospel procession or as an Advent gathering litany.

From the Music of Taizé comes *Maranatha Alleluia I*. After introducing the responses "Maranatha" and "Alleluia" and having the assembly repeat them, the cantor chants the gospel verse in two parts to which the assembly responds first with "Maranatha" and then "Alleluia." The form with the verses for each Sunday is:

First Sunday
Cantor: Lord, let us see your kindness
All: Maranatha
Cantor: and grant us your salvation
All: Alleluia

Second Sunday
Cantor: Prepare the way for the Lord; make straight his path
All: Maranatha
Cantor: all shall see the salvation of God
All: Alleluia

Third Sunday
Cantor: The spirit of the Lord is upon me
All: Maranatha
Cantor: I am sent to bring Good News to the poor
All: Alleluia

Fourth Sunday and Immaculate Conception
Cantor: I am the servant of the Lord
All: Maranatha
Cantor: may God's will for me be done
All: Alleluia

Eucharistic Acclamations. Acclamations for the eucharistic prayer during Advent may be the simple settings used during Lent such as the *Danish Mass* or Haugen's *Mass of Remembrance*. Or use the setting planned for the Christmas season without the harmonies and instrumentation. The well-known *Mass of Creation* by Marty Haugen, written in minor key, works well throughout the Advent-Christmas season. Other settings worth considering for Advent-Christmas are *Eucharistic Acclamations* by Bernadette Farrell (1987, Oregon Catholic Press), *Mass of Light* by David Haas (1988, G.I.A.

Publications, Inc.), *Eucharistic Acclamations 2* by Paul Inwood (1986, Oregon Catholic Press) and *Morning Star Mass* by Lynn Trapp (1988, Morning Star Music Publishers). Forms of the memorial acclamation more appropriate in Advent are A: Christ has died; Christ has risen; Christ will come again and B: Dying, you destroyed our death.... Lord, Jesus, come in glory. As the memorial acclamation in his *Mass of Remembrance,* Haugen has used the refrain of his popular *We Remember,* which celebrated the three comings of the Lord.

The Lord's Prayer is best recited. If it is sung use a chant form.

Suggested tropes of the Lamb of God litany for the fraction rite, which include the O antiphon names for the Christ, are: Hope for all, Bread of Promise, Wine of Peace, Sun of Justice, Holy Wisdom, Flower of Jesse, Key of David, Radiant Dawn, God is with us, King of Kings. These tropes could be applied in the fraction litanies of Haugen's *Mass of Creation* and *Mass of Remembrance,* Haas's *Mass of Light,* and Trapp's *Morning Star Mass.* Paul Inwood's *Jesus, Lamb of God* (1982, Oregon Catholic Press), which can be used with his *Eucharistic Acclamations 2,* draws upon some of these metaphors; if a longer litany is needed, more verses could be written. In *Jesus, Lamb of God* by Bernadette Farrell (1991, Oregon Catholic Press), verses five through eight are appropriate for the Advent-Christmas season.

General Intercessions. The people's prayer in the general intercessions during Advent is most appropriately, "Lord, you are our hope." The prayer can be recited or chanted to the same tones as "Lord, hear our prayer." Another possible prayer response is the refrain of Haugen's *My Soul In Stillness Waits* or even just the last phrase ("truly, my [our] hope is in you").

Gathering and the Penitential Rite. The song of gathering should inform the community that this is Advent, our season of longing, of preparation, of joyful anticipation of the Lord's coming. For continuity use one song throughout the season. Begin singing *a capella* on the first Sunday and intensify the urgency each week by adding an instrumental melody line the second Sunday, a harmony the third Sunday, and using the complete accompaniment on the fourth Sunday. *O Come, O Come Emmanuel* or Marty Haugen's contemporary version *My Soul In Stillness Waits* are both good choices to signal the Advent season. Rather than singing all the verses each week or just the first two or three verses, choose two or three verses in addition to verse 1 that reflect the readings for the day.

Another hymn that expresses longing for light to overcome darkness and for the kingdom to be fulfilled is *Creator of the Stars of Night.* Marty Haugen has written a contemporary text that is highly recommended; it can be found in his collection *Night of Silence* published by G.I.A. in 1987.

Form C of the penitential rite may follow. Use Marty Haugen's *Mass of Remembrance* setting of the second set of invocations, which speak of the three comings of Christ. The Kyrie of *Morning Star Mass* has invocations specific to Advent. Or compose invocation texts for each Sunday, drawing upon images of the readings, and have the assembly respond with a lyrical or chanted kyrie. Refer also to Pastoral Note 1 for the shape of the gathering rites.

Note that the Gloria is neither sung nor recited during Advent; it is THE song of Christmas.

Other Hymns and Songs are chosen from the Advent music repertoire to reflect the readings of the day. If a seasonal psalm is being used, then the proper psalm of the day becomes one of these. The preparation of the gifts is one time to make use of these selections.

The community should know at least one or two settings of the Canticle of Zachary and the Canticle of Mary, for singing not only during Advent but also for Morning and Evening Prayer and Communal Reconciliation. Some suggestions are:

Canticle of Zachary

Canticle of Zachary	ELLACOMBE
Canticle of Zachary	FOREST GREEN
Canticle of Zachary	HURON (David Haas)
Good Morning Zachary	Ed Gutfreund
Morning Canticle	Frank Andersen

Canticle of Mary

Canticle of Mary	Michael Joncas

Canticle of the Turning	STAR OF THE COUNTY DOWN/Rory Cooney
Evening Canticle	Frank Andersen
Great Is The Lord	Paul Inwood
Magnificat	David Haas
My Soul Flies Free	ST. BRENDAN/Steven Warner
My Soul Rejoices	Owen Alstott
My Soul Rejoices	Ault, Balhoff, Caesar, Ducote
Tell Out My Soul	David Haas

In addition to the Canticle of Mary, other sound Marian songs for the Fourth Sunday of Advent and Immaculate Conception include:

Sing A Maid	FLIGHT OF EARLS/M.D. Ridge
O Holy Mary	Owen Alstott
The God Whom Earth and Sea and Sky	EISENACH/Fortunatus

The song at communion may be related to the gospel but should also have a community focus. The proper psalm, if it is appropriate, can be sung during communion. Other examples of songs that can be used throughout Advent at communion are:

Bread of Life (Advent verses)	Bernadette Farrell
Come to Us	David Haas
Jesus, Wine of Peace	David Haas
Now In This Banquet (use Advent Refrain)	Marty Haugen
Taste and See	Bob Hurd (verses from Magnificat)
We Remember	Marty Haugen

The concluding song or Song of Sending Forth should reflect the parish Advent focus for mission; how are we preparing ourselves and our world for the coming of our Savior? Some suggestions are:

Come to Set Us Free	Bernadette Farrell
Lord of Glory	Tim Manion

Prepare the Way	Taizé
Prepare Ye the Way	James Moore
Ready the Way of the Lord	Bob Hurd
Sing Out, Earth and Skies	Marty Haugen
The King Shall Come	MORNING SONG/John Brownlie
Wait For The Lord	Taizé

PASTORAL NOTES

1. *The Gathering Rites*. Advent is a season of vigiling, of quiet reflection and waiting in joyful hope. The gathering rites should support this, setting a mood for quiet thoughtfulness and expression of anticipation. At this time of year especially we long for the light to overcome the darkness. Incorporating lighting the candles of the Advent Wreath into the gathering rites would be very appropriate. The Order for Blessing an Advent Wreath on the First Sunday of Advent is found in chapter 27 of the *Book of Blessings*.

Begin with the ministers gathered at the Advent Wreath. Sing the first verse of the gathering song. Pray the Advent Wreath prayer and light the candle or candles. Resume the song as the ministers go to their places.

If the lighting of Advent Wreath candles is made part of the gathering rites, it is sufficient as the penitential rite to allow several moments of silence for reflection before the opening prayer. Alternatively, use the third form of the penitential rite, the litany of praise for God's mercy in Christ. The second set of invocations, which speak of the three comings of Christ, is most appropriate for Advent.

2. *Silence*. Make good use of silence during this season of expectation, watchfulness, and reflective preparation. The ministers can encourage a bit of silence as a beginning if they gather silently around the Advent Wreath or quietly take their places. Observe sacred silence following the readings and the homily and again after communion.

3. *Eucharistic Prayer*. Use of one eucharistic prayer throughout the season is highly recommended. The text of the second eucharistic prayer for Masses of Reconciliation speaks of Jesus who comes in God's name, is the Word of salvation, and the way leading to peace. It concludes with the image of all humanity gathered around the banquet table of the kingdom.

4. *Preface*. The first preface for Advent, used on the First and Second Sundays, can be modified to include among the comings of Christ not only the Incarnation and the Parousia but also the coming of Christ as present to us now. The text, inserted as the fourth paragraph of the preface, is:

> but even now he comes among us, in every age, indeed, in every person, that we might welcome him in faith and bear witness to love to the blessed hope of his kingdom (from Advent Preface I/A, Italian Sacramentary).

On the third Sunday of Advent and throughout the week until the Eve of Christmas use the second preface of Advent.

5. *Blessing*. Use of one text for the final blessing will also serve to give continuity to the season. Recommended are Solemn Blessing 1: Advent or Prayer Over the People II or 23.

Other Liturgies of Reconciliation.
Though Advent is a season of preparation and joyful anticipation, it has also traditionally been a time for re-ordering priorities and changing the focus of life patterns. Communal celebration of reconciliation according to the second form of the rite should be scheduled once during the season, for example during the second or third weeks following the Sunday gospels of John the Baptizer's call to repentance. Various texts and even sample services are provided in the *Rite of Penance*, chapter 4 and the Appendix, Part II. Times for the first form of the rite, individual confession, should also be scheduled throughout Advent.

Liturgy of the Hours: Evening Prayer (Vespers).
Advent as a season of vigil is an appropriate season to begin celebrating evening prayer in the parish. The little book *Morning and Evening Prayer in the Parish* by Laurence Mayer published by Liturgy Training Publications in 1985 gives the background of communal Christian prayer and pastoral notes for application. *Praise God in Song* is a collection of services with music by Michael Joncas, Howard Hughes, and David Isele edited by John Melloh and William Storey published by G.I.A. in 1979. Newer collections composed for Evening Prayer and offering texts and settings for the liturgical seasons are *God of Light Be Praised* published by World Library Publications, division of J.S. Paluch Company in 1995, and *Pray Without Ceasing* (Liturgical Press, 1996).

Consider celebrating vespers on the memorial of Saint Lucy (13 December). Lucy was a young woman of Syracuse in Sicily who was martyred during the persecutions of the emperor Diocletian because she wanted to make her world a better place especially for the poor and oppressed. Her name means light. She is the patron saint of Sicily. But she is also honored in northern countries where at this time of year the nights are long and cold. Lucy the light-bearer is remembered for bringing light into the darkness.

Begin with the lighting of the candles of the Advent Wreath and tapers held by each participant. Sing *Joyous Light of Heavenly Glory* by Marty Haugen as the Evening Hymn. Use the Advent Thanksgiving for Light from *Praise God in Song*. As the psalm use Psalm 27: *The Lord Is My Light* by David Haas. The reading 1 Corinthians 4:5 may be followed by silent reflection or a brief homily. Then the gospel canticle, the Magnificat, is sung. Frank Andersen's chantform can be found in the collection *Lead, Kindly Light* (1992). Other settings of Mary's Canticle are listed under music for the Fourth Sunday of Advent and Immaculate Conception. The prayers of intercession and the Lord's Prayer follow. As the concluding song use *At Evening* by David Haas.

Paraliturgy and Devotions: Advent
Festival of Lessons and Music. This service, which comes to us from the Anglican tradition, traces through the Hebrew Scriptures our creation, need for redemption, and the promises of a savior. Both the preparation and celebration of this worship service are opportunities for ecumenical cooperation. The service is outlined in the *Book of Occasional Services*. If it takes place in the evening, it begins with the Lucernarium or lighting of candles as in Evening Prayer. Then follows the bidding prayer, which is related to the prayer of the faithful. Nine lessons and Advent psalms, hymns, and

canticles are the central and major component of the service. The service concludes with a collect and the Advent solemn blessing. This outline may be adapted to meet the needs and resources of the parish. The bidding prayer or intercessions may follow the lessons and songs as it would in the Liturgy of the Hours. Fewer of the readings may be used but the reading from the third chapter of Genesis is always included.

The nine readings are chosen from:

Genesis 2:4b-9, 15-25;
Genesis 3:1-22,
Isaiah 40:1-11;
Jeremiah 31:31-34;
Isaiah 64:1-9a;
Isaiah 6:1-11;
Isaiah 35:1-10;
Baruch 4:36-5:9;
Isaiah 7:10-15;
Micah 5:2-4;
Isaiah 11:1-9;
Zephaniah 3:14-18;
Isaiah 65:17-25.

If a gospel reading is desired, it is from Luke 1:15-25 or Luke 1:26-38.

Solemn Celebration of the Rosary. On the Sundays of Advent and especially on Immaculate Conception, those who wish may gather to celebrate the Joyful Mysteries of the rosary. Scripture readings to accompany the mysteries are:

1. Annunciation of the birth of Jesus to Mary by the Angel Gabriel, Luke 1:26-38;

2. Visitation of Mary to her cousin Elizabeth, Luke 1:39-47;

3. Nativity of our Lord and Savior Jesus Christ, Luke 2:1-7;

4. Presentation of the Infant Jesus in the Temple, Luke 2:22-32;

5. Finding of the Child Jesus in the Temple by Mary and Joseph, Luke 2:41-52.

For Marian songs and hymns, see the suggestions for the Fourth Sunday of Advent and for the Immaculate Conception. Add to those *O God Hear Us*, a setting of Mary's Canticle by Bob Hurd.

REFERENCES

Adam, Adolf, 1979. *The Liturgical Year. Its History and Its Meaning After the Reform of the Liturgy*. Chapter 6. Christmas and the Christmas Cycle. Pueblo Publishing Company (The Liturgical Press, Collegeville, MN).

Advent. *National Bulletin on the Liturgy*, vol 29, no 146. Fall, 1996.

Advent IV. *Liturgy: Journal of the Liturgical Conference* vol 13, no 3, 1996.

Bishops' Committee on the Liturgy, National Conference of Catholic Bishops, 1987. *Celebrating the Marian Year*. Publishing Services, United States Catholic Conference, Washington D.C.

Brown, Raymond E. 1988. *A Coming Christ in Advent*. The Liturgical Press, Collegeville, MN.

The Christmas Cycle. 1991. *Liturgy: Journal of The Liturgical Conference* vol 9 no 3.

Days of the Lord: The Liturgical Year. Volume 1: Advent/Christmas/Epiphany, 1991. The Liturgical Press, Collegeville, MN.

Griffin, Eltin, ed., 1986. *Celebrating the Season of Advent*. Fowler Wright Books Limited, Herefordshire, England.

Hynes, Mary Ellen, 1993. *Companion To The Calendar*. The Seasons: Advent pp. 2-6. Liturgy Training Publications, Chicago, IL.

Nocent, Adrian, 1977. *The Liturgical Year*, Volume 1: Advent, Christmas, Epiphany. The Liturgical Press, Collegeville, MN.

O'Gorman, Thomas, J. ed., 1988. *An Advent Sourcebook*. Liturgy Training Publications, Chicago, IL.

Simcoe, Mary Ann, ed., 1983. *Parish Path through Advent and Christmastime*. Liturgy Training Publications, Chicago, IL.

Talley, Thomas, J., 1986. *The Origins of the Liturgical Year*. Part Two: The Day of His Coming, Pueblo Publishing Company,

The Readings of Advent

Russell Hardiman

THE READINGS OF ADVENT

The season of Advent becomes Paul's "acceptable time," when the primary focus of the season is on the consequences of our attitudes to time, the way we consider it, and the way we are conscious of celebrating it. For the purposes of this chapter we shall consider the theology of the liturgical year, with particular emphasis on the relationship of the key periods of Advent, Christmas, and Epiphany. Then we shall illustrate the main goals of Vatican II in the proposal for a cycle of readings over several years and how the major principles are illustrated in the Advent-Christmas readings and how, on an ecumenical level, the major churches share the same readings.

PROCLAIMING THE WORD IN ADVENT-CHRISTMASTIDE

Since the earliest generations, Christians have given witness to the continuing tradition, inherited from their Jewish heritage, and publicly acknowledged by Jesus in the synagogue at Capernaum, when he proclaimed the Isaiah passage as being fulfilled in their hearing even as they listened (cf. Lk 4).

Paul himself encouraged his coworkers in the task of proclaiming the gospel to pay particular attention to the public reading of Scripture: "...devote yourself to the reading of scripture, to preaching and teaching" (1 Tim 4:13).

Vatican II proclaimed that "the primary duty of priests is the proclamation of the Gospel of God to all" (*Ministry and Life of Priests* no. 4). Proclamation covers a range of activities of the church from personal witness, to sacramental witness, to sacramental ministry, to pastoral care, but it is especially a priority in concern for preaching the Word of God. Advent is a prime occasion to preach of the fulfillment of God's plan as people listen to the Word.

In our generation, the U.S. Bishops' Committee on the Liturgy published a major document encouraging the ministry of preaching. They entitled it *Fulfilled in Your Hearing*. Published in 1982, it grew out of a concern for the quality of preaching in the church and, in so far as that concern is still a priority in the church today, it deserves to be better known, and it can still serve as a model for preaching during Advent and Christmastide. This document defines the homily as: "a scriptural interpretation of human existence which enables a community to recognize God's active presence, to respond to that presence in faith through liturgical word and gesture, and beyond the liturgical word and gesture, and beyond the liturgical assembly, through a life lived in conformity with the Gospel" (#29).

This is the vision expressed in the postcommunion prayer of the Roman Midnight Mass for Christmas, when the commitment beyond the assembly itself is phrased, "may we share his life completely by living as he has taught."

Vatican II credited the liturgical year with an almost sacramental title when it stated that "recalling the mysteries of redemption, she opens to the faithful the riches of the Lord's powers and merits, so that these are in some way present for all time" (*Constitution on the Sacred Liturgy*, #102).

The Council Fathers also stated that the liturgical year sets forth "the whole mystery of Christ from the incarnation and nativity to the ascension, to Pentecost, and the expectation of the blessed hope of the coming of the Lord."

It is important that we emphasize in our celebration the whole mystery of Christ, not a pageant or crib tableau, not a passion play, not a historical celebration, much less just an opportunity for a nostalgia trip down the memory lane of childhood.

The focus is on the celebration of the paschal mystery, the total incarnated life of Jesus as human, from womb to tomb, to resurrection and ascension to glory from where he has sent the Holy Spirit upon the church to raise us up with him.

Whenever texts and prayers such as prefaces, eucharistic prayers, orations, and blessings summarize the paschal mystery they always mention the passion, death, resurrection, and ascension of Jesus, almost as if it were a code phrase to summarize his whole life. We avoid anything that does not give the full emphasis in incarnational theology to the mystery of Jesus' total life, and we do not portray Christmas as if it were all about a baby. Paul teaches us in the Midnight Mass reading that the Christ of Christmas is the Christ of Easter, "who sacrificed himself to set us free from all wickedness and to purify his people" (Titus 2:11–14: Midnight Proper 1).

This sense that the Scripture is used to interpret life is the motive behind the actual selections used for both the Advent and Christmastide readings. Beyond the understanding of the context of a particular text and beyond any attempts at an exposition of that text, the reader and homilist must interpret life itself by illuminating what God does in the depth of human existence.

Several readings from Paul in the Advent selections (Advent 1A, Advent 2A, Advent 4A and B) give interpretations of the scriptural method of interpreting human existence to see the hand of God in the events of daily life.

When we read the Scripture we do not read it as a historical text from the past but as the divine revelation for the present age while we look forward to its promised fulfillment. The opening prayer for the Vigil Mass for Christmas expresses this well, even if it is a shame that most people never hear it:

> God our Father, every year we rejoice as we look forward to this feast of our salvation.
> May we welcome Christ as our Redeemer,
> and meet him with confidence when he comes to be
> our judge,
> who lives and reigns...

LITURGICAL YEAR

Arising from the specific Judeo-Christian concept of celebration, the linkage of past, present, and future events are seen as facets of the one continuous presence of God and God's word. Consistent with the Hebrew word *DaBaR*, we celebrate God's presence, an active and ongoing presence of the almighty not just a sequence of isolated events in past history.

This perspective raises questions as to how the liturgical year is different from a calender of feasts. A calender of events would give a perspective of separate, discrete, unconnected events, but the liturgical year is deeper. The liturgical year is the *Year of Grace*, as Pius Parsch's famous five-volume study was entitled. God's presence, God's revelation and salvation are eternal, so that when we read of events in the past, or pray for fulfillment for ourselves now, or when we look forward in expectation to the coming in glory, these three planes are really one. The three dimensions interact and interweave but our consciousness is of the *now*, how God is revealed to us this day.

PAST PRESENT FUTURE

The nuances of the classic Judeo-Christian sense of celebration are well illustrated both in the pattern of prayer in the eucharistic prayers as well as in the flow of themes specifying Christ's coming celebrated in Advent.

The chronological flow is obviously past, present, and future. In Advent, however, the trend is the opposite—starting with remembering the future, in the sense of the focus on the full completion of God's mystery and plan in the Second Coming of the Messiah. There are frequent mentions of the return of the Son of Man in the gospels—and we hear many of them in the lectionary selections at this time, both in the last weeks of Ordinary Time as well as in the Solemnity of Christ the King and the First Sunday of Advent. The opening prayer of the First Sunday of Advent calls us to take Christ's coming seriously, that Christ may find an eager welcome at his coming and call us to his side in the kingdom.

Every Memorial Day, we can see the differences between the secular and the theological understanding of celebration. The secular model focuses on the past to remind the present generation that they too inherit the fruits of the sacrifice of others. The element of future is only vaguely shadowed. In contrast the theological sense of celebration presumes that past, present, and future are all on the same plane in the one plan of God.

VIGILANCE IN WAITING

The Advent season's focus is on a key element of the spirituality of the liturgical year that flows from this theological perspective of the mystery of Christ celebrated in salvation history with its promise of fulfillment and the hope of eternal life. In Advent, the characteristic quality becomes one of vigilance and wakefulness to be ready for the coming of the Son of Man. In his public ministry Jesus is recorded in the gospels as saying frequently that the Son of Man will return. However vague this may be it became prominent in the early Christian community.

In the early church "Come, Lord Jesus" (*Maranatha* in Aramaic) was the community's prayer, so it is no surprise that several Advent readings are from passages in the epistles that are dominated by the theme of the imminent return of Jesus: 1 Thessalonians (Advent 1A and 3B), 2 Peter (Advent 2B), James (Advent 3A), Philippians (Advent 2C and 3C). The epistles are mostly chronologically older than the gospels but the preoccupation with the second coming is also very much a part of the gospels.

The memorial acclamations at the heart of the eucharistic prayer all express the same threefold sense of Christ's coming: past, present, and future. The text of Acclamation I: "Christ has died, Christ is risen, Christ will come again" is formulated differently in Acclamation III by paraphrasing Paul's words in 1 Corinthians: "When we eat this bread and drink this cup, we proclaim your death, Lord Jesus, until you come in glory." This same tension between past, present, and future, which is the characteristic of Christian vigilance, shows through in the missioning rites on the first Sunday of Advent. The post-communion prayer invites us to see that our communion teaches us to love heaven and that the promise and hope of heaven guide our way here on earth. The solemn blessing that day is even more specific in linking the triple dimensions of Christ's coming. It would be a useful reinforcement to use this solemn blessing on all the Advent days not just on the first Sunday.

On the first Sunday of Advent the distinctive theme is set by the gospel reading: the Lord's coming at the end of time. In Year A the words of Jesus are stark. Four times his call to "Stay awake, therefore" (Mt 24:42, 44) is expressed. In Year B we hear Mark's version of the invitation to "Be constant on the watch; be on guard" (Mk 13:33–37). In Year C Luke's message is "Be on your watch, pray constantly" (Lk 21:36).

CONTEMPORARY PREOCCUPATIONS

The lessons of history confirm that "millennialism" is a phenomenon that recurs when the major epochs of measuring time reach the crucial turning points. This was clearly seen as we moved from the second to the third millennium, and it poses for us the continuing challenge to put an authentic Christian interpretation on time and the liturgical celebration of time.

Advent serves as the micro example of the macro issue because the distractions of the secular-commercial style of Christmas make it extremely difficult to celebrate Advent in its true spirit. We shudder at the trends of commercialism bringing Christmas themes into advertising from October onward and swallowing up the Christmas and New Year festive season with the post-Christmas sales campaigns.

John the Baptist was countercultural in his challenge to stand up and be counted in producing the appropriate fruits (Advent 2A). Twice in the Advent season John holds center stage in the call to prepare for Christ's coming: on the Second Sunday the focus is on his preaching and on the Third the focus is on this ministry.

As Jesus looked for fruit that will last, the old joke that "what Jesus looks for is spiritual fruits not religious nuts" calls us to be positive in Christian witness and not merely negative in any carping criticism of the secular trends when trying to emphasize the profound Christian spirit of the Advent season.

There is a difference between preaching *on* the Scriptures and preaching *from* the Scriptures, and this season is a definite challenge to be conscious of relating the Scriptures to the present. The art of the homily is to show the bridge that links the reflection of God's actions in the past to seeing God's presence in the events and happenings of our world.

GENERAL PRINCIPLES OF THE LECTIONARY

As far back as 1963 the Vatican II Constitution on the Liturgy urged a deepening of awareness of the Scriptures:

> The treasures of the Bible...be opened up more lavishly, so that richer fare may be provided for the faithful at the table of God's Word. In this way a more representative portion of Holy Scripture will be read to the people in the course of a prescribed number of years. (*CSL* no. 51)

This single paragraph of Vatican II has had the greatest ecumenical impact over the past thirty years or so to the extent that a generation of Christians has been sharing a common heritage in proclaiming and preaching the Word of God.

The 1969 *Roman Lectionary* (*Ordo Lectionum Missae*: Vatican City, Polyglot Press) was adopted by the Episcopal Church in USA in 1970 and the Presbyterian Church the same year. The Lutherans initially stuck with their one-year lectionary cycle but in 1974 they published a three-year lectionary. The growing acceptance of the *Roman Lectionary*'s principles and format culminated in the production in 1982 of the *Common Lectionary*. Nearly a decade of worship use and continued consultation resulted in the *Revised Common Lectionary* being published in 1992. Raymond Brown called this ecumenical acceptance "Catholicism's greatest gift to Protestantism."

GENERAL THEMES OF ADVENT SCRIPTURE READINGS

Because the gospels dominate in setting the theme or thrust of each set of readings, the "spin" of each Sunday is determined by the gospel. The Introduction in the revised lectionary describes each Sunday as having a distinctive theme (no. 93).

1 Advent: The Lord's coming at the end of time

2 Advent: The preaching of John the Baptist

3 Advent: The ministry of John the Baptist

4 Advent: The events that prepared for the Lord's birth, the Annunciation and Visitation

The Old Testament readings take on a special coloring in Advent. They are prophecies about the promised messiah and the characteristics that would indicate the Messianic Age (ibid. no. 93). They seem freestanding witnesses though they are chosen in a typological relationship with gospel partners to show the continuity of God's promise in the Hebrew and Christian Scriptures. Often the focus is on Jerusalem as the continuing symbol of God's promise. What is proclaimed of Jerusalem is often code for what is God's plan. In the Hebrew Scriptures this was especially true in the image of being led back from exile to rebuild Jerusalem, but in the Christian Scriptures their reflection after the destruction of the city and temple leads to transferring the focus on Zion to a focus on the church. The opening prayer of Advent 3 prays:

> Father of our Lord Jesus Christ,
> ever faithful to your promises
> and ever close to your Church ...

Of the twelve Old Testament Advent readings, seven are from Isaiah, and in Year C other prophets are selected: Jeremiah, Baruch (Malachi), Zephaniah, and Micah. The final selection is from the book of 2 Samuel (Advent 4B) about the promise to David.

The psalm selections, as always, are chosen as a reflection on the intent of the first reading and to encourage the communitarian sense of God's presence with us. About six of the psalms are Songs of Ascent, which were sung going up to Jerusalem for worship at the temple. The choice of psalms is identical in the *Roman Lectionary* and the *Revised Common Lectionary*, with the Magnificat text used as the psalm on five occasions.

The New Testament readings "from an apostle serve as exhortations and as proclamations, in keeping with the different themes of Advent" (no. 93). St. Paul points out in Romans 15:4–9 (Advent 2A) that the Scriptures give examples of hope shown by those who trusted in God: "Everything that was written long ago in the scriptures was meant to teach us something about hope from the examples scripture gives of how people who did not give up hope were helped by God"(Rom 15:4).

Similar passages from Romans are used on four occasions and once from 1 Corinthians, and once from Hebrews. Beyond the reading of Jewish history, Paul also invites us to remember the future, and consequently we have readings that are dominated by the expectation of the imminent return of Jesus: twice from 1 Thessalonians (Advent 1A and 3B) and twice from

Philippians (Advent 2C and 3C). The same eschatological tension is found in the reading from 2 Peter (Advent 2B) and the passage from James (Advent 3A). James' call for patience until the Lord's coming is illustrated by the farmer's patience in waiting for harvest.

Principles of the Two Lectionaries

The principal difference in the two lectionaries is the approach to the Hebrew Scriptures, treating them holistically rather than treating them in a typological sense for a specific gospel passage. This respect for the Hebrew Scriptures is taken to a logical conclusion in the *Revised Common Lectionary* by having continuous readings from the Old Testament in the Sundays of Ordinary Time (after Epiphany and after Pentecost) where the *Roman Lectionary* has continuous readings from epistles of Paul and other epistles.

The remarkable consensus as to selections in the *Roman Lectionary* and the *Revised Common Lectionary* shows how the readings confirm the general principles enunciated by Vatican II (*CSL* no. 51). Where there are differences they reflect the approach to citing the Hebrew Scriptures where *RCL* treats the text more holistically. This usually means that the *RCL* segments are simple excerpts rather than a series of selected verses, which illustrates the practice of reading from the Bible rather than from an edited lectionary.

With selections from the Old Testament the *RCL* provides an alternative reading when the Roman reading is from a Deuterocanonical book, for example Advent 2 Year C when Baruch is given as an alternate from Malachi.

The major feature of the structure of the lectionaries is illustrated by how a particular gospel is assigned to specific cycles. The cycles are read in order beginning with Matthew, followed by Mark, followed by Luke, with John not having a specific cycle but being prominent in Lent and Easter of all cycles. The crunch comes in knowing which cycle is celebrated in which calender year. The generic rule is that any year that is divisible by three uses Year C. Thus, calendar year 2001 is divisible by three and so we read Year C. Then we begin again the sequence with Matthew in Year A 2002 and Mark in 2003.

As always the gospel determines the major thrust of the set of readings with the Old Testament passage chosen to relate to the gospel, and the psalm chosen to extend or deepen the insight of the first reading. The New Testament readings, being reflections of the shared life of the early Christian community, serve as a commentary for the connection of faith and life appropriate for today's community.

The sets of readings for Advent and Christmastide exemplify the principle of the choice of readings for the major seasons or feasts. The principle of thematic reading (*Lectio Selecta*) means that passages are selected from individual books of the Bible to link up with the particular feast, and all three readings, with the psalm, are unified around that feast. On the other hand, the principle of continuous readings (*Lectio Continua*) in Ordinary Time incorporates readings from the gospel of the cycle linked with the Old Testament reading, while the second reading is semicontinuous from the letters of St. Paul, with the result that the readings are not designed with a single focus but are in fact parallel tracks leading toward the mystery of God's presence.

In the key seasons, the Sundays are never displaced for another feast, but it can happen in Ordinary Time. The threefold distinction of feasts (solemnities, feasts, memorials) allows for the Solemnities of Our Lord in the cycle of feasts to displace Sundays of Ordinary Time.

The *RCL* readings, where they are different from the Roman readings, are generally longer and hence more likely to situate a passage in its proper context. In churches where reading from the Bible is the norm, rather than from a printed Lectionary with the edited selections, the longer passages perhaps help to provide a fuller framework for the significant verses. It is imperative that the homilist and the reader look up the context of the passages; otherwise pericopes may be left to stand alone, as Gerard Sloyan says with wit: "like the mule without pride of ancestry or hope of posterity" (*Liturgy 90*, Jan 1991:13).

LIVING ADVENT

Just as we can preach *on* the Scriptures rather the preach *from* the Scriptures, it is possible to preach about Advent rather than to live it. It certainly does help to have a sense of the overarching plan of the season and its specific topics. These include the unified vision of God's plan in salvation history, reflected in the concern for Jerusalem in the past and now focused on the role of the church in the present. The qualities of the Messianic age as outlined by the prophets need to be reinterpreted as the signs of the times in our day so that, like John the Baptizer, we are called to be witnesses to speak for the light. We take heart from John's assurance that the Messiah will come to baptize with the Holy Spirit and with fire.

The Hebrew concern for identity, ancestors, bonding, and heritage shows through in the pattern of genealogies. The purpose of those passages is to relate the connectedness of Jesus to the promise of the Lord. Nowadays the individualism that is so rampant is an obstacle to an acceptable sense of belonging to a group where the benefits accrue to the individual and to the community of which they are part. The Advent-Christmas season is an antidote for the modern malaise. The challenge is to keep the Christmas spirit, and its community focus, alive throughout the year.

The Advent Wreath

Russell Hardiman

Perhaps the introduction of the revised sacramentary, with the *Pastoral Commentary on the General Introduction on the Roman Missal,* may provide a new context and renewed impetus to continue to foster the renewal of attitudes, values, and personal spirituality along with the rites, texts, and structures.

In the early years after Vatican II we saw a plethora of over sixteen-hundred documents legislating the liturgical reform but it is questionable whether the full intent of the reform has been achieved. Just because there has not been, in recent years, a similar flow of new texts or new books does not mean that the renewal has been achieved, or that there is no longer any need for ongoing education for liturgical ministry. Perhaps the strongest illustration of that ongoing need is to point out that the areas where the goals have not been fully achieved are precisely in those areas where the new rites presume an integration of ecclesiology, theology of worship, and a pastoral sensitivity to the faith level of individuals such as occurs in the *Rite of Penance,* the *Rite of the Christian Initiation of Adults,* the *Book of Blessings,* and the *Order of Christian Funerals.*

It used to be said by social commentators that it took twenty-five years for new ideas to be passed on from one generation to the next. If this assertion is true, then we can but hope we are well on the way and then the ideal of Vatican II may be achieved: that the liturgy is the summit toward which the activity of the church is directed and at the same time is the fount from which the power flows (*SC* no. 10). Perhaps the widespread acceptance of the Advent Wreath could illustrate the difference between legislating from the top down and reception from the bottom up.

THE CELEBRATION OF ADVENT

The word "Advent" comes from the Latin *adventus,* which means coming. The coming of Christ at Christmas is the obvious sense of that coming, but it has to be seen in the full understanding of Christ's incarnation, with the emphasis on his life in the Spirit, shared now through his Body, the church, and his promise to come again in the fullness of time. That translates into three senses of Christ's coming: past, present, and future. In our celebration of Advent all three dimensions are woven together.

In Roman times the advent of the emperor, or of a god, was celebrated with particular festivities and customs. The close parallel we may make today could be something like a royal visit, or the appearance of a pop star. The expectation shapes the sense of preparation and intensifies the ordinary activities in anticipation of the future event.

THE ADVENT WREATH TODAY

The Advent Wreath has enjoyed a remarkable resurgence of interest in the last few years. What was once something of esoteric interest to liturgy buffs has now become a common sight in parish churches, schools, religious common rooms or dining rooms, and even family homes. What is a further indication that it has finally arrived is the fact that wreaths now are commercially available off the shelf. We can but hope it does not become one more bauble in the garish display of Christmas decorations. The interesting aspect of this phenomenon is that the Advent Wreath has never been mandated in official liturgical books. In fact, its only formal mention in liturgical books is the Rite of Blessing in the *Book of Blessings.* Yet, its widespread acceptance and use show that it appeals to popular imagination.

The Advent Wreath makes its impact on the level of symbol, for it is a form of symbolic communication.

That is its strength. Symbols have the inherent ability to function on a variety of levels and to trigger off a sequence of messages. This quality is what the experts call "heuristic," the chain reaction of images, messages, memories, and meanings triggered off by the perception of the symbol.

The use of the Advent Wreath has been an interesting story of acceptance by experience. No authority has ever legislated for its use or mandated conditions about how it is to be used. Yet, in spite of this—or maybe, because of it—the actual experience of how the Advent Wreath helps to focus symbolically on the mixture of themes that is Advent has been the best advertisement for promoting its use. Its acceptance is an example of the adage that if something has worked for generations, or centuries, then there must be something of perennial value in it.

Perhaps the impact of the Wreath is tied up with its ability to say different things to different people. Undoubtedly this is because of the different levels of perception of the Christmas story and the way it can make an appeal to the emotions of the people in different ways. We should not be afraid to let the symbols speak.

INTERPRETING SYMBOLS

The modern science of semiotics, or semiology, offers us new insights into explaining our traditions and how they have their effect. We can use a vital distinction from communications systems theory to help classify and integrate many interdisciplinary insights.

We can interpret and explain symbols historically, in the sense of illustrating their origins and historical adaptations down to our age (semantics). We can analyze them in a comparative way, contrasting them and their effects in a cross-cultural pattern of what is similar in various cultures (syntactics). We can reflect on them experientially according to the operative meanings we attribute to them or the actual way we feel about them. from the experience of their impact (pragmatics).

In this article we will trace, at the semantic level, the origins of the Advent Wreath. This will also shed light on what is common in secular Roman feasts, Germanic and Nordic customs, as well as Christian adaptations, all of which are included in the syntactic phase. Finally, in reflecting on the Wreath's impact we analyze the pragmatics of what happens.

ORIGINS OF THE WREATH

Like so many Christian customs, especially Christmas traditions, the Advent Wreath is an adaptation of a pagan custom. However, with St. Paul, we can say now is the acceptable time, now is the time of grace, and consequently seek to maximize the pastoral possibilities of any situation. It is time to baptize some of the secular influences in the Christmas season, to seek to christen the commercial trends associated with the season by uplifting the concern for decorations and so capitalize in a positive way on the emotional pull of the season.

In its pagan origins the wreath is associated with the custom of putting candles around a wheel during the time of the winter solstice (December 21-23 in the northern hemisphere). This custom was a prayer that the sun might come around again. Similar traditions and customs with lights have become part of our Christian tradition, where the symbolic connection with Christ the Light of the World is readily made. In this category is the very observance of Christmas on December 25, the time of pagan Roman festivals at the time of the solstice. The adaptation of a Teutonic custom of placing lights on the top of a pine tree, has successfully been adapted to be the basis of our traditions of Christmas trees and Christmas lights.

The Advent Wreath is usually constructed around a circular base. This circular base is traditionally taken to symbolize the ever-renewing cycle of the seasons, and so the never-ending cycle without beginning and without end stands for the relationship of our place in time and eternity, in much the same way as the wedding band is taken to mean never-ending love.

The four candles stationed equally around the perimeter of the Wreath represent the four Sundays of Advent. The candles are lit in sequence to represent the themes of the different Sundays and to highlight our personal preparation to meet Christ in the various ways he comes to us.

The colors of the candles, and also of any special ribbons that may be attached to them, are usually violet or purple, with one candle being rose. The purple color is associated with the traditional color of a penitential season, symbolizing the spirit of repentance and renewal to which we are called. The rose color is associated with the Third Sunday, which has something of change of focus and spirit, inserting a theme of joy along with the themes of longing and penance. In some circles today among liturgists, there is a body of opinion that encourages the ancient British custom of using a blue shade for Advent, on the grounds that the purple shade is associated with the penitential spirit of Lent, and the spirit of Advent is not identical with that of Lent, so that difference may be expressed visually by a different shade. The call to cast off the old way of life and put on the new is perennial, but it can be reinforced with a variety of images.

The Wreath is usually surrounded or covered with evergreens, traditionally explained as a symbol of the hope of new life or eternal life in Christ represented by the evergreens, branches of pine, spruce, holly, or one of the European varieties still green in midwinter. Another explanation is that the evergreens remind us that God's love for us never changes.

LOCAL ADAPTATION

It seems to me that the use of the evergreens runs the danger of causing the Wreath to be a source of mixed or conflicting messages. When they start to look a bit droopy or bedraggled, especially in warmer climates, one wonders what happens to the message about the never changing quality of God's love.

Some people seek to overcome that problem by using plastic leaves and vines, which safeguards the green appearance. Again, one must question what image is projected then. Perhaps what is needed at this point is experimentation with various local plants or shrubs.

Regardless of whatever floral or leafy verdure is used, the primary analogue of the Advent Wreath is in Jesus himself, who is the light come into the world that we might have life and life in its fullness. Like all good symbols, the Advent Wreath can communicate on a variety of levels and appeal in different ways to the emotions and memories. Whatever use is made of the Wreath, may its use be a constant reminder of the various ways Jesus comes to us and the occasion of putting Christ into Advent so that Christ comes all the more at Christmas.

The Season of Christmas

Russell Hardiman

DESCRIPTION

> Next to the yearly celebration of the Paschal Mystery, the Church holds most sacred the memorial of Christ's birth and early manifestations. [*GNLY* no. 32]

> By means of the yearly cycle the Church celebrates the whole mystery of Christ, from his incarnation until the day of Pentecost and the expectation of his coming again. [*GNLY* no. 17]

These brief quotes are from the document *The General Norms for the Liturgical Year and the Calendar*, first published in Rome in 1969. At the time more publicity was focused on "when the saints go marching out," which was the conclusion many journalists drew when they misinterpreted how the inclusion of certain saints in the universal calender of the church would depend on the historically verifiable facts about life and death. The fact that we have never recovered the lost ground in the place of the veneration of the saints in the life of the church illustrates also how difficult it has been to recover the primacy of the respective seasons in the church year.

DEEPENING CHRISTMAS GOODWILL

We still suffer from the common misconception that Christmas is more important than Easter, perhaps because people can relate more readily to the image of a cuddly baby than to understanding what being raised from the dead may mean. This is important, because in our Christian celebration of Christmas we do not focus so much on the baby as on the adult Jesus, who was born into our world human like us in all things but sin, and has given us the hope of life in its fullness, not merely in the sense of eternal life in the future but in the sense of life to the full, which begins even now. In this sense the Christ of Christmas we celebrate is the Christ of Easter we proclaim with St Paul:

> The grace of God has appeared, offering salvation to all. It trains us to reject godless ways and worldly desires, and to live temperately, justly, and devoutly in this age as we await our blessed hope, the appearing of the glory of the great God and of our Savior Christ Jesus. It was he who sacrificed himself for us, to redeem us from all unrighteousness and to cleanse for himself a people of his own, eager to do what is right. [Titus 2:11–14]

This passage from St. Paul is the reading for the Midnight Mass of Christmas [Proper I in the Revised Common Lectionary]. Amid the many images of darkness and light, which are a recurring image in the Christmas texts, this passage becomes the microcosm of the macrocosm contrast we face in trying to proclaim a positive interpretation of the call "to put Christ back into Christmas." This call is far more profound than simply using Christmas cards with a religious motif, or always writing Christmas out in full instead of abbreviating it to Xmas. The call is to celebrate profoundly the true spirit of Christmas, which need never deprive us from entering fully into the joy and conviviality we all wish to associate with the feast. The key to dispelling any sense of wowserism or being judged to be too secular in the spirit of Christmas is to have the vision or perspective of faith in the readings and prayers of the season, a perspective that guides us to be countercultural in a positive, not carping, way.

This vision is carried through all the year by the use of the prayer of Pope Leo when we mix the drop of water in the chalice with the wine. Originally written for Christmas Day Mass this prayer calls to mind the hope we have to share the divinity of him who humbled himself to share our humanity. Originally this prayer was one of praise of God for both the creation and the restoration of the human race and asking that, as Jesus has shared our weakness so may we share his glory. With another of the early Church Fathers, St. Irenaeus, we acclaim that the glory of God is the human person fully alive, and the full Christmas message is the epitome of that hope.

This incarnational dimension is vitally significant for the world today. Ecological and environmental issues are rapidly growing in the consciousness of people as we face a new millennium under the threat of global warming or nuclear holocaust. However, the balanced appreciation of the interconnectedness of all of God's creation is too important to be the claim of only the fringe "green movement." The Christmas message is one of salvation for our world, human and natural. Christmas brings out the best in everyone's aspirations, touching even the family reunions, the neighborhood get-togethers, and the office parties. The struggle is to carry the goodwill into the new year and beyond, rather than remove it with the decorations.

Because people have their own memories of Christmas family traditions, which help shape their experience, it is difficult to assert the theological primacy of the Easter season over the Christmas season. In fact, both the commercial world and popular tradition give the impression that Christmas is the most important feast. It is not surprising, therefore, that there is such a gulf at the pastoral level of celebrating Christmas.

HISTORY OF CHRISTMAS

It is not totally clear how the delineation of the Christmas cycle came about, with the consequence that in historic eras and in our own day, we have a range of different, if not conflicting, themes being celebrated. There are two schools of thought explaining the vagueness about the origins of Christmas and on which day it was celebrated.

One theory, often associated with the school of comparative religions and with the historical research of Dom Bernard Botte, OSB, predicates the connection of December 25th in the Christian substitution of the Mithraic feast of the Birth of the Unconquered Sun (*Natalis Solis Invicti*).

The pagan feast was associated with the winter solstice and the transformation from the shortest day of the year to the growing length of days. As a Roman custom, following the Julian calendar, this meant several days of festivity culminating on December 25th. As an Egyptian custom, following a different calendar, the culmination of the festivity came to be January 6th. The Christian interpretation of the return of the sun transformed the title *Sol Iustitiae* to now mean Christ as the new Sun of Justice, being proclaimed as the light of the world. Thus the adaptation of pagan solstice feasts concerned a native Roman feast of early times, or an imported Mithraic feast after the first century of the Christian era.

The second theory is based on various computation theories about the date of birth and death of the patriarchs, and is associated with the research of Anton Baumstark, Thomas Talley, Louis Duchesne, and Andre Wilmart. The heart of this theory is the Semitic belief that key figures, such as the patriarchs, were born and died on the same date. This theory interweaves biblical data with computations about the birth of John the Baptist, and of Jesus.

This theory involves John's being conceived in the autumn equinox (September 24th) and born at the summer solstice (June 24th). Since the Lukan account of the visitation journey occurs when Elizabeth is six months pregnant it presumes the conception of Jesus is at the time of the spring equinox. In the presumption of the same date of conception and death it affirms March 25th at the spring equinox as the time of his conception and death at passover. In the lunar-based calendar this puts the equinox on March 25th and therefore the birth on December 25th.

If the death of Jesus is calculated by a solar-based calendar, giving a fixed date for Pascha, this would result in April 6th being the date of death and, logically, the date of birth is brought back to January 6th. This became the major feast of the manifestation in eastern areas of the church, which wrapped the nativity and other facets of Jesus' public manifestations into the one feast. This also illustrates why even today Orthodox Easter is celebrated at a different date from the rest of the Christian world, differing by as little as a few days to almost a whole month according to the calculations of the lunar and solar calendars.

Commentators point out that the likelihood of a

winter date for the Roman census is remote, because of issues of transport, food, accommodation, and especially weather. These factors would seem to indicate that the data of the gospel accounts are not strictly historical in the modern sense of factual, but are more in the way of theological interpretation of the divine and human elements in these significant events.

Actually, the earliest specific reference to December 25th is found in the civil calendar of 354 C.E. This is built on a earlier list, from 336, concerning the anniversary of the deaths of the bishops of Rome and Roman martyrs, when the date December 25th is assigned as the birth of the Christ in Bethlehem, and that is observed as the beginning of the liturgical year.

Regardless of the merits of the respective arguments for these two hypotheses, the trend for centralization, which is associated with the era of Christianity becoming the religion of the empire in the fourth century, facilitated a rapid acceptance of this new feast. The result was that by the end of the fourth century, both throughout the West and in many Eastern Churches, there was now a feast that focused attention on the person of Christ, and not simply the work of the God-man.

The spread of the feast of the Incarnation was intensified by the Christological debates of the fourth and fifth centuries, especially the great ecumenical councils of Nicea (325), Constantinople (381), Ephesus (431), and Chalcedon (451). The feast became the occasion for affirming the full and authentic understanding of incarnation as central to Christian faith.

This original content of the new feast was directed at the manifestation of the God-Man as the Word made Flesh. This manifestation included:

- both his conception and birth;

- his manifestation to the Gentiles (portrayed in the gospel story of the three Magi);

- his manifestation to the disciples (portrayed in the portents and wonders in the scene of the baptism of Jesus); and

- his manifestation in the first "sign" of his power (portrayed in the miracle at Cana of Galilee).

Significantly all these manifestations are celebrated in the feasts of this Christmas season in the 1969 Roman Calendar.

EASTER AND CHRISTMAS PARALLELS

The multiple level of presenting the saving actions of God in Christ born into our world reflects a common connection between the development of the Easter cycle, with its sequence of feasts for the events of the last week of Christ's life, and the development of the Christmas cycle with its multiple feasts.

With the Easter cycle this meant that from the primitive Easter Vigil were developed earlier commemorations of Christ's suffering and death on Good Friday, the institution of the Eucharist on Holy Thursday, and the entrance into Jerusalem, which gave rise to Palm Sunday. In a similar way the celebration of the resurrection of Christ eventually led to the Ascension being celebrated forty days after Easter, and the sending of the Spirit being celebrated fifty days after Easter. With the passage of time the experience of the increasingly independent feasts tended to separate the continual presence of the risen Christ in his body the church into a historicized form of a mini-biography of Christ in the multiple feasts.

This loss of the unified sense of the paschal mystery of Christ tended to be even more severe in the development of the Christmas season. Whatever were the factors in the choice of the day for celebrating Christ's birth, the goal of presenting the saving action of Christ led to the emphasis on the different manifestations referred to above. Likewise, the tendency to separate the different scriptural scenes of the life of Jesus before his public ministry led to a further narrowing of the understanding of the presence of the risen Christ in his Spirit in the church to a focus on the emotional pull of an infant. Elsewhere in this volume is an article on the development of the devotion of the Christmas Crib, which illustrates how St. Francis found an imaginative way of giving ordinary people a sense of "being there." Even today many people have the image of Christmas as being the birthday of the Baby Jesus rather than the celebration of the Messiah born into our world, human like us.

THREE CHRISTMAS MASSES

Apart from the spread of feasts of the Christmas Cycle the major novelty of this cycle is the custom of three

Masses on Christmas Day. The origin of this custom has a quaintness all its own. Originally, in the fourth century, there was only one Mass on Christmas Day, which was celebrated in St. Peter's by the pope with his retinue in the pattern of stational liturgies of the era. After the declaration of the Divine Maternity of Mary, at the Council of Ephesus in 421 C.E., the Basilica dedicated to Mary was built on the Esquline Hill, was eventually given the title of St. Mary Major, and became the venue for another Christmas Mass.

The origin of Mass at midnight *"ad praesepem"* (at the crib) is also associated with the exporting of Jerusalem-based customs to other areas. In the Holy Land, the Christians would gather in the basilica that the Emperor Constantine had built to enclose the cave of Christ's birth. They celebrated Eucharist at night over the cave of Christ's birth in Bethlehem, then processed to Jerusalem and celebrated another Eucharist in the morning. The Roman midnight custom developed into having a papal Mass at St. Mary Major, after which the pope prayed at the replica of the Bethlehem crib built under the church and then retired for a brief night.

The origin of the Dawn Mass actually has little to do with Christmas. In Rome it is celebrated at the Church of St. Anastasia, down near the Tiber, on her feast day, December 25th. When the Byzantine Greeks conquered Rome they made this church their imperial church, so when the pope celebrated with the Greek community out of deference for the Emperor, the custom arose of this early morning Mass so he could be at St. Peter's for the Day Mass.

There were concerted attempts to unify the liturgical practices of the Holy Roman Empire in the ninth century. Under Alcuin's orchestration the translation and export of the Roman liturgical books meant that the papal practice of three Masses at Christmas became the standard in the Latin liturgical books. Subsequently, once private Masses had become the norm, the tradition of three Christmas Masses became normal for all priest celebrants.

LECTIONARY

Even now with the Vatican II lectionary the Christmas Masses are essentially the same as the historical precedents, with the addition of an Old Testament reading. It is significant that the *Revised Common Lectionary* also provides three sets of readings for Christmas, simply referring to them as Proper I, II, and III for all the three cycles but without any attribution of time.

The sequence of feasts continues throughout the twelve days of Christmas, sometimes with a generic set of readings used for all three lectionary cycles (as on Solemnity of Mary and Epiphany), sometimes with specific readings for each cycle (as on Holy Family and Baptism of Jesus). The development of different feasts, different theological images could offer insight into the choice of texts where options are available. The range of texts does not offer a mix and match smorgasbord, choosing bits and pieces from multiple sources. Rather the integrity of the individual sets needs to be respected so that the interplay of key images or themes is expressed as they were originally intended.

Further insights into the individual feasts and detailed commentary and background on their readings, and their use, are offered elsewhere in this volume. Spending time with this article would enable the preacher or reader to be familiar with the thrust of the biblical passages proclaimed as more than "compliments of the season," but the Good News of life to the full.

THE CHRISTMAS SEASON'S PASTORAL POTENTIAL

For many people, their lack of understanding of the liturgical year, with its theological priority given to the Easter Season over the Christmas Season, means that there can be a populist emphasis on Christmas Day alone. Certainly in the secular world and in the media, the emphasis is on the culmination at Christmas Eve and Christmas Day after weeks, even months of preparation. The extension beyond Christmas to Epiphany is swallowed up in post-Christmas sales, or soon lost in the revelry of the New Year festivities or holiday season, be it in summer or winter climates.

The historical framework of the emergence of a feast of Christ's nativity offers us encouragement in seeing how the Christian community has adapted to cultural and political environments. If the Christian presence could impact on previous eras, we can look back in thanksgiving and go forward in faith that the new millennium also will be impacted upon by the Christian hope that is the heart of the Good News.

WORSHIP ENVIRONMENT

The art and environment emphasis in Advent and Christmastide should complement one another. The simplicity of Advent prepares the way for the effusiveness of the Christmas spirit. Even so, the countercultural element of Advent decoration can still be carried over to Christmastide by a due deference for the spirit of the season in a profoundly Christian sense. Further ideas for facilitating this mutual relationship could be explored by reflecting on the articles on the origins of the crib, and on the worship environment in Advent, elsewhere in this volume.

If the parish has a prominent Advent Wreath stand, with a space for a Christ candle, it may remain in the same place as in Advent or be placed near the crib, or tree. You could replace the purple or rose candles with white candles, as well as have a more prominent Christ candle. However, be careful not to confuse this stand and candles with the Paschal Candle, which would presumably be near the baptismal font, outside the Easter Season.

Using indigenous flora and symbols would help incarnate the message of Christmas. Special use of prominent local color, whether of flowers or shrubs or trees, could help overcome the issues in transplanting seasonal flora from another climate and could perhaps engender some local customs or "superstitions" of their own.

The relationship of Advent and Christmastide is shown especially in the timing of the change of seasonal decoration. Resist the temptation, due to the busy character of the season or the preoccupations of the school calendar, to bring Christmas decorations in before Advent is over. In the years when the fourth Sunday of Advent is just prior to December 25th this pressure may be even greater, but it could be overcome by unified planning.

Thought has to be given to the placement and accessibility of the crib for popular devotions and visits. While some commentators discourage its placement in the sanctuary or near the altar, in a very small building—one with little likelihood of a side chapel, or the priority of space to cope with overflow crowds—the crib could well be linked to the pulpit, or even the altar, as a visual expression of how the Word incarnate "pitched his tent among us" and is with us still. A parish policy is appropriate to decide when the Magi make their appearance, preferably not in the quaint fashion of a daily incremental movement coming to arrive at the grotto for the Epiphany feast. Likewise, a decision needs to be made to keep the crib in place (and carols in use) for the whole Christmas season.

A dream, even fantasy, of mine for years as been the use of a reflectorized profile/shadow form of crib scene. This could go on a church porch under spotlights, or on the corner of the fence or wall where vehicle headlights would illuminate it. It could act as a visual reminder to travelers and motorists to help to put true meaning into Christmas.

It is almost a given to presume every place will have its own Christmas tree in a prominent position, whether inside the church or on the grounds, appropriately decorated in lights or crowned with a star. If outdoors, it might be a more powerful witness to the Christian message if it were surmounted by a cross, to challenge people to think of the other dimension of the Christ child. Inside the church, a contrasting relationship between the crib and the tree surrounded by wrapped gifts could be made implicitly by juxtaposition or explicitly with a sign, asking "which is yours?" contrasting a secular and faith view of Christmas. Opportunities for donations to parish charities or ecumenical outreach would be appropriate, if done discreetly.

MUSIC

The very special character of Christmas is both a strength and a weakness. It can develop into the occasion when a special effort is made as regards music with the formation of a special choir for the occasion, or for the setting of new goals for the choir, which may result in the production of a Christmas concert. The choice of music is of crucial importance.

Pastorally, Christmas is the key opportunity because so many people do come to church, and caution is advised lest the fringe people's goodwill be further alienated by any sense of not being able to take part in the singing of carols that they recognize. Familiarity in ritual is important, and it is vital, pastorally, to welcoming their stuttering faith in a way that allows them to feel able to join in joyfully. This is not the time for Christmas concerts by the choir that exclude others. If a children's group has been formed for the music during the Liturgy of the Word, think carefully what message is projected, if the children are then placed behind the "regular choir members" for the remainder of the Mass.

Policies need to be discussed at a parish level by all involved in liturgical planning to set realistic goals for the local community. This would include the times and nature of Christmas Eve Masses, the objectives in mind as to what groups are targeted at particular Mass times, the priority given to choices of carols and music that truly are a common repertoire, the levels or occasions the choir or specialized musicians can contribute, the manner in which carols would be used throughout the season, etc.

Unifying the season could also be accentuated by the use of a seasonal responsorial psalm, which would tie the individual celebrations together, and obviate the problems in small communities of the resources needed for topical psalms at every Mass.

In many communities carols have now become a form of secularized Christmas, more like a concert of individual artists with some group participation, but often without Scripture readings or profound Christmas spirit.

A parish or school may choose to have a special service of carols, close to Christmas Day—the evening of the Fourth Sunday of Advent would be most appropriate—rather than weeks before the 25th of December. The tradition, maintained in Anglican practice, of Nine Lessons and Carols, could be a model of combining the reading of Scripture with well-known carols, even to encourage indigenous carols using local images and features.

Organ preludes and unaccompanied organ can help establish the festive, and solemn, nature of the occasion. A strong organ postlude or trumpet voluntary can appropriately round off the well-planned liturgy and let everyone exit together, rather than allow many to slip away during an extended recessional hymn, and not share Christmas good wishes with others.

EUCHARISTIC PRAYERS AND PREFACES

The proper prefaces for the many separate feasts dictate the daily choice. The prefaces are very strong in their summary of why we give thanks to God through Christ, each with profound insight into the true spirit of the season.

The Christmas prefaces are not specifically attributed to any time frame, but from their concepts preface I could perhaps be applied to Midnight Mass, III to the Dawn Mass, and II to the Day Mass. The prefaces give profound yet brief summaries of why we give thanks on this feast; because the eternal word has brought to the eyes of faith a new and radiant vision of glory (I), we recognize in Christ the revelation of God's glory seen as one like us (II), and a new light has dawned upon the world and humankind has become one again with God (III).

Holy Family does not have its own proper preface, but Christmas II with the phrase "revelation of your love" recognized in the humanity of Christ could be linked with the ideal that human love is the first taste of the love of God experienced by most people.

New Year images are not found in any of the Christmas prefaces, so choosing to maintain the spirit of the octave would be valid in any, or the prefaces of Our Lady, especially P 56 on the Motherhood of Mary, would express the liturgical title of the feast.

Both Epiphany and the Baptism of Jesus have proper prefaces that continue the paschal mystery emphasis of the feasts as sequential manifestations of the divinity of Jesus in his humanity.

The choice of eucharistic prayer should be on the basis of pastoral goals more profound than brevity or speed. A community of mature biblical foundation may be the right venue for a judicious use of Eucharistic Prayer IV with full proclamation of this summary of the history of salvation especially in the manifestations of Jesus in his humanity. In similar places of mature formation in faith the special Communicantes for

Christmas as part of the Eucharistic Prayer I (Roman Canon) would be appropriate.

The Eucharistic acclamations are numerous in their musical settings. To add a Christmas flavor, choosing the Latin *Venite adoremus* from *Adeste Fideles* may be easy for some communities, or sing it in English. Marty Haugen's *We Remember* could be chosen to affirm that we celebrate our redemption in Christ's death rather than in the focus on the infant Jesus only.

PRESIDENTIAL PRAYERS

The Christmas Masses may present problems because of the different time frames celebrated. Ensure that the true Vigil Mass and the evening anticipated Masses are differentiated in all appropriate ways. The text of each prayer is developed according to the primary theme connected to the time of day: the image of light in the darkness for Midnight Mass; the need for us to share the life of Christ who is the light of the world, used at the Dawn Mass; the need to be faithful to the plan of God made real in the birth of Jesus, used at the Mass During the Day. Remember to choose the appropriate time.

The time frames of the three Christmas Masses will determine which opening prayer is used, but it is to be hoped that the relevant time frame is continued in the prayer over the gifts, and prayer after communion as well.

CREED

The rubric about genuflecting at Christmas Masses at the words "and was made flesh" is more honored in the breach than in the observance. The likelihood of its being remembered just this day is remote.

It may help to draw from the Easter Vigil format: instead of reciting the Creed in its full text, project it in a dialogue format and challenge people to put Christ into their Christmas and live out his message.

PEACE CEREMONY

Of all seasons, our peace ceremony in these feasts is more than a casual gesture of greeting. Precisely before being in communion with God in Christ's Body and Blood, we profess that we are in communion with one another as Christ's Body the church. We share the peace of Christ, not merely as the vague compliments of the season, but in the ongoing hope that one day we can make its fullness come true for one another.

BLESSING

The use of the solemn form adds to the specialness of the occasion. It becomes a missioning, or sending forth, that the grace and peace that is Christmas may be with us beyond this day for all our lives.

PASTORAL NOTES

1. The objective of the Christmas Day Mass opening prayer is "that we may bring your life to the waiting world." The spirit of the Christmas goodwill is almost universally shared, if somewhat in a shallow way. It behooves us in our planning to draw on that goodwill and nurture its aspiration, rather than antagonize or alienate it, by the positive emphasis we can bring in interpreting our era and our local issues in the light of Christmas hope.

2. The maintenance of the spirit of the Christmas season for all its twelve days and through the Baptism of Our Lord is a strong, desirable goal. Thought and planning are necessary to unify the season rather than let it become a flat post-Christmas overflow. To this end, concentration on integrated musical choices would dovetail with the specific readings, prefaces, and presidential prayers.

3. In planning special music events, ensure that an inclusive, welcoming spirit is expressed, both in the ecumenical sense of embracing all faiths, as well as in the outreach sense of inviting those who would not go to formal churches but wish to acknowledge Christmas especially for their children.

4. The suggestion to use a dialogic form of profession of faith as the way of saying the Creed could be extended to the whole season. By astute wording at the introduction, each of the successive forms of the manifestations of Christ's divinity, which are celebrated in the individual feasts, could be amplified to acclaim the

Father of salvation, the Son of our hope, and the Spirit of our empowerment, in making connections between our faith and its relevance to contemporary life and issues.

5. Because of the conflict with the populist sense of January 1 as New Year's Day, some attention is needed to include positively the issue of New Year's resolutions. Let the homilist encourage people to be reflective, to be realistic, rather than provoke another wave of depressive failure. Let intercessions pick up St. Augustine's thought that if each year we dealt with one fault then we would soon be perfect.

Pope Paul VI began the tradition that New Year's Day be observed as the World Day of Peace. His appeal to the leaders of the world is now being acted upon in some ways. Look for the current pope's statement for this day; search the press or news services for items that could be referred to in homilies or bulletins to spread the notion further.

6. The feast of the Baptism of the Lord is more profound than a facile switch to announcing parish baptism practices or moralizing about baptism and original sin. As the final sequence of the human, public manifestations of Jesus' divinity it concludes the Advent-Christmas season and invites parallels with the ninety days of the Lent-Triduum-Easter seasons soon to start again, when all the church is called to live its baptismal commitment in Christ's Spirit.

7. The crib is undoubtedly one of the most popular aspects of Christmas traditions. From great cathedrals to country chapels, from stately homes to simple cottages, one common link is the presence of some form of crib.

St. Francis of Assisi is attributed with instigating the custom of the crib, and perhaps its popularity universally is an indication of the appeal to human sentiment so deeply appreciated by the saint known as "il Poverello." In his tiny room in the monastery at Greccio, perched on a vertical cliff face, St. Francis painted a scene of Bethlehem in 1223.

The practice was spread by the Franciscans, with their strong connections with the Holy Land and their propagation of devotions redolent of the pilgrimage to the Holy Places, such as the Stations of the Cross. Other religious orders helped to spread the custom after the fourteenth century. In the baroque era, the crib setting became an intricate scenic landscape with the introduction of numerous secular figures. Anyone who has done a "crib crawl" through the churches of Rome will recall the marvels of design and detail, with wells pumping real water, and hundreds of figures, even down to hens and chicks.

In some countries crib making developed into a major folk art, especially in wood carvings in places such as Portugal, the Tyrol area, southern Italy, and Sicily. The custom of having a home crib became popular after the seventeenth century and has lasted to our day as a form of folk religion and homely piety.

At school many children are encouraged to make their own crib figures and then take them home. There are now available many commercial forms of crib, from paltry plastic models to quite elaborate settings with individual carvings.

As a way of helping us realize the true spirit of Christmas, the custom of the crib is to be encouraged as one way of showing our God is Emmanuel—God with us.

REFERENCES

Sacred Congregation of Rites (1984) *Norms governing liturgical calendars.* (Liturgy Documentary Series 6) Washington: United States Catholic Conference.

(1985) *The Liturgical Year: Celebrating the Mystery of Christ and his Saints.* Washington: United States Catholic Conference.

Irwin, Kevin W. (1986) *Advent Christmas: A Guide to the Eucharist and Hours.* (The liturgical seasons) New York: Pueblo Publishing Company.

Sourcebook for Sundays and Seasons: An Almanac of Parish Liturgy. Chicago: Liturgy Training Publications (various authors, various years).

The Readings of Christmas

Russell Hardiman

To understand the structure of the Christmas season is to have an insight into the theological sense of our celebration. The four weeks of Advent emphasize the coming of Christ at all levels—his historical coming at his birth, the sense of his presence now among us through his Spirit, and the future coming in the fullness of time.

The celebration of his human birth was not a key concern in the early centuries, when they were more preoccupied with the prospects of his return, which was believed to be imminent and the call was to be ready always. Once the realization sank in that his return was delayed—and is still to be determined—the celebration of his birth developed primarily as one of the phases in the major manifestation of his incarnation into and presence in our world.

These manifestations were gradually interwoven from a variety of liturgical traditions or adaptations of contextual feasts of the contemporary pagan world. The upshot was that the season of Christmas, after the celebration of his nativity, was to include his manifestation to the Gentiles, symbolized in the Magi, his manifestation to the world in the theophany of his baptism, and his manifestation in his first miracle at Cana.

The sets of readings assigned to this season are not a totally new composition in the 1969/1981 editions of the *Roman Lectionary*. They are frequently adaptations of the historical texts gleaned from the extant liturgical books of earlier centuries. These adaptations have further light shed on their use, their interpretation, and their spirit by the prayers that accompanied them, including the presidential prayers, especially the collect or opening prayer—which expressed the significance of that day's gathering—as well as the prefaces or memento insertions into the eucharistic prayer.

The Old Testament readings of Christmas and Christmastide are dominated by the Book of Isaiah. Every major feast has an Isaiah passage (eight readings) while the "newer" texts for Holy Family, Solemnity of Mary and the Sunday after New Year have readings from Sirach (twice), Numbers (once), Genesis (once) and 1 Samuel (once).

The second readings are almost all from the Pauline corpus, especially the pastoral epistles: Titus (three times), Ephesians (twice), Colossians (once), Hebrews (twice), and Galatians (twice). There are also two readings from Acts and two from 1 John.

The gospel acclamations, naturally, are mostly from the gospels of the day or related texts, but also are frequently from the second reading. The unusual element is that twice texts are used from nonscriptural resources, even though their origins are not attributed.

The gospels are naturally mainly from those gospels that have major nativity narratives. Luke's stories and details are used six times, with Matthew's propensity to fulfill the prophecies of the Hebrew Scriptures providing four texts. John's prologue is used twice. Mark is used only for the B Cycle on the Baptism of the Lord, as are the specific Matthew or Lukan texts in cycles A and C respectively.

The familiarity of many of the infancy narrative stories may well be a counterweight to the impact of those readings, so much deliberation is need to ensure that their proclamation can have the greatest impact. The familiarity of the story's character, the dialogue, and the outcomes may actually be a help because not so much exegesis or contextualization may be needed as with the other texts. The opportunity presents itself to work at the objective of moving the text from the past to the present, truly to proclaim to the listeners how this Good News touches us in our contemporary world and gives us the message of goodwill for our day.

DECEMBER 24 VIGIL MASS

It is a shame that the texts of the actual Christmas Vigil are rarely used because of the tendency to use any Masses on the Christmas Eve as occasions for a passion-play type pageant of the nativity story, complete with amended gospel passages, or simply to use the readings of the Midnight Mass. It is a shame that the true spirit of Christian vigils or waiting can be overlooked in the preoccupation with getting to Mass for Christmas, regardless of the time, or of the community that celebrates it.

To celebrate a completion or conclusion of the Advent season of expectation with its own texts and special character would be a step in the direction of encouraging the true Christmas spirit, as the prayer over the gifts says:

> Lord as we keep tonight the vigil of Christmas,
> may we celebrate this Eucharist with greater joy than ever
> since it marks the beginning of our redemption.

Old Testament Reading (Isaiah 62:1–5)

The Old Testament reading becomes an opportunity for reflection on the history of the Chosen People and how God has always shown faithfulness to the covenant. The original historical context of the passage is at the time of the return from the exile (539 B.C.E.) when the pagan King Eyras becomes the instrument in the fulfillment of the dreams of the people to return to their homeland. In fact, they returned to a place of desolation, to find the Temple in ruins, and hostility from the surrounding peoples (not unlike the return of the Jewish people to the modern state of Israel a half century ago).

In the years before and after the return from exile a feature of Jewish intercessory prayer was to praise and thank God for the Covenant of Promise and subtly to remind God that the criterion of promise was in the status of Zion or Jerusalem as synonyms for the Temple. This pattern of *Berakah*, *Todah*, or *Birkat-ha-mazon* prayers in the developing Jewish patterns of prayer is highlighted elsewhere in the volume (cf. article on the eucharistic prayer). The significant aspect is how in Christian tradition the intercession for Jerusalem was transformed into prayer for the church, that it may become witness to the culmination of the history of salvation in the birth, death, and resurrection of Christ, Jesus of Nazareth.

This passage becomes richer and richer in the way traditional images are used to portray God's relationship with the people. The images of "My Delight," "The Wedded," the analogy with marriage all resonate with other Hebrew texts like Hosea and parts of Isaiah (chs 54 and 61), and with the scene of Christ's baptism and transfiguration, with my "Beloved" son being revealed, and are redolent of the metaphor of the church now being portrayed as the Bride of Christ. These resonances in the scriptural tradition are climaxed in the words "You will be called by a new name, one which the mouth of the Lord will confer." This heritage of the significance of names and how God's action with key people is the message of hope for the people is taken even further in the gospel reading of the genealogy of Jesus, where Matthew, writing for people of Jewish background, portrays the birth of Jesus as fulfilling the promise of the covenant.

The Responsorial Psalm, Psalm 89

This psalm takes the theme of the reading further by reflecting on the intimate relationship implied in the covenant promise. The chosen verses pick up on the promise to David to establish a dynasty forever, setting up a throne through the ages. This future king will say "You are my father, my God, the rock who saves me…. and for him my covenant shall endure." In the Christmas context of celebrating Christ's birth the words of response lead us beyond the day itself to the grateful vision for all of life. "I will sing forever of your love, O Lord." This is the way Christians can "find their joy every day in your name" (v. 17).

New Testament Reading, Acts 13:16–17, 22–25

The New Testament reading is the same line of Jewish heritage and how salvation history is interpreted. At the synagogue at Antioch in Pisidia (not the Syrian one) Paul appeals to those members of God's people who acknowledge that the God of Israel chose their ancestors in the past. He highlights the era in Egypt, and the Exodus from there to the Promised Land, the era of David the King, "a man after my own heart." Paul claims Jesus as the fulfillment of God's promise, heralded by John the Baptist, who recognized there was someone greater than he yet to come. It is a style of interpretation similar to how Matthew interprets the genealogy of Jesus.

Gospel Acclamation

The gospel acclamation is unusual inasmuch as it is one of a handful of occasions when a non-biblical text is chosen. No reference is given to its origin. Even so, its character is strongly that of a vigil, where its opening word is "tomorrow." It is directed to the feast itself, just as two of the three Christmas Mass acclamations include the word "today."

This focus on the time frame needs to be seen in its proper light. It is time as *"Kairos,"* the graced time, rather than time as *"Chronos,"* the sequence of days. In the celebration theme of liturgy or proclamation of God's word, the linkage of past-present-future is always as one plane of God's action and presence. Our human time frame may have ways of marking time as twenty-four-hour days, but the focus is on the eternal presence of God's action, rather than a day-by-day diary.

Gospel, Matthew 1:1–25 or 18–25

The genealogy of Jesus from Matthew is also used on the feast of the nativity of Mary (September 8). Genealogies in the Bible are a special literary genre, with an interpretive meaning rather than a scientific historic one, in the modern sense of historical fact. Perhaps this interpretative view can be inferred in the Vigil reading, which includes verses 16 and 17, including the conveniently rounded out formulae of fourteen generations in each of three eras into which the saga is divided. The three generations can be epitomized in the titles "Son of Abraham," "Son of David," and "Christ," as paraphrases for the divine election that guided the story of God's people.

The key point is in the culmination of a sequence of the names in the bestowal of the child's name with its unique meaning: Jesus, the one who will save the people from their sins.

The context of the dream of Joseph, the husband of Mary, is resonant of other biblical figures for whom dreams are often the occasion of God's self-revelation and the announcement of a special mission. Matthew's concern is to connect the miraculous origin of Jesus, conceived by the Holy Spirit and born of Mary, with the status of Joseph as Mary's husband, through whom the connections of the genealogy are valid because Joseph takes Mary to his home to be his wife and Mary's son bears the name revealed by God's angel.

All of the readings unite in testimony, not so much as to the origins of Jesus, but to the good news of Jesus as the Christ of God, foretold and promised, now revealed and present in our world. By the way we become the living gospel of Good News, then, the glory of God is continuously being revealed so that all the world sees the saving power of God.

CHRISTMAS MIDNIGHT MASS

Midnight Mass at Christmas is the favorite experience of many people. Some lament the fact that, frequently nowadays, the evening Mass or Masses are brought forward by several hours and yet there is no true Midnight Mass. Actually, the official Latin title of this Mass would be more accurately translated as "Mass during the night," so decisions about early evening Masses may be made with this motivation in mind. More likely, however, it is because of the huge numbers of families with children who like the thought of an evening Mass (not evening understood as a vigil) so the morning family festivities can go through unimpeded by the constraints of including Mass as well.

The jokes abound about people calling the rectory to ask what time the Midnight Mass is, but perhaps there is a lesson here too. If the convenience aspect of getting Mass in on Christmas Eve goes on unabatedly, it is possible that we could finish up with something like the medieval distortion that was to last over a millennium whereby the Easter Vigil was celebrated on Saturday morning, losing all its connection with the images of contrasting light and darkness. The successful restoration of the Easter ceremonies to be a true vigil—in many places truly going through until dawn—offers us insight into how powerful is the experience of the awesome rites in the drama of night and day. Maybe we will have future generations clamoring for a return to the "real atmosphere" of Christmas, a night Mass truly at midnight.

This analogy with the Easter Vigil is not totally out of place here, for it does remind us of the basic Christian attitude for celebrating Christmas. Even in commemorating the birth of Jesus the goal of Christian celebration is to welcome Christmas with an Easter faith. We need to counterbalance the tendency of evening Masses to become birthday celebrations for the Baby Jesus, complete with cake and candles (how many? three? one for each millennium, or one for each of the Trinity?).

Our opening prayer of the Midnight Mass reminds us that "We welcome him as Lord." "By our communion with God made man, may we become more like him who joins our lives to yours," as the prayer over the gifts says. Like every Sunday, Christmas too is a mini-Easter mixed in.

First Reading, Isaiah 9:1–7

This passage may be more familiar to some from its place and melody in Handel's oratorio *The Messiah*.

Its tenor from the early chapters of Isaiah is of reassurance to the people in exile that the deported people will one day be transported back. The "Day of Yahweh" is portrayed in contrasting terms of light and darkness, a contrast appropriate for the context of its proclamation. The images of overcoming oppression and transforming the effects of the conquered status are further illuminated by a sequence of titles that come from coronation texts of the Egyptian pharaohs—but the child born for us will have qualities superior to all these images from the world of Isaiah's listeners. As Christian liturgy applies these titles to Christ we affirm his place as the savior of the world, the true light in the darkness.

Responsorial Psalm, Psalm 95

Once again the response of the psalm, with its use of the phrase from the Lukan message of the angels to the shepherds, gives an insight into its usage and function with the word "today." Naturally, the time element zeros in on the birth of our savior, but it is the savior Christ the Lord, not merely the cuddly baby with all the emotional pull the crib scene evokes. This links up with the phrase of the opening prayer, "we welcome him as Lord."

Second Reading, Titus 2:11–14

This reading for the Midnight Mass is not quite as replete with the Easter-vision of the other Pauline speeches or passages of the other Mass texts. It is more a statement of the Christian base for the moral life inherent in or demanded of the acceptance that God's grace had been revealed and made salvation possible for the whole human race. Even so, it is consistent with the other Pauline passages in its message that our vision in faith hinges more on the understanding of our relationship in grace to the adult Christ as savior, rather than on an imaginative clinging to the infant Jesus.

Paul's affirmation is a clear statement of the divinity of Christ: "our great God and Savior Jesus Christ" (v. 13). The Christmas connection is in the fact that he offered himself to ransom us from our sins and to purify a people. This connection with being a people in Christ's name and for God's purposes leads us to the individual responsibility for the pattern of Christian life we are called to live in this present life, while awaiting the future fulfillment. The Christmas vision surely flows into the new year and, indeed into all life.

Gospel Acclamation, Luke 2:10–11

The gospel acclamation is a direct preview of the coming gospel scene. It is the heart of the angel's message to the shepherds and to our world. *Today* is the focus, not for the time frame directly of December 25th, but from our Christian way of celebrating the past in the present while awaiting the future.

Gospel, Luke 2:1–14 or 2:15–20

Luke shows his attention to detail as he includes precise, factual details about the context of the Roman occupation of Palestine during which the events of Christmas took place. In this way he shows himself faithful to his stated purpose at the beginning of his two books, that he had carefully traced the sequence of events from the beginning so that Theophilus and his readers could see how reliable was the instruction they received (Luke 1:3–4).

One danger in the familiarity of the Christmas story is that people may easily switch off, thinking they know it already. However, just as children may never tire of their favorite bedtime stories and may even insist that nothing be changed, the familiarity can be a level of savoring the flavor of this key story—the authentic good news combining glory to God and peace to God's people on earth.

The Isaian reading used several titles associated originally with the Egyptian pharaohs. Now in the angelic proclamation of Good News, a title is bestowed: savior. Luke uses this title of Jesus fourteen times in his gospel and forty times in Acts. To highlight Jesus as savior "today," at Christmas, is to remind ourselves that, while we know the story of the divine salvation as it occurred in the past, that salvation is ours to share now and in its fullness forever.

CHRISTMAS DAWN MASS

Ever since the restoration of the restored Easter Vigil in 1951, the principle that the texts and symbols change with the time of day of the celebration has been clear. This is true of the Easter Vigil in the night, not in the day, in Morning and Evening Prayer, in Sunday or holy day vigils.

For the sequence of Christmas Masses, the priority is not merely the "rightness" of celebrating three Masses, or the convenience of "saying" the three Masses back to back in succession, but adverting to the times of community celebration and using the texts historically associated with the time of celebration.

In the era of convenient electric lighting, very few people—or even very few religious or monastic orders—rise and direct their total activity by the sunlight available. Some groups in isolated rural areas may still be directed largely by the movement of the earth around the sun, but for the majority, convenience overcomes the natural obstacles.

All this means the interplay of light and darkness, which are major thematic elements of the Midnight and Dawn Masses, may well be obscured by the choices made. The opening prayer of the Dawn Mass sets the tone of the double sense of light coming into the world:

> Father, we are filled with the light
> by the coming of your Word among us.
> May the light of faith
> shine in our words and actions.
> ...open our hearts to receive his life
> and increase our vision with the rising dawn,
> that our lives may be filled with the glory and his peace....

First Reading, Isaiah 62:11–12

The Isaian reading continues the context and theme of the Vigil passage, for it is from further along in the same chapter. Again, the context is the return from exile and how God's faithfulness to the covenant is epitomized in God's care for Zion/Jerusalem. This passage is part of a poem used as a conclusion of these chapters in Isaiah and also chanted subsequently on the pilgrimages up to Jerusalem.

What Yahweh proclaims to the ends of the earth, to its remotest parts, is the essence of Christmas celebrations: your savior comes. Once again the focus of the present tense is a continuous present. Our faith in our savior is not founded merely on the nativity story of this Christmas but on the presence of God in all of history, with its message of hope for all times and all places. The message to be proclaimed by the Lord "to the daughter of Zion" is a message to the new people of God. The message is from the Lord Yahweh as the source and origin of God's creative power and redemptive action, now visible in the birth of Jesus the Christ.

The practice of new titles or names being assigned continues in this passage, with a difference now. In the Vigil Mass section the titles are assigned to the child born for us, the son given to us. In this Dawn Mass pericope the new titles are assigned to the Chosen People, who are now to be the "The Holy People," "The Lord's Redeemed," "The Sought-After," "City-not-forsaken." The relationship of God and God's people is one of encouragement, support, and affirmation, but we still have our responsibilities.

Responsorial Psalm, Psalm 96/97

The responsorial psalm is a paean of praise for the triumph of the Lord Yahweh. The image of light dawning is prominent both in the response itself and in verses 11–12. "Light shines forth for the just and joy for the upright of heart." These words are the illumination of our vision in faith, the spotlight of Christmas focus to challenge us in our gifts to the Giver of the greatest gift, the Savior. Truly we can make our own the refrain used over centuries. "A light will shine on us this day: the Lord is born for us."

Second Reading, Titus 3:4–7

As at Midnight Mass the letter to Titus provides the basis for our responsibility to live out our lives in light of God's gift to us. Paul emphasizes that the revelation of our Savior was not based on any righteous actions we ourselves have done, but solely on God's own compassion.

The practice of initiation of new Christians into the family of faith, celebrated in a Christmas (and Epiphany) Vigil as well as Easter Vigil, may be the connection that explains the origins of such a specifically baptismal passage for this Mass. We have been saved "by means of the cleansing water of rebirth and by renewing us with the Holy Spirit which has so generously poured over us through Jesus Christ our savior." Whatever may be the truth of the Christmas baptismal practices, at the very least this text underscores yet again the paschal character that unifies our Easter-Christmas vision, to celebrate the savior who pours out his risen Spirit on us as we memorialize his birth into a human family that gives hope to all human families as they see eternal light dawn for their children (baptism rite). The dawning should grow within us all throughout life.

Gospel Acclamation, Luke 2:14

The gospel acclamation continues the link from the Midnight Mass to the Dawn Mass by a reprise of that gospel, with its message revealed by the angels. It is the only text of the four Christmas gospel acclamations that does not have a specific time reference in it, but the glory to God and the peace to his people on earth are the perennial fruits of Christian worship.

Gospel, Luke 2:15–20 or 1–7, 8–20

The connection between the Midnight and Dawn Masses is strongly emphasized in the way the two logical gospel passages are directly following one another. The witness to the birth of Christ has been proclaimed first to the shepherds by the heavenly angels. Now the shepherds become the first of all those who follow Christ.

The simple shepherds become the first evangelists, the ones who did not doubt the revelation of the savior wrapped in swaddling clothes, for there was nothing unusual about that, but perhaps they were encouraged by his "being" in a manger, for such a pastoral scenario made them feel quite at home. They showed their alacrity, as they hurried away, in much the same style as Mary herself had gone with great haste to visit Elizabeth.

Luke carefully manages his witnesses by pointing out that all who heard of these events were astonished at what the shepherds had to say. Like the woman at the well, like the disciples after the resurrection, like the observers of the Christians in Antioch, other people become engaged, interested, and active when ordinary people evangelize their ilk.

CHRISTMAS DAY MASS

Old Testament Reading, Isaiah 52:7–10

The Old Testament reading is again from the prophet Isaiah, another lyrical poem of enthusiasm in the promise that the Lord Yahweh will restore Jerusalem. In the time of the exile this was the background to the pattern of prayer, whereby thanksgiving and praise of God led to intercession that the promise of God would be reflected in the special care for Jerusalem.

Salvation comes with the announcement of "Your God Reigns," of "Your God is King." This common acclamation of God in the psalms is also our Christmas greeting and thanksgiving. As we again proclaim the profound sense of the Christmas message, we bring to the world the news that leads to the claim "how beautiful upon the mountains are the feet of the messenger." Our world needs the true Christmas message of how the Messiah is being born into our world.

Responsorial Psalm, Psalm 98

This psalm is part of the sequence of Psalms 96, 97, and 98 being used for the Christmas Masses. Their similarity is in the invitation to sing to the Lord for the fidelity to the covenant. Now indeed "all the ends of the earth have seen the saving power of God" (response, v. 3a) and we share in that joy and enthusiasm. Christmas is a message of unity and goodwill to all the nations of the world, but we share the responsibility as Christians to live its true spirit.

Second Reading, Hebrews 1:1–6

This reading is the opening passage to Hebrews, the source of the gospel acclamation for Holy Family and the Solemnity of Mary. Its use several times shows that its key message is that God spoke to the people in various ways through the prophets, but now God has spoken through his Son. Jesus is seen as the fulfillment of creation and the fullest form of revelation. As the perfect copy of God's nature (v. 3) the message is encouragement to all that being fully human is the path to becoming sharers in Christ's divine life.

Gospel Acclamation

This gospel acclamation is one of the unusual times, like the Vigil, when the phrase is not a specific biblical text. Still, it is appropriate for the Christmas context because it affirms that today a great light descends upon us. This image of light and illumination refer directly to the language and imagery of the Johannine prologue to follow.

Gospel, John 1:1–18 or 1:1–5, 9–14

This gospel is the theological reflection of John, so different from the factual details of the infancy narratives in Matthew and Luke. While some people find this passage abstract, this conclusion perhaps reflects the lack of scriptural culture to interpret the many biblical references that portray the birth of Jesus as the fullness of God's creation, redemption, and salvation. To pitch his tent among us is the expression of intimacy implied in the phrase "he dwelt among us," sharing life in all its daily dimensions.

FEAST OF THE HOLY FAMILY

The Sunday between Christmas and New Year was designated the Feast of the Holy Family in the Vatican II mandated reform of the liturgical year, eventually published in 1969.

In itself the feast has a certain natural affinity with the Christmas season, but it is possible that its celebration can descend to the maudlin sentimentality about the pious example of the Holy Family as the epitome of the idealized slogan "the family that prays together stays together." This feast has only existed for roughly a century, first being optional and used as a votive Mass. It was assigned as a feast for the universal church only in 1921, which confirms the Feast of Christ the King as the only feast in the calendar more recent.

A further tension about this feast is the difference between the reading laid down in the 1969 *Roman Lectionary* compared to the *Revised Roman Lectionary* of 1981. The revision was more an expansion of the Instruction, the general introduction with its rationale, theology, and principles, rather than substantial variation of its content. The 1969 texts underwent significant change for the Feasts of the Holy Family and the Baptism of the Lord, both in this season, and for the Ascension and Pentecost.

The earlier texts originally gave common Old Testament reading, psalm, New Testament reading, and gospel acclamation, which were used for all three years of the cycle, and specific gospel texts for Years A, B, C which came from Matthew 2, and Luke 2. The 1981 lectionary offered full sets of texts for each cycle of the three-year lectionary. Where the difficulty now arises is that the new rubrics offer the 1969 texts as alternatives that could be chosen over the 1981 specific cycle texts, provided that the appropriate gospel passage was used. It is a pity there is no provision made for a cut-off point, presumably allowing for new books to be printed with all texts in their specific sequence, so that beyond the cut-off point the 1969 texts would be treated as Cycle A and the alternatives would definitely apply in Cycles B and C. The problem now is that the options available obscure the principles of whose competency it is to make the choices necessary, and how these choices can be communicated to the assembly and the respective ministers who use them.

The context of the Vatican II feast day incorporated into the Christmas octave underlies how this feast draws its key significance from our celebration of the incarnation. The focus is on Christ's sharing our humanity in order that we might share his divinity, as the prayer expresses the concept each time water is placed in the wine. That prayer was originally written for Christmas by Pope Leo the Great, and offers us insight into our sense of celebrating the incarnation. Though the gospels give us incidents in the infancy narratives, or the Lukan passages about the childhood of Jesus, the fact is that, beyond these texts, the gospels offer very little detail about the "hidden life" of Jesus before his public ministry. It is a subtle way of reinforcing that it is the adult Christ who is our savior.

The feast is not primarily to be the occasion for reminiscences about family life, even in the context of the season when the focus on family is at its most positive.

It is not even about the childhood of Jesus and what joy he may have been for his parents, though Luke's two passages do not assert that was always so. The emphasis is on the peace and harmony that are the fruit of listening to the Word of God, and putting it into practice, the quality of Mary most praised by Jesus.

The opening prayer was specially written for this feast:

> Father, help us to live as the holy family,
> united in respect and love.
> Bring us to the joy and peace of your eternal home
> by recalling the quality of life we should all live.

As baptized members of God's family in Christ's Spirit we can perhaps minimize the alienation some fellow family members in the church may feel when the emphasis on family life—in an unreal, idealized way—may create the impression that there is no welcome for single mothers, separated or divorced parents, blended families, or single people of any description.

YEAR A

First Reading, Sirach 3:2–6, 12–14

The Book of Sirach or Ecclesiasticus is not used very often in the lectionary. The text for today, which can be used in other years as well, is a commentary on the Fourth Commandment—Honor your father and your mother. The first section consists of a series of parallelisms, the Semitic practice of saying the same thing twice over, in this context affirming one quality of fathers, then a similar quality affirmed of mothers. The second section is about the reverse cycle of parenting, when the elderly parents may be dependent on their children. These prescriptions about the attitudes toward aging parents can be very challenging in the contemporary world, when the culture of youth or ageism means that disability in elderly parents is seen as an inconvenience or problem.

Responsorial Psalm, Psalm 128

The responsorial psalm is one of the selections offered in the Rite of Marriage where the image of the wife as being a "fruitful vine" and of children as being like "shoots of the olive" may be the idealized form of family life. The response offers the key insight, in the full meaning of "fear of the Lord" as a positive relationship with the Creator and the motivation and source of empowerment to "walk in his ways."

New Testament Reading, Colossians 3:12–21

This reading is Paul's full challenge to live out our baptism. Baptism makes us members of the family of God's chosen race and his saints, and at all levels of relationships within that family we have responsibilities of mutual acceptance, forgiveness, fraternal support, and gratitude to God and one another. The final verses are not for point scoring about single responsibilities but for mutual recognition of need and leadership in appropriate ways.

Gospel Acclamation, Colossians 3:15–16

The gospel acclamation is taken from the above passage from Colossians. Normally this acclamation refers forward to the gospel but this passage is the basis of the family of faith; whereby we are called to be one body in Christ and the Word of God is our motivation to live it out.

Gospel, Matthew 2:13–15, 19–23

The Year A gospel is naturally from Matthew, whose infancy narrative gives us the source of many rare things we are told about the infant, or child, Jesus. Writing for a community with many people of Jewish background, Matthew continues his pattern of revealing the parallels between the actions of God in the time of the Hebrew Scriptures and now in Christ's time.

The Joseph scenario in Exodus is a parallel for the scenario of the dream of Joseph the husband of Mary; the death of Herod as a parallel to the death of pharaoh, and the occasion to return to his own land. Matthew deftly shows that it is not a mere detail that Jesus should live in Nazareth, for the only other time in his gospel that Jesus is connected with Nazareth is when Peter denies he knows Jesus of Nazareth. In this subtle way the story of the holy family of Nazareth takes on Paschal overtones of the sacrifice of Jesus, which makes this boy more than a mere child, but rather the mediator who reveals the covenant.

YEAR B

If the decision is made to choose the respective reading for Year B, instead of the available alternative to use the reading of Year A, then there is a certain obvious unity in these texts. This theme is in the continuity of the Hebrew and Christian Scriptures whereby we can learn from the ancestors in faith. This set of alternative readings moves the focus of the feast of the Holy Family away from a pietistic model of family life to an emphasis on the person of Jesus who, in being presented in the Temple fulfills all the prescriptions of the Law and, even as an infant, reveals something of his mission.

The presentation in the temple is understood by some people as a feast of Our Lady, in spite of the title for the Feast being "Presentation of the Lord." This confusion may have arisen from the placement of this title among the Joyful Mysteries of the rosary, with the resultant twist towards a Marian interpretation. Whether the full text, Luke 2:22–40, is used, or the shorter version, Luke 2:22, 39–40, the editing of the shorter version gives a clue to interpreting the heart of this passage in the messianic sign of contradiction, that a mere child, born of a human family, could grow and become strong, filled with wisdom, because the favor of God was upon him.

First Reading, Genesis 15:1–6, 21:1–3

The first reading is truly a composite passage with verses from two different section of two chapters. Genesis really begins the story of salvation through the covenant with Abraham in Chapter 11, but today we hear the story of Abraham and Sarah with their marvellous story of a son born against all odds. This aspect, and Abraham's willingness even to sacrifice his only son, are points of reflection in the Hebrews passage, so it becomes easy to see why Abraham is called, in the first eucharistic prayer or Roman Canon, "our father in faith." To put their trust in the Lord is credited as their act of righteousness.

Responsorial Psalm, Psalm 105

This psalm directly flows from the mention of the covenant with Abraham and his descendants forever. The versus of the psalm are a mini-summary of the story of salvation, calling to mind the marvelous works God had done for God's people over a thousand generations. The response is a direct invitation to us to remind ourselves yet again "the Lord remembers his covenant forever."

New Testament Reading, Hebrews 11:8, 11–12, 17–19

This is another composite text summarizing the key events that show why Abraham and Sarah are people of faith who obeyed because they trusted God's promise.

Gospel Acclamation, Hebrews 1:1–2

Also from Hebrews the opening verse in the acclamation shows how in the past God spoke to our ancestors through the prophets, but now he speaks through his Son.

Gospel, Luke 2:22–40

This gospel can be a longer or shorter version of the presentation in the temple with the prayer of thanksgiving of Simeon. His words, used daily in the Liturgy of the Hours in the *Nunc Dimittis* of Compline, include his pleasure that his eyes have witnessed the saving deeds of God, the revealing light for the Gentiles, and the glory of the people Israel. His time is described as "Now," our Christmas season's grace is "now," our daily prayer is for "now," because at all times we acknowledge that the grace and favor of God is among us.

YEAR C

Once again the choice is to be made whether to use the specific readings for Year C or to use the set from Year A. If the choice falls with using the unique readings of Year C it opens up the vista of the role and place of the Temple in the life of God's people as the major place of "*Shekinah*," the aura associated with the visible signs of God's presence in the Ark of the Covenant preserved in the Holy of Holies in the heart of the Temple. When Jesus asserts that he must be in his Father's house this is a coded reference to his divinity, in his role of mediating in a new way God's redeeming presence with the people.

First Reading, 1 Samuel 1:20–22, 24–28

Here is another composite text in the context of the period of the Judges when the Ark of the Covenant is stored, no longer in a tent, but in a stone building—at Shiloh. The sequence of the pericopes recounts the vow of the barren Hannah that, if she is blessed by Yahweh with a son, she will dedicate him to the Lord as a Nazirite. Then the story continues the next year on the feast of the Tabernacles, when Hannah chooses not to go up for the feast but will wait until she can dedicate properly the fulfillment of her vow. The third section is the narration of her devotion in the house of the Lord at Shiloh, where she offers the sacrifice of a bull, a measure of flour and of wine, before she hands over her son to Eli the priest, and dedicates him as her gift to the Lord who gifted her in his birth. In the original context this passage leads to the Song of Hannah, sometimes likened to the Magnificat of Mary.

Responsorial Psalm, Psalm 84

In our context of worship in the Lord's presence we take up Psalm 84 and make it the expression of our gratitude and thanksgiving. We use this song of Zion in praising Yahweh in his dwelling place in the Temple where the pilgrims could expect blessing and forgiveness. The response itself takes up that aspect. "Blessed are they who dwell in the home of the Lord." It is a call to all who are in God's family and call his name in faithfulness to God's promise.

New Testament, 1 John 3:1-2, 21-24

The New Testament passage is one of only two texts outside the Pauline writings in the Christmas season. We have two texts from Acts and two from 1 John. The first segment (1 Jn 3:1-2) is an invitation to reflect on what it is to be God's children and to live in hope for what the future glory will be. Among the conditions John would impose on Christ's faithful followers is to show that the Spirit God has given us truly lives in us, by following Christ's commandments to believe in the name of Jesus and to love one another as he told us to. This is at the heart of this feast of the Holy Family, the challenge to live with their faith and love.

Gospel Acclamation, Acts 16:14

This fundamental responsibility to live in faith and love is echoed in the words of the gospel acclamation with the phrase for Acts 16:14 "open our hearts, O Lord, to listen to the Words of your Son."

Gospel, John 2:41-52

The gospel is the second insight from Luke on the hidden life of Jesus, apart from the presentation in the temple and today's scene of Jesus being lost in the temple at the Passover feast and being found answering questions of the doctors and teachers.

As usual there are many resonances of the paschal call of Jesus, which may be lost in the familiarity of the story about a child lost for three days. Jesus goes down from Jerusalem to Nazareth and is subject to Mary and Joseph, and Mary, again, is portrayed as pondering or treasuring these things in her heart. Even the three days of his being lost is redolent of his three days in the tomb. Being in his Father's house is where Jesus asserts even what his parents would expect of him. Above all, the eyes of faith see that merely inquisitive interest might wish to know of more than two events in nearly thirty years of Jesus' hidden life, but even the evangelists concentrate more on the public ministry of Jesus. As living in Christ's family our call is to grow with him in human and divine favor. With Christ we find meaning in the daily realities of our life.

1 JANUARY, OCTAVE OF CHRISTMAS SOLEMNITY OF MARY, MOTHER OF GOD

Of all the feasts in the liturgical year, this day is perhaps the most confused and confusing of all. Even with a new title and new orientation in the 1969 reformed Calendar, which removed two concurrent feasts and themes, the day is still hopelessly overburdened with elements that are far removed from the popularist sense of celebrating New Year's Day.

The new designation still celebrating January 1st as the Octave of Christmas, continues the traditional sense of Christmastide lasting for twelve nights after Christmas, even if the secular world has left Christmas behind in the rush of post-Christmas sales, or is more attracted to the revelries of New Year's Eve. The Octave of Christmas now twins with the octave of Easter as the only remaining octaves in the church's calendar, a definite sign of the simplification that has taken place in recent times—even before Vatican II—when there were dozens of feasts with octaves.

The formal title for this day is the Solemnity of Mary

the Mother of God. As "solemnity" it ranks among the highest categories of celebrations in the ranking of occasions whether in the liturgical seasons or the calendar year. In itself this title is the oldest of all Marian feast days going back to the declaration of the Council of Ephesus (431 C.E.) of Mary as Mother of God (*Theotokos*). In fact, the pre-Vatican II feast of the Motherhood of Mary was set on October 11th by Pope Pius XI in 1931 on the occasion of the fifteenth centenary of the Council of Ephesus.

The earlier feasts of January 1, the Circumcision of Our Lord and the feast of the Holy Name of Our Lord, were both abolished by the renewed Calendar of 1969.

A further overlay of confusion has developed from the practice, first developed by Pope Paul VI, of designating January 1 as the World Day of Prayer for Peace. Since then, to coincide with the New Year, the Holy See releases intentions and themes nominated by the Roman Pontiff to encourage people to lift horizons on New Year's Day and include the pressing needs of the world.

A final source of confusion has arisen from the decision of episcopal conferences in different regions to revise the list of holy days of obligation. One solution has been to reduce the number of days from the previous list as in the Catholic countries of Europe (where as many as ten were observed in Italy, yet Good Friday was not a public holiday). The new guiding principle has been to keep one feast of Our Lord and one feast of Our Lady, and to move some feasts to be observed on the nearest Sunday. Thus, for example in Australia, this means Ascension is observed on the Sunday before Pentecost, Corpus Christi on the Sunday after Trinity Sunday, Christmas is observed as the holy day in honor of Our Lord, and the Assumption on August 15th in honor of Our Lady, and all others were suppressed. The irony of this is that New Year's Day is one occasion when people do come to Mass—more so than on the Sunday after Christmas—but not everyone can have access to Mass on August 15th.

All of this confusion is aggravated by the fact that many people come to Mass on January 1 thinking about their hopes and fears for the year ahead, yet the official readings and texts make little reference to the calendar day. In fact, it is not difficult to put a new year spin on certain elements, but it means distorting the literal context of the texts.

For example, the prayer over the gifts reads:

> God our Father, we celebrate this season
> the beginning of our salvation.
> On this feast of Mary, the Mother of God,
> we ask that our salvation
> will be brought to its fulfillment.

The words "the beginning of our salvation" obviously lend themselves to link both the birth of Jesus and the first day of the new year of grace in which our communion with Mary's Son will bring us salvation (prayer after communion).

Old Testament Reading, Numbers 6:22–27

This reading is the formula of blessing given to Moses to pass on to the people to invoke life and prosperity on God's people. These verses are one of the official texts for the solemn blessings given as optional in the *Roman Sacramentary.* In the original context in Numbers, this blessing comes just after the prescriptions about the Nazirite vow, a challenge to reflect that prayer for New Year blessings is not self-centered or self-indulgent but based on service above self for the sake of witness to the Lord Yahweh.

New Testament Reading, Galatians 4:4–7

The New Testament reading is a brief segment from Galatians, which provides the Christian experience of the profound sense of God's blessing because we are made the adopted children of God by the sending the Spirit of his Son into our hearts.

Gospel Acclamation, Hebrews 1:1–2

Like the Holy Family Year C, the acclamation takes up the opening verses of Hebrews, that in the past God spoke through the prophets but in our day God has spoken through his Son. Now in the new year too, God speaks to us in his Word incarnate in our world, so we learn to interpret how we encounter this revelation.

Gospel, Luke 2:16–21

The gospel is a veritable linkage of the Octave, for it uses the same text used at Christmas Dawn Mass with the shepherds' response to the angels' proclamation of the Savior's birth. Now, in addition to the verses about Mary treasuring these things in her heart, we hear the events of eight days later. The circumcision of Jesus and the conferral of his name had been separate feasts. Now we can still reflect on how, in the Hebrew culture, to invoke a name is to establish a relationship with that person. Each time we pray in the name of the Lord Jesus—and all our formal prayers have forms of conclusion in his name—we express our relationship in Christ and pray to him as the source of our true blessing, the one with the words of everlasting life, which is a good augury for New Year.

The Christian vision of peace can be the ideal that helps unify the major feasts of our tradition. The peace of Jesus' first Easter greeting, the peace of the Angel's Christmas announcement, the peace of universal goodwill that is readily expressed in the popular sentiment of Christmas—all of these are unified in our New Year greetings when the peace that is Christmas, our God with us, is shared all through the New Year.

JANUARY 6, EPIPHANY OF THE LORD

The feast of the Epiphany is one occasion that may need to be rescued from the danger of historicism, when the focus seems to be more on the Three Kings or the Magi, especially fostered by the practice of only adding their figures to the crib scene on this day, or worse, by moving them day-by-day from Christmas a bit closer to the crib. To counter the level of awareness arising solely out of the crib scene it may be helpful to encourage a theological vision of this feast that is truly connected with its origins.

The importance of the theological focus of this feast can be inferred from the practice now nearly universal after the 1969 calendar reform. Where January 6 is not a holy day of obligation and a public holiday, most countries now observe the Sunday after New Year as the feast of the Epiphany precisely to facilitate participation in its message by greater numbers of people. It is the church's way of saying this feast and its message are important.

Historically, it is clear that in most of the African and eastern parts of the Roman Empire January 6 became the original major celebration of the incarnation. This eastern influence was further carried into Gaul and Spain long before it also became a Roman feast. In the east the epiphany or manifestation of Jesus was linked also with his baptism and the miracle of Cana, as other manifestations or signs of the fulfillment of messianic promises. The Johannine gospel is renowned for emphasizing the connection between the public signs of Jesus' life and the manifestation of the divine glory of his role as Messiah (e.g., Jn 2:11; 11:4; 12:41).

Thus it is not surprising that in the east Epiphany was also considered an appropriate time for the initiation sacraments, perhaps based on the obvious parallel with Christ's baptism in the Jordan. As an extension of this initiation context, the formalization of the forty-day lenten period of preparation for the Easter sacraments tended to encourage a forty-day period before Epiphany, which brought its beginning back to November. Once December 25 became the major incarnation commemoration, the starting time of its preparation was left the same thus reducing to four weeks what became known as Advent.

Just as the extension of the Easter event through to Pentecost was originally a conceptual unity rather than a discrete separation of various feasts, spinning off to named days for the feasts of Ascension and Pentecost, likewise, the Christmas extension came to be seen as a conceptual unity developing the implication of the incarnation of the Word made flesh.

In the Middle Ages the feast became extended over the twelve days after Christmas, as is expressed still in the carol "The Twelve Days of Christmas" (and even in its contemporary parodies), as well as in Shakespeare's play "Twelfth Night" (which was written for that feast and its title was synonymous with its date).

In our current calendar this conceptual extension of messianic glory is still continued through Epiphany, the Baptism of the Lord as the conclusion of the Christmas season, and the transition to Ordinary Time. Here the Johannine readings of the Baptism of Jesus (Year A), the call of the disciples (Year B), and the Wedding at Cana (Year C) are assigned for the second Sunday of Ordinary Time. This neatly links up the flow from the major season of the Christmas Cycle with its preparation, highlight, and extension, into the intervening time before the major Easter season begins its ninety days with Lent. In season and out of season Paul calls us to live our baptismal calling living in the Spirit that makes us one in the body of Christ.

The Vatican II-inspired calendar of 1969 integrates this theological vision of the Christmas season, in which we celebrate the Savior's coming at Christmas and his manifestation in his humanity at Epiphany and the Baptism of the Lord. The opening prayer of Epiphany says:

> Father, you revealed your Son to the nations
> by the guidance of a star.
> Lead us to your glory in heaven by the light of faith.

First Reading, Isaiah 60:1–6

This reading for Epiphany is similar to the Christmas Vigil reading and the Christmas Dawn reading from Isaiah 62. All of them reflect the atmosphere of the exile period and the hope of the people for a restoration that will be a manifestation of God's faithfulness to his Covenant (a similar passage, from Isaiah 66, is read on Sunday 21 in Cycle C).

The geographical images are striking in their comprehensiveness: ships come from the west from the then powers of Phoenicia and Greece; the riches of the east come in caravan across the deserts of Syria and Sinai; the camels bring the riches of the people of Arabia, including gold and frankincense. These last goods are commonly associated with the gifts brought by the Magi in Mt 2:1–12 (today's gospel) but the primary thrust is on the worldwide network.

The overarching image is the light that overcomes the darkness, a light that will radiate out in the throbbing hearts of those who enjoy such a sight. In the original context the resurrection of Jerusalem is the goal, but the Christian tradition transforms the focus on Jerusalem itself to the church as the assembly of the nations coming toward the light.

This Christian perspective is at the heart of the manifestation of this feast, as Peter proclaimed to Cornelius and his family: "the truth I have now come to realize is that God does not have favorites but everyone of any nationality who fears God and does what is right is acceptable to him" (Acts 10:34–35). This passage is at the heart of the universal call of God to all peoples, and deserves not to be trivialized by mentioning only the word dromedaries/camels as if the whole message is simply applied to the coming of the Magi.

Responsorial Psalm, Psalm 72

The responsorial psalm picks up resonances of the Isaiah reading about the gifts of the kings and rulers, but, again, the message is more the vision of hope for all than the Magi story. God's plan is epitomized in the response "Lord, every nation on earth will adore you."

New Testament, Ephesians 3:2–3a, 5–6

This passage is a strong claim by Paul that the mystery was made known to him by revelation. What was now the revelation of the Spirit is that Gentiles have become fellow heirs with Christ Jesus through the gospel. He sees it as his role to show that there are no favorites in God's plan, and his ministry is to proclaim this to the Gentiles.

Gospel Acclamation, Matthew 2:2

The acclamation takes up the astrologers' part in the story of the Magi as they recount how they saw his star in the east and have come to adore the Messiah.

Gospel, Matthew 2:1–12

Today's gospel is a major story in Matthew's infancy narratives. For one who did not mention the annunciation or the nativity, or the angel's witness (as Luke did) Matthew has his own theological vision in his development from genealogy to the virginal conception of Christ, to the visit of the Magi and the flight into Egypt. Five times he makes specific connections with Old Testament passages being fulfilled in the events he narrates about Jesus' birth. This theological vision of God's plan being continually revealed should not be lost in the trivia about details of the Magi.

The Epiphany is not a past reality to commemorate but the living reality of God's salvation still being revealed in our world in our day. This affirmation of the mission of the church for all the world may be more than needed, so we can find "another way" back to the country of God's call and not limit it by nationalism or ethnic jealousies or religious strife. If the three kings are dead, long live the King of Kings and Lord of Lords.

BAPTISM OF THE LORD

Just as the Solemnity of Mary the Mother of God is the titular feast for the octave of Christmas, the Baptism of the Lord serves as the function as a quasi-octave of the Epiphany. These two feasts are linked as "manifestations" of the incarnation of the Word made flesh, extensions in a theological sense of the impact of the birth of Christ portrayed as more than a birthday party for the baby Jesus.

The mystery of incarnation reveals the word made flesh in Jesus Christ conceived through the power of the Holy Spirit. This mystery is at the heart of the liturgical season of Advent-Christmas-Epiphany, more than just remembering a birth. As a mystery it is something we know through revelation and whose understanding we can continue to develop by the way we live and celebrate it. This open-ended, spiral image is helpful to keep in mind on this feast day because, just when we bring the Christmas cycle to a formal conclusion, we also extend it into the next day, beginning the first week of Ordinary Time.

This is ordinal time, counted time in ordinal sequence, not time that is ordinary and doesn't matter. In fact, it does matter because the season ahead, with its symbolism of hope and growth expressed in the green color of the season, becomes the time when we can live out our baptismal commitment as members of Christ's body, the church. The Christmas season in general has highlighted the humanity of Jesus and now we are to share in his divinity by the way we live in the Spirit we share as adopted heirs of God. Among the unusual offering of three alternate opening prayers for this feast is the collect of Leo the Great used also for the drop of water in the chalice. It is a paschal journey for each of us through baptism to be transformed in Christ's Spirit. We share in that "wonderful exchange" of gifts at every Eucharist, and we look to the empowering of the Spirit shared in "Eucharist that we be faithful to our calling" (opening prayer).

The Baptism of the Lord has characteristics similar to those of the Feast of the Holy Family. Both are relatively new feasts incorporated into the Christmas cycle in the Vatican II reform of the Calendar published in 1969. In that first set of texts the Synoptic versions of the scene of the baptism of Jesus are divided up according to the principles of the lectionary cycles (Matthew in Year A, Mark in Year B, and Luke in Year C), and the same set of texts was published to be used in all three years, but also providing specific sets of readings to go with the unique gospel versions of the baptism of Jesus in Years B and C.

Even though these options are available some motivation or principle would need to drive the decisions as to which set is chosen for use in Years B and C. The theology of the manifestations of Jesus in his epiphany, in his baptism, and in the marriage feast at Cana should be the guiding light.

The remarkable fact is that the baptism of Jesus is included in some detail yet differently in each of the synoptics and also in John. Even the Last Supper does not receive such similar treatment in all four gospels. Perhaps this insight is saying that the manifestations of Jesus' mission and mandate from the Father are remarkable in themselves and are to be taken as a key factor. This implies that we should not interpret the baptism of Jesus in too narrow a sense and immediately turn it into a parallel with parish baptisms today. This feast may not be the time to emphasize parish baptismal policies, to facilitate the practice in the parish. The gospel accounts give us recollections of what happened, but we are to see the details as pointers that the signs and wonders at the Jordan are celebrated in the baptism we receive, and to which we are called to be faithful.

YEAR A
First Reading, Isaiah 42:1–4, 6–7
The passage from Isaiah 42 is a composite from the first Song of the Servant of Yahweh. This servant is to be God's witness to all the nations, which Christologically we now see fulfilled in Jesus of Nazareth. It is the response Jesus himself makes when he sends word back to John through his emissaries that the messianic signs are being fulfilled. At the synagogue in Nazareth he again illustrated this quality of eternal yet present fulfillment when he said to those who heard him reading Isaiah, "Today this scripture passage is fulfilled in your hearing."

Responsorial Psalm, Psalm 29
This psalm is David's hymn to the Lord of the storm, with may references to the power of Yahweh over the waters. We use as our own words the response "The Lord will bless his people with peace."

New Testament Reading, Acts 10:34–38
This passage is a brief section of two of Peter's speeches to the people of Jerusalem. The first part is the declaration he

makes before Cornelius' household that God does not have favorites. The second segment is like an early profession of faith, a summary of the life and mission of Jesus from his baptism onwards. The challenge is to hear it today as the "good news of peace." It is not enough to be able to recite the phrases of the Creed, or to be familiar with the events of the gospel, we need to be able to witness to God's presence being revealed in our lives.

Gospel Acclamation, Mark 9:7
This is Mark's summary of the baptism scene and the invitation to listen to the beloved Son.

Gospel, Matthew 3:13–17
The gospel is Matthew's account of the baptism of Jesus with all its resonances of the creative, redemptive, healing power of grace. The witness of the Holy Spirit as a dove is a key insight into reflection on how we are all to live in his Spirit.

YEAR B
First Reading, Isaiah 55:1–11
The first reading for Year B could be the Year A reading from Is 42, the first Song of the Servant of Yahweh, or it could be from Chapter 55, another text dealing with the metaphor of the new Jerusalem as the symbol for the fidelity of God to the covenant. The faithfulness of God to the Covenant is to be the "witness to the peoples, a leader and a master of the nations" (v. 3). This is the way the soul will live or that you may have life, as another version says. The sequence of images about the riches of God's blessings are not primarily about materialist gain but metaphors for the consequence of inclining the ear to listen to God.

Responsorial Psalm, Isaiah 12:2–6
The response this time is not actually a psalm; it is taken from hymns of thanksgiving from Isaiah 12. It speaks of thanksgiving for the fidelity of Yahweh, especially in the awareness that now in our midst is the Holy One of Israel. The actual response text is from the same passage and is a further extension of the pun on the waters of baptism in the phrase "you will draw water joyfully from the springs of salvation."

Second Reading, 1 John 5:1–9
This is one of the great passages of John's letters. In the gospel of John is the text to Nicodemus, "unless someone is born again of water and the Holy Spirit." This excerpt now is like a spiraling development of this central belief that everyone who believes Jesus is the Christ has been born of God.

Gospel Acclamation, John 1:29
This piece is also taken from John and witnesses to the passage where John saw Jesus approaching and proclaimed him the Lamb of God who takes away the sins of the world.

Gospel, Mark 1:7–11
The gospel is Mark's perspective on the baptism of Jesus. Without an extensive infancy narrative, as the other Synoptics used in Years A and C, this text is virtually the beginning of Mark's way of proclaiming the Good News of Jesus Christ the Son of God. The manifestation of Jesus' divine approbation is portrayed in special signs, not the dove of the Spirit and the voice of heaven, but, especially in Mark, how John saw the heavens torn apart. This connects with Isaiah's prayer that the heavens would be torn open and God would come down (Is 63:19) and Mark's inclusion of the events at the moment of the death of Jesus when the curtain of the Temple was torn from top to bottom (Mk 15:38). These visual and vocal acclamations of the designation of Jesus as the beloved are the entry point for Christians to acclaim Jesus as the Son of God who shares our humanity to empower us to share his divinity.

YEAR C
First Reading, Isaiah 40:1–5, 9–11
Once again the year A readings can be chosen or the specific set for Year C. The specific first reading (Is 40:1–5, 9–11) is from the beginning of the Book of the Consolation of Israel, already used on the second Sunday of Advent Year B, when the context is more on the preaching ministry of John the Baptist. The resonances of the person and ministry of John are clear, but the element of prime consolation is in the affirmation of the theophany that promises "here is your God." The many images of feeding the flock, gently leading them,

and carrying them are all verified in the later ministry of Jesus, but the key element is how God's manifestation is now, today, at the baptism of Jesus.

Responsorial Psalm, Psalm 104

The responsorial psalm continues the multitude of scriptural images for expressing the bounteous gifts of God. The unique resonance for this occasion is in the number of images that include water as the source of God's blessing. The strongest specific baptismal phrase is at the end with the prayer to send out the spirit of Yahweh and they are created, and in this way God renews the face of the earth. The tradition has turned this verse into an invocation of the Holy Spirit. For today, the response invites us to praise and thank God for the many examples of the plan for our salvation: "O bless the Lord, my soul."

New Testament, Titus 2:11–14; 3:4–7

The New Testament reading for Year C comes from the source of four readings in this Christmas season concluding today. This composite passage is an extended reflection on the manifestation of the "glory" of God, not just in the baptism of Jesus but in the call and hope we share to come to see God's glory by the Spirit he has poured out on us.

Gospel Acclamation, Luke 3:16

The acclamation is directly connected with the following Lukan account of the baptism of Jesus. It portrays the harbinger relationship of the ministry of John the Baptist with that of Jesus. He says that there will come another mightier than he whose baptism will be with the Holy Spirit and with fire.

Gospel, Luke 3:15–16, 21–22

This gospel is a composite text that develops the public ministry of John, but skips over the issue of his imprisonment before giving the briefest references to the baptism of Jesus. Here the unique thing is not the detail of the events at the time of Jesus' baptism but the events that took place after it. Luke specifically says that, it was after Jesus' own baptism, while Jesus was praying, that the theophanies of God's manifestation took place. Often in the Scriptures, as with Daniel, Ananias, Cornelius, and Paul, prayer precedes a revelation from God. In the instance of Jesus, the divine intervention is not so much in his physical baptism but in the prayer he lives in total relationship with his Father. As the next chapter of Luke develops, Jesus can claim that the Spirit of the Lord is upon him and has anointed him to proclaim the kingdom and that the messianic era has come (Luke 4:18). Jesus has publicly and visually fulfilled the Isaian prophecy.

FURTHER READING

(1991) *Days of the Lord: the Liturgical Year. Volume 1: Season of Advent, Season of Christmas/Epiphany.* Collegeville; MN: Liturgical Press

Adam, Adolf (1979) [translated by Matthew J. O'Connell] *The Liturgical Year: Its History and Its Meaning after the Reform of the Liturgy.* New York: Pueblo Publishing Company.

Irwin, Kevin W. (1986) *Advent Christmas: a Guide to the Eucharist and Hours.* New York: Pueblo Publishing Company.

Nocent, Adrian (1977) *The Liturgical Year. Volume One: Advent, Christmas, Epiphany.* Collegeville; MN: Liturgical Press.

Parsch, Pius (1962) *The Church's Year of Grace. Volume 1 Advent to Candlemas.* Collegeville; MN: Liturgical Press.

Talley, Thomas J. (1986) *The Origins of the Liturgical Year.* New York: Pueblo Publishing Company.

Whalen, Michael D. (1981) *Seasons and Feasts of the Church Year: An Introduction.* New York: Paulist Press.

The Paschal Mystery in the Christmas Season

Russell Hardiman

An overview of the Christmas season can help illustrate the distinctive character of the Advent emphases, the Christmas celebration, and its continuation throughout the Christmas season. These different facets of the season lead to an interweaving of the threefold dimensions of past, present, and future, referring to the coming of Christ:

• the second coming of Christ in the Parousia in the fullness of time (Advent I and II);

• the immediate preparations for his birth leading to the historic coming at Bethlehem (Advent III and IV);

• the immediate responses to the fact of the historical birth of Christ, with the focus on the veneration tendered by the angels and shepherds (Christmas Masses);

• the manifestation of the divinity of Christ in his role as the light of the world (the worship of the Magi at Epiphany);

• the public manifestation of the mission and mandate of Jesus as the beloved Son of the Father, in whom he is well pleased and in whom we are to believe (Baptism of Christ).

The opening prayer for Epiphany reads

Father, you revealed your Son to the nations by the guidance of a star.
Lead us to your glory in heaven by the light of faith.

Here there is a strongly drawn parallel that shows the linkages between past, present, and future whether celebrating in memorial the gospel events or our own journey in faith.

• the journey of the Magi	and	our journey to Christ
• going to meet the infant of Bethlehem	and	our meeting Christ the King in the glory of his second coming
• led by a star	and	our being led by the light of Christ come among us as the Bread of Life

LITURGICAL SOURCES

The sequence of the interlocking perspectives of past, present, and future is the common pattern of the prayer tradition of the church, especially in the presidential prayers (the opening prayer/collect; the prayer over the gifts; and the post-communion prayer). This interlocking perspective is the basis of praise for the marvels of God in the various themes or reasons for thanksgiving articulated in the prefaces singly, or in Eucharistic Prayers II and IV where there is, respectively, a brief or extended profession of faith.

This listing of liturgical sources may serve as a useful reminder as to the wellsprings from where we can draw nourishment and inspiration for a thirsting world. With the separation of the functions of "sermons" and "homily," we now acknowledge that a sermon is a religious exposition leading to increased faith but not necessarily tied to a worship context. A homily, by definition, is the breaking open of the Scriptures of a specific set of readings precisely to lead people to be nurtured in the ensuing sacramental action, especially and most frequently by the sharing in communion through the fruits of Christ's death and resurrection to empower us to give witness to the reign of God in our daily lives. As well as the actual Scripture readings, the biblical images and allusions are further expressed in the prescribed presidential prayers or the optional texts such as blessings or penitential rites and the choices for prefaces of the season. In short, there are other sources of inspiration and motivation than solely the Scripture readings, and homilists would be well advised to keep in mind the texts they use when praying publicly with, and for, the community of faith, as the above example of the Epiphany collect illustrates.

POSITIVE SECULAR CONNECTIONS

Another potential source for attention-gaining or pastoral application in liturgical leadership is the connection with the devotional elements and even the secular elements. We frequently advert to the need to be somewhat countercultural in seasons like Christmas and Easter, when the secular, commercial, and advertising values may be different from ours, but there is a level of pastoral sensibility needed on these occasions to make welcome the marginalized who come loyally to these feasts, to welcome home the ones who struggle with their life choices, and generally to show an attitude of inclusiveness at the key times of proclaiming that the reign of God is for all.

In the commercial focus on gift giving it is positive to assert the countercultural emphasis on the gift of divine life that is at the heart of Christmas celebrations. This is not the time to appear merely negative or sarcastic in the comments made of the plethora of activities people genuinely strive to achieve as their way to enter into the Christmas spirit. It would be more positive to affirm their efforts as the many entry points into the mystery of encountering the divine in the human. The next article in this volume deals with unwrapping Christmas among the myriads of wrappings.

This means it can be extremely difficult to ensure the separation of the commercial pre-Christmas splurge and the discrete emphases of the liturgical seasons: with the eschatological themes, Advent comings, and the Christmas extension beyond the actual day. In this regard, a positive attitude to the use of the crib as a Christmas symbol of universal appeal, and a parish policy to plan carefully its positioning and use in the Christmas season, may be priorities to set at this time.

REMOVING THE CRIB

In the past the focus of the Epiphany was shaped by the imaginative movement of the Magi gradually toward the crib. The weakness of this custom is that it reinforces the type of historicism so easily encouraged by the use of pageants at Christmas, Palm Sunday, Holy Thursday, or Good Friday. Nowadays it is hard to generate an appreciation of the significance of the feast of the Epiphany when most of the world thinks Christmas finished two weeks before.

The removal of the crib was traditionally associated with the octave day of Epiphany, hence January 13th. Nowadays that is even more unlikely because Christmas is three weeks old. Since the post-Vatican II reform of the church calendar has all but eliminated Octaves, except for Christmas and Easter, the time for the crib's removal has been problematic and by no means uniform. This is compounded by the influence of the secularization of the Christmas/holiday season whereby the lead-in to Christmas starts weeks earlier, even as early as October, but commercially ceases in the media and advertising by about 2:00 P.M. on Christmas Day. The post-Christmas sales have become all the rage, and St. Valentine's Day isn't far away.

Perhaps a countercultural movement could be appropriately asserted here to encourage a more theological basis to the crib devotion rather than to let it remain at the merely sentimental emotionalism associated with a baby's birth. Perhaps the Christmas feasts could be unified around the image of the crib. The crib might be a focal point in the environment of the church's decoration, including the Feast of the Epiphany and the Baptism of Christ, then removed when Ordinary Time begins.

This would be a way of saying that the humanity shared with us by Jesus revealed his divinity according to God's plan. Now, in the more low-key time of the liturgical year, our emphasis changes to our living out the paschal mystery in our daily lives, in our humanity to share fully his divinity. Green becomes the symbol of hope, the image of growth even in the distractions of the holiday season and vacations. We would be implementing Pius Parsch's vision of the seed from which grows the mighty tree of God's kingdom. These images of growth have been traditionally expressed in the Christmas Masses:

> God our Father, we rejoice in the birth of our savior.
> May we share his life completely by living as he has taught
> (Prayer after Communion, Midnight Mass)

> Father, may we follow the example of your Son who became man and lived among us.
> May we receive the gift of divine life through these offerings here on earth
> (Prayer over Gifts, Dawn Mass)

Unwrapping the Season of Christmas

Russell Hardiman

The spirit of the divine in the human is the goal of all our Christmas celebrations. The trick seems to be in encouraging people not to get sidetracked by the multitude of things to do but to see them as the levels by which they participate, or the entry points whereby they experience the mystery. The many secular customs and practices can be diversions or distractions but we would like to see them as the expression of the intention to put Christ into Christmas.

The rituals of Christmas are so very different; they speak to people in different ways; they appeal to one person more than another at different stages of their life; let us look to a deeper meaning of some of them.

Christmas in English, is a contraction of the old English expression "Cristes messe," that is the Mass of Christ, just as "Michaelmas" is the feast of St. Michael. Maybe we should start a campaign to pronounce it "Christ's Mass" to put the right emphasis.

I remember a letter to the editor, when someone had complained about the custom of writing Xmas. It was pointed out that the first letter of Christ's name in Greek is the "cross K or Ch" and it has the form of the Cross. So Xmas becomes in fact a profound tribute to the proper interpretation of Christ's suffering, death, and resurrection. Even more so we could advocate that instead of writing "Xmas" we substitute the "X" with the full "Chi Rho" ☧ symbol, which is the Christian expression of faith in Christ, rather than let an "X" become an unknown quantity; thus we invert the process and make the sacred out of the secular.

Unwrapping a single letter to reveal a more profound meaning is an invitation to be conscious of the many ways in which we can unwrap the meanings around about us.

Once I was at a tennis tournament at the local club, where everyone brought along a gift or item, and they became the prizes from which people chose their winnings after each match. Great interest was focused on one special parcel that looked huge. In fact it was a packet of jelly beans wrapped up in many layers of wrapping. It was interesting to see people's reactions, for the huge size seemed to attract people's attention as if size meant importance or value. It seemed to appeal to people's sense of greed.

It seems to me that this whole event, the wrapping of parcels and people's attitudes to the external wrappings is a symbol of Christmas. What was done by intention at the tennis club, our Western society does unwittingly when it comes to Christmas. For us it has become an event wrapped up with many meanings, some playfully misleading, some seriously distorting, some profoundly inspiring; but all of them inviting a further unwrapping of the meaning of this special time.

There are many wrappings, and each type of wrapping can make our Christmas appear to be something else than what it should be.

There is the wrapping of family festival. To be with family and folks for Christmas, people fly all over the world, but do those same attitudes continue all through the year?

There is the wrapping of a consumer orgy. The shops push Christmas with their cash registers in mind. I remember the fuss made in Queensland, Australia, where a minister of the government urged people to give only what they could afford. He was howled down by the chamber of commerce as being irresponsible!

There is the wrapping of an occasion for social merriment. Christmas is a time for office parties, commercial firms offering customers a drink, even neighborhood parties.

There is the wrapping of an occasion for a road blitz. Watch the TV news, follow the papers. The main emphasis is on the carnage on the roads, and the road toll dominates the news.

Then there is the wrapping of a Christian feast. Most would acknowledge the origin of the celebrations but does the main part get lost? Do the customs truly lead people in a personal response?

We have carols—carols by candlelight; the crib with all its figures; the Christmas tree and lights; symbol of Christ light of the world; Midnight Mass and its special atmosphere.

Yet is Christmas so wrapped up that its meaning is obscured?

What happens to all the Christmas wrapping? It must be one of the best businesses around: providing gift wrap that is just thrown away. The wrappings are not the gifts and should not be confused. Can we peel off the wrappings of our Christmas to get to the real Christmas?

We have to learn to unwrap our Christmas trimmings so that there is more than just a birthday party for the baby Jesus. We need to help that baby be seen as God, the Prince of Peace; in this way our carols are not just background noise, muzak, but we can say "Come, let us worship Christ the Lord"; so that the hundreds of millions gathered in churches everywhere for Midnight Mass/Christmas Mass would be ready to become fully human like Jesus; then the healing of our world could begin.

This is what our celebration of Christmas is really about.

Because Jesus Christ came into our world born as a human person, he has sanctified all human life, all our human activities.

Because we are human we learn through our senses, we express ourselves through our senses. Hence all our activities that involve sight, taste, touch, hearing, and smell are all valid ways of absorbing the Christian message, and expressing human joy and fellowship.

Our eyes should see beyond the wrappings and not be bedazzled by the lights, the streamers, the decorations. Rather they should lead us to see the one who is the light of the world.

Our ears should peel away the wrappings of sentimental music, not cringe at the sound of carols, of singing, or even of jingle bells. Rather they should lead us back to hear the Word of God, who has become one with us.

Our touch should not mistake the nice feel of glossy wrapping paper for the gift itself. Rather we should bend the knee before the one who is born the King of Israel or we should bow our heads as we recognize Our Lord and Our God among us now.

Our taste should not be over-satiated at this time, even with the array of goodies around us. Rather we should taste the Bread of Life, born into our world that we may have life with him.

Our sense of smell should not be distracted by the perfumes and aftershave lotions given as presents when anything at all will do. Rather we should recognize the odor of sanctity that our prayers can rise like incense in the Lord's sight.

In short, make sure the wrappings of Christmas do not confuse you. Make sure you do not mistake the wrapping paper for the gift itself, but see beyond the wrapping to the spirit in which it is given.

CHRISTMAS TRIMMINGS

Remember the poem "The Trimmin's on the Rosary" by John O'Brien, an occasion when the extra prayers seemed to take longer than the main act? It seems to me we could well do with concentrating on the "trimmings" of Christmas to make sure we don't lose sight of the main aspect of Christmas. After all, what is Christmas? What is the main point of it?

Why Celebrate December 25th?
There is no real proof that this is the actual day. Christians in the fourth and fifth centuries took over a Roman custom of a party around the time of the winter solstice; in fact in different areas they picked on different days: December 25, January 6, January 13. The important thing is not the actual date, but the wish to celebrate the fact of Christ's birth as a human person, like us in all things but sin.

Cards
They originated only in Victorian England, late last century as a way of exchanging greetings. Now, what an industry!

The Special Foods
No aspect of life is left out, even eating and drinking. I hope we do not say *especially* eating and drinking. The common tradition is the joy in gathering as family and friends for a special meal. The customs and traditions vary e.g., Panettone, Polish Bread, Plum Pudding.

The Christmas Tree
Again it is not even a Christian custom in its origin. It is an adaptation of a Germanic custom of using lights on a pine tree, virtually the only tree left green and in leaf during the northern European winter. In our usage now, we decorate the tree to remind us Christ is the light of the world—the incarnation in the unbelievable mystery whereby the human race is given another chance to live in paradise where the tree of life is planted.

Christmas Carols
These were originally medieval dances, but now they are so often the haunting reminder, so evocative of family memories and places. The carols were originally religious, now less so in the commercial ones, such as "White Christmas," "Rudolph," and "Jingle Bells." At least they urge us to reflect that the first Christmas was a silent night, a holy night, and all the faithful do come to adore Christ the Lord.

Christmas Presents
The customs of exchanging gifts traces its origins to the story of the Three Wise Men and their gifts. It is now so dangerously over-commercialized that we need to stop and reflect on what is the Gift that God has first given us: life and life in its fullness. Gifts are given now because the memory of Christ's birth becomes the mirror of the generosity of God in his gift of life to all creation.

Decorations and Streamers
Whether in the family home or the shops, in the city square, the mall, the main street; these decorations are a public tribute that this time is special. Rarely does public life acknowledge any religious sentiments, so it is one more way of saying Christmas is a unique time.

The Crib
What began as a personal painting on the wall by St Francis of Assisi in his monastery of Greccio in Italy has become a loving tradition. It is the visual reminder, whether in simple figures or an elaborate reconstruction of a whole village complete with animals and village characters, the well that pumps water, and so on. It is a trigger to the memory of what happened and why it is important. The simple facts of Matthew and Luke are transformed into the reflections of John—that to all who believe in him, he has given the power to become the children of God because the Word was made flesh. God became human.

May you recognize the gift of God himself, his Son given for us, and then may the grace that is Christmas, Immanuel—God with us, be truly yours not only at Christmas but always.

This is the prayerful hope expressed in the Midnight Mass:

> God our Father,
> We rejoice in the birth of our Savior.
> May we share his life completely
> by living as he has taught.
> (Prayer after Communion, Midnight Mass).

The Season of Lent

Jayne Newton Ahearn

DESCRIPTION

Lent is a preparation for the celebration of Easter. For the Lenten liturgy disposes both catechumens and the faithful to celebrate the paschal mystery; catechumens, through the several stages of Christian initiation; the faithful, through reminders of their own baptism and through penitential practices. (*General Norms for the Liturgical Year and the Calendar*, no. 27).

The annual observance of Lent is the special season for the ascent to the holy mountain of Easter. Through its twofold theme of repentance and baptism, the season of Lent disposes both the catechumens and the faithful to celebrate the paschal mystery. Catechumens are led to the sacraments of initiation by means of the rite of election, the scrutinies and catechesis. The faithful, listening more intently to the Word of God and devoting themselves to prayer, are prepared through a spirit of repentance to renew their baptismal promises. (*Ceremonial of Bishops*, no. 249).

HISTORICAL ORIGINS

Lent evolved out of the primitive Christian pasch; the earliest celebration of the passion, death on the cross, and resurrection of Christ. In the second century a two-day fast was already associated with the vigil of Easter. This was the paschal fast; the abstaining from the wedding feast until the bridegroom returns. In the third century the practice in the east was a six-day fast leading up to the vigil while in the West the practice of a two-day fast was maintained. Evidence into the fourth century indicates that practice was varied, with the duration of fasting being anywhere from six days to six weeks. It was Bishop Athanasius of Alexandria who encouraged the Roman church to follow the then eastern practice of fasting for six weeks (roughly forty days) leading up to Easter.

There are two theories about the motivation for the forty-day fast. One is that it began as a post-Epiphany fast, a fast that was a liturgical participation in Jesus' forty days of fasting in the desert after his baptism. The other is that it began as a period of preparation for catechumens leading up to their baptism; a preparation in which all the faithful assisted by prayer and example. Evidence for this origin comes from the *Apostolic Tradition*, which outlines catechumenal practice of the early third century. In fact, both motivations have contributed to Lent as we have it today.

By the mid-fourth century Lent was a recognized liturgical season. The Council of Laodicea prescribed that there be no celebrations of marriage during Lent and that saints could be commemorated only on lenten Saturdays and Sundays. Since the only reason for celebrating Mass on a weekday was the commemoration of a saint, this served as a prohibition of Mass on all but Saturdays and Sundays during Lent. Fasting was of prime importance. At that time, meals were eaten only in the morning and in the evening. In practice, fasting meant the morning meal was dropped. Forms of fasting included the dry fast (when only bread, salt, and water were consumed), and total abstinence from food.

THEOLOGY

Since Lent is a part of the unity of our celebration of the paschal mystery, you are invited to read first the "Historical Origins" and "Theology" sections of the "Holy Week and the Paschal Triduum" chapter, which appears later in this volume.

Lent is pilgrimage through the desert. Key passages from Scripture for Lent are Matthew 4, Jesus' sojourn in the desert after his baptism; Exodus 24:9–18, Moses on Mt. Sinai; and 1 Kings 19:3–8, Elijah's flight for his life into the desert. The desert is the place where no one lives; it is away from human habitation. However, it is a place where the demons live and to where evil is sent (the scapegoat of the Jews). The desert is also a place where God can be encountered. God invites or leads Jesus, Moses, and Elijah into the desert. It is in the desert that God acts; here is the place of the covenant with Israel. Thus the desert is both hostile and idyllic. It is a place where good and evil struggle; it is a battleground. In the desert both the conflict and the victory occur.

In Lent we are invited or led, or sometimes even driven (see Mk 1:12) into the desert. We symbolically withdraw from human habitation, from the concerns of the world, to reflect on our sinfulness and our need for forgiveness, to struggle with the demons. Prayer and fasting are sacramental; they are liturgical participation in the self-emptying (*kenosis*) of Jesus that culminated with his dying. And they are prophetic words in that by our actions we become what we do; we are formed for the demands of Christian life.

Lent, then, is symbolic of all Christian life. During Lent we practice intensely for our living through the entire year.

WORSHIP ENVIRONMENT

Lent is the season to get back to the basics. Clear out everything superfluous from the sanctuary, from the nave, and especially from the church entryway where tables and bulletin boards can become quite cluttered.

The environment for Lent is determined by:

a) the readings of the entire Lent/Easter season of the current liturgical year and;

b) the challenges to the community that the lenten readings pose and the responses they evoke and;

c) the initiations and conversions that are celebrated in the RCIA rituals during Lent and that culminate in the Easter sacraments.

It is, then, the task of the environment team to put into visual expression the transformation that the parish seeks as it journeys through Lent toward Easter.

The colors of the season are purples and greys. It is a season of desert and dryness with the promise of water, a season of darkness with the promise of light, a season of death with the promise of life. The ashes blessed on Ash Wednesday, placed in a large glass container, can be incorporated into the environment for the entire season.

Incense, symbolic of prayer and purification, can be used during the gathering rite, both in the entrance procession and at the penitential rite. Rather than the thurible, use a brazier that is carried in the procession and placed as part of the worship environment. During the penitential rite more incense can be added to the coals.

MUSIC

Responsorial Psalm. The seasonal psalms for Lent are Psalm 51, Psalm 91, and Psalm 130. The selection of one from among these is framed by the Scriptures in relationship to the needs and situation of the particular parish.

Psalm 51

Be Merciful, O Lord	Marty Haugen
Be Merciful, O Lord	David Clark Isele Option
Be Merciful, O Lord	Christopher Willcock
Be Merciful, O Lord	Michael Joncas
Create In Me	David Haas

Psalm 91

Be With Me, Lord	Marty Haugen
Be With Me, Lord	Michael Joncas
Be With Me, Lord	Christopher Willcock

Psalm 130

With The Lord There Is Mercy	Marty Haugen
With The Lord There Is Mercy	David Clark Isele
With The Lord There Is Mercy	Michael Joncas
With The Lord There Is Mercy	Christopher Willcock

Gospel Acclamation. During Lent, the Alleluia is not sung. Another acclamation is sung before the gospel is proclaimed. Some possibilities are:

refrain of *Praise to You, O Christ Our Savior*, Bernadette Farrell (one of the verses may be sung by the cantor as the gospel verse);

Glory To You, O Word of God (from *Mass of Light*), David Haas;

refrain of *Lord, To Whom Shall We Go?*, David Haas

Praise to You, Lord Jesus Christ (from *Mass of Creation*), Marty Haugen

Lenten Gospel Acclamation, Joe Regan

Eucharistic Acclamations. Acclamations for the eucharistic prayer during Lent should be simple settings. *The Danish Mass*, from which the Amen is best known, is a good lenten setting. Others are the *Mass of Remembrance* by Marty Haugen (use the lenten form for the Amen) and the *Community Mass* by Richard Proulx. Forms of the memorial acclamation more appropriate in Lent are: "Dying you destroyed our death...." and "Lord, by your cross and resurrection...." The Lord's Prayer is better recited; if it is sung use the chant mode arranged by Robert Snow. The Lamb of God litany for the Fraction Rite (breaking of bread, pouring of wine) should likewise be a simple setting. Those from Haugen's *Mass of Remembrance* and Owen Alstott's *Good Shepherd Mass* are good choices.

General Intercessions. The people's prayer in the general intercessions during Lent is most appropriately "Lord, have mercy." Musical settings for this response can be found in Michael Joncas' setting of evening prayer, *O Joyful Light*, or in the Music of Taizé, Kyries 1-11. Other music that could be used for the general intercessions include the refrain of Bob Hurd's *O God, Hear Us* and the Taizé ostinato *O Lord, Hear My Prayer*.

Gathering Rites and Penitential Rites. The penitential rite should be emphasized during Lent, and this can be done with music. As it is one of the gathering rites, music for the penitential rite and the gathering song will be considered together. Three alternatives for the gathering rite will be offered. The liturgy should begin in the same way for the first five Sundays of Lent.

1. People and ministers gather in silence. All kneel and the cantor sings the refrain from Paul Inwood's setting of Psalm 25, *Remember Your Mercy, Lord*. All sing in response. The presider leads the second form (B) of the penitential rite and says the absolution. Then all stand for the opening prayer.

2. A gathering song or antiphon is sung while the ministers process in. For example: *Remember Your Love*, verses 1-3 by The Dameans; *Remember Your Mercy*, by Paul Inwood, refrain only, sung ostinato; Taizé's *Salvator Mundi* sung ostinato; or *Tree of Life* by Marty Haugen. All kneel, and the presider leads the first form (A) of the penitential rite, that is, the *Confiteor*, and says the absolution. Then the *Kyrie* is sung and can be repeated two or three times. Finally all stand for the opening prayer.

3. People and ministers gather in silence or with song. All kneel and the deacon or cantor begins singing the first invocation of the third form (C) of the penitential rite. The people's response is also sung. A number of the Taizé settings of the *Kyrie*, numbers 1, 8, 9, and 11, provide chant tones for the cantor. Bob Hurd has a setting for the first set of invocations of Form C that is called *Penitential Rite*.

The Gloria is not sung during Lent.

Other Hymns and Songs. The song at the preparation of the gifts can be specific to the Sunday and reflect the readings. If the seasonal psalm is being used, then the proper psalm of the day may be sung at this time or at communion if it is appropriate. The song at communion can be related to the gospel but should also have a community focus. Some examples of songs that can be used throughout Lent at communion are: *To Be Your Bread* by David Haas, *Eat This Bread* by Taizé, *Behold the Lamb* by Martin Willett, and *Now In This Banquet* (using the lenten refrain) by Marty Haugen. Possibilities for the concluding song include *Lord Who Throughout These Forty Days* (tune: St. Flavian), *I Heard The Voice of Jesus* to the tune Kingsfold or the setting by Michael Joncas, and *Amazing Grace*. If *Amazing Grace* is used, consider substituting "saved and set me free" for "saved a wretch like me" in the first verse. Use the same song or silence to conclude the liturgy throughout Lent.

RCIA Rites. A good source for ritual music of the RCIA rites of Lent is David Haas' two-volume collection *Who Calls You By Name* published by GIA.

PASTORAL NOTES

1. The traditional practices of Lent: prayer, fasting, and works of charity, are to be encouraged. Fasting is action symbolic of our participation in Jesus' self-emptying (*kenosis*) and of our quest for the things that really matter. Food and drink are not the only things from which we can fast; except for the liturgy team, most parish business meetings need not be scheduled during Lent. These times then become available for prayer and for Bible study. Participation by the parish in a project like Operation Rice Bowl should be encouraged; this links our fasting with meeting the needs of those who must fast all the time.

2. One of the priorities of Lent is preparation for baptism. Be in close communication with the parish catechumenate team about the parish rite of sending for election, the three scrutinies, and the presentations of the Creed and the Lord's Prayer. Be sure that all involved have studied the *Rite of Christian Initiation of Adults*. The entire parish community should be kept informed of the progress of the catechumens toward baptism. They should be included every Sunday in the prayer of the faithful.

3. Refer to the music section above for suggestions about the penitential rite during Lent and the lenten gathering rites in general.

4. Make good use of silence: silence at the beginning or a silent departure, silence after the first and second readings, silence after the homily, silence after all have received communion.

5. The Johannine gospels of the third, fourth, and fifth Sundays in Year A may more effectively be proclaimed by several readers. This is true also for the Fourth Sunday Year C Lukan gospel. A source for these gospels and readings arranged for multiple voices is *This is the Word of the Lord* published by Ave Maria Press, Notre Dame, Indiana. In this case the texts for the readers should be in books worthy of liturgical celebration. Loose pages or a bundle of sheets held by a paper clip give the unspoken message that God's Word is temporary and disposable. When there are several books for the readings, only one is to be carried in the procession: the Book of the Gospels (or the lectionary).

6. Use of one eucharistic prayer throughout the season is highly recommended. In Year A, since the proper prefaces of the five Sundays are used, this may be followed by Eucharistic Prayer II, but they link equally well with the text of the first eucharistic prayer for Masses of Reconciliation. The prefaces for the First Sunday of Lent and for the Second Sunday of Lent may also be used in Year B and Year C since the gospel for those Sundays in all the years is the story of the Christ's temptation and of Christ's transfiguration, respectively. In Years B and C, the first eucharistic prayer for Masses of Reconciliation may be used with its own preface on the third, fourth, and fifth Sundays of Lent.

7. Likewise, use of one text for the final blessing will serve to give continuity to the season. Recommended are Solemn Blessing 5: Passion of the Lord, or Prayer over the People 4, 5, or 6.

OTHER LITURGIES

Reconciliation. Celebration of penitential services and of the sacrament of reconciliation is a priority of Lent (from Ash Wednesday to Holy Thursday). Communal celebration of reconciliation according to the second form of the rite should be scheduled once or even twice during the season, for example during the third, fourth, and fifth weeks. Various texts and even sample services are provided in the *Rite of Penance* (chapter 4 and the appendix). Times for the first form of the rite, individual confession, should also be scheduled throughout Lent. One appropriate time would be following the celebrations of the Stations of the Cross. The celebrations of the scrutinies with the elect can be powerful experiences of God's mercy and forgiveness and of God's power over sin for the entire community. If the scrutinies are not being celebrated because there are no persons to be baptized, the scrutinies can serve as a model for parish penitential services (refer to the chapter on the scrutinies later in this volume).

Liturgy of the Hours: Morning and Evening Prayer. Lent is an appropriate season to begin celebration of morning or evening prayer in the parish. The little book *Morning and Evening Prayer in the Parish* by Laurence Mayer published by Liturgy Training Publications in 1985 gives the background of communal Christian prayer and pastoral notes for application. *Praise God in Song* is a collection of services with music by Michael Joncas, Howard Hughes, and David Isele, edited by John Melloh and William Storey published by GIA in 1979.

DEVOTIONS AND PARALITURGIES

Stations of the Cross. Communal celebration of the Stations of the Cross takes place in the parish on Friday evenings or another weekday evening. Consider having a reading from sacred Scripture for each station. One list of readings for the fourteen traditional Clementine (1726) stations is:

1. 1 Peter 2:20–23;
2. 1 Peter 2:22–24;
3. Hebrews 2:17–18;
4. Luke 2:27, 34–35;
5. Matthew 25:34–36;
6. Matthew 25:37–40;
7. Luke 9:23–24;
8. Luke 23:27–31;
9. 1 Corinthians 1:21–23, 25;
10. John 13:36–38;
11. Isaiah 53:3–5;
12. Isaiah 53:6–7;
13. Isaiah 53:11–12;
14. Philippians 2:5–11.

It is becoming customary to commemorate a fifteenth station, the resurrection. A reading for this station is Philippians 3:10–16. Or consider celebrating fourteen scripturally based stations with Scripture readings, psalms, reflections, and prayers as presented in Tolbert McCarroll's *A Way of the Cross* or in *The New Scripture Way of the Cross* by Bill Huebsch based on the stations led by Pope John Paul II. Various models for celebrating the Stations and the devotion's historical origin are included later in this volume.

Solemn Celebration of the Rosary. During Lent those who wish may gather to celebrate the sorrowful mysteries of the rosary. The customary days are Monday, Thursday, and Sundays of Lent. On the Solemnity of the Annunciation, March 25th, which often falls in Lent, it would be appropriate to have a communal celebration of the joyful mysteries. A good resource for such a celebration is the book *Celebrating the Marian Year*, which is a collection of devotional celebrations in honor of Mary published by the National Conference of Catholic Bishops' Committee on the Liturgy in 1987. A reading from sacred Scripture is given for each mystery; intercessions are provided, and suggestions for music are made.

REFERENCES

Adam, Adolf, 1979. *The Liturgical Year: Its History and Its Meaning After the Reform of the Liturgy.* Chapter 5: Easter and the Easter Cycle of Feasts. Pueblo Publishing Company, New York (now a subsidiary of The Liturgical Press).

Baker, J. Robert, Evelyn Kaehle and Peter Mazar (editors), 1990. *A Lent Sourcebook: The Forty Days.* Book One and Book Two. Liturgy Training Publications, Chicago, IL.

Congregation for Divine Worship, 1988. *Circular Letter Concerning the Preparation and Celebration of the Easter Feasts* (first published in *L'Osservatore Romano*, 29 February 1988).

Days of the Lord: The Liturgical Year, Volume 2: Lent. 1993. The Liturgical Press, Collegeville, MN.

Freburger, Rev. William J., 1974. *This Is The Word of the Lord.* Ave Maria Press, Notre Dame, IN.

Huebsch, Bill, 1993. *The New Scripture Way of the Cross.* Twenty-Third Publications, Mystic, CT.

Irwin, Kevin, 1985. *Lent: A Guide to the Eucharist and Hours.* Pueblo Publishing Company, New York (now a subsidiary of The Liturgical Press).

McCarroll, Tolbert, 1985. *A Way of the Cross.* Paulist Press, Mahwah, NJ.

Nocent, Adrian, O.S.B., 1977. *The Liturgical Year.* Volume 2: Lent and Holy Week. The Liturgical Press, Collegeville, MN.

Sanchez, Patricia Datchuck, 1989. *The Word We Celebrate: Commentary on the Sunday Lectionary, Years A, B, and C.* Sheed and Ward, Kansas City, MO.

Simcoe, Mary Ann (editor), 1985. *Parish Path through Lent and Eastertime.* Liturgy Training Publications, Chicago, IL.

Taft, Robert, S.J., 1984. Lent: A Meditation in *Beyond East and West: Problems in Liturgical Understanding.* The Pastoral Press, Washington, D.C. pp 49-60 (originally published in *Worship* 57:123-134 [1983]).

Restoring Unity to the 90 Days: Lent as Preparation for Easter

Jayne Newton Ahearn

This article is one of a pair that will be completed in the Easter section under the title: "Easter As a Reflection On Lent." It proposes a unifying approach to the celebration of the seasons of Lent and Easter by adopting the process of the Rite of Christian Initiation of Adults for the entire parish.

THE PASCHAL MYSTERY

For Christians, the climactic and complete revelation of God was in the person of the historical Jesus of Nazareth. Jesus was the manifestation of God's gratuitous offer of Godself to humanity and was the manifestation of the free response of humanity to God through his total self-giving for others. The Jesus event is the foundational event that gives Christians meaning and identity. Because of Jesus' incarnation, passion, death, resurrection, and ascension, all humanity is offered a share in God's life. The mystery revealed by the historical Jesus event—God coming to us and saving us in God's Son—is actualized in every age by *anamnesis* (remembering). Because of God's promise and through the Holy Spirit, the person Jesus continues to be contemporary: present to us now, saving us now.

This is what the disciples experienced when they gathered after Jesus' death and burial—as soon as the Sabbath was over on the first day of the week—to remember the person Jesus and share bread and wine in his name. Together, they experienced the presence of Jesus as the risen One; together, they experienced the world as created anew; together, they experienced themselves as having a new identity and meaning. What they did together was both source and expression of their new life in Christ. So they and Christians ever since have repeated it Sunday after Sunday. Sunday embodies the entirety of the mystery of salvation.

This mystery—the paschal mystery—must be appropriated and entered into by each person in every age and place. This is the ministry of the church, which is done primarily through celebration of the liturgy. By its very name—*mystery*—we realize that we can always seek deeper understanding, find deeper meaning, approach through yet another facet. Hence the mystery that the first Christians celebrated on Sunday has through the centuries expanded into the liturgical year. The evolution of the liturgical year was useful because we are limited in our ability to focus on the entirety in any one celebration. However, the evolution of the liturgical year was also problematic since with the partitioning of our remembrance of the entire mystery came also a loss of continuity, the tendency to see seasons and feasts and even Sundays as individual celebrations with different "themes."

DEVELOPMENT OF LITURGICAL YEAR AND CATECHUMENATE

The season of Lent-Easter and the catechumenate (the means by which the church makes available the paschal mystery for appropriation) developed together co-dependently. By the early second century Christians were celebrating an annual Pasch: a night vigil of readings and fasting commemorating the passion and death of Jesus, which was concluded after midnight with the

Eucharist as the sign of the resurrection with its eschatological hope. The paschal fast of the vigil that was ended by the Eucharist began forty hours earlier and was an outward sign of participating in the death of Christ. The *participatio* theology, developed by Paul, understood the Christian as a participant in the acts of Christ (see Romans 6). It was no longer Christ who suffered, who died, who rose but Christ and the Christian who suffer, who die, who rise. This participation in Christ brings the paschal mystery to the present dimension. And access to the mystery is gained through baptism. Hence the annual paschal feast became the most solemn time for Christian initiation.

In the third century the season gradually began to take shape, extending back to include from two to six penitential fast days (depending on the local church). The celebration season also extended forward to include the time the Jews called Pentecost: the feast of weeks or the 50 days. From the writings of Tertullian and the Apostolic Tradition we know that by 215 C.E. there was a well-developed catechumenate with an intense preparation time proximate to baptism.

The turning point for the early church was the Edict of Milan of 313 C.E., which ended the persecution of Christians by Rome and gave Christianity a legal equality with other religions. Ultimately the Roman Empire took on the cause of Christ as its own. In the fourth century, then, the church became free to grow and develop. The catechumenate enjoyed its "golden age" from 350 to 450 C.E. The pre-baptismal preparation time expanded to six weeks or forty days (depending upon the local church). By 320 C.E. the baptized were joining with the catechumens in the instructions and practices of Lent: instruction and practices that were to support conversion. A number of bishops (Cyril of Jerusalem, John Chrysostom in Antioch, Theodore of Mopsuestia, Ambrose of Milan, Augustine of Hippo) preached for the benefit of catechumens before baptism and for the newly baptized during the days and weeks following baptism. Many of these homilies are still available to us. Those addressed to the newly baptized, were called mystagogical (meaning "studying the mystery") homilies, and were meant to help the neophytes understand the sacraments in which they now were participants. (Thus, this same period has been called the "golden age of sacramental theology"). The stational liturgies celebrated in Jerusalem during Holy Week (that is, liturgies celebrated at historic sites on the day they most likely occurred) were transported to other parts of the world by pilgrims, most notably a lady from Spain named Egeria who kept a detailed dairy of all she heard and saw. Thus were developed the unique liturgies of the week prior to the Easter Vigil, the liturgies of Holy Week. And the unitary feast of the Pasch was broken down into components: Holy Thursday, Good Friday, and Easter: the Triduum or Three Days.

From 500 C.E. on, a set of circumstances led to the gradual decline and finally the disappearance of the catechumenate. With more and more adults Christian, there were more infants than adults to be baptized. And Augustine's theology of original sin led to the conclusion that infants must be baptized as soon as possible after birth. By the time of the missions to the barbarians (500-700 C.E.), there functionally was no catechumenate to support the work of evangelization and conversion. All that was left was a ritual that had been used for the emergency baptism of sick or dying adults that was now being used with infants and disconnected from the liturgical year. This was indeed the case until 1972 when the *Rite of Christian Initiation of Adults* was promulgated.

CATECHUMENAL PROCESS

The catechumenate, during its golden age, supported a whole process that was called "baptism." This process was to lead to the establishment of new relationships for the individual with the church, with Christ, and with God. The person became a member of the church through initiation. The person also became a participant in Christ and was identified with Christ. This understanding was first developed by Paul. The person was reconciled with God through forgiveness of sin, was regenerated or created anew, adopted as a child of God, and had heaven opened to them—in Eastern terminology they were divinized. These new relationships could be established because the person freely accepted them as a gift. The acceptance involved a turning or conversion from faith in other gods to faith in God who saves us in Christ by Christ's paschal mystery. The practices of the catechumenate supported that conversion. It was recognized early on that conversion must be ongoing, must continue even after baptism. Thus practices supporting conversion, also called penance, were engaged in by the baptized especially during Lent.

The restoration of the adult catechumenate by the Second Vatican Council has contributed significantly to our perception of church as community, our understanding of grace as relationship with God, and our celebration of the liturgy throughout the liturgical year, (but especially Lent-Easter) as *anamnesis* of the paschal mystery—the mystery of our salvation by God in Christ. The catechumenate and Lent-Easter developed symbiotically. Each requires the other for its fullness. The RCIA is very specific about requiring the process of initiation to be accommodated to the liturgical year with the initiation sacraments celebrated at the Easter Vigil and the proximate preparation period coinciding with Lent (*RCIA* nos. 7, 16). It should also be true that Lent-Easter cannot be celebrated in its fullness without catechumens or at least the catechumenal process.

For the catechumens the First Sunday of Lent coincides with the Rite of Election.

> At this second step, on the basis of the testimony of godparents and catechists and of the catechumens' reaffirmation of their intention, the Church judges their state of readiness and decides on their advancement toward the sacraments of initiation.... This step is called election because the acceptance made by the Church is founded on the election by God, in whose name the Church acts. (*RCIA* no.119)

Those who are elected by God join the ranks of those throughout the ages who have been called by God to act as God's representative in some service or deed. Moses is an example of one who was elected (Ex 3:1–10). The church is charged with being the primary vehicle through which God is revealed to and acts in the world and at the same time the primary representative to God for the world (hence, the need for intercession for the needs of the world). Election bears great responsibility.

God does not always choose the most likely or most qualified person for the job. Recall that Moses was called to speak to Pharaoh on behalf of the Hebrews but he stuttered (Ex 4:10). After choosing a representative, God puts them to a test, allows them to endure a period of trial to prepare them for the job to be done. Abraham was asked to sacrifice his son, Isaac (Gn 10:1–18). Moses met severe resistance from Pharaoh as "The Lord hardened Pharaoh's heart" (Ex 4:21). Often the tests took place in the desert (wilderness away from settlements). Recall the temptation of Jesus. The Rite of Election begins the period of Purification and Enlightenment.

> The period of purification and enlightenment, which the Rite of Election begins, customarily coincides with Lent. In the liturgy and liturgical catechesis of Lent the reminder of baptism already received or the preparation for its reception, as well as the theme of repentance, renew the entire community along with those being prepared to celebrate the paschal mystery. For both the elect and the local community therefore, the Lenten season is a time for spiritual recollection in preparation for the celebration of the paschal mystery.
>
> This is a period of more intense spiritual preparation, consisting more in interior reflection than in catechetical instruction, and is intended to purify the minds and hearts of the elect as they search their own consciences and do penance. This period is intended as well to enlighten the minds and hearts of the elect with a deeper knowledge of Christ the Savior. (*RCIA* no. 138, 139)

These paragraphs clearly set the agenda for Lent as a time of conversion and preparation not only for the elect but also for the baptized. The scrutinies and the presentations are the liturgical rites of Lent that support the process for the elect.

> The scrutinies...are rites for self-searching and repentance and have above all a spiritual purpose.... The scrutinies are celebrated in order to deliver and elect from the power of sin and Satan, to protect them against temptation, and to give them strength in Christ who is the way, the truth, and the life. These rites, therefore, should complete the conversion of the elect and deepen their resolve to hold fast to Christ and to carry out their decision to love God above all.
>
> ...the elect must have the intention of achieving an intimate knowledge of Christ and his Church, and they are expected particularly to progress in genuine self-knowledge through serious examination of their lives and true repentance. (*RCIA* no. 141, 142)
>
> The presentations take place after the celebration of the scrutinies .... Thus...the Church lovingly entrusts to

them the Creed and the Lord's Prayer, the ancient texts that have always been regarded as expressing the heart of the Church's faith and prayer. These texts are presented in order to enlighten the elect. (*RCIA* no. 147)

The culmination of the process of Christian initiation is the celebration of the initiation sacraments of baptism, confirmation, and Eucharist at the Easter Vigil. In the midst of the community the elect profess their faith (the interrogatory form of the Creed) and are immersed into Christ's death and resurrection in baptismal waters. They share in the outpouring of the Holy Spirit and then, for the first time and with full right, they reach the culminating point: they share in the offering of the sacrifice as members of the royal priesthood and pray the Lord's Prayer in the spirit of God's adopted children.

How does this translate to the celebration of Lent by the baptized—especially in the absence of the catechumenate? The spirit of this season remains as one of purification and enlightenment in preparation for renewal of baptism at the Easter Vigil. In the ritual for Ash Wednesday of the Book of Common Prayer, the introduction to the blessing and giving of ashes is a call to the baptized to continuing conversion.

> Dear People of God: The first Christians observed with great devotion the days of our Lord's passion and resurrection, and it became the custom of the Church to prepare for them by a season of penitence (conversion) and fasting. This season of Lent provided a time in which (those who came to) faith (in Jesus) were prepared for Holy Baptism. It was also a time when those who, because of notorious sins, had been separated from the body of the faithful were reconciled by penitence and forgiveness, and restored to the fellowship of the Church. Thereby, the whole congregation was put in mind of the message of pardon and (reconciliation) set forth in the Gospel of our Saviour, and of the need which all Christians continually have to renew their repentance (conversion) and faith.
>
> I invite you: therefore, in the name of the Church, to the observance of a holy Lent, by self-examination and repentance: by prayer, fasting and self-denial and by reading and meditation on God's Holy Word. (*Book of Common Prayer* pp. 264-265)

In the article on the scrutinies in this volume it is proposed that the praxis of conversion of the RCIA is paradigmatic for all Christian life. The elements of this praxis include: 1) appropriating the meaning of the death of Christ, that is, embracing the cross, 2) responding to God's Word such that priorities and commitments are reordered, 3) engaging in biographical reconstruction, that is, changing our story because God's presence and action in it is recognized, 4) responding with praise and thanksgiving for that gift, and 5) continuing the process. Prayer, fasting, and acts of charity have, from early on (for example, as recorded in the *Didache* 50-90 C.E.) been the church's means of supporting conversion. Fasting and almsgiving are liturgical acts through which we participate in the death of Christ. The Sunday liturgies, if well prepared and celebrated, allow for reflection on the readings such that biographical reconstruction might occur and then lead to the response of praise and thanksgiving in the Eucharist.

A SAMPLING OF SUNDAY READINGS FOR LENT

The Introduction to the Lectionary (no. 13.1) gives an overview of the readings provided for the Sundays of Lent. The gospel is always pivotal but also stands in the context of the Old Testament and apostolic selections. On the First and Second Sundays of Lent the gospel accounts are of Jesus' temptation and transfiguration, respectively. Sundays Three through Five traditionally are the Johannine accounts of the Samaritan woman, the man born blind, and the raising of Lazarus—these are the gospels of the scrutinies, whether in Year A or any year in which they are celebrated, for in them we meet Jesus who is Savior.

However, if the scrutinies are not being celebrated (in the absence of a catechumenate) two sets of alternatives are provided in the texts of Year B and Year C. In Year B the Johannine texts offer the image of Jesus' mission being the example of God's love for the world and the preparation of the disciples to understand the approaching death of Jesus. In Year C, the gospel presents the Lukan texts on reconciliation. The Old Testament readings are about the history of salvation from the beginning to the promise of a new covenant. The story of Abraham and of the Exodus are heard on the Second and Third Sundays, respectively. The selections from the writings of the apostles support and augment the gospel and Old Testament readings.

Preparation for the liturgy begins with reflection on the readings. Then selection of composition of prayers and other texts, preparation of the homily, choices of music, and even designing of the worship environment all flow from the readings. Pastorally, each year we shape our approach to Lent through the last Sunday of Ordinary Time in the post-Epiphany period, regardless of which cycle of readings is used in that year. Then Ash Wednesday calls us to the forty days of continuing conversion in which we will once again appropriate the paschal mystery and which will culminate in a renewal of our immersion into this mystery in baptism during Holy Week and especially at the Easter Vigil. The movement is from recalling our election and the purpose for which we were called (Ash Wednesday, Lent 1, and the RCIA Rite of Election) through the period of trial or testing supported by a preview of the outcome (Lent 2) that invites us deeper and deeper into participation in the paschal mystery by being conformed more and more to Christ.

Our inner intentions are reflected by our acts and also formed by our acts. Here begins our reflection on how well we are doing that for which we have been elected by God. The task of the church is to be the continuing presence of Christ in the world and the sign that all humanity has been reconciled to God in Christ. Each one of us and the whole church is known by its deeds. This all seems an impossible task since we know we are always struggling with sin. The good news is announced by Paul in the letter to the Corinthians. Sin and its consequence, death, have been overcome. Thanks be to God who has given us the victory through our Lord Jesus Christ (1 Cor 15:57). This is our song of praise today as it will be at the Easter Vigil. Our lenten journey helps us to claim the gift of victory by conforming ourselves in deed, and thus in heart and mind, more and more to Christ.

Ash Wednesday

These are the familiar readings we hear each year. The call to continuing conversion is issued with trumpet blasts gathering all the people (Joel). Now...even now echoes the urgent cry to begin. Paul makes a statement of the task of the church. We are ambassadors for Christ, God as it were appealing through us (2 Cor 5:20). In order to do this we must be sharing in God's life: reconciled to God. The gospel (Mt) lays out the activities that will support our inner conversion: prayer, fasting, and acts of charity.

First Sunday of Lent

On this day the Rite of Election is celebrated. Our election by God is for the task of proclaiming by deeds that humanity has been reconciled to God in Christ. To the Romans, Paul writes that faith in the heart is linked to confession with the lips. The first reading from Deuteronomy describes the ritual by which the Hebrews were to make proclamation of God's deeds of salvation: to tell the story over offerings to God of the first fruits of the land and then to make merry over all the good things the Lord had given. The church does the same in the celebration of the Eucharist. Those elected by God are made fit for the task through testing. The gospel tells the story of Jesus' temptation, and notice that it is the Spirit who leads Jesus into the desert. We are all tempted by the desire for economic, political, and even religious power. Jesus, alone, resisted. But in Christ, we too are victorious.

Second Sunday of Lent

We are continuing to struggle through our testing. Paul, to the Philippians, exhorts us to imitate Christ by embracing the cross. This is a frightening prospect, for we, like Abram and Peter, James and John, are terrified of the darkness. The first reading (Gn) tells the story of God making covenant with Abram, and the gospel (Lk) is the account of the transfiguration of Jesus, a preview of the glory that is ours in the new covenant established by Jesus' paschal mystery. The glory of God is encountered in the midst of the darkness. Paul says we must continue to stand firm.

Third Sunday of Lent

The continuing urgent call to reform is contextualized in God's mercy and patience. In the gospel, Jesus' challenge to reform now is contrasted with the parable of the fig tree, teaching us that God is also patient and nurturing (Lk). Paul uses the passage by Moses and the

Israelites through the Red Sea as a type for baptism. But, says Paul, though God rescued the Israelites he was not pleased with most of them, and the same is true for the baptized who do not live out their baptismal commitment. Like the Israelites, we may not make it through the desert—the place of testing (1 Cor). On this day the first scrutiny is celebrated. We are drawn into consideration of the mystery of sin by the first reading and the gospel. In both the innocent suffer the consequences of sin along with the guilty. It is God who intervenes through Moses "I have come down to rescue them" (Ex 3:8). The first reading is the "burning bush" experience of Moses, which is the paradigm for *mysterion* or experiencing the presence of God. Because of his encounter with the living God (The God whose name is I AM) Moses is forever changed. We can be forever changed if we turn to the power that God has over sin and is available to us in Christ.

Fourth Sunday of Lent

We are told yet again that ours is the ministry of reconciliation (2 Cor, overlaps with the Ash Wednesday reading). The means by which we proclaim reconciliation with God is in the Eucharist—the proleptic sign of the new creation. In the first reading (Jos) the Israelites at last enter the promised land and celebrate Passover because God forgave them. The gospel is the well known (but don't think you really know this story ... there are always surprises) Lukan story of the "prodigal son" or "the merciful father" in which the reconciliation is celebrated by a sumptuous banquet. Today the second scrutiny is celebrated. Those preparing for baptism are experiencing the saving power of Christ. The accusation against Jesus was that he welcomes sinners and eats with them. Sometime in the week ahead would be a good time for the parish celebration of the sacrament of reconciliation so that those who have not been coming to the Table might once again be welcomed and eat with Christ.

Fifth Sunday of Lent

We are invited to become part of something new by embracing the paschal mystery. In the desert, life-giving waters will flow (Isaiah). In our lenten desert where we have wrestled with the beasts, we will soon encounter the fullness that is God.

For the elect, today is the third and final scrutiny. The gospel (Jn) is the story of the woman caught in adultery who encountered God in Christ and came away a new person. Though we now stand on the brink of Holy Week, that most sacred and awesome commemoration of our Lord's passion, death, and resurrection, the readings are quite joyful. Back on the Sunday before Ash Wednesday, Paul thanked God for the victory we have over sin in Christ. That victory came because Jesus was faithful to God even to death. That victory is ours as we participate in Christ: his suffering, death, resurrection, and ascension. Today Paul to the Philippians continues praying to share in Christ's sufferings and even to be formed into the pattern of his death so that he may also know the power of the resurrection and share life on high in Christ Jesus. That continues to be our prayer.

PRESIDENTIAL PRAYERS

The selection of opening prayer and of the eucharistic prayer is made within the context of the readings. The function of the opening prayer is to complete our gathering as the Body of Christ and prepare us for the readings. In effect, it serves as an introduction to the readings.

Eucharistic Prayer for Masses of Reconciliation I is most appropriate for use throughout the entire season. In it are to be found threads from many of the readings. This prayer has its own preface, which is superior to most of the Lenten prefaces available for use. The prefaces titled "First Sunday of Lent" through "Fifth Sunday of Lent" are composed for use only when the readings are from Year A.

A CLOSING EXHORTATION

So that Lent is indeed a time of preparation for baptism and the renewal of baptism, parish policy should be publicly proclaimed that baptisms will not be celebrated during Lent. This may cause some initial confusion, and even pain, but it is more theologically coherent with the spirit of the season rather than just responding to the perceived preferences of parishioners' timetables.

REFERENCES

Parish Path through Lent and Eastertime edited by Mary Ann Simcoe, Liturgy Training Publications, Chicago, 1985 (Includes an introduction to the seasons, orientations to the readings and prayers, notes on preaching, also deals with the RCIA music and worship environment).

Celebrating the Easter Vigil edited by Rupert Berger and Hans Hollerweger, Pueblo Publishing Company, New York, NY, U.S.A. 1983. (Provides content, form, and advice for celebrating the vigil as well as overviews of the Sunday readings of Lent which lead into the vigil.)

The Three Days: Parish Prayer in the Paschal Triduum by Gabe Huck, Liturgy Training Publications, Chicago, 1981/1992.

On Becoming A Catholic: The Challenge of Christian Initiation by Regis Duffy O.F.M., Harper & Row, Publishers, San Francisco 1984 (A liturgical theology of the RCIA).

"The Praxis of Conversion," pp 13-34 in: *Initiation and Conversion* by Regis Duffy O.F.M., The Liturgical Press, Collegville, MN, 1985 (Develops the methodology supporting initial and continuing conversion).

The Scrutinies: Not for RCIA Only

Jayne Newton Ahearn

... how we celebrate and think about reconciliation and penance usually reflects for better or worse, our praxis and theology of initiation (Regis Duffy, 1984, p. 165).

Margaret Mary Kelleher (1986) gives insight into the reason for this in her application of Lonergan's discussion of acts of meaning to the liturgy. In the liturgical act, the ecclesial subject mediates itself.

> In its public worship the church, as it is realized in each local assembly, discloses a horizon, a corporate vision of what it means to live as a Christian. This vision is mediated by the symbols of the liturgy and made available to the community. It is a public spirituality disclosed in the liturgy and offered to individuals for their personal appropriation.... Individuals become themselves in relation to a horizon which is initially received from the communities to which they belong.... Since the church is a community, it plays a significant role in offering a horizon to those who are in the process of becoming Christians.

What the church does in the liturgy expresses what the church is and what it is becoming.

PENANCE AND RECONCILIATION

Before looking at how the way we celebrate initiation expresses the meaning of the church and at the same time forms individuals concerning reconciliation and penance, it is necessary to distinguish between and clarify the two (cf. Mannion, 1986). Through the death and resurrection of Christ and resulting gift of the Holy Spirit, all of humanity was reconciled, restored to unity, united with God. Individuals appropriate this through baptism, which then is the primary experience of reconciliation, and continue to express/experience reconciliation in the Eucharist. Post-baptismal reconciliation restores baptized Christians who have become separated through serious sin from the communion of the church. Penance is a translation of the Greek word *metanoia* or conversion. Conversion begins in the process of Christian initiation but continues throughout the life of a Christian. Conversion is interior—a change of heart—but is expressed through deeds that become a way of living. It is the mission of the church, the community of the reconciled, to draw in those still in need of reconciliation. At the same time, the church needs to acknowledge, through the deeds of penance, its incompleteness, its own brokenness and sin, and that it is continually in the process of conversion. James Dallen (1990) says that the church must experience itself both as penitent and as reconciling community.

SCRUTINIES MODEL PENANCE AND RECONCILIATION

Conversion and reconciliation are first experienced through the process of Christian initiation. Thus the process of the Rite of Christian Initiation of Adults (RCIA) is paradigmatic. The praxis of conversion of the RCIA becomes the same for the rest of Christian life. (Do not be misled by the term "praxis of conversion." Remember that people engage in practices but conversion is God's work). Elements of this praxis include:

1. appropriating the meaning of the death of Christ: that is, embracing the cross:

2. responding to God's Word such that priorities and commitments are reordered:

3. engaging in biographical reconstruction: that is, changing one's story because God's presence and action is recognized:

4. responding with praise and thanksgiving for the gift: and

5. continuing the process (Duffy, 1985).

The celebration of the scrutinies exemplifies this praxis. The elect both engage in and are being formed for future penitential practice.

> The scrutinies...are rites for self-searching and repentance and have above all a spiritual purpose. The scrutinies are meant to uncover, then heal all that is weak, defective or sinful in the hearts of the Elect: to bring out then strengthen all that is upright, strong and good. For the scrutinies are celebrated in order to deliver the Elect from the power of sin and Satan, to protect them against temptation and to give them strength in Christ who is the way, the truth, and the life. (*RCIA* no. 141)

At the same time, as the baptized celebrate with the elect, they experience themselves as penitent and as reconciling community. This means we need to "carry out the celebration in such way that the faithful in the assembly will also derive benefit from the liturgy..." (*RCIA* no. 145).

For the baptized, the elect are a witness to the power of Christ's healing and reconciling through the church. Or as Kelleher (1985) says, through these liturgies, the church mediates itself.

CELEBRATING THE SCRUTINIES

The context of the scrutinies is near the end of the initiation process, which may have already been a long journey of conversion. The Rite of Election has been celebrated, which ends the catechumenate proper and begins the intense "retreat-like" period, coinciding with Lent, in which the elect step back and reexamine their story. They are already part of the household of faith and called Christian. But they are in between, having moved from what they once were but not having reached what they hope to become. In a few weeks they will be baptized, confirmed, and for the first time celebrate the Eucharist. The scrutinies are celebrated within the Sunday liturgy, and there are ritual Masses proper to their celebration.

The scrutinies take place after the homily in the Liturgy of the Word. They begin with prayer in silence followed by intercessions. Then there is the exorcism, which is in two parts: the first prayer is addressed to God, the second to Jesus. Between the two parts there is an option for the presider to impose hands on each elect. Following the exorcism, a song may be sung, and then the elect are dismissed to continue their reflections.

Readings are Central

Robert Duggan (1988, 1989) and Mark Searle (1988) have written commentaries on the three scrutinies. This chapter draws on their work as well as this author's experience with celebrating the rites. The readings used are always those of the third, fourth, and fifth Sundays of Lent, Year A. Both Duggan and Searle point out the importance of all the readings, but the gospels are pivotal: the Johannine stories of the Samaritan woman at the well, the healing of the man born blind, and the raising of Lazarus from the dead. In these can be seen a progression from individual sin to social sin to radical sin and death. In each case, the elect are invited into biographical reconstruction as they review their own story in relation to the gospel story. They ask: How has Christ quenched my thirsts? What are the thirsts/hungers that I need Christ to fill? How has Christ enlightened me? What are the things I still refuse to see/acknowledge? How/where has Christ already freed me/brought me new life? From what do I still need to be freed? What are the dead things in my life? Out of such reflections come both the acknowledgment of sin and the recognition of Christ's power over sin. And this, in turn, allows them to pray eucharistically: what God did through Christ for the Samaritan woman, for the blind man, for Lazarus, and as God has done for me in the past, so let God through Christ do for me now so that my future will be changed.

Duggan (1989) suggests that a process of discernment be used with the elect so that the prayers of the scrutinies will reflect their needs. This process can take the shape of a preparation and reflection time for elect and sponsor in which the gospel is read several times; they identify with characters in the story, explore feelings and reactions, and finally answer the questions posed above. The sponsor reports the results of the reflections to the liturgist who then composes the intercessions and chooses the exorcism prayers.

The opening prayers for these liturgies all recall the choice by God of the elect and look forward to their rebirth in baptism. They use images of water, light, and life and are joyful in spirit. During the silent time of prayer following the homily the assembled faithful pray

> that the Elect be given a spirit of repentance, a sense of sin and the true freedom of the children of God. (*RCIA* no. 152)

This sacred silence and prayers flow out of the gospel and other readings and into the intercessions. It is the homily that helps all to make the connections (such as the elect have already made in their preparation time) and enables prayer. So, the role of the homilist is crucial.

Intercessions

The intercessions follow the pattern of the prayer of the faithful with an invitation to pray by the presider, petitions by a cantor or other minister, and a response such as "Lord, have mercy" sung or recited by the people. Responses specific to the gospel text can also be used: for example: "Lord, give us living water," "Lord, be our light," and "Give us Lord, a new heart." There are formularies given for the prayers but there is also the freedom given to adapt them.

The invitations to pray set the tone of the prayers as asking for assistance and healing as the elect move toward the sacraments. These are not prayers of guilt. Two sets of intercessions are offered for each scrutiny: the first is generic, the second relates to the gospel of the day ("that like the woman of Samaria, our elect may review their lives before Christ and acknowledge their sins..." RCIA no. 153B).

In each there are prayers for the elect:

> that they may ponder the word of God in their hearts and savor its meaning more fully day by day ... (*RCIA* no. 153A)

> that they may humbly confess themselves to be sinners ... (*RCIA* no. 153A)

> that faith may strengthen them against worldly deceits of every kind ...(*RCIA* no. 174A)

and also for their families:

> that their families also may put their hope in Christ and find peace and holiness in him... (*RCIA* no. 153A)

There are also prayers for the church embodied in the local community:

> that we ourselves in preparation for the Easter feast may seek a change of heart, give ourselves to prayer, and persevere in good works... (*RCIA* no. 153A)

> that we who are faced with the values of the world may remain faithful to the spirit of the Gospel... (*RCIA* no. 167A)

and for the world:

> that throughout the whole world whatever is weak may be strengthened, whatever is broken restored, whatever is lost found, and what is found redeemed... (*RCIA* no. 153A)

There are supplications for the working of the Holy Spirit (the reconciling force):

> that the Holy Spirit, who searches every heart, may help them to overcome their weakness through his power... (*RCIA* no. 153A)

> that they may be filled with the hope of the life-giving Spirit and prepare themselves thoroughly for their birth to new life... (*RCIA* no. 174B)

The response of thankfulness is clearly requested in one example:

> that they may always thank God, who has chosen to rescue them from their ignorance of eternal life and to set them on the way of salvation... (*RCIA* no. 174A)

Exorcism

Of the exorcisms *RCIA* no. 144 says:

> the Elect, who have already learned from the Church as their mother the mystery of deliverance from sin by Christ, are freed from the effect of sin and from the influence of the devil. They receive new strength in the midst of their spiritual journey and they open their hearts to receive the gifts of the Savior.

The first prayer addresses God as powerful, merciful, source of life. The saving deeds of God through Christ are recalled: those deeds of the gospel stories

...through your Son you revealed your mercy to the woman of Samaria: and moved by that same care you have offered salvation to all sinners. (*RCIA* no. 154B)

.... you led the man born blind to the kingdom of light through the gift of faith in your Son. (*RCIA* no. 168A)

Then this same God is called upon to

...protect them from vain reliance on self (*RCIA* no. 154A)

...defend them from the power of Satan (*RCIA* no. 154A),

...free these Elect from the false values that surround and blind them (*RCIA* no. 168A),

...enable them to pass from darkness to light (*RCIA* n. 168B).

God's action will result in transformation for future mission:

...that they may serve you faithfully in peace and joy and render you thanks for ever (*RCIA* no. 154B)

...so that they may bear witness to their new life in the risen Christ ... (*RCIA* no. 175A).

The second prayer is addressed to Christ, Lord Jesus Master, fountain, true light that enlightens the world. Supplication is made for the gifts of strength, of healing, of life and of the Spirit:

In your love free them from their infirmities, heal their sickness, quench their thirst and give them peace...stand by them now and heal them (*RCIA* no. 154A)

Through your Spirit, who gives life, fill them with faith, hope, and charity ... (*RCIA* no. 175A).

Again, these gifts will fit the elect for their mission as Christians

...that they may come to worship the Father in truth ... (*RCIA* no. 154A)

...let them prove to be staunch and fearless witnesses to the faith (*RCIA* no. 684A).

The rite suggests that a psalm be sung after the exorcism and lists eleven as examples of what is appropriate (*RCIA* nos. 154, 168, 175). Of those, only a few have familiar musical settings. Psalm 51 has been set by Bob Hurd, *Create In Me*; David Haas, *Create In Me a Clean Heart*; and Marty Haugen *Be Merciful O Lord*. Psalm 130 has settings by the Dameans, *Remember Your Love*; by Marty Haugen, *With the Lord There Is Mercy*; Tim Mannion, *With Our God There Is Mercy*; and Michael Joncas, *With the Lord*. Psalm 139 is best known as *You Are Near* by Dan Schutte but has also been set by David Haas as *You've Searched Me, Lord*. These psalms express confidence and trust in placing our sinfulness before God because God will heal. Other possibilities for song that have been tried and found to work include the well-known *Amazing Grace* and *I Heard the Voice of Jesus*.

Dismissal

The texts for the dismissal of the elect offer assurance that God is and will be with them as will the support and prayers of the community (of which they are already a part). They also look to the future. For example, *RCIA* no. 169, Form B:

My dear friends, this community now sends you forth to reflect more deeply upon the word of God which you have shared with us today. Be assured of our loving support and prayers for you. We look forward to the day when you will share fully in the Lord's Table.

After the elect have departed, the liturgy continues with Eucharist which is the sign of reconciliation.

Symbol and Gesture

That these rites take place in the midst of the Sunday Eucharist assembly with its various ministerial roles adds greatly to their power. The presiding priest, the sponsors, the assembly, and the word proclaimed all mediate the presence of Christ. The elect both identify and are identified with the Samaritan woman, with the man born blind, with Lazarus.

Posture and gesture combine with the various roles to convey meaning. During the rite, the elect and their sponsors come before the assembly and the presider. If the worship space allows, placing the elect and their sponsors in the midst of the assembly (for example, taking places down the center aisle) may shift the tone from judgment to healing ministry. The elect are invited to kneel during the silent prayer (*RCIA* no. 152), which indicates their penitential attitude.

Kneeling by all at this time could signify the solidarity of the baptized with the elect in their continuing need for conversion. The sponsors, as representative of the entire community, are with the elect and place hands on their shoulders during the intercessions (*RCIA* no. 153). They could continue this contact during the exorcism prayer.

The baptized stand during the intercessions: the elect stand but they could also remain kneeling. The presider says the first part of the exorcism prayer with hands joined, then for the second part he extends his hands over the elect as an epicletic gesture. The entire assembly might join in this gesture since the Spirit resides not only in the priest but also in the baptized.

The imposition of hands on each elect, though optional, has proved its power and is not to be passed by, unless the presider will not do it effectively. This is not a tap on the head but prolonged touching while the presider prays silently for the individual.

SCRUTINIES FOR THE WHOLE CHURCH

As signs of the journey of conversion toward the reconciliation of baptism, the scrutinies allow the church to experience itself as penitent and as reconciling community. Furthermore, they can be models for celebration of ongoing conversion (penance) of the baptized as well. Jim Lopresti (1987) has addressed the question of whether baptized Christians preparing for full communion in the Catholic church should celebrate the scrutinies. He concludes that since these persons are in extraordinary circumstances—not fully initiated in the Catholic church—"confession" is inappropriate for them and they should celebrate the scrutinies using texts that take into account that they are baptized. The 1988 American version of the RCIA does provide for the celebration of a scrutiny as part of the optional rites for baptized but uncatechized adults (*RCIA* nos. 464-470).

In the last 25 years, the attitudes of Catholics about sin and reconciliation have changed. The shift has been from focus on the individual to focus on the community (Hater, 1985). The experience of communities of the RCIA is probably contributing to this change. In 1990, James Dallen wrote yet again on the current rites for reconciliation and concluded that they are in need of revision because they are not meeting the pastoral need. When celebrated carefully and well the scrutinies do certainly meet the need to celebrate ongoing conversion as well as provide (when celebrated within Mass) the experience of reconciling reconciled community.

REFERENCES

Dallen, James, 1990. "Reconciliation in the Sacrament of Penance." *Worship* 64(5): 386-405.

Duffy, Regis A., O.F.M., 1984. *On Becoming A Catholic: The Challenge of Christian Initiation.* Harper & Row Publishers, San Francisco.

Duffy, Regis A., O.F.M., 1985. "The Praxis of Conversion," In: *Initiation and Conversion,* pp. 13-34. The Liturgical Press, Collegeville MN.

Duggan, Robert, D., 1988 "Coming to Know Jesus Christ: The First Scrutiny." *Catechumenate* 10(4): 2-10.

Duggan, Robert D., 1989. "God Towers Over Evil. The Second Scrutiny." *Catechumenate* 11(1): 2-8.

Hater, Robert J., 1985. "Sin and Reconciliation: Changing Attitudes in the Catholic Church." *Worship* 59(1):18-31.

Kelleher, Margaret Mary, 1985. "Liturgy: An Ecclesial Act of Meaning." *Worship* 59(6):482-497.

Mannion, W. Francis, 1986. "Penance and Reconciliation: A Systemic Analysis." *Worship* 60(2):98-118.

Lopresti, James, 1987. "Scrutinies or Confession?" *Catechumenate* 9(4):15-19.

Rite of Christian Initiation of Adults, 1988. Liturgy Training Publications, Chicago. (by authority of the Bishops' Committee on the Liturgy, National Conference of Catholic Bishops).

Searle, Mark, 1988. "For the Glory of God: The Scrutiny for the Fifth Sunday of Lent." *Catechumenate* 10(1):40-47.

Holy Week and the Paschal Triduum

Jayne Newton Ahearn

DESCRIPTION

During Holy Week the Church celebrates the mysteries of salvation accomplished by Christ in the last day of his life on earth, beginning with his messianic entrance into Jerusalem. (*Circular Letter Concerning the Preparation and Celebration of the Easter Feasts* [PCEF] no. 27)

On Passion Sunday (Palm Sunday) the Church enters upon the mystery of its crucified, buried, and risen Lord, who by his entrance into Jerusalem, gave a glimpse of his own majesty. Christians carry branches as a sign of the royal triumph that Christ won by his acceptance of the cross. Since Saint Paul says: Provided we suffer with him in order that we may also be glorified with him (Rom 8:17), the link between these two aspects of the paschal mystery should stand out clearly in the liturgical celebration and catechesis of Palm Sunday. (*Ceremonial of Bishops* [CB] no. 263)

The greatest mysteries of the Redemption are celebrated yearly by the Church beginning with the evening Mass of the Lord's Supper on Holy Thursday until Vespers of Easter Sunday. This time is called "the triduum of the crucified, buried and risen" (St. Augustine): it is also called the "Easter Triduum" because during it is celebrated the Paschal Mystery, that is, the passing of the Lord from this world to his Father. The Church by the celebration of this mystery, through liturgical signs and sacramentals, is united to Christ, the Spouse, in intimate communion. (*PCEF* no. 38)

Christ redeemed us all and gave perfect glory to God principally through his paschal mystery: dying he destroyed our death and rising he restored our life. Therefore the Easter Triduum of the passion and resurrection of Christ is the culmination of the entire liturgical year. Thus the solemnity of Easter has the same kind of pre-eminence in the liturgical year that Sunday has in the week. (*General Norms for the Liturgical Year and the Calendar* [GNLYC] no. 18)

HISTORICAL ORIGINS

As they reflected on the meaning of Jesus' death on the cross and on post-resurrection experiences of the risen Christ, the first Christians gathered on the first day of the week, Sunday, to remember his death and encounter Christ risen. Sunday was the original feast day, the day of the Lord, the day of resurrection, the first day of the new creation, the day of gathering to celebrate the Eucharist. Most of the first Christians were Jews who continued to go to the synagogue and to keep the Jewish feasts. The quote by Paul in his first letter to the Corinthians—"Christ our Passover has been sacrificed"—is probably from a Christian Haggadah and is evidence that annually a "Christianized Passover" was being celebrated.

From writings that we have, we know that early in the second century a controversy arose over the date on which the Easter Vigil was to be celebrated. Thus we know that an annual commemoration of the Lord's passion, death, and resurrection had evolved and was being celebrated as a major Christian feast. By the early third century the church's liturgy had developed such that the Easter Vigil was preceded by a period of preparation, especially by those who were to be baptized, and that baptism was celebrated at the Easter Vigil.

Hippolytus, in the *Apostolic Tradition* (215 C.E.), gives a description of the liturgy of baptism which, through context, is presumed to be the Easter Vigil. This celebration took place in the night between Holy Saturday and Easter Sunday.

The next step in the development of Holy Week and of the Paschal Triduum began in Jerusalem. Pilgrims came to Jerusalem from all over the Christian world to visit the sacred sites, especially during the week before Easter. It became the custom to go to the sacred sites to commemorate events of Jesus' last week with prayer and liturgical participation (*not* historical reenactment) on the day they occurred. On the Mount of Olives on the Sunday before Easter there was a procession with palms. In the chapel of the cross (on the site of Golgotha) on Friday there were prayers and veneration of fragments of the true cross. Eucharist, when it was celebrated, was celebrated in the cathedral.

During their journey some pilgrims kept diaries recording where they went and what they did (not unlike travelers today). Most notable among diary-keepers is Egeria, who chronicled her entire Holy Week experience in Jerusalem near the end of the fourth century.

Pilgrims who had been spiritually uplifted by their Jerusalem experiences wanted to have these celebrations back home. (Again, this occurs today: we often bring home with us ideas for liturgy that we have experienced at other parishes or at conferences or workshops.) Thus liturgical celebration of Jesus' last week spread and became part of the church's calendar.

THEOLOGY

The annual Christian paschal feast began with the community's lived experience of the mystery of the passion, death, and resurrection of Jesus Christ and evolved through reflection on the meanings of the mystery (Taft, 1990). The earliest meaning that emerged was passion (*passio*).

The paschalization of Jesus in his death and subsequent reinterpretation of Jesus' death were the first steps of evolution. Jesus was identified with the paschal lambs and called Lamb of God. His death was a sacrifice that was salvific.

In the mid-first century Paul wrote to the Corinthians: "For our paschal lamb, Christ, has been sacrificed. Therefore, let us celebrate the feast, not with the old yeast" (1 Cor 5:7). Paul may be quoting from a Judeo-Christian Haggadah. The references to celebrating the feast and to the fresh batch of dough may indicate that Passover was being celebrated with a Christian interpretation. But there is something new here: Jesus is the Lamb who returned to life. Unlike the sacrificed lambs whose blood saved a people from death on one night, Jesus' death saved all peoples in all times. It was once for all.

The paschal homily, based on the reading from Exodus 12, by Melito, Bishop of Sardis (138-160 C.E.) places Christ at the center of all salvation history. The one who hung upon the tree is the same one who created heaven and earth and the same one who was raised from the dead and has the power to save all. Melito says the words of the mystery of the Hebrew Exodus have been made clear: "how the sheep was sacrificed and the people saved.... For in place of the lamb was God, in place of the sheep man: in the man was Christ who contains all things."

The paschal feast was enriched by the addition of passage (*transitus*) to passion (*passio*) as the meaning of *pascha*. In the Platonic tradition, third-century Alexandrian theologians such as Origen spiritualized events, giving them inner meaning. Philo, an Alexandrian Jew, had moralized the Passover imagery. Christians expanded on this: The angel of death passed over the Jews: the Jews passed through the waters to new life: Jesus passed through death to life and from earthly life to the Father: the Christian passes from sin to the new life of grace.

Combining the spiritualization of the Alexandrian school with the Pauline theology of *participatio* exemplified by Romans 6 ("Or are you not aware that we who were baptized into Christ Jesus were baptized into his death? We were indeed buried with him through baptism into death, so that, just as Christ was raised from the dead by the glory of the Father, we too might live in newness of life"), produces a paradigm shift making the Christian a participant in the acts of Christ. Access is gained to the mystery through baptism. It is no longer Christ who suffers, who dies, who rises but Christ *and* the Christian who suffer, who die, who rise. Or as Paul expresses it: "It is no longer I who live, but Christ living in me." The living now of the Christian life, the participation in Christ, brings the paschal mystery to the present dimension.

What we do every Sunday and most intensely in Holy Week and the Paschal Triduum is to participate liturgically in the great salvific events of Jesus' last week on earth. This is not historical re-enactment, a sort of "You Are There." Rather it is remembrance or *anamnesis*: the actualization now in the life of the community of the paschal mystery.

WORSHIP ENVIRONMENT

Since these liturgies: Passion Sunday, Holy Thursday, Good Friday, Easter Vigil, Easter Sunday, are unique, there are two general principles that need to be taken account of.

These liturgies arose as *stational liturgies*: liturgies celebrated at different sites and with processions to move from one site to another. In Rome, the days of Holy Week were celebrated in a different church each day. Study of the liturgies as we have them today reveals that they are meant to be celebrated in a stational manner using different locations for the different parts and having processions that move from one location to another. The richness of these liturgies will be diminished if their stational character is not respected.

The worship environment prepared for the church for the Easter Vigil is the environment of the *entire fifty-day Easter Season*. It should express for the parish community the "to" or resurrection side of the paschal mystery as in "from death to life." (The lenten worship environment expresses the "from" side of the conversion process. Thus the lenten environment is transformed at Easter.)

Assessment must be made of the particular needs of your parish. Examples are: the need to be a more united community, the need to provide shelter for the homeless in the neighborhood, the need to deal with the loss of a pastor, the need to respond compassionately to parishioners with AIDS, the need to accept and nourish children at our liturgies.

The Easter environment will express the life-giving response of the community: the response of faith of those who have heard the gospel and experienced the saving power of Christ.

PASTORAL NOTES

1. Study well the sacramentary, the lectionary, the circular letter from the Congregation of Divine Worship on the Preparation and Celebration of the Easter Feasts (available from your Office of Worship) and the *Rite of Christian Initiation of Adults*.

2. Clarifying the relationships of the feasts may help with some practical questions. Passion/Palm Sunday is still Lent although it begins Holy Week. Thus the Gloria is not sung and the lenten gospel acclamation and eucharistic acclamations are used. Lent continues until the celebration of the Mass of the Lord's Supper on Thursday evening. This begins the Paschal Triduum, which is one celebration that lasts over three days. On Holy Thursday the Gloria is sung but the gospel and eucharistic acclamations are still those of Lent. On Good Friday and Holy Saturday no sacraments are celebrated. (Exceptions are anointing of the sick and the individual rite of reconciliation.) The gospel acclamation at the Good Friday liturgy of the Word is the one used in Lent. At the Easter Vigil a festive Gloria is sung, the Alleluia (THE Easter Song) returns as the gospel acclamation, and the eucharistic acclamations should be the festive ones for all of Easter season.

3. The Paschal Triduum is a unitary celebration that lasts over three days. From the greeting and sign of the cross at the Evening Mass of the Lord's Supper until the solemn blessing of Easter and dismissal with twofold Alleluia at the Easter Vigil is one continuing liturgy. There is no final blessing or dismissal on Thursday, Good Friday has neither a greeting and sign of the cross nor final blessing and dismissal, and the Easter Vigil has no greeting sign of the cross. Preparation and celebration of the Triduum must keep this integrity in mind. One way to emphasize the unity of the celebrations is with a common antiphon or song. Suggestions will be made in the "Music" section.

4. The times of the celebrations: It seems that to encourage participation in these liturgies they must be scheduled when people can come. The Holy Thursday and Easter Vigil celebrations are to be in the evening. In fact, the Easter Vigil is not to begin until it is dark, and is to conclude before sunrise. The problem may be with the celebration of the Good Friday liturgy, which is pre-

scribed to be at 3:00 P.M. Many people are at work at that time. It would be pastorally advantageous to schedule the liturgy in the evening, at the same time as on the previous and succeeding days. Such uniform scheduling also enhances the sense of unity of the feast.

5. The gospels of Passion Sunday: the passion narratives of either Matthew, Mark, or Luke, and the Good Friday passion narrative from the gospel of John, are to be proclaimed by three voices. A source for these gospels and readings arranged for multiple voices is *This Is The Word of the Lord*, published by Ave Maria Press. In this case the texts for the readers should be in books worthy of use in a liturgical celebration. Loose pages or a bundle of sheets held by a paper clip give the unspoken message that God's Word is temporary and disposable. When there are several books for the readings, only one is to be carried in the procession: the Book of the Gospels (or the lectionary).

6. A homily is to be part of each celebration. However, on these days the readings, symbols, and actions should carry the weight of the mystery. A brief homily (three to five minutes) helping to link the life of the community to the heart of the mystery celebrated in symbol and action is what is needed.

7. On Good Friday and on Holy Saturday, too, the church observes the paschal fast. This is not a penitential fast as was kept in Lent. This is a sacramental fast through which we commemorate and participate in the Lord's death. We abstain from food, and we abstain from the sacraments.

8. We do these liturgies once each year. Thus we forget from year to year how we prepared and how what we prepared was received. Note keeping and evaluation are essential.

MUSIC

Pastoral Note 2 above summarizes the use of the Gloria, the gospel acclamation, and the acclamations for the eucharistic prayer. In Pastoral Note 3 it was recommended that music be used to enhance the perception of the three Triduum celebrations as one liturgy. Antiphons in the ostinato style from Taizé such as *O Christe Domine Jesu; Jesus, Remember Me;* and *Adoramus Te Christe* can be used as people gather, as the acclamation during the proclamation of the passion, and as a processional song (transfer of the Eucharist, veneration of the cross). Another approach is to use a common song for communion.

David Haas's *Now We Remain* could be used at every liturgy, even for the communion on Good Friday. Additional songs that could be used in this manner include two from Marty Haugen, *Tree of Life* and *Triduum Hymn: Wondrous Love,* which has verses for each of the three days. *Tree of Life* has additional verses for each Sunday of Lent as well.

Also from David Haas is the *Song of the Body of Christ* set to an old Hawaiian melody. The refrain is a powerful reminder of what we are doing in these gatherings: "We come to share our story, we come to break the bread, we come to know our rising from the dead." If this song is chosen for use, omit singing verse 5 ("alleluia is our song") until the Easter Vigil.

OTHER LITURGIES

Chrism Mass

At this Mass celebrated during Holy Week, the bishop of the diocese blesses the oil of the sick and the oil of catechumens and together with the presbyters consecrates the holy chrism. These oils are used in the sacramental life of the diocese. They symbolize the link of the parish with the bishop in the sacramental ministry. And the Mass at which they are blessed, which is concelebrated, is a diocesan sign of the unity of the church. Parishioners should be encouraged to participate in this Mass, and several should go as representatives of the parish to receive the holy oils from the bishop and bring them to the parish community.

A rite for the reception of the holy oils blessed at the chrism Mass has been prepared by the Task Group on American Adaptation of the Roman Missal (a rite appears in this volume). It is meant to be celebrated at the beginning of the Evening Mass of the Lord's Supper.

Liturgy of the Hours

Morning Prayer can be celebrated Monday through Saturday of Holy Week

RCIA

On Holy Saturday morning, the rites preparatory to

baptism: the ephthetha, recitation of the Creed (if the Creed was presented) and presentation of the Lord's Prayer (if that was deferred)—are celebrated. These can be in the context of the parish Morning Prayer. In some dioceses, anointing with the oil of catechumens may also be used as a preparatory rite. However, since this anointing symbolizes the need of the catechumens for God's help and strength throughout the conversion process, pastorally it is more desirable to celebrate the rite several times during times of acute doubt, stress, and challenge.

Reconciliation

Ample opportunity should be given during Lent for the celebration of penitential services and the sacrament of reconciliation. During the third, fourth, and fifth weeks of Lent, communal celebrations of the sacrament may be scheduled. There should be no scheduled celebrations of reconciliation during the Paschal Triduum so that these days may be given completely to the proper mysteries of the Triduum itself.

DEVOTIONS AND PARALITURGIES

Stations of the Cross

On Good Friday, it is customary to celebrate the Stations of the Cross. However, this should not appear to be the principal liturgy of the day. Some other hour in the day, other than 3:00 P.M., would be appropriate for an ecumenical service of Stations.

Commemoration of the Three Hours

It is customary in many places for Christians of many traditions to gather together from noon until 3:00 P.M. on Good Friday and, in word and song, meditate on the seven last words of Jesus.

REFERENCES

Berger, Rupert and Hans Hollerweger (eds), 1983. *Celebrating the Easter Vigil*. Pueblo Publishing Company, New York (now a subsidy of The Liturgical Press).

Brown, Raymond E. 1986. *A Crucified Christ in Holy Week*. (Essays on the Four Gospel Passion Narratives). The Liturgical Press, Collegeville, MN.

Congregation got Divine Worship 1988. *Circular Letter Concerning the Preparation and Celebration of the Easter Feasts* (first published in *L'Osservatore Romano*, 29 February, 1988).

Days of the Lord: The Liturgical Year, Volume 3: Easter Triduum and Easter Season, 1993. The Liturgical Press, Collegeville, MN.

Freburger, Rev. William J., 1974. *This Is The Word of the Lord*. Ave Maria Press, Notre Dame.

Huck, Gabe, 1992. *The Three Days: Parish Prayer in the Paschal Triduum* (revised edition). Liturgy Training Publications, Chicago.

Huck, Gabe and Mary Ann Simcoe (editors), 1983. *A Triduum Soucebook*. Liturgy Training Publications, Chicago.

Jeffrey, Peter, 1992. *A New Commandment: Toward a Renewed Rite for the Washing of Feet*. The Liturgical Press, Collegeville, MN.

Neumann, Don A, 1991. *Holy Week in the Parish*. The Liturgical Press, Collegeville, MN.

Nocent, Adrian, 1977. *The Liturgical Year*, Volume 2: Lent and Holy Week. The Liturgical Press, Collegeville, MN.

Nocent, Adrian, 1977. *The Liturgical Year*, Volume 3: The Paschal Triduum and the Easter Season. The Liturgical Press, Collegeville, MN.

Ramshaw, Gail, 1990. *Words Around the Fire*. (Reflections on the Scriptures of the Easter Vigil). Liturgy Training Publications, Chicago.

Simcoe, Mary Ann (ed), 1985. *Parish Path Through Lent and Eastertime*. Liturgy Training Publications, Chicago.

Stevenson, Kenneth, 1988. *Jerusalem Revisited: The Liturgical Meaning of Holy Week*. The Pastoral Press, Washington, D.C.

The Passion of Our Lord Jesus Christ for use in Holy Week. 1984. (texts from the New American Bible). Catholic Book Publishing Company, New York.

Video

This Is the Night 1993 Liturgy Training Publications, Chicago.

Rite for Receiving the Holy Oils

Jayne Newton Ahearn

This rite is for use at the Evening Mass of the Lord's Supper on Holy Thursday

PREPARATION

1. In the sanctuary or near the baptismal font should be a place visible to those assembled where the Holy Oils will be placed. There should be a lighted white candle at or near this place.

2. The oils should be in crystal or cut glass vessels of such design and quality that they speak of the importance of their contents.

3. The parish representatives who received the oils from the bishop at the Mass of Chrism are the ones who bring the oils to the community. They gather at the back of the worship space.

4. A lector narrates.

PROCESSION OF THE OILS

The liturgy begins with soft instrumental music (e.g., *Veni Sancte Spiritus* by Christopher Walker or *O Lord, Hear My Prayer* by Taizé) or singing in the ostinato style (e.g., *O Christe Domine* or *Jesu, Jesus, Remember Me* both by Taizé).

The lector makes the introduction:

United with the faithful and priests of our diocese several days ago at the Cathedral of _____ our Bishop _____ consecrated the holy chrism and blessed the oils for use in the anointing of the sick and in the preparation of catechumens for baptism.

Tonight we receive these holy oils for use in the celebration of the Church's sacraments during the coming year. These holy oils are a symbol of our unity with the bishop and all the faithful of our diocese.

Now, in turn, the oil of the sick, oil of catechumens, and holy chrism are brought in by their presenters who hold the vessel high for all to see.

For the oil of the sick the lector says:

Behold the Oil of the Sick blessed by our Bishop _____ and sent to us to bring consolation and healing to all who suffer.

The presenter places the oil of the sick in the place prepared.

For the oil of catechumens the lector says:

Behold the Oil of the Catechumens blessed by our Bishop _____ and sent to us to strengthen our catechumens in preparation for their baptism at the Easter Vigil and throughout the coming year.

The presenter places the oil of the catechumens in the place prepared.

For the oil of holy chrism the lector says:

Behold the Sacred Chrism,
oil mixed with sweet perfume,
a sign of life and salvation.
Consecrated by our Bishop _____
and sent to us, the Sacred Chrism will be used to anoint the newly baptized,
to confirm Christians in their likeness to Christ
and encourage their witness to faith,
and to preserve those who are ordained
for their work of sanctifying.

The presenter places the oil of holy chrism in the place prepared.

The liturgy continues with the procession of the ministers: incense bearer, cross bearer, servers bearing lighted candles, deacon bearing the Book of Gospels, concelebrants, and presider. The Gloria can be used as the processional hymn.

After reverencing the altar, the presider incenses the altar and the holy oils.

When the Gloria concludes, the Mass continues with the opening prayer.

The Season of Easter

Jayne Newton Ahearn

DESCRIPTION

The fifty days from Easter Sunday to Pentecost are celebrated in joyful exaltation as one feast day, or better as one "great Sunday." These above all others are the days for the singing of the Alleluia. (*GNLYC* no. 22)

The celebration of Easter is prolonged throughout the Easter season. The fifty days from Easter Sunday to Pentecost Sunday are celebrated as one feast day, the "great Sunday." (*PCEF* no. 100)

The Church celebrates the paschal mystery on the first day of the week, known as the Lord's Day or Sunday. This follows a tradition handed down from the apostles and having its origin from the day of Christ's resurrection. Thus Sunday must be ranked as the first holy day of all. (*GNLYC* no. 4).

HISTORICAL ORIGINS

The feast referred to in the New Testament as Pentecost (*Pentekoste*) was the Jewish feast of weeks, a thanksgiving for the wheat harvest celebrated seven weeks and one day (fifty days, the fiftieth day) after the feast of unleavened bread.

In intertestamental times this feast also became associated with a recalling of the covenant of Sinai made between God and the Jews through the Ten Commandments. It was during the gathering of Jews in Jerusalem for the celebration of Pentecost that Acts places the outpouring of the Holy Spirit upon the apostles. On Pentecost the church became a visible sign in the world.

By about 150 C.E. the word Pentecost had taken on a uniquely Christian meaning. Pentecost had become the fifty-day extension of Easter Sunday, a fifty-day season of Sundays. Irenaeus wrote in about 200 C.E. that there was no kneeling during the fifty days of Pentecost (or Easter) because the Christian community was "feasting" the resurrection. And Tertullian, about twenty years later, wrote in his treatise *On Baptism* that after the Easter Vigil, Pentecost was the most appropriate season for baptism. He associates resurrection, ascension, and the Holy Spirit with Pentecost. In *De Corona*, Tertullian says that because Sunday is the day of resurrection, fasting and kneeling are forbidden.

Up until the mid-fourth century the entire Pentecost season was concerned with feasting the resurrection, ascension of Jesus, and descent of the Spirit. The theme was that of chapter 16 of John's gospel: Jesus had to go so that the Paraclete could be sent. On the fiftieth day, the day of Pentecost, both the ascension and giving of the Spirit were celebrated. This is evidenced in the writing of Eusebius in the early fourth century. In her diary of liturgical experiences in Jerusalem in 384 C.E., the pilgrim Egeria describes the Pentecost Day celebration as including a station at the site of the ascension.

However, the unity of the feast was already beginning to break up. A few years earlier in Antioch the Ascension was commemorated on the fortieth day after Easter Sunday following the Lukan chronology of Acts 1:3. When Augustine wrote of Pentecost as a separate feast in the early fifth century, he indicated that this was the case "all over the world." However, in Rome, which was more conservative, the separation of Ascension and Pentecost Sunday did not occur until around 450 C.E.

THEOLOGY

The passion, death, and resurrection of Jesus Christ began a new age: the age of a new creation when God and humanity are reconciled in Christ: the age of God's presence with humanity through the Spirit of Christ dwelling in the church. The mystery of our life in God through Christ in the Spirit is celebrated primarily in the Sunday Eucharist of the believing community.

Sunday came to symbolize the many facets of the mystery that continued to be revealed through reflection on the experience of life and prayer. A primary time for such reflection was and continues to be Pentecost, the Season of Easter. The mystagogy of Pentecost is the mystagogy of Sunday. (Read *On Sunday* elsewhere in this volume.)

Pentecost is a day and a season: a week of weeks and one day beyond. As Sunday is the first day and the eighth day of creation, signifying the age of fulfillment and completion; so, too, is Pentecost a week of Sundays and an eighth Sunday, the Great Sunday.

Jesus' earthly mission was completed not only by the resurrection but also by his ascension and sending of the Holy Spirit.

> But I tell you the truth, it is better for you that I go. For if I do not go, the Advocate will not come to you. But if I go, I will send him to you. (Jn 16:7)

> And I will ask the Father, and he will give you another Advocate to be with you always..... I will not leave you orphans: I will come to you. In a little while the world will no longer see me, but you will see me, because I live and you will live. On that day you will realize that I am in my Father and you are in me and I in you. (Jn 14:16, 18-19)

These lines from John's gospel express the experience of the early Christian community that the risen Lord was present among them in some way that brought them into union with God and made the victory of Christ their own. Pentecost is a time for feasting, not fasting, for the Bridegroom is with us. Pentecost is a time not for kneeling in penitence but for standing in praise, for through Christ's death our sin is forgiven, through Christ's resurrection we rise, and through Christ's ascension we are uplifted to God's right hand.

Jesus' mission was completed: the mission of the church was begun. By the Lukan chronology, the Holy Spirit was given on the Jewish feast of Pentecost. Pentecost means fifty, which is the jubilee: the year of favor when all debt is forgiven: that time which Jesus, as the one empowered by the Spirit, was sent to proclaim (Is 61:3; Lk 4:19). Forgiveness of sins and the reconciliation of humanity with God and one another is the sign of the new creation and the work of the Holy Spirit.

The immediate result of the outpouring of the Spirit in Acts was that people of the many nations gathered for the Jewish feast were able to hear and understand the message of salvation preached by the apostles in their own language. The barriers to communication between human beings, symbolized in the Tower of Babel story, are removed through the Spirit's unifying power.

The new creation is also the meaning of the post-resurrection appearance of Jesus to the disciples on Easter Sunday evening. He greets them with peace, breathes on them, and says: "Receive the Holy Spirit. Whose sins you forgive are forgiven them, and whose sins you retain are retained" (Jn 20:22-23).

As God's spirit blew over the waters on the first day of creation, so does Jesus' Spirit infuse the new creation. The Spirit brings unity from diversity. Inherent in this is the mission of the church, the ministry of reconciliation (recall Paul's words in 2 Corinthians proclaimed on Ash Wednesday).

The church is to be a sign of the unity of humanity with God and to offer that salvation to the world. This new age when God's Spirit would be poured out on all humanity was foretold by the prophet Joel. This prophecy is recalled by Peter in the Acts:

> In the last days it will be, God declares, that I will pour out my Spirit upon all flesh, and your sons and your daughters shall prophesy, and your young men shall see visions, and your old men shall dream dreams. Even upon my slaves, both men and women, in those days I will pour out my Spirit.... (Joel 2:28-29; Acts 2:17-18)

The new covenant is the new age of the church.

Baptism is the way to accept that offer of salvation and participate in the death and the life of Christ and the mission of the church. When Peter finished his Pentecost speech, "those who accepted his message were baptized, and about 3,000 persons were added that day" (Acts 2:41).

Thus Pentecost is a time for Christian initiation.

The first day was created when God separated light from the darkness. When God raised Jesus from the darkness of death, the rising sun (Son) gave light to the first day of the new creation. All those new creatures born in baptism are children of the light enlightened by Christ.

Being enlightened or finding new meaning through participation in the paschal mystery of Christ was the experience of the two disciples on the road to Emmaus on the first day of the week. They were discussing events of the past (the death by crucifixion of the one they thought might have been the Messiah) and finding neither hope nor faith. A stranger joined them (the risen Christ who is the promise of God's future) and helped them through the Scriptures to reinterpret their past. Finally they recognized Jesus in the breaking of the bread (the Eucharist), and their present was changed. They rushed back joyfully to Jerusalem to share the news of their experience with others. Like Cleopas and his companion, Christians each Sunday and throughout Eastertide celebrate the totality of the Christ event present among us now.

MYSTAGOGY

The Masses of the Easter season are the main setting for the period of postbaptismal catechesis or mystagogy of the neophytes. These are occasions for the newly baptized and newly received to gather with the community and share in the mysteries.

The readings of Year A are particularly suitable for reflecting on their new, personal experience of the sacraments and of the community, but in every year the homily and the general intercessions should take into account the presence and needs of the neophytes (*RCIA* nos. 237 and 238).

The new participation of the neophytes in the sacraments and their presence at the eucharistic liturgy has an impact on the experience of the community as a whole. In welcoming them and celebrating with them, the faithful derive a renewed inspiration and outlook (*RCIA* no. 236). With the neophytes they, too, reflect upon what it means to live after death, to look into the empty tomb.

Mystagogy is the least practiced of all the stages of the adult initiation rite, and it presents the biggest problem. Is that because we as a community do not take the time to reflect on our experience of death and of life in Christ?

The paradigm of the Mass as well as of the Christian life is also the paradigm of mystagogy. It is the story of the two disciples on the road to Emmaus, which is heard on the Third Sunday of Easter in Year A. These two are really struggling with life and its meaning in the face of a horrible death. Through reflection on the Scriptures and the sharing in the breaking of bread, they come to an understanding. But they had to do the work of relating their story to the story of Scripture (God's story). The understanding was the grace of the paschal mystery, which requires that suffering accompany liberation, revelation, and new life.

The readings of the Easter season Sunday liturgies help us to do what those two disciples did. We hear again and again the stories of how the early believers had gradually unfolded what the Jesus event meant...and we are still doing that today. In fact, the word mystery means that there is always more to be revealed and understood.

The motivation for the Johannine gospel, which figures prominently in the Easter Season, is "so that we will believe." And this is especially true of the accounts of encounters with the risen Christ. Peter and John, Mary Magdalene, the disciples, and Thomas come to faith through their experiences of Jesus who died and now lives.

The neophytes have just participated in the death of Christ in baptism. But all who have been baptized must learn how to live after death. People who have had "near-death" experiences or who are dying can teach us. We must learn to take joy from the simple pleasures. We must take on a different set of values.

We have died in Christ: yet we live between that death and physical death. We are living in the "between," in the "already, not yet." The new age has begun and we are part of it, but it has not been completed.

Our Easter song is "*Alleluia, He Is Risen.*" But we still have to peer into the empty tomb and learn to live with Jesus' absence. The neophytes face this more acutely as the emotional high of the Easter Vigil and first weeks of Easter dissipates and they find that life has not really changed as much as they thought it would. They have to deal with the loss of relationships from their pre-initiation life while they may not find they are fully accepted by their adopted community. They may be victims of the "elder brother syndrome" as long-time parishioners resent them for the fuss and attention they have received. ("I have been here all the while and done everything you asked, yet you never gave me a goat so that I could have a party with my friends.")

It is the Sunday gathering of the believing community for the Eucharist that is the key. As Ray Kemp has said: "When the going gets tough, it is time to have another Emmaus experience."

WORSHIP ENVIRONMENT

1. The liturgical color is white. Gold, silver, and rich, multicolored brocades are also fitting for the Easter feast.

2. The symbols of the season are the cross (from the Good Friday liturgy), the Easter (Paschal) Candle, and the water of the baptismal font.

3. The water of the font, blessed at the Easter Vigil and called "Easter water," remains and is used throughout the Easter season for baptisms and for the rite of sprinkling. (Judicious additions must be made every few days to replace water lost through evaporation.) If your font is one that is portable and usually is hidden in a corner, it should occupy a prominent place in the midst of the community during the Easter season.

4. The Easter Candle remains near the altar or ambo and is lit at every liturgy. Or, if your font has been brought into the midst of the community, the Easter Candle may be associated with it.

5. The sanctuary and nave are decorated for all of the Easter season as they were for the Easter Vigil. Palms, other green plants, Easter lilies, flowers, hangings in pastel colors (yellow, pink, light blue, light green, pale orchid), butterflies, all speak of new life. If the Good Friday Cross, draped with a yellow or white cloth, is part of the environment, there should be no other cross or crucifix in the sanctuary.

6. The neophytes (those newly baptized or received into the church) with their sponsors should occupy a special place in the assembly for the Masses of the Easter season (*RCIA* no. 238).

MUSIC

Responsorial Psalm. The seasonal psalms for Easter are Psalm 118 and Psalm 66. One of these could be used for the entire season. Or Psalm 118 may be used for Sundays 1 through 5, and Psalm 66 for Sundays 6 and 7 as well as for Ascension.

Psalm 118

Alleluia	The Dameans
Alleluia—Let Us Rejoice	David Haas
Let Us Rejoice	Marty Haugen
Psallite Deo	Taizé
Surrexit Christus	Taizé
This Is The Day	Michael Joncas
This Is The Day	Christopher Willcock
This Day Was Made By God	Christopher Walker

Psalm 66

Let All the Earth	Marty Haugen
Let All the Earth	Christopher Willcock

Gospel Acclamation. The song of Easter is ALLELUIA. Use a strong, festive setting of the Alleluia to greet the presence of the risen Christ in the gospel.

Alleluia (2 different settings)	Howard Hughes
Alleluia, Praise the Lord	Gutfreund
Alleluia no. 7	Taizé
Alleluia—Let Us Rejoice (refrain)	David Haas
Celtic Alleluia	O'Carroll/Walker
Praise His Name (refrain)	Michael Joncas

Eucharistic Acclamations. The most festive setting of the acclamations of the eucharistic prayer known by the parish community should be used throughout the season. Examples include the *Coventry Acclamations* by Paul Inwood, the *Mass of Creation* by Marty Haugen, and the *Mass of Light* by David Haas. The most appropriate form of the memorial acclamation for Easter is "Christ has died, Christ is risen, Christ will come again." In Inwood's setting, the alleluia is added.

The Lord's Prayer may be sung using the setting that is familiar to the parish community. *The Mass of*

Creation includes a setting of the Lord's Prayer. In their settings for morning and evening prayer, David Haas's *Light and Peace* and Michael Joncas's *O Joyful Light* offer settings of the Lord's Prayer of both the traditional text and of the ecumenical (ICET) text.

A lyrical setting of the Lamb of God litany is appropriate. *The Mass of Creation* and the *Mass of Light* offer possibilities. Or consider David Clark Isele's setting from the *Holy Cross Mass,* which has been very popular through the years.

General Intercessions. The people's prayer in the intercessions during Easter is most appropriately "Lord, hear our prayer." Most well known is the Byzantine chant form. Alternatively, see the possibilities for the general intercessions presented by James Hansen in the collection *Litany: When the Church Gathers.*

Gathering: The Sprinkling Rite and Gloria. During the Easter season the liturgy should begin with the commemoration of baptism through the sprinkling of water blessed at the Easter Vigil (see Pastoral Note no. 1 below).

Acclamation to the Thanksgiving Prayer

Alleluia (refrain of *O Filii et Filiae*)

Springs of Water	David Haas
(in *Who Calls You by Name*)	

Song for Sprinkling

Flow River, Flow	Bob Hurd
Saw Water Flowing	Randall DeBruyn
Water of Life	David Haas
We Shall Draw Water	Paul Inwood

The Gloria may be sung during the sprinkling. In that case the acclamation to the prayer of thanksgiving over the blessed water becomes: Glory to God in the highest.

The Gloria

Give Glory to God	John Foley S.J.
Glory to God (Mass of Light)	David Haas
Glory to God (Mass of Creation)	Marty Haugen
Glory to God	Peter Jones
Gloria Psallite Mass	Michael Joncas
Gloria	Joe Zsigray

Other Hymns and Songs. The song at the preparation of gifts can be specific to the Sunday and reflect the readings. Suggestions can be found within the treatments of each Sunday. If the seasonal psalm is being used, then the proper psalm of the day may be sung at this time or at communion. The song at communion can be related to the gospel but should also have a community focus. Some examples of songs that can be used throughout Easter are:

Communion

Behold the Lamb	Martin Willett
Now We Remain	David Haas
One Bread, One Body	John Foley S.J.
Song of the Body of Christ	David Haas
We Have Been Told	David Haas

Concluding Hymn

Alleluia, Sing to Jesus	Hyfrydol
Canticle of the Sun	Marty Haugen
Crown Him With Many Crowns	Diademata
Jesus Christ Is Risen Today	Easter Hymn
Paschal Procession	Christopher Walker
Sing A New Song	Dan Schutte
Sing to the Mountains	Bob Dufford
This is the Feast of Victory	Festival Canticle

Some of these are also appropriate as gathering songs.

PASTORAL NOTES

1. Gathering Rites. Keep in focus what happened at the Easter Vigil: commemoration of the Lord's passion, death, and resurrection, celebration of our passage through the waters of baptism to new life. Our participation in the paschal mystery of Christ continues throughout Easter's fifty days.

How might the sprinkling rite be celebrated throughout the Easter season? The font containing water blessed at the Easter Vigil remains in a central location along with the Paschal Candle and the cross. The liturgy begins with the presider going to the font, greeting the people (the sign of the cross is displaced to the time of sprinkling), and inviting them into the thanksgiving over blessed water for example:

> Dear friends, this water, consecrated at the Easter Vigil, will be used to remind us of our baptism. Let us praise and thank God for the life and Spirit he has given us. (Texts may be found in the *RCIA* no. 215 D and E.)

The concluding prayer, adapted for the sprinkling rite, is:

> You have called your children to this cleansing water, that we may share in the faith of your Church and have eternal life. May this water remind us of our baptism, and let us share the joy of all who have been baptized this Easter.

Water from the font is transferred to a portable container, and the presider circuits the entire worship space sprinkling everyone. During the sprinkling the Gloria, or another song, may be sung. As people feel the water, they make the sign of the cross.

After he has sprinkled everyone, the presider ends up at the chair. From there he either says the opening prayer or, if the Gloria has not been sung, says the absolution and briefly introduces the Gloria; for example, "Let us give glory to God."

2. Profession of Faith. Another way to highlight the character of Easter as celebrating new birth into the risen Christ is to use the interrogatory form of the Profession of Faith. The Profession of Faith has its origin in the baptismal liturgy where it was intimately related to the immersion of the one being baptized into the water. To each question: "Do you believe," the one being baptized answered: "I do believe." This was followed by one of the three immersions.

Our other name for this is the Creed. In Latin, it means "to give the heart to." Thus the Creed is not just words to be recited but an act by which the person gives their heart and life over to life in God. The text for the baptismal form of the Profession of Faith follows.

> My brothers and sisters,
> with all the Church, let us profess our faith and trust in God as we say: We do believe.
>
> Do you believe in God, the Father almighty,
> creator of heaven and earth,
> of all that is seen and unseen?
> *All reply:* We do believe.
>
> Do you believe in Jesus Christ, his only Son, our Lord,
> light from light,
> who to secure our salvation came down from heaven,
> was conceived by the Holy Spirit,
> and born of the virgin Mary,
> was crucified, died and was buried,
> rose from the dead,
> and is now seated at the right hand of the Father?
> *All reply:* We do believe.
>
> Do you believe in the Holy Spirit,
> the Lord and giver of life,
> who is worshiped and glorified with the Father and Son?
> *All reply:* We do believe.
>
> Do you believe in the holy catholic Church,
> the communion of saints,
> the forgiveness of sins,
> the resurrection of the body,
> and life everlasting?
> *All reply:* We do believe.
>
> God, the all-powerful Father of our Lord Jesus Christ,
> has given us a new birth by water and the Holy Spirit,
> and forgiven all our sins.
> May he also keep us faithful to our Lord Jesus Christ
> for ever and ever.
> *All reply:* Amen.

3. Posture and the Eucharistic Prayer. In keeping with the spirit of Easter season as the great feast of the resurrection, I recommend you follow the ancient practice of the church and invite all to stand throughout the eucharistic prayer and communion. (Tertullian, in *De Corona*, states that fasting and kneeling for prayer was forbidden during Easter season and this was made part of church law by the Council of Nicea, canon 20.)

4. Blessing. The solemn blessing for the Easter season (no. 7) can be used every Sunday. Conclude the words of dismissal with the threefold alleluia to which all reply: "Thanks be to God, alleluia, alleluia, alleluia!"

5. Baptisms. Where the parish policy discourages baptisms during Lent it becomes publicly obvious that the Easter season is the most appropriate time for celebration of the baptism of infants and for the celebration of confirmation and first Eucharist of children baptized as infants. This Easter season would also be an ideal time to encourage celebration of baptisms during Mass.

OTHER LITURGIES

Liturgy of the Hours: Morning and Evening Prayer

If you began celebration of Morning Prayer or Vespers during Lent, don't stop now! The Easter season is the time to praise God at sunrise for the risen Son and commemorate baptism with a liberal sprinkling of Easter water. It is a time to thank God at sundown for Jesus, the Light that no darkness can overcome, singing to the Easter Candle, "O joyful light, O Sun divine, of God the Father's deathless face." If you didn't begin in Lent, why not start now?

DEVOTIONS AND PARALITURGIES

Solemn Celebration of the Rosary

During Easter those who wish may gather to celebrate the glorious mysteries of the rosary. The customary days are Wednesdays, Saturdays, and Sundays of Easter (also Sundays of Christmas and Ordinary Time). Occasions when this would be particularly appropriate are April 16th, St. Bernadette Soubirous; Ascension (Thursday); May 24, Mary, Help of Christians; Vigil of Pentecost.

Scripture readings to accompany the glorious mysteries of the rosary are:

1. Resurrection of our Lord from the dead
    Luke 24:16a
2. Ascension of our Lord into heaven
    Luke 24:50–53
3. Descent of the Holy Spirit upon the apostles on Pentecost
    Acts 2:14
4. Assumption of the Blessed Virgin Mary into heaven
    Song of Songs 2:8–14
5. Coronation of the Virgin Mary
    Revelation 12:1-6 or *Lumen Gentium* 69:2

On the Feast of the Body and Blood of Christ, the new Eucharistic Mysteries may be celebrated. Scripture readings to accompany these are:

1. Feeding of the Israelites with manna
    Exodus 16:2–4, 12–15
2. Ratification of the Covenant in the Blood of Sacrifice
    Exodus 24:3–8
3. Miracle of the multiplication of the loaves and fishes
    Luke 9:11–17
4. Institution of the Eucharist
    2 Corinthians 11:23–26
5. Appearance of Christ on the road to Emmaus
    Luke 24:13–35

REFERENCES

Adam, Adolf, 1979. *The Liturgical Year: Its History and Its Meaning After the Reform of the Liturgy.* Chapter 4. "Sunday as the Original Celebration of the Paschal Mystery" and Chapter 5. "Easter and the Easter Cycle of Feasts." Pueblo Publishing Company, New York (now a subsidiary of The Liturgical Press, Collegeville, MN).

Bishops' Committee on the Liturgy/National Conference of Catholic Bishops, 1987. *Celebrating the Marian Year.* United States Catholic Conference Publishing Services, Washington, D.C.

Brown, Raymond E., 1991. *A Risen Christ in Eastertime.* The Liturgical Press, Collegeville, MN.

Congregation for Divine Worship, 1988. *Circular Letter Concerning the Preparation and Celebration of the Easter Feasts.* (first published in *L'Osservatore Romano*, 29 February, 1988).

Huck, Gabe, Gail Ramshaw and Gordon Lathrop (editors), 1988. *An Easter Sourcebook: The Fifty Days.* Liturgy Training Publications, Chicago, IL.

Nocent, Adrian, O.S.B., 1977. *The Liturgical Year, Volume Three: The Paschal Triduum and The Easter Season.* The Liturgical Press, Collegeville, MN.

Porter, H. Boone, 1987. *The Day of Light: The Biblical and Liturgical Meaning of Sunday.* The Pastoral Press, Washington, D.C.

Sanchez, Patricia Datchuck, 1989. *The Word We Celebrate: Commentary on the Sunday Lectionary, Years A, B, and C.* Sheed and Ward, Kansas City, MO.

Simcoe, Mary Ann (editor), 1985. *Parish Path Through Lent and Eastertime.* (second edition) Liturgy Training Publications, Chicago.

Passover and the Easter Season

Russell Hardiman

THE CALCULATION OF EASTER

Over the years in my classes and occasionally from the pulpit, I have delighted in asking the question as to how Easter varies and how it is calculated. Almost invariably, the majority have no idea but usually there is someone who can trot out the definition, inculcated in memory since school days: the first Sunday after the first full moon after the twenty-first of March (the spring Equinox). This means that the earliest that Easter can fall is about March 23rd and the latest it can fall is about April 24th.

The definition connecting the Sunday with the full moon is in some way connected with the calculation of the Passover as being the fourteenth day of the Jewish month of Nisan, for often Passover coincides with our Holy Week, but sometimes it does not. Likewise, Oriental Rite churches and Orthodox churches are often celebrating Easter at different times from western rites. The crux of the confusion seems to hinge on when precisely is the full moon. In any month the moon appears to be full for several nights in a row. The question arises as to which night is deemed to be the full moon. My personal theory, for which I have yet to find any authoritative source as validation, is that the full moon is judged to be when moonrise and sunset occur simultaneously.

The calculation of Easter was the source of great controversy in the early centuries of the Christian church. The issue was whether Christians would celebrate the resurrection on the Sunday (the first day of the week) or at the occasion of the Jewish passover, the fourteenth day of Nisan. Hence, the faction supporting the Jewish observance were called the *Quartodecimani ordecimani*, literally those who followed the fourteenth day. Eventually, about the third century the Christians felt strong enough to move beyond their origins to assert their own beliefs, and this became the standard of the known world in the fourth century when the first Christian Emperor, Constantine, declared Sunday to be the rest day of the Empire.

The Rabbi emeritus of the Perth Hebrew congregation, Dr. Coleman, manages to get a letter published in "The West Australian" newspaper every year. Invariably he makes the connection with the observance of the Passover for the Jewish people as a time of hope for the fulfillment of God's promise with the invitation to people of goodwill to pray for the fulfillment of that promise. An admirable sentiment, especially for Christians who take seriously the shared tradition of Judeo-Christian prayer for the fulfillment of God's covenant.

What will happen in years when the two feasts are nearly a month apart or even Christian churches cannot agree when to celebrate the major feast of their common year?

All in all, this confusion underlines the importance of the declaration of Vatican II, now almost two generations old, in which the Council Fathers acknowledged the problems inherent in the moveable feast of Easter and indicated that they saw no inherent problems with the proposal for a fixed date for Easter.

> ...recognizes the importance of the wishes expressed by many concerning the assignment of the Feast of Easter to a fixed Sunday and concerning an unchanging calendar.....the Church has no objection only in the case of those systems which would retain and safeguard a seven day week including Sunday, without the introduction of

any days outside the week. (Appendix to the Constitution on the Liturgy)

A VISION FOR A UNIFIED EASTER

The vision of a unified Lent-Easter Season opens up a vista of a single ninety-day celebration of the paschal mystery of Christ. We prepare for forty days by reminding ourselves that in our baptism we have been baptized into Christ's death, and passover with his resurrection to be raised up to the fullness of life in the power of his risen Spirit. We extend that celebration for fifty days, a week of weeks, to the Pentecost day when the Spirit comes upon the gathered disciples and overcomes them to go out and proclaim the risen Lord. There is a balance between the private or individualistic sense of penance and the communal experience of living in God's Spirit. We ask ourselves what kind of Christians we must be to be faithful to our call for the sake of the community that is to witness to the reign of God revealed by Christ.

Early in Lent (First Sunday, Year C) we hear Paul's words: "The word, that is the faith we proclaim, is very near to you, it is on your lips and in your heart. If your lips confess that Jesus is Lord and if you believe in your heart that God raised him from the dead, then you will be saved" (Rom 10:8–10).

On Pentecost Sunday (Year C) we also hear from Paul: "...if the spirit of him who raised Jesus from the dead is living in you, then he who raised Jesus from the dead will give life to your own mortal bodies through his Spirit living in you" (Rom 8:10–11).

In the texts, from one end of the ninety-day season to the other, we have a profound insight into our Christian tradition of proclaiming God's word, of sharing in God's creation, redemption, and salvation.

Our ritual practice of the triple signing of the cross at the beginning of the gospel reinforces the words of Paul with the prayerful reflection on the vision of faith that leads us to life in God's Spirit promised by Jesus. We pray that God's word, coming to us in the gospel, may be the inspiration for our mind, the expression on our lips, and the motivation in our heart. We memorialize looking back to the *past*, conscious of the risen Spirit of Jesus with us *now* and in the expectation of the completeness of our life in Christ in the *future*. The gesture, while simple in itself, is a powerful expression of the integration of our external actions with our internal attitudes and beliefs.

Each cycle of the lectionary repeats these fundamental principles of Christian belief, as we hear how the early Christian community was so strengthened by the resurrection appearances of Jesus that they could strongly proclaim their belief in his presence.

We **hear** of six appearances of Jesus, which all result in a dramatic response of new-found faith.

We **hear** seven sermons of Peter, which all start with confronting the reality of the death of Jesus before proclaiming what Peter now sees as his personal responsibilities.

We **hear** twice of the preaching of Paul and Barnabas, confident in their mandate to preach the Good News to the Gentile world.

We **hear** eleven vignettes of the early Christian community with its steady growth, its decisions about the community life and service.

We **hear** three images Jesus used of himself in proclaiming himself the Good Shepherd.

We **hear** nine segments from the discourse of Jesus after the last supper, in which John portrays Jesus' promise and prayer for his followers.

This plethora of scenes could appear bewildering (almost like the twelve days of Christmas) unless we have an overview of the structure of the lectionary cycles. This overview enables us to see both the forest and the trees and to appreciate how their relationship constitutes the picture. When we can see the individual trees we can also appreciate the forest they create by their ritual relationship.

There are many general and specific principles of lectionary selection that are reflected in the specific details of each cycle;

•For the only time in the whole church year there is no Old Testament reading;

•The first reading in the Easter season is taken from the Acts of the Apostles. This allows for a close scrutiny of the life of the early church;

•The sermons of Peter especially are highlighted;

•The second reading is assigned from different New Testament writings that give insight into the needs or life of the first generations of believers in different contexts;

• In Year A we have the first letter of Peter assigned, normally regarded as a commentary for a baptismal service: so appropriate for the neophytes after Easter;

•In Year B, we read from the first Letter of John, which reflects the experiences and tensions of the community after several generations;

•In Year C we have a series of visions from the Book of Revelation, which were confidence boosters in times of struggle by referring to the hope of ultimately sharing in the victory won by the Lamb;

•The gospel passages are almost all from John (even when Luke is used, it is not in Year C);

•The first three weeks' gospels give the post-resurrection appearances of Jesus and the response he evokes;

•The fourth Sunday is dominated by images from the Good Shepherd passages of Jn 10;

•The final Sundays give significant excerpts from the Last Supper Discourse that feature the life Jesus expects when his disciples would be filled with the Spirit he promised.

In preparing for proclaiming the word the study of the individual elements of any year's cycle could be very helpful. For those with little time or inclination for such detailed reflection, perhaps we may prompt readers to look further and deeper in the synopsis of each week of the whole Easter season in the chapter *Restoring Unity to the 90 Days: Easter as a Reflection of Lent* by Jayne Ahearn, which appears next in this volume.

Restoring Unity to the 90 Days: Easter as Reflection of Lent

Jayne Newton Ahearn

Or are you unaware that we who were baptized into Christ Jesus were baptized into his death. We were indeed buried with him through baptism into death, so that, just as Christ was raised from the dead by the glory of the Father, we too might live in newness of life. (Romans 6:3–4)

These words of Paul, which we heard at the Easter Vigil, are the fruit of his reflection on his own experience of dying and rising in Christ. During the forty-day lenten journey we sought to be conformed more and more to the image of Christ: to participate with Christ in the cross and the resurrection. From the Easter Vigil we go forth to the fifty days of Easter to reflect on our own experience of dying and rising in Christ to find its meaning for our life.

ORIGINS OF EASTER SEASON

In the early third century the annual paschal feast began to expand. Forward extension coincided with the time the Jews called Pentecost. Pentecost was a joyous feast of thanksgiving for the wheat harvest, celebrated seven weeks plus a day (a week of weeks, hence also called the Feast of Weeks) or on the fiftieth day after the feast of unleavened bread.

For Christians these days became a time for reflecting on and celebrating the paschal mystery as revealed in a multiplicity of scenarios. They understood the Jesus event as having initiated a new covenant between God and humanity, beginning a New Age.

The promise of God through Joel was seen as fulfilled by the experience of those gathered in Jesus' name on Pentecost (the Jewish feast).

Then afterward I will pour out my spirit upon all humankind. Your sons and daughters shall prophesy, your old men shall dream dreams, your young men shall see visions. Even upon the servants and the handmaids, in those days. I will pour out my spirit. And I will work wonders in the heavens and on the earth... (Joel 3:1–3a and see Acts 2:17–21)

The pouring out of the Holy Spirit resulting in those so anointed being able to heal, preach, and speak in tongues was the sign of the new covenant. By 150 C.E., Pentecost was a Christian feast. Irenaeus (200 C.E.) refers to Pentecost as one day: the Sunday that was the fiftieth day after Pascha. Tertullian (210 C.E.) refers to Pentecost as a season of fifty days.

In fact, Pentecost was both. Pentecost celebrated the resurrection, post-resurrection appearances and presence of the risen Christ, the ascension and enthronement, the coming of the Holy Spirit, and the second coming of Christ. But, as was the case for the paschal feast itself, this unitary feast became partitioned. By about 450 C.E., Ascension and Pentecost were separated in the Roman liturgy.

THE CATECHUMENATE

For those newly baptized (the neophytes) the days following the Easter Vigil, the days of Pentecost, were the time for reflecting on what had happened to them, on what it means to live in the paschal mystery. This reflection was called "mystagogia." During the golden age of the catechumenate from 350 to 450 C.E., homilies were given for the benefit of the neophytes that helped them to appropriate the meaning of the sacraments they had celebrated and the meaning of the life they now lived. We still have available to us many of these mystagogical homilies, those of Cyril of Jerusalem, John Chrysostom in Antioch, Theodore of Mopsuestia, Ambrose of Milan and Augustine of Hippo. (See for example: *Mystagogy* by Enrico Mazza from Pueblo Publishing and *The Awe-Inspiring Rites of Initiation* by Edward Yarnold, from Liturgical Press).

MYSTAGOGY IN THE RESTORED CATECHUMENATE

The third step of Christian Initiation, the celebration of the sacraments, is followed by the final period, the period of postbaptismal catechesis or mystagogy. This period is a time for the community and the neophytes together to grow in deepening their grasp of the paschal mystery and in making it part of their lives through meditation on the Gospel, sharing in the eucharist and doing the works of charity. (*RCIA* no. 244)

The neophytes are, as the term "mystagogy" suggests, introduced into a fuller and more effective understanding of mysteries through the Gospel message they have learned and above all through their experience of the sacraments they have received.... Out of this experience, which belongs to Christians and increases as it is lived, they derive a new perception of the faith of the Church, and of the world." (*RCIA* no. 245).

Since the distinctive spirit and power of the period of postbaptismal catechesis or mystagogy derive from the new, personal experience of the sacraments and of the community, its main setting is the so-called Masses for neophytes, that is, the Sunday Masses of the Easter season. Besides being occasions for the newly baptized to gather with the community and share in the mysteries, these celebrations include particularly suitable readings from the Lectionary especially the readings for Year A. (*RCIA* no. 247)

The period of baptism for the newly initiated is a time to become fully integrated into the Christian community. It corresponds to the Easter season and is a time for deepening their grasp of the paschal mystery, which they have now personally experienced. Here in the period of mystagogy neophytes and faithful walk together. Christians here on earth are always in the period of mystagogy, and the stance we take during the Easter season is a sign of that.

The Masses of the Easter season are also a sign of that. The Masses of the Easter season are the main setting for mystagogy.

The readings, themselves the reflection of early Christians on the lived experience, support our reflections. As in the lenten cycle of readings, where Year A readings are specific for catechumenal celebrations, the Easter readings of Year A are the ones originally used for post-baptismal catechesis. Our revised lectionary offers two sets of alternatives for communities where there is no catechumenate. And the Eucharist renews our participation in Christ's paschal mystery.

CELEBRATING THE EASTER SEASON

The Easter/Pentecost season expanded out of the annual commemoration of Jesus' passion, death, and resurrection, the *Paschal Feast*. To restore unity to the celebration requires making the Easter season a time of mystagogia or reflection on the experience of Lent, on our participation in Christ's passion and death, and on the experience of the risen Christ among us.

We live in the new age begun when the offering made in Jesus' death was accepted in God's raising him from the dead and pouring out the Holy Spirit to reconcile/restore broken humanity. What are the implications for us of a risen Christ? Where do we meet this risen Lord? How have we been transformed by our immersion into the paschal mystery? What is our experience of reconciliation? How have we been empowered by the Spirit: what are the gifts we have received?

For all this mystagogia to take place, Easter has to be more than one Sunday. Easter has to be a week of Sundays and a Sunday.

The worship environment established for the Easter Vigil (which should have grown out of that for Lent) must remain throughout the fifty days. Cross, paschal candle, and baptismal font are the major components of the environment along with altar and ambo.

The water in the font blessed at the Easter Vigil is used every Sunday for the renewal of baptism in the sprinkling rite.

The responsorial psalm of Easter Sunday ("This is the

day the Lord had made: let us rejoice and be glad," Ps 118) might well be used throughout the season. And since Alleluia is the Easter song, a strong, festive Alleluia (e.g., *Celtic Alleluia* by O'Carroll and Walker, Oregon Catholic Press) should be sung—the same one—right through to Pentecost Sunday.

READINGS, Year C

The readings, out of which all preparations for the liturgy flow, support our own reflections by providing the reflections of the early church on the meaning of the Jesus event.

> Until the third Sunday of Easter the Gospel selections recount the appearances of the risen Christ. The Gospels of the fifth, sixth and seventh Sundays of Easter are excerpts from the teaching and prayer of Christ after the last supper. The first reading is from the Acts of the Apostles, arranged in a three-year cycle of parallel and progressive selections. Thus, the life, growth and witness of the early Churches are presented every year. The selections from the writings of the apostles are Year A: The First Letter of Peter, Year B: the First Letter of John and Year C: the Book of Revelation. These texts seem most appropriate to the spirit of the Easter season, a spirit of joyful faith and confident hope. (Introduction to the Lectionary no. 14.1)

Easter Sunday

We are invited to enter into the experience of the empty tomb and the risen Lord. "Christ our Passover has been sacrificed" is part of an early Christian passover text quoted in the second reading used today from 1 Corinthians. The alternative second reading from Colossians says "we have died, we have been raised with Christ." Both of these remind us that the experience of Jesus and the experience of the early believers is our experience, too. That experience of Jesus as the Passover in its historical context is given in the first reading from Acts, and the historical events familiar to his listeners are interpreted by Peter, and given meaning in light of the post-resurrection experiences of the disciples.

This is the kerygma, or Good News, upon which the church's faith is built and to which the church—those chosen by God who eat and drink with the risen Lord and are commissioned to preach—gives witness.

The gospel recounts the experience of the first witnesses of the resurrection. Their responses varied from confusion and fear to belief. Like them, we enter the empty tomb. What is our response? The sequence or hymn in poetic imagery gives the meaning of Easter as Mary Magdalene might have proclaimed it. What is our hymn?

Second Sunday of Easter

How do we know what it means that Jesus rose from the dead? John's gospel tells us that the disciples began to know when they gathered together on the first day of the week—that first Easter Sunday. They were forgiven in Jesus' greeting "Peace be with you" (recall that they had all abandoned and denied Jesus). They were then empowered to extend that forgiveness to the world. Their experience of the risen Christ was one of reconciliation with God that renewed creation (He breathed on them and said: "Receive the Holy Spirit"; recall the creation story in Genesis—the Spirit hovering over the waters—and in Genesis 2, God breathed life into the human).

The absent Thomas doubted what the others believed until he gathered with them and shared the experience of the risen Christ.

The reading from Acts tells us that we know that the new creation has begun by the signs and wonders—the healings and the adding of believers—worked through the apostles. Recall the reading from Isaiah 43 on the Fifth Sunday of Lent, which promised that God would do something new. And we know because, as the second reading tells us, the experiences of the early Christians have been written down.

Third Sunday of Easter

Experience of the presence of the risen Christ calls forth a response. In the gospel the apostles have gone back to their former occupation, fishing. As he did once before, Jesus calls them, this time to ministry. Through the sharing in a meal of bread and fish (John's eucharistic image) they are to proclaim the reconciliation of humanity with God in Christ (the meaning of Jesus asking Peter three times if Peter, who denied Jesus three times, loved him).

The first reading from Acts recounts how the apostles, in spite of a ban, preached and taught the reconciliation given through Christ and testified to by the gift of the Holy Spirit. Revelation presents us with a vision of heavenly worship by all creation: praise and adoration of God and the Lamb who was slain, worship in which we participate sacramentally in the Eucharist. What is our response to the presence of the risen Christ?

Fourth Sunday of Easter

One of the earliest metaphors used by the Christian community to express their experience and relationship with Christ was the shepherd. As the one through whom reconciliation of all humanity was made, Jesus gathers all together and gives them eternal life (never being separated from God).

Paul and Barnabas are continuing the work of the shepherd in the first reading. They preach the message of reconciliation first to the Jews in Antioch, but when they are rejected they bring the good news of salvation to the Gentiles. Revelation presents a vision of the heavenly pastures with life-giving waters (the new creation, again recall Isaiah 43) to which (are shepherded) all those gathered together from every race and nation and washed in the blood of the Lamb. The way to eternal life is beset with trials, persecution, and rejection but Jesus is the one who leads us. There is no resurrection without suffering and death. Recalling our lenten journey, how have we experienced Jesus as shepherd?

Fifth Sunday of Easter

We reflect on the paschal mystery from another perspective. It was in love for humanity that Jesus accepted the cross, and it was in love for his Son that God glorified him in the resurrection. It was love that carried Paul and Barnabas through the hardships of their missionary journey. It is love that binds the Father and the Son so that not even death could separate them. It must be love that binds the community of disciples so that others will know of God's love for humanity.

The reading from Revelation sets before us the vision of the new creation where, through the church, the new Jerusalem, God lives among humanity.

Sixth Sunday of Easter

Jesus' Easter gift is peace, the peace that comes in unity with God and one another. It is the gift of reconciliation won on the cross. The gift is mediated by the Holy Spirit. As the Holy Spirit is the binding force between Father and Son so is the binding force between God and humanity. The Spirit works through the church, making the church a sign of the reconciliation for all humanity.

The first reading from Acts recounts the dissension and controversy between the Judaizers, who wanted to follow Mosaic law, and orthodox Christians, and how the church dealt with the problem by calling the first council.

The imagery of the Revelation reading is of the heavenly Jerusalem, the city of the fulfilled kingdom of God. The recurring number twelve, the product of four—the directions on the earth, above the earth and under the earth—is symbolic of all of creation.

Ascension

Where Christ has gone, we too, shall follow. Christ's exaltation is part of the paschal mystery in which we participate. Ephesians, the letter on the church, presents the church as part of the plan of God for the salvation of the world, to be Christ's presence and carry on the mission of Christ, until all has been gathered up in Christ.

Both the first reading from the beginning of Acts and the gospel are Lukan versions of the ascension. The disciples are given the mission to preach penance (a change of heart) for the forgiveness of sin, and the promise of the Holy Spirit to empower them in that mission.

Seventh Sunday of Easter

On Ash Wednesday, we heard that the ministry of the church is reconciliation. The gospel is from Jesus' priestly prayer: Jesus praying for the unity of all believers with God through his living in them so that the world will know of God's love for them.

The first reading recounts the death of Stephen, the first martyr, who prays to God to forgive those who stone him. It was the account of this death that was the model for the gospel accounts of Jesus' death, for there were many witnesses to Stephen's death including Saul, while Jesus was abandoned at his death. Coming full circle, it was later Saul, reborn as Paul, who wrote that the church's ministry is reconciliation.

The Revelation reading is an exhortation to the church to continue in its ministry, bringing all who desire to baptism. And it is a promise, "I am coming soon," and a prayer in response, "Amen. Come, Lord Jesus."

Pentecost

Our time of mystagogy is almost at an end. The gospel (which we heard also on the Second Sunday of Easter) and the first reading from Acts are two versions of the coming/giving of the Holy Spirit. One takes place on the evening of the first Easter Sunday, the other takes place fifty days later. Recall that Pentecost was both fifty days and the fiftieth day during which the entire Easter mystery—resurrection, presence of risen Christ, ascension, coming of the Spirit and second coming—were celebrated. In Year C, the Year of Luke, the emphasis is on reconciliation and thereby the renewal of creation accomplished through Jesus' death and resurrection.

It is the outpouring of the Spirit that is the sign of the new creation, for the Spirit mediates reconciliation (John's gospel, also the psalm). It is the work of the Holy Spirit to bring unity from diversity (Acts and 1 Corinthians).

All that we have reflected upon and celebrated these fifty days we did only in the Spirit. Our participation in the paschal mystery of Christ is possible only in the Spirit. We cannot say *Jesus is Lord* except in the Holy Spirit.

PRESIDENTIAL PRAYERS IN YEAR C

The selection of opening prayer and of the eucharistic prayer is made within the context of the readings.

The function of the opening prayer is to complete our gathering as the Body of Christ and prepare us for the readings. In effect, it serves as an introduction to the readings.

The first preface for Easter is used at the Easter Vigil and on the First Sunday of Easter. Thereafter, exclusive of Ascension and Pentecost which have their own prefaces, the preface is selected from among the five prefaces for Easter.

The fourth Easter preface: The Restoration of the Universe through the paschal mystery, most closely reflects the readings of Year C which emphasize reconciliation and the new creation. These prefaces may be used with any one of eucharistic prayers I, II, and III.

However, Eucharistic Prayer III seems most closely to reflect the spirit of the Year C of the Easter season. The anamnesis recalls the entire paschal mystery.

> Father, calling to mind the death your Son endured for our salvation, his glorious resurrection and ascension into heaven, and ready to greet him when he comes again...

in offering

> Look with favor on your Church's offering, and may this sacrifice, which has made our peace with you, advance the peace and salvation of all the world.

Blessing and Dismissal

Use of a solemn blessing is suggested throughout the season. To maintain continuity with the lenten season and reflect the spirit of the readings, perhaps the blessing for Easter Vigil and Easter Sunday could be used during the rest of the season as well, exclusive of Ascension and Pentecost. In that case, the first invocation might be modified:

> May almighty God bless and protect you during this season of Easter.

As Alleluia is the Easter song, the words of dismissal and the community response are capped with a threefold Alleluia.

REFERENCES

"Easter's Fifty Days" in *Liturgy, Journal of the Liturgical Conference*, vol 3 (1) 1982. (Features 12 articles on various aspects of the Easter season).

Parish Path through Lent and Eastertime edited by Mary Ann Simcoe, Liturgy Training Publications, Chicago, 1985. (Includes an introduction to the seasons, orientations to the readings and prayers, notes on preaching, and also deals with the RCIA, music, and worship environment).

Celebrating Liturgy Supplement edited by Peter Scagnelli, Liturgy Training Publications, Chicago.

Mazza, Enrico. *Mystagogy: a Theology of Liturgy in the Patristic Age.* New York: Pueblo, 1989.

Yarnold, Edward. *The Awe-Inspiring Rites of Initiation: The Origins of the RCIA.* 2nd edition. Collegeville: Liturgical Press, 1994.

THE PASCHAL MYSTERY
in Ordinary Time

On Sunday

Jayne Newton Ahearn

The day on which Christians gather, Sunday, the Lord's Day, with all that it means and symbolizes, is something new and unique to Christianity. Sunday did not arise from the Jewish Sabbath, nor was it mandated by Christ. Sunday results from the reflections of the community on its experience.

In fact, it should be noted that all of the earliest writings we have from, and about, the Christian community are already interpretive of the community experience particularly as it gathered to do what we now call liturgy. Some of these writings are included in the canon of Scripture: the Pauline writings, the gospels, and the Acts of the Apostles (50-100 C.E.).

Others sources are patristic: the *Didache* (50-70 C.E.) the letters of Ignatius, Bishop of Antioch (110 C.E.), and the *First Apology* of Justin Martyr (150 C.E.).

HISTORICAL ORIGINS

Almost all of the early writings that say something about the community's gatherings, from the *Didache* and the Acts of the Apostles, to the letter of Pliny to the Roman emperor Trajan (112 C.E.) to Justin Martyr, place them on Sunday. And by the time Justin writes his descriptions addressed to the pagan Roman emperor, what is happening at the Sunday gathering is not very different from what Roman Catholic Christians are doing on Sunday now:

• there was proclamation of the word;

• there was thanksgiving made over bread and wine for God's gift of "knowledge and faith and immortality ... revealed through Jesus Christ" (already called Eucharist in the *Didache* 9 and 10);

• there was shared eating of that bread and wine;

• there was service exemplified in many ministerial roles at the liturgy;

• there was a concern for the needs of the world expressed in intercessory prayer and giving to the sick and poor.

In the beginning there was Sunday alone: the community gathered to hear the word and make Eucharist on Sunday. Sunday was all that was needed because it was everything. By the time Justin wrote in the mid-second century, Sunday had already emerged as a symbol of the richness of the Christian experience of life in God: an experience that can be expressed using many metaphors.

During the fourth century, after the Edict of Milan, which made Christianity a state religion, the liturgical calendar developed quite rapidly. This development extended more and more the meaning of Sunday, looking at its many dimensions, without diminishing Sunday itself.

SUNDAY AND GOD'S TIME

Sunday transcends and fulfills all days in that reality that is beyond time. The Judeo-Christian tradition understands God as the Creator that stands apart from creation and exists outside of time (as time is a characteristic of creation). The only way human beings can encounter God is through God's entrance into time in the events of our history. Thus we believe that God has revealed Godself to us in the real events of history.

For the Jews, the Exodus was the foundational event that formed them as a people with a unique relationship to God.

For Christians, the climactic and complete revelation of God was in the person of the historical Jesus of Nazareth. What Jesus did determined the person who Jesus became. Jesus was the manifestation of God's gratuitous offer of Godself to humanity and of the free response of humanity to God through his total *self-giving* for others. We call this the Jesus or Christ event: this is the foundational event that gives meaning and identity to Christians. Because of Jesus' incarnation, passion, death, and resurrection, all humanity is offered a share in God's life, *that reality which is beyond time*. This is salvation.

In history, the Jesus event was *once for all*. For us who dwell in time, it is past. But for God who transcends time, it is always now. The mystery that the Jesus event reveals, God coming to us and saving us in God's Son, is actualized in every age by *anamnesis* (remembering).

Anamnesis is done through the proclamation of the Word, telling the story of the person Jesus. Because of God's promise and through the Holy Spirit, the person Jesus continues to be contemporary. Jesus is present to us now; Jesus saves us now.

This is what the disciples experienced when they gathered after Jesus' death and burial—as soon as the Sabbath was over on the first day of the week—to remember the person Jesus and share bread and wine in his name. Together, they experienced the presence of Jesus as the risen One: together, they experienced themselves as having a new identity and meaning. What they did together was both source and expression of their new life in Christ, so they repeated it Sunday after Sunday.

SUNDAY IS ITSELF A SACRAMENT OF THE GOSPEL

On that first Sunday, in the presence of the risen Christ, the community of disciples broke into the new age begun by the Jesus event.

The Judeo-Christian tradition conceives time as linear. From the beginning of creation, the beginning of time, creation has been evolving and time has been moving toward an ultimate goal. That goal is unity and perfection in God.

Jesus talked about and preached about that goal. He called it the reign or the kingdom of God. He said the kingdom of God was near and he called that Good News (the gospel).

• in parables, Jesus described God's kingdom: always with an unexpected and disconcerting outcome. In deeds, Jesus acted out the kingdom;

• he healed both body and spirit; he shared table with prostitutes and tax collectors as well as with his friends (they were all his friends).

• in the beatitudes, he taught that the kingdom belonged to those who appeared to be the marginalized, the outcasts, and the failures of human society.

• he taught that the law of God's kingdom is love.

• in the end, Jesus became the parable of the kingdom, the crucified Lord. Through the death and resurrection of Jesus, God inaugurates the new age, the kingdom of God.

The account of Easter evening in John's gospel (written around 90-100 C.E.) begins with the disciples gathered in a locked room. Jesus appears in their midst and greets them with peace. Then he breathes on them and says "Receive the Holy Spirit." The gospel writer in this way expresses the community's experience of a new creation and of being made new. As God's spirit blew over the waters on the first day of creation, so does Jesus' Spirit infuse the new creation. Jesus' offer of peace to this group of friends, who had abandoned him in his hours of greatest need, expresses the forgiveness of God's kingdom: the new creation where all the broken pieces are put back together again.

In the Lukan version of this Easter evening appearance, Jesus wishes peace to his disciples, tells them not to be frightened because he is really Jesus alive, and then eats with them to prove it. He eats with them on other occasions too, including a picnic breakfast on the beach of the Sea of Galilee. Recall that in the Synoptic accounts of the Last Supper, Jesus does not share in the final cup, saying that he will not drink with them again until the kingdom of God. One of his kingdom parables was that of the wedding banquet—already a familiar image for the messianic kingdom. So eating with the risen Lord was a sign of the kingdom and that the kingdom was already happening.

Another metaphor for the kingdom of God that was applied to the Christian Sunday experience was the *eighth day*. God had worked on creation for six days and then rested on the seventh. Thus it was proposed that there would be six ages in creation's history before a final age of rest. A new creation or a new age would begin on the eighth day. The Holy Spirit breathing on the disciples in John's gospel and descending upon them at Pentecost in the Acts is the sign of the new creation, the kingdom of God. It is also life-giver to the church. Sunday is the Day of the Spirit and the Day of the church. The church, empowered by the Holy Spirit is the sign of God's kingdom here, now. Good News! The Sunday gatherings of early Christians were recorded to be joyful occasions and filled with hope.

SUNDAY, A MINI-EASTER

Sunday renews the fullness of the feast of feasts, our death and resurrection with Christ. The church is sign but not fulfillment of the kingdom. The return of Christ was, and is, eagerly anticipated. Meanwhile Christians live in the now between the faith-bearing past and the hoped-for future. Christians can live in the between because they share in God's life and are immersed in God's love through their participation in the death and resurrection of Christ.

The church came to celebrate the Eucharist on the first day of the week because that was the day they first experienced the presence of the risen Lord in their midst. Sunday becomes associated with the resurrection. All four gospels specify that the resurrection was on the first day of the week. But more than that, Sunday Eucharist becomes the means of unity with the risen Christ and with one another.

Ignatius of Antioch wrote to several Christian communities that were having problems of disunity arising particularly from celebration of more than one Eucharist (Judaizers were celebrating Eucharist on Saturday). He stressed the power of the Eucharist to both signify and effect union of the members with Christ and with one another.

Paul developed the metaphor of the Body of Christ before Ignatius wrote. In his first letter to the Corinthians, also a community suffering from divisions, Paul likens each person in the church to a part of one body. Each member is needed if the body is to function. Those who make up the church are no longer individuals but part of the one Body of Christ. The Body of Christ in the Eucharist makes the Body of Christ, the church.

The *Didache* echoes this using the metaphor of the grain scattered on the hills and gathered into one loaf. Through the Eucharist Christians maintain their participation in Christ. And for Paul, the way to begin this participation is through baptism. To the Romans he writes: "Are you unaware that we who were baptized into Christ Jesus were baptized into his death? We were indeed buried with him through baptism into death, so that, just as Christ was raised from the dead by the glory of the Father, we too might live in newness of life" (Rom 6:3–5).

Baptism as participation in Christ's death and resurrection and as entry into the communion of the Body of Christ was a part of the Sunday experience.

Sharing in Christ's resurrection makes each Christian a new creation. To create the first day God separated light from the darkness. The first day of the new creation brought about by Christ's resurrection is a Day of Light. The new creature born in baptism is a child of light: is enlightened. (Justin calls baptism illumination.) Because he rose from death and darkness, Christ is the light of the world and the rising sun. The day of resurrection of the Son is called Sunday.

Being *enlightened* or finding new meaning through participation in the paschal mystery of Christ is the experience of the two disciples on the road to Emmaus on the first day of the week. They are discussing events of the past (the crucifixion of the one they thought was the messiah) and in those events finding neither hope nor faith. A stranger join them, the risen Christ, the promise of God's future, and helps them to reinterpret their past. Finally they recognize Christ in the breaking of the bread and their present is changed. Their priorities are rearranged in favor of God's kingdom as they turn around and speed joyfully to Jerusalem to share the news with others.

Just as those two disciples at Emmaus did, Christians celebrate each Sunday the totality of the Christ always present among us now.

Sundays in Ordinary Time

Jayne Newton Ahearn

DESCRIPTION

Apart from those seasons having their own distinctive character, thirty-three or thirty-four weeks remain in the yearly cycle that do not celebrate a specific aspect of the mystery of Christ. Rather, especially on the Sundays, they are devoted to the mystery of Christ in all its aspects. This period is known as Ordinary Time. (*General Norms for the Liturgical Year and the Calendar* no. 43, *Ceremonial of Bishops* no. 377)

The Church celebrates the paschal mystery on the first day of the week, known as the Lord's Day or Sunday. This follows a tradition handed down from the apostles and having its origin from the day of Christ's resurrection. Thus Sunday must be ranked as the first holyday of all. (*GNLYC* no. 4, *CB* no. 228)

By a tradition handed down from the apostles and having its origin from the very day of Christ's resurrection, the Church celebrates the paschal mystery every eighth day, which, with good reason, bears the name of the Lord's Day or Sunday. For on this day Christ's faithful must gather together so that, by hearing the word of God and taking part in the eucharist, they may call to mind the passion, the resurrection, and the glorification of the Lord Jesus and may thank God, who "has begotten them again unto a living hope through the resurrection of Jesus Christ from the dead" (1 Pt 1:3, see Second Sunday of Easter, cycle A). Hence the Lord's Day is the first holy day of all and should be proposed to the devotion of the faithful and taught to them in such a way that it may become in fact a day of joy and of freedom from work. Other celebrations, unless they be truly of greatest importance, shall not have precedence over the Sunday, the foundation and core of the whole liturgical year. (*Constitution on the Sacred Liturgy* no. 106)

THE LECTIONARY AND AN APPROACH TO LITURGY PREPARATION

During the portion of the liturgical calendar called Ordinary Time, the gospel readings proceed more or less continuously through one of the three synoptic gospels. This principle of continuous reading means we read from Matthew's gospel in Year A, Mark's gospel in Year B with a long segment from John chapter 6, and St. Luke's gospel in Year C.

The first readings are selected from the Old Testament (Hebrew Scriptures) to harmonize or relate to the gospel. The second reading again is a more or less continuous reading of one of the Pauline epistles or other New Testament writing. Thus the second reading may or may not relate to the first reading and gospel.

Remember that the only theme of any Mass is the paschal mystery of Christ. However, the preparation of the liturgy for any particular Sunday should not be done in isolation from the Sundays preceding or following. There should be a continuity and a flow from Sunday to Sunday.

A way to achieve this is to divide the Sundays of Ordinary Time into blocks or units and prepare by blocks of Sundays rather than by individual Sundays. The content and structure of the gospels help to determine the blocks of Sundays.

Read the chapters in this volume by Jerome Neyrey, S.J. and Paddy Meagher, S.J. to appreciate more the craft and the style of writing of each of the evangelists' narrative. This will help locate each reading in context.

PRESIDENTIAL PRAYERS

To provide continuity and flow from Sunday to Sunday, it is proposed that one preface and eucharistic prayer be used for all the Sundays within a block. The same practice applies to the final blessing.

PENITENTIAL RITE

One set of invocations for Form C of the penitential rite may be used throughout a block of Sundays. The invocations may be composed to draw on images from the readings within that unit of time.

MUSIC

Responsorial Psalm. One significant way to provide continuity between Sundays within a unit or block is with a seasonal responsorial psalm.

Gospel Acclamation. The proclamation of the gospel is the high point of the Liturgy of the Word. It should be introduced by a strong Alleluia that accompanies a well choreographed gospel procession. Use the same gospel acclamation during Ordinary Time until Advent.

Alleluia from *Mass of Light* (provides verses for use in ordinary time)	David Haas
Alleluia, Your Word	Lucien Deiss
Celtic Alleluia (provides a large selection of verses which can be chosen to reflect the gospel)	O'Carroll/Walker
Sing Praises To The Lord	Christopher Walker
Word of Truth and Life from *Mass of Creation*	Marty Haugen

Eucharistic Acclamations. A strong, solid setting for the acclamations of the eucharistic prayer, not as highly festive as those for Easter and not as sober as those for Lent, should be used throughout the rest of the year.

Marty Haugen's *Mass of Creation* has become quite popular in some areas. It includes the Holy, Memorial Acclamation A, Doxology for the presider, Great Amen, and Lamb of God. *Eucharistic Acclamations 2* by Paul Inwood are easily learned by the community since the people sing what the cantor has just sung. These acclamations include the Holy, Memorial Acclamations B and C, Doxology for the presider and the Great Amen.

Another set of acclamations worthy of being learned and sung are the *Eucharistic Acclamations* by Bernadette Farrell. This set includes the Holy, Memorial Acclamations A, B and C, Doxology for the presider, and the Great Amen.

The St. Louis Jesuits' settings for the Holy, Doxology for presider, and the Great Amen have become standard for Ordinary Time use in many parishes. Though a memorial acclamation is not provided in this set, acclamation C can be set using the melody of the Great Amen. *Anamnesis II* by Tom Conry can be used with the Jesuits' acclamations.

A Community Mass by Richard Proulx is found in *Worship III*. *Mass of Freedom* by Maggie Russell provides the Holy, Memorial Acclamations A and B, the Great Amen, and Lamb of God. It can be found in *As One Voice*.

A word has to be said about the Great Amen. The doxology is the conclusion of the eucharistic prayer and is properly said or sung by the presider alone. The Great Amen is the acclamation of the people that affirms all that has been said in the eucharistic prayer. The practice has arisen in some places that the people join the presider in the doxology. This presumably is because they feel the need to acclaim and affirm in prayer but are only given a weak Amen by which to do this. If the community is provided with a good, strong Amen they will leave the doxology to the presider. Try Tom Conry's Amen which is no. 171 in the old *Glory and Praise*.

The Lord's Prayer. During Ordinary Time the Our Father is best recited.

The Lamb of God. This should always be sung and it should continue until all the bread has been broken and all the wine has been poured into communion cups.

The simple setting, that is, "Lamb of God, you take away the sin of the world," is repeated with the conclusion "have mercy on us" until the fractioning is completed. The last time the conclusion is "Grant us peace."

Such settings of the Lamb of God include Proulx's in *A Community Mass* and Russell's in *Mass of Freedom*. Paul Inwood has written a Lamb of God that can be used with his *Eucharistic Acclamations 2*. It has three differing verses to be sung by a cantor to which the people respond "Jesus Lamb of God, have mercy on us."

The length of the verses ensures that it would last through the fraction rite in the average-size parish. Other settings of the Lamb of God provide tropes, which are essentially other names by which Jesus is called upon. Examples are Bread of Life, Word Made Flesh, Wine of Peace, King of Kings. The cantor sings the tropes and the people respond "have mercy on us." These can easily be extended as long as needed.

Settings in this style of Lamb of God include Marty Haugen's *Mass of Creation*, David Clark Isele's *Holy Cross Mass* and Bernadette Farrell's *Jesus Lamb of God* in the collection *God Beyond All Names* from Oregon Catholic Press.

General Intercessions.
The people respond with prayer at the invitation to pray for the proposed intentions: in other words, the prayer in silence and the vocalized response *is* the prayer of the community. This prayer is in the form of a litany, which is best sung. Some settings can be used throughout the rest of the year.

God of Mercy from *Mass of Glory*	Bob Hurd
Hear Our Prayer	Ernest Sands
O Loving Father	James Moore
O God Hear Us	Bob Hurd

Some parishioners may also know the response sung by the Iona Community: By our work and by our prayer, may your kingdom come (*Music of Iona*).

The Gloria.
The Ordo calls for the Gloria to be sung or said every Sunday. Since the Gloria is a hymn of praise it really should be sung: otherwise omit it. The liturgy team should make the decision of when the Gloria is best used and when it is better omitted. Keep the setting simple during Ordinary Time.

In the following, the community sings the entire hymn:

Gloria from *Mass for Congregations*	Carroll T. Andrews
Gloria From *A Community Mass*	Richard Proulx.

In these, the community sings an antiphon and a cantor or choir sings verses:

Glory To God from *Eucharist*	Michael Anderson
Glory To God from *Mass of Freedom*	Maggie Russell
Glory to God from *Mass of Creation*	Marty Haugen

Sprinkling Rite.
If the Rite of Blessing and Sprinkling Holy Water is used, the Gloria may be sung during the sprinkling or one of the following:

Song of Fire and Water (If we have died to ourselves...)	Marty Haugen
You Will Draw Water	Tom Conry
We Shall Draw Water	Paul Inwood

Other Hymns and Songs.
Some songs and hymns can be used repeatedly during a block of Sundays since they relate well to the readings within that block. These hymns and songs will also serve to tie the Sundays together. Hymns and songs that are more specific to the readings of the Sunday need to be chosen with knowledge of the music capability of the parish, and with awareness of the ritual function of the individual part of the Mass, and the flow of the seasons.

WORSHIP ENVIRONMENT

1. The liturgical color for Ordinary Time is Green. Green has many shades. Combine several shades of green for vestments and altar linens. Or have two sets, each one a different shade for use at different times within the year: one for June through August and the other for September through November. The change of the seasons will offer inspiration to express the rhythm of life.

2. The major symbols for Ordinary Time are:

• **WORD:** the book from which the word is proclaimed and the ambo from where it is proclaimed.

Attend to the book. Is the book worthy of its symbolic function? Is there a Book of the Gospels? If so, from what are the first and second readings proclaimed?

• **EUCHARIST:** the altar, bread and wine.

Attend to the bread and the wine. Does the bread we use for Eucharist look and taste like bread? Is it bread that can be broken? Are there enough breads for the communicants at any one Mass without presuming to use hosts from the tabernacle? Is the wine of good quality and pleasant to the taste? Is the parish committed to the symbolism of sharing from one cup? Is the decantering planned with sufficient chalices? Are there enough communion ministers? Are there enough communion stations?

3. Are the furnishings worthy of their function in the liturgy? Do they need cleaning, refinishing, repairs? Is the church clean and tidy? Does it reflect the pride of the parishioners in their place of worship?

Attend also to the vessels and other things associated with the liturgy. This includes the plates for bread, the cups for communion, the chalice and/or container for the wine on the altar, the censer and incense boat, and candle sticks. Are they clean, polished, in good repair?

4. This is a good time to reread the document *Art and Environment in Catholic Worship*. Are we using the liturgical space or is it using us?

5. Is the place where the community gathers to celebrate Sunday Eucharist a welcoming place? Is it clean, neat, and comfortable? What about the entry area? The pews and under the pews?

PASTORAL NOTES

1. The Sundays of the year that fall outside of the seasons of Advent, Christmas, Lent, and Easter are called Sundays in Ordinary Time. For Christians, Sunday is never ordinary. The word ordinary in this case refers to ordinal or counted, as in second, third, fourth, and so on.

2. Sunday is described as "a day of joy and freedom from work." However, this does not mean a sabbath rest. Rather Sunday should be freed of usual work so that Christians may spend time working for the coming of the kingdom. This would include such activities as visiting those in prison, those who are homebound, those who are sick in hospital, providing meals for the poor, working on projects to build homes for the homeless, as well as engaging in Bible studies and community prayer.

3. Because Sunday is the nucleus and foundation of the liturgical year the Sunday celebration takes precedence over any other sort of celebration. The proper character of the Sunday celebration is to be observed with fidelity and devotion. "This has a particular application to the practice, frequently involving a Sunday, of assigning a special theme to a particular day: for example, dedicating a day to the promotion of peace and justice, vocations, or the missions. In such cases the liturgy to be celebrated is the Sunday liturgy...." (*Ceremonial of Bishops* no. 229).

REFERENCES

Adam, Adolf, 1979. *The Liturgical Year: Its History and Meaning After the Reform of the Liturgy*. Pueblo Publishing, New York (now affiliated with The Liturgical Press, Collegeville, MN). (See Chapter 7, "Ordinary Time.")

Beaumont, Madeleine (translator), 1992. *Days of the Lord: The Liturgical Year*. Volume 4 Ordinary Time, Year A. The Liturgical Press, Collegeville MN.

Bishops' Committee on the Liturgy, National Conference of Catholic Bishops, 1987. *Celebrating the Marian Year*. Publishing Services, United States Catholic Conference, Washington, D.C.

Nocent, Adrian, O.S.B., 1977. *The Liturgical Year Volume Four*: Sundays in Ordinary Time. The Liturgical Press, Collegeville MN. (See especially Chapter 1, "The Organization of Ordinary Time.")

Sanchez, Patricia Datchuck, 1989. *The Word We Celebrate: Commentary on the Sunday Lectionary, Years A, B and C*. Sheed and Ward, Kansas City, MO.

Reading Matthew: From Womb to Tomb with the Messiah

Jerome Neyrey, SJ

OVERVIEW OF MATTHEW'S GOSPEL

All the good stories have a beginning, middle, and end. Biographies too have a recognizable structure: from womb to tomb. So readers of Matthew might well expect that the story of Jesus comes to us in a carefully crafted manner that highlights certain aspects of Jesus' life and ministry, especially his birth, public life, and death. If we compare Matthew to the typical biography in antiquity, it too begins with announcement of the parents and family of the hero: Joseph belongs to a clan ("son of David") although he does not enjoy the wealth and power of his ancestors. Jesus' genealogy, a regular feature of biographies, contains a "who's who" of Israelite history (Abraham, David, Solomon, Hezekiah, etc.), indicating Jesus' noble blood lines. Typically, too, the heavens rejoice at this birth: the new star indicates that a special hero, indeed a new king, has been born on earth. From Matthew we learn nothing about Jesus' upbringing and education. But we quickly discover that Jesus demonstrated all of the four classical virtues: prudence, justice, courage, and temperance. All of his words and deeds demonstrate how noble, wise, bold, obedient, and honorable he was. Like biographies, Matthew's account tells us of his passion and the remarkable things that accompanied his death and exaltation. It is not farfetched, then, to consider Matthew's document as an encomium of praise to Jesus, for it contains all of the standard elements of just such a testimony of honor, precisely in the order in which the ancients expected them.

Yet readers of Matthew quickly discern other shapes and structures in the narrative that are also useful for interpretation. Matthew portrays Jesus speaking at great length, unlike Mark's presentation of him. And Matthew gathered his words and made them memorable in five lengthy discourses.

Sermon on the Mountains (chapters 5-7)

Missionary Discourse (chapter 10)

Parables of the Kingdom of God (chapter 13)

Discipline with the Church (chapter 18)

Discourse on Final Things (chapters 23-25)

Each of these collections of Jesus' sayings conveniently ends with remarks such as

"When Jesus had finished saying these things ...." (7:28)

"When Jesus had finished instructing his twelve disciples ... " (11:1; see 13:53; 19:1; 26:1).

Moreover, clever readers will pay attention to the alternation of Jesus' words and deeds. Each collection of sayings seems to be juxtaposed with a collection of his deeds. For example,

the Sermon on the Mount is balanced by a collection of ten miracle stories (chapters 8-9);

the Missionary Discourse, by a series of controversy stories (chapters 11-12);

the Parables, by a series of miracles and controversies (chapters 13-16);

the Discourse to the Church, by Jesus' actions on the way to Jerusalem (chapters 19-20). After all, like most of the great prophets, Jesus is "mighty in word and deed." We might even say that his actions and deeds illustrate most of his words. Hence he teaches as much by example as by precept.

Much of the importance of Matthew's gospel rests upon our appreciation of the fact that Matthew represents a profound development in the understanding and preaching of Jesus. By that I mean, Matthew writes late in the first century (80-90 C.E.) and contains clues about the way Jesus was preached by earlier generations. Matthew's gospel is but the final draft of an ongoing reflection about Jesus and contains diverse and even conflicting points of view about him. We can detect some of the sources used by Matthew, and when we compare Matthew with them, we can see the drift of a distinctive "theology" articulated by him.

Such a way of reading the gospels, of course, should sound familiar: after all the enlightened Vatican II delegates stated just such a process as typical of the way each of the gospels came into its final form:

> The Sacred authors wrote the Gospels: selecting some things from the many which had been handed on by word of mouth or in writing, reducing some of them to a synthesis, explicating some things in view of the situation of their churches, and preserving the form of proclamation but always in such fashion that they told us the "honest truth" about Jesus. For their intention in writing was that either from their own memory and recollections, or from the witness of those who themselves "from the beginning were eyewitnesses and ministers of the word" we might know "the truth" concerning these matters about which we have been instructed (cf. Lk 1:2–4). (Vatican II, *Dei Verbum*, no. 19)

Thus, we can discern how a venerable and old preaching about Jesus (the "Q" material) has been adapted and updated to make the gospel message relevant to later, different times. No longer is the message restricted to "the lost sheep of the House of Israel" (10:6): "all nations" are to be taught the gospel. No longer is the perfect keeping of the traditional law and customs related to it held a paramount value (5:17–20): disciples will observe all that Jesus has commanded (28:20), which will contain many reforms of Jewish piety and practice. In addition to material from the "Q" source, we know that Matthew's group also had access to Mark's gospel and accepted most of its values and strategic pastoral moves, such as God's impartiality to Jew/Gentile and slave/free as well as the importance of prayer as the primary form of Christian piety.

This means that we might hear "contradictions" or "inconsistencies" in Matthew because the old sits side-by-side with the new: but we can make sense of them by remembering that the evangelist

selected some of the many things he knew,

reduced some to a synthesis, and

explicated the tradition in terms of the needs, context, and situation of his community

In this, Matthew has presented us with a clear example of "pastoral theology" namely, the heralding of Jesus in terms that a new group with a new history and culture can understand.

If Matthew's gospel contains diverse points of view on certain key issues, such as membership in the group, how can readers safely follow the thread? How can they learn the Matthean point of view?

Like all good writers, the evangelist invites us to study closely the beginning and ending of the story, for those two key rhetorical places contain the clearest articulation of the major themes, values, and statements of the author. Hence, when we begin the gospel, we should let ourselves be schooled by Matthew's story of the infancy of Jesus so as to become sensitive and familiar with his dominant themes. In this, writers resemble symphonic composers: the opening bars of Mozart and Beethoven signal the dominant theme, key, and tonality of the whole piece.

In chapter 1-2, Matthew immediately heralds that Jesus belongs to an ancient covenant tradition that is quite different from that of Moses and priestly Temple traditions. Jesus is "son of Abraham and son of David" with whom God made covenants of promise, not covenants of law. God acted in total freedom to choose and bless Abraham and David, and so demonstrated how surprising and even unconventional God's favor is. It is not restricted to Israelites, much less observant ones (see Gal 3:6–9). Christians interpreted the Abraham and David covenant as suggestive of a blessing of all nations, that is, of an inclusive and impartial acceptance by God of all peoples, regardless of gender, geography, or generation (see Mt 8:11).

Hence it is not surprising to find in the genealogy four women who are "foreigners" (Tamar: Gn 38; Rahab: Joshua 2; Ruth: Ruth 1:4; Bathsheba: 2 Sam 11:3) and each of whom had some marriage or sexual cloud over them. Of course, Matthew could hide this information, as most of us would if writing our own family histories. But by including it in the very opening of the gospel, Matthew seems to be making the point that in Christ Jesus God shows no favor to Jews over

Gentiles, or to saints over sinners. Furthermore, Jesus' very name means "savior": "he will save his people from their sins" (1:21). What better way to signal Jesus' legitimate commerce with sinners and his offer of God's mercy and forgiveness than to indicate in his blood lines that such a strategy has always been God's way. Israel's history has always included such signal events and unusual persons.

Confirmation of these two major points can be found in the conclusion of the story. The risen Lord commissions his disciples to preach to all nations, thus echoing and emphasizing the inclusive theme made in Mt 1. Moreover Jesus proclaims a "baptism" for sins that includes the echoes of this earlier heralding of him as agent of the forgiveness of sins and as the savior of his people from evil. "Baptism," moreover, seems to replace "circumcision" as the official rite of initiation in Jesus' clan. Inclusiveness and new purification, then, are the hallmarks of Matthew's point of view.

The beginning and ending of the story both highlight another theme. Although Jesus is God's Son and the king of Israel, he lives a life constantly threatened by enemies. Yet God acts as his savior and deliverer. Hence, at his birth Gentile Magi (more foreigners) acclaim him as king, although all Jerusalem was troubled at the news and Herod sought to destroy the boy. But, by God's providence, he escapes the death visited on the innocent children of Bethlehem. Likewise at the end of his life, Jesus is again acclaimed as king (e.g., title over the cross), is again rejected by his own (27:25), and put to death. But God again rescues him and enthrones him as Lord of Creation. Hence, beginning and ending both tell us of God's favor and power: favor to include the excluded and to rescue the oppressed. As God worked toward Jesus, so this same God turns to the followers of Jesus and promises them life, membership, and blessing.

Besides the clear articulation of key themes in chapters 1-2 and 26-28, Matthew articulates many signature themes in the course of his narrative. For example, Matthew immediately heralds Jesus as the bringer of wholeness and healing to all peoples, just as Isaiah prophesied (Mt 4:12-17): hence readers wait for the presentation in narrative form of Jesus' healing and blessing actions (chapter 8-9). One of the hallmarks of modern readers of the Bible is our historical consciousness. We are acutely aware that our experience colors our perception: we are very sensitive to the formative influences of us and other peoples. This holds true for ancient authors, with the result that we can more fully understand communication from them when we know their historical and social times, location, audience, and experience. Matthew is generally said to be written in an urban environment with significant Jewish and non-Jewish populations (Syria or Antioch are good guesses). He wrote after the cataclysmic Roman-Judean war, which ended in the destruction of the temple in 70 C.E. His gospel reflects considerable conflict between the disciples and their Jewish neighbors, especially those who begin to make the Law or Torah the focus of Jewish life after the destruction of Israel's Temple. Moreover, Matthew the author seems to be a scribe, for he is quite literate (maybe 5% of that population was literate) and thoroughly conversant with the Jewish Scriptures: he understands typical Jewish issues and modes of argument. Although he suggests significant reforms for Jewish traditional piety, by no means does he suggest that Jesus or the disciples have turned their back on Israel. Rather they would present themselves as the reformed and enlightened ones, who would truly know the secrets of the kingdom of God. Thus Matthew writes at a time of crisis and upheaval, for a mixed Jewish-Gentile audience, balancing both a strict reform of Jewish piety and an expanded membership in God's covenant community with decided loyalty to the Scriptures and selected traditions of Jewish piety rather than to the Temple.

Matthew's gospel contains the most extended set of instructions from Jesus on discipleship, and for this reason it has been prized in the history of the church precisely as a "church" gospel. Discipleship for Matthew is considerably more systematized and articulated than it is in Mark, his source.

ELEVENTH SUNDAY IN ORDINARY TIME: YEAR A Mt 9:36—10:8

We resume the gospel of Matthew in Ordinary Time with a passage that links Jesus' own ministry with that of his disciples. In chapters 8-9, Matthew gathered many of Jesus' healing miracles so that their concentration might help us understand better what such miracles signify. Matthew earlier interpreted Jesus' healings in terms of what Isaiah said: "He took our infirmities and bore our diseases" (Mt 8:17). And after more miracles, he compared Jesus to a "shepherd" concerned for his sheep (see the responsorial psalm for today: we are all the sheep of God's flock). The miracles, then, remind us that Jesus represents God's power and concern for our physical well-being. God's favor is not simply grace for our souls, but also healing and health for our bodies. The miracles, moreover, were performed for Gentiles as well as Jews, females as well as males, and slaves as well as free. Thus God shows no partiality, but has mercy on all. We understand, then, why Matthew boldly announces how Jesus traveled about "all the villages" and "cured every sickness and every disease" (9:35). And so, we are reminded of the basic thrust of all the miracle stories: they tell us about the impartial and inclusive concern of God for all peoples and they dramatize that God's blessings and favor include our physical well being here on earth. God intends our well-being!

But today's gospel balances two things. First we see Jesus himself finishing his own ministry of preaching and healing. We remember how the miracles encode God's inclusive and impartial compassion. But how will this be manifested after Jesus' career? How will God's benefaction continue and be expended to all? Jesus prays in 9:37–38 for more laborers to join him in the harvest, that is, for disciples to share his ministry: he commands us to pray that God send out more workers. This prayer seems immediately fulfilled by the subsequent commissioning of the "twelve disciples" to continue Jesus' work. He gave them the same powers he enjoyed: "…authority over unclean spirits to cast them out, and to cure every disease and every sickness." Thus, God intends the great benefaction released to continue in the life of the church. Disciples too will "cure the sick, raise the dead and cleanse the lepers."

Oddly, Jesus tells them to stay on familiar turf and not to go to non-Jews or to their Samaritan neighbors. We do not understand the rationale for this restriction, but in the course of the whole gospel, Jesus' own actions eventually override it (15:21–28), and he explicitly commands the disciples to "…make disciples of all nations" (28:19). Nevertheless, we do well to focus on the thrust of Jesus' commissioning here, which is the extension of his saving ministry both in time and space. If future generations are to expect continuation of God's blessings in their midst, there is, then, no sense of a golden age long past, when things were better. On the contrary, God's favor and Jesus' power continue to be effective and abundant today.

The disciples are commanded to do their ministry freely and without pay: "You received without payment: give without payment." This probably has more symbolic meaning than literal sense. Just as Jesus acted out of compassion to help and heal and dispensed freely and generously God's benefits to all, so the disciples should imitate the utter gratuitousness and abundance of God's favor. This may be the gospel's way of criticizing the costliness of Temple offerings. Yet what makes symbolic sense in the gospel hardly constitutes practical advice for those who will live a life of ministry and service. This may explain why Luke records for his community the remark of Jesus that the laborers are worthy of their hire and should be fed and housed by those whom they serve. In this Luke seems more practical than Matthew the idealist. Yet the point is well taken: God sends rain and sun on the good and bad alike: God is generous and full of benefits for all. This hallmark of God's utter gratuity in blessing all should also be symbolized in some way in the life of today's church. How important it is for us mortals to realize finally that God means to fill us with blessings and not to despoil us. This might help us to reread the first reading from Exod 19:2–6 in which we hear the grand record of God's continual and generous outpouring of blessings and favors.

TWELFTH SUNDAY IN ORDINARY TIME: YEAR A Mt 10:26–33

Last Sunday we began to read the second of the five great "Sermons" that Jesus delivers in Matthew (we heard the first sermon on the 4th-7th Sundays of Ordinary Time). This sermon contains detailed instructions on the missionary conduct of the disciples. The gospel balances that grand sense of the outpouring of

God's favor in last Sunday's gospel with sharp warnings today that the mission does not automatically succeed and may prove very hazardous to the disciples. Jeremiah the besieged prophet exemplifies the plight of prophets who speak an unpopular word: his example in the first reading reminds us of the challenges often facing those who preach repentance and justice or even witness to them. Is this not all the more the case with Jesus' own ministry: great success in healing, followed by rejection and persecution?

As we delve into today's gospel, we hear not just about future trials and dangers, but about God's providential concern and protection, which may be the more important issue for us. Three times in today's gospel we are told to have courage: "Have no fear of them! (10:26)": "Do not fear those who kill the body..."(10:28): and "So do not be afraid" (10:31). Why? Because "secrets" are known! What secrets? Probably all the good deeds that disciples constantly do and that meet rejection or end in hostility from others. Although lives of service and ministry seem never to be rewarded by our peers or the people whom we serve (after all, we do not do such for money or respect), the "secret" is known by God and will eventually come to light. Disciples are compared to sparrows, for whom God providentially cares. If God acts so solicitously for just one of them, how much more jealous will God be for our welfare? What counts is loyalty and faithfulness: hence, Jesus says "tell in the light...proclaim from the house tops." What counts is courage and steadfastness in the face of adversity.

This gospel, although it originally spoke to disciples formally commissioned by Jesus for public ministry, can be understood as addressed to all disciples who today enjoy a ministerial role in God's household as spouses and parents. The same gift of knowing God's constant providential care is extended to them: their "secrets" are known to God and the hairs of their heads too are counted. For it would be too limiting to Jesus' inclusive ministry to see the service of the gospel restricted only to a handful of formal missionaries. Did Jesus not pray: "The harvest is great...ask the Lord of the harvest to send out laborers" (9:37–38)? Not only should they see God's providential care surrounding them, but they too should take to heart the demands of faithfulness and loyalty, no mean items in our rapidly changing world.

THIRTEENTH SUNDAY OF ORDINARY TIME: YEAR A Mt 10:37–42

Today's gospel, the third selection from the Mission Sermon, concludes Mt 10. Although ostensibly addressed to those sent on mission, the selection for today seems to speak more generally to all who would be disciples of Jesus. In the first part of the material, we find three parallel statements: "they who do such-and-such, are not worthy of me":

(1) "who loves father or mother more than me" is not worthy of me;

(2) "who loves son or daughter more than me" is not worthy of me;

(3) "who does not take up the cross and follow me" is not worthy of me .

It helps to put these remarks in context. If the gospel is spread, which is the thrust of the whole Mission Sermon (10:5–13), then men and women would be expected to accept or reject it (10:14–15). Yet Jesus envisions a more complicated situation. The gospel will meet with outright hostility (10:16–25), and threats to one's person and life. Hence, there follows an exhortation "not to fear" (10:26–33). Finally, one of the prime sources of opposition to the gospel is identified: family pressure to maintain the old ways and the ancient traditions (10:34–36), which Jesus seems bent on reforming. Matthew shifts from addressing those who preach the gospel to those who hear that preaching and follow it. These people are the adult children living in traditional extended families where exquisite pressure could be put on individuals to conform to family ways. Jesus envisions would-be disciples involved in very divisive conflicts within their families, which seem to result in the kind of banning or shunning of children we noticed earlier in the longest of the "Beatitudes" (5:10–11).

Traditional families regularly control the beliefs and behaviors of their adult children with threats of dispossession and shame. In the face of these threats we hear Jesus' exhortation to love the gospel more than father, mother, son, and daughter (10:37). This is followed by the more general demand that disciples "take up the cross and follow Jesus" (10:38). The shame experienced in the conflict with one's family becomes honor from Jesus. One is "worthy" of Jesus: to follow Jesus would require courage, virtue, and boldness, all virtues highly prized in Jesus' world. Once more, we receive a powerful exhortation to hold dear the greatest of all treasures, Jesus. His companionship is worth more than family and wealth.

The concluding part of the Mission Sermon is clearly addressed to the audience of the preaching, not the preachers themselves. It sanctions and supports reception of the gospel. In typical Semitic fashion, Jesus casts the message in parallel terms:

Who welcomes Jesus welcomes the one who sent Jesus, namely, God.

Who welcomes God's prophets and preachers of the gospel receives the same reward that the preacher enjoys.

Who welcomes a righteous person (i.e., member of Jesus' circle), receives the reward of the righteous.

"Welcoming" clearly means full and wholehearted reception, not mere mental assent. Moreover, "welcoming" entails a complex social interaction: it involves those who receive the gospel in a meaningful relationship, not just with the preacher, but with Jesus who sent the preacher and with God who sent Jesus. "Welcoming" means "giving" to the preacher, namely, a ready ear, table fellowship, hospitality, and the like: yet Jesus assures them that they will share in the great rewards that preachers will enjoy. We should probably read the saying about the "cup of cold water given to one of these little ones" as a reference to the poor and socially insignificant preachers of the gospel, those who have been the focus of the bulk of the Mission Sermon. The point is, any "welcome," even so meagre as a cup of cold water on a hot day, will be respected by Jesus and rewarded. But preacher and those preached to are linked in terms of Jesus' reward for loyalty and faithfulness. "Receiving," we should note, characterizes this final exhortation: as we receive, either the gospel or its preacher, we are truly receiving in many senses: welcoming and accepting a great gift, a share in the reward of the preacher, and finally a special repayment for extending hospitality. In receiving we truly receive.

Receiving might be the clue to understanding the first reading and the psalm for today. In receiving the prophet Elisha into her home, the Shunammite woman was blessed not only with the presence of a holy person, but her hospitality resulted in the birth of a child, one of God's greatest of blessings to us. In receiving Elisha, she received still more favor from God. Hence, we say in the psalm: "I will sing of the goodness of the Lord." For God is gift to us, always. Receiving God's friendship and call means receiving all of God's favor. For God delights in giving, not taking.

FOURTEENTH SUNDAY IN ORDINARY TIME: YEAR A Mt 11:25–30

Alas for prejudice. Most of us fail to see beyond appearances and do not recognize the value or goodness before us. Alas for secrecy. Sometimes we are just not "in the know," which may well be our fault. Today's readings serve as timely reminders for us to open our eyes and grasp as fully as possible just what stands before us and not to reject that reality for imaginary and unreal fantasies.

In Zechariah, the nation is called to rejoice and revel in its deliverance. Wonderful, but hardly simple. Israel's king comes, but not like typical monarchs clothed in power, prestige, and pomp. The victorious king arrives surprisingly in a modest mode: "humble and riding on a donkey." How sad if the nation will accept a victorious ruler only if he conforms to their ideas of success and honor! So it is with Jesus. Although victorious over the demons and conqueror of disease and illness, yet he seems too ordinary to many, too much like other human beings. His own kin and neighbors could not see past appearances to his status as God's authorized warrior and prophet (Mt 13:54–58). Jesus has God's power and he enjoys God's authorization as Messiah, but he comes to us as a peasant and artisan, as one not interested in power and advancement of self: "Learn of me for I am gentle and humble of heart." We are certain in our faith that God always provides for us salvation and blessing, but how hard it is to be free of illusions and deceptions about what that will look like. It could even be that my very spouse or my children or my parents bring me God's word and blessing. How hard it is to see the good in another! How difficult to allow what is familiar to provide a heavenly blessing!

Jesus says more about perceptions. He praises God for hiding "these things" from the wise and intelligent and revealing them instead to infants. This curious statement probably does not mean that God deliberately restricts access to wisdom and knowledge to anyone (see Romans 1:19–20). Rather, it should be read as a positive affirmation of just how wonderful is the surprising gift of God here and now; it rests on God's constant strategy of reversing expectations that we mortals put on what God should and should not do. God, who freely bestows divine blessings, is not bound by our sense of what is fair or just. Not that God is unfair or unjust, rather God shows favor to the lowly, the poor, the oppressed, and the needy. As Mary sang in her Magnificat, it belongs to God to surprise us and to include the excluded and to reverse our sense of who deserves God's favor and who belongs in God's family. Hence, we celebrate today the surprising behavior of our God to "choose the weak to shame the strong" (1 Cor 1:26), to choose the younger son over his elder brother (Jacob over Esau, Joseph over his brothers, David over his brothers). God's ways are not humans' ways: God acts to include what was excluded by us mortals, to enrich what was despoiled, to raise what was brought low.

FIFTEENTH SUNDAY IN ORDINARY TIME: YEAR A MT 13:1–23

Today's gospel comes from Matthew's collection of Jesus' parables in chapter 13, which will be the source of our gospel reflections for the next three Sundays. Now we hear the first of the parables, which in many ways sets the tone and the theme for all the subsequent ones. This parable talks of a sower sowing seeds and of God's word, which powerfully and surprisingly works for success. Despite all the hazards that seeds face when sown, a bountiful and rich harvest is assured. But what of the sowing? what of the sower? what of the seed?

The gospel contains first a parable by Jesus and then an allegorical explanation of it. Let us focus first on the parable. Jesus, himself a peasant, addresses other peasants, the bulk of whom were themselves farmers. The scene appears to be very formal: Jesus in a boat and a vast crowd on the shore waiting to hear from him. Rather than imagine the kind of stillness that exists when our preachers begin their homilies, let us picture an "audience" waiting to be entertained as well as instructed. The scene has more in common with the expectations of a political event than a religious instruction. Let us not be too formal and solemn. Jesus' audience could just as well get up and leave when the preaching got boring. They stayed to listen because he constantly challenged them.

Jesus begins by talking "politics," that is, he speaks about a most important topic of his day, the "kingdom" of God, which must surely be different from the kingdoms of Herod and Caesar. "The kingdom of God" poses key questions for Jesus' audience: Who is God? What does God do that is different from other kings? What does God want? Important, solemn, and formal? Yes. But then Jesus encodes this formal teaching in a joke, namely, a parable. He describes a daffy and incompetent farmer, rather like the cartoon characters we see on TV: all of the sower's gestures are exaggerated, and his strategy, if he has one, is intended in Jesus' story to be ridiculed and laughed at. This farmer simply does not know how to farm: three out of every four seeds are wasted, that is, thrown helter-skelter where they can't possibly produce a crop.

A true farmer would go broke in one season doing this. He would surely lose his land and end in disaster. And his smart farmer neighbors would laugh at his folly. And so Jesus' audience begins by laughing at the stupidity of the farmer in the story. All he can do is sow one good seed out of four (note: experts indicate that a 5-1 return on grain sown would be typical). But the laugher dies down when we remember that Jesus is describing "the kingdom of God."

Scholars generally agree that "allegories," that is, stories with a one-to-one correlation of items stem from the efforts of the early church to interpret Jesus' cryptic "parables." Parables tend to make but one point only, and that one a shock or surprise. It seems clear that the interpretation of the parable in 13:18–23 is just such a moral allegory created by the later church of the original story in 13:1–9. Matthew gives us a clue to this: he labels the earlier material "the parable of the sower" (13:18), not "the parable of the seeds." It appears that the later church created the allegorical "explanation" which shifts the focus from "sower" to "seeds."

A single point, with a shock! The "parable of the sower" makes a dramatic single point with a strong jolt to it. God becomes the stupid sower: God "wastes" three quarters of the seed on unpromising soils. God is either stupid or prodigal. Ah, now Jesus has truly engaged his audience. The "kingdom of God" is seemingly foolishness and prodigality. But then, might not God's foolish but prodigal spreading of the seed explain the ministry of Jesus? To whom did God send him? The elite? The rich and powerful? The saints?

His name "Jesus" means "savior" of his people from their sins (1:21): God sent him as light to those in darkness, even if they are Gentiles (4:15–16): he is "physician to the sick" (9:13), who are the sinners and non-observant people in Galilee, the Decapolis, Tyre and Sidon, as well as Jerusalem. God's Christ is sent prodigally to all peoples. Thus Matthew continues to tell us, albeit in parabolic form, of God's impartiality and inclusivity. Let us imagine that the laughter among Jesus' hearers over a stupid farmer becomes a deep smile of satisfaction at hearing a true gospel message of God's prodigality to all, especially the lowly, which includes poor peasants.

Modern westerners as well as ancient easterners want "relevance" from the words of Jesus. Apparently they think that the interpretation of "the parable of the sower" as "the allegory of the soils" make a relevant pastoral point and indeed it does. In the face of such staggering generosity from God, humans are faced with life and death choices. Outright rejection of the word sown, unfaithfulness in holding on to the word, even smothering of the word with materialistic concerns—these are the unfortunate but real fates that Jesus' gospel meets (recall the rejection of the missioners in 10:16–33, on the Twelfth Sunday in Ordinary Time). The allegorical interpretation, then, shifts the point of the parable away from God's surprising generosity to human moral responsibility. The allegory exhorts us to courage and faithfulness so that we who hear the word of God today may endure to produce a staggering harvest: Jesus indicates an unbelievable return 100-1 or 60-1 or 30-1.

SIXTEENTH SUNDAY IN ORDINARY TIME: YEAR A Mt 13:24–43

Last Sunday we meditated on a "parable" of Jesus and the church's "allegorical" interpretation of it. The same structural distinction applies to today's gospel. Jesus tells a second parable about seeds and sowing, this time about a field of wheat in which weeds have been sown. In the request for an explanation, we find a detailed allegory which, I think, nearly misses the point of the parable. But let us examine first the parable.

If parables aim to make only a single point and a surprising or shocking one at that, then it seems unlikely that Jesus' audience-catching "parable" refers to God's wheat and Satan's weeds. The parable indeed depends on the radical contrast between wheat and weeds. But let us put this parable alongside other parables, which tell a shocking and radical message. Let us begin by remembering that ancient Israelites and Judeans were mandated by the biblical law to plant a field in only one seed: all wheat or all barley (Lev 19:19). Yet Jesus tells a parable about the "kingdom of God" in which a man knowingly puts a "mustard seed" into a field already planted with grain (13:31). At the very least, this signals "unkosher" behavior that is utterly forbidden and shocking! Yet Jesus says that the holy "kingdom of God" is like unholiness!

Jesus would seem to be challenging his audience once more to question their accepted notions of what God is doing. His was an exceptionally traditional and conservative culture, in which there was little space for reform or change or newness. But God is doing precisely this in sending Jesus to the poor, unclean, sinful, and non-Jews: God acts in new and surprising ways to bring into the center those forced by tradition and custom to the periphery. According to Jesus' gospel, God is acting freely to do something new and different.

How shocking to describe God as an "enemy" deliberately sowing a worthless seed in a perfectly good field of wheat. But when we compare Jesus' remarks here with another passage from Matthew's gospel, this does not sound so strange to Christian ears. In Mt 24:43 Jesus compares his surprising return at the end of time to that of a thief who comes in the night to break into a house. We recall how often the New Testament likens Jesus' coming to that of a thief in the night (1 Thes 5:2; 2 Peter 3:10; Rev 3:3). Hardly a flattering image! Now when we compare today's parable with 24:43 we note the following parallels: (a) an "enemy" (who is God) and a "thief" (who is Jesus), (b) both act at "night" (the period when only evil is abroad), (c) to sow weeds or to break in. In both cases the implication would be: humans must be awake and alert to seize the moment, upon which so much rests. God-as-enemy sowing the weed-of-the-gospel, while unusual, does not sound so strange when we consider that Jesus describes himself as a thief who breaks into a household.

We might ask why Jesus chose such a shocking image of God. I suggest that is has to do with Jesus' admission that in the eyes of the observant Pharisees and priests, he appears to be utterly deviant in his presentation of God's plans and purposes, namely, when he tinkers with Sabbath observance, eats with sinners, prostitutes, and tax collectors, and touches the dead and the unclean. They would judge his frequent transgression of their customs and laws as "evil." Jesus is, on occasion, called a deceiver who leads the people astray. In their eyes, then, Jesus is like the mustard seed sown where it ought not to be. Comparably, I suggest that Jesus' parable today about "the kingdom of God" rehearses the same theme: the gospel that Jesus preaches is likened to a weed sown in the field of Israel's traditional faith. This suggests a certain sense of humor on Jesus' part as he takes the public criticisms of himself and makes them into the vehicle of the truth of his gospel. God, he reminds us, does not always play by the kosher rules of Lev 19:19; God can elect Gentiles into the covenant as well as Jews; God can send Jesus to sinners and tax collectors, as well as to saints; God directs the sun and rain on just and unjust. If we learn anything from Jesus' "shocking" parables, it is that God acts in new, surprising, and inclusive ways.

The first reading today echoes the same theme. It describes the impartial care of God for everything. God, just sovereign over all, is "mild in judgment and governs us with great leniency." Human interpretations of what God should do (i.e., strict judgment: "an eye for an eye") restrict God's freedom to act prodigally and foolishly toward sinners. We sing the same theme in today's psalm: "Lord, you are good and forgiving."

What, then, of the allegory? As in the case of the parable of the sower, it shifts the focus from God-the-sower to the hearers-as-seeds. In this allegory, we find an elaborate one-to-one correspondence between parable and allegory:

sower = Son of man

field = world

good seed = subjects of the kingdom

weeds = subjects of the evil one

harvest = end of the world

reapers = God's angels

Again, the powerful and shocking parable seems much reduced to an obvious moral when read this way. True, it sounds very pastoral and touches human lives, but it also misses some of the punch and shock of Jesus' gospel.

SEVENTEENTH SUNDAY IN ORDINARY TIME: YEAR A Mt 13:44–52

Ah, wisdom! Solomon asks for it and gets it. But what is "wisdom"? Today's gospel presents us with three more parables to conclude our reflection on the third of Matthew's great Sermons (chapter 13). And in them we find glimpses of gospel wisdom.

In the first parable, Jesus again shocks us by comparing the "kingdom of God" to a man finding treasure in a field and surreptitiously buying the field. What we must remember is that it was very unusual for a farmer to sell his field at all: land remained in the hands of the family, whose total livelihood came from working the fields. We are shocked to hear that a farm could be sold. Moreover, Jewish law would consider this an illegal sale, if an opportunist took advantage of an unknowing seller. Remember, this is not the economic capitalist system of the modern West, but a stable agricultural world where family interests come first. Hence, we have the kingdom of God compared to a dishonest opportunist! Jesus has done it again. He once compared God's kingdom to unclean leaven kneaded into flour, to an unkosher mustard seed sown into a field of grain, to a weed sown in a field of wheat. Yet, shocking as this seems, praise goes to the opportunist who seizes the moment in this new system to gain God's kingdom.

In the second parable, the "kingdom of heaven" is compared to a merchant. Again, let us remember that merchants were considered in antiquity as a kind of thief: they buy cheap and sell dear. This sounds okay in our capitalist world, but was considered a form of theft in antiquity. But how shocking of Jesus to compare the kingdom of God with a publicly disrespected person, who might truly be a sinner. But like the opportunist in the first parable, he acts boldly and decisively in the dispensation of Jesus' preaching to seize new "wealth," namely, God's mercy and compassion.

Thus both parables tend to make a single, shocking point: the kingdom of God is a new and surprising moment when old conventional wisdom does not apply. Old wisdom that limited God's actions in strict forms of justice simply does not account for Jesus' bold offer of mercy and covenant fellowship even to Gentiles and sinners. A new, but shocking, dispensation arrives with Jesus, which challenges so many of our traditional and conventional ideas of what God should or must do.

A third parable is told that in its most compressed form continues the "shocking" portrayal of God by Jesus. The kingdom of God is like a large net cast into the sea that collects all sorts of fish, both those worth saving for sale and others that are worthless. But the point is: God's actions in Jesus are like that net, which reaches out to Jew and Gentile, saint and sinner. Just as the prodigal sower in 13:1-9 sowed the word of the gospel to all sorts of soils, so the impartial mercy of God is extended to all. Lest we think, however, that God has no standards or principles, the parable continues with a clear reminder that although "many are called, few are chosen." A genuine scrutiny awaits all of us. Just as John the Baptizer once commented on the division of wheat and chaff, the wheat gathered inside the barn and the chaff thrown away (3:12), so Jesus repeats the same message. Some fish will be saved in buckets and brought inside, while others will be thrown away as of no use.

God welcomes all, sows the gospel to all: but human response matters greatly. Actions in response to God's grace truly count: look again at the bold behavior of the man who finds the treasure or the merchant who finds the prized pearl: they acted to grab for the treasure that God put in their paths. "Wisdom" in regard to the kingdom of God, then, has to do with letting God do new and surprising things in our midst and having the insight to recognize God's surprise. "Wisdom" has to do with acting decisively to secure the treasure of God's grace that we find.

EIGHTEENTH SUNDAY IN ORDINARY TIME: YEAR A Mt 14:13-21

The readings today are likely to give us an appetite as we come to pray, for they talk of fine foods (wine, milk, etc.) and breads in abundance. Isaiah proclaims God's invitation to come to a sumptuous banquet table though we have no money.

God, of course, intends us to understand by this that divine grace and favor extend to our material lives and to our human bodies, as well as to our souls (recall that we pray for "daily bread"). But God feeds our hearts and minds as well: hence Isaiah reminds us to "listen" to God and so we will have good things to eat. Hearing God's word and holding to it will mean for us "an everlasting covenant" where God will take pains to feed us with creation's very best gifts.

In Matthew's gospel selection, Jesus performs one of his great miracles, the feeding of more than 5000. Of course we ought to see this as an intensification of Isaiah's prophecy of God's banquet of rich foods for God's covenant people. The continuity between God's actions of old and those done in Christ should confirm in our hearts faith in God who acts continually on our behalf to fill us with good things and who acts to give us not just fragmentary benefits, but "wine, milk...good things to eat" and so much that we have twelve baskets of leftovers. Let us rejoice in this reminder of God's continual sustenance and nourishment. How badly we need to remember all that God intends for us, namely, that God is "giving" to us, not "taking" from us. God means fullness, not emptiness.

Yet another dimension of Jesus' feeding miracle can

nourish us when we recognize it. As all the gospels present him, Jesus does not abide by the conventional rules of his culture. He does not keep the strict Sabbath of the Pharisees, nor does he fast as they do, nor does he pay tithes on his food as they do. He does not perform the customary washing rituals before eating, nor does he separate himself from sinner and non-observant people as did the proper religious people of his day. Why? Simply because God authorized him to act as an inclusive agent of mercy: by not keeping the old ways, Jesus indicated that the boundaries of God's covenant community were more open than strict observers thought.

Matthew interpreted Jesus' eating with sinners as the act of a "physician" toward those in need (9:13) and his refusal to keep the washing rituals as a sign that Jesus was not a boundary guardian, but a boundary breaker. As "Savior of his people," he ate with all sorts of people, Jews and Gentiles as well as saints and sinners.

The very fact that the feeding occurred in a "wilderness" prompts our reflection that Jesus is "out of place" eating there. Let's not imagine that the ancients enjoyed picnics in the park or on the beach as we do: they ate at home, where they could be sure of the proper observance of kosher rules. The "wilderness" has no water, and so the customary washing of hands before eating is impossible there. The size of a crowd of 5000 means that no one can be sure that the people seated alongside them are "kosher," that is observant Jews: recall the criticism of Jesus for being careless of the people with whom he ate. Moreover, five loaves and two fish appear, but Jesus and the disciples have no way of knowing if they are "kosher," that is, if the proper tithes have been paid on them to the Temple. In short, every detail of the scene suggests a studied disregard of the old rules for eating. And this is surely one of the main points of the story. Jesus impartially offers God's covenant blessings, food in this case, to all people regardless of ethnic background or spiritual status. God refuses to be constrained by human rules that limit divine freedom to act generously on behalf of all sorts of peoples. Thus, the feeding continues the presentation of God's bold and novel actions of impartiality and inclusivity that extend favor and blessing to all.

NINETEENTH SUNDAY IN ORDINARY TIME: YEAR A Mt 14:22–33

In the core readings today, we see a mysterious presence. Elijah, after fleeing for his life, comes to a mountain where he would encounter God. Like all of us, the prophet thinks that God must surely come with high drama and striking power, either in a mighty wind or earthquake or fiery lightning. But look as he can, the prophet does not find God in these presumed forms. At last, "there came the sound of a gentle breeze," and the prophet covers his face and approaches his God. The responsorial psalm may help us grasp the rich meaning of this. It prays that God "show us" something: but it begs to be shown "mercy and love," which are gentle and peaceful things, not violent like cyclones, earthquakes, and lightning. God's voice is one "of peace" and God's help is "near for those who revere God." For, encounter with God should be good and renewing, and not terrible and terrifying. And so "justice" will march before God and "peace" follow in God's steps—images of a world in harmony. God, moreover, will come in many forms. How wise the person who lets God be God and awaits God's manifestation, in whatever form it comes.

In the gospel, Jesus functions as the mysterious presence that brings peace and security. The narrative simply tells the basic facts: the disciples are on the sea, separated from Jesus, rowing hard in a heavy sea: Jesus, on the other hand, remains on land and goes up a mountain to pray. The story initially emphasizes separation from Jesus and great need. In the critical scene, the gospel states that when Jesus draws near the disciples, he means to "pass by them." We do not read this as "by-pass," that is, trying to avoid them, such as we bypass business districts on our expressways. Rather "pass by them" echoes the behavior of God in appearing to Moses in Exod 34:6. "Pass by them" indicates a decided strategy of presence with the disciples, not avoidance. Yet it is mysterious and paradoxical, like all of Jesus' actions. Most of the disciples think a "ghost" approaches, which generally means harm from an aggressive spirit world. But Jesus brings God's peace, and so he tells them "Do not be afraid." With his presence, the terrible storm ceases. The separation from

Jesus is now filled with his healing and saving presence. If Elijah found God in a gentle breeze, the disciples found Jesus' mysterious presence in the midst of crisis. God's saving power is not confined to only one sphere or manner.

A passing word about Peter here seems warranted. Matthew's gospel indicates that Peter is singled out for special grooming. He receives special revelations (16:16) as well as unique instructions (15:15; 17:24–27); he is privy to some of Jesus' greatest moments, the raising of Jairus' daughter, the transfiguration, and the prayer of Jesus in the Garden. His walking on the water here fits into this consistent pattern. Peter is not just a disciple whose authority and legitimation rest on a mandate from the earthly Jesus. He appears to be a "charismatic" leader as well, one favored with exceptional revelations and powers, which in the early church served also as criteria for authority. Let us not forget that Matthew says that "he started walking toward Jesus across the water." That is, he actually did the miraculous journey—up to a point. His fear and sinking may serve to cut him back down to size, but he is presented to us as a figure designated to be a leader by his powerful revelations and actions. Jesus' rescue of him foreshadows the forgiveness Peter will receive when the risen Jesus appears to him and reconciles him after his triple denial of Jesus. Nevertheless, we sense that leadership in the early church tended to be a combination of criteria, if not a competition between authorization by Jesus and legitimation through charismatic activity.

TWENTIETH SUNDAY IN ORDINARY TIME: YEAR A Mt 15:21–28

Today's gospel must surely rank as one of the strangest in Matthew's narrative. Jesus leaves Galilee and thus a land nominally Jewish, and travels north to the villages of Tyre and Sidon. Innocent enough, until we recall how unorthodox it was for Jews to travel to Gentile territory (Acts 10:28). Moreover, in the Mission Sermon in chapter 10, Jesus forbade his disciples to leave Jewish lands: "Go nowhere among the Gentiles, enter no town of the Samaritans" (10:5). In today's narrative, moreover, Jesus clearly articulates his understanding that God commissioned him to deal only with Jews: "I was sent only to the lost sheep of the house of Israel" (15:24). I was sent = sent by God. So, what are we to think of Jesus outside the land of Israel, in commerce with non-Jews, and not keeping to God's will?

We are invited in this traditional story to see the disciples of Jesus wrestling with the issue of "change." Obviously an old tradition survived indicating that Jesus and his disciples ministered only to Jews. Paul reflects this when he suggests that until his commissioning, Peter and the others preached only to Jews, for Paul claims to be the original apostle to the Gentiles, which seems to be a bit of self-serving exaggeration on his part. Matthew would argue that the "change" came earlier, namely in the ministry of Jesus: or rather, he seems to argue that later "change" is rooted in the very ministry of Jesus. The issue here embraces more than Jesus' dealings with women in general, for at stake is the very inclusion of non-Jews in God's covenant. Hence, it may be wise to examine the behavior of Jesus as dramatically exaggerated to grasp the enormity of the "change" being made. Thus, we should see this gospel as a piece of theatre: the characters are very sharply drawn, and the dialogue contains heightened and provocative language. The sharp exchange between Jesus and the woman dramatizes in a melodramatic way the enormity of the change taking place.

A very needy woman, albeit a Canaanite, comes to Jesus begging for God's favor for her daughter. Jesus ignores her (in accord with expected custom of Jews having no dealings with non-Jews). The disciples curiously enough favor yielding to the woman's request, if only for the sake of peace. Jesus postures theatrically, not to insult the woman, but to underline the dramatic point at stake: (in the past) God did not want this extension of blessings to non-Jews. The persistent pleading of the woman takes a more heightened form: she calls Jesus "Lord" and bows low to his feet. In any other context in the gospel we would interpret these actions as manifestations of great faith. Why not here? The drama is not over, as Jesus once more insists on the gravity of the issue: to accede to her request would be like taking the "bread" of God's blessings from the table of the children and giving it to dogs. Surely, this exaggerated statement simply brings home the enormity of the change that is about to take place. Jesus then acquiesces: he confirms her "faith" ("great is your faith") and he grants her a favor normally reserved to Jews. The drama is complete: a theatrical reversal has occurred.

How did Jesus change his mind? What principles did he use? How did he justify altering his explicit commission from God? Jesus recognizes "the signs of the time," so to speak. It is evident that this woman is "inspired": she seeks God's blessing—surely a good thing. She comes directly to Jesus, "Son of David" and heir of God's kingdom. She demonstrates the most remarkable persistence in prayer, something that Jesus himself praised in his parables (Luke 18:1-8). Despite his "traditions," Jesus recognizes that God works a new thing here, and so he acknowledges the "faith"/gift of this woman and changes his mind and his ways. This same pattern of "recognizing the signs of the time" warrants Peter's willingness to baptize Cornelius and his family (Acts 10:4-48). Failure to change in this instance would have meant that God was not in fact impartial toward all people, something that the gospel heralds from its very beginning. Thank God that Jesus could read the signs of the times.

TWENTY-FIRST SUNDAY IN ORDINARY TIME: YEAR A Mt 16:13-20

As in the gospel from last Sunday, Jesus and his disciples travel north of Galilee to the villages around the non-Jewish town of Caesarea Philippi. Consider just the name: "Caesarea" and "Philippi." This cannot be a Jewish town. It is hardly accidental that the greatest confession of faith in the gospels occurs outside of Jewish territory, a hint, perhaps of the destiny of the church to be inclusive of Jews and Gentiles. At the midpoint of his ministry, Jesus asks his disciples about his identity: what have they learned about him as a result of his powerful words and deeds? Many think him a prophet, a wise conclusion in light of his mighty sermons and miracles. But Simon Peter speaks for the group a new word that sums up Jesus' significance for them: "You are the Christ, the Son of the living God." If we think of the ministry of Jesus as that of a "sower," then Jesus reaps a remarkable harvest of faith here with this confession by Simon Peter and the group. This one seed did not fall prey to birds, thin soil, or thorns.

Matthew's gospel differs from that of Mark, Luke, and John at this point in that it records a unique series of remarks by Jesus to Simon Peter. First, Jesus credits Simon Peter with a special gift of faith from God to confess Jesus as he did: "Flesh and blood did not reveal this to you but my Father in heaven." Simon Peter, then, is blessed by God with special gifts of insight and revelation now and on many occasions: he regularly gains special information from Jesus (15:15 and 17:24-27). Jesus, moreover, recognizes this special favor shown to him and gives him the special name, "Peter," which means rock or foundation stone for the church. We generally think of Jesus himself as the cornerstone or foundation of the church-as-Temple, and the apostles as the pillars (Eph 2:20; Gal 2:6). If, as scholars generally indicate, Matthew's remarks about Peter are important in the period when the evangelist wrote his gospel, then we can make more sense of Jesus' statement: "The gates of the underworld will not hold out against you." This indicates that Peter will have successors and so Death ("Underworld" does not mean Hell, but the realm of Death) does not stop the command of Jesus when Peter dies.

John's gospel records a prediction by Jesus of Peter's very death (Jn 21:18-19), so we are sure that Jesus is not predicting that Peter would never die. Rather, Jesus is credited with saying that despite death, there will always be a leader among the disciples, a "rock" on whom they can find safety. In giving Peter "keys," we should remember that keys lock and unlock chests, rooms, and storehouses, as is mentioned in the first reading from Isaiah about the investiture of Eliakim as major-domo of the palace. Hence, Peter gets authority to welcome in and usher out, that is to include and to exclude. We generally see this as legitimation of the pastoral practice of the early church to forgive sins and to hold them (see 1 Cor 5; see Mt 18:15-20): it also extends to issues of membership—who will be allowed in (non-Jews?) and who will be excluded (unbelievers?). In Acts 10:46-47; 11:17; and 15:7-11 Luke credits Peter with the use of just such keys to welcome into the circle of disciples Cornelius and his household.

Any full appreciation of this gospel passage must include several things. In Mt 23, Jesus issues a scathing critique of Pharisees and other leaders. He explicitly forswears, it seems, establishing a fixed or hereditary leadership for his disciples: "Call no one your father on earth, for you have one Father—the one in heaven. Nor are you to be called Teacher, for you have one teacher, the Messiah. The greatest among you will be your servant" (23:8–11). Yet, the risen Jesus commissions the Eleven disciples to go make disciples of all nations and to teach Jesus' message. Both of these important pieces of Matthew's gospel need to be seen alongside the honoring of Peter in today's story. Clearly Matthew does not envision the establishment of what we call the papacy; yet neither does he imagine the disciples as leaderless and without a shepherd. Taking the whole of Matthew's gospel, we delight in not being left as orphans, for our Shepherd ensures that we have adequate leadership. Yet the shape of that leadership seems to be still in process during Matthew's time. Eleven disciples are commissioned to preach and teach: in fact, the Eleven are given "keys" just as Peter was (18:15–20). God, moreover, remains Father, and Jesus is still Christ. They are our Shepherds and Leaders. Earthly guides especially among the disciples of Jesus are but our "servants," not our masters (Mt 20:25–28). The good news in all of this can be summed up in today's responsorial psalm: "You do not forsake the works of your hands." We are not left orphans.

TWENTY-SECOND SUNDAY IN ORDINARY TIME: YEAR A Mt 16:21–27

Last Sunday we heard Jesus praise Simon Peter as "rock" for the gift of revealed faith bestowed on him by God. Today Jesus calls Peter a "rock of scandal" for his refusal to accept a new revelation about his cross. The smart way to understand today's gospel, then, is to keep comparing and contrasting it with last Sunday's.

First, Peter understood the glorious part of Jesus' ministry, his powerful words and deeds: hence, God gave him faith to acclaim Jesus as "the Christ, Son of the living God": but the fullness of Jesus' identity includes also that of "Son of man," which refers to the figure rejected on earth and vindicated in heaven (see Dan 7:14). Peter's great faith, noble as it is, simply lacks an important element: he needs to become Jesus' disciple in the second half of the gospel and follow him to his cross and empty tomb.

Second, Peter gets in Jesus' way, literally: he would stop Jesus from any talk and thought about "suffering grievously...being put to death." Hence, Jesus calls him a "stumbling block," no longer a rock of foundation.

Third, although Peter has been portrayed as a "follower" of Jesus, the Lord ironically tells him to get out of the way: "Get behind me!" This might mean "Get out of my way!" as well as an ironic way of saying "Become a true follower and receive this new revelation."

Finally, although praised for receiving God's revelation, Peter now seems to resist God's new revelation. By standing in Jesus' way, "You do not think God's thoughts, but human ones." Even Simon Peter, proclaimed a leader on our behalf in the previous gospel episode, actually becomes an obstacle to the fullness of Jesus' saving ministry. We read today's gospel story best when we see it as the mirror reading of last Sunday's narrative.

Yet what shall we make of this? Where is there gospel here for us? Students of the gospels generally accept that the ministry of Jesus consists of two distinct parts. First, in Galilee Jesus gathers a circle of disciples, teaches them about God's new kingdom, and illustrates this through his powerful healings and teachings. Thus, power, fullness of blessings, glory, and success attend Jesus—at least in the first half of the story. But a second part remains, similarly authorized by God and equally enriching for the disciples, as Jesus begins to teach on his way to Jerusalem his "way" of discipleship in its fullness, which includes his saving death and resurrection. "Christ" and "Son of God" mean honor and glory and success, yet Jesus is also "Son of man," which refers to the figure in Daniel 7 who was rejected on earth but vindicated by God in heaven. He is, moreover, "prophet," like Jeremiah in the first reading, a figure sent by God on a very difficult mission, including rejection and death (see Mt 23:29–34). Among God's messengers we include victorious kings like David as well as suffering prophets like Jeremiah. What a mistake to say that God can only have one kind of agent or messenger.

Thus the first thing Jesus does as he begins his way to Jerusalem is to predict his own fate as a rejected prophet. Those, moreover, who would follow him must likewise imitate him in this: "If any want to be followers of mine, let them take up their cross and follow me." This generic statement contains less a prediction of suffering and misery as qualifications for discipleship, for Jesus basically calls for loyalty and faithfulness. Discipleship, if genuine and true, must be inclusive of the whole of Jesus' life and teaching, his glory as well as his shame. Disciples have often rephrased this as: if you want to be at the empty tomb with Jesus, you must stand with him on Calvary: or, if you want to wear his crown, you must shoulder his cross.

TWENTY-THIRD SUNDAY IN ORDINARY TIME: YEAR A Mt 18:15–20

Our gospel comes today from the fourth of Matthew's great Sermons, or collections of Jesus' sayings. All of chapter 18 has to do with life inside the church, in particular, how the disciples are supposed to handle sin and evil. Even among the authentic disciples of Jesus we do not find a perfect church, but a group of sinners always needing guidance and forgiveness.

Jesus teaches the disciples a certain procedure for dealing with sin and evil in their midst. We seem to hear almost procedural rules to follow in settling a dispute. The occasion is clear: "If your brother does something wrong...." Notice, it is a "brother," probably not a blood brother, but a brother-in-Christ, a fellow believer whom we now call our "kin" because all disciples become "brother and sister and mother" in the circle of Jesus' disciples (Mt 12:45–50). Unlike typical procedure in the village, the offended person does not make a public fuss and seek satisfaction or vengeance: "Go, have it out with them alone." No face should be lost, no lasting feud started. But if this strategy does not work, then the disciple should instigate a formal proceeding by securing evidence from several witnesses. If this does not succeed, only then are they to make it public and report it to the community of disciples. Obviously we are dealing with a very serious matter. And if this still does not work, they are to treat the offender like a pagan or tax collector. Should the process work, "you will have won back a brother": but if it does not, the group will be purified of a pollution in its midst.

Two things need to be remembered as we appropriate this gospel. First, in teaching the "Our Father," Jesus insists that we forgive others: "If you forgive others their trespasses, your heavenly Father will forgive you yours: if you do not forgive others, neither will you Father forgive your trespasses" (6:14–15). "Mercy," not "sacrifice" is what God desires (9:13; 12:9). Moreover, next Sunday's gospel will give us a long instruction on forgiveness (Mt 18:21–34). What, then, do we need to imagine going on in Mt 18 that demands "repentance"? Why not just "forgive" the offender?

Matthew 18 begins with a solemn warning against scandal and harm that can destroy (18:6–8). Better for the group that such corrupting offenders be cast into the sea with a millstone around their necks; better that the offending eye, hand, or foot be cut off. This is radical talk in the face of a presumed radical situation. Not all situations of wrongdoing and sin are this grave; the shepherd goes in search of the lost sheep and returns it to the safely of the flock (18:10–14). Jesus, despite our efforts to reduce his complex message to simple procedures, teaches two values: "holiness" and "mercy." "Be ye holy as I am holy" says God (Lev 11:44–45), a truth repeated in the New Testament (1 Peter 1:16). "Holiness" has to do with "wholeness"; God is all life, all goodness, all justice. God does not allow, we are led to imagine, anything less than complete holiness in the divine presence (see 1 Cor 6:9–10), and Jesus teaches that we are to love God with our whole heart, mind, and soul (Mt 22:37). But let us note that only repentant (and forgiven) sinners enter the presence of the holy God—only the dead who are raised to life enter, only those mortals with all their frailty who are transformed by grace come into God's presence. In short, Jesus' initial message remains his missionary theme: "repent and believe in the gospel." Matthew makes clear that God's mercy is abundant and ever-present, but sinners must repent of their sins to be clothed in God's and the church's mercy. But what if... what if a sin is very grievous (sexism, racism, injustice?) and what if the sinner refuses to repent? Today's gospel, we suggest, envisions just such a situation of very serious sin and refusal of repentance.

What are we to do? In so grave a situation, Jesus

reminds us of a value to guide our actions: the holiness of God. Sinners, such as we envision above, corrupt not just themselves, but threaten the group's character. Sinners who refuse to see serious evil in their actions or who see it and refuse to repent still threaten the rest of us. Matthew records very measured steps to seek the freedom and holiness of the sinner. After all, the aim of the Jesus' mission is the saving of men and women from their sins. His very name means "Jesus," that is "he will save them from their sins" (1:21). The holiness of the group and God's holiness serve as beacon lights for us, balancing the value of "mercy" and "forgiveness." They never cancel each other out: both are true and both are lasting.

As strong as this sounds, let us see this as part of the "good news" of the gospel. We all accept warnings on labels that certain products are hazardous, cause cancer, and may poison us. We consider these labels as beneficial to us: we know where we stand. We appreciate how dangerous certain things truly are. Such knowledge does not depress us. On the contrary, it serves to underscore the values of life, health, and well-being in ourselves and others. So with Jesus' remarks today. We have clear warning labels that some sins are truly "mortal" (they cause cancer of the soul) and, if left untreated, can kill. They need not, of course: such is the value of warning labels. If we heed the warning, we can avoid the disasters. Perhaps the best way to read today's gospel is to begin by asking ourselves if others have pointed out to us any "mortal" danger in us or any wrong that is killing our relationships. Have we heard in faith this call to repentance? Are we ignoring the warning labels? Moreover, as Ezekiel testifies in the first reading, one of God's greatest gifts to us is our freedom to choose: we live as moral persons who can will and do what is righteous, but alas can also do the opposite. Our very human dignity as free people who decide our destinies is affirmed in the gospel today.

TWENTY-FOURTH SUNDAY IN ORDINARY TIME: YEAR A Mt 18:21–35

If last Sunday's gospel spoke of times when the call to holiness and repentance meets with refusal and thus separation from the group, this gospel passage balances it as it instructs us that the hallmark of Jesus' disciples is forgiveness, as God has forgiven us. It would, of course, be a mistake to juxtapose these two messages so that we prefer one to the other: Matthew indicates that Jesus said them both: and to reinforce their importance, they occur side by side. As Macbeth once said: "Two truths are told...." Not one, but two: and they are often hard to hold together.

Peter, ever the pipeline of important information for the early disciples, asks Jesus a key question: "How many times must I forgive? Seven times?" Now seven is no arbitrary number: since "seven" days make one week, it probably signifies plenty, if not "completeness." Jesus says, "Not seven, but seventy-seven times," which in a peasant and illiterate culture must sound like an infinitely large number. Clearly, it is not a literal, but a symbolic number: therefore, we realize that the occasions for forgiveness are numberless and we should not keep an accounting list. Jesus' remark sounds broad and unqualified. Yet given the fact that this episode follows Jesus' instructions about a process for dealing with serious sins and unrepentant sinners, we would do well to qualify these remarks and keep them in context. They are important and true, but "two truths are told..." (Mt 18:15–20 and 18:21–35).

To confirm his remark to Peter, Jesus tells a parable, which to peasants would sound like utter fantasy because it is so foreign to their world. It is about debt and the forgiveness of debt. As a backdrop to this, let us remember that Jesus' peasant environment was brutally beset by taxes, so severe that many small landowners were driven into debt and then into insolvency. Peasants either have debts themselves or they surely know a neighbor with them, and they all know that those who hold the debts never cancel them. So when the audience hears Jesus' parable about two debtors, they probably think that the king who forgives the large debt is either a fantasy figure or a fool: nothing in their experience supports this. Rather, they understand the second half of the story all too well. The servant to whom a small debt is owed by another servant fits into their mental landscape: they expect foreclosure, not debt remission. They might even go so far as to say, "Well, that's the way it is! The foreclosing debtor is doing nothing particularly unusual or evil!"

As usual, Jesus' parables work by surprising us and turning our world upside down. The king owed the large amount and who (foolishly?) remits that debt would be acting entirely too strange for Jesus' peasant world: he does not cling to his honor and demand what is owed him. Yet this dishonorable? foolish? and fanciful monarch typifies "the kingdom of God." And the debtor servant who refused to cancel a small debt owed him is not characteristic of the kingdom of God, in spite of the fact that he may be typical of earthly kingdoms. Jesus seems to be saying in parable form what he stated bluntly after the "Our Father": "If you forgive others ... your heavenly Father will forgive you: but if you do not forgive others, neither will your Father forgive you" (Mt 6:14–15). In short, God's mercy stands out: disciples of this God must be "chips off the old block." Indeed, taught by God's gift of mercy to us, we know what forgiveness is and can thereby imitate our God.

Yet, lest we prove false to the total parable of Jesus, we note that the servant owed but a small amount did not imitate God's forgiveness of the great debt he himself owed. As his fate he loses what advantage he already had (forgiveness of his debt) and will be held accountable for his recalcitrant behavior. God is no fool: God's ways are always just, even when God shows mercy. It would be utterly naive to think that our actions have no consequences and that somehow it will all work out fine for us, despite our refusals to follow the gospel. "Seventy-seven times!" Of course, but within a context of trying to be an authentic disciple! Indeed, as the psalm reminds us, "The Lord is kind and merciful, slow to anger and rich in compassion." But the Lord is also just and holy.

TWENTY-FIFTH SUNDAY IN ORDINARY TIME: YEAR A Mt 20:1–16

With today's gospel, Jesus' "way" ends on the outskirts of Jerusalem, and he teaches us one last item of his "way" of doing things. He tells a parable, which by now we have come to expect will turn our expectations and values on their heads. We recall that Jesus could very well have had firsthand experience at being a day laborer, such as are described in the parable. His father is a landless peasant, an artisan. The family land, if it is still in family hands, lies down in Bethlehem, but Joseph and his family live far away in Nazareth. And the family trade is that of artisans, not farmers. It is entirely probable that Joseph and Jesus served as day laborers in their villages, earning "daily bread."

How would peasants hear this story? They recognize the system: landless peasants gather in village squares and hope to be hired for a day's wage (i.e., a "denarius"). Lucky ones are chosen and so have work to earn bread for their families. Alas for those not chosen, who wait and wait with no prospects. It would be a truly good day for all concerned if all laborers found work, as they eventually do in the story. Yet no peasant would imagine that all laborers would be paid the same amount: this violates all sense of peasant justice and fairness. Hence, we expect that the audience, while thoroughly understanding the story up to a point, would quickly agree with the outbursts of those who grumbled. The narrative says that they "envied" those with equal wages, which literally means that they had an "evil eye" toward them, for they seem to be getting something (wages) that is undeserved. Let us imagine that peasants would not think this strange either. The envious "evil eye" was a cultural fact of life in Jesus' world.

When it dawns on the audience that Jesus is speaking about God and the "kingdom of heaven," then the peasants' world is turned upside down. Jesus does not speak about earthly wages at all. In fact, he might even be delivering a critique of the system of debt that causes peasants to lose their land and become day laborers. At a very minimum, Jesus proclaims a God whose ways are not those of this world, as Isaiah reminded us in the first reading. God acts as a generous benefactor, not as an extractor of taxes or debts. God acts inclusively (all seeking work are eventually hired) and impartially (all receive a "living wage"). God's kingdom, then, does not operate according to a model of exploitative economics or in a manner that shows rank favoritism. This is truly good news for us. For we can count on a generous God, showing kindness to all, including us sinners who come late. God's freedom to act in new and bold ways to secure justice for all stands out once more as a dominant theme of Jesus' message.

TWENTY-SIXTH SUNDAY IN ORDINARY TIME: YEAR A MT 21:28–32

Once again, Jesus tells a parable that, if we listen carefully, contains a striking message. To make sure that we listen in the same way as Jesus' peasant audience would, we need to remember how important "respect," "face," and "reputation" were in the ancient world. A father who could not control the behavior of his sons lost face in the eyes of his neighbors: he was a fool (see 1 Tim 3:4–5). Children, even adult offspring, were expected to "Honor father and mother," as enshrined in the law of Israel. This respect or honor has often been called the pivotal value in Jesus' world, which undergirded all social relationships. And honor and respect are what Jesus' parable is all about.

For the moment, let us abstract from the setting into which Matthew has located this parable. Scholars generally agree that each evangelist has a different reason and strategy for placing deeds and words of Jesus where we find them. The core of the parable simply states that a father, presumably in public where everyone can observe his actions and those of his sons, gives one son a command: "Go and work in the vineyard today." To the utter shock of the father and the amazement of those who observe this, the son refuses to work and thus brings bitter shame upon his father:

"I will not go!" It matters not in the eyes of the onlookers that he subsequently went, for the damage has already been done. The father looks utterly foolish before his family and neighbors, for he cannot control his sons and they refuse to honor him. We cannot imagine a worse fate for this father in Jesus' time: he has lost the most precious thing he could hope for, the respect of his son and confirmation of that by the family. Yet this father goes to a second son and gives the same order. This time the son says the appropriate public response: "Certainly, sir!" On the surface, he renders respect and honor to his father: from the exterior, all seems well. But the second son did not go into the vineyard to do the father's bidding. Both sons "say one thing and do another," but in the eyes of peasants only the first son shamed his father.

Obviously two sons are contrasted, two behaviors held up for praise or blame. Ordinary hearers of Jesus' word would probably think well of the second son, for he did not shame his father in public. On the other hand, the public loss of face caused by the first son constitutes an unforgivable offense. Yet precisely here Jesus turns upside down the cultural expectations of his day, for he praises the first son and shames the second.

Let us put this cryptic parable back in Matthew's context, for the evangelist sees it being applied to a very specific situation with a precise application. The audience consists of the religious elite ("chief priests and elders of the people"). The fictive occasion, according to Matthew, takes place immediately after Jesus' criticism of the Temple and his defense of his authority to the religious elite of Jerusalem to "do these things." In other words, the situation bristles with conflict of the highest order, as Jesus delivers a relentless critique of the religion of his day. In the midst of this we find today's parable about two sons. Hence just like the persons addressed by Jesus, we should evaluate the two sons. Although the chief priests and scribes seem to have gotten everything else wrong, they correctly respond that the first son, heinous as his shameful behavior was, did the right thing. Jesus then connects this with his ministry and the values he espouses. He compares the first son with "tax collectors and prostitutes," shameless people who publicly flaunt Israel's customs and laws, but who hear Jesus' call to repentance and change their lives. Implied, then, is the equation of the chief priests and religious elite with the second son: they made a grand protestation of religion, but something is lacking: performance. Their glorious Temple and its elaborate rituals of worship appear honorable and holy: but they are failing on the most important issue: seeking and doing the will of their heavenly Father. In another place Jesus criticizes the elite for "neglecting the weightier matters of the law, justice, mercy, and faith" (23:23). Hypocrisy comes to mind, although the term is not used here.

What, then, are we to make of the parable? As always, Jesus continues to remind us that God's inclusive mercy extends to all, to tax collectors and prostitutes as well as the religious elite. All are called to holiness; all are invited to the Lord's vineyard; the master makes no distinction among persons. Balancing this image of an impartial heavenly Father, Jesus reminds us that two responses are possible to the invitation to life. More important, we are cautioned not to judge by appearances. For, we surely do not know what is going on beneath the surface. To appearances, many of Jesus' audience and us as well make snap judgments that "certain people" cannot be doing God's will and have no place in the heavenly kingdom, for they are sinners. Only God can read hearts. Only God can know what happens after failure and refusal. Only God knows who repents and seeks to labor in the vineyard. Yet, as the parable warns, all of us from the religious elite on down need to examine our total performance in regard to worship of God. For it may be only a facile "yes!" with no follow-through: it may be all for show. In short, we are urged to see how total and whole our response is, lest it verge on hypocrisy.

Imagine, now, that some people in Jesus' audience might be "tax collectors and prostitutes," with whom he often seems to have taken meals. They, of course, would hear the parable as a grand affirmation of what the psalm proclaims: "Remember your mercy, Lord...do not remember the sins of my youth." How welcome they must feel in his presence: how rich and true a faith in God's impartial blessings they must have. For it belongs to God to "guide the humble in the right path and teach his way to the poor."

TWENTY-SEVENTH SUNDAY IN ORDINARY TIME: YEAR A Mt 21:33–43

Today's gospel should be read in the light of last Sunday's parable. In Matthew's narrative, they follow each other and share similar imagery and a common theme, thus reinforcing each other. Let us, then, be smart readers and compare the two parables. In both, a "vineyard" figures largely, which Isaiah indicates stands for the people of Israel. In both, the owner went to great pains to clear land, plant vines, build facilities, and wait for a delicious harvest. In both, the owner is grievously disappointed: one son fails to do his father's will and labor in the vineyard and in today's story the tenants refuse to honor the owner and give him his just share of the harvest. In both, the owner of the vineyard rises up in judgment. There is, then, a sharp edge to both stories: in their current context they both critique the religious elite of Jesus' day for failing to render to God the things that are God's.

Today's parable, however, goes much further in allegorizing the situation of Jesus. God = Father or Owner; vineyard = Israel; second son or tenants = religious elite. The parable introduces a series of servants who are "seized, thrashed, and killed," whom Matthew suggests are the prophets sent of old (Mt 23:34). Now enters "a son," who is heir and who endures a shameful death. At this point, today's story veers away from the focus of the previous parable of the two sons. There is no talk here of sinners repenting and entering the kingdom of heaven. Instead we hear a gruesome tale of retribution: the father who was shamed by the death of his son at the hands of the tenants "brings those wretches to a wretched end." Often scholars consider this an allusion to the destruction of Jerusalem's temple in the Roman-Jewish war of 70 A.D. Nevertheless, strict justice is not the point of the parable. The owner seeks out new tenants, whom Matthew probably considers to be the Gentile converts streaming into the church. Thus the owner continues doing what the landlord does: he cultivates a vineyard and seeks suitable people to work in it and share its bounty with him.

Indubitably there seems to be a cryptic reference to Jesus, the special son who is sent by the father, but slain by the wicked tenants. Yet, perhaps the story engages us more fundamentally if we keep focusing on the father-owner of the vineyard. If we are correct in understanding that Jesus keeps talking about God in terms of God's impartial generosity, surprising election of outsiders, and great mercy and forgiveness, then let us continue this stream of thought. The father-owner refuses to be frustrated, even by the tragic fate of his son: he finds new tenants. Jesus then steps out of the allegory to make a bold comparison. Quoting Ps 118, he states: "The stone rejected by the builders has become the keystone." In the context, we hear that God's elect stone, rejected by the Temple elite, has become the key or foundation stone of a new temple (see 1 Peter 2:7). God will not be frustrated by human sin and so acts to build a new system in which divine mercy can draw near to humans and they can find safety and life in God's service. "It is the Lord's doing." It is God's grand plan to build a new temple and thus establish a new system of worship in Christ.

The readings might take us in various directions. We might well examine ourselves as to whether we are "giving to God the things that are God's," namely worship, faithfulness, loyalty, and the like, lest we be like the religious elite of Jesus' day or like the smug son who said "yes" but did nothing. Better, perhaps, to be nourished once more with Jesus' gospel message about God: generous, forgiving, just, and loyal. God's purpose of sharing life with us will not be frustrated by sin and disobedience. For God can always build a new building with the stone rejected by the builders. Yet, both themes arise from the day's gospel—a vineyard and a patient owner, sin and justice—yet from the ruins, a new temple and new bonds of loyalty and life. It is surely unprofitable for us to judge others and assess the fairness of God's just judgment of them. Rather, the good news of today's gospel may lie in our willingness to accept God's servants, to stop the rejection, and to forestall the death of the son. In doing so, we truly hold on to our inheritance in God's vineyard and maintain a rich relationship with our generous God.

TWENTY-EIGHTH SUNDAY IN ORDINARY TIME: YEAR A Mt 22:1–14

Matthew's editorial genius is never more evident than in the way he has stitched the last two Sunday's gospels with that of today. We have a continual story of a vineyard, invitation (and rejection), generosity, and just judgment. The first reading from Isaiah sets the stage by describing a sumptuous banquet, not just for a chosen few, but for "the nations." God means to provide "food rich and juicy…fine wines" for all. Matthew chose this prophetic word with Jesus' parable of the grand banquet. The audience in the narrative continues to be the religious elite, whom Jesus sees as giving loyalty to God but not doing God's will and rejecting his messengers. They constitute the object of his parable, just as they have in the previous two.

But let us again abstract from the immediate context and listen to what Jesus says, for it need not be confined to so conflictual a context with these specific opponents. A king prepares a wedding banquet. Obviously, those invited are the king's nobles. Since such invitations would involve those invited in some sort of reciprocal hospitality (see Luke 14:12–14), only the top stratum of society is in view. But they shame the host: the invited guests refuse to come and, what is worse, make up lame excuses. Let us remember that no elite in a kingdom could fail to know that the monarch's son was soon to be married. The issue is hardly "last minute conflicts," such as cause us to cancel appointments. The power of the parable depends on our appreciating that the nobles publicly shame the king by refusing to join him at the wedding of his son. An insult has been given, despite the seemingly polite excuses. An unthinkable and serious harm been given to the king, on a par with the insult of the father by his first son in 21:28–29. The insult moreover, is manifested in the way the invitees treat the king's messengers: "They seized his servants, maltreated them, and killed them." Make no mistake, the situation is utterly insulting and humiliating for the king.

As is the case of the vineyard story last Sunday, the shamed king has his satisfaction. But that is hardly the end of the story or its main point, for the monarch still wants a hall filled with guests to share the feast in honor of his son. Hence he sends other messengers to gather "anyone you can find," which command they fulfilled by collecting everyone they could find *bad and good alike.*" The king's pleasure is realized: guests pour into the house. If we are correct in seeing Jesus continuing to talk about God, then we learn of God's determination to share the riches of his table with all, Gentiles as well as Jews, slaves as well as free, females as well as males, and sinners as well as saints. The inclusive and impartial deity opens the banquet of his favor and presence to all. How shocking it would have sounded that *bad and good alike,* would receive a festal garment upon entering so as to grace the presence of the monarch and his son. But alas, the king finds a guest without this garment. And he is rightly insulted by this new refusal of the guest to accept the garment and grace the occasion. Although invited and welcomed by the incredible generosity of the king, the guest refuses to respond properly and show the appropriate gestures of gratitude and respect. In doing so, he insults the king with shameful excuses and shameless treatment of his messengers, so the king justly acts again. The guest, so richly honored by the king but so scornful of this blessing, is cast out of the wedding.

As with the other two parables, we find ourselves in a world where great generosity is shown us, where important and irrevocable choices are required of us, and where our human actions have decisive consequences. This is a moral world, yet one bathed in generosity and kindness. God, ever the rich host, invites us to a feast, not just the saints in our midst, but "bad and good alike." Welcome into the king's palace, rich foods, royal entertainment, and festal garments are provided for us. For God is never stingy with us. But are we wearing that new garment? It's there at our fingertips, it's provided for our use, it's expected of us. What sort of response are we giving so generous a host? Will God recognize us as belonging at the feast? Will we be dressed for the occasion—at God's expense of course? God's incredible generosity and inclusivity confronts our life choices and actions. Blessed are they who can pray today's psalm: "The Lord is my shepherd...who has prepared a banquet for me." Alas for those who refuse the care of the Shepherd.

TWENTY-NINTH SUNDAY IN ORDINARY TIME: YEAR A Mt 22:15–21

After hearing Matthew's collection of parables dealing with God's generosity and how God is honored or shamed by those blessed by him, we turn to a series of open controversies between Jesus and the various elites of Jerusalem. Yet let us not ignore "God" in all of these: for throughout these controversies, Jesus continues to speak explicitly about God. It greatly aids us to recognize the rather formal structure of Jesus' series of controversies in Jerusalem, for they conform to a recognized pattern. In Jewish lore about academic contests, we read of a regular set of difficult questions asked of a prominent Rabbi, namely, four typical questions:

1. questions about the core of the Law

2. questions about the application of specific laws

3. questions about the interpretation of the Scriptures

4. nonsense questions that reduce arguments to laughter.

Although our lectionary this year does not contain all of these question-contests, we are invited to view two of them in this light:

1. questions about the core of the law = what is the greatest commandment? Matthew 22:34–40—30th Sunday in Ordinary Time.

2. questions about specific application of laws = issue of tribute to Caesar. Matthew 22:15–21—29th Sunday in Ordinary Time.

Taking our clue from this carefully choreographed contest, we see Jesus successfully deflect the challenges of the Pharisees, along with those of the Scribes and the Sadducees. There can be no doubt who knows best the laws and lore of Israel: Jesus wins convincingly over all other claimants. He is a most honorable teacher, wise and clever. The topic of the controversy with the Pharisees in today's gospel presents us with a special problem: the issue of tribute to Caesar. Jesus makes his very adversaries produce the hated coin used to pay this tribute, on which Caesar's image usually appears either as a divine person or as one sanctioned by heaven. They, not Jesus, have the detested coin with its blasphemous image. But winning the argument is much less interesting than Jesus' remark. In one sense, he sidesteps the whole issue, indicating that there are legitimate honor claims made by Caesar, whom Jesus merely mentions on his way to the real topic. Jesus the peasant realizes that Caesar has many legions with which to collect taxes. Inasmuch as the Pharisees are "seeking to trap" Jesus, we admire his nimble footwork. But Jesus says more: "Render to God what is God's." He deflects one challenge, but then issues his own challenge to them: render to God what is God's.

At this very moment Jesus does not tell the audience what "belongs to God." Yet that must be the real point of this episode. If we back up a moment and review the previous three Sunday's gospels, we have part of the answer about what "belongs to God." God asked one son for faithful service: such loyalty "belongs to God." God sent messengers to those who cultivated his vineyard to give him his just due in kind: such justice and fairness is owed God. Finally God generously invited people to his palace to feast in honor of his son: it takes little imagination to envision what belongs to God here. Thus, in the light of God's persistent gifts of blessings and favor, those so blessed should render to God what is God's, namely, faith and faithfulness, honor and obedience, gratitude and service.

But let us examine the subsequent stories in Matthew's account to see what belongs to God. Next, the Sadducees ridicule the tradition that God raises the dead (22:23–33). Jesus rebukes them by pointing out how wrong they are for not rendering to God what is God's, namely the will and the power of God to vindicate those faithful to God by raising them from the dead: "You are wrong, because you know neither the scriptures nor the power of God" (22:29).

Following this, when asked about the greatest commandment, Jesus says that loving God totally, with wholeheartedness and complete service, as well as loving one's neighbor as oneself are the first and foundational law. Total and faithful "love" constitute rendering to God what is God's. And finally, Jesus insists that it belongs to God to show favor where God wills. Hence "the Lord," who is God, said to David's "Lord," who is his son, the Messiah, "Sit at my right hand" (Ps 110:1; Mt 22:44). It belongs to God to send Jesus his Son as the world's savior: it belongs to God to stand by that Son, raising him from the dead, undoing the rejection and shame shown him on earth, and enthroning him at God's right hand in heaven. True rendering to God what is God's will mean total acceptance of God's Christ as Lord and Savior and thus complete loyalty to God's plan of our salvation.

If Jesus' principle is valid, how many other things rightfully owed God ought we to render to God? The psalm says it broadly today: "Give the Lord glory and honor." That is, sing a song of gratitude for blessings received: tell the world of God's generous kindness: give God the credit for our happiness and success: proclaim to all that "God is king." Our very worship of God this Sunday is the key and beginning to what Jesus meant by "render to God what is God's."

THIRTIETH SUNDAY IN ORDINARY TIME: YEAR A Mt 22:34–40

As we saw in our discussion of last Sunday's gospel, Jesus continues to be challenged by the religious elite of his day with hard questions. Another enemy comes up "to disconcert" Jesus with a difficult question: "Master, what is the greatest commandment of the Law?" It is ironic that a Pharisee would ask this, for the New Testament presents them as quite concerned about many commandments and customs: the washing of hands and pots, the keeping of the Sabbath, fasting, and tithes. So far, no one would ever guess that Pharisees concerned themselves with the core of the law or its principles. Alas, they treat them all equally, which devalues the central core.

Jesus had earlier hinted at his understanding of the core of the Law when he said "In everything, do to others as you would have them do to you. For this is the law and the prophets" (7:12). Now a more formal answer is required of him. Without hesitation Jesus states that "love" of God and neighbor form the core of the Law and the traditional worship of Israel. So much for an answer, but what does it mean? If we labored to discover what it means to render to God what is God's, it should not come as a surprise that we must struggle to learn what "love" means. Jesus immediately tells us that "love" entails a completeness: whole heart, soul, and mind. It is an open-ended commitment, vast in its scope and endless in its duration. After all, God's love for us is precisely this: a permanent, total, complete laboring for our well-being.

"Love," moreover, shows itself in deeds. Verbal expressions of love, while important, must be realized in deeds of love (recall the failure of both sons to match words and deeds in 21:28–30). On this score, we are blessed with a biblical tradition that spells out in great detail what such deeds of love look like. One of the key descriptions of this sort of love-in-action can be found in the first reading of today from Exod 22 where the covenant with God is explained. "Love" entails justice, as simple as that: "Do not molest the stranger or oppress him...do not be harsh with the widow or the orphan...take no advantage of the poor to whom you lend resources...be just and fair with all." "Love," then, deals with the justice of our most basic relationships.

We render not only to God what is God's, but to others what is their due. In one sense Exod 22 does not itself spell out what loving "justice" looks like: it only says that we should not "molest" or "be harsh with" the needy and vulnerable. Jesus later supplies the concrete details when he rewards those who feed the hungry, clothe the naked, succor the sick, etc. (25:34–36). Whatever "love" means, it shows itself in deeds: not just any deeds, but deeds of justice.

Thus, while we applaud Jesus' cleverness in besting his adversaries, let us not ignore the rich content of his response. "Love" for us is based, as Exodus reminds us, on the fact that we are first loved by God, the slaves in Egypt are made free, the strangers wandering in the desert are tended by a faithful shepherd. Because we all have such deep experiences of being so totally respected and cared for by God, we are thereby empowered and encouraged to show this same kindness to others, especially the needy in our midst. And "love's" twin sister is justice: "love" shows itself in deeds, not words.

THIRTY-FIRST SUNDAY IN ORDINARY TIME: YEAR A Mt 23:1–12

Matthew portrays Jesus concluding his controversies with the Jerusalem elite by means of a collection of critical sayings, which were probably spoken elsewhere at diverse times, but which the evangelist brings together here to make a sustained critique. Although addressed to specific people in one concrete situation (the Pharisees), over the ages the kinds of criticisms made by Jesus have been applied to a host of people within the church, giving rise to our modern disdain for Pharisaism or legalism. What is the brunt of Jesus' remarks? Let us begin by remembering that Jesus himself is a reformer in his culture. God authorized him, as well as the ancient prophets, to speak a reforming word to Israel in general, but often specifically to the priestly and royal elites. As a reformer, Jesus attends either to things ignored by the elites or to excesses in their structures and organizational zeal. Jesus often spoke about the heart and things within human life, in contradiction to Pharisees who seem to have paid more attention to surfaces, boundaries, and things external. Recall how Jesus in the "Antitheses" calls for total purity of body and spirit, inner and outer (5:21–48). Recall how Jesus criticizes people who place rules and structures above the physical needs of people, whether it be activity on the Sabbath that saves or playing the physician to the sinners. We hear now the full scope of what Jesus would reform.

Jesus starts off, not trashing all authority, but indicating its rightful place in the lives of disciples. The Scribes and Pharisees occupy the chair of Moses: they have legitimate, if misused authority. Yet Jesus the reformer does not call for the overthrow of all authority.

Most basically, he warns his disciples not to imitate bad examples of it in people whose exterior actions are overly strict or hypocritical. Recall, moreover, that Jesus speaks in the traditional Semitic style of exaggeration. This kind of dramatic speech indeed makes a point, but let us remember that it is an exaggeration. "They tie up heavy burdens but do not lift a finger to move them." This refers to Jesus' perception that the Pharisees had so rationalized the law of Israel that it covered most of the aspects of daily life in significant detail. Such a complete specification of law sounds like a "burden" and stands in contrast to the "yoke" of Jesus, which is easy and mild.

Worse than this, the Pharisees are accused of being excessively public in their religious observance, and for the wrong reasons. They "attract attention" by "broader" phylacteries than are called for and by "longer" tassels on their prayer shawls. As self-styled leaders, they expect marks of respect, such as places of honor and first seats and reverential greetings. These externals are hardly in themselves so very wrong, but they indicate a concern only for externals with a corresponding masquerading of attitudes and motives.

As we noted above, Jesus does not attack the principle of legitimate authority or authorized leadership. The issue rests with how that authority and leadership are used. In the second part of today's gospel, Jesus seems to restrict severely the way a reformer would see authority practiced. His disciples have no Rabbi, but only Jesus the Teacher: "you are all brothers." They have but one Father, who is in heaven; and on earth they may not assume the title or role of "teachers," that is, people who expand the Law into heavy and constrictive systems. Anyone who exalts himself will be humbled, while the humble will be exalted. This is strong reforming language, no less filled with exaggeration than was the first part of the discourse. God in heaven and Christ alone are our leaders, teachers, and shepherds! Clear enough. But this critique of the excesses of ambitious leadership should be read in balance with other statements by Jesus in Matthew's gospel about leadership within the church.

Jesus once summoned the Twelve whom he had chosen and authorized for specific ministries of preaching and healing (10:1, 5–10). Moreover, he acknowledged the grace of God shown to Simon Peter and declared him the foundation stone of his group (16:16). He told the Twelve who had left all and followed him that they would sit on "twelve thrones judging the twelve tribes of Israel" (19:28). Finally, the risen Jesus commissioned these select disciples to "Go, make disciples of all nations, teaching them to observe all that I have commanded you" (28:19). It would be simplistic to conclude from today's gospel that Jesus thoroughly and permanently dismissed all leadership for his circle of disciples. How, then, should we read these remarks?

THIRTY-SECOND SUNDAY IN ORDINARY TIME: YEAR A Mt 25:1–13

Our gospel today contains the first of three parables that compose the last part of Matthew's fifth and final Sermon (24:1—25:46). As we shall see, no student of any one of these parables should ignore the other two when trying to understand even one of them. Matthew intends us to see all three of them as parallel, not only in the sequence in which they occur, but also in the basic message they convey.

Moreover, although we begin with 25:1–12, the parable of the wise and foolish maidens, this itself is connected with previous remarks about faithful and unfaithful servants in 24:45–51. There Jesus blesses the loyal servant who attends to duty and is found faithful when the master arrives home (24:46–47). But woe to the wicked servant who interpreted the "delay" of the master to mean that he would never return—and so, freed from any fear of judgment, that servant began to "beat fellow servants, eat and drink with drunkards." Thus Matthew balances one story about faithful and unfaithful male servants whose loyalty is tested as they await their master with the parable about contrasting dutiful and slothful female servants awaiting the return of the bridegroom. Both genders are clearly in view. Both face the same situation. Both have options of loyalty and faithlessness before them. And both reap comparable rewards and punishments.

Yet something else occurs in today's story of the maidservants. A certain deception seems to be practiced by the slothful ones. They count on the master arriving during daylight or at twilight: as maidservants, they surely know what is expected of them and should have made preparations for all sorts of possible scenarios. The event, moreover, is nothing less than the wedding of the owner of the house, which must demand attention and preparation. Let us read the foolish maidens, then, as deceptive servants who masquerade as dutiful ones.

Their "folly" is not absentmindedness, but a shameful act of deception and failure of duty. Should the master come on time, they are likely to escape notice and censure. But the master is delayed: a long time passes, darkness, then midnight. When the household jumps from sleep to attention, the deception is as painfully clear as the light in the vessels of the faithful servants. The dutiful servants are not to be faulted for refusing to share their oil, for the point of the story is the unmasking of deception and the unveiling of the gravity of failing to make preparations. The bridegroom welcomes the faithful into his banquet, shuts the outer door, and begins his festivities. The returning maidservants cannot get in, which is precisely the point. There is a tide in the affairs of mortals when decisions made are fixed and decisive: consequences follow. How stinging, then, is the rebuke of the bridegroom: "I do not know you." They are not members of his household anymore: he does not recognize in them the marks of a loyal and faithful servant.

Where shall we put our emphasis? On the symbolism of the oil? What it might stand for? On "light," which true disciples are to show to the world (5:14–16)? Or on the praise and blame that the master awards, his reward for honorable faithfulness and his recompense for deceptive slothfulness? "Oil" may be something as general as "decisive action" in hearing the gospel, such as the merchant showed when he found the pearl of great price (13:46). If we take the parable in 25:31–46 as a guide, "oil" might be the complex of deeds of service and justice that we show the needy and lowly. But knowing that still does not absolve a reader of the requirement of faithfulness and loyalty. Friends of Jesus are not simply those who start out well, but those who remain true disciples through thick and thin.

Discipleship is a lifetime affair with the concerns of God, not a quick weekend away. How hard, then, for us modern people who have such difficulty with lasting commitments to hear the call to faithfulness in the gospel. Let us reread the first reading about Wisdom, the pursuit of which resembles the honorable behavior of the faithful maidservants.

THIRTY-THIRD SUNDAY IN ORDINARY TIME: YEAR A Mt 25:14–30

A curious thing occurs in the readings today. In the first reading from the end of the book of Proverbs, a dutiful female is praised for using her time and energy profitably. She is balanced in the gospel by the praise of two males who likewise act prudently in the light of the kingdom. Inasmuch as male and female servants were compared and contrasted in 24:46—25:12, this same pattern seems to be repeated in today's readings.

Yet let us be careful not to convert a powerful parable into a bland allegory. Let us listen once more with peasant ears and see how Jesus might be shaking up the expectations of his audience. We need to bring to this story some of the awarenesses of typical peasants in Jesus' time to see how he might be playing with those expectations. Peasants were conservative and traditional people: they cannot afford to take risks or to try something new. Farming, especially the subsistence level which characterized Jesus' Palestine, is unforgiving of mistakes and novelty. Moreover, peasants knew quite well what was expected of them in terms of behavior: they were carefully socialized from birth to know the code of their culture. Their "honor" and reputation rested on living up to those expectations. Two pressures, then, would constrain peasants to play it safe and do the conventional thing. Peasants simply would resist bold and unusual behavior.

One further item: we must recall that merchants were unsavory people whose livelihood came from exploiting others (see gospel for the seventeenth Sunday). Usury was forbidden by the Bible. In fact, any sort of "investment" and any kind of quick increase in wealth would have been met with great suspicion of ill-gotten gain. The peasant world simply did not imagine, much less countenance, anyone getting ahead.

In the story, an absentee master entrusts differing degrees of wealth to each of three servants. No command was given them about what to do with the funds. They are simply "entrusted" with it, perhaps simply to guard it, which would make eminent sense in a conservative peasant world. Each of the three interprets the master differently and so does differing things with the wealth. Eventually the master returns and demands an audit. Then the fun begins for the audience. The first two servants come forward and boast how they had greatly increased the master's wealth. In peasant ears, this sounds evil: trade is suspect and usury-investment is forbidden. Moreover, these servants were exceptionally successful at their task, gaining ten times or five times the amount left by the master. Yet the master praises them, something that shocks peasant ears. Praise? For scoundrels? Just who is this master? A thief? The parable tells us that he is "a hard man, reaping where you have not sown and gathering where you have not scattered." Let us not be mistaken—the master himself sounds like a thief: he takes where he has not labored. It sounds as though we are hearing a story about thieves and criminals. Something is terribly wrong.

Worst of all, the one person who by conservative peasant standards did the "right thing" is chastised and dismissed. He did the thing most peasants would do: he buried the master's wealth for safekeeping. He did not risk the ruin of the master by devious and forbidden investments. According to the code of his times, this servant did the honorable thing by his master. But horror of horrors! The master rebukes him, dispossesses him of whatever he has, and turns him out. Why are the wicked servants praised and the faithful one chastised? What is going on?

"The kingdom of heaven is like...?" Like nothing we have ever experienced! And thereby lies the power of the parable. The old ways, safe and sure, no longer work. Something new has happened that calls for "strange" action. The old ways of synagogue and Temple are no longer the sure, much less the only paths to God's favor, especially when God's reforming prophet Jesus steps on the stage. In the eyes of many Jesus himself was a deviant who led the people astray: many claimed that he had a demon. And his ways in the eyes of some were evil ways, for example, not keeping dietary laws, Sabbath observance, or ritual observances. Is "Jesus" the "hard man" who ostensibly does illegal actions? Could praise be lavished on those who break with the past, with family expectations and synagogue regulations? Are disciples expected to be "different," like their master?

The parable grabs us insofar as we view it, not as moral allegory about proper use of abilities and opportunities, but as a shocking call to act in unconventional ways to seize hold of the gospel. How often have we heard Jesus praise people who acted to seize the prize? An unjust steward is praised for his bold and decisive action (Luke 16:8); a merchant, for selling all he had to buy the pearl of great price (Mt 13:45–46); a crafty person for purchasing a farm with hidden treasure (Mt 13:44). What counts is action in the face of the gospel opportunity: decisive, bold, risky action. The deceptive maidservants should have acted just this way to insure that they had sufficient oil. Only, now the "wicked" servants are praised for their bold action, not the faithful ones.

But what actions? Just as we had great difficulty in making concrete what actions Jesus envisioned in regard to having "oil" in one's lamp, so we are not entirely sure what constitutes bold and decisive action in the face of the gospel. It may be "repent and believe in the good news" or "feed the hungry and clothe the naked." Maybe we are wasting our time trying to be precise about what to do when the gospel demands that we start doing something, anything "productive." Today's responsorial psalm only tells us that "Happy are those who 'fear' the Lord and walk in his ways."

CHRIST THE KING
Mt 25:31–46

The King, the last of the three parables in Mt 25, occurs as today's gospel. The third of anything often serves as the climax of the sequence: the punchline or hidden meaning of a story generally comes at the end. Hence, we turn to the parable of the sheep and the goats expecting that it will both clarify the previous ones and illumine what it means to take bold and decisive action in the light of the gospel. The reason for the choice of this parable for the Feast of Christ the King is immediately apparent from the opening lines, "When the Son of man comes in his glory...he will take his seat on his throne." What does this king do? Separate the good from wicked, as he separates sheep from goats. But who qualifies as a "sheep"? Who a "goat"?

All true parables, we have seen, contain a surprise or upsetting of conventional expectations. And today is no exception. At first, the plot line seems quite straightforward. Some people are credited by Jesus with feeding him when hungry, clothing him when naked, receiving him as a stranger, visiting him when in prison, and attending him when sick. Nothing in the gospel story has prepared us for this: we have never seen Jesus hungry, thirsty, sick, naked, or in prison. And the "sheep" in the story confess that they, too, never did see Jesus in any of these situations. Then why are they singled out for praise, especially praise for doing something they denied doing? In the logic of a peasant world they may actually have acted foolishly in feeding the hungry, clothing the naked, etc. In a peasant context, one would do this for one's kin, but not for strangers. Moreover, it would be foolish to "take the bread belonging to the children and give it to dogs." One's family would lose the clothing and food it so desperately needs in a subsistence peasant world. After all, "charity begins at home." Hence, we receive our first surprise: the king praises those who appear to have acted foolishly in dispensing the family's meager resources on utter strangers. And to compound the problem, they were certain that they were not doing it to Jesus! The Lord adds another surprise: he goes about in disguise! They can't see him because he does not want to be seen—at least in kingly fashion. What a confusing world Jesus creates!

After praising and rewarding the "sheep," the king turns to the "goats." He banishes them from his sight because they did not feed him when hungry, clothe him when naked, comfort him in sickness, etc. If we were correct in suggesting that those who did feed, clothe, comfort, etc., were acting quite foolishly according to a peasant assessment of duties and exchange, then these people who did not feed, clothe, comfort, etc., a stranger would have been acting correctly—that is, according to peasant custom. They saved their resources for their kin: they lived up to their basic duty to family members. The king censures them for this, much to their chagrin. When they ask for an explanation, they are even more confused. The king confesses that he has gone about in disguise and that the peasants were not supposed to recognize him. All of a sudden, old certainties crack, clarity splinters, chaos seems to reign. What kind of a "kingdom" is it when those who act "foolishly" are praised in contrast to those who acted "prudently"? What kind of "King" is he who goes in disguise, precisely to fool his subjects? Once more, the gospel turns our world upside down.

Several reactions are possible for us readers. We may see this climactic parable as but one more in a series of stories that have attacked smug attitudes toward the gospel and demanded radical, swift action. It may be the one that best dramatizes Jesus' own sayings such as "last is first and least is greatest." It may clarify just how "foolish" Jesus was to ask people to take up a cross and lose their lives by following him. The gospel, alas, does not call for "more of the same," but a change in our lives: repentance or "change of mind." Or, we may now legitimately ask if the "oil" of the maidservants or the "investing of wealth" by the entrusted servants is better understood in terms of a gospel that emphasizes justice to the needy. Are the deeds that really count those "foolish" ones of care for the outsiders and comfort for the afflicted? After all, would we not characterize Jesus' own ministry as feeding the hungry and comforting the sick? Did he prefer Jews to Gentiles? Did he make any distinctions between slave or free? Male or female? Rich or poor?

It's the king's disguise that is so difficult to understand. Of course, none of us would ignore Jesus if we clearly saw him. But he says that he is in our midst always, not to deceive us, but simply present in ways that our customs, prejudices, and the like prevent us from recognizing. This means that disciples cannot afford the luxury of being totally sure who is holy or worthy or deserving. Yet before we become distraught, we remember that most of the people who saw the miracle-worker Jesus did not accept him in his power and grandeur. Most of the people who heard his powerful, prophetic words did not take him for anything but a false prophet. Jesus, in power and with persuasive signs, did not always touch hearts. How much less would a suffering Christ impress us? How great a problem would a lowly Messiah and an insignificant Galilean pose for us?

This last gospel of Ordinary Time indeed puts an end to this year. It clearly summarizes the good news of Matthew's gospel in that it articulates how God's constant benefaction and justice for the poor will come about, namely, though the gospel actions of Jesus' disciples. It also proclaims the value of such loving works of justice: "Come, blessed of my Father, take your inheritance…" And it gives great value to our simple actions: "When you did it to the least of these brothers, you did it to me." Moreover, the king knows that such action may seem "foolish" to many: but we celebrate with our king a kingdom where impartial kindness and generosity are poured out to all, irrespective of appearances. We glory to be part of a kingdom where last becomes first and least greatest.

Matthew's Gospel in the Lectionary

Paddy Meagher, SJ

When we study the readings chosen from Matthew we are given a particular emphasis in the lectionary. We note that the majority are taken from Jesus' teaching. There are five major collections of teaching in the gospel. These collections are clearly demarcated by means of the concluding verses (7:28—8:1; 11:1; 13:53; 19:1 and 26:1). There are seventeen texts from these five collections. Along with these, there are three other teaching texts. There are only three texts about his cures and "works of powers." From the tense Jerusalem days there are five conflict texts, and the remaining five texts deal with the person of Jesus more directly (3:13-17; Jn 1:29-34; 4:12-23; 11:25-30 and 16:13-20). Two of these texts could be grouped with the teachings (4:12-23 and 11:25-30). Consequently, we have a rather one-sided presentation of the gospel, as so much of the narrative has been omitted.

THE NARRATIVE OF MATTHEW

General Structure

We shall approach the gospel from various viewpoints. Matthew has carefully sculpted the first part of the gospel (chapters 1-13). Only in chapter 14 does he follow Mark's order of events and geographical skeleton. Into this he incorporates chapter 18, an instruction on aspects of life in the community, and contributes some scenes from his own source like Jesus' paying the temple tax and the parable of the laborers in the vineyard. In the Jerusalem section Matthew adds some scenes to Mark's narrative (parables of the two sons and the wedding banquet). Apart from his reinterpretation of Marcan scenes in the light of the problems in his church, what is characteristic of Matthew in this section is his long collection of prophetic woes against Jewish leadership (chapter. 23) and his parables aimed at his community and the need to be prepared for the Day of the Son of Man (24:45—25:46). Matthew has reinterpreted aspects of the Passion and written his own account of the resurrection appearances.

The Ministry of the Messiah and his Community

After the careful presentation of Jesus as the Messiah with a detailed account of his teaching (chapters 5-7) and his works of compassion and power (chapters 8-9), Matthew indicates that this ministry is to be continued in the community of faith. Therefore, he adds at this point the instruction to the Twelve about their future ministry (chapter 10). Their ministry is to mirror Jesus' ministry, which he described in the previous chapters. He has framed the early description of this ministry by two summaries of its details. "He went about all Galilee, teaching in their synagogues and preaching the gospel of the kingdom and healing every disease and every infirmity among the people" (4:23 and 9:35).

The ministry of the Twelve is introduced by a moving passage. Jesus contemplates the people of his time, sheep without a shepherd, lost and leaderless, and is filled with compassion for them (9:36). This leads him to want others to share in his ministry (9:37-38).

Responses to this Ministry

Having concluded his instruction to the Twelve, an instruction that echoes both the circumstances of his own ministry and the needs and problems of the early community, Matthew reflects upon the responses to Jesus' ministry (chapters 11 and 12). The responses are largely negative. Jesus has been a failure. John the Baptist is puzzled. Jesus praises his ministry (11:1–6, 7–15). The contemporary generation heeds neither John nor Jesus. The cities of the lakeside where most of Jesus teaching and works of power took place are unrepentant (11:16–24). In prayer Jesus himself ponders this reality (11:25–27) and continues his mission to the little ones (11:28–30). Matthew continues to narrate the responses and to detail the conflicts, the intent to destroy Jesus and the negative propaganda about the one said to be aligned with the prince of spirits (chapter 12). Jesus faces the conflict as the servant of God intent on God's work (12:15–21).

There are two groups in these chapters who listen and respond, the "little ones" (11:26) and "those who do the will of the Father in heaven" and make up Jesus' family (12:46–50). These crises in Jesus' ministry reflect a reality of his own life and reflect an ongoing crisis for the community. Will the kingdom of God actually come or will evil have the last word? Why do some abandon the community? What ought the community to do to those members who are insincere disciples? Gathering a series of parables Matthew answers these questions. The parables speak of various aspects of the future coming of the kingdom and final judgment (chapter 13).

Galilee to Jerusalem and in Jerusalem

Up to this point, the gospel is a great tour de force by Matthew. This is a rich presentation of ministry and its consequences. Matthew follows Mark (6:1—10:52) quite closely in his preparation for Jesus' question to the disciples about his identity and the consequent teaching about his passion and discipleship (13:54—20:34). We shall not comment on the narrative. Matthew has paid special attention to the life within the community and aspects of the life of disciples. In chapter 18, he gathers teaching into a communitarian discourse. The other major appearance of the hand of Matthew is in the Jerusalem ministry before the Passion. Since Matthew's community is under great pressure and in serious conflict with communities who follow the Judaism of some groups of Pharisees, the conflictual nature of the days in Jerusalem is highlighted. The harsh polemical denunciation of the scribes and Pharisees owes more to the situation of the community than to the life of Jesus. Also there are serious problems in the community. Members are not living the gospel. This issue is again at the forefront of the concerns of Matthew's Jesus at the end of the ministry. He gives repetitive warnings to the community to live the gospel and be ready to welcome the Son of Man (24:45—25:46).

Narrative of the Origin of the Messiah

I have outlined some aspects of the unfolding of the narrative in the gospel, omitted in our lectionary readings to a large extent. We do not expect the lectionary in Ordinary Time to include the opening and final chapters of the gospel, for the infancy narrative is used in Advent-Christmas and the Passion/Resurrection is used on Palm Sunday and Easter. We must make some comments. Matthew must establish in a way acceptable to his Jewish world that Jesus is the legitimate Messiah. In the opening narratives, the major theme is that Jesus is the fulfillment of God's promises. He is the authentic Son of Abraham and David. He goes to great lengths to establish this by means of the genealogy and account of the dream to Joseph, Son of David, who must name the child and so incorporate him within the David family. Matthew presents this Messiah as the savior of his people (save his people from their sins: 1:21; cf. 26:28—only in Mt). He is also the fulfillment of God's promise of a savior in and through whom God will be with us to save, the Emmanuel.

The Jews rejected Jesus. Both their leadership and the people reject him most forcefully in the Passion narrative (26:63–65; 27:24–25). However, many Gentiles accepted Jesus. Surely, these two facts speak against him being the Messiah. This problem Matthew tackles in the second chapter in an allusive way. He has the story of Moses (endangered at his birth by Pharaoh; fleeing and returning; the pharaoh as the murderer of children), and of Israel (Israel in Egypt, Israel as God's Son,

Rachel-Jacob weeping at the exile, Balaam and the star of the Judah King) in the background. Jesus is also endangered at the beginning of his life and at the end (Herod and the Leadership). God saves him and makes him the new Israel, the Son and Messiah in whom all people will find hope.

PERSON OF JESUS

The Father on the Son

In turn we can study how Matthew paints a picture of Jesus from the words and attitudes of different people:

• the authoritative voice of God's approval;

• the authoritative statements of the author;

• the approaches of the individuals and the crowd;

• the opponents of Jesus; and

• the way Matthew interprets the self-awareness of Jesus.

The most authoritative is God's attitude. There are two major texts, and in each, God is responding to a major decision taken by Jesus. When John objects to baptizing Jesus, Jesus persuades him by pointing out that they must fulfill God's will (3:15). This basic orientation in his life is followed by his designation by God as the beloved Son entrusted with a unique mission. God says: "This is my Son, the Beloved, with whom I am well pleased" (3:17). The basic attitude of Jesus to God's will is reinforced in the narrative of his conflict with the power of evil (4:1-11).

The second incident is at the turning point in his ministry. The disciples and Peter recognize that he is not another prophet. They confess that he is "Son of the living God" (14:33 and 16:16). When Jesus commits himself to death as the outcome of his fidelity to his mission Peter rebukes him. Jesus makes it perfectly clear to Peter that his option is diametrically opposed to God's will (16:22-23). Matthew signals to the reader that the movement of the narrative has changed with his "from that time on, Jesus began to proclaim...". In this context God again appears in a special type of narrative and says: "This is my Son, the Beloved, in whom I am well pleased" (17:5). He adds, for the sake of the disciples, "listen to him." The other special "word" of God about Jesus is the earthquakes that accompany his death and the subsequent revelation at the empty tomb (27:51-53; 28:2-6). This apocalyptic feature is only in Matthew.

The Narrator on Jesus

The author makes another series of authoritative statements himself. He relates Jesus and his ministry to chosen texts from the long story of God's action in the history of Israel. These texts are called *formula quotations* in many studies. There are thirteen such texts (1:23; 2:5b-6, 15b, 17-18, 23b; 4:14-16; 8:17; 12:17-21; 13:14-15, 35; 21:4-5; 26:56, and 27:9-10). Not all refer directly to Jesus. In these texts he is identified with:

• the promised savior (the Emmanuel) who will save his people from their sins;

• the promised shepherd of Israel; the Son called from Egypt;

• the Nazorean; the promised light which dawns in the darkness for the Gentiles; and

• the servant who shoulders our ills.

Matthew uses another particularly rich servant text as an interpretation of Jesus. He is the chosen and beloved servant, endowed with the Spirit who has the strength of gentleness in his ministry. He proclaims God's kingdom to the Gentiles and is their hope (12:17-21). Jesus is the inspired prophet who uncovers God's mysteries (13:35). He is also the humble messianic king (21:4-5).

Matthew has another way of focusing attention on Jesus himself. His narratives are concise, and usually all props are omitted. Jesus' words and actions are in the spotlight. We notice this when we compare his narratives with Mark and Luke. Some examples include the cure of the leper (8:1-4), his touch of Peter's mother-in-law (8:14-15), and his encounter with the demoniacs (8:28-34). This characteristic stands out with great clarity in the scene of Jairus whose daughter is already dead, and that of the hemorrhaging woman (9:18-26).

An aspect that Matthew highlights is the compassion of Jesus. He narrates that "he had compassion for them [crowds from towns] and healed their sick"(14:14). Earlier he had remarked that when he saw the crowds "he had compassion on them, because they were harassed and helpless like sheep without a shepherd" (9:36). This compassion found tangible expression in his healing ministry. Apart from the actual accounts of healing, Matthew intersperses his narrative with summaries of healing. He prefaces the Sermon on the Mount with a general overview of healing. The narrative runs: "...people brought to him all who were ill with various diseases, those suffering severe pain, the demon possessed, those having seizures and all the paralyzed and he healed them" (4:24).

In a later account after healing Peter's mother-in-law, Matthew narrates: "that evening they brought to him many who were possessed with demons. He cast out spirits with a word and cured all who were sick" (8:16). This ministry was interpreted as an expression of the Servant's ministry (8:17).

When asked to confirm his identity as "the one who is to come," Jesus offered the following credentials. He said that "the blind receive their sight, the lame walk, the lepers are cleansed, the deaf hear, the dead are raised and the poor have the good news brought to them" (11:5). Was it because people had forgotten the long story of God as compassionate that Jesus added: "blessed is anyone who takes no offense at me" (11:6)?

Two thumbnail sketches, like two engravings, are drawn of Jesus' Galilean ministry. One at the lakeside (14:34-36) and the other on a mountain (15:29-31). All types of sick people surround him. After Jesus had begun to speak of his passion (16:21), his ministry of healing recedes. However, we find him surrounded by his "people" in the Temple. Matthew recounts how the blind and lame came to him there and he cured them (21:14). We know that these groups typify his "friends" since Jesus himself invites them to come to him: "Come to me all you who are weary and burdened."

Various People on Jesus

Various individuals and the crowd take stances in relationship to Jesus. He is a religious person. Therefore they will address him or approach him within the expectations of the period. The more powerful statements about Jesus are made with the knees than with the lips. In the gospel many figures kneel before Jesus:

- the wise men (2:2, 8, 11);
- the leper (8:2);
- the leader of the synagogue whose daughter had died (9:18);
- the disciples in the boat (14:33);
- the Canaanite woman (15:25);
- the mother of John and James (20:20);
- the women leaving the tomb with fear and great joy (28:9); and
- the eleven on the mountain in Galilee (28:17).

Matthew also closes some narratives with a response of wonder or with a question about the "who" of Jesus of Nazareth (8:27; 9:8, 33)

The more appropriate address used by people who approach Jesus for help is "Lord," with Son of David occasionally added (8:2, 6, 8, 25; 9:28; 14:28, 30; 15:22, 25, 27; 17:15; 20:30-32; cf. 21:9). Peter also addresses him as Lord (14:28-30; 16:22; 17:4; 18:21). The relationship of the use of this term to the risen Jesus is found in the angels' words at the empty tomb: "See the place where the Lord laid" (28:6). Jesus uses the title of himself in some important texts, reflecting the early church's attitude to him (12:8; 21:3; 22:43-54).

The first disciples are the pagan soldier and his companions. They witnessed the "earthquake" and "what had happened" and filled with awe confessed: "Truly this was the Son of God."

The Opponents on Jesus: Demons, Leaders, People of Nazareth

The people of Nazareth are a surprise opponent. Unable to figure out how the particular man from their town could be a prophet they are scandalized by him (13:54-58). In the narrative, therefore, they join the groups described in chapters 11 and 12. The spirit world is fearful and acknowledges that God's sovereign power works through the "Son of God" (9:29). The religious leadership accuses him of blasphemy when he forgives sins (9:3), and they smear his name when they witness exorcisms. The fellow is in cohorts with the prince of demons! (9:34; 12:24). They are angered and shocked by his acceptance of praise and his exercise of prophetic authority in the Temple (21:15-16, 23-27). They attempt to force him into grave error (22:16, 35). Finally, they pursue him to death (12:14; 21:46; 26:3-5).

When face to face in the trial scene they are forced to

ask him the major question. Are you the Christ, Son of God? Hearing his affirmative response—the only time he affirms his identity in this way—they condemn him because of blasphemy. The irony is that he also reveals that he is the Son of Man whom they will see seated at the right hand of God and coming in the clouds of heaven as judge! (26:63-65). They force Pilate to crucify "the Christ" and at the cross, mocking Jesus, taunt him about his claim to be "King of Israel and Son of God" (27:41-43).

Jesus on Jesus

We can also approach the picture of Jesus from his own consciousness. A word of caution is needed. We are only aware of Jesus' self-awareness through Matthew's interpretation.

Jesus' first words draw out attention to his sense of obedience to God and his final words to his awareness of great authority. He said: "We must fulfill all righteousness " and "All authority in heaven and earth has been given to me" (3:15; 28:18). The personal prayer of Jesus is "Father, holy be your name, your kingdom come, your will be done." The great symbolic reality "the kingdom of God/of heaven" encapsulates the whole meaning of his life. Therefore, we must always reflect on Jesus in the context of the great story of the activity of God. He had been involved in the past, and now was involved through Jesus and would be into the future, establishing his sovereign rule over human history.

The picture of Jesus in the gospel is the picture of the Son who is both obedient and aware of unique authority and responsibility. The theme of obedience holds together the major decisions of Jesus' life. The great moments of "testing" are the symbolic expressions of this. In the symbolic narrative of his tests by Satan, the Son is only concerned about the "every word which comes from the mouth of God" and worship uniquely given to God (4:4, 7, 10). As his passion becomes a reality he commits himself and rebukes Peter most sternly (16:21-23). As the passion begins to unfold Jesus announces it: "You know that after two days the Passover is coming and the Son of Man will be delivered up to be crucified" (26:2; only in Mt). At the supper, he surrenders himself "for many for the forgiveness of sins" (26:28; only in Mt). In the garden in Matthew, he explicitly submits to the will of his Father three times (26:39, 42, 44).

Besides this careful obedience which is the true witness to and expression of his being Son of the Father, there is the explicit awareness of authority and its actual exercise. However, the authority is coupled with a profound humility (11:28-30; 12:18-20; 21:4-5—Jesus' messianic entrance into the city) and the pervasive sense of being the servant who offers his life as a ransom for many (20:28). This authority has its source in the relationship of Jesus as Son to his Father (11:27). The Father gives all authority to Jesus of Nazareth and to the risen Lord (11:27a; 28:18). With this authority, he reveals the Father (11:27b). Therefore, he is the authentic and genuine interpreter of the Law and of God's will. In all the texts in which aspects of the Law are involved, he is the authoritative interpreter (5:21-48; 6:1-18; 12:1-14; 15:1-20; 19:1-12).

The most important aspect of Jesus' self-awareness in Matthew is his relationship to God as Father. He shares this relationship with his disciples who are taught to pray the "Our Father." Apart from Jesus' address to God as Father in his prayers (11:25-27; 26:39, 42), he speaks of "the will of my Father" (7:21; 12:50; 18:14), and of appearing before the Father in heaven (10:32, 33; 18:10, 19). Comments on many of these texts can be found on the relevant Sunday.

Jesus normally refers to himself by the title "Son of Man." This designation occurs when he speaks about the special characteristics of his ministry (8:20; 9:6; 11:19; 12:8, 32; 13:27; 16:13; 18:11; 20:28). He also uses it to announce his passion, death, and resurrection (12:40; 17:9, 12, 22; 20:18; 26:2, 24), and especially his return as the universal Judge (10:23; 13:41; 16:27-28; 19:28; 24:27, 30, 37, 39, 44; 25:31; 26:4). These texts reveal a depth of conscious responsibility and a depth of relationship with the Father and God's plan for human history. The designation "Son of Man" evokes a sense of mystery.

DISCIPLESHIP

This is a major theme of each gospel. Jesus entrusts his Twelve with a universal mission. He describes it in terms of "making disciples" (28:19; cf. 13:51–52). There are two major elements in the process of becoming and living as a disciple. One was to be dedicated to the Father, Son, and Spirit and the other was to following all of Jesus' teaching (28:19-20). We shall highlight some aspects.

First we recall the great faith figures of this story:

- the centurion (8:10, 13);
- the sick woman (8:22);
- the two blind men in Galilee and in Jericho (9:27-31 and 20:29-34);
- the Canaanite woman (15:28).

In contrast Jesus' own disciples are consistently chided because they are "of little faith" (6:30; 8:26; 14:31 and 16:8; 17:20; cf. 15:16 and 28:17). This refers to a faith that crumbles and is inadequate in the face of certain challenges in life. The hallmark of the disciple is to do the will of the Father, and nothing can replace this major orientation (7:21; 12:50). This creates the relationship between the disciple and the Father. In the Sermon on the Mount, Matthew places his mark on the tradition of Jesus' teaching. In it there is a repetitive reference to "your Father in heaven" (5:16, 45, 48; 6:1, 4, 6, 8, 9, 14, 15, 18, 26, 32; 7:11, 21). The norm for the disciple's way of living is to be authentic children of the Father and to be like the Father (5:45, 48). Their way of life is to lead others who witness it to praise their Father (5:16).

Jesus calls his disciples to a "greater righteousness" (5:20). His teaching has characteristic marks. He emphasizes the interior attitudes that ought to be the norms for behavior (5:21-48; 15:11, 16-20). He opens out horizons for human behavior that cannot be demarcated. The only norms really are the potentialities of the human as created in the image and likeness of God who, because of the resurrection of Jesus, are children of the Father.

Matthew pays special attention to the community and its life (chapter 18). There are obvious problems within the community that we find reflected in this chapter and in some parables (e.g., 13:20-22) and in a special way in the warning in the parables of judgment (13:36-43; 47-50; 22:11-14 and 24:45—25:46). There were various forms of laxity and a lack of awareness of the responsibilities of discipleship. Aspects of his criticism of the religious attitudes and practices of Jewish leadership reflects also sinfulness of the community (e.g., 6:1-18—the three major works of piety ; 23:1-12 —leadership).

We shall not comment in detail on Jesus' actual teaching. This can be found in the commentary on the readings, which include so much of the special Matthean teaching material.

JUDAISM—PHARISEES AND SCRIBES

Any attentive reader will note how harshly Jesus speaks to and about the non-priestly religious leadership. The priestly leadership was finally responsible for his death and yet are not the focus of his prophetic critique. We just mention the major texts (6:1-18; 12: 22-45; 15:1-20; 16:1-4, 5-12; 19:3-9; 22:15-22, 34-40 and chapter 23). This group is an evil and adulterous generation (12:39-45; 16:4), the snakes, brood of vipers (3:7; 12:34; 23:33), the hypocrites (6:2, 5, 16; 15:7; 22:18; 23:13, 14, 15, 23, 25, 27, 29), fools (23:18— note that Jesus warned against using this term! [5:22]), and deceptive teachers and blind guides (16:5-12; 15:14; 23:16, 24).

Reading chapter 23 we are shocked at the vehemence of Jesus' criticism of these groups whom his contemporaries admired. At this point we have to stress that Matthew's gospel, like all the gospels, is deeply influenced by the situations of the community for which it was written. Matthew's community was struggling for its identity as well as against the persecutions and denials of the credentials of Jesus as the Christ by groups affected by Judaism of the post-destruction period. The Pharisees and Scribes were the architects and the leaders of post-Temple Judaism. They are severely condemned. The community also suffered persecution from these groups as we find reflected in some texts (e.g., 5:11-12; 21:35-36; 22:6; 23:34; 24:9-12).

MATTHEW'S CONTRIBUTION

We could describe this contribution in terms of authentic religion. The contrast figures are named Pharisees and scribes. However, they represent that human tendency to socialize and accommodate religion to the prevailing values in a culture and a human vision and standards. We as Christians do the same. The most startling scene in the gospel is the judgment scene (25:31-46). The consistent sensitivity to and service of the least as the expression of genuine love for God always shocks us. This text is addressed to Christians. The Pharisees are also criticized for similar reasons. They are concerned with tithes on the small herbs, cleansing cups, plates, and hands, and protecting the observance of the Sabbath. However, human need, justice, mercy, and faith and the rapacity and extortion within their hearts are overlooked (23:23-24, 25-26; 15:4-6; 12:1-14 [12:7, 11-12]). Exterior observance hides inner emptiness and hypocrisy (6:1-18; 15:1-9; 23:27-28). We forget and neglect the map of the heart and the desires and movements of the inner depths of our person (5:28: 6:21; 15:11, 18-20). We forget that the Father sees the heart. Our left hand is so conscious of what our right hand is doing! Jesus tears the mask off the "Lord, Lord" syndrome and looks to the heart that searches for God's will.

Social status and personal importance play such major roles in human lives. Not only the Jewish teachers are caught up in this snare but also the leaders of the Christian community (23:1-12 and 18:1-14; 20:24-27). Jesus stands among his community as the servant (8:17; 12:18-19, and 21:27).

The socially accepted norms for relationships with the neighbor are inadequate for the disciple of Jesus (5:46-47). Discrimination even on religious grounds is quite unacceptable (9:10-13). Prayer and the unwillingness to forgive are incompatible (6:14-15; cf. 5:23-24).

Wealth replaces real religious commitment in the lives of the "Pharisees and scribes" whom Matthew attacks (23:25). It also lessens the commitment and trust of his Christians (6:24, 25-33), prevents them from hearing Jesus' call (19:16-22), or smothers the seed of faith as it attempts to grow (13:22). True religion (seek first the kingdom of the Father) and anxiety and concern for wealth are in such deep tension.

YOUR KINGDOM COME, YOUR WILL BE DONE

Finally, overarching the whole gospel is the great story of the activity of God placing the stamp of his sovereignty onto human history. The kingdom of heaven is the symbol of this great story. Jesus of Nazareth as Christ and Son was and remains the servant of God who alone brings about his reign. His own personal prayer was "Your kingdom come." All his activity was an expression of his filial commitment to the Father and his way of sharing in this activity. His involvement will culminate when he returns as the Son of Man. The Father has given him universal authority. He created the community of faith to continue the proclamation of the kingdom of God. This community is not to be identified with the reign of God but is a servant of this reign.

The conflict with the power of evil, which came to expression in the machinations, blindness, hypocrisy, and evil of the leadership and the weakness of his people and infidelity of is disciples, continues today. The community of faith itself is affected. During Jesus' life people had to take a stance. They could either enter the kingdom or exclude themselves. To enter and remain within the realm of God's sovereignty is God's gift. However, the believers have the responsibility to hunger and thirst for righteousness, to become "little ones," to discern continuously the deeper orientations of their hearts, to serve those in need, to forgive, to exclude no one from their love, and, in short, to "obey all that Jesus has commanded" (28:20).

Jesus has spelled out the conditions for being within the sovereign embrace of the Father (5:2-10; 5:20; 6:33; 7:21; 13:23, 44-46; 18:3, 23, 35; 19:14; 23-34; 25:31-46). The tragedy to which Jesus returned so often in Matthew is the exclusion from the sovereignty of God and from life (7;19; 8:11-12; 12:32-37; 13:41-43; 21:31, 43; 24:51; 25:11-12.30, 41-46).

We leave Matthew's gospel with a task, empowered by the risen Lord who is with us. This is God's task, the task accepted by Jesus and handed on to us. We are to bring out of the Christian treasury "what is new and what is old" and to "go and make disciples of all nations." A major way to fulfill this responsibility of cooperating with the dynamic activity of God and his Son is to be salt and light to the world so that others "seeing our good works" may give glory to the Father. To give glory to the Father would be to enter under the sovereignty of God who is holy and faithful.

The Gospel of Matthew

The Overture	**The Christ Entrusted with Mission**	
Baptism of the Lord	The Option of God's Chosen One	Mt 3:13–17
Second Sunday	I am not... He is...	Jn 1:29–34
Third Sunday	Light in the Darkness	Mt 4:12–23
The Great Teacher	**His Vision of Human Life**	
Fourth Sunday	Glimpses of the Divine in the Human Face	Mt 5:1–12
Fifth Sunday	The Salt of Social Responsibility	Mt 5: 13–16
Sixth Sunday	Seek Him–Observe his Law–All Heart	Mt 5:17–37
Seventh Sunday	The Other and Our Journey to God	Mt 5:38–48
Eighth Sunday	It is Easy for the Birds of the Air	Mt 6:24–34
Ninth Sunday	Stock Taking	Mt 7:21–27
The Great Teacher	**Teaching by Example**	
Tenth Sunday	Not... but ... Attitude to Life	Mt 9:9–13
The Faith Community	**The Responsibilities it Must Share**	
Eleventh Sunday	The Layperson Gazes at Society	Mt 9:36—10:8
Twelfth Sunday	Prophetic Responsibility	Mt 10:26–33
Thirteenth Sunday	The Sword	Mt 10:37–42
The Great Teacher	**Mission a Failure?**	
Fourteenth Sunday	Jesus and Failure	Mt 11:25–30
Fifteenth Sunday	Fruitful Seed–Good Soil	Mt 13:1–23
Sixteenth Sunday	Judgment and Hope	Mt 13:24–43
Seventeenth Sunday	The Heart's Treasure	Mt 13:44–52
Who Do People Say I Am?	**Preparing for the Answer**	
Eighteenth Sunday	Jesus, The Compassion of God	Mt 14: 13–21
Nineteenth Sunday	An Epiphany. It is I... If it is You...	Mt 14: 22–33
Twentieth Sunday	Open Communities of Faith	Mt 15:21–28
Messiah Who Is Crucified	**Peter and Jesus**	
Twenty-First Sunday	To Love the Church	Mt 16:13–20
Twenty-Second Sunday	The Spirituality of Jesus	Mt 16:21–27
The Great Teacher Again	**Life in the Community of Faith**	
Twenty-Third Sunday	Ecclesial Responsibility	Mt 18:15–20
Twenty-Fourth Sunday	Seventy Times Seven	Mt 18: 21–35
Twenty-Fifth Sunday	The Last have a Story to Tell	Mt 20: 1–16
The Messiah in the Temple	**Authority, Conflict and Rejection**	
Twenty-Sixth Sunday	Unmoved	Mt 21:28–32

Twenty-Seventh Sunday	A Window onto another World	Mt 21:33–43
Twenty-Eighth Sunday	Three Weddings and Two Funerals	Mt 22:1–14
Twenty-Ninth Sunday	Streetwise	Mt 22:15–21
Thirtieth Sunday	First Links in the Chain	Mt 22:34–40
Thirty-First Sunday	The Ecclesial Community and Ministry	Mt 23:1–12

The Coming of the Son of Man — Be Ready. How to be Ready?

Thirty-Second Sunday	The Closed Door	Mt 25:1–12
Thirty-Third Sunday	Winners and Losers	Mt 25:14–30
Christ the King	The Poor You Will Always Have with You	Mt 25:31–46

THE BAPTISM OF JESUS: Mt 3:13–17

The Option of God's Chosen One

The catechesis for this liturgical year comes from the interpretation of Jesus Christ and his ministry by Matthew's church. We begin this Sunday. The focus of our attention is upon God and Jesus at the threshold of his ministry.

The reading of Is 42:1–4, 6–7 reminds us that all genuine interpretations of Jesus must place him within God's great purposes for human history. It also creates a rich background for Jesus' ministry. Isaiah indicates to us that the initiative exclusively belongs to God. He chooses, enables, and gifts the servant. He determines the purpose of his ministry. This purpose concerns the quality of human life and its transformation. He describes the qualities of the ministry of the servant. In his commitment to God's work he will be compassionate, courageous, persevering, and faithful. Isaiah 42:1–4 will be quoted by Matthew later as he reflects upon Jesus' qualities in his ministry at a time of crisis (Mt 12:18–21).

The psalm (28/29) celebrates God who sent Jesus and Jesus the Lord sent by God.

We turn to the gospel. The Christian interpretation of John's prophetic ministry, urgently calling for repentance and issuing harsh warnings at the turning point of God's involvement in our history (3:1–6), forms the immediate background to Jesus' ministry.

Jesus' baptism by John is not the focus of attention. What happens before the baptism and after it are important. Though each gospel in its own way underlines the fact that John and his ministry are subordinate to Jesus, Matthew carefully explains the reason why Jesus was baptized by John. This was a problem in at least some of the early communities. The narrator draws our attention to Jesus' saying. He accepts this baptism because this is God's will and plan. In this way, Matthew has told us from the beginning that all of Jesus' ministry will be his response to God's will (all righteousness). We turn to the event after the baptism. The religious experience, which is described with rich symbolism, informs the reader (community) that Jesus and his ministry are at the very center and culmination of God's plan, his past saving actions and promises.

The opening of the sky-dome indicates an extraordinary moment in God's continuous action in our history. Jesus sees the Spirit given to him by God for his ministry. We as readers hear God who affirms that Jesus is the person to whom he has entrusted a unique responsibility. No longer does God act through the friend of God (Abraham), the one to whom he spoke face to face (Moses), the chosen king (David), or the special divine spokespersons (prophets) but through the final and greatest mediator (the Son, the beloved). The gospel of Matthew is not concerned with Christian baptism or with the Trinity. The gospel draws out attention to the need of the salvation of the human family, to God's commitment and purpose, and especially to Jesus of Nazareth, his ministry and response to God.

The writer of Acts in the short extract from the opening of Peter's address to the devout Roman official Cornelius guides us in our understanding of this passage common to each gospel (Acts 10: 34–38). Notice how he underlines: (a) God's choice of Jesus for ministry; (b) God's gift of the enabling Spirit; (c) God's continuous presence in that ministry; and (d) the essential quality of Jesus' mission "to do good" and come to grips with the power of evil by healing those destroyed by evil.

The purposes of today's liturgy are the following: to remind us of the enormous background to Jesus' ministry, namely, God's historical commitment; Jesus' essential mission ("Good News of Peace" [Acts 10:36]) and his fundamental disposition of availability to his Father.

SECOND SUNDAY OF ORDINARY TIME: YEAR A Jn 1:29–34

I Am Not…He Is

In the liturgy, the church puts a bridle upon us and again draws our attention to Jesus and his mission, interpreted this week within the tradition attributed to John. Another sketch of the mission of God's Servant taken from Isaiah (49:5–6) creates a preparatory background. The prophet reminds us that all mission originates in and is defined by God. The unknown Servant's mission reaches beyond religio-ethnic boundaries to embrace all the human family—"light to the nations" and "ends of the earth."

When we read John's gospel we must be clearly conscious how the faith that arose from the experience of the risen Jesus is read back and permeates the account of his Palestinian ministry.

Our text (John 1:29–34) is the second part of the Christian account of the Baptist's witness to Jesus. Initially the leadership had questioned him on whether he was the Christ, Elijah, or the expected prophet. Each question met with a denial. He identified himself with a preparatory voice whose baptism is also preparatory (1:19–38). A far greater emissary of God is to come.

The next day John saw Jesus. We have a series of testamentary statements about Jesus and his mission. In the midst is the disclaimer we met last week. John again clearly states that he and his mission are subordinate (1:30–31[cf.1: 6–8, 15;1:19–28; 3:25–30]).

There is no real progress in the quality of the testimonies, just an accumulation of tradition and reflections. We can list the three major statements: "Here is the Lamb of God who takes away the sin of the World"; "He … is the one who baptizes with the Holy Spirit"; and "…this is the Son of God." The text implies in various ways that John's testimonies have God's own sanction.

We begin with the final statement. In the gospel the basic significance of Jesus being Son of God is that he is able in a unique and authentic way to reveal the Father (Jn 1:18) by speaking the Word of God and doing the Work of God. In this manner, he is the source of eternal life. He is the Lamb of God (a phrase whose precise reference and meaning remain a puzzle) because through him God takes away the fundamental brokenness and evil that afflicts and destroys the world. (We note the use of the singular "sin.") To baptize with the Holy Spirit signifies that Jesus is the source of radical transformation, permanent renewal, and ceaseless life (Jn 3:3–8; 4:7–15; 7:37–39; 20:22).

I judge that in liturgical catechesis we need to nourish a deep sense of pride in Jesus Christ and what he brings to human life. We need to develop a sense of the immense gift God has given us, a sense of profound wonder and joy. We must emphasize that Jesus Christ is one who shared our history. We need to seek words and images that respond to the search and yearnings of contemporary believers.

We add a brief comment on 1 Cor 1:1–3. We have a series of valuable descriptions of the faith community, namely the church. This community is God the Father's creation (sanctified/called) by means of bonds to Jesus Christ. The community is also described as consisting of "all" who in every place call on the name of our Lord Jesus Christ—namely all who acknowledge Jesus Christ as their Lord. Here we find the basis for profound respect for all Christian denominations. There is a further description. The community of faith consists of all "whom God has called" into the fellowship of his Son, Jesus Christ Our Lord (1:9).

THIRD SUNDAY OF ORDINARY TIME: YEAR A Mt 4:12–23

Light in Darkness

Leaving John's gospel we return to Matthew and in a way stand still. The focus of our liturgy is again the nature and dimension of Jesus' ministry. We can broaden our reflections to include the mission today of the community of faith.

The Isaian reading (Is 8:23—9:3) has been chosen to indicate the origin of the text quoted in Matthew 4:15-16, not because of its historical meaning. However, it expresses the common Old Testament theme of God's promise and commitment to relieve oppressed people and to ensure change and hope. This aspect is meaningful as Jesus' ministry is a special expression of this commitment. Much of the northern Kingdom of Israel (Zebulun, Naphtali, the Way of the Sea, land beyond the Jordan, "Galilee of the Gentiles"[=dominated by Gentiles]) was subjugated by the Assyrians (modern Iraq) in 732 B.C.E. and divided into three provinces. The prophet promises that God will free these areas through an ideal king (Is 9:6-7), and the people will experience prosperity, joy, and peace.

The responsorial psalm (Ps 26/27) is a lively prayer of hope. The response taken from the psalm echoes the major theme of the liturgy: "The Lord is my light and my salvation."

A major section of our gospel reading is Matthew's insightful faith grasp of the deeper significance of Jesus' responsibilities and therefore the task of faith communities today. Our lectionary omits the important and highly symbolic presentation of Jesus' uncompromising response to his mission (4:1-11—a lenten reading). In the face of proposed sinful compromises in his life, he states and restates in three different ways that the only criteria for all his decisions will be fidelity to God, the Father. The theme of "to fulfill all righteousness" (3:15) is restated in a forceful way.

Matthew tells us that with John's arrest Jesus returns to Galilee and leaves his home (Nazareth, cf. 2:19-23) and settles in a new town. For Matthew this change of permanent residence (recall Abraham's setting in a new land) symbolizes a radical shift in Jesus' career and self-understanding. Matthew highlights events in Jesus' life, and they become occasions of deeper faith reflection on his person and mission by means of a rereading of texts from the Old Testament. Scholars refer to these as Formula Quotations (see 1:23; 2:15, 17-18, 23; 4:14-16; 8:17, 12:17-21).

Matthew has underlined two themes. First Jesus comes as a re-creative presence and power within a desperate, broken, and lost world. This is symbolized by the light that dispels darkness, which itself is a symbol of the most extreme form of dehumanized existence, namely death. "To sit" signifies to live in such a situation. The second point is related to his inclusion of the phrase "Galilee of the Gentiles." The darkness is universal beyond any ethnocultural boundaries, and Jesus' mission is to embrace all.

With this as background, Matthew summarizes what Jesus brings to his world and our world. "The Kingdom of heaven" (=God—a peculiar Judeo-Christian phrase common in Matthew) signifies that special presence and purpose of God embodied in the gift of Jesus Christ that opens up such new potentials, hopes, and changes for our human family. People are challenged to recognize, acknowledge, welcome, and accept both the fractured nature of their human life and human society and God's gift (=repent).

We pause here. Pastors with their communities need to assess their own faith community and the larger world to see what are the types of darkness that are damaging human and faith life. Can Jesus Christ dispel that darkness? What does he call believers empowered by him to do to come to grips with the "darkness"?

Our gospel shows us that believers are to share Jesus' tasks, as the concise, paradigmatic, and stylized narrative of the call of the pairs of brothers indicates (4:18-22). The narrative usually is interpreted in the sense of the vocations of ordained ministry or consecrated life. However, the leaving of nets, boats, and father can symbolize a conscious commitment to a quality and intensity to Christian life and witness within the normal circumstances and obligations of human life.

We note that 4:23—a summary of Jesus' ministry and repeated nearly word for word in 9:35—forms with 9:35 a major compositional frame for Matthew's principal presentation of Jesus' ministry in word and action.

The Corinthian problem (1 Cor 1:10-13, 17) is a particular form of divisive factionalism. The religiocultural background concerns the type of importance given to personalities and to their ability to speak in public—the style, language, and the way to organize arguments and to persuade. Paul is not concerned with building a following. Eloquence can be an obstacle to the proclamation of the gospel, especially the scandal of Jesus crucified. The Christian community, Christian ministry, Christian institutions, and Christian programs must ask themselves the question: Are we emptying the cross of Christ of its power? Good human values can be subversive of the gospel.

THE FOURTH SUNDAY OF ORDINARY TIME: YEAR A Mt 5:1–12

Glimpses of the Divine in the Human Face

We can misunderstand the gospel text. The list of qualities can easily be judged to picture emaciated human persons, men and women who are just shadows of greatness, men and women who repel rather than attract as they mirror the negative, the defeated, the losers in life's struggles or just do-gooders.

What I suggest is that we rummage in our memories, recall TV interviews and stories from life, recall ordinary men and women, check through lists of great figures of our history…and find women and men, young or old, great or unknown people who have enabled us to glimpse authentic examples of these qualities of which Jesus speaks.

A word of caution. We will be able to choose people who are poor in spirit, merciful, peacemakers—probably not the Nobel Peace Prize winners. And normally there would also be a shadow on their lives as normally people do not embody the full richness of any of these qualities. The qualities have a rich potential beyond any one example since these qualities open up the horizons of the human potential and reflect the divine in whose image we are created. These qualities describe Jesus of Nazareth who alone had no shadow falling across his person though many only saw dark shadows and so destroyed him.

We can all recall stories of men and women who are "poor in spirit," "meek," hungering and thirsting for a better society. The Nelson Mandelas, the Mother Teresas, the Archbishop Romeros, some among AIDS patients, refugees, workers in refugee camps, judges, doctors, police personnel, adolescents, teachers, sports persons, single parents, prisoners, an old lady in a nursing home, nurses, an abused migrant, a taxi driver, our mother or father. They enable us to see these qualities lived out among us in various degrees of intensity. Such men and women humanize our lives, reflect the mystery of God, reassure us, and guide us.

The qualities are interrelated. They are different expressions in life of the openness of the human person to transcendence in the midst of the ugly and beautiful, the generous and mean, openness of mind and narrow prejudice, and good and evil.

Some of the descriptions of the qualities are probably too biblical for us to understand correctly. The "meek" are those who have the strength not to be arrogant. The poor in Spirit are so rooted in human richness and open to transcendence that they do not need to be arrogant, proud, aggressive, and self-assertive. They can be vulnerable. Those who mourn have allowed sacred anger before evil to find expression in deep sensitivity and concern for the suffering world. The motives of the pure in heart become ever more transparent, truthful, and focused, shedding manipulation, hidden selfishness, and doublespeak. Those who hunger and thirst for justice amaze us by their consistent and persistent dedication to authentic human values, human structures in society, and the human dignity of any type of person. All these attempts to describe these qualities are helpful and yet deficient. They describe the potentialities of the human as we grow into the image and likeness of God. Those who are merciful or peacemakers in Jesus' sense are prophets within contemporary society. These qualities are related to the newness made possible by Jesus' death and resurrection and the creativity of the Holy Spirit.

The beatitudes are not commandments. We must not moralize them. Jesus sketches a vision of authentic human life made possible by the re-creative power of God. He draws also a self-portrait. This vision has to compete with other sets of beatitudes that appear to enhance the human yet are deceptive. There are very appealing and deceptive cultures of death propagated in our culture.

A few "scholarly" remarks. The Sermon on the Mount (chapters 5–7) begins with the description of its setting (4:23–25) and the classical opening of authoritative teaching, echoing Moses on Sinai. The first eight sayings follow a fairly set pattern:

Blessed are;

the category; and

the promised future reward.

The rewards are variations of the same idea adapted to be appropriate to the category. In the last beatitude we have both variations in the pattern and the clear influences of the painful experiences of the community. Note how the believers are expected to be prophetic in their way of life.

The reading from Zephaniah (2:3; 3:12-13) introduces us to types of believers who are praised by prophets and psalmists. The "humble of the land" are the humble and lowly people who seek God with fidelity. They are contrasted with arrogant, proud, deceitful, and lying leaders (3:3-4).

Paul would surely not have found "beatitude" Christians among the faction-ridden community in Corinth. Self-sufficiency, self-assertion, worldly competitiveness, and boosting were destroying the community. The reflection on the cross, on Christ/Christ crucified as a scandalous and unintelligible expression of the wisdom and power of God, has been omitted (1 Cor 1:18-25).

The conclusion of that reflection needs to be quoted to understand how Paul illustrates his main point by recalling the origins of those God has chosen as Christians in Corinth. Paul concludes: "For God's foolishness is wiser than human wisdom and God's weakness is stranger than human strength" (1:25). Not only is Christ crucified an expression of the thoroughly disconcerting wisdom and power of God but also God's choice of "nobodies" to be his chosen ones in Corinth (1 Cor 1:26-31). In that church there was a small group of middle class Christians and very few, if any, upper middle class. The majority was daily wage earners or slaves. This fact rules out boasting. In addition, "who they are before God" is God's gift given through Christ. The small selection is a sobering reminder to Christians in faith communities who allow social status, wealth, and education, etc., to inflate egos.

FIFTH SUNDAY OF ORDINARY TIME: YEAR A Mt 5:13-16

The Salt of Social Responsibility

Our liturgical catechesis opens with a sharp critique tinged with sarcasm (Is 58:7-10). The anonymous prophet subjects ritual duties to a close and critical examination. The example of public worship is the public fast that was supposed to be an expression of devoted commitment to God and a manner of intercession for his blessing, help, and guidance. The prophet strips away the appearances of godliness and devotion —the fast is accompanied by social injustice, selfishness, quarreling…(Is 58:3-4). Our reading describes authentic religion and the essential conditions that must accompany genuine religious observances and worship. We could put attendance at Mass, charismatic prayer meetings, special days of prayer in the place of the fast. What is the quality of social responsibility of observant Christians? The psalm (Ps 12:4-9) praises and gives assurance of God's blessing to all who live with a keen sense of social responsibility.

We may be surprised with this choice of a reading to form the background to our gospel (Mt 5:13-16). The beatitudes do not immediately conjure up social responsibilities and ways of acting that are so concrete, practical, and demanding—"share bread with the hungry, bring the homeless poor into your home, not hide yourself from your own kin.…" Note these are examples. There are many more possibilities. Jesus uses two images, that of salt and light with secondary images of a city on a hill and a lamp. He also uses a complementary pair of words, namely earth and world. These indicate the endless horizon of human life that disciples need to influence effectively. No milieu is outside of God's purpose and concern.

Salt is like the many preservatives that are used in foods. In that period, it would have been the major preservative. Were it to lose its basic quality then nothing could be done but dump it as useless. The disciples gifted with the qualities described in the beatitudes are to be transforming influences within the world. Otherwise, they are useless, dead branches on a fruit tree.

As we do not build a city on a hill or light a lamp to hide it, so the gift of discipleship is a responsibility. The disciples are to live as disciples of Jesus within the day-to-day circumstance and responsibilities of life. The "good works" to which Jesus refers would be all the ways of living, celebrating, thinking, speaking, acting, and deciding that embody the qualities of the beatitudes. Our liturgy underlines the social responsibilities and sensibilities of discipleship.

The purpose is that others witnessing this manner of life "will give glory to your Father in heaven." A transformation of others is implied when they acknowledge the values, the vision of human life, and the obligation to live according to such values.

There is an important mention of "your Father." At significant places Matthew's Jesus draws on the fact that the disciples, when acting in conformity with his teaching, are revealing God as Father and acting as his true images.

Our liturgy is an occasion to develop the different dimension of the ministry of laypersons who, immersed within the flow of life in its diversity and complexity, are to be salt and light. The genuine celebration of the Eucharist is inseparable from this ministry.

Lay ministry is at a low ebb in Corinth where too many are influenced by deceptive cultural values and attitudes that value human pretensions. Paul uses their experience of his initial ministry, which had been very productive, establishing the faith community, to illustrate his insistence on the scandal of God's wisdom and power (1 Cor 2:1-5). Paul had been dogged by opponents in northern Greece and humiliated in Athens before arriving in Corinth (Acts 16-17). In a simple and plain way, he placed before them the message of the crucified. God's Spirit and power drew men and women to believe. Are there lessons here for pastoral ministry that may tend to rely too much on technology?

SIXTH SUNDAY OF ORDINARY TIME: YEAR A Mt 5:17-37

Seek Him, Observe his Law with the Whole Heart

What would be valuable in the celebration of our liturgy would be the creation of an attitude toward obedience and God's will. The celebration of the gift of the Torah by the psalmist could provide some guidelines (Ps 118/119). This is the longest psalm, repetitive, and yet rich in its joyfulness, its appreciation of genuine obedience, humble in its awareness of human waywardness. It is urgent in its sense of human need to be guided, enlightened, enabled, and grateful for God's revelation of his will. The few verses chosen as the responsorial express some of these attitudes.

The instructions given by Ben Sirach may not help so much (Sir 15:15-20). The teacher makes some uncomplicated reflections on human moral freedom excluding a type of intimate tendency to evil and affirming moral responsibility. We need to qualify the simple affirmation, "If you choose, you can keep the commandments, and to act faithfully is a matter of your own choice"(15:15). Years of experience forced biblical writers to acknowledge the need of deep inner healing (new heart, spirit, metanoia). Today, psychology (social, cultural, and personal) makes us aware of the many ways human freedom may be diminished and the healing that is required.

The gospel is a long text (Mt 5:17-37) and needs to be subdivided. The first section (5:17-20) acts as an introduction to a major section of the instruction (5:21-48). The author's Jesus makes a type of apologia. He absolves himself of any accusation of not being fully committed to the revelation of God (Torah and prophets). He lays emphasis on his attitude to the Law as the expression of God's will. Dismissing any intention to abolish he insists that he is intent that God's purpose is fully realized. His interpretations of the Law draw out their full intent.

He is also committed to wholehearted and careful obedience on the part of his disciples and the leaders of the community entrusted with the role of teachers. Meticulous obedience is a hallmark of the true members of God's People and the children of the Father (5:16, 48). This point is made by means of an exaggerated comparison. The disciples' obedience to God's will (righteousness) must have traits that the contemporary leadership of the Jewish people, the scribes and Pharisees of Matthew's time, lacked. We grasp the meaning of this cautionary statement from a series of texts. We can read quietly the polemical denunciation in chapter 23 and observe Jesus' insistence on interiority.

We need also to attend to the great commandment:

• the place of the Sabbath (12:1-14);

- the laws of purity and association (9:10-13; 15:10-20);
- his critique of their ways of interpreting the Law (15:1-9; 19:3-9); and
- the lack of transparent sincerity in life (12:22-24; 16:6; 22:15-22; 34-40).

With this background, Jesus takes up important aspects of interpersonal relationships:

- anger—insults—mockery (5:21-22);
- male lust (5:27-28);
- men and divorce (5:21-32); and
- honesty (5:33-37).

The problems associated with retaliation, aggression, and love for the enemy are reserved for next Sunday.

Looking at these small pieces we note that a major interpretation of an aspect of the law attracts to it a number of other sayings more or less associated with the theme. The sayings in 5:23-24 and 5:25-26 are linked together and to 5:22-23. The idea of looking at a woman lustfully has attracted the linked sayings about the right eye and hand (5:29-30; cf. Mt 19:8-9 a second use). Matthew repeats the teaching on divorce at more length (19:3-9).

Jesus forces us to look at a whole range of ways we can seriously injure others. Murder is physical and obvious. He points to slander, calumny, and detraction, nasty gossiping, putting people down, spreading rumors, spiteful innuendoes, and the more basic cynical, critical, and quietly arrogant attitude we can harbor inside. Henri Nouwen wrote of an inner disposition of welcome in contrast to hostility.

In a type of turnabout we are asked to look at the hurt feelings and hurts others have against us. Jesus has taken hold of the many expressions of hostility and in imaginative ways insisted upon reconciliation. Reconciliation is more important than worship and remains an urgent obligation in the face of final judgment (5:26).

Jesus' teaching about sexual relationships concerns men. However, the patriarchal structure of society conditions so much of his teaching. Lustful hearts belong to all of us. Again with an example, he radicalizes God's teaching about sexual relationships. The present pope reflected on rape in marriage. Using examples, in each section Jesus leads us to the root of a major aspect of God's will for interpersonal living. The images of gouged eyes (right = best) and amputated hands are to underline the imperative of seeking God's will from deep within our being.

Taking oaths, invoking God's name or what is associated with God and serves as substitutes for God's name, were commonplace in the culture. To ensure truth in specific instances modern society insists on statements/witness given under oath. In abolishing all oaths, Jesus demands honest communication. He banishes the distinction between communication that must be true, and false or partially true communication. There is a radical demand for honesty. He does not explain how to do this.

There is adequate matter here for Christian reflection on the radical nature of God's will in our relationship to each other and from group to group.

The reading from Paul is hard to make head or tail of because we have a few verses (1 Cor 2:6-10) from the middle of a complex reflection (1 Cor 2:6-16).

SEVENTH SUNDAY OF ORDINARY TIME: YEAR A Mt 5:38-48

The Other and Our Journey to God

We reflect more on our reading from Leviticus (19:1-2, 17-18), not only to appreciate the grandeur of the Jewish vision of human society, but also to be aware of a formative influence on Jesus of Nazareth. We draw attention to the moral sensitivity about obligations to one another.

The foundation for moral behavior is God himself. He has made Israel (the human family) his own family by means of:

- the primary gift of creating us in his image and likeness;
- by the liberating and creative action of the Exodus; and
- by the Covenant of election.

Therefore, the author states: "you shall be holy, for I the Lord your God am Holy." They are called to a life of godliness. In their life's journey, they are to approximate increasingly the very image of God.

We list some of the ethical commands that are not included in the reading and which concern others. These include:

- to purposefully leave grain and grapes at harvest for the poor and alien to glean (19:9–10);
- not to rob, deal falsely, and lie to one another;
- not to swear falsely, defraud, and keep back daily wages;
- revile the deaf, or
- mistreat the blind.

The law-giver mentions also:

- not to give unjust judgments;
- be partial to the poor or defer to the great in court cases;
- not to slander others,
- not look the other way when a neighbor is in danger;
- not to hate in your heart your kin; or
- take vengeance and keep a grudge (19:11–18).

Further on, God instructs his people about their behavior to resident aliens: you shall not oppress them; the alien shall be as a citizen (equal); and finally you shall love the alien as yourself (19:33–34).

The recurring authoritative and motivational phrase is "I am the Lord your God," which, with the few references to redemption from Egypt, reminded them that ethical behavior was rooted in the Covenant relationship.

The psalm (102/103) celebrates the wonderful reality of God's steadfast love and mercy in the face of our sinfulness. The psalmist looks at the forgiving love of God from various angles and by mean of various images. We pray: "He does not deal with us according to our sins, nor repay us according to our iniquities." In this prayer, we are binding ourselves to match his forgiving love in our dealings with the other who offends or acts as enemy to us. The psalm looks ahead to the gospel's teaching about love of the enemies rather than back to the ethical teaching of Leviticus about love of neighbor.

These readings create a background for aspects of the gospel. In the first group of sayings (5:38–42) the Jewish legal principle was a wise juridical maxim that allowed proportionate retaliation and curbed a disastrous spiral of vindictiveness. Jesus also wants to curb the spiral of vindictiveness and vengeance. His teaching looks simple and seems utterly impractical. He says simply "Do not resist an evildoer." The examples concern personal offenses or injustices. The final example, dealing with begging and borrowing, is of a different nature. If a person gave their cloak (outer garment) when sued for their coat (inner garment) they would be left naked. Maybe we receive some guidance to the meaning of Jesus' teaching from a person like Nelson Mandela and the Truth Commission. We see the disaster caused by the spiral of violence, hatred, bitterness, injustice in the Apartheid era, in Northern Ireland, Palestine, and Yugoslavia. We know that slander and calumny also can result in a spiral of vindictiveness. We know that resistance to violence and injustice are imperative in some circumstances. We must confront the wisdom of Jesus, an attitude of nonviolence that is prophetic and re-creative, rising out of inner strength, forgiveness, and extraordinary trust in God. Do we only understand when we have followed this path?

We look at the second collection of sayings (5:43–48). The reading from Leviticus warns us against thinking that Jesus' religious tradition taught hatred of the enemy. However, the curse tradition in the psalms and verses similar to the following could influence the popular religious mentality and behavior: "Do I not hate those who hate you, O Lord? and do I not loathe those who rise up against you? I hate them with perfect hatred; I count them my enemies" (Ps 139:21–22). Together, our cultures, and we ourselves, create boundaries, some very rigid, that determine trust, acceptance, mixing, and forgiveness.

To love our enemies is parallel to praying for persecutors—even a person's godless attitude or actions are no excuse to exclude wanting only good for the person. The motivation echoes the norm in Jesus' Jewish tradition. To love enemies is to be like the good Father and to be genuine children. Tax collectors and Gentiles in Matthew's gospel are the ungodly par excellence. So much more is expected of Jesus' disciples since he broke down all barriers between humans and lived a love that was committed to the good of all.

We return in the final verse to the "Be you Holy as I

the Lord your God am Holy." In the Sermon on the Mount Jesus drew out the implications of our being sons and daughters of his Father. Our key prayer is "Our Father...." We address our God as Father so often in our Eucharist. The crowning and culminating prayer of our Eucharist is "through him (Jesus Christ), with him and in him in the unity of the Holy Spirit all glory and honor is yours, almighty Father, for ever and ever." To love, which also embraces any type of enemy, is fully true to this prayer.

Paul's religious tradition based moral behavior on God's holiness. After discussing the major problem of some members, namely their attitudes to the ministry of Paul and Apollos—a very fine speaker (1 Cor 3:1–15), Paul returns to their pretensions, quarrelsomeness, and pride (1 Cor 3:16–23). He motivates appropriate Christian community life with the rich images of the community as the Temple of God in which the Holy Spirit dwells. He also wants them to have a mentality that recognizes and acknowledges the gifts given by God. The greatest is their union with Christ and through Christ with God.

We have here a solid basis for building community and breaking down the barriers that education, wealth, status, caste, and ethnic attitudes can erect and prevent community coming into existence.

EIGHTH SUNDAY OF ORDINARY TIME: YEAR A Mt 6:24–34

It Is Easy for the Birds of the Field

There is one of Jesus' pithy sayings not included in our gospel but part of the small thematic collection to which 6:24 belongs. The saying is: "For where your treasure is, there your heart will be also." There are three contrasting pairs. Jesus speaks of treasure that is passing, corruptible, and in danger and one that is permanent and secure. He contrasts the healthy and unhealthy eye and light/darkness. Finally he draws attention to the master who is despised and hated and the one who is loved and to whom servants are devoted. God and wealth are the masters from whom we must choose. There is inherent in these sayings a question to the faith community. Its message, the way it lives, the quality of its worship, the characteristics of its ministry, its witness to God and the God to whom it witnesses, the gospel it proclaims, the human values it affirms, promotes, and guards: are all these of such a quality that young and old find genuine treasure for the heart? The treasure or "the master" needs to be appealing and challenging, subverting the deceptive treasures or false "masters," enriching and enabling the human person, human life, and society. The faith community witnesses to Jesus Christ and his gospel in such a way that believers and others meet a "master" or find a treasure whom they can love and to whom they want to be devoted. There is plenty of competition in the market of life to fire and capture the human heart.

The main theme of the liturgical readings stretches human credibility and asks us to cross the bridge to a vibrant and concrete life of faith and trust. Isaiah verbalizes the apparently reasonable and bitter complaint of God's distraught people whose sacred city is in ruins and the majority of whom have been taken into exile (Is 49:14–15). Obviously God has forgotten and forsaken the city that symbolized his protective fidelity and power. The reassurance and demand for trust is graphically expressed in terms of the impossibility of a mother forsaking her unweaned baby. The prophet gives the same assurance by means of the image of God on whose hand the picture of Jerusalem is tattooed (49:16).

The psalmist (Ps 61/62) is most emphatic in his protestations of utter trust in God. The images of an enormous hard rock, a fortress, and a secure refuge symbolize his reliability. Isaiah would want Israel to share the psalmist's prayer: "For God alone my soul waits in silence, for my hope is from him."

The dearth of basic necessities, namely food, drink, and clothing is not a normal preoccupation of most Americans. There is too much choice. I write this, however, in Southern Ethiopia. Here women may have to walk an hour to get water. After heavy rain I saw women with mugs filling 5 litre plastic containers with water lying or flowing by the road!

The church today in the Ethiopian parish was packed at both Masses, three to four thousand people. The tattered, hand-me-down, patched clothes of the barefooted children were a sign that parents here ask the question: "What will we wear?" This is a relatively prosperous area of small farmers.

However, food, drink, and clothes signify basic everyday, pervasive human preoccupations. When we are going to work each day on the bus or train or driving, what preoccupies us? When we wake, are showering, and having breakfast what planning are we doing? In the night as we go to sleep what runs through our mind?

Jesus would ask whether God, his will, and the type of family, human society, socioeconomic structure, cultural values, provisions for the needy have any place in our daily preoccupations, concerns, and efforts. Jesus goes further. He shows the concerns of God expressed in the parallel phrases of the only prayer Jesus taught: "your name be holy, your kingdom come and your will be done," are to be the primary orientation of our lives. When Jesus uses the term "first" in the command, "seek first for the Kingdom of God and his righteousness" (his will), he means that this orientation is to pervade and determine all other concerns. This orientation is not the first in a series but is unique.

The examples of God's care for the birds and beautiful but transient wildflowers may not convince. They are evocative images. Basic is Jesus' faith statement: "Your heavenly Father knows what you need...." He also underlines the radical difference he expects in a disciple who believes in the living God and the "Gentile." Later in the gospel Jesus will learn to his surprise that some Gentiles are the models of faith: "Truly I tell you in no one in Israel have I found such faith" (8:10; cf.15:28).

A phrase occurs here for the first time that characterizes the experience of Matthew's Jesus of his disciples, "you of little faith"(6:30; 8:26; 14:31; 16:8; 17:20; cf. 28:17). In today's gospel Jesus does ask for vibrant faith. He asks his disciples to grow to live the prayer they pray to the Father.

We conclude our reading of Corinthians today. Last Sunday we saw that a major cause of friction and immaturity in the community was the way they evaluated, esteemed, and compared their leaders (1:3–4:21). Paul had taken up this problem (3:5–15). He returns to it (4:1–5). Leadership in the community is equated with service and fidelity to the role assigned by God (3:5–6; 4:1–2). He instructs his community to put an end to their propensity to compare, judge, and condemn.

NINTH SUNDAY OF ORDINARY TIME: YEAR A Mt 7:21–27

Taking Stock

Matthew's extensive survey of the major characteristics of the life of disciples is drawing to a close. There is a characteristic conclusion in 7:28. Jesus has pushed the boundaries of the ethical potential of human life. We have listened to the greater teacher, and may be fascinated, puzzled, or frightened by the path of life he has placed before us. He has some final words of warning.

As a background, selective instructions (Dt 11:18, 26–28, 32) from one of Moses' concluding exhortations (Dt 11:18—12:1) have been chosen from the long repetitive exhortation (chapters 6-11). They must write his words in the depths of their being so that they guide their life. Their future will depend above all on obedience to the great command of single-minded and exclusive devotion to God and the other directions God gave them about their manner of religious, socioeconomic, and political life as his people.

The psalmist (Ps 30/31), expressing deep trust in God's power and mercy, prays for his saving assistance. Not a very apt psalm.

In the gospel (Mt 7:21–27) Jesus contrasts two groups of people. We can describe them as the "Lord, Lord" group and the "do the Will of my Father" group.

He develops his description of the first group. These people have been apparently devoted disciples. In Jesus' name they have spoken prophetic words, exorcised, and healed. However, they have not done the will of the Father. Therefore Jesus calls them "evil doers" [lawless ones]. Jesus' sarcasm reminds us of Paul's description of deceptive disciples who speak in tongues, prophesy, have great spiritual understanding and insight, and yet lack love (1 Cor 13:1–3). We must not approach these contrasts of either Jesus or Paul with logic. They are rhetorical. Nothing can substitute for the basic orientation and search to do God's will or live in love. In 25:31–46 Matthew will spell out love's concrete deeds and the Father's will. Is there here a warning especially for those in ordained or non-ordained ministry and who are close to the institutional church, in special prayer groups, attached to Catholic institutions? Jesus returns to the two groups with his brief illustrative stories contrasting the hearers/doers and the hearers/non-doers and rock and sandcastles.

Throughout this collection of teaching Jesus has not dealt with church laws and regulations. His basis is the dignity of the disciples as daughters or sons of God. He has been concerned with basic orientations in life covering various spheres of relationships to others, basic attitudes and values, and our relationship with God. He has drawn out the implications of our being created in God's image and our union with himself as the risen Lord and eldest Brother. He has pushed the potentialities of the human person in the sphere of ethical living and opened a never-ending horizon where the measure is God the Father. In our gospel Jesus has stressed the disciples' responsibilities and highlighted genuine discipleship. To live as disciples we need to be nourished by Jesus Christ in the Eucharist and humbly to journey with repentant, trustful, and joyful hearts.

We begin reading Romans this Sunday. Because of the peculiar arrangement of the lectionary we begin toward the end of an extended reflection that began in Romans 1:18 (1:16-17) and ends at 4:25. Christian theologians often return to our text (Rom 3:21-31). We read only selective verses. Paul has argued that left all to themselves and with the help of their religious systems and beliefs, the whole human race is under the power of sin and lacks the glory of God (3:9, 23). This applies also to Judaism. However, as God had promised through the prophets, his fidelity and transforming power have become effective for all in and through Jesus' atoning death. He underlines heavily that God's initiative rises from his utter graciousness and that our transformation is his gift alone. For our part, we must surrender all our pretensions, and our "goodness" and efforts, and receive the gracious gift of God as pure gift. Paul calls this response to God's initiative faith. He also emphasizes the universality both of God's gift and faith's importance. He uses various terms from different symbolic worlds to describe what God has done in and through the Jesus event. Here sacrificial terms are used. Though the terminology is foreign to many contemporary Christians yet the fundamental graciousness of God, the gratuity of his gift, and the centrality of faith are rich themes.

TENTH SUNDAY OF ORDINARY TIME: YEAR A Mt 9:9-13

Not…But Attitude to Life

Throughout the Sermon on the Mountain Jesus extends the horizon of the ethical life he expects of his disciples. The measure for the daughters and sons of the Father (5:48) is no less than the Father's ways with the human family. In our gospel today we meet Jesus in the company of sinners, whose lives fall far short of the ideal (Mt 9:9-13) The restraints of the lectionary and the choices made may impoverish our reading of Matthew. Only one text has been chosen from the important chapters 8-9. These describe in Matthew's special way the other side of Jesus' mission as Messiah, namely healing and saving deeds.

In the gospel Jesus alludes to a text from Hosea (Hos 6:6). Therefore, the liturgy has chosen Hosea 6:3-6 as a background text. An Assyrian (modern Iraq) invasion of northern Palestine, Syria, and Lebanon has created great political turmoil in Judah and Ephraim (=Israel). Kings and their courts have made decisions about alliances, invasions, and tribute without seeking to know God's will. Our text is a piece of a larger text (Hos 5:8—6:6). With forceful irony the prophet condemns their futile political strategies and sinfulness (5:8-13) and announces God's utter disappointment with the ephemeral nature of their repentance (morning cloud/dew) and his consequent judgment. In a famous verse, he outlines what God desires: "For I desire steadfast love and not sacrifice, the knowledge of God rather than burnt offerings" (6:6; cf. Micah 6:8; Is 1:16-17; Amos 5:24 for similar classical texts). Loyalty to the Covenant expressed in seeking God's will is essential to all religion. Even the sacredness of devotion to God expressed in ritual is secondary. Jesus' interpretation of the text differs from Hosea's meaning. However, both use paradox in different situations to highlight genuine religiosity and godliness (Mt 9:13 and 12:7).

The psalmist expresses the same point with sarcasm Ps 49/50), insisting on the quality of life and not mere ritual sacrifices.

In our gospel, two scenes are juxtaposed. Our text does not clearly state that the meal took place in Matthew's house, as in Mark and Luke. In the first scene we read a concise call-narrative. The narrator strips away all inessential elements. The sovereignty of Jesus' command (invitation) and Matthew's response stand out alone. On the Third Sunday we read two similar call-narratives, concerning Simon Peter and Andrew, together with James and John.

The second scene is an objection or conflict narrative. The narrator gives a brief description of a situation—Jesus and his disciples are at table with tax collectors and sinners. This gives rise to a pointed objection voiced by Pharisees to the disciples but not directly to Jesus. The narrative so far has created a background for Jesus' sayings. These are important. There are many narratives in the gospels where the narrative serves as the background for sayings of Jesus.

The Pharisees, devout Jews, had a point. A man of God, a religious teacher ought not to associate so intimately (meals in that culture were important events) with irreligious groups whose life or type of work implied consistent disobedience to God's Law. Within our contemporary society, there are boundaries and taboos based on social, cultural, ethnic, or religious grounds related to close association. At times a believing community can isolate or restrict association with certain types of people. Only yesterday, I was in a type of home where everyone is HIV-positive. There are eighty-five children between nine and a few months. I experienced fear to associate with these children.

Jesus transgressed boundaries in various ways. In this case we are dealing with sinners in a society where religion and God are not excluded from, but form, major elements in the very texture of daily life. Unfortunately religion can build walls of discrimination and remove the compassion and mercy of God from its center. Our Catholic communities can have problems with divorced and remarried Christians, Catholics disillusioned with the institutional face of the church, people with sexual orientations and relationships, de facto partnerships, AIDS victims. Some of the renewal and enthusiastic movements within Christian communities are open to the tendency to "religious elitism." They may be described in Jesus' language as "the righteous," "the healthy." Some Christians in their own inner world, conscious of sinfulness and burdened with guilt, exclude themselves from close association with Jesus.

The more important saying is the final statement in which Jesus spells out his own consciousness of the purpose of his life: "For I have come to call not the righteous but sinners." This statement must be heard again and again when we reflect on the severe judgment texts in Matthew (chapters 13, 18, 24–25).

There is a paradox and striking contrast here and in the other two sayings. It is in the paradoxical contrasts that we learn how Jesus uncovers of the mystery of God and sinners. Normal conventional and "good" religiosity and laws do not capture the indefinable ways of God and the mystery of his mercy and compassion with us as we journey. We all are always sinful as persons and communities. Both need to "go and learn."

The reading from Romans (4:18–25) is the conclusion of a longer argument about Abraham's faith (4:1–25). In the background is the narrative of God's promise of a son to the aged and childless couple. Abraham (Sarah overlooked) is a model for all, being a person who trustingly surrenders to God's graciousness and mysterious life-giving power. This leads Paul to describe the great expression of this life-giving power, namely the resurrection of Jesus. He adds a creedal statement in which the death and resurrection, namely the central events of Jesus' life, are together seen as the source of forgiveness and transformation. Jesus seated with sinners also expresses this power and invites us to believe and not object.

ELEVENTH SUNDAY OF ORDINARY TIME: YEAR A Mt 9:36—10:8

The Layperson Gazes at Society

We could build our liturgy around the theme of who we are because of the gift of our Christian vocation and its consequent responsibilities. These responsibilities arise both from the gift of God and our awareness of what is happening in society around us.

As a first step we reread a major text from Jewish religious experience of the gift of their vocation (Ex 19:2–6). God spells out the purpose of the Exodus liberation event. Our text forms a frame and is preparatory to the great manifestation of God on Sinai, the gift of the Covenant Law and the actual making of the Covenant (19:16–25; chapters 20–23 and 24:1–14).

God recalls the whole extraordinary saving event using the image of an eagle. He himself is the eagle (cf. Dt 32:11). The writer describes the purpose in a series of phases. God "brought Israel to himself" to be their God and that they be his people. Therefore, he describes them as the people who are his treasure from among all peoples. We think of a very wealthy person with a jewel of inestimable value. The same idea is repeated in two other ways to underline the idea of personal choice and uniqueness. Israel is a kingdom and a nation—but very special. The terms "holy" and "of priest" (priestly) underline the idea of being set apart and so special, chosen, and treasured. Early Christian writers used the major ideas of this text to describe the Christian vocation (1 Pt 2:5, 9; Rev 1:6). This gift implies a responsibility. Moses emphasized loyalty to the Covenant through obedience. Peter underlined the responsibility to live exemplary lives and proclaim God's mighty acts of mercy.

The psalmist invites us to acknowledge God and his gifts (Ps 99/100). He refers to the Covenant God as the shepherd of his people and draws special attention to his enduring Covenant loyalty and fidelity. Christians must be concerned that so many cannot pray such a prayer because of their broken lives caused to a large extent by the damage to life in modern society.

In the gospel (Mt 9:36—10:8) the Twelve represent the chosen people, the new community of believers. The Twelve remind us, as members of this community, of God's choice and the gift of belief in Jesus Christ and our being God's family.

Before developing our reflections on the gospel, we need to pay attention to Matthew's composition. In 4:23 and 9:35, he makes a concise summary of Jesus whom he presents as the authoritative teacher and then as the healer with power, the servant and the master who dominates evil (chapters 5–7 and 8–9). Up to this point, Jesus has been alone in his ministry. Matthew now involves disciples in his ministry. Chapter 10 is an extended instruction to the disciples on ministry as he reminds us in 11:1 ("When Jesus had finished instructing the Twelve disciples..."). This is Matthew's way of teaching his Christian community that they are now responsible to continue Jesus' ministry. We are their heirs. We shall highlight some major points.

The first point, and one that needs attention and time, is the careful examination of modern society. Matthew's Jesus gazes at his world. He is aware of the effects of sin, disease, religious formation, hypocrisy among religious leaders and in religious practices, the lack of compassion, the alienation of groups, the weakening of marriage commitment, the ravages of enmity and vindictiveness, corruption within the temple, religious arrogance. Matthew emphasizes his basic response in terms of compassion. He relates this to God's concern by his reference to "sheep without a shepherd" (Ez 34:1-16).

We may find it difficult to see and accept the diseases that affected modern society, family and public life, the adolescent, adult, and aged. Effective lay ministry within human society, the neighborhood, business, family, humanitarian organizations depends on at least two factors: a consciousness of need, and compassion that arises from seeing contemporary society through the eyes of the Father and Jesus Christ.

When Jesus speaks of the harvest and laborers we must not restrict this to forms of consecrated life and ordained ministry. We do not interpret Jesus' deep concern primarily in terms of these types of ministry of the church in the world.

The actual summary descriptions of ministry (10:1, 6-8) mirror the ministry exercised by Jesus and described in chapters 5-9. The restriction placed on his disciples, who are ordered to concentrate exclusively on "the lost sheep of the house of Israel"(cf. 15:24), does not apply. This is an aspect of a polemical issue that preoccupied Matthew in his concern to demonstrate that Jesus is the authentic Messiah promised to Israel. The responsibility of the faith community is to all people and in a special way to those most in need. Cure the sick, raise the dead, cleanse lepers, cast out spirits must be reinterpreted. The major concern is that human society reflects increasingly a society that is imbued with transcendental values—a society that acknowledges God and the authentic dignity and destiny of the human person and human communities. In 10:8b-10 Jesus' historically conditioned instructions stress the urgency of the task before the faith community. We pray for committed laypersons who will take a Christian vision into human society as leaven, salt, or light.

In the text from Romans—again a disconnected piece of a larger reflection (5:1-11), Paul skillfully builds the foundations for Christian hope. The gift of the Spirit who dwells at the depths of our person ("poured into our hearts") is the assurance that Christian hope is not a delusion. This gift is a powerful expression of God's love for us (Rom 5:5). Paul will return to this point in 8:14-30 and 8:31-39. The mention of God's love leads him back to Jesus' death and its consequences, God's love and Christian hope. Note the structure of Paul's argument. He develops the greatness of God's love for us while we were still sinners, ungodly, and enemies. This love is expressed in and through Christ's death.

If such was God's love for us when we were sinners, how much greater will God's love be for us in the future, who are now justified and reconciled. He distinguishes between our present relationship to God (justified/ reconciled) and our final and permanent relationship (will be saved). This history of God's love is the firm and utterly reliable basis for living in hope. Many Christians—bishops, priests, and consecrated included—are fearful of death, unsure of the utter fidelity of God and do not glow with a profound sense of hope. It is worth it to listen quietly and prayerfully to our fears and uncertainties and Paul's joyful hope. He boasts in God, caught up with the great mystery of his reconciling love in Jesus Christ. Part of lay ministry is to share this hope with so many who live in fear of death and its symbolic expression in aging, sickness, and experiences of helplessness, unemployment, retrenchment.

TWELFTH SUNDAY OF ORDINARY TIME: YEAR A Mt 10:26-33

Prophetic Responsibility

Many Christians listening to the gospel (Mt 10:26-33) would be at least puzzled by it and wonder about its relevance. Jesus here addresses the subject of Christian responsibility to give a prophetic witness to the effective role of God's will in all aspects of human life and public life. This would mean to witness to the vision that Jesus spelled out of human life, to transcendent values, to the dignity of human life, to societal obligations to disadvantaged group, to uncover the evil of racism, various forms of fascism. An authentic Christian voice and Christian action will receive a very mixed response in contemporary society. The many forms of the culture of death confront the culture of life.

To pause and listen to Jeremiah (Jer 20:10-13) has a value. He has to come to grips with the conflicts his prophetic witness has stirred up in public life and among the major players in the socioreligious and politico-economic spheres of life. Our reading is the latter part of his sixth complaint to God (cf. 11:18-23; 12:1-6; 15:10-28; 18:18-23; 20:7-13; 20:14-18. These are quite unusual texts). Jeremiah had to denounce the religious, political, and economic leaders for the many forms of public sinfulness. This led to reproach, derision, imprisonment, and attempts to murder him. In our text he describes the attitude of his persecutors and states his deep trust in God, whom he urges to punish his opponents. A small hymnic piece is included, praising God who protects the life of the needy. If we read the beginning of this complaint and the others we will realize that he comes to trust with great difficult and reluctance.

The psalm (Ps 68/69) is a long and rather typical prayer of a persecuted person in which moods and thoughts change. The Jeremiahs and suffering figures of each age could identify with the psalmist and share the prayer.

We turn to our gospel. The first theme is public witness and its inherent dangers. We note the repetition of the word "fear," the thematic word in 10:26-31 with which this small collection begins (10:26) and ends (10:31). Using a type of proverbial saying about what is covered or secret ultimately becoming public, Jesus urges his disciples to witness in the public domain to what he has taught to a relatively small and intimate group of disciples. We note the stark contrasts used to urge widespread and confident witness (in dark—in light and whispered in the ear—shout from rooftops). Such witness will create conflict. Jesus himself was murdered. The disciple is neither to fear to live and witness to the gospel in public nor to run from the consequent dangers. Behind Jesus' statement is the presumption that the disciple has the responsibility to witness in the public domain whatever be the negative consequences. The disciple has this responsibility before God, whose power exceeds that of any human person, group, or institution. Life and death are in God's hands.

Jesus reassures the disciples of God's loyal commitment. Using the images of God's care for sparrows and our hairs, he forcefully states the great biblical theme of God's promise "to be with you."

From reassurance Jesus returns to the theme of the responsibility of the disciples to acknowledge him, his gospel, and his vision within contemporary society and adds both the themes of reward and caution. We draw attention to the implied relationship between Jesus and the Father, whom he names as "my Father." This will be the major theme of the Fourteenth Sunday's liturgy.

There are individuals and groups within the Catholic community and Christian churches involved in advocacy campaigns and public witness to Christian values. Some groups and individuals, however, often need to hear the beatitudes and Jesus' teaching about vindictiveness, reconciliation, love, and compassion, as they tend to be self-righteous at least. We could mention some pro-life campaigns, heresy-hunting among Catholics, and other such groups.

Jesus urges upon all his disciples the responsibility of public witness in all areas of human life, human endeavors, and institutions. The communities, individuals, and groups are to leaven society with the vision of Jesus Christ and genuine transcendent and human values. We could hope that many women and men would share Jeremiah's experience. He stated: "If I say: 'I will not mention him, or speak any more in his name,' then within me there is something like a burning fire shut up in my bones, I am weary of holding it in, and I cannot" (Jer 20:91). May the fire lead to humble witness.

It is difficult to justify the choice of the fragment from Romans (5:12–15) proposed for our liturgy. Romans 5:13 used to be "used" to prove original sin. Maybe this mistake explains the choice! These verses are the introduction to the reflections on the gratuity of God's saving action in and through Jesus Christ (cf. 5:15). Paul reads the Genesis narrative to affirm the universality of the dominion of sin and death originating with human sinfulness and affecting all because all personally sin and so are under death's dominion. He will compare this universality, which originated with the Adam figure, to the universality of grace, the gift of righteousness (transformation) and eternal life originating in the obedience of Jesus and God's utter graciousness.

THIRTEENTH SUNDAY OF ORDINARY TIME: YEAR A Mt 10:37–42

The Sword

We could start our reflections today imaging a large and sharp sword. The sword symbolizes conflict, division, and destruction. Though the lectionary omits Mt 10:34–36 we must begin with these sayings. We are forced to take stock of this paradoxical and programmatic saying (10:34), which is spelled out in the following sayings (10:34 and 10:35–36, 37, 38, 39). Jesus begins with: "Do not think that I have come to bring peace to the earth; I have not come to bring peace, but a sword."

Discipleship brings division and conflict even into the heart of the family (10:35, 36 cf. Lk 12:51–53). Last week we reflected on the conflict that is consequent upon public witness to the gospel. We need to be careful not to identify Jesus' saying with the conflicts that do arise in families because of fundamentalist approaches to the gospel, bigotry and elitist self-righteous posturing by some "Christians." However, genuine commitment to Jesus Christ, speaking the truth in love, the pursuit of the essential values intimately related to living faith can, unfortunately, be very divisive.

Matthew adds other sayings that define the cost of genuine discipleship (10:37–39). These sayings with variations were judged important descriptions of authentic discipleship. We find them in each gospel at least once (Mt 10:37–39; 16:24–26; Mk 8:34–35; Lk 9: 23–25; 14:26–27; 17:33).

Recalling the character of commitment in marriage may help to grasp Jesus' teaching and how compelling it ought to be. Marriage entails a commitment that demands exclusivity and reordering of blood relationships. A husband can not love his parents or family more than his wife. The bond between a man and woman involves the promises to share the joys and all the sorrows and pains of life, shared carrying the cross of married life—in sickness, or in suffering. To grow in mutual love each must increasingly let go of the "self." We could reformulate one of Jesus' sayings "...the husband who loses his life for his wife's sake will find it."

The devotion of discipleship must relativize all the sacred bonds, as the blood bonds created by family life.

The disciple of Jesus must share in the painful consequences of following Jesus, who was crucified because of his gospel. To live according to and witness to it will have many painful consequences. Christians do have to face discrimination, nasty remarks, difficult decisions, unpopular stances, unselfish service of the needy. (I write this at the time when three Missionaries of Charity [Mother Teresa's Sisters] were murdered in Yemen.)

Finally, any deep and permanent commitment that creates a relationship to others demands a long journey of losing our selfish self. We can live our lives with closed hearts, eyes, ears, and hands.

We note what Jesus is stating about himself. He mediates the mystery of his Father to us with such intensity and depth that he can ask of his disciples total devotion. He could not ask less.

The next collection of sayings (10:40–42) explains the choice of the first reading (2 Kgs 4:8–11, 14–16). A wealthy Shunamite woman and her husband go out of their way to be hospitable to Elisha the prophet. Not only is he a welcome guest at their table during his journeys but also an extra room is built and furnished for him. Elisha is keen to reward them (4:11–13). His servant points out that the elderly couple has no son. The "prophet's reward" for the devout couple is a son (4:17). The reading is only the introduction to a larger story of the death of this son and Elisha's power to raise him.

The psalm (88/89) is a wonderful prayer of praise of God's everlasting loyalty, steadfast love, and fidelity. Creation and the Covenant with David are the particular expressions of his faithful love. However, the psalm is not so appropriate as a response to the reading or to the themes in the gospel.

We return to Jesus' concluding sayings. The historical context concerns the hospitality offered to Jesus' itinerant disciples in the early years of the Jesus movement (church) and the promise of blessings. A broader context would be the type of acceptance given to the disciples.

The first saying (10:40) appears in many forms in the gospels (Mk 9:37; Mt 10:15, 40; 18:5; Lk 9:48, 10:16, 18:17; Jn 12:44–45; 13:20). What we wish to highlight is the bonding implied between the disciple, Jesus himself, and his Father ("the one who sent me"). When the disciples live and witness to the gospel they are mirrors of God to our contemporary world. The honor is inseparable from the responsibility.

The rewards promised for simple hospitality shown to disciples (a cup of tea) could act as a reminder. Christians need to be open to collaborate in many spheres of life with women and men committed to human welfare and human dignity whatever be their beliefs. It also reminds Christians to be appreciative and to acknowledge so many good and committed people who do not share Christian faith. The instruction to Christian witnesses ends here with Matthew's characteristic concluding comment, which is a bridge to the continuation of his narrative presentation (11:1).

Paul's reflections—on the basic responsibility that flows from the ways we have been bonded to Jesus Christ—are rich (Rom 6:3–4, 8–11). My first comment is about Paul's method in teaching. The exhortation he gives runs "so you must consider yourselves dead to sin and alive to God in Christ Jesus" (6:11). We must pay attention to the little word "so" or to his "therefore." Many priests moralize in homilies. Paul builds a solid basis for his ethical exhortation. In this case, he describes the dignity and wonder of Christian existence and our insertion into the mystery of Christ.

In our text and the verses foolishly omitted (6:5–7) Paul develops the nature of the relationships between what Jesus Christ did or God did in his death and resurrection, and the believer. We have his famous creation of new words—buried with, united, like a fetus with its mother—with Christ in the likeness of his death; co-crucified with; died with Christ and co-alive with Christ. Because of this union Christ has both radically freed us from the dominion of sin and death and given us the gift of a new way of life. This is a sure pledge of a full share in his resurrection. Therefore, we, who are united so deeply with Christ, must live as dead to sin and alive only to God.

FOURTEENTH SUNDAY OF ORDINARY TIME: YEAR A Mt 11:25–30

Jesus and Failure

The biblical opening phrase "at that time" guides us initially in our reflections on the gospel. We must go back and follow Matthew's patterns of narrative. In a masterful manner he has presented Jesus as the anointed of God in ministry (chapters 5–7 [Teacher]; chapters 8–9 [Healing, etc.]). This ministry has to be continued through the believing community, which is the new Israel and is symbolized by the Twelve. Therefore, Jesus shared the ministry and instructed them at length (10:1–11). In 11:2, Matthew takes us back to the Messiah's ministry through a comment about John the Baptist having heard what the Messiah was doing. Jesus summarizes his ministry in 11:4–5. This is followed by a series of accounts about responses to the ministry:

- The questioning of John the Baptist with Jesus concluding "Blessed is anyone who takes no offense at me" (11:2–6);

- The cantankerous generation who take strong offense at both John and Jesus (11:16–19); and

- Capernaum, the center of his ministry, and the neighboring towns that remain unmoved by "the deeds of power done in you"(11:20–24).

This is the background for the gospel. Largely, Jesus has been a failure unable to break through the strong defenses of people. He has even been mocked as a "glutton and drunkard, a friend of tax collectors and sinners" (11:19). How does Jesus handle the situation according to Matthew? He could indulge in fault finding. His prayer to the Father could look as if he sidesteps the issue and takes refuge in a type of fatalistic attitude to God's will!

Jesus prays to the Father, Lord of heaven and earth, from whom he has received his mission. This has been to proclaim repentance and God's Kingdom (4:17) and good news to the poor, to take upon himself our infirmities (8:17), to call sinners (9:13) and bring good news to the poor (11:5). In this ministry he has learned that many are not interested. They closed their hearts to God's Word. He looks at the experience from his Jewish faith perspective where everything that happens is within the sovereignty of God, the Lord of heaven and earth. Therefore, Jesus speaks of God hiding and revealing. He affirms that there are the two contrasting categories, the wise/the intelligent and infants, the nobodies of society.

At the close of the extended narrative of Jesus' "great works," he cured a mute person whose muteness was attributed to an evil spirit (9:32–34). The people's reaction is, "Never has anything been seen like this in Israel." In contrast the Pharisees (cf. Introduction), representative of the wise and intelligent, throw scorn on Jesus, saying: "By the ruler of the demons he casts out the demons" (9:34; cf. 12: 22–45 for further examples). The rebukes in 11:16–19 and 11:20–24 are addressed to the wise and intelligent.

We all need to pause and find out to which category we belong. So much in our contemporary culture would both blatantly force and insidiously entice us to have the mentality of the wise and intelligent. Jesus continues his reflection (11:27). In this crisis, he expresses forcefully his consciousness of his mission and his awareness of its unique and crucial character. We must keep our reflection within the context of his mission. All has been entrusted to him, the obedient son (7:13–17; 4:1–11). The "all" refers to the coming of the Father's Kingdom. Jesus' disciples, the people, the Jewish leadership cannot grasp who Jesus is and what is his mission unless the Father enables them, as he alone knows the Son. Jesus' own responsibility is to reveal the Father in ways that he only is able to do because he is sent by the Father. Keeping the crisis in mind, the contrast between the wise/intelligent and those of no importance or status and Jesus' responsibility to reveal the Father, we study the final sayings (11:28–30). When we analyze the text, we note that Jesus addresses a particular group ("all who are weary and carrying heavy burdens"). Two motives are expressed for accepting the invitations ("for I am gentle and humble in heart" and "my yoke is easy, my burden light"). Jesus makes a simple promise ("I will give you rest"/"you will find rest").

The first reading (Zech 9:9–10) has been chosen to serve as a background to Jesus' self-description as meek and humble in heart. In a series of oracles (Zech 9:1— 11:17) the prophet celebrates God as the divine warrior who makes war and defeats his enemies and restores his people. In our text, the prophet pictures God as the victorious warrior who enters Jerusalem with peaceful intentions. The choice of a donkey symbolizes a humble way to enter. However, God remains the powerful and victorious warrior.

The psalm (Ps 144/145) praises God as king who is

gracious, merciful, compassionate, and loyal, and whose dominion is universal. The text may help us to correct any sense of Jesus as effeminate, being a pushover, a dreamer. A text that could be read with this self-description is Matthew's comments about Jesus when he uses Is 42:1-2 at another moment of another crisis (Mt 12:18-21). The description unites authority and compassion, authority, and an attitude of humble service (cf. Mt 20:22) and inner authority with no aggressive pretentiousness.

The yoke was a symbol for the Law. The group addressed would be the ordinary people who are often burdened by religion and life. The rest that Jesus promised would be meaning in life, hope, dignity, and forgiveness. The new yoke is his gospel. Three points deserve attention. First is the picture of Jesus, a very attractive picture reflecting the compassion, commitment, and loyalty of the Father. Many people today are burdened by aspects of institutional religion and by secular and consumerist ideologies. The challenge to the church community and its ordained ministers is to mirror the person and message of Jesus found here. The faith community, its leaders, and institutions are not to serve the aims of institutions, authority, or any theology but to serve the gospel and before all others those who are weary and burdened. We pray for the whole church. We also pray for socialized Christians within and on the margin of the community who do not want to hear the gospel. We pray also to recognize those good people, at times alienated from the church, who belong to the "infants" who do hear and live the gospel though they are not found "in" the church.

The lectionary omits from the reading of Romans a very rich section (6:12—8:8). A few verses (8:9, 11-13) from the first part of 8:1-17 have been chosen. This choice highlights the inherent weakness in the second readings of our lectionary. To choose these few verses from such a rich reflection (8:1-17) is an impoverishment making Paul's thought unintelligible to the normal Christian. The presence of the Spirit of God who is also the Spirit of Christ within the believer is an assurance and a task. The gift of the Spirit assures the believer of sharing fully in the gift of the life of the risen Lord (8:11). Their task is to allow the Spirit to guide them and enable them to live the freedom and the newness of life gifted to them by the Spirit (8:2, 12-13, cf. 6:4).

FIFTEENTH SUNDAY OF ORDINARY TIME: YEAR A Mt 13:1-23

Fruitful Seed and the Good Soil

There is a contrast between the major affirmation in the reading from Isaiah (Is 55:10-11) and the implications of Jesus' evocative story. As rain and snow are effective and produce new life, so God's Word is certainly creative and effective. However, Jesus is aware that God's word spoken by him is rejected by many and quite ineffective. Isaiah persistently invited all disheartened and dejected people in the Exile to be open to God's promised saving actions. He reassured them that his Word of promise would be effective (Is 55:1-13).

The psalm (Ps 64/65) celebrates God's goodness shown in an abundant harvest and the increase of livestock. Both readings add little to our liturgy.

To understand the gospel readings for the following three Sundays we must again backtrack. They are taken from the long collection of parables (13:1-53). In Matthew's gospel this is Jesus' third set of instructions. This collection is an extended response to the negative and conflictual situations narrated in chapters 11-12. We have summarized chapter 11. All of chapter 12 is unfortunately absent from the lectionary. After two accounts of conflict, involving human need and the sacredness of the Sabbath, Matthew tells us that Jesus withdraws, and the Pharisees plot how to destroy him (12:14). Drawing on Isaiah 40:1-4 Matthew paints the moving picture of Jesus as the authentic Servant (12:15-21). Except for the final contrasting scene (10:46-50) the rest of the chapter describes unremitting hostility by the Pharisees to Jesus. He vigorously uncloaks their malice and their obduracy in spite of the obvious evidence of the presence of God's Spirit, their inner evil (evil tree-evil fruit), and their hypocritical insincerity. Jesus calls them a "brood of vipers," an "evil and adulterous generation," and a generation infested with evil. Contrasted to them are the disciples who are intimately bonded to Jesus like a mother, brothers, and sisters because they do "the will of my Father in heaven" (12:46-50).

We have arrived at a point in the gospel where obduracy, rejection, conflict, and nastiness are the dominant responses to Jesus' proclamation of God's kingdom. This also reflects a major aspect of the experiences of the community to whom Matthew writes. They are in conflict with and rejected by Jewish groups dominated by the Judaism promoted by groups of Pharisees.

When we study Jesus' parables we need to be conscious that we are listening to him speaking to the people of his time, this voice reinterpreted to other audiences in the early preaching and to those who collected the parables. Finally, the gospel writer again reinterprets them for his communities.

The parables are the response of Matthew's Jesus to this situation. Whatever may be the appearances and whatever be the opposition, God will bring about his kingdom. This problem does not concern us today. History has taught us that the Christian churches are not passing phenomena, and the impact of Jesus Christ and the gospel has not been and will not be negligible on human history. Matthew has a second concern. How many people exposed to the gospel, including "believers" in his community, will resist Jesus' message?

The line in our reading to which we could pay special attention is the challenging and cautionary command "Let anyone with ears listen!" (13:9). What is the quality of our listening to the Word?

An attentive reader will notice the illogical nature of the sequence of sections. Jesus teaches from a boat (13:2). He seems to be there until 13:36 though in 13:10, the disciples have come to him and he teaches them apparently in private. We are never to sure to whom Jesus is speaking.

The opening parable is about seed and soil and not the sower. The way of sowing and preparing fields would be quite foreign to us. Last week in an interior village in the southern Ethiopian highlands I watched a farmer sow in this way. The parable describes the vicissitudes of the seed dependent on the nature and quality of the soil.

To pursue our reflections on the quality of our listening to God's Word we shall attend to Jesus' allegorical explanation of the parable and his response to the question of the disciples who appear from nowhere. The allegorical explanation most probably arose in the early church. It does not belong to Jesus' historical teaching. There are two contrasting groups—the path-seed group who hear the Word and do not understand. These would be the Jewish opponents to the community. Their opposite number are the genuine believers who hear and understand and bear fruit—the good soil group. The intermediary groups are transient members of the community. One group—rocky ground-seed — joyfully hear the Word but their joy and enthusiastic fidelity fade and die in the face of difficulty and opposition that arise because they have become disciples. The other disciples—among the thorns-seed—prove to be sterile disciples because Jesus' gospel is drowned by their dominant passion for wealth, status, power, and success. This category deserves attention, for many Christians are in danger of finding themselves among this group. What are the reasons for the exodus of many adolescents and young adults from the believing community? Is it that they do not hear the Word presented in ways intelligible to them or something in modern culture?

Is there some possible light thrown on the present exodus from communitarian faith life and institutional expressions of Christian faith in Jesus' comments about why he uses these provocative and evocative stories whose meaning is somewhat ambivalent? Is there an atmosphere created in contemporary Western culture, a type of secular ideology, a form of personal autonomy, and an immersion in acquisition that removes openness to the transcendent, to community, and to inner humility? Has something happened to the human heart, to the inner human eye, and to the inner human voice? Are not many unable to understand with the heart and hear in the gospel the Word that responds to the deeper, richer longings and needs of the human person? Are Christians willful and so remain socialized Christians and live with a veneer of the gospel? These are questions that our gospel opens up for the believing community and its ordained ministers.

The few verses from Romans open an enormous vista before us. One aspect is the disastrous consequences of human sinfulness. We see these consequences today in the massive ecological devastation, actual and potential. The other aspect is the meaning of raising of the crucified Jesus by God. The resurrection of Jesus is such a profound and re-creative act of God that its full impact will only be understood when the whole cosmos is affected. Sin destroyed the human and the cosmos. The resurrection of Jesus and the Spirit recreate the human and the cosmos.

SIXTEENTH SUNDAY OF ORDINARY TIME: YEAR A Mt 13:24–43

Judgment and Hope

The few verses chosen from the book of Wisdom (Wis 12:13,16–19) are meant to serve as a counterbalance to the severe judgment scenes in the parables (13:24, 30 and 36–43). The verses highlight God's mildness and forbearance with evil people though he could destroy them with swiftness and ease. However, these verses belong to a passage that reflects great religious immaturity and the strong cultural conditioning of God's word. The writer justified ethnic cleansing and racialism. He builds an argument to justify the destruction of the Canaanite people and Israel's gradual acquisition of Canaan. Israel interpreted their conquests and acquisition as God's action. God punished the sinful Canaanites in order to give Israel the land (Wis 12:3–18).

Were I to celebrate the Eucharist in a community this Sunday I would build the liturgy around the psalm (Ps 85/86). This is a rich and poignant prayer for help. There is an interplay of earnest pleas, confessions of trust, the description of human experiences of God's greatness and loyalty, and an ancient confession of faith (Mt 8:6,15:5 and Ex 34:6; 33:19; Num 14:18; Ps 103:8). The psalmist gives brief accounts of present suffering, his desires for ever-greater fidelity ("give me an undivided heart to serve your name") and an attitude of gratitude. We all experience times of distress and pain, often severe and prolonged. Many Christians also search for ways to pray in such situations. The psalm could be a valuable example of prayer.

We turn to the gospel (13:23–43). It is a collection of parables—the pair of thumbnail sketches underlining the potential power of the small (13:31–32, 33) and the parable of the weeds among the wheat and its allegorical explanation (13:24–30 and 36–43). Before giving the explanation Matthew brings the teaching in parables to the crowds to its first conclusion (13:34–35), and Jesus retires to a house (13:36), a technique used by Matthew to limit teaching only to the disciples.

Jesus uses the following formulas to introduce his parables: "The Kingdom of heaven may be compared to…"/ or "… is like yeast…." We can expand the concise formula in this way. There is an aspect of the reign of God that is similar to an aspect of this story. We have to decide what in the story has been used to illustrate some reality related to God's reign. For Matthew's community the parables of the very small seed (not smallest) of mustard becoming a large shrub and the little yeast causing more than 50 pounds of dough to rise are clear reassurance. The opposition of orthodox Jews will not curtail the spread of God's reign, identified to an extent at least with the growth of their community. Is there a sense of ennui among many Christians confronted with the enormous problems that face human society, both here and in other countries? Is there an indifference, a quiet sense of hopelessness, a sense that the gospel is irrelevant? I read a quotation in an Italian book about the area in Ethiopia where I am at present. French and Italian Capuchins with the assistance of many Ethiopians have built a vibrant Catholic community here. The quote is from Edmund Burke: "No one has ever committed a greater error than the person who has done nothing only because he or she was able to do so little." Could not the yeast and mustard seed that gradually transform human life and values be the small contributions of each believer in the community of faith? Does Jesus strengthen our resolve to contribute to the coming of the kingdom? Note in the parable of the mustard seed the obvious exaggerations. Matthew's Jesus uses hyperbole. There is also a reference to an image found in Ezekiel (Ezek 17:22–23).

The parable of weeds sown among the wheat could be read as a critique of those movements within religious communities that want to cut off the dead branches. They are keen to weed out those who are not "true believers" and establish elitist groups and movements. All such human tendencies are unable to live with the ambiguous character of religious communities.

However, the focal point of the parable is the moment of harvest and the separation of weeds and wheat and their disparate fates, the furnace or the barn.

This could function as a reassurance to sincere and dedicated disciples and as a warning to others.

There is a series of parables in Matthew where judgment, separation, and radically different fate are the central points (cf. Seventeenth and Thirty-Third and Thirty-Fourth Sundays). The contemporary Christian rightly has problems with judgment and the worldview presumed in its description (cf. 13:40–43). Some Christians have problems because they have vague beliefs about life after death. Others have problems with the descriptions, with the black and white nature of judgment, the permanence of punishment, the picture of hell, and the impact of the descriptions of judgment on the image of God.

Most Christians will agree that we are able to be culpable of deliberate and gross evil and we can persist in gross moral evil. I judge most would agree that a person can choose an orientation in life, for at least a considerable period, which is radically a denial of transcendence or transcendent values and by which he or she causes havoc and destruction. The affirmation of genuine human evil and adequate responsibility is expressed in the judicial system and sentences of real life imprisonment. Some Christians have little problem with the death penalty for specific crimes (for others!). Most Christians would also be aware of the extenuating circumstances and insights into criminal behavior and a criminal mentality provided by areas of psychology and sociocultural anthropology.

Can we make religious sense of the descriptions of judgment? They are valuable affirmations of the horrible reality of true evil, of the human potential to do evil, and the fact of terrible human evil and of genuine ethical responsibility. They act as one useful catechetical motivation to do good and a caution about the nature of evil and our ethical responsibilities. They also affirm the efforts of genuine discipleship. They confront us with the mystery of God, whom we cannot manipulate. We stand answerable to God. Our freedom is a serious responsibility. The descriptions use white and black categories—there is no grey. If reward is described as eternal, then punishment must be eternal. This is a consequence of the nature of God and belief in the afterlife. We cannot conclude from these parables that human are actually punished forever. The mystery of God and Jesus Christ would argue against that.

The major theme Paul develops in chapter 8 is hope. We are children of God and therefore heirs, heirs of God and joint heirs with Christ (8:17). In 8:18–25 he has further developed this idea. In the short reading of this Sunday (8:26–27) he reminds us of the role of the Spirit in relationships to this hope for which we groan inwardly (8:23) and wait in patience (8:25). The Spirit dwells at the core of our being. This spirit is the Spirit of the risen Christ and the dynamic pledge of our future resurrection and the flowering of our adoption into God's family (8:23). Therefore, Paul affirms that the Spirit makes up in an extraordinary way for our inability to be present to the core of our existence and effect our total redemption. Only God knows the core of our being and this inner yearning and creative power of the Spirit, who alone can yearn fully according to God's will. This whole faith reality is a further reassurance that our hope does not disappoint us (Rom 5:5). Many misunderstand this passage because they do not read it in its context.

SEVENTEENTH WEEK OF ORDINARY TIME: YEAR A Mt 13:44–52

The Heart's Treasure

In one of the more impassioned and lyrical passages in his writing, Paul uncovers his inner world. He writes: "And the life I now live in the flesh (my human life) I live by faith (surrender) in the Son of God, who loved me and gave himself for me" (Gal 2:20). Our liturgy invites us today to examine and discover our heart's treasure.

Solomon was by no means an exemplary king (cf.1 Kg 11). Today we meet the young king in a moment of greatness. In his early life, he followed the example of his great father and walked in the Law of Moses. Therefore God appears to him in a dream and invites him to ask for a gift. We are reminded of many popular folktales with a similar story line. Having confessed humbly his own ignorance and readiness to be guided, Solomon asks for an understanding mind so that as king he may discern between good and evil in his government of God's people. God gifts him with outstanding wisdom and showers on him endless gifts. The fundamental choice of Solomon could not have been more appropriate. To discern between good and evil—this he states as his consuming passion in life.

The psalmist is another model (Ps 118/119). A few verses are selected from the 176 verses that celebrate God's law. The Lord is his portion; that is, his delight is God's Word/Law/Statutes. The Law is a treasure more precious than wealth and the finest gold. His radical choice is for good over any form of evil or disobedience. His heart's treasure is God's Law.

A few comments on the gospel text before we interpret the meaning of the parables. Jesus addresses only disciples (Mt 13:36). There is a special concluding brief scene (13:51–52). The teaching (13:44–53) is only found in Matthew. We have another pair of twin parables (13:44 and 45–46; cf.13:31–32 and 33). The brief parable and allegory of judgment makes the same major points as the larger parable and its allegorical explanation, which we studied last Sunday. The writer uses a phrase to express the horror of those condemned, namely "weeping and gnashing of teeth." This phrase recurs in Matthew's descriptions of judgment scenes (8:12; 13:42, 50; 22:13; 24:51; 25:30). His furnaces of fire and the weeping and gnashing remind me of the sheer horror on the face of the condemned figures in Michelangelo's Last Judgment. The gestures express profound regret and a sense of sheer hopelessness.

The twin parables are an expression of our theme of the heart's treasure. The common features are the finding of a precious object, the selling of all present possessions, and the purchase. The note of joy is not repeated and yet is significant. We have classical examples of this type of madness:

• the poor man of Assisi;

• Mother Teresa entering a Calcutta slum with nothing but a sense of God and a few companions;

• Archbishop Romero aligning himself with simple, poor, and oppressed people;

We have other examples: of heroic fidelity in marriage, or people who make conscious options to serve those with AIDS. Preachers need to search for examples within their believing community and in humanist groups.

Each of us, as believers, is invited to examine the nature of our Christian commitment—what degree of passion and madness do we find? Is Jesus Christ and his gospel like a lodestar? Does he enable us to navigate in our journey of life? Do Jesus and his gospel gather up the many threads of our life and form them into a meaningful pattern? These gospel parables are about our fundamental choice in life, the dominant value that sheds light on our major choices, attitudes, and commitments. We may need to splurge again, selling all to buy what is priceless!

Jesus made the same point in his earlier teaching about our treasure, the two masters, and the preoccupying anxiety for our daily needs. He had urged his disciples to seek above all the kingdom of God (6:19–20; 24:25–33; Eighth Sunday).

Most Christians need at some point to withdraw for a more extended time of prayer and quiet to achieve adequate inner space and freedom to examine and discover what actually is the treasure of their heart. Where does the person and vision of Jesus come on the list of actual priorities? I wonder whether the Christian community provides adequate occasions and places for such stocktaking.

The gospel ends with a simple question. We may be surprised with the affirmative response. Jesus' final words could be reexpressed in terms of being youthful in old age or of tradition being tempered by the questions and wisdom of modernity.

Normally the phrase about a scribe "who has been trained for the kingdom of heaven" would be applied to ordained ministers. However, this phrase includes the many laypersons involved in lay ministry. We can think of leaders in education and teachers, members of parish councils, members of boards of trustees of Catholic institutions, catechists—all of these have the responsibilities to be Wisdom figures, committed to Christ and to the authentic Christian tradition and aware of the problems raised in the modern world so that they can contribute to God's reign today.

The reading from Romans is the final argument about Christian hope (8:28–30). Paul describes Christians from two perspectives. They are those who are committed to God the Father through their faith in Jesus Christ and surrender to the interior action of the Spirit ("those who love God"). They are also all whom God himself has called (cf.1:7).

He unpacks what he means by "called according to his purpose." At the center of his plan is his Son, Jesus Christ. Paul describes the gospel as "the gospel of his Son, descended from David according to the flesh, and declared Son of God in power according to the Spirit of holiness by his resurrection from the dead" (1:3–4). He later states that God sent his own Son in the likeness of sinful flesh that we become children of God, heirs of God, and fellow heirs with Christ. God's plan concerns his Son and us. He is to be the big brother of an immense family. He explains the historical steps in the process as far as we are concerned in these terms. He predestined us, he called us, he justified us, and he glorified us. In the letter, the final step is still in the future for us. We have been justified and reconciled (5:8–11). We have been gifted with the Spirit (5:6; 8:1–2, 9–14) and with the newness of life (6:4; 8:9–17) and are children of God (8:14–17). Our resurrection will be the climax. This is already a definite part of God's plan. We have a very solid basis for hope.

EIGHTEENTH SUNDAY OF ORDINARY TIME: YEAR A Mt 14:13–21

Jesus, the Compassion of God

Today we face one of the limits of our lectionary selections. Though the gospel text (Mt 14:13–21) is apparently a complete narrative, yet its significance depends on the following narrative (Mt 14:22–33), which we shall listen to next Sunday. I shall make some introductory comments on the text and then develop a theme that surfaces in the gospel (Mt 14:14) and is a rich thread running through Matthew.

Jesus intended to withdrawn into solitude and to a solitary place by a boat (rowed by Jesus!) when he heard of John the Baptist's senseless murder (Mt 14:3–12). Note there is no reference in Matthew to any disciples accompanying him. His solitude ends with the "invasion" of crowds of people whom he welcomes with compassion and a day of healing ministry.

The major part of the text is the description of provision of abundant food in a deserted place in the evening for about five thousand men, "besides women and children"—quite a crowd! The disciples suddenly appear and function as a mere foil for Matthew's presentation of Jesus. The disciples cannot provide food. This aspect is underlined in the brief dialogue. Their only function is to serve the food. The writer focuses our attention on Jesus, who ordered the crowd to sit, blessed the bread and fish (forgotten in the rest of the narrative), and gave them to the disciples. Then our attention is drawn to the enormity of what has happened: all ate and were filled; twelve baskets full; the size of the crowd. There is no comment on the crowd's reaction, the effect on the disciples, or on Jesus. The text immediately continues with Jesus' dismissal of the disciples and crowd and his own withdrawal to prayer (14:22–23).

Our actual text with its Old Testament allusions is an epiphany in which Jesus and his mission are manifest in their relationship to God and his saving power and purpose. God's presence with Israel in the desert, manifested in the gift of manna to the whole people for the whole 40 years of the journey, forms the background. All attempts to read the text as a lesson in sharing and similar popular interpretations must rewrite the text. With chapter 14 we have entered upon the dynamic of the self-manifestation of Jesus. This reaches a climax when Peter in the name of all the disciples identifies Jesus (Mt 16:13–16), and Jesus teaches about his passion (16:21–28; cf. 21st and 22nd Sunday).

The Old Testament reading (Is 55:1–3) is rather pointless. God wants to persuade exiled and discouraged people to accept his plan for the restoration of Israel and the Covenant. At coronations and major national events, kings feed the whole population freely. This image is used to symbolized Israel's acceptance of God's plan. Come to the feast!

The psalm (144/145) celebrates God's graciousness, steadfast love, mercy, trustworthiness, and compassion. These qualities are shown in God's responsiveness to human need. This leads us to a study of Jesus who manifests the compassion of God to those in need. We begin from our text. Matthew narrates that "he had compassion for them (crowd from towns) and healed their sick" (Mt 14:14). Earlier he had remarked that when Jesus saw the crowds "he had compassion on them, because they were harassed and helpless like sheep without a shepherd" (9:36).

This compassion found tangible expression in his

healing ministry. Apart from the actual accounts of healing, Matthew intersperses his narratives with summaries of healing. The Sermon on the Mount is prefaced with a general overview of healing. The narrative runs: "...people brought to him all who were ill with various diseases, those suffering severe pain, the demon possessed, those having seizures and the paralyzed and he healed them" (4:24).

In a later account after healing Peter's mother-in-law, Matthew narrates that "that evening they brought to him many who were possessed with demons. He cast out the spirits with a word and cured all who were sick" (8:16). This ministry was interpreted as an expression of the Servant's ministry: "He took our infirmities and bore our diseases" (Mt 8:17). When asked to confirm his identity as "the one who is to come" Jesus offered the following credentials. He said that "the blind receive their sight, the lame walk, the lepers are cleansed, the deaf hear, the dead are raised, and the poor have good news brought to them" (11:5). Was it because people had forgotten the long story of God as compassionate that Jesus added: "blessed is anyone who takes no offense at me"(11:6)?

Two thumbnail sketches, like two engravings, are drawn of Jesus' Galilean ministry. One at the lakeside (14:34–36) and the other on a mountain (15:29–31). The sick of all types surround him. After he has begun to speak about his passion (16:21), his ministry of healing recedes. However, we again find Jesus surrounded by his "people" in the Temple. Matthew recounts that "the blind and the lame came to him in the Temple, and he cured them" (21:14). We know that these groups typify his "friends" since Jesus himself invites them to come to him: "come all you who are weary and over burdened."

This picture of Jesus urgently invites all Christians to be seriously involved in alleviating the loneliness, sickness, handicaps, isolation, and needs of so many. Various groups offer openings like the Vincent de Paul Society, homes for the aged, meals on wheels, support groups for AIDS victims, shelters for the women and children. Many may find their way back to regular worship through serving God in their neighbor.

The stunted reading from Paul's great concluding hymn (Rom 8:31–39) is a shame (Rom 8:35, 37–39). A sensitive presider will ensure the reader proclaims the whole hymn as the second reading. Paul celebrates the utter reliability of God's love. The context is his long reflection on Christian hope that began in 5:1 and concludes here. There is passion, conviction, and wonder in the hymn and a masterly use of rhetoric.

NINETEENTH SUNDAY OF ORDINARY TIME: YEAR A Mt 14:22–33

An Epiphany—"Fear Not! It Is I…If It Is You…"
The presider would be wise to read the full text from which the first reading is taken (1 Kg 19:1–18). The chosen verses (1 Kg 19:9, 11–13) describe only Elijah's experience of God in his mood of dejection and fear for his life. Hunted by the idolatrous and peeved Queen Jezebel, Elijah had fled to a solitary place. God strengthened, nourished, and commanded him to retrace Israel's steps and return through the wilderness to Mt. Horeb (19:1–9). Having arrived, God demanded to know why he had come to Horeb. Elijah explained his desperate state. God seemed unmoved and commanded him to stand on the mountain of the Lord for He was about to pass by (19:11). We recall Moses on Sinai/Horeb (Ex 19:24–34). The normal symbols of God's presence, the mighty and tempestuous wind, the earthquake and blazing fire are not the symbols of his manifestation on this occasion and for this author. The intimation of God's presence on the mountain was "the sound of sheer silence" (NRSV) or a gentle little breeze. Some authors translate the Hebrew as the sound of a "light whisper" or "a still small voice." The narrative at this point only wants to indicate God's presence by a special symbol. The revelation of his future mission was made to Elijah who emerged from the safety of the cave after the sound of sheer silence (19:13b–18). In the gospel, Jesus is presented as the icon or manifestation of the Father's power.

The psalm (Ps 84/85) is an inadequate response or comment on the theophany to Elijah. In response to an urgent plea for forgiveness and deliverance by a community (84:1–8) a prophet, priest, or psalmist answers in God's name. God will certainly save and restore those who fear him and manifest his great qualities as the Covenant Lord, namely his steadfast faithfulness, saving power, and righteousness.

Last Sunday we did not focus our reflection on the meaning of the feeding narrative. We underlined the theme of Jesus as the expression of God's compassion. We want to link the feeding narrative to the following scenes. In the feeding narrative at the key point, we are told "he looked up to heaven, and blessed and broke the loaves." This echoes the early Christians' celebration of the Lord's supper. However, more important, due attention is focused on God's power, which is revealed through Jesus. The enormity of the feeding underlines this revelation of God's power with strong echoes of the Manna experience.

The presence of Jesus with his Father is emphasized in the following incident in which Jesus withdraws to the mountain to pray. Matthew remarks: "When evening came, he was there alone." This prayer forms the background for the following self-revelation, the dialogue with Peter, and one of the richest confessions of faith in the gospel (14:33). The prayer is integral to his mission. The following interaction with the disciples and Peter is symbolic of the relationship of the risen Lord Jesus and the community of faith in Matthew's time and today.

Contrasted to Jesus alone all night in prayer Matthew briefly describes the state of "the boat"—battered by waves and far from land because of a strong contrary wind. This is the situation until the early hours of the morning. Note the strong wind persists until Jesus climbs into the boat (14:30, 32).

The emotion that dominates the scene, with Jesus approaching the disciples "walking on the sea" and Peter walking towards Jesus, is deep fear. This is that fear that blinds and can corrupt faith and destroy it. Fear is such a prevalent and destructive force in our lives. We may not recognize the faces of fear, which are the cancer of living faith and which make our commitment to Jesus Christ and his gospel so lukewarm and ineffectual in personal, family, and public life.

Jesus' words to the terrified disciples are rich in meaning. The "It is I" gathers up the meaning of the feeding event, the prayer, and the walking across the water. Jesus is the one to whom the Father "has given all things." The Father manifests his power through Jesus and reveals Jesus as the Son of God. The disciples will acknowledge this as they "worship" him (14:33). Jesus' command "Do not fear" is probably the command repeated most frequently in the Bible. The believer in all types of strange, terrifying, hopeless, and extraordinary situations is called to unwavering trust. The living Lord calls us also to trust. So often must Jesus say silently to us in our lives: "do not fear."

The account continues. Peter voices a tentative faith insight. "If it is you then command me to come to you on the water." Peter has overcome his fear. He has began to understand the "It is I." Jesus' simple "come" launches Peter onto the water. However, fear gets the upper hand. Peter has a lot to learn about Jesus. We all walk in Peter's footsteps across water during our lives and so often sink as doubt, suffering, and problems weaken our faith. Peter again models for us with his urgent plea, "Lord, save me." How often in our journey to become more authentic Christians do we experience both the strong and reassuring hand of Jesus and that mild rebuke? We could say that Jesus invites us to grow through his words "you of little faith, why did you doubt?"

The whole account is about the deeper reality of Jesus of Nazareth, the risen Lord, alive among believers today. He is indeed the person to whom the Father has given all, the Son whom the Father alone knows and is revealed by the Father. He is finally the Son of God who reveals the Father and enables us to "walk on water."

When we say simply from our hearts, "you are the Son of God," we entrust ourselves to Jesus Christ whose presence and power drives out fear, calms storms, and enables us "to walk on water," namely live and witness to the gospel in our daily lives. "Take heart, it is I, do not fear." We do not need to repeat Peter's hesitant "If it is you."

We have developed the themes attached to Matthew's frequent use of worship (14:33), little faith (14:32), and Son of God in the Introduction.

We begin a new section of Romans. Paul had suffered a lot at the hands of his own people in the large Diaspora world. His most intense suffering arose from the rather general and bitter rejection of Jesus Christ by his people. They refused to accept him as the Messiah. He went to great pains to explain this rejection (chapters 9–11). We witness the opening paragraph of his reflection (9:1–5) in which he pours out his anguish.

God has gifted them and had planned to gift the world through them. Had God failed? He will develop his thoughts around the premises of God's unfailing loyalty and fidelity and human responsibility.

TWENTIETH SUNDAY OF ORDINARY TIME: YEAR A Mt 15:21–28

Open Communities of Faith

Within an exhortation to the exiles who had returned to Judah (Is 56:1–8) in which the prophet urges obedience with special mention of Sabbath observance, he also addressed two groups normally excluded from God's people. Do we see a prudish streak in our lectionary, as the comments on the inclusion of eunuchs have been omitted (56:4–5)? The text observes that foreigners, who seriously commit themselves to the Lord, observe the Covenant, and specifically the Sabbath, will be fully accepted. This is symbolized by their presence in the Temple and the wholehearted acceptance of their prayers and sacrifices. The reading creates a background for our gospel.

The psalm (Ps 66/67) reinforces this idea of God's openness to all. The psalmist pleads with God to be gracious to his people and allow his face to shine on them (cf. priestly blessing, Num 6:24–26). His desire is that all nations may in this manner witness God's saving power and praise him. He also invites all nations to be joyful in God's presence and praise him because God's ways, not only with Israel, but also with all peoples, are fair and equitable.

The community is now prepared to enter the fascinating narrative of Jesus faced with the persistent and shrewd Canaanite woman. We shall first outline the dramatic quality of the narrative. There are three "characters": Jesus, the persistent woman, and the embarrassed disciples. The Canaanite woman shouts at Jesus her urgent plea for her daughter. He is quite unmoved and makes no reply. Embarrassed by the situation, the disciples urge action. Replying to them, Jesus excludes the Gentile world from the scope of the mission given to him by God. This saying is the first major point in the narrative ("I was sent only to the lost sheep of the House of Israel" [cf. 9:36; 10:5–6]). Our attention now moves to the kneeling woman urging him to help. Jesus reiterates his stance in a careful and offensive way: "It is not right to take the children's food and toss it to the house dogs." We get the impression that his stance has hardened. The resourceful woman with respect ("Lord") counters with a shrewd reply. We could be surprised with Jesus' sudden reversal of his position. However, the dramatic narrative of a determined quest and the obstacles placed in the way all highlights the faith of this non-Jewish woman. This faith is the focal point.

However, there is another theme running through the narrative. Matthew consistently portrays Jesus as the authentic Messiah, faithful and committed to Israel. His own people alone bear responsibility that they have not believed and accepted him (cf. 13:54–58—Nazareth; 12:22–45—Pharisees; 11:16–19, 20–24—this generation/chosen cities). What characterizes the few Gentiles who enter his life is their unusual faith. We did not read the accounts of the Centurion and the amazement of Jesus who praised of his faith ("Truly I tell you, in no one in Israel have I found such faith"[8:5–13]), and his comments about inclusion and exclusion from the Kingdom (8:11–12). In the immediate context Matthew contrasts this Gentile woman to the Pharisees and Scribes as "blind guides to the blind" (15:1–14) and even the dull disciples led by Peter (15:15–16 and 15:12).

The woman is a model to the believers with her two prayers ("Have mercy on me, Lord, Son of David..." and "Lord help me"), her posture of worship (she knelt), her persistence, and her humble faith.

As a faith community, we could be challenged to recognize the rich faith life of Christians of other denominations and other religions. We need to be open, also, to Christians of our own community of faith whose mode of living this faith is not expressed in some of the traditional and time-honored rich ways. She also interrogates us. Do we desire, trust, and believe with her grit? The text also reminds us of the universal nature of the Catholic faith community enriched by the religious experience of peoples from all races and backgrounds.

We read some verses from the end of Paul's reflections on the mystery of Israel's rejection of Jesus Christ and the inclusion of the Gentiles among God's People. We wonder again about the wisdom of the selections from the letter. The major part of the complex argument has been overlooked (9:6—11:12). What can people make of such a fragment (11:13-15, 29-32)? Paul's desire is that his mission among the Gentiles and its success will jolt some of his own people to believe. He judges that ultimately the Jewish people will accept Christ (11:28-31). This event will be a sign of the culmination of God's saving plan. All his reflections depend on a belief in universal disobedience and universal mercy.

TWENTY-FIRST SUNDAY OF ORDINARY TIME: YEAR A Mt 16:13–20

To Love the Church

We could fruitfully reflect on some aspects of the church and the ministry of the Holy Father. We need to be careful to distinguish between the major aspects of our text and the socioecclesiastical structures of the church, the papacy, and the Vatican. All of these are in not included in Jesus' statements.

The confession of Peter in the name of the disciples is a central point. Peter takes this role on a number of occasions and gets into trouble on some (14:28; 15:15; 16:16, 22; 17:4; 19:27). We need to remember that the disciples in the boat have made a similar confession (14:33). This confession is a gift of God as Father who alone knows the Son (11:27). The role of this confession in relationship to the following sayings indicates that Matthew understands it as an expression of the faith of the church after the resurrection. The confession states that Jesus is at the center of God's saving plan. The church is built on this core of Christian faith.

In his gospel, Matthew consistently indicates that Jesus as the Messiah of Israel created a community of faith that is the authentic People of God. In this text with its focus on Peter and in the ecclesial discourse (chapter 18) Matthew uses a Greek equivalent for the sacred community of the People of God (*ekklesia*/church [16:18; 18:17]). Therefore the sacred community is before all else the community that believes that the Father has given Jesus Christ "all saving power in heaven and earth" (28:18; 11:27). The essential role of the Holy Father is to nourish, teach, celebrate, and protect this faith. We note the careful parallel between Simon Peter's confessional statement about Jesus' unique role among prophets ("you are....") and Jesus' statement about Peter's unique role ("you are Rock and on this rock...") among the disciples. Furthermore, Jesus actually gives a symbolic name to Simon bar Jonah. It would be better to keep the symbolism and not use Cephas. Jesus promises that he will build "my church" on this solid rock. The community as God's sacred people is also ensured that the power of evil/death will never be able to destroy it (Gates of Hades; gates = power). The positive aspect is that the community will be the bearer throughout human history of saving action of God worked out in and through Jesus Christ (cf. 28:18-20).

The image of "keys" signifies authority as the reading from Isaiah reminds us (Is 22:19-23). The image of Peter admitting people to heaven, standing at the gates, keys in hand, is a wrong understanding of the text. Peter is given teaching authority within the community of faith (cf. Mt 23:13; Lk 11:52. Note Jesus' concern about authentic teaching in 16:1-12). Binding and loosing is a Jewish expression related to authoritative teaching. Jesus is the model for the use of this authority. He interpreted his religious traditions in his day according to the will of his Father. He gave to all the eleven disciples and the "whole" church authority to teach in his name (28:29; 18:18). God has given to Peter an irreplaceable responsibility.

The difficulty for contemporary Catholics is to be able to distinguish and discern the teaching ministry of the Holy Father and the many organs of the large bureaucracy of the Holy See whose influence can depend on many circumstances and human factors.

In our liturgy, we can be grateful for the Holy Father's place within God's plan where God is present and active through the greatness and frailty of the human. We pray with and for him. We can also recall nearly two thousand years of the mysterious actions of Jesus Christ and the Spirit guiding, nourishing, and protecting what Jesus named "My church." Matthew's gospel ends with that wonderful promise "I am with you always, until the end of the ages" (28:20).

The first part of our text indicates popular estimations of Jesus by his own people. They related him to current religious expectations of promised figures through whom God would restore Israel to its former greatness as an independent socioreligious people. In the narrative prior to our text Matthew has narrated the epiphany of Jesus as healer (15:29-31) and as God's messenger (15:32-39). The Pharisees, again asking for a "sign from heaven," are taunted that they can read the heavens/sky to judge weather conditions but not the ministry of Jesus. Therefore, they deserved to be branded as an evil and adulterous generation and as deceptive teachers (16:1-12). Jesus' disciples are again described as "men of little faith" (16:8) who need to be jolted to understand (16:12).

The psalm is a rich and vibrant prayer of thanksgiving (Ps 137/138). The psalmist acknowledges God's loyal and faithful commitment, his power and readiness to hear prayers and to gift others with strength. I do not see how the psalm serves as a fit responsorial.

Paul's long reflection on Israel's rejection of the Messiah comes to a magnificent climax (11:33-36). He is aware that he cannot fathom the depths of God's saving plan, the irrevocable nature of election, the mystery of sin and Jewish rejection of the Messiah, and the breadth of God's mercy. He cannot fathom God in our history. Having reflected, argued, probed, suggested, and dreamed, he must finally acknowledge the inscrutable mystery of God. "From him, through him and to him are all things. To him be glory forever"(11:36)! After all our thinking and speaking about God we must remain in wonder and humble silence.

TWENTY-SECOND SUNDAY OF ORDINARY TIME: YEAR A Mt 16:21-27

Jesus' Spirituality

Last week we noted a similarity between Peter' confessional statement and Jesus' response in which Peter is given a singular responsibility in the community of faith to be built by Jesus. Peter could not be further removed from Jesus' spirituality in our reading today (Mt 16:21-27).

I am unsure of the purpose of the choice of a few verses (Jer 20:7-9) from Jeremiah's sixth complaint to God (20:7-13). In one of the more shocking complaints against God, Jeremiah uses language that could be interpreted in this sense. God has treated Jeremiah like a man who seduces and rapes a young woman (20:7). The reason Jeremiah is so disturbed is that his prophetic role implies constant threats and harsh judgments against his people who respond with contempt and derision. As much as Jeremiah may wish to shut up and escape his vocation, he is gripped by God's word. Maybe the reluctant Jeremiah reflects Peter and disciples who wish to avoid the consequences of being disciples of the crucified Jesus.

The urgent and deep longings of the psalmist (Ps 62/63), his experiences of God's power, loyalty, and protection that led him to praise and confidence, are moving. Many could identify with this rich prayer. However, I fail to see its place in the liturgy.

In the gospel, our attention is drawn to Jesus. We watch him accept his destiny from his Father ("The Son of man must..."). We witness his anger as he rebukes Peter, and we hear his stark words addressed to all his disciples. We discover an essential aspect of his spirituality. Within his actual world Jesus lives, speaks, and acts in accordance with the mind of his Father (set his mind on divine things). He must be ready to sacrifice his own life. Before all Jesus must deny himself and take up the cross to be the true and genuine Son to the Father. He is bound by the "must" of the consequences of seeking only God's will within a sinful world.

Our reading opens with the phrase "from that time on, Jesus began to explain to his disciples" (16:21). We are reminded of the opening of his Capernaum-based ministry: "From that time on Jesus began to proclaim..."(4:17). A new stage in his life has begun in which he will pay close attention to the education of his disciples (chapters 17-20) and be under more and more tension because of opponents (chapters 21-23). He openly speaks of his passion for the first time (16:21; cf. 17:12; 17:22-23; 20:17-19). We need to recall that in the post-resurrection period teachers and writers elaborated on Jesus' historical awareness and statements about his death and God's future for him as the just suffering person (cf.17:12 for a simple statement).

Peter's attempt to assume again the role of leadership ("Taking him aside he began to rebuke him...") earns the harshest rebuke in the gospel. We ought to be stunned. The "Rock" has become "Satan." Instead of "follow me" Jesus tells him abruptly to "get behind me, Satan!" Two visions of reality clash, God's and an all too human perspective.

Instructing his disciples, Jesus reveals both his own inner value system and what he expects of his disciples. Note that he addresses all disciples ("any one who wishes to come after me, let them..."). The stark reality is that a disciple ought to be ready to make any sacrifice in order to be faithful to him. Fidelity to him is at the heart of the being and life of a disciple. When Jesus uses the term "soul"/"self"/"life" (psyche) he refers not just to human life but to life as determined by discipleship. He reassures his disciples that all sacrifices and lifelong efforts to be faithful will be richly honored at the close of human history (16:27).

Throughout the gospel as Jesus describes one or other aspect of discipleship, we can only be daunted by the uncompromising nature of his teaching. What is important is not to water down his vision of the way of life of those " who follow me" with all its extreme demands. We are called to follow, repent, and journey along, humbly following Jesus, gentle and meek in heart.

Paul takes up the theme of discipleship also in his brief exhortation (Rom 12:1–2). The final part of the letter is a variegated ethical exhortation that responds to the needs of the Roman community (12:1–15:13). Three brief texts are included in the lectionary (12:1–2; 13:8–10, and 14:7–9). In today's reading, Paul lays foundations for an appropriate Christian life. The experience of God's immense and unfathomable mercies, which have been described earlier (1:16—11:36), are to motivate the community. They are to commit themselves totally in the service of God. This is compared to a worthy burnt offering. He insists on inner transformation and the radical break with the culture of selfishness and self-interest (cf. 6:2–12; 8:5–13). The consequences will be that in the hurlyburly of daily life they will be free and therefore able to discern God's will. Aspects of God's will are taken up in the next two Sundays.

TWENTY-THIRD SUNDAY OF ORDINARY TIME: YEAR A Mt 18:15–20

Lay Responsibility

There were various ways a person could incur blood-guilt. In various texts Ezekiel underlines personal responsibility (chapters 18 and 33). In our text, he reflects on his own responsibility as a prophet (cf. 33:7–9). In the earlier part of the text, he describes the responsibilities of a sentry when there is an invasion. He can incur blood-guilt if he is silent and does not warn the people. Using the same image of a sentry, he developed the same idea earlier (3:16–21). This aspect of speaking out is used as a background for the necessary speaking out of our gospel.

The psalm (Ps 94/95) is well known to all who pray the Daily Office. Its setting would be the Temple and could be a synagogue. After the lively prayer of praise motivated by God's greatness as creator and Covenant Lord, a priest or prophet admonishes the community. As they hear God's Law read, they must be ready to listen and obey. This would be the desired disposition for the Christian who sins and is taken to task by another Christian or the community.

We have passed over some significant texts in Matthew. The lectionary omits all of chapter 17. The Father's confirmation of Jesus' commitment to his passion and the significance of his related teaching on discipleship (Transfiguration text) are an important event. The disciples reveal their little faith and the people their blindness in the context of the healing of the epileptic boy. Jesus pays the temple tax after some reservation and clarifying his stance.

The first part of Jesus' fourth major instruction (18:1–14) has valuable reflection on some ills that afflict a Christian community. Matthew refers to status, influence, and power, and also obstructing or showing a lack of concern for the faith life of marginal members.

Our gospel (18:15–20) is concerned with both Christians' responsibility for the spiritual health of the community and for members whose sin is able to damage the community. In the context, three sayings about the risen Lord's presence and activity within the community and its exercise of authority have been included.

The text begins with a description of the procedure to be followed. It is not sure whether the text deals explicitly with a grave personal injury/offense to a member ("against you"). The problem could be grave damage to the community as such by the serious public behavior of a member ("against you" is an uncertain reading, cf. Lk 17:3).

Jesus describes the relationships between members

within the community in terms of being brother/sister to each other (cf. 12:46-52). The reason for taking a few other members if the person is unrepentant is to prevent misrepresentation by either party and to have witnesses if the whole community has to be involved. The aim is first of all reconciliation and repentance and also the protection of the life of the community from disruption, unresolved antagonism or the erosion of its ideals and unity. The process guards against arbitrary or hasty decisions and favors a mature sense of responsibility and sensitivity to the offending member.

The excommunication of the offender where necessary has two aims—to protect the life of the community and lead to the reintegration of the offender (cf. 1 Cor 5: 1-6, 11-13 and 2 Cor 2:5-11; 4:2-16). We need to remember that membership within defined groups, including religious groups, was of significant importance in the period of the early church. Solidarity, identity, and security were involved. Excommunication would have little significance for many today.

The final sayings underline both the disciplinary authority and the responsibility of the community. As Peter has special authority, the community also has authority and responsibility. Matthew does not clarify how it was exercised. A saying probably dealing with a group in the community at prayer (18:19) and another about community in mission and Jesus' presence with them (18:20) have been reinterpreted to bolster the affirmation of community responsibility and authority.

In today's parish life, this text and 18:1-14 open up many areas of responsibility for laypeople. The quality of life of the community of faith is to be the shared responsibility of those in ordained ministry with the laity. There is a mutuality in their responsibilities. Lay ministry of catechists, reconciliation, contact with those on the periphery of community, concern for the sick and the alienated need to be reinforced. Such ministry is integral to the Christian vocation. The life and health of the faith community is the responsibility of everyone.

The Romans text reminds all Christians and all with responsibilities within the community that the law of love is the heart of all Christian life. At times love leads to sensitive correction and reconciliation. Love always leads to deep concern for "brothers and sisters" in Christ. The instructions in Mt 18:1-14 are also expressions of love.

TWENTY-FOURTH SUNDAY OF ORDINARY TIME: YEAR A Mt 18:21-35

Seventy Times Seven

The appropriate place to begin our reflection for this Sunday's liturgy is the psalm (Ps 102/103). The psalmist celebrates the mystery of God within our lives. He prays: "Bless God, who forgives your sin and heals every illness, who snatches you from death and enfolds you with tender care, who fills your life with richness and gives you an eagle's strength." This mercy of God for us as sinners is celebrated in particular. We quote a few more apt verses: "The Lord is tender and caring, slow to anger, rich in love" (cf. Ex 34:6). "God will not accuse us long, nor bring our sins to trial, not exact from us in kind what our sins deserve. As far as east is from west, so God removes our sins." Commenting on the utter brevity of our lives, the psalmist affirms the permanence of God's love. Earlier he had used the enormous space between heaven and earth to image the greatness of God's steadfast love. We need to be soaked in a sense of the mercy of God, feel profound gratefulness in our hearts, and confess simply that we are forgiven sinners.

We can also learn from a simple admission of the psalmist, namely "the Lord knows how we are made, remembers we are dust." We must face our frailty because the challenge to forgive others and the difficult and long journey to forgiveness uncovers for us the many shadows within our hearts. We wish to punish, to hold on to hurt, to take revenge or vindicate ourselves.

The wise teacher urges control of anger and emphasizes the necessity of forgiveness (Eccl [Sir] 27:30—28:7). He piles up motives: God's pardon; that prayers and sacrifices be accepted; judgment and death; the comparison between God and a mere mortal....

We return to the psalm. Another theme that recurs is our obedience. The psalmist conditions the continued experience of God's merciful love on obedience: "God's love is for all ages...for those who keep the Covenant who take care to live the Law."

The rich tradition of God's boundless mercy for sinners had nourished Jesus (meals with sinner). He knew of the major obligation to obey the way of life spelled out by God. A major aspect was forgiveness of each other. The prayer to the Father is one witness to this teaching (6:12). Matthew adds a comment to the prayer: "For if you forgive others when they sin against you, your heavenly Father will also forgive you; but if you do not forgive others, neither will your Father forgive your sins" (6:14-15).

Jesus returns to this area of community life in his ecclesial instruction (18:21-35). Peter is again the spokesperson. His proposal is very generous. The seven times represents many many times. The text may presume that the offending member of the community asks for forgiveness. This is explicit in the Lukan traditions (17:3-4). The text focuses on the obligation of the offended party. Jesus allows for no limits. We must always forgive.

The importance of this imperative in God's vision of human society and of the church built by Jesus Christ is illustrated in the graphic and shocking parable. As usual, stark contrasts characterize the story. The 10,000 talents is an enormous sum. A talent would be equivalent to 15 years wages of a normal laborer. In his compassion the king released his servant and canceled his debt. For a paltry 100 denarii the governor violently attacked another servant and threw him into prison. The consequences are horrible. The experience of compassionate mercy had no impact on the merciless person. What shocks us is that Jesus identifies his Father with the harsh king. We would want to erase the final verse: "so my heavenly Father will also do to everyone of you, if you do not forgive your brother or sister from your heart" (18:35). We need to pray a sincere "Lord have mercy" as we so often fail. To say to God "Our Father" has some very frightening implications. The severity is meant to be pedagogical. It is meant to remind us of this primary responsibility in our Christian community life. Such forgiveness must also embrace any another human person who has offended us.

We conclude our reading of Romans this Sunday (14:7-9). In his mixed community with members coming from diverse socioreligious backgrounds Paul urges the members to be tolerant, respectful, and sincere and to stop quarreling and condemning others (14:1-10).

He goes on to instruct them about creating scandal and urges them to care and build community (14:11-23).

The small fragment (14:7-9) describes a basic attitude for all. Eschewing selfish freedom and self-interest, all must be devoted to the Lord above all else. Because of his life, death, and resurrection his Lordship spans our whole existence.

TWENTY-FIFTH SUNDAY OF ORDINARY TIME: YEAR A Mt 20:1-16

The Last Have a Story to Tell

The last have a story about God and it may be worth listening to this story. We first hear from a prophet and a person whose prayer also tells a story.

The prophet wishes to arouse in a people, exiled from the land, a sense of hope in order to remove their despair (Is 55:1-13). In the few verses of the reading, he urges them to repent and turn confidently to their Lord. The only motive he places before them is the inscrutable ways of the Lord (Is 55:6-9). God's mercy and the power of his word are incomprehensible. His re-creative plan is beyond their imagination. Their experiences and their concrete circumstance in Exile tell a different story about their God—a story of anger, indifference, and powerlessness.

The psalm (Ps 144/145) is a wonderful symphony of praise with variation played around the reasons for joyful praise. The psalmist also tells a story of God who is loyal, compassionate, attentive to need and prayer, awesome in his creative and re-creative acts. We select a few verses: "The Lord is good to all, and his compassion is over all that he has made"; "the Lord is just in all his ways and kind in all his doings." The summary of his experience is the rich confessional statement: "The Lord is gracious and merciful, slow to anger and abounding in steadfast love"(cf. Ex 34:6). The whole psalm could be fruitfully prayed in the liturgy.

We have seen these brief "stories" of the inscrutable and utterly loyal and committed God. The gospel tells the story about God of "the first" and "the last" (Mt 20:1-16). The whole of chapter 19 has been skipped. In 19:1 Matthew tell us: "He left Galilee and went to the region of Judea beyond the Jordan." The disciples continue to be puzzled by their master, his attitude to divorce (19:10–12), the symbolic meaning of "children" (19:13–15), his skeptical evaluation of wealth, discipleship, and salvation (19:16–22, 23–26). His promise to all who have lived in renunciation "for my name's sake" is certainly reassuring (19:27–29). However, Jesus persisted in puzzling them with his topsy-turvy vision of God, discipleship, and life (cf. 19:30).

The parable in our gospel reading (20:1–16), the first of a series of parables selected for Sunday liturgies, is framed by paradoxical sayings. We find these sayings: "But many who are first shall be last, and the last shall be first" and "But the last will be first, and the first will be last" (19:30 and 20:16; cf. 18:4). The sayings do not really catch the major points in Jesus' story.

A few introductory notes. This is a parable, and so it is meant to shock and evoke a change of perspective. It was normal in Jesus' time, even today in major Indian cities, to find daily laborers gathered at certain places to be employed for the day. In Jesus' time the wage had to be paid by evening. The normal daily wage for a laborer was a denarius, enough to keep a reasonably large family for a day. Those employed at intervals during the day were assured of a reasonable wage. The parable is concerned with the two groups at either end of the spectrum.

We must put aside questions of social justice and follow the logic of the parable as parable. The first groups are shocked—they had to wait so long, nursing their hope of two denarii! The story they tell of the landowner is full of bitterness and anger. The last would tell a different story. Jesus himself is telling the story of God who acts utterly gratuitously, a gratuity that is a scandal to us when we reflect. We all know the stories of the wicked man or woman who calls for a priest on their death beds. I wonder what the every-Sunday-at-Mass Christians think and feel at the funeral a week later!

In the second part of Jesus' comments on the wealthy young man who refused the invitation to discipleship, Peter asks about the consequences of leaving all and living as disciples. He asks bluntly: "What then will we have?" Jesus' response includes the Twelve and all disciples. Earlier Jesus had insisted that renunciation and "being saved" were gratuitous gifts—"for God all things are possible" (19:16). The parable and its allegorical interpretation (20:14b–16) return to the theme of salvation (end of day and wages) and gratuity.

The story "the last" tells to practicing Christians is a story of the utter gratuity of God's gifts and especially of the ultimate and greatest gift of salvation. The good Christian may show the mentality of "the first" and expect earned rewards from a God who is obligated to them. To be able with joyous and humble hearts to pray the psalm of our liturgy and to realize that we must pray this type of psalm that praises God's goodness in such an unabashed and generous manner is an antidote to all religious smugness. We want to find ourselves among the last and be able to share their story.

We begin to read Philippians today (Phil 1:20–24, 27). Paul is in prison. The Philippian church has sent gifts and Epaphroditus to assist him. Initially he reflects on his experience in prison (1:12–26). His major concern is the proclamation of the gospel. His imprisonment has had two beneficial effects that increase his joy. Many more people know about Christ by the sheer fact of his imprisonment because of Christ. Also, many more disciples have been strengthened and preach the gospel with new boldness and without fear. Some, he admits, do this out of base motives (1:12–18).

He turns to himself. Unsure of the outcome yet he is convinced that God will ensure that he is released for further ministry among them. What concerns him is his fidelity to Jesus Christ, the gospel, and his ministry. Faced with the possibility of death, he is aware of an inner conflict. Death would mean total union with Christ. For this he longs with his whole being. Release would mean being able to strengthen his communities. Their need is greater than his personal option. In his future ministry, he will continue to live, as he has for years, only for Christ.

The lectionary has included the beginning of his instructions about Christian life and especially the paramount importance of unity as the expression of "a life worthy of the gospel of Christ" (1:27—2:18). The depth of Paul's attachment to Christ and his dedication to his people must inspire today's listeners.

TWENTY-SIXTH SUNDAY OF ORDINARY TIME: YEAR A Mt 21:28–32

Unmoved

We join Jesus in the Jerusalem Temple confronted by and confronting the major leaders of his people (Mt

21:28-32). He had moved into Judea (19:1) and continued to teach his disciples (19:2—20:16). Then he began the final part of his journey to Jerusalem announcing to the twelve his impending death there (10:17-19). Zebedee's sons, their mother, and the jealous and angry ten failed to understand him. This saying summarizes his attitude: "the Son of Man came not to be served, but to serve, and to give his life as a ransom for many" (20:20-28 and 20:28). He approached Jerusalem accompanied also by the two blind men whose earnest desire had moved Jesus to compassion (20:29-34).

The sequence of events on his first day in Jerusalem provides the background to the consecutive readings chosen for the next five Sundays and today's gospel (21:28-32). Jesus' humble entrance into the city accompanied by a large and enthusiastic crowd created a great stir ("the whole city was in a turmoil asking, 'Who is this?'" [21:10]). The prophet from Nazareth had arrived. He cleansed the Temple of sinful commerce, cured the blind, lame in the temple, and accepted the "children's" acclamations (21:12-16). He left behind a group of angry chief priests and scribes, scandalized by the events, his presumption of authority, and the healings (20:15-17).

The next day on his way to the city and Temple Matthew narrates an incident with great significance. A hungry Jesus cursed a fig tree, which withered instantly (21:18-20). The prophet who had come to the center of his religious world and God's people will only find the barrenness of a blind and willful leadership.

The immediate context for our text (21:28-32) is the confrontation between the religious leadership and Jesus about his authority and its source (21:23-28). From 21:23 until 24:1, he remains in the temple. Jesus confronted this group with their closed hearts and increasing readiness to destroy him. If they would commit themselves about the source of John's authority, Jesus would answer their questions. Caught in a cleft stick they refused. Jesus also refused. Then he posed another question by means of the story of the two sons whose response to their father was so different. The key phrase in the story is "later he changed." The tragedy that Jesus faced with the leaders of his people is summed up in the phrase "you did not change your minds and believe him"(cf. 3:7-10).

They had refused John, and they refused Jesus. However frustrated Jesus might be, he could do nothing. The invitation "repent" had been rejected often in his life and now brazenly by the religious elite (4:17, cf. 9:34 and 12:34; 11:16-19; 11:20-24; 13:54-58; 15:6, 12-14; 16:1-4; cf. 12:38-42). The text, very Matthean in character, reminds us that public sinners found in John and Jesus genuine prophets.

The first reading (Ezek 18:25-28), concerns the cases discussed by the prophet when dealing with personal responsibility (chapter 18). It does not really fit into the gospel situation. The repentant wicked person of Ezekiel, the prayer of a repentant person (Ps 24/25) eager to learn how to live according to God's Law could mirror the repentant tax collectors and prostitutes who are entering God's kingdom.

What could be significant for a faith community in these reading? To see Jesus making no headway and facing growing opposition and danger is useful. There are women and men of God who also face the sinfulness of "reputable" people with authority in civil, political, religious, and socioeconomic spheres of life. Many suffer for their integrity.

We also must face ourselves. We could look at some of the difficult changes in our lives. We find it painful to change an attitude, to allow ourselves to hear God's word, to move from indifference to involved commitment in the service of others, to begin to actually pray personally, to move from social forms of ordained ministry and Christian life to personal conviction.... In so many ways during these twenty-six Sundays, we have been exposed to Jesus and Jesus' teaching. What has been the fruit?

The reading from Philippians (Phil 2:1-11) is a classical and great text that tells the "hidden" story of Jesus' life, the essential story. Whatever may have been the concrete forms of selfishness, ambition, conceit, and self-seeking in the faith community at Philippi, we all recognize the seriousness of the problems caused by such attitudes. Such destructive attitudes and behavior plague so many groups, parish communities, and committees. Paul appeals to their union with Christ, his love, their communion of life created by the Spirit, and the great human qualities of compassion and tenderness.

However, his real appeal and assault upon our narrowness, self-seeking, and pretentiousness is the story of the inner life of Christ Jesus. Paul begins (possibly he has used a current Christian hymn) with that hidden decision that was so fundamental. He knows in faith that Jesus is the Lord and Son who came from the mystery of God. He also knows the account of the life of Jesus of Nazareth from early disciples. The first decision was not to exploit (NRSV—a good translation) what he shared in the mystery of God. Using a blunt contrast Paul opposes the way of being proper to God (form of God) and a human way of being (form of slave/servant). Two decisions are interrelated. Jesus did not use equality with God but he emptied himself. Then Paul moves to Jesus' human life—a human life in no way different from others. Paul chooses one incident in Jesus' life as expressive of his inner person, namely his death. His core decision was that he humbled himself. This found genuine expression in his obedience to the Father unto death. This death and his humble obedience had a special quality—"death on the cross" obedience and humility. We need to remember the horror and utter shamefulness of being crucified naked in public. The next part of the hymn gives an account of the great reversal. We note the opening "therefore." As Jesus was the person who made the crucial decisions in the first part, now God controls the story.

In contrast to abasement, we have exaltation to the highest place. This would be God's right hand. This is re-expressed in terms of God granting Jesus "the name that is above every name." This refers to Jesus' status alongside God. The universal obeisance and acclamation highlight the greatness of the status. We have a scene from a royal court. The name is ultimately stated, namely, Lord. No other name is so expressive in the context of the earlier decisions: "he did not judge to exploit," "he emptied himself taking the form of slave," "he humbled himself, becoming obedient to death on a cross."

The whole great Judeo-Christian story begins from God the Father and ends with all humanity and creation before God the Father. Therefore, our liturgy, which celebrates this story, culminates in the "through him, with him...all honor and glory be yours, almighty Father." The hymn also concludes that the whole Jesus' story is to be "to the glory of God the Father."

TWENTY-SEVENTH SUNDAY OF ORDINARY TIME: YEAR A Mt 21:33–43

Windows Onto another World

There is a clearly recognizable thread running through the readings held together by the image of the vine/vineyard/its tenants. The meaning of the gospel for a Christian community in North America today is more difficult to define.

Isaiah's text is a literary masterpiece (Is 5:1–7). It is a combination of a love lyric (5:1–2), a court scene (5:2–4), and a prophetic oracle of judgment (5:5–6) with the explanatory conclusion. Having prepared the vineyard with such care we can imagine the disappointment of the owner, as he tastes the sour grapes. This leads to a court case between God and the vineyard with the people as judges, judges of themselves! God pronounces the judgment—the destruction of Israel. Finally, the prophet draws attention to Israel's sins—all related to many forms of socioeconomic injustice.

The psalm (Ps 79/80) is a community prayer of lament, probably of people in the North or the remnant left after the exile of 721, a horrible example of ethnic cleansing. They rehearse and recall the election, exodus, settlement, and expansion of the people in the land. However the present situation is so desperate, a ravaged land is all that is left. Therefore, the people cry in their desperation to God to tend again the vine and restore his people.

While the psalm is a cry of a repentant and trusting people, following Isaiah Jesus develops the theme of God's judgment upon Israel (Mt 21:33–43). Throughout Matthew we have noted how the situation within his community or the conflict between his community and the larger Jewish community led by groups of Pharisees have influenced the way Jesus has been interpreted. This is true in a special way of chapters 21–25.

The background to our text (Mt 21:33–45) would be some of these elements: The destruction of Jerusalem, the persecution of leading members of the Jesus movement, the Jewish rejection of Jesus as Messiah and his death, his acceptance by some Jews and Gentiles who constitute the believing community and the constant conflict with contemporary Judaism (70s and 80s).

Matthew follows Mark's order of events once Jesus has entered Jerusalem, adding some texts and modifying others. Earlier Matthew had strung parables together in series of three (13:24–33, 13:44–47). There are three parables also here (21:28–32 [only in Mt]; 21:33–45; 22:1–14). The parable has become an allegory. We expect that trouble will begin once the absentee landowner sends servants to claim his share of the produce from the tenants. Both groups are met with great violence. Matthew is referring to the way the Jewish prophets had been treated in the past and how Christian prophets are being treated now (cf. 23:31, 34–35). The son as heir is murdered: a clear reference to Jesus' death. In Matthew's version the leaders answer Jesus' loaded question. As in Old Testament parable stories, the response is a sentence of judgment on the audience. In 70 C.E. Jerusalem was destroyed and many of the religious leaders put to death. Matthew's Jesus takes up their response quoting Ps 118:22–23. The action of the builders is contrasted with God's action. While they reject Jesus (stone), he is the cornerstone in God's saving plan. A major theme had been intimated in the account of Herod's attempt to murder Jesus as contrasted with the Gentile adoration of him. In the light of this, Jesus concludes that the kingdom of God will be taken from the Jewish people and given to the community who believes in Christ. There is also the warning that the rejection of Jesus as God's Messiah and the Son will have catastrophic consequences (21:44, "broken to pieces and crushed by the stone").

As the text ends (21:45–46) we realize that Jesus and the leadership are on a collision course. The crowd's acceptance of him as a prophet of God can only temporarily protect him.

A community today can profitably remember the integrity of Jesus as he lived the gospel he taught. Bonhoeffer wrote of the cost of Christian discipleship and was murdered because he lived the gospel. Jesus' fidelity to his Father also cost him his life. Recently I was with a group of men in a jail. They were discussing parts of Jesus' teaching in Matthew. One said simply, "They had to kill him!" Jesus' own life reminds us that his gospel is countercultural, a scandal to many attitudes, visions of life, and ways society is structured and life is lived. In various ways the gospel is silenced and marginalized, and genuine and sincere Christians made to suffer. We face the great conflict between good and evil played out in so many ways. God calls us both to discern and be aware and to opt more clearly for all that is good. We are entrusted with a vine or vineyard!

I am puzzled by the choice of the verses from Philippians (4:6–9). The natural start of the paragraph is 4:4 or 4:8. The exhortation in 4:8–9 prevents the Christian from being myopic. There are so many people committed to great human visions who are not Christians. We must not only acknowledge all these good people and co-operate with them but be influenced by all that is good, noble, and enhancing of the human in our society. Paul is concluding his letter. Therefore he gathers insights and appeals for an ever deeper and richer life.

TWENTY-EIGHTH SUNDAY OF ORDINARY TIME: YEAR A Mt 22:1–14

Three Weddings and Two Funerals

A vibrant note of hope pervades the first reading (Is 25:6–10) and the psalm (Ps 22/23). The use of rich and appealing imagery conveys hope. In chapters 24–27 the prophet dreams of the future. The context would have been a situation of great difficulties, grief, shame, and humiliation for the faith community. Such darkness apparently energized the prophet, who spoke with great clarity and certainty about God's future action. He used images. On his royal mountain God prepares a sumptuous banquet for all. The writer knew of wine as he described the wine to be served as "well-aged wines strained clear." Death is swallowed up. The grief of all and the shame of Israel are banished. The prevailing mood will be joy, as the persistent hope of the people has not proved a delusion: "This is the Lord for whom we waited."

This mood of confidence and hope spills over into the psalm. The person who composed the prayer has experienced the saving hand of God. In the first part (23:1–4) we see God as a shepherd through the eyes, as it were, of a sheep who finds rich pasture, plenty of water under the shepherd's guidance. Even in the dangerous valleys, the sheep experienced no fear. In the next part (23:5) the psalmist's experience of God and his trust are compared to a guest whose host welcomes him warmly and respectfully (oil) and provides a great meal (his cup overflows). A special joy is the envy evoked in his enemies who were not invited! The whole experience is summed up in the confession: "goodness and kindness (mercy) will follow me every day of my life."

The mood of hope and joy fades now as few of the invitees in Jesus' parable have cause for joy (Mt. 22:1–14). We must make some comments on this text. Rightly, Matthew says "once more Jesus spoke to them in parables." There are really three partial "parables" in the text. The link is a wedding banquet, a king, and invitees. There is the story of the refusals of the invitations and the consequences (25:1–7); the story of all the people on the roads invited to the banquet, good and bad (25:8–10); and the story of the speechless fellow who is wearing his working clothes! (25:11–14). There is a "funeral" for him and for invitees who violently refused the royal invitation. The first two stories are related, as the refusals lead to new invitations. The second also prepares for the third with the comment about "both good and bad." Matthew or his tradition has reworked a parable found in Mark and Luke. If we join 22:8–10 to 22:1–7 we note a war intervenes (22:7)!

The stories are partially allegories. The first refers to the rejection of Jesus as God's anointed by the Jewish leaders and to the destruction of Jerusalem, temple, and people by the Romans in 70 C.E. An original parable would have indicated Jesus' awareness of opposition and ultimate rejection. The second story tells of the acceptance of the gospel and Jesus by people originally not expected to belong to the chosen people.

It reflects the fact that the community is made up of unlikely people, Jews and Gentiles. An aspect that we find recurring in a series of "parables" is the presence within the community of good and evil. We have seen the earlier parables of wheat and weeds/righteous and evildoers (13:24–30; 36–43) and of good and bad fish (13:47–50). Ahead of us are stories of wise and wicked slaves (24:45–51), wise and foolish women (25:1–13), and the sheep and goats (25:34–46). Our gospel witnesses to the sinfulness of Matthew's community.

The final mini-parable ought to puzzle. In the text the man without his tails has been forced in off the street! The story concerns the sinful lives of some within the community. This is a serious warning. The members of the community have the responsibility to live according to Jesus' teaching. The text is quite frightening. The heavies grab the unfortunate and unsuspecting "guest," bind him up, and throw him out headfirst. Outer darkness is "hell." This warning will be spelled out more fully on the Thirty-Third and Thirty-Fourth Sundays.

The reassuring image of God in Isaiah and the psalm could be developed in the liturgy. The gospel creates problems. The reality of final judgment does not normally function well as a motivation for a committed Christian life. Fear is a poor motive in good religion. In the New Testament the symbol of putting on new clothes signifies the new identity of a Christian. Matthew's improperly dressed person at the banquet symbolizes a Christian who does not live up to his or her vocation in some major way. The liturgy could develop again the theme of responsible Christian life.

We read selected verses from Paul's final expression of gratitude to the Philippian church. It had again come to his aid in need (Phil 4:10–20; cf. 4:12–14, 19–20). Paul is in prison (1:12–13). The church sent Epaphroditus with gifts and to assist him in prison (2:25–30). Paul had allowed this church to help Paul financially more than any other. There was a special bond between them (1:3–8; 4:15–17). Paul makes a brief autobiographical reflection of his attitude during his life of ministry, years of many sufferings and great danger and toil (cf. 2 Cor 11:23—12:12; 2 Cor 6:3–10). The gratitude and returns he is unable to make to them he leaves in the hands of Jesus Christ and the Father.

TWENTY-NINTH SUNDAY OF ORDINARY TIME: YEAR A Mt 22:15–21

Street Wise

Perhaps the better place to begin is with a negative. The gospel provides no real basis for reflection on the questions concerning the relationship of church and state, the sacred and the secular. The choice of verses from Is 45:1–8 and the royal psalm (95/96) may suggest this theme apart from Jesus' final saying in the gospel (22:21).

Around 539-38 Cyrus finally broke Babylonian power and decreed that all exiled people who wished could return to their native land, places of worship could be rebuilt (some state finance was available), and religious objects were to be returned. The prophet celebrates this situation. Cyrus is seen as chosen by Israel's God, enabled by his power to conquer his enemies and guided to discover all their hidden treasures and wealth. The writer gives the reasons for this choice. Cyrus is to know that Israel's God alone is God. All the nations are to acknowledge Israel's God. Israel/Jacob, God's chosen people, are to be freed. We would be very suspicious today of any dictator, king, president, or prime minister who claimed to be commissioned by God. Israel interpreted the secular events in the light of their belief in God, the Covenant, and their election.

The psalm (Ps 95/96) is an exuberant call to all nations and people to acknowledge God's universal sovereignty—God who alone is creator is the Lord, King, and Judge of all.

This faith vision of sociopolitical and economic reality is true. The whole of human history is within the will or embrace of God. We find it difficult to express this in a realistic and adequate manner. God is not outside of our history. God does not at times intervene and tamper with our history. However, we have no appropriate language because God's "presence" and "activity" are so enormous and mind-boggling and apparently negligible. We probably are more aware of God's absence as we watch world or national news and see the state of the world and the power of evil. We have no adequate image to tell the truth as all images and language diminish rather than enhance God's presence to all within the world.

We turn to the gospel. Jesus has navigated through the shoals of hostility in the first hour of his second day in Jerusalem (21:1—22:14). The day will be long (21:23—26:1). The next hour will be taken up preventing his opponents entrapping him. The Pharisees attempted this through their disciples and the Herodians (22:15-22). The Sadducees try unsuccessfully (22:23-32). Finally the Pharisees regroup and through a specialist in the Law have another try (22:34-40). When the Pharisees prepare for a further assault (22:1) Jesus takes the offensive (22:41-46).

Shamed by his skill we are told that "No one was able to give him an answer nor from that day did anyone dare to ask him any more questions" (22:46). Today we read of the first attempt to trap Jesus.

The question concerns the head (poll) tax (*kensos*) that symbolized Roman hegemony. This sign of colonial domination was resented by the people yet they, including the Pharisees, paid it. Some nationalists would refuse. Note that the group has a denarius with them in the Temple area! If Jesus urged refusal, the Romans would act, if he urged payment the people would be offended.

An approach to our text would be to heighten our awareness of Jesus' normal Jewish life. He is caught up in the web of sociopolitical problems of his day and forced to be a shrewd person. The group approached with flattery that was a type of bait to stir Jesus into a clear mistake. Their praise is actually a valid description of him as a teacher. People of good will did judge that he was a sincere teacher who taught the way of God in a genuine way. Others did not sway him because he did not pay attention to social status and sought only God's will.

Jesus did not spare the group as he unmasked their hypocrisy. The denarius they showed him would have had the head of Caesar and the inscription: Tiberius Caesar, son of the divine Augustus, high priest.

He did not answer their question about the Law and the civil tax directly. In the situation, he accepted the civil administration and the normal working of civil society. Much of Jesus' teaching undermined many aspects of sociopolitical and economical structures of both Roman administration and Jewish society. His vision of human society was a direct critique of his society.

The emphasis in the text would be on the second part of the final answer. In a way he was already enunciating the great commandment: he affirmed God's place in all human life, human decision, and visions of reality. In the context, his opponents, by rejecting Jesus, were not giving to God what is God's. A possible area of reflection would be the place given to God in normal human life.

We commence to read the first Christian writing that has been preserved. Paul commends the Thessalonian community in a prayer of gratitude. Note he addresses this prayer and all his prayers to God the Father. He singles out their vibrant and energetic love and the constancy of their hope. He begins to recall his experiences among them when he proclaimed the gospel. Signs of the Spirit's presence and Jesus' power, possibly healings, accompanied his proclamation. He also mentions their experience of him as a person. He will develop this idea. There were many charlatans wandering around who sold supermarket religion and philosophy in that world.

THIRTIETH SUNDAY OF ORDINARY TIME: YEAR A Mt 22:34–40

First Link in the Chain

We listen to an ancient voice in our first reading who could be speaking to our world (Ex 22:20–26). The passage is taken from the Book of the Covenant (20:22—23:33). The legislator is concerned that Israel as God's people create and preserve a human society that is just. Therefore, he gives his attention to those who are particularly vulnerable and who are so easily oppressed. He lists them: the resident alien, the widow and orphan, the poor who need to take loans to survive, and the poor who are forced to pawn even essential clothing. We have the refugee, displaced persons, the migrant workers, immigrants, the aged, pensioners, the street youth, the addicts, AIDS patients.... These are some of the people who are neighbors to us. We also have nations who are burdened with immense debts and debt repayment. These also are neighbors to our nation. We know of racial prejudice, exploitation, or discrimination of migrants and migrant workers in many countries. An ancient voice spoke in the name of God who identifies himself as the compassionate God. He legislated about some human obligations to the neighbor.

In forbidding absolutely any worship of any other god and attaching to it the severest penalty, the legislator reformulated the first commandment: "I am the Lord your God who brought you out of Egypt...you shall have no other gods before me" (Ex 20:2–3).

The psalmist celebrates this God (Ps 17/18). Traditionally this long psalm is attributed to David who prayed it when he was rescued from enemies. The images of God are related to warfare—rock, fortress, deliverer champion, shield, and stronghold.

We reenter the tense world of Jesus in the Temple. There is none of the friendliness we find in Mark 12:28–34. His major opponents have heard that he had silenced the Sadducees, leading priestly authorities. Therefore they gather again and an expert in the Law attempts to trap Jesus. Probably his opponents, who are intent on testing him (only Satan and Pharisees test Jesus; 4:1–3; 16:1, 19:3; 22:18) wanted to trick him to say something disrespectful about the divine Law.

In his reply Jesus adds a second commandment and describes it as being "like the first." The meaning is clear from his concluding remark. All of God's revealed word—the Law and prophets (5:17; 7:12; 11:13; 22:40)—hangs on these two commandments. The second is like the first because it is inseparable from it and as indispensable.

The word "love" often needs to be reexpressed. I have found "committed loyalty/loyal commitment" to be useful expressions. The total person is to be involved in single-minded loyalty to God, and the whole person committed to the good of the other.

Matthew has spelled out various aspects of the relationship to others expected of disciples (Mt 5:21–48; 18:1–35; cf. 25:31–46). He also included this in the list of obligations mentioned by the rich young man (19:18). How this primacy of God and neighbor is to be enfleshed in our basic orientations in life is left to us to discern. Such undivided loyalty to God and to the neighbor enhances us as human persons. Our selfishness is slowly burnt away. We celebrate today Jesus Christ's vision of the human person, the hopes of human society, and our religious potentialities. We grieve at the shadows—some so dark—that hang over our world and our lives. We repent and humbly ask to travel along this path.

As I was writing these comments I went to a five-star hotel in Delhi and began to pray some psalms. The first line was "Blessed are they who consider the poor and sick" (Ps 41:1). Watching the coming and going, hearing music from the bar and restaurant, I was aware of a totally different ethos, an alien world. I also thought that the good reputation of God, his credibility, depended so much on the way women and men genuinely love the neighbor.

Within the context of his prayer of gratitude, Paul continues his account of the conversion of a group of Gentiles who made up the church in Thessalonika. The story of their conversion and the events accompanying it (Acts 17:1-9) have been retold in other parts of Greece. In the final verse (1:10), we have the earliest written reference to Jesus being raised by God, being the Son of God, and the hope that he will return as Savior. This is also the first account of the conversion of Gentiles.

THIRTY-FIRST SUNDAY OF ORDINARY TIME: YEAR A Mt 23:1-12

Ecclesial Community—Ministry

We shall begin from a part of Paul's apologia (1 Thess 2:7-9, 13). Why our lectionary begins halfway through a text is beyond me (1 Thess 2:1-12). Paul reflects with the community about their experience of his ministry. He affirms that he has placed no obstacles in the way of the gospel of Christ. His own attitudes, his way of life, the sufferings he endured recommend him and the gospel of God he preached. He singles out deceitfulness, flattery, greed, manipulation, insensitivity, and seeking cheap popularity as vices of popular teachers. He reminds them of what he had suffered in Philippi (Acts 16) and among them (2:1-2). He recalls how he did not use the "rights" of apostolic authority. He compares his ministry to the ways a mother (2:7-8) and father care for their children (2:11-12). He underlines his deep affection and his desire "to share with you not only the gospel of God but our own selves" (2:8). He draws attention to his daily life as an ordinary worker, earning his/our living (2:9). His ministry placed no obstacle before the Word of God, rather he enabled them to accept the gospel as God's Word (2:13). We can read this text in dialogue with our gospel (Mt 23:1-12).

Malachi's indictment of the priests in Jerusalem (Mal 1:6—2:9) serves as a fitting backdrop to Jesus' indictment. Again our lectionary has used the "cut and paste" method of selecting a text (1:14—2:2, 8-10 [verse 10 belongs to the following oracle 2:10-16]). He denounces the priests on two accounts. First, they offer in sacrifice what are polluted, namely blind, lame, sick, and stolen animals. With biting sarcasm, he asks what the governor would do were they to offer him such a gift (1:6-14a)! Second, they are irresponsible teachers of the Covenant tradition (2:8-9). He affirms the great majesty and power of God, revered by all nations (1:14), places before them the model of Levi (2:4-6), threatens dire curses upon them (2:1-3), and describes the role of a priest teacher. This we shall quote: "For the life of the priest should guard knowledge, and people should seek instruction from his mouth for he is a messenger of the Lord of hosts" (2:7). Essential to their life is "to lay it to heart to give glory to my name" (2:2).

The beautiful psalm of humble trust (Ps 130/131) does not add to our theme. A realistic and honest attitude enables the psalmist to trust—a calmness like a weaned child resting quietly in its mother's arms.

We turn to the gospel. In chapter 23 we must remember that we have some polemical sayings in which Jesus critiqued the religious leadership. However, the ongoing conflict between Matthew's community and post-70 C.E. Judaism, concentrated around the synagogue and the leadership of the Pharisees and scribes, has greatly influenced the chapter. It also reflects some inner community problems.

We begin with the words of Matthew's Jesus to the community about its inner reality. Behavior is to flow from this reality. The community is a communion of brothers and sisters united around one Father and one teacher and master, Jesus Christ (23:8-10). Following the example of the unique teacher, greatness is expressed in humble service of others (23:11-12; 20:28, 20:25-27; 18:2-4). The Christian community must resist the influence of cultures and societal pressures and not allow status, hierarchy, and honorific titles to damage that essential mark of the true church. This is the ecclesial communion of all who believe, share one hope, and whom God calls to love. Clergy and laity under social pressure can compromise equality and mutuality, with the distinctive responsibilities of ordained and lay ministry.

The second aspect of Jesus' teaching is his critique of leadership—a critique of the absence of communion, equality, and mutuality. He singles out the propensity of teaching authority to bind burdens on others and shirk their own obligation to live what they teach. He draws attention to the ways culture and social pressure can cause status, honor, esteem, and recognition to dominate the lives of religious leaders. There is an anomaly in the text. Jesus both acknowledges their authority to teach and the binding nature of their teaching (23:2–3) and the burdensome character of their teaching (23:4; see 11:28–30; 5:20–48).

An aspect of today's liturgy would be addressed to all who exercise ordained ministry. Malachi, Paul, and Jesus address them. Many of the clergy are aware of being responsible for Christian communities: local church, parishes, chaplaincies. For how many is their responsibility to Christian communities the major aspect of their consciousness?

ALL SAINTS NOVEMBER 1: YEAR A Mt 5:1–12

Glimpses of the Divine in the Human Face

The Beatitudes have been chosen for this feast because they paint the portrait of authentic disciples of Jesus. We can misunderstand the gospel text. The list of qualities can easily be judged to picture emaciated human persons, men and women who are just shadows of greatness, men and women who repel rather than attract as they mirror the negative, the defeated, the losers in life's struggles, or just do-gooders.

What I suggest is that we rummage in our memories, recall TV interviews and stories from life, recall ordinary men and women, check through lists of great figures of our history…and find women and men, young or old, great or unknown people who have enabled us to glimpse authentic examples of these qualities of which Jesus speaks.

A word of caution is necessary. We will be able to choose people who are poor in spirit, merciful, peace makers—probably not the Nobel peace prize winners. And normally there would also be a shadow on their lives as normally people do not embody the full richness of any of these qualities. The qualities have a rich potential beyond any one example since these qualities open up the horizons of the human potential and reflect the divine in whose image we are created. These qualities describe Jesus of Nazareth who alone had no shadow falling across his person though many only saw dark shadows and so destroyed him.

We need to search for the saints of our age. The Nelson Mandelas, the Mother Teresas, the Archbishop Romeros, some among AIDS patients, refugees, workers in refugee camps, judges, doctors, police personnel, adolescents, teachers, sports persons, single parents, prisoners, an old lady in a nursing home, nurses, an abused migrant, a taxi driver, our mother all enable us to see these qualities lived out among us in various degrees of intensity. Such men and women humanize our lives, reflect the mystery of God, reassure us, and guide us.

The qualities are interrelated. They are different expressions in life of the openness of the human person to transcendence in the midst of the ugly and beautiful, the generous and mean, openness of mind and narrow prejudice, and good and evil.

Some of the descriptions of the qualities are probably too biblical for us to understand correctly. The "meek" are those who have the strength not to be arrogant. The poor in Spirit are so rooted in human richness and open to transcendence that they do not need to be arrogant, proud, aggressive, and self-assertive. They can be vulnerable. Those who mourn have allowed sacred anger before evil to find expression in deep sensitivity and concern for the suffering world. The motives of the pure in heart become ever more transparent, truthful, and focused, shedding manipulation, hidden selfishness, and doublespeak. Those who hunger and thirst for justice amaze us by their consistent and persistent dedication to authentic human values, human structures in society, and the human dignity of any type of person. All these attempts to describe these qualities are helpful and yet deficient. They describe the potentialities of the human as we grow into the image and likeness of God. Those who are merciful or peacemakers in Jesus' sense are prophets within contemporary society. These qualities are related to the newness made possible by Jesus' death and resurrection and the creativity of the Holy Spirit.

The beatitudes are not commandments. We must not moralize them. Jesus sketches a vision of authentic human life made possible by the re-creative power of God. He draws also a self-portrait. This vision has to compete with other sets of beatitudes that appear to enhance the human yet are deceptive. There are very appealing and deceptive cultures of death propagated in our culture.

A few "scholarly" remarks. The Sermon on the Mount

(chapters 5-7) begins with the description of its setting (4:23-25) and the classical opening of authoritative teaching, echoing Moses on Sinai. The first eight sayings follow a fairly set pattern: (a) Blessed are; (b) the category; and (c) the promised future reward. The rewards are variations of the same idea adapted to be appropriate to the category. In the last beatitude we have both variations in the pattern and the clear influences of the painful experiences of the community. Note how the believers are expected to be prophetic in their way of life.

To accompany this reading we have a vision from Revelation. In the midst of one of the visions of judgment (Rev 6-8) when six of the seven seals have been broken there is a pause. Earth and the sea are about to be seriously damaged. The elect must be sealed with the seal of the living God. We are told that 144,000 are sealed, 12,000 from each of the tribes. They represent the Christians as the chosen people of God. This group is juxtaposed by a vision of God's court and the immense multitude from every nation of our history gathered before God (= throne).

THIRTY-SECOND SUNDAY OF ORDINARY TIME: YEAR A Mt 25:1-13

The Closed Door

The theme running through the liturgical readings is "to watch and be ready." As the liturgical year draws to its close the community looks ahead to the culmination of our human life when we "stand before the Lord" at our death. The mood fluctuates between joy and apprehension, with big caution signs appearing on the road.

The Liturgy of the Word begins with a text from a pressing exhortation to rulers to seek wisdom (Wis 6:1-16). Our reading (Wis 6:12-16) draws attention to the need to love wisdom, to seek and pursue her, to desire and watch for her, and to be attentive to her. The writer assures the elite that they will find her if they sincerely seek because she herself seeks out such people. The reading has been chosen probably because of the emphasis on seeking and watching in the gospel and so being prepared.

The psalm (Ps 62/63) emphasizes the aspect of yearning and longing. A person in the Temple prays for help. He expresses urgent longing (vv. 1-2) and praise based on confidence in God's help (vv. 3-8).

The gospel story is rather straightforward (Mt 25:1-13). We shall situate it in Matthew's narrative. Jesus leaves the Temple after the series of conflicts and his denunciation of his opponents (21:23—24:1) and predicts its destruction. At this point the final discourse begins (24:3—26:1). There are two major themes indicated by two questions his disciples asked him as he sat on the Mount of Olives: (1) "What will be the sign of your coming (24:29-25) and of the end of the age" (24:3-28). All of chapter 24 is omitted while all of chapter 25 is included in the lectionary.

A series of themes and similarities bind the section together (24:36—25:46). The hour of the coming of the Son of Man (24:29-31) is sudden, unexpected, and unknown (24:36, 37-41, 43, 44, 50; 25:13) Also his coming will be delayed (24:48; 25:5; 25:19) and his arrival sudden (24:50; 25:6). Because of this uncertainty and the crucial nature of the Son of Man's final coming there is a persistent exhortation to be awake and ready (24:42, 43, 44, 46; 25:13). The point of each text is in some way linked to the idea of being ready (24:36-44; 24:45-51, and the three "stories" in chapter 25).

Throughout we find contrasting groups or figures (a faithful and wise slave/ a wicked slave [24:45-50], wise/foolish women [25:1-12]; good and trustworthy slaves/ a wicked and lazy slave [25:14-30] and right and left hand groups [25:3, 4, 6]. In each case there is permanent reward or punishment and radical separation (cf. also 24:40-41). We have come across this phenomenon of contrasting groups and fates in earlier parables [13:36-42; 47-50; cf. 7: 24-27).

Anyone familiar with marriages in some Asian countries will be able to picture the scene of a group of women (and men) with torches (or their modern counterparts), accompanying the bridegroom to the marriage hall. His arrival is quite unpredictable.

The important point is the state of the women at his arrival. One group is in the shopping mall looking for oil at midnight—or at a gas station. When they return the door is shut, never to be opened. The owner's only response to their pleas to be allowed in is "I do not know you." We are forced back to the conclusion of the basic instruction to disciples (chapters 5-7). The "Lord, Lord" cry is met with "I never knew you; go away from me, your evildoers"(7:21–23). We also turn to Jesus' final words in the gospel: "...teaching them to obey everything that I have commanded you" (28:20).

We begin to approach the end of Jesus' ministry. The gospel reminds us that we are to journey in life not only listening to his teaching but also striving to obey and mold our attitudes and lives according to it. "Not those who say Lord, Lord will enter the Kingdom of God but those who do the will of my Father"(7:21). Such men and women are his mother, sisters, and brothers (cf.12:46–50).

I wonder whether one of the reasons why so many drift away from the Christian community is that they do grasp the challenge of Christian life, or they do not want to feel like hypocrites, or they are not willing to accept such a commitment.

In our text, the bridegroom is Christ. The delay represents the passing years from 30 to the 80s and the awareness that the time of the Second Coming is unknown. The arrival of the groom is the final judgment. The wise women are the Christians who have striven to live the gospel. The marriage hall is eternal life (heaven). The women in the shopping mall—late night shopping!—are those who have seriously neglected their Christian way of life. Do such warnings and caution signs motivate those who still worship regularly?

The Thessalonians about 50 C.E. were concerned and grieved with a feeling of hopelessness about Christians who had died (1 Thess 4:13–18). What would happen to them at the return of Christ? They expected his return soon! Paul argued that Jesus, who died and rose, would enable dead Christians to share his resurrection: "through Jesus God will bring with him those who died" (4:14). With culturally conditioned images, he described the coming of the Lord. First the dead will rise. Then Christ will transform those who are alive and all will be "with the Lord forever." The living will have no advantage over the dead.

THIRTY-THIRD SUNDAY OF ORDINARY TIME: YEAR A Mt 25:14–30

Winners and Losers
We are again among the winners and losers in the game of life. The media have sensational stories of losers. Usually they had been winners. The winners in life's games are glamorized. In our gospel, we read of winners and a loser who gets the lion's share of attention. We are confronted again with words of caution, dire threats, and consequences.

Reading Matthew, we gather the impression that the evangelist and teachers were clearly unhappy about the quality of discipleship of a considerable number within the community. In Jesus' earlier collection of parables the theme of severe judgment is prominent (13:14–50) and again in this final instruction (24:36—25:46). The menacing description of punishment as "weeping and gnashing of teeth" occurs six times (8:12; 13:42, 50; 22:13; 24:51; 25:30). The Sermon on the Mount ends with a severe cautionary warning (7:21–27) and watchfulness dominates this last instruction. The believer who is unwilling to forgive will meet an iron-faced God (18:35) and all hypocrisy is mercilessly unmasked. Much of the seed sown proves to be fruitless (13:18–23). Therefore, the gospel again confronts us with the simple question about the quality of our Christian life. In addition, are we investing well the gift of discipleship God has entrusted to us. Is it a blue chip investment?

I was surprised by the choice of the first reading (Prov 31:10–13, 19–20, 30–31 [It is worth reading the full eulogy of the noble wife]). The passage is dangerous since the writer looks at woman, her role, and nobility from the perspective of his patriarchal culture and the status of the social elite. The key to his appreciation is the fact that this wife is one "who fears the Lord" (31:30), namely lives according to Torah. This theme reverberates in the short and exquisite psalm (127/128). Everyone who fears the Lord and walks in his ways is blessed. With images that would resonate in that culture, the psalmist describes the blessings.

The same theme of blessings as a reward for fidelity and diligent management can be read into the way the wealthy man rewards his "slaves." However, the emphasis in the parable falls on the unfortunate third slave. We shall look at some aspects of the parable. The motif that calls forth the parable was the conclusion of last Sunday's gospel, "Keep awake for you know neither the day nor the hour" (35:13). The reason is that we, as members of Christ's community, are like the servants entrusted with the property of the rich man. Note how each is given an amount proportionate to their ability (25:15). As in such popular tales, one figure will act in a peculiar way. The master delayed in returning. The descriptions of the first and second slaves as investors (25:16-17), their rending account and being rewarded (25:20-24) is repetitive. The peculiarity of the third draws our attention, surprise, puzzlement, and maybe anger toward the wealthy man.

We only learn late in the parable of the slave's fears that explain his strange way of securing the one talent. Seeing the wealthy man through his eyes, we lose any respect we had for him. His actions seem to confirm the slave's opinion. This is not a very appealing image of God! Whatever may be the character of the master the slave is condemned as wicked and lazy and in terms of his own worst fears. The punishment is very, very severe. The master is like a Mafia boss who eliminates a worthless gang member! The proverb (25:29) just makes matters look more unjust.

Matthew seems to be quite frustrated. His Jesus returns to the topic of responsible discipleship and dire threats. The theme of the unexpected and unknown time of the return of the Son of Man forms the basis for Paul's exhortation to his Thessalonian community (1 Thess 5:1-6 [cf. 5-11]. The gospel had not spelled out how the believers could live as responsible and faithful disciples. Matthew presumes the earlier teaching to be the charter. Paul mentions explicitly faith, love, and especially hope (5:8-9). He wants his community to encourage and build each other. Though Paul warns, his exhortation affirms the hope and fidelity of the community.

The liturgy needs to emphasize the aspect of hope and the fidelity of so many Christians. Those who need to see the caution signs and hear the warnings probably are not celebrating the liturgy—a pastoral challenge to reach out. However, fear probably will not attract men and women to the Lord.

THIRTY-FOURTH SUNDAY OF ORDINARY TIME: YEAR A Mt 25:31-46

Christ—the King

We have an example of a "cut and paste" use of Scripture again. The purpose of the few verses (Ezek 34:11-12,15-17) from long prophetic oracles (34:1-16, 17-31) is to introduce the use of Shepherd as a symbol for God. The text also provides a background for the idea of the shepherd as judge separating lean sheep (good people) from fat sheep (an oppressive elite). God pronounces stringent censures on Israel's king (34:1-10). He promises to assume the role of the shepherd (a common symbol of a king) who would gather again the exiled and dispersed people, lead them to the land and care for them in every possible way (34:11-15). As a bridge to an oracle of judgment Ezekiel's God distinguishes between the needy among his people (lean, strayed, injured, and weak sheep—cf. 34:16-19, 20-22) and the oppressive and self-seeking leaders (fat and strong sheep—cf. 34:16, 18-19, 21). He cares or punishes (Ezek 34:17 and 20-23). Many authors weave the idea of God as the consistent protector of the broken, the oppressed, the widow, the orphan, the alien, and the poor as a major thread throughout the long narrative of God and Israel. Legal texts and the prophetic teaching accentuated this motif.

The psalm (Ps 22/23) only takes up the theme of the caring shepherd, and host, not the shepherd "who feeds with justice" (Ezek 34:16), namely punishes the self-centered and insensitive (cf. Twenty-Eighth Sunday).

As we approach the gospel, we need to recall that on this Sunday the community honors Christ the King. The overture of Matthew's gospel introduced the king of the Jews who frightened Herod the King and all Jerusalem and who divided "Jews" against wise men from the East (Gentiles). As it ends, a crucified and mocked man has this charge hanging at his head. "This is Jesus, the King of the Jews" (27:37). The people as a whole had taken responsibility: "His blood be on us and on our children"(27:23).

As he died, nature was convulsed and death surrendered its dominion to the power of life (27:51-53). As Lord of the universe, he sent women and men into all nations to create a new community, disciples of Jesus Christ. This community would live his gospel in the world, empowered by him who remained among them and in history (28:18-20). Men and women were divided in their attitudes to him from his origin to his death. Men and women are divided until today. Now the division arises because of others in whom he remains within our history. Jesus' response to his angry disciples as reported in the scene of his anointing at Bethany contradicts a major saying in our gospel. Jesus said "...for you always have the poor with you, but you will not always have me" (26:11).

To the surprised group "who are blessed by my Father," the King of the account says: "I was hungry.... I was thirsty...." (25:35-36). To their further amazed objection he continues: "Truly I tell you, just as you did it to one of the least of those who are members of my family (my brothers) you did it to me" (25:40). In the poor, Jesus remains among us.

We give a few clarifications of the text. This is a narrative of the Son of Man's return and judgment told with apocalyptic stage props. We have the usual stark contrasts. Sheep/goats; right/left hand; blessed of my Father/ accused; kingdom prepared from foundation of the world/eternal fire prepared for the devil and his angels; you gave me food/you gave me no food....

There is an understanding of Jesus explicit or implied. He is the Son of Man and universal king and therefore the Messiah. He is Son of the Father and present in the needy. He is shepherd, judge, and Lord. These responsibilities belonged to his God in his religions tradition.

There are various conflicts in the gospel. There are conflicts between good and evil within the universe (cf. 4:1-11). Matthew narrates the conflicts between Jesus as God's prophet and Son and men and women who are called the adulterous generation and hypocrites. He also gives an account of the conflict within the community of disciples between wheat and weeds. These conflicts come to an end in this scene. In the midst of these the kingdom of God comes. There are two phrases whose meaning is disputed. Does "all nations" refer to nations as such, to all people or to Gentiles or just Christians? Who are "the least of these my brothers?" Does the phrase refer to any needy person or only to needy Christians or needy missionaries (cf. 10:40-42)?

To the extent that the narrative goes back to Jesus those addressed would be human persons and the needy would be any other person. In Matthew's gospel members of his community are addressed. The least would be both members of the church and others. At another level, the "nations" could refer to Gentiles and the way they receive those who preach the gospel.

For us the scene recalls the primacy of the love commandment and the primacy of those in greater need. We need to re-interpret the categories used. The sick and prisoners are probably not the marginalized now. We end our journey face to face with the God of the poor, the humble man of Nazareth alive in the needy of society. Genuine faith in Jesus, Son of God, comes to its authentic expression in day-to-day sensitivity and service of the poor.

Paul's vision of the end of history crowns our liturgy and the year (1 Cor 15:20-26, 28). Paul is clarifying doubts and a major misunderstanding of the resurrection of Christians (1 Cor 15). Any denial of the resurrection implies a denial of Christ's resurrection (15:12-19). However, faith in Christ risen is an integral element of the earliest creed, Christian experience, and the gospel (1 Cor 15:1-11).

Paul states the universality of death, its human origin (Adam), and its human cause. Parallel to this is the universality of resurrection and its human origin, Christ. He sketches a timetable, as it were, for the resurrection and the universal dominion of God. First is the resurrection of Christ, the first fruits. At his coming, this is extended by the resurrection of all who belong to Christ. Christ's dominion over all evil, especially death, precedes his personal submission and the gift of the kingdom to God. He stresses Christ's universal dominion over all evil, human, earthly and cosmic, using contemporary categories and cosmology.

As we celebrate Christ the King, we remember that the Son to whom the Father has entrusted all sovereignty has not the ultimate sovereignty. His Father is sovereign. The Son subjects himself to God who must remain "all in all." We remember the hymn in Philippians and the final doxology of every Eucharist. How fitting that the year end with the great doxology.

The Location Is Everything: The Craft of Mark's Gospel

Jerome H. Neyrey, S.J.

In the liturgy, we tend to read Mark and hear his gospel in segments. Except for the Passion Narrative, which is read in its entirety on Passion (or Palm) Sunday, Mark's story comes to us in a highly excerpted fashion. This could create problems for preachers and audiences, because of the immediate loss of context and location, as they and we lose our sense of where we are in the story. So to offset this loss of context and location, we offer the following sketch of the Marcan narrative and its structural markers. There is no reason any more for preachers or audiences to say "Where are we? I'm lost."

Mark carefully crafted his gospel about Jesus into five sections. Each highlights a specific activity of Jesus and heralds him according to a special name. These observations can be useful for a prayerful reading of Mark and especially for an insightful preaching of his gospel. Knowing where a certain Sunday gospel fits into Mark's larger scheme allows readers and preachers of Mark to grasp more clearly the particular aspect of the crafted message of the evangelist in this section. The five basic parts of Mark's gospel are:

(1) Jesus, the Warrior, who battles and defeats God's enemy, Satan (1:1—3:35);

(2) Jesus, the prodigal Sower, who spreads God's blessings to all people in all places (4:1—8:30);

(3) Jesus, the Master, who teaches "his Way" while on the way to Jerusalem (8:31—10:52);

(4) Jesus, attacked, but victorious over those who challenge God's reform (11:1—13:37);

(5) Jesus, martyred, but vindicated by God (14:1—16:8)

I. Mark 1:1—3:35: Jesus: Warrior, Liberator, and Holy One

Lectionary Readings from Mark

3rd Sunday in Ordinary Time:	Mark 1:14–20
4th Sunday in Ordinary Time:	Mark 1:21–28
5th Sunday in Ordinary Time:	Mark 1:29–39
6th Sunday in Ordinary Time:	Mark 1:40–45

Mark begins his narrative with the theophany of God to Jesus at the Jordan (1:1–11). Clearly Jesus did not come to John the Baptizer because he needed repentance, as did the other pilgrims. Matthew tells us that John even protested when Jesus presented himself for the washing rite (Mt 3:14–15). So we look for another meaning to this event.

All theophanies in Scripture are commissionings. Abraham, Moses, Elijah, Isaiah, and Jeremiah all were favored with a revelation from God, which served as their commissioning as prophets and agents of God. So it is with Jesus. God's appearance to him at the Jordan indicates certain things: (a) Jesus enjoys God's favor, and so we should think of him as a saint or holy person, and (b) God puts the Holy Spirit into Jesus, so we know that he acts with divine power and in accord with God's will.

It is profitable to compare this theophany-commission of Jesus with the remarks in Isaiah 42:1–9, where the Servant of God, who enjoys God's favor, is authorized to bring justice and healing to a needy world. Thus we begin the story knowing important things about Jesus: he is holy and has a "holy" spirit. John the Baptizer even speaks of him as "the stronger one" (1:7), that is, a person who has God's power. Jesus, then, is God's warrior, "well pleasing" to God and designated as God's champion in the battles to come. All of this is immediately challenged and defended in Jesus' temptations in the desert (1:12-13). There Jesus, the Holy One, battles the Evil One, Satan, and proves to be the "stronger one." He continues to enjoy God's favor, as God's angels minister to him. The Holy Warrior has begun the war with a great victory.

Mark casts the first public action of Jesus in the synagogue as a "battle" (1:21-28). Jesus' holiness is attested to by his presence at the village synagogue on the Sabbath. Because he knows God's holy word and will, he teaches with "authority," which here refers to his authorization to act with power. But Mark highlights here the conflict between Jesus and the unclean spirit as the major point of the story. The unclean spirit acknowledges that Jesus comes to wage war, "Have you come to destroy us?" (1:24). He knows, moreover, that they are in opposite camps: Jesus is "the Holy One of God," while he is an "unclean spirit." When Jesus acts with God's power to silence and then subdue him, Mark informs us about Jesus the Warrior of God and "stronger one," who liberates God's oppressed people from the dominion of God's enemy, Satan.

Furthermore, this first miracle of Jesus is meant to be programmatic for Jesus' ministry: time and again in 1:21—3:35 Jesus will heal and cast out demons (1:29-31, 32-34; 2:1-12; 3:1-6, 9-12) or bring cleanness to unclean people (1:40-44) or battle "unclean" spirits. In each and every instance Mark would have us continue to appreciate that Jesus is God's Warrior! Holy One! Liberator!

The ministry of Jesus, the "Holy One," also consists of a reform of Jewish purity concerns. Because Jesus was told by God that "with you I am well pleased," we trust Jesus' subsequent violation of many of the purity concerns and practices of synagogue Judaism. When Jesus touches the unclean leper, he extends God's cleanness even if he breaks the taboo of touching the unclean. When Jesus forgives sins, he demonstrates that he has God's authority to deal with uncleanness in a new way (2:10). When Jesus eats with unclean toll collectors and sinners (2:15-16)—something that a holy person should not do—we know that he is God's "physician," sent to heal such uncleanness (2:17).

Finally, when Jesus does what was forbidden on the Sabbath, he reforms synagogue notions of what pleases God: he offers life, not death, and good, not evil. Thus Mark tells us that, not only is Jesus a holy Warrior battling Evil, but he is God's agent of holiness and wholeness who reforms the old customs of dealing with uncleanness. God's kingdom, then, consists of liberation from Satan's oppressive power and cleanness from all stain. Jesus is God's authorized agent (warrior, physician, reformer) commissioned to effect these dramatic changes in human lives.

Yet Mark would not let us forget that from its very beginning Jesus' ministry is a constant battle. He not only confronts and silences Satan and other unclean spirits (1:25, 34; 3:11), he engages in endless controversy with people who stand against God's reforms of the purity codes of the day. In 2:1—3:6 Mark assembled and arranged five such controversies, as the diagram on the facing page indicates.

Purity Controversies in Mark's Gospel

A. 2:1-12 CONTROVERSY with SCRIBES over SIN
- location: "And again he entered Capernaum..." (2:1)
- form: *healing* (of paralytic) and embedded *controversy* (forgiveness of sin)
- question: "Which is easier to say, 'Your sins are forgiven' or 'Take up your pallet and walk'"
(2:9 – note alternatives presented)
ISSUE: Jesus deals with "uncleanness" (sin) in a new way

    B. 2:13-17 CONTROVERSY with PHARISEES over EATING with SINNERS
    - eating with sinners
    - explanation: " ...those in need" (2:17)
    ISSUE: Jesus' new dealings with unclean sinners

    C. 2:18-22 CONTROVERSY with PHARISEES
    - eating (non-fasting)
    - explanation: new sacred time/new kosher practices
    ISSUE: outline of a "new purity system"

    B'. 2:23-28 CONTROVERSY with PHARISEES over EATING
    - eating untithed foods on Sabbath
    - explanation: "...when David was in need" (2:25)
    ISSUE: Jesus' new interpretation of sacred time/sacred things

A'. 3:1-6 CONTROVERSY with PHARISEES over SABBATH OBSERVANCE
- location: "again he entered the synagogue..." (3:1)
- form: *healing* (withered limb) and embedded *controversy* (work on Sabbath)
- question: "Is it lawful to do good or to do harm, to save life or to kill"
(3:4 — note alternatives presented)
ISSUE: Jesus deals with "clean" time in a new way

In 2:1—3:6, Mark presents here a cluster of five "controversies" over purity concerns, which he considers an alternate form to the "battle" that Jesus wages against unclean spirits. The central three controversies focus on eating: *with whom* one eats, *when* one does not eat (i.e., fast), and *what* one eats. The first and last conflict stories are combinations of controversy and healing elements. Jesus' actions affect both body and soul, for God's kingdom regards the whole person. As well as God wills the liberation of the heart from slavery to the Evil One, God also wishes holiness of body, which means bodily wholeness. These controversies, then, continue the liberating work of God's Warrior and the purifying mission of God's Holy One. Yet Mark would remind us that Jesus was ever in conflict.

God's kingdom may be a reign of peace, but it can come only after a battle. But what a champion God's people have in Jesus, Reformer, Holy One, and Warrior!

Like most good storytellers, Mark is attentive to beginnings and endings. This first section of his narrative **begins** with a story about Jesus, the stronger one who has God's holy Spirit and who battled Satan (1:1–13). And it **ends** with a parallel story in which **people contest** this judgment about Jesus, only to be proved wrong (3:22–30). The following diagram should aid our appreciation of how the themes and issues announced at the **beginning** are reconsidered and definitively answered in the **ending** of this section.

Beginnings and Endings in Mark's Gospel

1:5 *(Overture/Introduction)* | 3:21–35 *(Conclusion/Resume)*

1. preaching baptism of repentance for *forgiveness of sins* (1:4):
"repent and believe" (1:15)

1. all sins and all blasphemies *will be forgiven* (3:28–30)

2. correct response:
confessing their sins (1:5)

2. wrong response: they say he is possessed of Beelzebul (3:22)

3. Jesus the warrior: "there comes after me a 'stronger one'" (1:7)

3. Jesus the warrior: "no one can enter a 'strong' man's house . . . unless he binds the strong man" (3:27)

4. which spirit?
"He will baptize you with the Holy Spirit" (1:7) he saw the Holy Spirit coming down upon him (1:10) Led by the Spirit (1:12)

4. which spirit?
whoever blasphemes against the Holy Spirit has an eternal sin, for they said "He has an unclean spirit" (3:29–30)

5. God's verdict of him "My beloved son, in whom I am well pleased" (1:9)

5. their verdict of him
"he is possessed of Beelzebub" (3:22)

6. the Kingdom of God is at hand (1:15)

6. a kingdom divided cannot stand (3:24) he has an end (3:26)

Mark leaves nothing to chance. Since it was clear that many people did not accept Jesus as God's holy prophet, he uses 3:22–30 as an opportunity to answer those criticisms and to herald again his foundational message about Jesus. How should we think about Jesus? Saint or sinner? Whose agent is he? Servant of God or minion of Satan? Is he holy or unclean? Mark told us in the *beginning* (1:1–13) crucial information about Jesus, namely that God was well pleased with him and put the Holy Spirit upon him, and that he proved stronger than Satan. And so when Jesus' enemies contest this, claiming that he is only an agent of Beelzebub who has an unclean spirit, we know that they are wrong. One more challenge to Jesus has been repulsed. He is truly the victorious one. He is, moreover, always the liberator, for his task is "to bind the 'strong man' [Satan] and enter his house and plunder his goods" (3:27). Jesus remains, then, the "stronger one" who rescues those possessed by Satan and restores them to God's kingdom. As the one who enjoys God's "holy" Spirit, Jesus can extend that holiness to others, whom he instructs in God's reformed ways of wholeness and holiness.

II. Mark 4:1—8:30
Jesus, the Prodigal Sower:
Faith, the Eventual Harvest

Lectionary Readings from Mark

11th Sunday of Ordinary Time:	Mark 4:26–34
12th Sunday of Ordinary Time:	Mark 4:35–41
13th Sunday of Ordinary Time:	Mark 5:21–43
14th Sunday of Ordinary Time:	Mark 6:1–6
15th Sunday of Ordinary Time:	Mark 6:7–13
16th Sunday of Ordinary Time:	Mark 6:30–34
22nd Sunday of Ordinary Time:	Mark 7:1–8, 14–15, 21–25
23rd Sunday of Ordinary Time:	Mark 7:31–37
24th Sunday of Ordinary Time:	Mark 8:27–35

Mark's second section of the gospel *begins* with a programmatic story, whose details serve as clues to the new images and themes he develops. Three times Mark notes that Jesus is teaching (4:1-2), a very public action. So many people—holy and sinful, strong and weak—gather around him that he has to sit in a boat (4:1). Jesus then speaks a series of parables, most of which have to do with some agricultural theme: sowing seed (4:3-9), soils (4:14-20), secrecy of growing seed (4:26-32), and the mustard seed (4:30-32). There is even a certain logic to this collection, which begins with sowing and ends with harvest. But it is the first parable (4:3-9) that interests us, because Mark intends it to be a summary of the identity and mission of Jesus in this part of the narrative.

Not surprisingly, Jesus tells the parable of a sower to an audience of peasant farmers. At first this sounds like an outrageous story about a stupid farmer who does not to know how to plant. This dumb farmer wastes three of every four seeds by throwing them on the places least likely to grow. He sows the seed first on the path, where birds devour it, then on rocky ground, where it withers, and then among thorns, which choke it. His audience must be roaring with laughter at Jesus' description of a dumb farmer who will shortly lose his land because of his stupid sowing practices. And this is the point where Jesus' story bites. But who is this "dumb sower"? anybody we know? or possibly God? or even Jesus, God's agent?

This "dumb" sower might just be a "prodigal" sower. This "stupid" sower just might be a benefactor. The secret of the parable turns on Mark's insistence that we see God or Jesus in the role of the sower. Jesus spreads God's word to the most unlikely people and in the most unlikely places. God's impartiality and inclusivity are what are "stupid" here! Jesus' mission to the unclean, the sick, and the sinful is what is "dumb" here! Hence, Mark would have us rename this parable, from "the stupid sower" to the "prodigal sower." God's prodigal extension of blessing, grace, and benefaction to all peoples is the issue.

This programmatic parable of Jesus then becomes the motif for a careful reading of the following miraculous acts of Jesus. Mark would have us see all of Jesus' travels in 4:35—8:30 as illustrations of the "prodigal" sowing of the gospel message to all places, either across the Lake of Galilee or in the region of Tyre and Sidon or in the Decapolis or in the villages of Caesarea Philippi. The sower of God's grace is not confined to Jewish territory. Furthermore, Mark would have us interpret the various people to whom Jesus extends God's healing mercy as further examples of the divine prodigality. God's healing and blessing extend to males and females (5:1-20, 21-43), to Jews and Gentiles (5:1-20; 7:24-30, 31-37), to slave and free. Jesus' two feedings are "prodigal" offerings of seed-food to all present, male and female, saint and sinner, Jew and Gentile (6:30-44; 8:1-10). No one, Mark insists, is excluded from God's inclusive and impartial mercy. Thus the "stupid" sower is really a "prodigal" farmer, he casts his seed everywhere to everyone.

The beginning parable, moreover, presents us with a series of images that are thematic for the next part of the narrative. If the sower sows a "word" (4:14), then we should pay attention to who "hears" the word of Jesus and who "sees" him with faith and understanding. "Some," we are told, only "see but do not perceive, hear but do not understand" (4:12). Mark would have us keep tabs on who hears Jesus or hears about him (5:27; 6:2, 14, 55; 7:14, 16, 25; 8:18) and who sees him. Of course, as the parable of the soils warned us

(4:14–20), not all will hear correctly and become Jesus' disciples. Despite Jesus' injunction, "Let all hear who have ears" (4:9) and then his warning "Take heed how you hear" (4:24), there are many deaf ears.

The most telling example of this failure of eyes and ears occurs when Jesus returns to his hometown. They have heard of his "wisdom" and "the mighty works wrought by his hands": but when they hear Jesus themselves, "they took offense at him" so that he marveled at their unbelief (6:1–6). Being a blood relative of Jesus does not insure membership in his circle: for earlier we saw that his relatives thought him mad and came to snatch Jesus from the public and take him and hide him at home (3:21). Now the same relatives and friends shame him and refuse to accept his new role as sower of God's powerful word. They are replaced as his "kin" by others who believe in him and listen in faith to him (3:31–35). Unfortunately, other examples of deaf ears abound in the gospel. For example, Herod "heard of it, for Jesus' name had become known": but he does not act upon his hearing about "these powers at work in him" (6:14–16). The Pharisees too have heard of his great deeds, but they demand to see a special sign, a mark of unbelief (8:11–13).

Yet God's plan secretly and silently advances, so that an eventual harvest of faith is assured. The initial evidence of this comes in the agricultural parables in 4:26–34. First we hear of the secret growth of the seed (4:26–29): the farmer indeed labors, but he cannot recognize, much less control, the sprouting of the seed and its maturation. Growth and harvest come from God (see 1 Cor 3:6–7). And what a harvest it is: rich, full, and surprising. Next we are told of a mustard seed (4:30–32) which begins as "the smallest of seeds," yet produces "the greatest of all shrubs," so large as to house an aviary. Again, in defiance of human logic or power, God provides startling growth and success.

Mark dramatizes the success of God's sowing of the gospel when Jesus symbolically heals deaf ears (7:31–37) and blind eyes (8:22–26). The two miracles are crafted carefully to have similar structure and so a reinforcing message:

Parallel Miracles and Messages in Mark

7:32–37 (deaf mute)

32. And they *brought to him* a man who was deaf and had an impediment in his speech. And *they besought him to lay his hand* upon him.

33. And *taking him aside from* the multitude *privately*, he put his *fingers* in his ears and *spat* and touched his tongue.

34. And *looking up* to heaven, he sighed and *said* . . .

36. And he charged them *to tell no one* . . .

8:22–26 (blind)

22. And some *brought to him* a blind man, and *besought him to touch* him.

23. And *taking* the blind man by the hand, he led him *out of* the village: and when he *spat* on his eyes and *laid his hands on him.*

24. And *looking up,* he *said* . . .

26. And he sent him to his home, saying, *"Tell no one."*

Jesus' great liberating power now serves to bless eyes and ears so that they may see and hear, not just the stuff of the world, but God's gospel. These miracle stories symbolize once more the sowing of the seed, and they both articulate the great and successful harvest that must attend this action of God.

Finally, the harvest of faith is reached when even the incredulous disciples see clearly that "You are the Christ" (8:27–30). Mark sets the scene in Caesarea Philippi, far north in the Galilee: because of its two Greco-Roman names ("Caesar" and "Philip"), we are urged to see this as Gentile territory.

Jesus then asks the disciples two questions: "Who do the outsiders say that I am?" and "Who do the insiders say that I am?" Presumably by this time in the narrative, all the peoples of upper and lower Galilee have either seen Jesus or heard of him: the prodigal sowing is complete. But what results? what harvest? Many outsiders are correct in recognizing in Jesus' miracles the power of God: thus the miracles serve as credentials to identify Jesus as "Elijah...one of the prophets" (8:28). This would correspond to a rich harvest, "thirty or sixty-fold" (4:8a). The insiders, however, acclaim him "the Christ" of God (8:29), which parallels the "hundredfold" harvest (4:8b). And so the climactic events narrated here summarize much of the point of the narrative:

- (a) the word/seed has been sown on all types of soil:

- (b) many have seen or heard this "gospel," for the sowing is radically inclusive:

- (c) furthermore, many take the word to heart in faith and yield a successful harvest of discipleship:

- (d) thus God is ever in control of events, giving grace and insight and insuring success.

And so when we follow the logic of the parable of the sower (4:3–9) we are schooled to see Jesus sowing God's word of life in all sorts of places and to all kinds of people. No one is denied sight of Jesus or hearing about him. And his mission, despite conflict and obstacles, wonderfully yields a harvest of disciples of faith, who see and hear and confess him truly as God's Christ.

Scholars long ago pointed out that Mark is incorporating here a very old collection of miracle stories about Jesus. As Mark gathered data for his preaching about Jesus, he was acquainted with a double strand of miracle stories whose shape is indicated in the diagram below.

The *miracles* are the sowing of God's grace and benefaction. They serve as the clear signs of what God wills for us: protection from malevolence, healing of bodily ills, rescue from death, fully fed bodies, and access to God's word. The way, moreover, in which the miracles are extended geographically in Galilee, Tyre and Sidon, and the Decapolis, mirrors the "prodigality" of the sower Jesus extends God's benefaction to all.

To this double chain of miracle stories, Mark added the parallel *controversies* between Jesus and the Pharisees.

Parallel Collections of Miracles and Controversies

1. crossing the sea (4:35ff.)
2. stilling of storm (4:35–41)
3. unclean females: woman with hemorrhage/Jairus' daughter (5:21–43)
4. feeding of 5000 (6:34–44)
5. healing of deaf mute (7:31–37)
6. controversy with Pharisees over purity rules and bread eating (7:1–23)

1. sea crossing (8:10a)
2. walking on water (6:45–51)
3. unclean females: Syrophoenician woman and daughter (7:24–30)
4. feeding of 4000 (8:1–10)
5. healing of blind man (8:22–26)
6. controversy with Pharisees over a sign: warning about their "leaven" (8:11–13, 15)

The issue centers around the Pharisees' "teaching" or their "bread"/"leaven." Their teaching, it may be argued, does not support the inclusiveness that Jesus promotes. For they would impose restrictive purity rules concerning the washing of vessels and proscribed foods: both sets of rules tend toward exclusivity, as they draw clear distinctions between what may be eaten with whom and in what conditions. Thus the controversy in 7:1–23, although ostensibly about washing and foods, functions as an indicator of who may share table and fellowship, either Jesus' inclusive or their exclusive strategy. In this regard, the controversy reinforces the general theme of inclusivity and prodigal sowing.

Returning once more to the thematic parable of 4:3–9, we attend to the repeating motif of "seed," "sowing," "growth," and "harvest." As every farmer knows, the end product of all this labor is bread. Mark knows this too, and he programs us by the parable to look out for "bread talk."

- Multiplication of BREADS for 5000 (6:38-44)
- Non-understanding of BREADS (6:52)
- Eating BREADS with unwashed hands (7:2-5)
- Children's BREAD and the dogs (7:27-28)
- Multiplication of BREADS for 4000 (8:4-10)
- Multiplication of BREADS recalled (8:16-21)

"Bread" is physical bread that hungry people eat as gift of God's benefaction. But "bread" in Jewish traditions also serves as a metaphor for wisdom or teaching. And so Jesus' gift of bread is also an invitation to accept his gospel and teaching. Eating his bread, then, is similar to hearing his word and seeing his deeds: it should produce faith and discipleship. Later, when many hearers of Jesus track him down, Jesus acts as a "shepherd" toward these "lost sheep" (6:34). His shepherding takes two forms: first he "began to teach them many things" (6:34b), and then he fed them abundantly with bread (6:35-44). Thus "teaching" and "bread" are almost interchangeable symbols of Jesus' benefaction.

Thus Mark has crafted a clever story of Jesus' activity in the guise of a "prodigal sower." By using this parable in the *beginning* of this section, he has programmed us to attend to the inclusive and impartial gift of God's benefaction. We note how Jesus sows this gift to Jew and Gentile alike, as well as to male and female. No person or place is excluded from the ministry of this stupid, prodigal farmer. But not all soils receive the seed and yield a harvest: not all who see and hear Jesus become disciples. Yet in the *end*, God's plan proves successful and there is finally a great harvest of faith, when Jesus' closest associates demonstrate remarkable insight (8:27-30).

Thus we might summarize Mark's second section by noting the interrelation of the double helix of "sower sowing" and "soils receiving the seed:

Sower (sowing):	Soils (receiving the seed):
a prodigal sowing replicated in:	the fate of the seed reflected in:
a) Inclusive geography	a) eyes which see/ears which hear
b) inclusive miracles	b) growth and spread of Jesus' gospel
c) inclusive giving of bread	c) harvest of insight, faith, confession.

III. Mark 8:31—10:52
The "Way" of Jesus, on "the Way" to Jerusalem

Lectionary Readings from Mark

25th Sunday in Ordinary Time:	Mark 9:30-37
26th Sunday in Ordinary Time:	Mark 9:38-43, 45, 47-48
27th Sunday in Ordinary Time:	Mark 10:2-16
28th Sunday in Ordinary Time:	Mark 10:17-30
29th Sunday in Ordinary Time:	Mark 10:35-45
30th Sunday in Ordinary Time:	Mark 10:46-52

When the third section of Mark's narrative begins, Jesus and his disciples are far north of Galilee, in the villages of Caesarea Philippi. From there he begins his way to Jerusalem, and so this section reflects a "way" or travel motif. But "on the way" (8:27; 9:33-34; 10:17, 32, 46), Jesus teaches his "'way' of discipleship." We recall that Christianity was called "the Way" (Acts 9:2, 24:14). But the "way of Jesus" taught in 8:31—10:52 will focus on the "way of the Cross" as the pattern of discipleship.

Mark records that on the way to Jerusalem Jesus made three predictions of his rejection and vindication. These three predictions, however, are each misunderstood by the disciples. And so Jesus issues further clarifying remarks to explain the meaning of his "way." Thus the shape of this part of the story may be grasped by appreciating the following pattern: statement, misunderstanding, and clarification.

statement	8:31	9:30–31	10:32–34
misunderstanding	8:32	9:32	10:35–40
clarification	8:33–9:29	9:33–10:31	10:41–45

Jesus begins by stating that he must be rejected, to which Peter objects. This prompts Jesus to issue a clarifying statement that summarizes the value of discipleship (8:33—9:1). True disciples will imitate Jesus by rejecting the values of their world, and by "denying" themselves and "losing" their lives for his sake. Those who honor Jesus in this way will be honored in turn by him. But "whoever is ashamed of me, of him will the Son of Man be ashamed" (8:38). Thus discipleship, accepted or rejected, has radical consequences. This is indeed a hard saying, and it demands some warrant: for it goes against the grain of all that people know. How do we know that Jesus is correct in these demands?

When Jesus and his three elite disciples ascend a mountain, miraculous things begin occurring (9:1–8). First, Jesus is metamorphosed in form, with his garments becoming more brilliant than any earthly process could make them. Next, the prophets Elijah and Moses appear to and converse with Jesus. We would probably best understand these heavenly figures as prophets who were rejected by their contemporaries, but vindicated by God. Thus Elijah and Moses are types of martyrs whom God rescues, and thus serve to indicate Jesus' own future.

Finally, God stages another theophany and proclaims a sacred word about Jesus: "This is my beloved son: listen to him" (9:7). If we were correct in understanding God's theophany at the baptism (1:1–11) as a commissioning of Jesus for his career as a warrior, liberator, and sanctifier, then this theophany would be authorizing Jesus in terms of his way of the cross in Jerusalem and his "way" of discipleship. Although at the transfiguration Jesus says nothing to the disciples, yet God commands them: "Listen to him." To what should they attend? What did God command them to pay attention to? Mark would have us think back to what Jesus just said about discipleship in 8:31–38 and ahead to what he will speak when they leave the mountain (9:9–13). The transfiguration, then, functions as God's commissioning of Jesus for the second half of the gospel story, namely, his journey to the cross and the pattern of discipleship encoded in his special "way."

In many other places Jesus has articulated some aspects of his "way." Not everything to do with his "way," however, is part of the "way of the cross." Let us recall what Jesus has been saying about his "way" and how as a reformed "way," it differs from the teachings of the synagogue. In general, Mark records Jesus presenting his way as an antithesis to the way of the synagogue: hence Jesus' disciples can distinguish themselves as those who do not do what the synagogue does:

- they fast — we don't (2:18–20)
- they keep strict Sabbath — we don't (2:23–28; 3:1–6)
- they wash hands, etc. — we don't (7:1–5)
- they do korban — we don't (7:11–13)
- they keep kosher — we don't (7:18–23)
- they keep elders' tradition — we don't (7:10–13)
- they divorce — we don't (10:1–9)
- they sacrifice in temple — we don't (11:15–18: 12:29, 33)

But when Jesus is "on the way" to Jerusalem, we find more pointed teaching about imitating him. Disciples should adopt his values and structure their social lives after his pattern. Hence they should learn to value what Jesus values. For example, status in the group consists in being "last of all and servant of all" (9:35). What, then, is the "way" of Jesus like?

- way of the cross: dishonor, shame (8:31, 34–36)
- way of prayer and fasting (9:23, 28–29)
- way of low status (9:33–36)
- way of non-sectarian stance (9:39–40)
- way of hospitality to missionaries (9:37, 41)
- way of concern for pollution (9:42–49)
- way of accepting children (10:13–16)
- way of the Ten Commandments (10:17–20)
- way of loss of wealth, honor, and status (10:23–31)
- way of non-pursuit of honor, status (10:35–37, 42–44)

Certain emphases and patterns become apparent from this list. First, Jesus does not compete for honor, wealth, and power like all the other people in the villages. In fact, the "way of the cross" despises such and turns to God as the only value. Jesus' triple announcement of his rejection and loss of honor in Jerusalem clashes with the disciples' squabble for honor and prestige. Mark notes that the disciples "did not understand" Jesus' second passion prediction (9:31–32), probably because they are too busy "discussing with one another who was the greatest" (9:34). Mark juxtaposes the third passion prediction (10:33–34) about the loss of honor with the secret request by James and John to have the honor of sitting at Jesus' right and left hand (10:35–40). Their request constitutes a radical "misunderstanding" of his "way." In clarification, Jesus presents his own behavior as the model to be followed: "The Son of Man came not to be served but to serve, and to give his life as ransom for many" (10:45).

Second, honor is tied to wealth, for wealth can buy elegant clothes, horses, chariots, villas, and banquets. So when a man of wealth comes to Jesus and asks him about "inheriting eternal life" (10:17), Jesus reminds him first of the basic piety to God expressed in the Ten Commandments (10:19), which the man has kept from his youth. Jesus then extends to this ideal candidate for discipleship his "love" and tells him to forgo his wealth and the honor it brings and to follow Jesus' way of non-honor (10:21). Like the seed choked by the thorns of delight in the world and its riches (4:19), this candidate "proves unfruitful." The stage is then set for Jesus' teaching on the perverse desire for honor that is bound up with wealth. "How hard it is for those who have riches to enter the kingdom" (23), for they tend to be focused on themselves and their status and reputation, and cannot imagine that a good use of wealth is to "give [it] to the poor" (10:21) and to be servants of others, as Jesus is (10:45).

The disciples, however, have either voluntarily left all to follow Jesus or been disinherited of it for their allegiance to him: losing whatever wealth they had as peasants and artisans, they are "rich" in honor in God's eyes and promised a great inheritance (10:29–30). For "true honor" in God's eyes has nothing to do with worldly reputation. And so, Jesus concludes, "the first are last, and the last are first" (10:31).

One final theme about the "way of Jesus" is articulated. As we have seen, Jesus regularly offers a reform of the cultural purity regulations of Judaism. This theme returns in 9:38–42, 43–48. First Jesus speaks against the tendency to exclusivity typical of sectarian groups to think that they are the few elite, who should jealously guard their name and boundaries. It matters not if outsiders use Jesus' name to heal, but do not thereby promote Jesus and his circle. What counts is the fact that once more the seed is sown in all soils and that God's liberating power rescues the enslaved. Yet Jesus is concerned with purity and boundaries, for he then warns against scandal and harm caused to others, which corrupts them (9:42). Such people are so great a threat to the holy group that it should act immediately to protect itself. Likewise, individuals are called to holiness, such that, if a hand or eye or foot "causes you to sin," better to cut it off (9:43–48). A strategy of inclusivity is balanced with a doctrine of holiness. A new purity system is emerging.

Throughout this gospel, *beginnings* and *endings* have been important narrative clues for understanding the themes and motifs of the story. This section of the gospel *begins* with Jesus' first declaration of what constitutes his way (8:31–38). Peter expresses reluctance to follow and imitate Jesus: and so Jesus caustically commands him "Get behind me" (8:33), that is, "Reform and conform! Follow in my pattern!"

The *ending* of this section on the "way" of Jesus consists of a healing of blind Bartimaeus (10:46–52). Jesus stops and "calls him," which is a metaphor for being invited to be a disciple (10:49). Unlike Peter, Bartimaeus "sprang up" and came to Jesus. And when healed, he joyfully "followed him on his way" (10:52). Discipleship in the "way" of Jesus, once rejected by Peter, is now gladly assumed by a blind man. In terms of Mark's presentation of Jesus, this section highlights his role as teacher of an authentic and reformed "way" of serving God. Authorized by God in the transfiguration, Jesus proclaims the "way of the cross," and faithfully follows that path. He presents himself as a model to be imitated and promises to his disciples the same reward and vindication that God will bestow on him.

IV. Mark 11:1—13:37
Jesus in Conflict: Challenge and Counter-challenge

Lectionary Readings from Mark

31st Sunday in Ordinary Time:	Mark 12:28–34
32nd Sunday in Ordinary Time:	Mark 12:38–44

As we have noted, Mark tends to give narrative clues at the *beginning* and *ending* of sections to help us focus our attention. This fourth part of the story *begins* at a highly significant place, "...the Mount of Olives" (11:1). Not only does this mountain play a symbolic role in the speculations of Israel about the coming of the Messiah, it literally faces the Temple across the valley. Thus the narrative *begins* with the Temple in view. It *ends* back where it *began*, on "...the Mount of Olives" (13:3). And here the talk is focused on the Temple across the valley: "Do you see these great buildings? There will not be left here one stone upon another, that will not be thrown down" (13:2). And so, Mark instructs his readers and hearers to focus on the Temple and what Jesus says about it and does to it.

The Temple is the physical locus of most of the events in this section: Jesus enters Jerusalem, but immediately "went into the temple" (11:11). On the following day, he returns to the Temple (11:15). The next day, as he was "walking in the Temple" (11:27) he is challenged about his actions performed the previous day in the Temple. He then speaks a parable whose punchline is the remark about "the very stone rejected by the builders has become the head of the corner" (12:10 = Ps 118:22), which must refer to the cornerstone of a new temple. All four controversies in 12:13–37 take place in the Temple, as do the critical remarks about the moneys being put into the Temple treasury (12:41–44). Finally, the apocalyptic discourse in Mark 13 has as its occasion and focus Jesus' prediction of the destruction of the Temple (13:1–2, 3, 4, 14).

The following list indicates Mark's studied concern for the Temple, which should indicate to us its importance.

11:11	"And he went in Jerusalem, into the Temple ..."
11:15	"And he went into the Temple and began to drive out those who bought and sold in the Temple ... he would not allow any one to carry a vessel through the Temple.
11:17	"My house shall be a house of prayer for all the nations"
11:27	"By what authority to do these things?" (= 11:15–19)
12:11	"The stone rejected by the builders has become the cornerstone"
12:33	"To love God ... is worth more than all whole burnt offerings"
12:35	"... teaching in the Temple"
12:41–43	remarks about Temple treasury and the ruin it causes on the poor
13:1	"He went out of the Temple"
13:2	"... there will not be left a stone upon a stone, which will not be thrown down"
13:3	"... seated on the Mt. of Olives, opposite the Temple"
13:14	"When you see the 'abomination of desolations' standing where it ought not to be ..."
14:58	(false witness): "I will destroy *this* temple made with human hands and in three days I will build another not made with human hands"
15:29–30	"Aha, you would tear down this temple made by human hands and build one in three days ..."
15:38	"And the curtain of the temple was torn in two ..."

To understand Mark's focus on the Temple, we need to know more about the significance of temples vis-à-vis their cultures and populations. All temples, including the Jerusalem Temple, are more than mere buildings. They embody and express a political and social arrangement: they symbolize a system. When land is made sacred by becoming a temple, there must needs be a special group of people to erect and maintain the buildings, officiate at feasts and services there, and function as wise mediators with the gods or God. This implies a vast expenditure of money for personnel, buildings, offerings, and the like. Temples quickly acquire vast wealth, for lands and taxes are dedicated to their construction and maintenance: they often serve as treasuries and banks. They express, moreover, the political will of the ruling elites. In short, they are not simple "religious" shrines, but elaborate systems engaging large numbers of priests, special offerings, guards and attendants, and official ideology sanctioning their operation. It is this system that Jesus engages by his actions in the Temple, which are highly provocative and revolutionary actions.

Thus when Jesus enters the Temple (11:15–19), he does not merely "cleanse" it, but fundamentally challenges its system and stops its operations. These are not reforming, but revolutionary actions. First he stops the system of sacrificial offerings by driving from the Temple those who sold there (11:15b). Then he denies the Temple its revenue when he overturns the tables of the money-changers, who exchanged Roman coins with idolatrous images for kosher Jewish coins (11:15c). Poor peasants and artisans, who constitute 95% of the population, no longer had to pay this entrance fee to enter the sacred precincts. He prohibits people from carrying anything across the Temple, which must surely be sacrificial offerings, such as grain, doves, wine, animals, and the like (11:16). Thus Jesus appears to have stopped the old system of petitioning and propitiating God. He strikes a blow at the very raison d'être of the Temple.

Moreover, he proclaims a new ideology, which vitiates the heart of the temple system: "My house shall be a *house of prayer* for all the nations" (11:17 = Is 56:7). "Prayer" does not require a sacred place, with a special clergy and an elaborate system of offerings. Neither does it require vast expenditures of wealth, nor embody a political ideology of honoring the deity of the city or region. For, Jesus' new place of prayer will be "for all the nations," not just the Judeans. Whatever purification, forgiveness of sins, or thanksgiving is offered to God should be done in some other way, namely, through the "way" of Jesus (1:8; 2:1–12; 9:29; 14:24).

The following listing suggests the shape of the new *system* heralded by Jesus:

- new ritual: prayer and charity, not sacrifice (12:33)
- new temple: Jesus himself as replacement of temple and cult (12:10)
- new membership: impartial membership to Jew and Greek (11:17)
- new definition of holiness and purity (1:8; 2:1–12; 7:1–23)
- new institutional emphasis: promotion of kinship (i.e., satisfaction of human needs) over political interests (i.e., Temple tithes, taxes, and donations) (11:15; 12:41–42)

Therefore, Jesus challenges the old system and offers a new one in its place. His threat was so great that "the chief priests and the scribes...sought a way to destroy him" (11:18).

All subsequent materials in this section dealing with the Temple are also grouped together by the repeated motif of controversy. Jesus challenges the Temple elite (11:15–19) and now they challenge him (11:27–12:37).

Earlier, in 2:1—3:6, we saw how Mark presented a series of five controversies between Jesus and his adversaries. Now we find a comparable collection of controversies. It greatly helps us to appreciate what is going on here if we know the shape of the "controversy game" played by Judeans, which we can call "the four questions."

> Our Rabbis taught: Twelve questions did the Alexandrians address to Rabbi Joshua bar Haninah.
>
> Three were of a scientific nature, three were matters of aggada, three were mere nonsense, and three were matters of conduct. (b. Niddah 69b)

It seems that the same four kinds of questions apply to the controversies between Jesus and his opponents in Jerusalem.

1. scientific nature	= basic principles of the Law/Torah= Mk 12:28–34
2. aggada	= biblical exegesis= Mk 12:35–37
3. nonsense	= ridiculing an opponent's position= Mk 12:18–27
4. matter of conduct	= specific application of the Law = Mk 12:13–17

First the Pharisees "try to trap Jesus in his talk"

(12:13) when they ask him about "matters of conduct," that is, whether "it is lawful to pay taxes to Caesar" (12:14-15). This question concerns "matters of conduct," namely, the specific application of the law. Second, Sadducees ask him a "nonsense" question about the resurrection, trying to ridicule his position (12:18-27). Then one of the scribes asks a "scientific" question about the basic principles of the Law, "which commandment is the greatest?" (12:28-34). Finally, Jesus himself asks the fourth question, the "aggada" question which has to do with biblical exegesis (12:35-37).

These are not the only controversies in this section. After Jesus' challenge to the temple system, the chief priests and scribes return the challenge and demand to know "by what authority you do these things, or who gave you authority to do them?" (11:28).

It greatly helps us to know the standard form in which challenges were typically made in antiquity:

- a) *claim*,
- b) *challenge*,
- c) *response*, and
- d) *public verdict*.

Jesus made a bold *claim* against the Temple system with his actions and words in the Temple (11:15-19): this *claim* is now challenged (11:27-28).

Jesus delivers a fitting *response* by answering a question with a question (11:29-32), which serves to silence his opponents. The controversy form structures each of the subsequent "four questions" asked in the story. From this we learn that Jesus defends the honor of God with great effect. After all, it is God who authorizes him to act in this way and to teach what he teaches. Hence, *challenges* to him are actually *challenges* to God. We learn, moreover, how successful Jesus is in conflict, an important item when we next face his arrest, torture, and execution. Has his success run out? Is there no *response* to this ultimate "challenge" to him?

But for the moment, Mark portrays a very bold and feisty Jesus whose honor is always defended. People need to follow a winner or a hero. And the portrayal of Jesus here certainly fills that prescription. He is, moreover, God's authorized agent, even to the point of terminating the system of the old Temple, a strategy that in that culture could only be interpreted as folly or sinfulness.

Yet Jesus succeeds. By his successful answers to the "four questions," he proves himself to be the epitome of victory: he can withstand chief priests, Sadducees, and scribes and answer the hard problems posed by the Jerusalem elite. He deserves to be acclaimed the winner.

Something quite curious, however, occurs in many of these controversies that articulates a remarkable message about God's power to raise the dead. Jesus made the proper retort to his challengers, "Render to God the things that are God's" (12:17). But what belongs to God? Mark provides an answer. Immediately prior to this controversy with the Pharisees, Mark records a parable about an absentee landlord who owned a vineyard. The rebellious tenants beat some of the owner's servants (12:3); others they "wound and treat shamefully" (12:4); others they kill (12:5). When the owner sends them his "beloved son" (12:6), they murder the heir. What will the owner do? Not only does he shame the tenants (12:9), but he honors his son who was shamed (12:10-11).

Most commentators interpret this as an allegory of Jesus' career: the owner/God sends his beloved son/Jesus sent to the vineyard/Israel, who reject and kill him. But God vindicates his son by making "the stone rejected by the builders" into the cornerstone, that is, by raising Jesus. "This was the Lord's doing!" Hence, if we "render to God what is God's," then we are confessing faith in God who vindicates his faithful ones and raises them from death.

Moreover, if we read further, Mark continues to clarify what it means to "render to God what is God's." The next incident describes the challenge to Jesus by the Sadducees, whom Mark hastens to describe as those "who say there is no resurrection" (12:18). They ridicule the idea of afterlife and resurrection, and thus hope to discredit Jesus further. But in Jesus' response to them, he literally renders to God what is God's, when he says, "You know neither the Scriptures nor the power of God" (12:24). Jesus then argues that God is the "God of the living," not the dead (12:27), and so he proclaims that God's plan and strategy are to give life to the dead. All, then, should "render to God" the plan and power to raise the dead.

Mark speaks once more about this doctrine of the resurrection when Jesus asks about Ps 110, "The Lord said to my lord, 'Sit at my right hand'" (12:36). Christians quickly saw in Ps 110 a prediction of Jesus' resurrection and enthronement (see Acts 2:36; Heb 1:13). Thus Jesus concludes his controversies with a final remark on what belongs to God, who is the Lord, to raise "my lord," who is Jesus, and enthrone him in his resurrection. It belongs to God to raise the dead.

V. Mark 14:1—16:8
Jesus, the Vindicated Martyr

Lectionary Readings from Mark

Passion Sunday:	Mark 14:1—15:47
Vigil of Easter:	Mark 16:1–8

As we have come to learn, Mark tends to bracket sections of his gospel with corresponding *beginnings* and *endings*. In this last part, Mark *begins* the narrative with the account of the anointing of Jesus by a woman (14:3–9). Jesus interprets her gesture as a prophetic act: "She has anointed my body beforehand for burial" (14:8). Mark *ends* this section with women "going to anoint" the dead body of Jesus in the tomb (16:1–8). But the two anointings focus our attention on the chief issue, the death of Jesus.

In the first anointing, Mark narrates a scene that epitomizes so many of the reforming actions of Jesus. He is eating once more with unclean people, this time as the guest of "Simon the leper" (14:3). A women enters and touches Jesus, not unlike the culturally improper touching of the unclean woman in 5:24–31. We are not told if she is a family member or not, but it is surprising in that culture to have women attending meals where non-kinship males are feasting together. She is roundly shamed by some males there for her gesture (14:4), but equally honored by Jesus for it. In fact, Jesus proclaims a timeless honor for this woman: "Wherever the gospel is preached in the whole world, what she has done will be told in memory of her" (14:9). Jesus is constantly portrayed as transcending the cultural conventions of his world.

Mark then narrates what we have come to call the Passion Narrative, the immediate events of the last day of Jesus. In one sense this "last day" balances the "one day" in the life of Jesus with which Mark began his gospel (1:12–39). Thus the evangelist treats us at the *beginning* of Jesus' career to "one day" in the basic ministry of Jesus, which was programmatic for all of Jesus' speaking and acting. He repeats this motif at the *end* with the "final day" in his life, which also contains basic information about Jesus' identity.

One way of making sense of the various events in the Passion Narrative is to understand how they are crafted to proclaim a certain message about the death of Jesus. They are not just historical memories, but interpretations of those events and preachings about them. What was the problem? The ancients simply do not view death as we do: we have an "explanation" of death as the result of disease or old age, which accords with our scientific understanding of health and the body. But for the ancients death encoded many other meanings. Adam, created deathless in God's image and likeness (see Wisdom 2:23), died as a result of eating the forbidden fruit: "The day you eat it you will die" (Gn 2:17). Death, then, is caused by someone: in the case of Adam and other sinners, by God. But God's enemy might also wage war on God's creatures and harm them and take them prisoner. This is what Paul meant when he said that "Death reigned" (Rom 5:14) and "Sin reigned" (Rom 5:21). Thus dead persons are in some way presumed to be the object of some cosmic action, either by God (and so death is a just punishment) or by the Evil One (and so death is unjust slavery).

What, then, would folks make of the story of a man rejected by the religious elite of his day, tried and sentenced by the imperial courts of justice, and executed as a slave? To say the least, Jesus' death demands some explanation and interpretation.

To the casual eye—the eye of an outsider or unbeliever—Jesus must be sinful and so is justly punished by God. He must have committed some crime, and so is validly executed by the legitimate legal authorities. He must, like all the children of sinful Adam, be under the power of Death and the Evil One. He cannot, then, be God's "Holy One" or the Christ or the Son of God or the Son of David. Or so it seems.

To the eye of faith, however, and in the view of the believer, his death was holy, providential, undeserved, and beneficial. This is the interpretation of Jesus' death that Mark would have us consider. Mark's narrative, then, contains a number of regular theological motifs that express the Christian point of view of Jesus' death:

1. Jesus is utterly *innocent*, hence his death is *not* the punishment for a sin or crime.

2. His death happens *according to the Scriptures*, which means that it is under God's providence and control: it was foretold: it enjoys a unique place in God's plan of our salvation.

3. Jesus dies in *obedience* to God, *not* in rebellion against God's will.

4. He dies as a *saint*, praying to God and close to God.

5. His death has *beneficial* effects on others, because it is a *salvific* death.

6. He dies because *Evil always attacks good*, just as in the case of the prophets.

7. God by no means abandoned him or punished him: just look at the evidence of *God's presence and benefaction* at the moment of his death.

8. His death is a *status transformation ritual:* he is enthroned as "king" and reigns from the wood.

1. Mark repeatedly attests to the *innocence* of Jesus. When arrested, Jesus declares that he is no robber to be arrested with clubs and swords, for "day after day I was with you in the temple teaching, and you did not seize me" (14:49). He is no secret villain, but speaks and acts openly for all to hear. Later we are told that two sets of "false witnesses" arose to accuse Jesus, but their testimony proved contradictory (14:55–57). He had done nothing evil or sinful that could be proved. Finally Pilate recognized that Jesus was handed over to him "out of envy" by the Jerusalem elite (15:10), not because of any crime. Pilate demands of them a valid reason to execute Jesus, "What evil has he done?" (15:14), for which there is no answer. Because Jesus stands *innocent* of all sin, crime, or evil, his death can not be a just requital: we must look for another reason.

2. When Mark narrates that Jesus dies *according to the Scriptures*, he intends to show that God was truly involved in this death, but in control of it: it happens according to God's plan of salvation and in fulfillment of God's providence. This is what Jesus means when he says at the Last Supper, "The Son of Man goes as it is written of him" (14:21) and again at his arrest, "But let the Scriptures be fulfilled" (14:49). Jesus predicts the defection of his disciples, citing Zech 13:7, "It is written, 'I will strike the shepherd and the sheep will scatter'" (14:27). This prediction is fulfilled in 14:50. His prediction about Peter's denial (14:30) finds its fulfillment when Peter says, "I do not know this man" (14:71). At that moment the cock crowed and "Peter remembered how Jesus had said to him, 'Before the cock crows twice, you will deny me three times'" (14:72). Finally, Jesus makes a grand prediction before the Jewish court of his vindication by God, "You will see the Son of man seated at the right hand of Power and coming with the clouds of heaven" (14:62). This saying of course, blends remarks from Ps 110 ("seated at the right hand of God") and Dan 7:13–14 ("coming on the clouds of heaven"). It is a bold statement of faith in God to rescue and vindicate him, which is fulfilled in the resurrection. Mark uses this motif most emphatically in the crucifixion scene, where Jesus is said to die fully in accord with Ps 22.

The evangelist records Jesus' death after the pattern of the suffering, righteous person of the psalms. He does not die the victim of some plot, but in accord with God's plan and conformed to the pattern of the righteous saints of the Scriptures.

3. Mark stresses in the Garden scene that Jesus' death happens in *obedience* to God's will. The narrative tells us that Jesus was praying a particular prayer, the "Our Father," one element of which prayer is highlighted: "Not what I will, but what thou wilt" (14:36). This prayer makes explicit once more what Mark has been insisting upon throughout the gospel, that Jesus' destiny is according to the will of God (8:31). In the ancient world, obedience to one's father would be acclaimed the highest virtue a son could demonstrate.

4. Jesus, moreover, dies as a *saint*. Not only has he demonstrated obedience, the premier virtue of Jewish piety, but he is presented to us as one who is constantly praying. We noted above that Jesus prays intensely in the Garden. He begins his sojourn there with snatches of Ps 42:5, "My soul is sorrowful unto death" (14:34).

Thus Jesus is presented as a person who knows the sacred prayers of his culture and actually prays them. When by himself, Jesus prays the "Our Father" (14:36). Mark tells us that Jesus prayed this prayer three times (14:39, 41), thus emphasizing the basic posture and attitude of Jesus as a holy person who constantly prays to God in distress. Finally, we should consider the dying words of Jesus in 15:34 as another prayer: for what Jesus says is not simply an emotional cry but formally a prayer, namely, the first line of a famous psalm prayed by those who suffer innocently. It would be a mistake to imagine that Jesus cried out in despair, which means a total lack of faith and hope in God. Nothing could be further from the truth. Rather, as Jesus prayed Christian prayers in the garden (the Our Father [14:36], he prays traditional Jewish prayers at his death (Ps 22 = Mark 15:34). Thus, Jesus is ever presented as a *saint*, who prays constantly to God.

5. Jesus' death, moreover, is presented to us as a *salvific* act, which brings God's *blessings and benefaction* to us. As Jesus said earlier, "the Son of man came…to give his life as ransom for many" (10:45). "Ransom" means the payment of a price to release slaves from captivity. Later, at the Last Supper, Jesus declares that his blood is both a covenant and an atonement sacrifice: "This is my blood of the covenant which is poured out for many" (14:26). Blood in a covenant sacrifice (Exod 24:3–8) is sprinkled both on God's altar and on the people. By this blood the people are consecrated and made holy: they become "blood brothers and sisters" of God, that is, kinfolk of God. Blood in an atonement sacrifice (Lev 16:14–16, 18–19) is sprinkled on the ark of the covenant and the altar, to signify that God passes over sins and cleanses his people. Thus early Christians used a variety of metaphors to tease out the rich saving effects of Jesus' death, by comparing it to "redemption," "covenant," and "atonement." All three suggest the depth of blessings we receive from Jesus' salvific death.

Twice Jesus is mocked as he hangs on the cross. One group taunts him by saying "Save yourself, come down from the cross" (15:30), while others mock him, saying, "He saved others: he cannot save himself" (15:31). These words sting only when we realize how truly they touch the key issue: he does save others! *Salvation* is what he is all about! Thus they are ironic attestations of the truth: he is savior! he does save! And his greatest act of salvation will be his death on the cross. This is dramatized for us immediately by what happens to Jesus' very executioner. When the centurion saw the way Jesus died (15:39), he was gifted with faith to proclaim: "Truly this man was God's son." Here is an earnest example of the inclusive saving benefaction that God will extend to all.

6. Why does Jesus die? It is not enough to say that he dies in obedience to God's plan or in accord with the Scriptures. It was part of the cultural scenario of Jews and Christians that God's prophets were all rejected and killed (Mt 23:31–35; Acts 7:52). Such was the fate of John the Baptizer, killed by the monarch whom he reproached (Mark 6:18, 26). It was the experience of Elijah and Moses, who appeared to Jesus at the transfiguration and "were talking with him" (9:4). And it is the sad fate of Jesus "the prophet" (14:65). Thus Mark and those in his world would interpret Jesus' death as another example of *Evil attacking good*, similar to the attack by the Devil in 1:12–13.

7. It would be unthinkable that God had abandoned Jesus or was distant from the scene. The God who was near in the theophanies of the baptism (1:9–11) and the transfiguration (9:7) *remains near* as the "Beloved Son, with whom I am well pleased," dies. Mark narrates the evidence for this by the strange but miraculous event that accompanies Jesus' death: "The curtain of the temple was torn in two, from top to bottom" (15:38). This could only be God's action: the direction of the tear is from heaven to earth, which further confirms it to be an act of heaven. It signifies, moreover, the truth of Jesus' claims that the former Temple and its system no longer enjoy God's favor. Jesus is no blasphemer or fanatic in his posture toward that great religious symbol. Now God steps in to confirm that Jesus spoke the truth. God, then, is by no means far from Jesus, but hears his prayer (Ps 22) and begins to answer that prayer with vindication of the Christ.

8. Finally, in the eyes of unbelievers and outsiders, Jesus experienced a status degradation ritual, such as criminals experience when convicted and sentenced to prison. Yet in the eyes of disciples and insiders, Jesus' passion and death are ironically a *transformation* ritual that *elevates his status.* Irony is the key. People act so as

to shame and humiliate Jesus when they clothe him in a purple robe, put a crown of acanthus on his head, bend the knee to him, and acclaim him "king" (15:17-19). Mark says that they "mocked Jesus" by these actions. But in God's irony, these are the very actions whereby Jesus is transformed and enthroned as Son of David and King. He truly ascends his throne and begins his reign by this ritual. Thus the title is put over the cross: "King of Jews" (15:26), for Jesus ironically assumes his kingly role by this humiliation. After all, we have been schooled through the gospel to learn that "last is first" and "least is greatest" (10:31). Ironically Jesus becomes king precisely when he is disowned and despised. For when deemed "foolish," he is truly "wise"; when "weak," he is "strong"; when "shamed," he is "honored."

Jesus' ironic death does not end the story. Having told the account of the martyrdom of a holy man, Mark must tell us of God's vindication of this faithful servant. This gospel, however, does not contain a typical resurrection appearance by Jesus, such as we find in Matthew, Luke, and John. Yet the fragmentary remarks in 16:1-8 serve to herald that the dead martyr is alive and vindicated.

Some women attend Jesus' burial and "see where he was laid" (15:47). Later, one of them, Mary Magdalene, comes with still other women to this tomb "to anoint him" (16:1). They assess their problem on the way: "Who will roll away the stone for us from the door of the tomb?" (16:3). The answer is implied in the subsequent events. God has sent "a young man dressed in a white robe" (16:5), who has apparently opened the tomb. But his true task lies in heralding the phenomenal news: "You seek Jesus of Nazareth, who was crucified. He has been raised!" (16:6). Mark would have his readers know that the faithful servant of God, who went to his death in obedience to God and prayed to that God constantly in his passion, has been vindicated by the loyal God.

The heavenly herald only echoes what Jesus himself had predicted earlier in the narrative "The Son of man must suffer many things...be killed, and after three days rise again" (8:31). This prophesies not just the death of the martyr, but also his vindication. We are correct in seeing his resurrection as God's vindication for several reasons. First, when Peter objects to these future events, the master declares that he speaks "the thinkings of men, not those of God" (8:33). The "things of God" are precisely Jesus' death and resurrection. Next, at the transfiguration, when God metamorphoses Jesus into glory (9:3) and declares him to be his "beloved son" (9:7), Mark insists that it is God who authorizes Jesus on the way of the cross, and it is God who will vindicate Jesus in comparable glory after that passage. The presence of Elijah and Moses, we noted above, probably represent prophets who were rejected by mortals, but vindicated by God. Later in the narrative, Jesus tells a parable in which the son of the owner of the vineyard, the heir, is slain by the tenants (12:6-8). The owner responds to this challenge with a judgmental action against those who slew his son (12:9).

But the narrative continues with a citation of Ps 118 that indicates that God goes one step further and vindicates the martyred "beloved son": "The very stone which the builders rejected, has become the head of the corner: *this is the Lord's doing!*" (12:10-11). The discourse about God's power to raise the dead is hardly over. For when the Sadducees, "who say there is no resurrection" (12:18) ridicule that doctrine, Jesus silences them by saying: "You are wrong, you know neither the Scriptures nor the power of God" (12:24). Since God is "the God of the living," it belongs to God to raise the dead. Finally, when Jesus asks about the proper interpretation of Ps 110 in 12:35-37, we should hear this in the light of the Christian proclamation of the resurrection. It belongs to the ancient and widespread Christian understanding of Ps 110 to see it as a statement about the resurrection of Jesus (see Act 2:34-36; Hebrews 1:13). "The Lord said to my lord: Sit at my right hand." The first "Lord" is God, who speaks to David's "lord," who is the Christ: God commands the Christ to "sit at my right hand," that is, to be vindicated, raised up, and enthroned besides the living and faithful God. The note of vindication is very strong in the Christian understanding of this psalm, for the full citation of it includes a note that in the vindication of the "lord," "his enemies will be put under his feet."

One final consideration concludes Mark's understanding of the resurrection as Jesus' vindication. We noted above how Jesus seemed to be in endless controversy with his enemies throughout the gospel. Yet in 2:1—3:6 and 11:15—12:37 Jesus himself is able to delivery the riposte to the challenges against him. Not so in his passion: finally his enemies succeed in overpowering him. But a riposte must and will be given, but not by Jesus himself. That is the irony of the mocking remarks to him on the cross: "Save yourself and come down from the cross" (15:30) and "He saved others: he cannot save himself" (15:31). This sarcastic challenge will be answered, but by the One who alone saves the dead, namely God. Thus the prophecy of Jesus that began his ordeal as a martyr, 14:28, is fulfilled in virtue of the heavenly herald's announcement:

Mark 14:28
"... after I am raised up, I will go before you to Galilee"

Mark 16:7
Go, tell his disciples and Peter that he is going before you to Galilee: there you will see him, as he told you

Thus the narrative comes full circle. It began with God's theophany to Jesus and its declaration of divine favor and commissioning (1:9–11). It was punctuated in the middle by a second theophany in which God reaffirmed his favor on Jesus, and authorized his way of the cross to Jerusalem (9:2–7). And it concludes with a final statement by God that Jesus is both the "Holy One" and a triumphant warrior. For by raising Jesus from the dead, God vindicates his holiness and truthfulness and aids him in the battle to defeat the last enemy, Death. Such is the destiny of all who are faithful to God—vindication and the reward of eternal life.

The Gospel of Mark

Paddy Meagher, SJ

INTRODUCTION

While holding second position in the biblical canon of the books of the New Testament, the gospel of Mark is usually acknowledged by biblical scholars as the first gospel text in written form.

It is disconcerting, however, that we do not know who the author is, when he wrote or to whom he wrote, and, finally, why he wrote a gospel. We have hypotheses, and so there is a measure of disagreement among those who write about the gospels. We do know that the gospel as a narrative presentation of Jesus' adult life is an interplay of various levels of historical reality and their interpretation by believers.

First of all, there is Jesus' historical life and the way his contemporaries, friends and enemies, interpreted him within the Jewish religious belief system:

• Holy One of God, or blasphemer;

• a person with God-given power, or an agent of the evil spirit;

• one who does everything well, or sinful and disobedient to the Sabbath law.

Jesus also had his own faith consciousness, which was related to his understanding of God as Father and the reign of God.

Second, we have the initial and ongoing interpretation by the major witnesses of Jesus' life's work and teaching, and particularly his death. Their experience of God having raised Jesus led them to believe that he was the Christ, Son of God. This interpretation by witnesses is also conditioned by the needs of the early believing communities, whose faith and community life they nourished and strengthened. At this stage narratives are formed (Passion narrative, accounts of healings, exorcisms, controversies) and teaching gathered thematically (parables, on riches, on scandal).

Finally, from all the available matter "Mark" composes his gospel with an eye to the needs of his community according to his aims and ability. This is the final stage of interpretation. Now 2000 years later we continue the process, attentive to Mark's gospel in its socioreligious and cultural context, our contemporary world, our own journey of faith, and the God who speaks to us within, in the world and through the gospel.

Any structural analysis that would artificially divide the work as if it had a table of contents is likely to be an imposition on the gospel. We suggest ways to help read and understand the gospel.

• From a geographic point of view Mark takes us from the Jordan (1:2–13), to and around Galilee (1:17—7:23; 8:10–26 and 9:30–49), beyond Galilee (7:24—8:9 and 8:27—9:29), and finally to Judea, beyond the Jordan (10:1–31) and toward Jerusalem (10:32—11:10). Then Jesus remains in and around Jerusalem and the temple until his death (11:11—16:8).

• There are also "thematic" blocks of material, some easier to describe than others: a type of survey of a very successful ministry (1:21–45) contrasted with a series of conflicts (2:1—3:6 and 3:20–35) that highlight characteristics of Jesus' ministry and opposition to him.

• This is followed by stories of reassurance and caution (4:1–34, parables) and a series of demonstrations of great power, and faith (4:35—5:43) again contrasted by rejection (6:1–6).

- Interspersed at significant moment are the steps in the story of the disciples' paradigmatic call 1:16-20 (four men): choice and mission of the "twelve" (3:13-19) and the sending of the "12" (6:7-13).

- There are also significant summaries (1:32-34 and 3:7-12) that heighten the sense of Jesus' magnetism and saving power.

The next section (6:14—8:26) is not so easy to divide and describe.

- We hear of the popular debate about Jesus' identity (6:14-16) and have to wait until 8:27-30 for an initial clarification by Peter.

- In between we have the two feeding narratives (and walking on the sea) and the disciples' inability to understand how these events reveal the identity of Jesus (6:30-51 and 6:52; 8:1-10 and 8:14-21).

- Intermingled are a typical Marcan summary of healing (6:53-56; cf. 3:7-12 and 1:32-34), two healings (7:24-37) and disputes with Galilean religious leaders about purity laws and signs (7:1-17 and 8:11-13) with clarifications for the crowds and disciples (7:24-37).

- A shadow casts its foreboding shade over this section. There is future danger illustrated by Herod, who had murdered the *prophet* John the Baptist (6:14,16,17-29 and 8:15).

A transition to the next development in the gospel is the gradual healing of a blind man (8:22-26), which can be linked to another transitional event, the healing of the blind man in Jericho (10:46-52). Like the blind man of Bethsaida the disciples gradually "see" and therefore can identity Jesus as the Christ (8:27-30) and also ought to share the fearlessness of the Jericho blind man and accompany Jesus to his destiny in Jerusalem (10:32 and 10:52).

This section of the gospel (8:27—10:52) is marked by

- the three sayings about Jesus' future passion, death, and resurrection (8:31-32a; 9:31-32; and 10:32b-34);

- the gross inappropriate behavior and reactions of the disciples (8:32b—33 [Peter]; 9:32 and 33-34 [greatness] and 10:35-40 [1st places]);

- the pointed instructions on radical aspects of discipleship (8:34—9:1; 9:35-37; 10:40-45);

- the significant scene related to Jesus' passion-resurrection and John the Baptist (9:9-13).

The tone of the gospel narrative does change with 8:31-32a. A major interpretative event, symbolic in character, is linked to Jesus' readiness for his passion-death-resurrection. The Father reaffirms Jesus' unique mission as "the beloved Son" (the initial affirmation was in 1:10-11) and commands the disciples, represented by Peter, James, and John to "listen to him" (9:2-8).

This section of the gospel collects the explicit teaching material in Mark about various aspects of discipleship (9:38-50; 10:1-12, 13-16, 17-31). The major focus of 8:27-10:52 is discipleship.

The final days of Jesus' life are spent in Jerusalem. Most incidents in chs 11-12 are located in the temple. Jesus is presented as a prophet condemning:

- corrupt worship, symbolically predicting the destruction of Jerusalem and temple (11:12-21: the cursed fig tree and cleansing of the temple);

- the obduracy of the leadership (11:27-33);

- the consequent destruction of Israel as God's People because of their rejection of him (12:1-12);

- the hypocrisy and greed of religious teachers, and by contrast, recognizes the authentic religiosity of a poor widow (12:38-44).

There is an atmosphere of confrontation and danger. Jesus is also the genuine teacher who insists on "giving to God what belongs to God" (12:17) and who knows, and is able to interpret his religious tradition found in the Scriptures (12:18-27, 28-34 and 35-37).

A feature of Mark is the different ways Jesus' foreknowledge is described. In the final collection of teaching (chapter 13) there is comparatively little teaching in a gospel that often refers to Jesus as an authoritative teacher and his teaching forces the disciples to look toward the future.

There is an interplay in Chapter 13 between the teaching of Jesus prior to his passion and the interpretation and development in the early years of the community, prior to the destruction of Jerusalem in 70 C.E. The content draws attention to the judgment on Jerusalem, periods of false messiahs, persecution and civil unrest, the final coming of the Son of Man, a coming known only to the Father, and exhortations to the disciples and early believers to be faithful, to guard against deception, and to live in hope.

The passion narrative is particularly stark with little relief given to the picture:

- the growing brutality undergone by Jesus;
- the frailty and the denial by his disciples;
- the rejection and mockery by the leaders of his people and the crowd; and
- a death.

Jesus' anguish, loneliness, and suffering is relieved by:

- a Gentile military officer's utterance "Truly the Man was God's Son";
- the presence of a group of devoted women disciples;
- the courage of Joseph, a righteous leader of the people.

The above survey has given some indications of the unfolding plot in Mark's narrative of Jesus Christ, Son of God. As we read each scene and follow the development of the gospel we ought to pay attention to the way Mark presents the main character, Jesus, and then the supporting characters, the disciples and the twelve, Jesus' family, the socioreligious and political leaders (Pharisees, scribes, Herodians), Herod, the high priest, chief priests, Pilate, Roman officials, and the crowds.

We also need to be attentive to individual people: unnamed possessed people, a leper, the blind and mute, an anonymous sick woman, the Canaanite woman, Jairus, Peter's mother-in-law.

We must pay careful attention to changes of place and time, beginnings and endings of scenes, and to the selected details in narratives with the dramatic tension created by contrasts. We need to note small details: the insights the narrator shares with the reader, what the reader knows and the characters do not know, the irony in some scenes, and emotions expressed or described. We need to ask who does, or says, what to whom, how, when, where, and ask what are the consequences.

Themes worth attention are the gradual portrait of Jesus that emerges, the importance of his passion and death, and the relationship between the understanding of Jesus as the Christ, King, and Son of God, and the way "Son of Man" is used by Jesus alone when talking of his specific mission, his passion and death, and his coming in glory.

Two major themes running throughout the gospel are the concerted opposition to Jesus, people intent finally to destroy him (3:6a, a strange observation so early in the gospel; 11:18; 12:12; 14:1) and the dismal account of his disciples, lacking understanding and so fearful that they all desert him (4:13, 40; 6:57; 7:18; 8:14–21; 8:33; 9:33, 37; 10:13, 24; 10:35–40, 41; 14:32–42, 66–72). We also note how at times Jesus privately teaches his disciples.

We must pay attention to Jesus' single-minded concern for the *human person* and human needs. We need to remember that he lived in a peasant society with few urban centers, under colonial rule, in a society where there was a fusion of religion and culture, "politics" and all aspects of life, and that the Temple was the center of religion and culture. Jewish identity, always in danger because of the colonial influence and a Hellenistic worldview, was affirmed and preserved by a deep concern to ensure ritual purity endangered by pollution (dirt, unclean foods, disease, Gentiles, blood, breaking the law), the observance of the Sabbath as a major symbol of identity, and by following the cycle of feasts and devotional practices (fasts, prayer, tithes).

Jesus belonged to a conservative society where honor was greatly valued and protected, and holiness was often identified with external realities. We will find that he was deeply religious, and that the focus of his life was God and the kingdom of God, but he broke socially accepted boundaries of religiosity to be true to God, the deeper purpose of the Law, and to the dignity and needs of the human person.

We continually need to remind ourselves not only of the two thousand years that separate us from the gospel but also the great distance between our culture and our worldview and the culture, religion, and world of Jesus and Mark.

THE GOSPEL STRUCTURE IN LECTIONARY YEAR B

As regards the use of Mark in the lectionary, a schematic outline would help to identify the major elements traceable in the sequence of Sunday readings, which also includes a substantial segment from John 6 and so a word of introduction to this passage may help.

Block 1
Sunday 2 Narrative: First Disciples   Jn 1:35-42

Initial Ministry of Jesus
Sunday 3 Narrative: Programmatic Statement
    Choice of Four Disciples   Mk 1:14-20
Sunday 4 Narrative: Authority of Jesus—
    Teacher and Exorcist   Mk 1:21-28
Sunday 5 Narrative: Healings—
    Popularity and Ongoing Mission   Mk 1:29-39
Sunday 6 Narrative: Leper—
    Ever greater acclaim   Mk 1:40-45

Block II
In Conflict—Clarity of His Mission
Sunday 7 Conflict Narrative:
    To Forgive Sins   Mk 2:1-12
Sunday 8 Conflict Narrative:
    Fasting - New Era   Mk 2:18-22
Sunday 9 Conflict Narrative:
    Sabbath—To Affirm the Human   Mk 2:22, 3:6
Sunday 10 Conflict Narrative:
    To Remove Reign of Evil   Mk 3:20-30
    Correction Narrative:
    True Family   Mk 3:31-35

Block III
Sunday 11 Parables:
    Yet the Kingdom will come!   Mk 4:26-34

Block IV
Key Role of Faith
Sunday 12 Narrative:
    Have You No Faith?   Mk 4:35-41
Sunday 13 Narrative:
    In Praise of Faith   Mk 5:21-43
Sunday 14 Narrative:
    Amazed at Unbelief   Mk 6:1-6

Block V
Aspects of Mission
Sunday 15 Instruction:
    Preaching Repentance   Mk 6:7-13
Sunday 16 Narrative:
    Key Role of Compassion   Mk 6:30-34

Block VI
Bread of Life–Challenge of Faith
Sunday 17 Narrative:
    Wrong Type of Prophet   Jn 6:1-15
Sunday 18 Discourse:
    I am the Bread of Life   Jn 6:24-35
Sunday 19 Discourse:
    The Living/Life Giving Bread   Jn 6:41-51
Sunday 20 Discourse:
    Live because of Me   Jn 6:51-59
Sunday 21 Narrative:
    The Choice   Jn 6:60-70

Block VII
End of Galilean Ministry
Sunday 22 Narrative:
    Religion of the Heart   Mk 7:1-8, 14-15, 21-23
Sunday 23 Narrative:
    He has done all things well   Mk 7:31-37

Block VIII
Passion—Discipleship
Sunday 24 Narrative:
    Passion Sayings: Discipleship I   Mk 8:27-35
Sunday 25 Narrative/Passion Sayings:
    Discipleship II   Mk 9:30-37
Sunday 26 Sayings:
    Aspects of Discipleship I:
    Obstacles to Faith   Mk 9:38-49
Sunday 27 Conflict/Corrections Narratives:
    Aspects of Discipleship II   Mk 10:2-16
Sunday 28 Narrative:
    Aspects of Discipleship III:
    Problem of Wealth   Mk 10:17-22
    Dialogue: Renunciation   Mk 10:23-30
Sunday 29 Narrative/Passion Sayings:
    Discipleship III   Mk 10:35-45
Sunday 30 Narrative:
    A Model Disciple   Mk 10:46-52

Block IX

In Jerusalem

Sunday 31 Narrative:
    The Great Commandment   Mk 12:28–34

Sunday 32 Narrative:
    Contrast of Scribes– a Widow   Mk 12:38–44

Sunday 33 Sayings:
    Coming of the Son of Man   Mk 13:24–32

Sunday 34 Dialogue:
    Christ the King   Jn 18:33–37

John Chapter 6

Readings from John 6 are incorporated into Mark's narrative after the miracle of the loaves and the fishes, and are used to develop the image of the Eucharist in the life of the church. To understand John 6 we need to remember a number of points:

- the narrative is rooted in the historical ministry of Jesus;

- the account is influenced in a decided manner both by the common resurrectional faith in Jesus of Nazareth (1:45) as the Christ, Son of God (20:31); and

- the particular faith interpretation of Jesus in John's gospel.

He is the one sent by God the Father:

- "seeing and hearing" the Son is to "see and hear" the Father (1:18; 3:11; 3:32; 6:46; 8:38–40; 12:49–50);

- being one with the Father in his mission and prior to his mission (1:1–2,18; 3:34–35; 4:34; 5:17, 19–20, 36; 6:28–29; 8:16, 28–29; 9:4, 25, 30, 37–38; 12:44–45; 14:9–11, 20, 24 and Chapter 17);

- the Word is able to reveal the Father;

- anyone who believes in Jesus as the one sent, as the witness to the Father, as speaking and acting in the name of and as commissioned by the Father, has eternal life and will be raised up on the last day;

- anyone who does not believe is in the dark, judged and destined for judgment (3:18–21).

In the gospel the Jews are Jesus' enemies and models of disbelief even to the extent of excommunication (chapter 9). John is referring to that large Jewish community who had rejected the claim that Jesus was the Christ and were harassing the Christian community to whom "John" wrote. Therefore the gospel, especially in chapter 2 and chs 5–12 is *very* polemical. The Jews in this context are *not* the Jewish people as we understand them down the centuries and today, but refers to the particular context of the Jewish-Christian tensions after the destruction of the temple.

Jesus' acts of healing (chapter 4, 5, 9, 11) and the feeding of the crowd (chapter 6) are signs (Cana is the first) that point beyond the actual deed to the more radical reality of Jesus as sent to reveal the Father and bring LIFE.

The instructions related to some of these deeds (chs 5, 6, 9, 10, 12) both clarify the revelation and emphasize both believing, as well as the staunch and growing disbelief and opposition of "the Jews" who are portrayed as symbols of all who refuse to believe. The instructions (discourses) are related to the signs evolving over time and reflect both the growing faith interpretation of Jesus Christ by the Johannine group, and the needs and difficulties in the evolving Christian community. In this gospel Jesus is typically quite reflective as he instructs the people.

The liturgy chooses five units of Chapter 6, omitting the disciples' experience of Jesus on the lake (Jn 6:16–21), some transitional verses that explain how the people cross the lake (6:22–23), and some reflections on the unwillingness and consequent guilt of the people (Jews) to believe in Jesus despite his efforts to reveal God and his commitment to his mission (6:36–40).

SECOND SUNDAY OF ORDINARY TIME: YEAR B JN 1:35–42

Who Is Jesus?

Our gospel spells out for us the attitude with which we can listen to the gospel story of Jesus told by Mark in the following Sundays and the goal we can keep before us as we listen Sunday after Sunday to the Word about Jesus Christ.

The gospel opens with three persons, John the Baptist, Jesus, and an anonymous pair of John's disciples (one will be identified as Andrew, Simon Peter's brother). If we look back the evangelist has introduced John to us in a tense scene where he is being interrogated about "who he is" and the significance of his baptizing ministry (1:19–28). John categorically rules out any claim except to be a special prophetic voice, precursor to one far greater. Jesus is introduced to us by John in a series of pregnant testimonial statements (1:29-34).

Jesus is the person through whom God will redeem the world from the domination of sin (Lamb of God). Jesus' existence is touched with mystery ("One who is before me") and he is to be the source of the transforming power of God, the Holy Spirit. Finally he is the person uniquely able to reveal God (the Son of God, cf. 1:18). He will be addressed by the disciples as *teacher*. John will gradually indicate that he is *the* teacher; having seen the Father and remaining with him he can witness to the Father.

The two anonymous disciples symbolize the reader (listener) of the gospel. They hear John's witness: "Behold the Lamb of God." This is a condensation of all that John had said about Jesus in 1:29-24 and is one way to describe him. The phrase probably evokes aspects of the "servant of God" (Is 53:7) and the Paschal Lamb, the cultic and liturgical symbol of God's redemptive action in the face of the universal power of sin ("sin of the world").

The disciples of the Baptist (note Jesus' initial disciples in John's gospel are disciples of the Baptist and not fishermen at work) hear his witness and follow Jesus. Discipleship is then described in terms of an eagerness to seek and to know the mystery of Jesus ("where do you live / dwell?"—the word used has a symbolic sense of Jesus' dwelling with the Father) and to commit oneself to experience the person of Jesus ("Come and you will see"). They came, saw, and remained.

The evangelist does not elaborate. There is silence except for the strange remark: "It was 4 P.M.," probably a way of indicating that this was the occasion of momentous change in their lives. There is also symbolic meaning attached to "see" and "remain": indication of faith and commitment.

However the nature of their experience is told indirectly in the next small scene. Andrew goes and immediately finds his brother and says: "We have found the Messiah." This term means "anointed of God." Earlier the reader has learned that Jesus is indeed the anointed of God, being "the Father's only Son, full of grace and truth" (1:14). Nathanael will describe Jesus as "Son of God and King of Israel." All these "titles" intend to state the intimacy of the relationship between Jesus and the Father of whom Jesus is the ultimate and complete witness.

The gospel ends introducing the reader to Simon, who will be a significant person in Jesus' community (21:15-19). This is indicated by Jesus giving him a symbolic name. Jesus also begins his ministry at this point.

The liturgy draws attention to the theme of being a disciple. In the gospel the following aspects are underlined: listening to a witness, seeking, seeing with the inner eye/heart, and being with. The anonymous disciples are the models. Andrew shares the experience with another—another aspect of a disciple's life.

The story of Samuel (1 Sam 3:3-10, 19) being called to his prophetic mission draws attention to the disposition of inner readiness: "Speak, Lord, for your servant is listening" and the psalmist reinforces these dispositions with his prayerful "Here I am..." and "I delight to do your will, O my God; your law is within my heart." We can pray to God for "an open ear" and ready heart.

THIRD SUNDAY OF ORDINARY TIME: YEAR B Mk 1:14-20

The Story Begins

This Sunday we begin the narrative presentation of Jesus' ministry, and for the next three Sundays we read Mark and then take up this gospel again after the Easter season. Our Sunday by Sunday reading/listening to Mark's story of Jesus Christ is like watching a weekly serial on TV—the plot gradually unfolds, characters come and go, we move in time and from place to place. Through his account of Jesus, Mark wants to communicate with us.

We need to recall the Baptist's ministry: a movement of religious renewal is set in motion, an atmosphere of expectation created—"The one more powerful than I is coming after me. I am not worthy..." (1:7-8) and the major character is introduced in a dramatic and graphic way—the vocational epiphany at Jesus' baptism (1:9-11). Jesus is entrusted with tremendous responsibility, empowered with the Spirit, revealed as the prophet of all prophets ("Son" and "Beloved"). He proves himself to be eminently trustworthy to enter into that great struggle with the greatest power of evil on God's terms, namely as the faithful Son (1:12-13). We must be conscious that the story/narrative of Jesus is part of the greatest story—namely God the Father's committed presence within world history; one great account of this recreative presence is the complex account Jesus inherited and with his own people knew from the regular reading of the Torah and Prophets and celebrated in prayer and worship in the synagogue.

Our reading has one scene (1:16-20) and a type of summarized survey and interpretation of Jesus' whole ministry (1:14-15).

John's ministry has come to an abrupt end, and Jesus moves to Galilee. As the prophet of prophets he begins in a public and authoritative way to speak in God's name and about the way God views human life and what God promises and expects of his people. Mark uses three loaded terms that interpret each other—"good news from/about God" and the "time is fulfilled," which means that "God's kingdom is near." Mark uses a special term for "time," namely, *kairos*, referring to the decisive moment in our religious history and in human history. In and through Jesus of Nazareth we come face to face with God, creator and Lord of human destiny, re-creator of the human heart and so human society. Being a crisis occasion men and women are challenged to "repent" and to "believe," namely, to look into the face of God, listen to the voice of God, see the plan of God in the deeds and teaching of Jesus and his way of being human. This poses a challenge to our deeper selves, calls for a movement away from what corrupts, demeans, destroys, and diminishes our humanness and to entrust ourselves, our inner self, to the living and life-giving God. We are asked to look into the eyes of God and to give our deeper selves in trust, being ever more and more possessed by God. This is to "believe the good news."

The following scene is an idealized, typical, and summarized type of account explaining what it means to be a disciple/believer in Jesus the Lord. This means an open-ended commitment to Jesus Christ (symbolized by the leaving behind of boats, nets, family) and an involvement in God's concerns and action for human history by an attachment to Jesus Christ, which has priority over all other necessary commitments that are part of human life. We are invited to have a "follow me" attitude at the heart of our personal life, an attitude that becomes ever more the determining factor in our attitudes, decisions, ways of living. This is not a scene describing the vocation of priests and religious but the type of commitment of all authentic believers who wish that God's action in history and Jesus' vision of human life and his gospel be effectively present in more and more aspects of modern life.

We do not want to be reluctant Jonahs, cajoled by God to proclaim his word of truth, stirring human hearts to be conscious of evil and responsible for it in their society, and so to act to re-create human society. We could use Ps 25 as a prayer asking God's guidance for us who listen to Jesus' words and that we see the need to ensure that his vision be alive in prophetic ways in modern life.

FOURTH SUNDAY OF ORDINARY TIME: YEAR B Mk 1:21-28

"They Were Astounded…"

The narratives for the next two Sundays will draw our attention forcefully to Jesus as gifted with extraordinary religious authority and power. This Sunday's narrative is framed by two exclamations in response to Jesus' teaching and his power to exorcise a possessed person. We read: "They were astounded at his teaching" (1:22) and "they were all so amazed that they kept asking one another" (1:27). The reasons are given: first because "he taught as one possessing authority," which is taken up again in terms of "new teaching and with authority" (1:27—though "with authority" could be linked to the exorcism). Second they are at a loss because he "commands even unclean spirits and they obey him" (1:27). Mark wants the listener to be captivated by Jesus as a person with genuine religious authority.

Our liturgy has, therefore, chosen the passage from Deuteronomy in which Moses promises Israel that God will send another great prophetic teacher of whom God promises, "I will put my words in the mouth of the prophet who shall speak to them everything I command" (Dt 18:18). The verses chosen from Psalm 95 bring to our attention our responsibility to "listen to the Word" and "not to close our hearts."

The people who had gathered for worship and to listen to God's word in the synagogue recognize Jesus' authority and compare it with the routine way of teaching of their traditional religious guides. We are not told what is the difference in the light of 7:1–13 (conflict about not washing) and the way Jesus is presented by Mark. I suggest that Jesus' authority in speaking God's word rises from his inner experience of God and his profound fidelity to God. Not only priests but parents, teachers, leaders of prayer groups, Christian writers, and those critical of others in the church are challenged to ensure they speak God's word with an authority that rises from personal experience of God and a fidelity to his Word—at times human words are judged to be authentic Words of God!

Mark also narrates in a dramatic fashion Jesus' first open conflict with evil, experienced in that culture in terms of a person possessed by a destructive (unclean) spirit. Because of modern medical knowledge, our awareness of psychic diseases, and our worldview, we do not attribute to the action of malign spirits phenomena that Jesus' contemporaries believed to be caused by spirits. However, we do know how evil can possess persons and how people are destroyed themselves and can destroy others because they are dominated by "evil" in the form of addictions, false values, ambition, power, money, excessive work.

The unclean spirit speaks to Jesus. The original listeners to the gospel would have picked up the desperation of the spirit (the piercing shout and the "come to destroy us") and the way the spirit attempts to ward off Jesus' power by what he says in 1:24—especially the use of his knowledge of the name "holy one of God": we can recall here how the Marcan Jesus faced the full power of evil at the commencement of his own public ministry and remained untouched and unaffected by this power (1:12–13). Therefore he could proclaim the Good News of God and his presence (1:13–15) and possessed the power of God's Spirit (1:10, 12).

In contrast to the spirit, Jesus is conscious of his God-given power manifested in his authoritative and simple words "Be silent, come out" and dramatically in the convulsions and the loud shout of the possessed person. Mark wishes us to observe religious power: "he commands...and they obey...."

This is the Lord whose Eucharist we share and who with his power over all evil is present to heal and free us. Again the Christian community is reminded of the source of God-given power that will enable believers to unmask "evil" especially when it is masked as apparent "good."

We leave our worship today impressed, maybe puzzled, by Jesus' power and authority. Mark finally tells us that "all over Galilee, in every place," people begin to speak of him.

FIFTH SUNDAY OF ORDINARY TIME: YEAR B Mk 1:29–39

Three Scenes

We have three brief scenes in our narrative thumbnail sketches of Jesus in his ministry and people's enthusiasm. Living in an urban setting or in the countryside we find it hard to imagine the type of popular enthusiasm a religious figure can evoke in small villages and towns—sports men and women, popular singers and musicians, TV stars, are the modern draw cards mobbed by crowds.

There is a strange simplicity and single-minded focus in each narrative, just the essentials with the spotlight unashamedly focused on Jesus. In the first scene Jesus heals Simon's mother-in-law. Note the simple narration of power—"He came and lifted her up, taking her by the hand" and "the fever left her and she served them": a homely scene, told from a man's point of view.

The sabbath ended at sundown and crowds gathered. Mark has narrated an exorcism, a healing, and underlined astonishment and the spread of fame. Now he impresses upon us the astonishing magnetism, authority, and power in a summary filled with superlatives (1:32–34)—"all who were sick or possessed"; "the whole city"; "he cured many (means all) of various diseases"; "cast out many demons" over whom he had total power, not allowing them even to speak. There is a graphic touch in "the whole city was gathered around the door." In Jesus of Nazareth God has entered into human history in a decisive way and a re-creative way. The small scene (it must have been very noisy!) reminds us of the reality of human suffering, and therefore the liturgy of the Word opens with the anguished reflections of Job on the brevity and oppressive pain of human life, described in such a picturesque way. We need to know/imagine the anxieties of daily laborers/slaves to appreciate the imagery. A few verses from Ps 147 recall that Jesus lives the prayer to the God who "gathers the outcasts of Israel," heals the brokenhearted and binds up their wounds...", "and lifts up the downtrodden..."—and in these ways exercises his power "to number and name the stars."

In the final scene (1:35-39) Jesus reveals aspects of his own inner life and vision and corrects his disciples. Mark reinforces the impression of Jesus' fascinating power in Simon's words "everyone is searching for you." He reminds us that Jesus is God's prophet and so must be alone with God—the very early hour and the quietness of the place create a sense of sacred time, space, and communion. Note the graphic description of the anxious disciples who are "hunting for him" and who seem to shatter his silence. The narrow vision of these eager men acts as a foil for Jesus to spell out the scope of his work, proclaiming God's presence and prophetic word (1:14-15) throughout the whole region in their places of worship and freeing people from the domination of evil. The short narrative in 1:21-28 is a model of Jesus' ministry.

In the liturgical celebration we may want to focus on one scene or allow the cumulative effect of the three interlocking scenes to enable the believing community to expand their inner grasp of who Jesus the Lord is now for them and respond to him from a deeper level of faith. He reminds the believing community of our obligation to "the broken" as a practical consequence of praying to the Father "your kingdom come." His proclamation of the kingdom of God led him to the broken.

SIXTH SUNDAY OF ORDINARY TIME: YEAR B Mk 1:40-45

Why is Jesus Mobbed?

The narrative of this event has a number of puzzling elements, and there are quite a lot of differences among interpreters. Jewish society was deeply concerned with sacral purity/impurity and had a complex system to prevent pollution and preserve ritual purity. Many types of scaly skin diseases were described as "leprosy," and there were strict rules about these diseases. The ritual priests had the responsibility to declare someone clean or unclean and, if unclean, to quarantine the person and later declare that the cured person was clean. "Lepers" were obliged to live isolated and to dress in a way that indicated their state of ritual uncleanliness. Cured "lepers" had ritual offerings to perform when declared clean. The few verses chosen from the elaborate laws about skin diseases (Lev 13-14) form a background to Jesus' cure. Unfortunately the psalm chosen is a penitential hymn and therefore implies that such skin diseases were related to personal sin.

The scene falls into two parts. The actual cleansing is a pointed, simple, and graphic account—and could be read as a small catechesis of prayer. We note both the posture of the leper "kneeling," in intensification of his urgent plea and the words in which the plea is expressed: "If you choose (are willing) you can make me clean." There is a presumption of power at Jesus' disposal. We also note that the priests declare that a person is clean. Jesus is being asked to heal. Jesus responds spontaneously in a remarkable way: "He stretched out his hand and touched him" (such a touch would contaminate, yet Mark is not interested in this detail), and simply affirmed his awareness of God-given power to heal. "I do will it. Be clean." Mark underlines the recreative power with the redundant statement, "the leprosy left him and immediately he was made clean."

Not so often does Mark comment on what in Jesus' inner world motivates him to act. However, many scenes in the gospel have paradigmatic elements that are not repeated, and we can state that compassion was a major motivation in Jesus' life.

We could reflect on the sovereign power of Jesus as Lord available to the believing community. Traditionally "the leprosy" has been seen as a symbol of human sin (the explanation the psalm uses). However, there are many ways in which we are all broken, "in quarantine" as it were because of various causes that dehumanize us. We are challenged by the leper's bold faith, "If you will you can...," and he can model aspects of prayer for us. The fact that Jesus enables the "leper" to rejoin his human community and family is an important feature in the narrative.

The subsequent scene is puzzling because of the strong, apparently negative, emotions attributed to Jesus, the man's flagrant disregard for Jesus' clear instructions, and the apparent negative consequences for Jesus, forced to go into hiding, as it were. However, there is another way to read the dramatic narrative.

Each healing/exorcism is authenticated in some way and draws an acknowledgment from the people who witness it. This response enables people to express their awareness that in and through Jesus God is present and active in their history. God's time (*kairos*) has come and he reveals himself. This is the focus of Jesus' life.

In our scene the leper enables others to experience the healing action of God through Jesus when the priest declares him to be clean and when he offers the prescribed public offerings. With great forcefulness in body language (Mark writes of a type of growl) and in words Jesus, faithful to religious regulations, sends the leper straight to the priest. We note the words "say nothing to anyone...." However, the man achieves the purpose of revealing God's action in a more dramatic way. Mark does not give the impression he disapproves of the man's actions. There is a type of tension between Jesus' instructions and the man's actions. The end result is that Jesus is "mobbed" and forced to stay in the thinly populated countryside. However, he is still like a magnet, drawing people to hear the good news and be cured. The chapter concludes with this picture of the magnetism of God's special prophet who calls us to "repent and believe the Good News."

EIGHTH SUNDAY OF ORDINARY TIME: YEAR B Mk 2:18–22

The New Creates Problems

The Liturgy of the Word is occasionally quite lean and this Sunday is one of those days.

The few verses selected from Hosea emphasize God's love as husband for unfaithful Israel—a love celebrated in Ps 103. This is meant to provide some background to the symbolic use of the bridegroom/marriage image to refer to salvation and Jesus' role. However, the reading does not really enrich the themes found in the gospel.

The gospel is a mild controversy narrative in which an aspect of the life of Jesus' disciples is critiqued. They fail to observe the pietistic practices of fasting that are part of the external religious life of two contemporary enthusiastic groups—disciples of the Baptist and the religiopolitical group named Pharisees. Apart from obligatory fasts, some individuals and groups observed more regular fasts, signs of penitence and devotion (Tobias 12:18–9; Mt 6:16–8; Lk 18:12).

It appears that Jesus' followers, probably like their teacher, did not practice certain external religious observances that some people would have expected. This provides Jesus with another opportunity to highlight his authoritative role and the nature of the situation that his ministry has created. With a certain humor he points out how foolish it would be to fast at a marriage celebration.

Jesus designates himself as the bridegroom and in the present moment as a "marriage banquet." In this way he is affirming with other imagery what he said at the outset of his ministry: a very special moment has come that mirrors God's long history of presence to Israel through major prophetic figures, and which now demands thorough repentance and commitment to Jesus' teaching and person (1:14–15). This theme of the "scandal" of newness and the need to question many aspects of traditional religion and a societal structure molded by the religion are implied in the two sayings that contrast so sharply with the new (unshrunk cloth, new wine) and the old (old garment, old wine skins). Traditional beliefs, practices, and structures are pointedly questioned by Jesus and his teaching.

For a community gathered to worship, a possible area of reflection could be the value of fasting and so likewise the esteem for the human body in our faith life. Fasting has become a "secular" practice—fasting for refugees and famine-stricken people and for health. Fasting is also a way to intensify a person's religious search and prayer life. Our text refers to fasting and Jesus' future death (the going away of the bridegroom).

Another area of reflection could be the tendency

among Christians to retreat from such theological ideas, such structures of life in the church and the church's response to problems in human society—major problems of human sexuality, human rights and dignity, racial questions, gender discrimination, injustice and poverty, and international trade practices. Such a retreat may appear to offer security but lends itself to limited involvement, pietistic practices, and shallow appeals to authority. The Christian presence in the world is to be a disturbing presence. The world, human problems, and concerns are to disturb the church. The continual search for new wineskins for new wine and not to patch old cloths, is a challenge to us.

NINTH SUNDAY OF ORDINARY TIME: YEAR B Mk 2:23—3:6

The Primary Value of the Human

An identity badge for Catholics about thirty years ago was not to eat meat on Friday. One of the central expressions of Jewish religious identity was, and still is, the observance of the Sabbath. The simple command in the *ten words*: "observe the Sabbath day and keep it holy as the Lord your God commanded you" (Dt 5:12) was hedged about with all types of rules to ensure its observance. Its weekly occurrence, the obvious way it distinguished Jewish villagers, townspeople, and urban community from outsiders, and the fact that it was anchored into God's creative act (Gn 2:3) ensured that it was a touchstone of religious observance, righteousness, piety, and identity.

In the reading from Deuteronomy (5:12-15) and the accompanying psalm (Ps 81) our attention ought to be drawn to the humanistic and religious significance of the Sabbath. We note the command that all, especially slaves, rest from work and also note the commemoration of the God who freed the enslaved people in Egypt.

The two conflict narratives in Mark are easily distinguishable (2:23-28 and 3:1-6) with the surprising conclusion (3:6). As with other conflict and controversy stories there is an expressed or implied critique of Jesus (often by a critique of his disciples) that acts as a dramatic foil and is followed by sayings, or an action of Jesus. There can be a concluding reaction by any observers. The important point is what Jesus says or does, because here we learn something more about Jesus and his mission.

In the first and second story, the conflict is not about Sabbath observance as such, but rather about priorities in authentic religious (faith) life and the criteria to judge the obligations of various practices, which embody true values. The actual needs of the human person have primacy and are the interpretive key to best practice and the way this obligates a person or group.

Religion in its structured and socializing forms, in its rituals and customs, is affected by cultural and historical factors like many other social realities, whether clubs, bureaucracies, political parties, business companies, hospitals, schools, and medical or educational bodies. The danger is to absolutize customs, rituals, laws, expressions of belief and structures, at the expense of the primacy of the human person and human needs. We could reflect on this aspect of our Christian life.

There are two other aspects in today's gospel. Mark's Jesus explicitly affirms his authority as a religious teacher, claiming as Son of Man to be "Lord even of the Sabbath." This is a provocative claim of extraordinary religious authority as the Sabbath law comes from God and is found in the key part of Jewish Scripture, the Torah. He exercises this authority in both scenes.

Further aspects of his authoritative role are implied in his anger, in the prophetic action of healing, and the implied judgment on the hardness of heart of the religious leaders.

Though we have reasons to question at times the exercise of authority in the church we cannot escape the authority of Jesus Christ, his prophetic insights and vision.

In reflecting on Sabbath we may also wish to reflect on another aspect of human life—our bodily reality and the need for rest, for time and space to be with God, with ourselves and our families, and to re-create our inner selves, truly a Sabbatical rest.

TENTH SUNDAY OF ORDINARY TIME: YEAR B Mk 3:20–35

Further Opposition

In our reading we hear a slogan used in a nasty slur campaign against Jesus, "He has Beelzebul and by the ruler of demons he casts out demons." We also are informed of a strange popular opinion about Jesus: "He has gone out of his mind." Both opinions are clearly derogatory.

The narrative itself is made up of three "pieces." The setting is a house (or Jesus' home) where Jesus and presumably his disciples (the text is vague) are besieged by a crowd so that they are not even able to eat (cf. 6:31). There are two reactions to this popularity, one domestic and the other public. His family—an undefined group—perhaps embarrassed or angered, attempts to put some order into the mess. We shall later read the scene of Jesus' rejection in Nazareth.

The public slur campaign draws a response from Jesus. It presumes that exorcisms are quite typical of his ministry (1:23-26, 32-34; 3:11-12; 3:15; cf. 5:1-20; 9:14-27). The explicit worldview of Jesus' time, as now in many contemporary African and Asian countries, accounted for many types of evil in terms of an alien spirit world that was antagonistic to real human good, and to God's power over his creation. It is hard to see how Gn 3: 9-15 and Ps 130 form an appropriate background for our reading. Probably the origin of satanic demons is implied in the condemnation of the "snake"—an idea that is foreign to Genesis 3. Exorcism by religious figures was a known and accepted phenomenon in Jesus' world.

Jesus is accused of being in league with evil power. In response he takes up a number of issues. With some short sayings he indicates the stupidity of the accusation (3:23-26) and challenges them to see the truth of the reality—a stronger person than "satan" has tied him up and plundered his house.

The basic attitude of Jesus' opponents is also uncovered in a saying that seems so strange—the eternal sin. People can sin in any way and speak about God in all types of erroneous and improper ways (cf. God's words to Job's accusers 42:7). However, in the face of the evidence of the goodness and power of Jesus' work and the religious atmosphere created by him, a prophetic teacher gifted by the Spirit (1:11-13,14-15), to accuse him of being a false prophet, magician, in league with evil is to harden the heart in its depths before God.

We need to avoid reading this passage in the light of conflicts between theological currents and stances in the contemporary church—on women in the church, social justice, use of magisterial authority, papal theology, issues of human sexuality and bioethics. However, every Christian and every community can reflect how ready they are to travel the difficult path of discerning God's presence and where God's voice is found in the church and in significant movements and voices in today's world.

The dispute (3:22-30) is framed by Jesus' domestic world (3:19b-21 and 3:31-34). "His mother and his brothers come" and from outside (presumably of the house, 3:19b) "they sent to him and called him."

Interpreters have to decide whether to link 3:19b-21 and 3:31-34 and judge whether his mother and brothers were at least upset, or unable to understand and accept Jesus' ministry. I judge that 3:31-35 does not continue the thought of 3:19b-21 and distinguishes mother and brothers from family. The saying of Jesus, paradoxical and using a clear contrast, sets two values in comparison, *family ties*, which in his society were major values, and *discipleship*, to underline in a paradoxical way the total primacy of God's will over or against all other values. Family ties and obligations would be judged both as essential, and as major values, sanctioned by God. Yet God's will is *the* value.

We can reflect on our own value system. What is the key value in our decisions even in our daily decisions? God's will? Do we truly mean it when we pray "Your will be done on earth as it is in heaven"?

ELEVENTH SUNDAY OF ORDINARY TIME: YEAR B Mk 4:26-34

Evil or Good

To listen to Jesus' two brief parables and see their relevance for ourselves as believers, or a believing community, we need to reflect on the ways evil, often masked and cloaked under the disguises of the "good," is present within our society and world today. We need to grow in a consciousness of the pervasive power of "evil." Evil has many facets: in selfishness, indifference, and the powerful structures of injustice. It creates an atmosphere, ethos, and value that when promoted skillfully, undermine human dignity and rights, deeper human values, truth, beauty, honesty, and love. We also need to understand the sense of individual and group powerlessness, discouragement, pessimism, and indifference that lead to withdrawal into our small worlds and securities.

Jesus' parables emphasize hope over pessimism and powerlessness in the ongoing struggle between evil and good, between "sin" and God. He speaks of the certainty as regards the effectiveness of God's presence and action in history despite all types of contrary impressions. The grain becomes a rich harvest, the smallest seed becomes the greatest of all shrubs with branches large enough for birds' nests!

The reading from Ezekiel (17:22–24), full of imagery, forms a background both to the image of the shrub and more importantly to the theology of God's immense power despite all odds. Ps 92 reminds us of his protective power in the lives of the righteous, those who seek and work for his reign.

We could reflect on how in our modern world God's Spirit is at work often silently and in a hidden way, in the ecclesial communities and individual believers, in striving for concrete expressions in sociocultural, economic, and political life for a far more human and just society that has great concern for truth and genuine human values. We need also to see how the same Spirit is at work in individuals, groups, and movements outside of the church or official religious influence and sponsorship. This recognition, the hope and reassurance given by Jesus Christ to us, would lead to involvement with patient realism and hope that enables us to handle discouragement and frustration, and to develop a commitment that grows. Our prayer "Our Father... your Kingdom come," invites us to be involved with courage and hope.

TWELFTH SUNDAY OF ORDINARY TIME: YEAR B Mk 4:35–41

No Faith

Our liturgy today invites us to reflect upon what happens to our relationship to God or Jesus Christ on the occasions of personal crisis, whatever may be the cause and nature of the crisis. Crises affect many types of relationships: the crises inherent in the growing and maturing processes affect a person's relationship to parents and siblings: within friendships, within marriage, and in business. Crises often spill over and weaken and destroy or deepen and cement relationships. One of the basic personal relationships of our life arises from our image of God. How has this relationship weathered the crises of our life?

The graphic reading from Job (38:1, 8–11) and the few verses from Ps 107 prepare us for the symbolic meaning of our gospel. God is the sole creator and master of the sea, and his power is discernible in a visible manner as he controls mighty storms: "He made the storm be still and the waves of the sea were hushed." His power and dependable love are visible as he saves sailors from death.

We now enter the boat with a weary Jesus (note in 4:1 Jesus had got into a boat). Sudden and dangerous storms are a feature of life on the Lake of Galilee. The tension in the narrative is created by the contrasting pictures of Jesus asleep on a cushion and the helpless disciples, terrified by the raging storm of wind and waves. We are not even told whether Jesus sits up. Only his words of rebuke are important: "Quiet, be still." If we glance at the exorcism in 1:25 we note the similarities. Power over demons and power over the sea are related. The conflict is resolved. There is a clear contrast between the raging sea and the wild wind, and the dead calm and no wind.

The key aspects of the narrative are Jesus' words to his disciples and their reaction. Jesus asks "Why are you scared? Have you still no faith?" The very presence of Jesus rules out the possibility of perishing and terror. The terrified disciples are now awestruck disciples who ask each other "Who then is this, that even the wind and sea obey him?"

Within the background of God and the sea, God and storms (see also Job 26:11–12; Ps 65:8), and Jesus' quiet sovereign words of power, Mark invites the believing community to be reassured. Jesus Christ their Lord is present, and on him they can depend whatever be the crisis that may lead them to question the goodness, the power, the fidelity, and the presence of Jesus as Lord in their lives in times of crisis. He will appear to be "asleep," yet he is there. We are challenged and invited to learn to reach out to Jesus Christ in the very midst of crises. We experience pain, doubt, helplessness, and we do grow in that trust that gives a maturing depth to our personal relationship to Jesus Christ and God the Father in the Spirit. Jesus is less an idea, less able to be controlled by us, less predictable, and so more authentically the Lord. As we look back over our journey of faith we may wish to share the prayer of the disciples, quiet awe, and a question to which we are never able to give an adequate answer: Who is this?

THIRTEENTH SUNDAY OF ORDINARY TIME: YEAR B Mk 5:21–43

A Man and Woman of Faith

The theme of last Sunday is continued. This week we can also appreciate the narrative skill of the writer and the beauty of the narrative. Were you to make a short play or use this for a sequence in a film, how would you go about it? Read the narrative in a rural setting of two thousand years ago.

There is a creative pause in the narrative of Jesus and Jairus as he is delayed on his way to the house by the woman. The tension is magnified because, *as* he is speaking in praise of the woman's faith, messengers come from Jairus' house with the tragic news that "your daughter is dead," and their sense of broken hope and futility is verbalized, "Why trouble the teacher any further?"

There is dramatic contrast between Jesus and his disciples. In the midst of the jostling crowds, Jesus asks "who touched my clothes?" This is an apparently stupid question, as the disciples point out: "You see the crowd pressing in on you, how can you say…?" Tension is created, and our attention is focused on the woman and Jesus.

There are other details we need to note. The woman's situation could not be worse: the nature of the disease—hemorrhages; time span—twelve years; medical experience—suffered much; financial situation—spent all she had; present state—no better, rather grew worse. We note also the inner conversation of the woman—"If I but touch his clothes…"—and the contrast between the years of searching for a cure and "immediately her hemorrhage stopped."

Jairus' situation is paralleled and could not be worse, as his daughter, at the point of death, is now dead. The contrast between the wailing women and Jesus' calm is described so graphically (anyone who has seen "social wailing" at death will appreciate the scene). Note their laughter. These details reenforce the reality of her death.

The selection from Wisdom (Wis 1:13–15; 2:23–24) provides some reflections on God as creator, his gift of human life, death, our creation in God's image, and the gift of immortality. The psalmist is faced with possible death and prays urgently and with grateful confidence (Ps 30).

The gospel narrative is not concerned with incurable sickness and death as such, but with the striking faith of the woman, the faith demanded of Jairus (and his wife), "Do not fear, only believe" and the power of Jesus faced with impossible situations. As a believing community we are challenged by the woman's vibrant faith and invited by Jesus in moments of crisis to hear his words to Jairus, "Do not fear, only believe."

We could reflect on a small phrase in the woman's story: "She had heard about Jesus." We are not told more except the effect upon her. She has come to the conclusion, "If I but touch his clothes…." She had a profound sense of God's power available to her through this holy man. Years of hearing the Word and celebrating the Eucharist are meant to enable us also to reach out in times of crisis—cancer, sudden death, drug addiction of a son or daughter, infidelity, a broken marriage, loss of employment, aging—to the power of God in Jesus Christ.

In the Jairus story we note the expression of futility by some of the family (servants) of Jairus, the incredulity of the professional mourners, and Jesus' invitation to Jairus, "Do not fear: only believe." We could reflect on the phrase "Do not fear," which in the biblical records is one of Jesus' and of God's more frequent commands. Fear really builds a wall between us and our God. Fear is a looking within our world, our own capabilities, our horizon of possibilities, and our cherished vision of life. "Do not fear, only believe" takes us out of this small world into the world of a faithful and loving God, and Jesus his Son, who is Lord of all.

FOURTEENTH SUNDAY OF ORDINARY TIME: YEAR B Mk 6:1–6

A Day of Disappointment

There is a note of realism, however disappointing, in

our gospel. We have followed the story of Jesus from 4:35—5:43 (5:1-20 was omitted), and we have seen his power and examples of faith. Now we face that all too common human reality of judging by externals, discounting, disparaging, belittling, discrediting, calling into question, and doubting. In the situation of a person sent by God such attitudes are expressions of disbelief, a vision and heart closed to the voice of God.

The narrative is simply constructed. Mark moves Jesus and his disciples to his hometown. This incident happens on the Sabbath when the rural community is assembled for common worship. Jesus teaches. Earlier his teaching has caused amazement because of Jesus' peculiar authority, or caused opposition because of its content. Now he is met with cynicism. Note that "astounded" and "amazed" are used to describe the negative reaction of his townsfolk.

The whole ministry of Jesus is called into question and deprecated—his wisdom and deeds of power and their source (note "been given him" and "being done by his hands"). It is important to note the open disparaging tone in the way they refer to Jesus, "this man." We would say "this guy—who does he think he is?" The belittling term ("this" in Greek) is used three times to refer to Jesus.

The reason is that they have grown up and lived with Jesus—one of the local carpenters (this type of work is not looked down on as such) whose mother and his extended family are known. (The text itself does not allow us to come to any conclusion about Mary's virginity.) How can they accept this man as a prophet and an authoritative teacher? Jesus is a cause of scandal to them—incredible that he could be a genuine prophet.

The people's attitude is related by the opening reading (Ez 2:2-5) to a long history of the rejection of prophets. A particular statement of God to the prophet is relived by Jesus: "…I am sending you to them…whether they hear or refuse to hear…they shall know that there has been a prophet among them" (2:4b-5). The psalm (Ps 123) is probably meant as an encouragement to the rejected prophet.

Jesus acknowledges the experience, narrated in his sacred tradition, of the rejection of the prophet by his own people. Probably the saying is a proverb and does not include his mother and family in the rejection and belittlement of his role and mission.

The attitude of the community hinders Jesus' usual healing ministry and shocks him. We could pause and remain in conversation with Jesus who is both shocked and pained.

We reflect today on that strange fact that God can only be present, address, invite, challenge, and guide us through human persons, human institutions, human rituals, and historical events, which all have at least an element of ambiguity. We must discern and open the deep levels of our person to the ways God comes to us. We need to learn from others' experiences and accept the limitations of the human. The spirit guides us in discerning the historical and culturally conditioned ways, in and through which God and Jesus Christ come to us today.

FIFTEENTH SUNDAY OF ORDINARY TIME: YEAR B Mk 6: 7–13

My Concern

There is a phrase used at the beginning of today's gospel that causes problems, namely "the Twelve." This term could lead us to restrict Jesus' instructions to those with ecclesiastical roles, and also to religious men and women, so excluding the largest part of the believing community. Traditionally the text would have been applied to the "professionals" (priests, sisters, brothers, bishops). Let us read the text as addressed to all who believe in Jesus Christ with special concern for the responsibility of the laywoman and man, or groups of laypeople.

The text is very conditioned by the concrete circumstances of that period, with its customs and culture. "Two by two" ensures that there are witnesses and protection (Dt 19:13). It is hard to go back to a rural world—only donkeys, horses, and carts as means of transport. For the majority walking was normal, and luggage was minimal and light. As the disciples would eat in the houses they visited, there was no need of "bread, bag, or loose change"; sandals and a "walking stick" were needed and no change of clothes, no extra shirt and pants ("spare tunics"). There were many itinerant teachers, and they normally received hospitality in a home in each village.

The immediate background to their mission is mentioned in 6:6b "then he went about among the villages teaching." The liturgy has omitted an important Marcan text (3:14–19) in which Jesus called "the Twelve" and appointed them apostles to be with him and share his ministry. In today's gospel he actually summons and sends out, giving authority over demons, twelve (men) of his disciples. The use of "the Twelve" indicates that the early community of believers understood themselves to be "the chosen people" and consequently entrusted them with the responsibility to be the community through whom God the Father, and Jesus as Lord, would continue in a special way through his risen Spirit, to be present in human history.

The responsibility entrusted to "the Twelve" is restricted to "authority over unclean spirits" in 6:7 but also includes proclaiming "that all should repent" and healing the sick (6:12–13 and 6:11). They use oil as a means to healing—quite common in many village communities and a practice of early Christian communities (James 5:4). What Jesus has been doing they are also to do (1:14–15; 1:38–39; 1:34; 3:10–11; 3:14–15). They are sent in God's name and, therefore, refusing them welcome or refusing to listen calls down on a village God's judgment, symbolized in shaking the dust of the place off their feet—a symbol of rejection.

All of this is so alien to our modern life, and quite unlikely to stir up a sense of concern and responsibility in the believing man or woman.

In our modern world there is indifference to the transcendent. Though many also search for the transcendent, there is a growing alienation from the churches and their regular expression of belief in worship, prayer, and the action of church-related associations. What is the role of the believing person? We acknowledge the damage done by issues of race, the debate on immigration, the lack of social justice, national foreign policies and business ventures, which increase poverty, injustice, and alienation for the poor and minorities in other countries and damage the environment, and destruction caused by drugs. Yet the "good life" is propagated by the media. What does the believing community say, looking at this society from the perspective of the gospel of Jesus Christ?

What are our demons that are destroying the human? Where, and in what ways, do we need to repent? What sickness needs to be cured by human care, concern, and commitment?

In the reading from Amos 7:12–15 (it is worth putting it in context by reading 7:10–17) we are reminded that the prophet is an unwanted person in human society—to speak "the truth in love" is not appreciated. The prophetic role is to speak on behalf of God, not to foretell the future, as it can be trivialized. The psalm (Ps 85) allows us to glimpse how God acts as a re-creative presence within our history.

SIXTEENTH SUNDAY OF ORDINARY TIME: YEAR B Mk 6:30–34

A Quiet Sunday

Today's reading is really only a transitional paragraph, functioning as an introduction to Mark's feeding of the five thousand (6:35–44; cf. 8:1–10, the feeding of the four thousand).

We have skipped two significant scenes. In one, at the court of King Herod, while various opinions circulate about Jesus' identity, Herod expresses his opinion that Jesus is the decapitated John the Baptist raised from the dead and come to haunt him (6:14–16). In a flashback Mark recounts the murder of John (6:7–29). The popular opinion about the identity of Jesus forms a frame around a section of the gospel (6:17—8:26) and will surface again at a crucial juncture (8:27–30). The disciples, sent into the villages and small towns, rejoin Jesus in 6:30.

As he continues the story of Jesus, Mark draws our attention to the person of Jesus and his religious reputation. What Jesus' family wanted to do earlier, namely get him out of the limelight (3:19–20), Jesus does now with his disciples and for the same reason—so many people coming and going that they "did not even have leisure to eat." Implied is the success of his commitment to the people as a man of God. However, Jesus' attempt to find quiet and rest for the disciples is frustrated. Mark is quite graphic, a few brush strokes and a picture is painted. "*Many* saw them going...they *ran* on foot from *all* the towns and arrived ahead of them"—a further indication of Jesus' tremendous power to attract.

Mark is not at all interested in the possible grumbling of the disciples at the spoiled picnic! All attention of the listener is drawn to Jesus: As *he* went ashore, *he* saw a great crowd and *he* had compassion…and *he* began to teach.

We should note that Jesus had compassion on the people and responded to their need. Priests and religious who are, or tend to be, compulsive workers should ask themselves about their motive. Workaholics do not find a model in Jesus; he responds to the needs of others, rather than use others to satisfy his own needs.

We shall pay attention to what stirred Jesus' compassion. The narrator reads his heart—"for they were like sheep without a shepherd." We need to go back to a rural setting two thousand years ago where flocks of "sheep" were not Merinos in a paddock but needed a shepherd to protect them from wild animals and to lead them in the search for pasture and water.

The image implies that the people are abandoned, without leaders and protection, and at the mercy of "wild animals." Mark does not elaborate in his gospel as to the religious and human state of Jesus' contemporaries.

In the first reading Jeremiah (Jer 23:1–6) both castigates the religious and civil rulers of the people—"the shepherds who shepherd my people" and promises a future genuine ruler who will ensure the dignity and rights of all the people. This future ruler ought to model himself on God, the Shepherd "whose goodness and mercy" is celebrated in Ps 23 where God is the attentive Shepherd and gracious host.

These readings form a background to the portrait of Jesus as the authentic Shepherd. The aspect we ought to concentrate upon is his compassion, the unselfish, sensitive, intelligent attentiveness to others and an appropriate responsiveness that will so often be costly—personal energy and time, to listen, to act, to organize, and to give of ourselves. Jesus allows himself to be moved to action by the people. He is not an observer. We believe that Jesus is the Son of God. To grasp what it means to be the Son of God we need to invert the statement, the Son of God is Jesus—the compassionate person surrounded by ordinary people.

At this point we could just recall how various people have seen Jesus:

- demons: "do not destroy us, holy one of God";

- a sick woman: "If I only touch his clothes";

- the leper: "If you will, you can make me clean";

- people in Nazareth: "Who is this guy?";

- disciples: "Who is this that the wind and sea obey him?";

- the crowds: "hurried to the place on foot."

What response do we make?

SEVENTEENTH SUNDAY OF ORDINARY TIME: YEAR B Jn 6:1–15

We Often Get It Wrong

We now interrupt the semi-continuous reading of Mark with an extensive reading from John 6, starting with today's gospel of the loaves and the fishes.

We begin by analyzing the small narrative to make sure we follow the plot, note the roles the characters play, and catch the point being made. The setting is quite elaborate—the lakeside and mountain. The characters are introduced: an enthusiastic crowd drawn, we are told "seeing the signs he was doing on the sick" (possible reference to 4:43–54; see 2:23; 3:2), the disciples and Jesus sitting among them. The time of the year is indicated, "near Passover" [We need to forget the feeding narratives of Mt, Mk, and Lk and read John].

The crisis is introduced by Jesus who, seeing the large crowd approaching, puts the question: "Where are we to buy bread for these people to eat?" The ensuing dialogue only heightens the crisis and underlines the impossible situation and the disciples' helplessness. In an aside, typical of John's gospel, the narrator ensures that the reader does not get an impression that Jesus is at a loss. Though Jesus is from Nazareth, in John he is always master of every situation even his arrest and death (6:15, 64; 5:34; 11:42; 12:30; 18:6; 19:33–37). He is always "*Word* made flesh."

The working out of the crisis is entirely in Jesus' hands. Note that he does everything, he himself distributes the bread and fish to the five thousand! The disciples just gather up twelve large heavy baskets full of the leftover bread. This detail adds to the extraordinary quality of the event called in John "a sign." Jesus has set himself up for...?

The *climax of the event* is the popular acclaim "This is indeed the prophet who is to come into the world" (cf. Dt 18:18). Jesus escaped into the hills by himself because he was aware of their plan to make him the long-expected religiopolitical leader (messianic king) who would rid them of the oppressive colonial rule of Rome and restore their sociopolitical identity, power, dignity, and prosperity.

The reading from 2 Kg 4:42–44 and Ps 145 depict a powerful and provident God and a great prophet, Elisha, who shows God's concern in the feeding of the people, and so they form a vague background for our gospel reading.

A new crisis is created, again by Jesus, who escapes and hides and leaves a genuine prophetic question. The sign is to lead those who witness it to penetrate into the person and purpose of Jesus, and also into the mystery of God and the human community.

The Christian churches, local ecclesial communities, are to be a prophetic sign in today's world as they "see the large crowds." Do they project images of institutional power and influence, of silence and lack of concern in light of major issues, social problems, and challenges; before a prevailing atheism; before a culture dominated by the culture of the supermarkets and large commercial chains? Jesus has a prophetic role with a leadership role, and this is to be shared by individual Christians, and Christian communities and the churches. There is great power, yet a power often misunderstood, misused, or forgotten. Does Jesus have to withdraw and go into hiding because of wrong expectations or wrong "uses" of him in our lives, or do we just simply neglect him?

EIGHTEENTH SUNDAY OF ORDINARY TIME: YEAR B Jn 6:24–35

The Search

The place to begin our reflections this week is not the biblical text but our local society and culture, and the "search" for significant meaning in life, and the source(s) of this meaning for young people, men and women in their working years, in retirement, and in old age. We could characterize the human search as a search for "the bread of life," aware that there is much "bread" offered by the media, popular culture, peer group, societal and professional expectations, the tourist industry and business. This "bread" is apparently good for health and genuine, yet is deceptive, a poor substitute for the real thing. There are many descriptions of "the good life," many types of "life" in the marketplace, sold by religions, political parties, clubs, popular philosophy, magazines, novels, and the media. All of these are disguised forms of human diminishment and dying. We allow these reflections to form a context in which to read our gospel.

The text is basically a Question/Answer session set in motion by an apparently innocent question of the crowd. The dialogue does not unfold logically but rather in an evocative manner, where words have levels of meaning and symbolic potential. The writer has also related the feeding narrative and the Manna incident (described in the selection of verses of the first reading [Ex 16:2–4, 12–15] and Ps 79) in a form of contemporary Jewish interpretative commentary on an Old Testament text. The crowd's questions either indicate a misunderstanding of Jesus, or provoke Jesus to lead them to new levels of meaning.

On one level there is a religious polemic where Moses and the Jewish religion are relegated to the past and evaluated as not life-giving.

There is another level of the text built around the symbols of "bread" and "life," "the bread that endures to eternal life," "bread that comes down from heaven and gives life to the world," "the true bread which God gives," and finally the identification of Jesus as both the source of, and the actual, "Bread of life." He is the bread of life himself and its source because of his relationship to God the Father, who has anointed him (genuine revealer) and sent him. This relationship of Jesus to God the Father is the key element, enabling Jesus to be the genuine "bread" that gives authentic life to believers. This is one of the key elements in discerning the "bread" offered in the contemporary world. Is it from God?

The life that is given is described as "eternal," a qualitative term rather than temporal. It is genuine life and is not characterized by continual thirst and hunger. In one sense the search is completed and in another the search continues accompanied by a profound peace. These are the criteria to judge the quality of life that is available for us as God's gift.

Finally we are challenged to believe in Jesus Christ, to surrender ourselves in such a way, and from such depths, of our religious personality that indicate a self-giving to Jesus Christ, the one who is able to satisfy the deepest yearnings of the human person and the human community.

The question to each of us is: Do we have a Jesus Christ who is worth such self-giving? Do parents and educators, the faith community through her bishops, priests, catechists, and theologians, in the church's writings, public statements, and lived value system—do these all witness to Jesus Christ in whom young and old can see "the Bread of life"(6:35)?

NINETEENTH SUNDAY OF ORDINARY TIME: YEAR B Jn 6:41–51

The Shadows Upon Jesus Christ

The narrative structure of the reading is quite simple. The listening crowd, identified as "the Jews," put together the ideas of 6:32–33 and 35 in the phrase "I am the bread that come down from heaven" and start complaining. They murmur: how can the son of Joseph claim "to come down from heaven?" The remaining verses are Jesus' reaffirmation of his unique role as revealer and source of authentic life to all who believe.

We could look at various points. There is an aspect of scandal about believing that Jesus Christ is the God-given *unique* source of "life to the *world*" (6:33).

There is the problem of the historical particularity of Jesus, his genuine human origin "whose father and mother we know," and the faith claim of universal saving significance.

There is the problem for people today of the Jesus Christ presented by the churches, the Jesus of popular religious art and devotions, of popular theology, where his divinity often swallows up his human life. The other side of the problem is where the church that proclaims Jesus Christ is perceived as an institution with its historical and cultural baggage and other factors that throw shadows upon his divinity. These problems make it very hard for many people of various cultures, various socioreligious backgrounds, and contemporary secular culture to recognize and believe in the Jesus Christ who does reveal the mystery of God and is the source of life.

Women and men, who believe and find in Jesus Christ the center of the deeper meaning of their lives and the basis of their hope can pause and be deeply grateful for the continued and hidden action of God the Father, through the Spirit, in the deeper recesses of their person. The Father "draws" believers to Christ: he teaches believers who "hear and learn" his teaching. In the verses omitted (6:36–40) we are also reminded that Jesus is the life-giver because the Father sent him and the Father willed that "all who see the Son and believe in him may have eternal life" (6:40). Jesus is always the one sent by the Father to reveal the Father and finally to enable us to share in the Father's life. Therefore in the Eucharist the climactic prayer is "through Christ, with him, and in him, in the unity of the Holy Spirit…all glory and honor is yours, almighty Father…."

Finally, we as believers look at Jesus Christ with profound appreciation because of who he is, and who he has been, and still is for us over years. Jesus continually speaks in various ways of his own intimate relationship to God—the perspective of mature Christian faith— Jesus is the one "who is from God" and so "he has seen the Father." He is sent, and the primary concern of his life is his Father's will. He is able to satisfy the deepest *longings* of the human spirit being "the Bread of life," or the "living and life giving bread" gifted by the Father ("come down from heaven"). His full identity with the human and his genuine human life is important. He is the source of that life that we share with God the Father now ("eternal life") and share endlessly ("live forever"). Therefore he is the source of human hope in the face of the ultimate reality of death.

Our Eucharist can be a great prayer of gratitude and praise to the Father and Jesus, his Son, in their Spirit.

TWENTIETH SUNDAY OF ORDINARY TIME: YEAR B Jn 6:51–58

I Live Because of the Father

Earlier in the instruction Jesus had identified himself with "the bread of God which comes down from heaven and gives life to the world" (6:33 and 6:35).

This gave rise to strong complaints (6:41–42). Jesus identifies himself also as "the living bread that came down from heaven" (6:50) and further develops this by saying "the bread that I will give for the life of the world is my flesh" (6:51). We also note that "to believe" earlier had been expressed in terms of "come to me." Now John uses the term "eat" to symbolize believing (6:51). The use of this word follows from the Old Testament account of Manna. Also the emphasis given to the idea of life/living rises from the contrast between the Manna and the ancestors who died, and Jesus as bread from heaven and the believers who will never die.

In a fashion typical of this gospel Jesus' statement "the bread that I will give for the life of the world is my flesh" gives rise to a strident reaction. This evokes Jesus' elaborate affirmation of himself as the essential source of authentic life for human persons and the crucial role of believing.

The powerful symbolism and use of contrast needs our attention. Obviously the Eucharist, as celebrated in John's communities, is the point of reference and so the discourse is clearly interpreted in light of the risen Jesus Christ.

However these verses also clarify with a graphic power both the primary place of Jesus Christ as the source of authentic life, and the key role of a faith that is vibrant, effective, and central in Christian life. There is an essential link among Jesus Christ, revealer of the Father, authentic human life and faith.

The first essential link is in the incarnate Jesus Christ who in his human flesh and blood becomes part of our history and so is *the source of life*. Why? The Jesus of flesh and blood is related to God the Father and draws his life, which is life *par excellence*, from the Father. This life is shared by him with those who believe. The crucial statement is "just as the *living* Father sent me and I *live* because of the Father so, whoever eats me will *live* because of me" (6:57). He is the source of life in the two "sacramental" ways we meet him: in the Word and in the eucharistic bread and wine. Using flesh/blood, true food/true drink symbolism, the writer underlines the importance of Jesus Christ, the one who dwelt/dwells among us as *the* source of life—the great nourisher.

In language so graphic that it scandalizes, the writer also emphasizes our responsibility to surrender to Jesus Christ as sent by God in a faith that rises from the deeper realms of our hearts. "To eat" and "to drink" are the symbols of such faith. The whole discourse invites us to reflect on the quality of our faith.

The gift that we receive is that reality we all ultimately seek—authentic and full humanness, to be the image and likeness of God. This is true life. This is expressed in a number of ways: the contrast between "no life in you"; "eternal life"; "will raise up on the last day" (6:53); the reality of the union that "they will abide in me and I in them"; and "they will live because of me."

In our text we also see Jesus in the image of the servant, the authentic human person "giving himself for the life of the world" (6:51). This is a reference ultimately to his death. We live the life given to us to the extent we are like Jesus, ever wanting to be responsive to the Father and being life-givers to others, even if the price demands deep sacrifice, "our flesh and blood."

The reading from Proverbs 9:1–6 and the prayer from Ps 34 focus our attention on the Eucharist as God's gift of life through Jesus Christ.

TWENTY-FIRST SUNDAY OF ORDINARY TIME: YEAR B Jn 6:60–69

Choice

Most of us become Christian as part of a process of socialization in our families as various values, customs, expectations, and ways of looking at life are handed on to us. As we grow we sift through what we inherit from family, church, school, and our own culture. Gradually these more or less consciously create our own basic attitudes, hopes, values, beliefs, and political options. As we mature as Christians the central issue is who is Jesus Christ for each believer. We can of course evade the issue all our lives, or for a long time. At the heart of being Christian, however, is the question of who is Jesus Christ for us.

Throughout these Sundays we have come across various opinions and attitudes about Jesus:

- misconceived enthusiasm: "take by force to make him king"(6:15);
- selfish use: "you seek me because you ate your fill of loaves" (6:26);

- disbelief: "you have seen me and yet do not believe" (6:36);
- scandal: "is not this Jesus, son of Joseph?" (6:24); and
- incredulity: "how can this man give us his flesh to eat?" (6:52).

In today's readings the issue of personal choice becomes the central concern.

The reading from Joshua (24:1-2, 15-18), a classical text in the faith interpretation of Jewish religious history, forms a background. Joshua challenges the assembled People, whom "God has enabled to conquer the land and take possession of it," to choose between this God who liberated and created them as his People, and the gods of their ancestors and of the people of Canaan. The reading can be divided into two parts 6:60-66 and 66-70, with v. 66 as a transitional verse.

There are difficulties because the text reflects, in a distant way, attitudes to Jesus in his own life, and more precisely and immediately the conflicting attitudes and decisions within the Christian community to whom John writes. This community is under much pressure from "orthodox" Jewish groups to abandon the community who believes Jesus is the Christ, Son of God and source of hope and the meaning of life.

We note negative attitudes among the disciples: a querulous complaint, an incredulity that leads to disbelief and finally rejection, and in one case betrayal (the reference to Judas, a "devil," is explained in 3:19-20). We are not sure to what actually the statement "this teaching is difficult" refers. We could understand it referring to the relationship of Jesus to God the Father, his unique role as revealer and source of authentic life—not specifically the eucharistic interpretation of the symbolic teaching of Jesus as "bread of life."

Another difficulty, a recurring difficulty in biblical texts, is the impression given that the reference to "spirit" (a gift of God) and the reiterated statement "No one can come to me unless it is granted by the Father" (6:65 and 6:44-45) absolves people of the responsibility for their disbelief. Actually, a deeper type of human sinfulness is implied—a heart closed to God, who is continually trying to draw all to the truth and to faith.

Jesus' teaching about himself and what he gives and does for us, as expressed symbolically in Chapter 6, is related to his whole life and mission, and specifically to the great events of his return to his Father ("the Son of man *ascending* [used because he spoke of bread from heaven which comes down] to where he was" [6:62]). His death, resurrection, and return to the Father are the climactic events that reveal that he is genuinely "the bread of life," gift of the Father for all. Shall these events also be met with incredulity?

We are also reminded that faith that leads to sharing in God's life is a gratuitous gift of God (We also have the problem of reconciling divine gratuity and human responsibility). The contrast between flesh (not related to 6:52-58) and spirit indicates that we must surrender a type of human self-sufficiency, whether it is the quiet and deep desire for autonomy, or whether it be an arrogance, that type of imprisoning rationalism that hardens the heart before God, and his self-revelation in and through Jesus Christ.

Finally, we have a model in Peter's words—"Lord to whom shall we go? You have the *words* of eternal life: We have come to believe and come to know that you are the Holy One of God." (There are many possible modern "teachers" who can fascinate and mold our basic options.) The phrase "Holy One of God" indicates that Jesus is the one sent by God who is both utterly faithful to God and reveals God, and therefore mediates life. There are a series of texts that give expression to these ideas (3:34; 4:42; 4:34; 1:41, 49; 5:24, 36; 6:30; 9:33; 11:27). The interesting point is the journey to a personal and deep faith implied in the synonymous phrase "we have come to believe/know...."

Let us pray for each other in our personal journey so that Jesus Christ is actually the Bread of Life, gift of the Father for us.

TWENTY-SECOND SUNDAY OF ORDINARY TIME: YEAR B Mk 7:1-8, 14-15, 21-23

From the Heart

After five weeks we rejoin Mark.

At times when we follow a TV serial we miss one or other event. In Mark we have skipped over the feeding story, the subsequent walking on the water (6:35-52) with its important ending: "They [disciples] were utterly astounded, for they did not understand about the loaves, but their hearts were hardened" (6:51b–52). We also skipped the impressive summary of the healing ministry (6:53–56). The remark about the minimal desire of the sick "that they might touch *even* the fringe of his cloak" and the result "and all who touched it were healed" reminds us of the woman with hemorrhages.

Conflicts about genuine religiosity with the religious teachers have been absent from the narrative since 3:22–30. We shall not discuss the question of what was the actual historical conflict Jesus had about purity and food laws. Our reading omits 7:9–13 in which an example is given of a human religious tradition which undermines God's will for the people—a way in which adults avoided supporting their parents. It also omits 7:17–20 in which Jesus explains the meaning of the saying in 7:14–15.

The narrative is quite simple:

• *the setting* in which the elements of the conflict are introduced (7:1–2);

• *an explanatory aside* about Jewish purificatory customs (7:3–4);

• *the accusation* against the disciples who do not conform to customs (7:5); and

• *Jesus' response* (7:6–8 and 9–13).

The audience then changes as Jesus addresses the crowds within a background of clean/unclean food, explaining that the source of defilement (sin) is inside, namely in the heart (7:14–15). The explanation of this saying is given only to the disciples privately (again their lack of understanding is indicated (4:12–13; 4:40; 6:52; 8:17–21). The heart is the source of real defilement. In a traditional way Jesus lists sinful attitudes and actions that arise from the core of a person and create real alienation from God. The heart is the core of a person for the Jew and the center of thought, intention, attitude, and action.

The first reading (Dt 4:1–2, 6–8) underlines the greatness of the gift of the Law, its adequacy to guide the people, the need for diligent obedience, and the witness value of such obedience. In the Law, God himself is near to his people. The psalmist also (Ps 15) celebrates obedience to this way of life. We note the emphasis on aspects of personal relationships.

Anyone acquainted with Islam, Sikhism, and especially the various form of Hinduism, knows that the categories of clean/unclean, profane/sacred, pure/impure have religious and cultural sanctions. Jesus' quotation from Isaiah "This people honors me with their lips but their hearts are far from me" and Jesus' comment "you abandon the commandment of God and hold to known tradition" could be points for reflection today.

The quality of our heart, the inner center of the human person, on which depends the genuine expression of our relationship with God, could be an area to which we need to pay attention. The pejorative phrase, "lip service," probably originates from this text. In the area of religion, priests and pastors, catechists and parents, religious and lay religious leaders do great damage to the gospel and the image of God the Father, and Jesus Christ, by whatever would fall under "lip service."

Another area of consideration is the danger that a particular cultural tradition, or a particular theology, or some traditional devotions assume such importance that they smother the Word of God. They also smother new theological expressions and searching, new liturgical prayers and rites, new efforts to re-express the depths of Jesus' ethical teaching in the face of the complexities of modern life and the structural character of sin. So many human precepts within the realm of religion can disfigure the authentic and fundamental teaching of Jesus Christ.

TWENTY-THIRD SUNDAY OF ORDINARY TIME: YEAR B Mk 7:31–37

He Has Done Everything Well

Unfortunately the semi-continuous reading in the *Roman Lectionary* omits the lively story of Jesus and the Syrophonecian woman (Mk 7:24–30) but it is included in the *Common Lectionary*. This narrative would be an apt occasion for Christian communities to reflect on their attitudes to believers of other religious traditions and to respect their life of faith and their belief systems, with their rites and rituals, places of worship, prayers, ethical teaching, and written records of the experience of God.

The actual narrative of the healing of the deaf man with the speech impediment (Mk 7:31–37) has a number of strange elements absent from other accounts of

Jesus' healing ministry, though some are found in contemporary narratives of healing. Though elements like putting fingers in the ears, the use of spittle, a heavenly look, groaning, and the use of a special word have a link to medicinal ideas (spittle) and magical practices, yet the whole tenor of the story is so unlike magical texts that the narrative probably only wants to lay emphasis on the difficulty of the healing, and consequently Jesus' extraordinary power. We also note that there are similarities to the narrative of the healing of a blind man in 8:22–26. The graphic elements would be intelligible to those who heard the story. The privacy motif probably also belongs to the idea of difficulty.

The narrator would want the reader to see the contrast between the urgent desire of the crowd who brought the man, the effort of Jesus, and the immediacy and total nature of the cure—able to hear and speak *plainly*. The command to the crowds of "silence!" and their total disregard of Jesus' demand heightens the sense of Jesus' power, a recurrent theme. The concluding astonishment and hyperbolic statement, "He has done everything well: he *even* makes the deaf (plural) to hear and the mute to speak" emphasizes again the "who" of Jesus. The listener to the gospel knows that Jesus is "Jesus Christ, Son of God" (1:1).

There are two areas for reflection and prayer. The first is the image of Jesus Christ projected by Christian communities, the more official church, by parents to their children, and by institutions managed by religious congregations. "He has done everything well." Is the Jesus Christ projected pro-human, pro-woman, pro-the elderly, pro-AIDS suffers, pro-battered wives, pro-rape victims?

The other related area is described in a symbolic way by Isaiah (Is 35:4–2) writing about God. God creatively changes the lives of the blind, deaf, lame, and mute. The psalm (Ps 146) expands on the same theme adding the widow, orphan, foreigner, oppressed, and hungry. In his ministry Jesus reveals this God, the God who is so deeply committed to the welfare of all people, and, in a special and scandalous way, those who are vulnerable in human society, those on the edges of society, those left behind by "progress." To work in shelters, in Vincent de Paul centers, the Salvation Army, detox centers, or with AIDS patients would probably help many Christians to find the face of God, and hear his voice, than would participating in liturgies and prayer meetings.

TWENTY-FOURTH SUNDAY OF ORDINARY TIME: YEAR B Mk 8:27–35

A New Step

This Sunday, as a Christian community, we are brought face to face with a basic attitude inherent in a mature Christian life. Deep within, we need to experience the love of Jesus Christ and make a decisive choice to allow our inner person to be molded by the life of Jesus of Nazareth. We would then desire our personal and public lives to reflect his options, which would affect our family and civic responsibilities, our professional and business life, and our political options. This leads to a choice in which the ethos of contemporary culture would be critiqued, and the values propagated by the media would be discerned carefully.

The Marcan narrative (chs 1–8) comes to a relative climax. Having been with Jesus, the disciples are challenged to identify him: "Who do you say that I am?" and are led into a world of values that can, at the least, puzzle them and actually scandalize them.

The readings of Twenty-Fourth, Twenty-Fifth and Twenty-Ninth Sundays have a similar pattern:

• Jesus speaks clearly of his suffering, death, and resurrection (8:31–32a);

• the disciples (here Peter) misunderstand the implications for discipleship (8:32b–33); and

• Jesus instructs the disciples (8:34–38).

The prior scenes are important:

• the second feeding (8:1–10), the demand for a sign by some Pharisees (8:11–13);

• the disciples' failure to understand the significance of both feedings (6:35–44 and 8:1–11);

• Jesus' harsh rebuke (8:14–21); and

• the gradual healing of a blind man, probably symbolic of the gradual process the disciples must undergo to at least recognize Jesus as the Messiah (8:22–26).

In various ways Mark has been filling in the picture of Jesus, recognized popularly as a great prophet

(6:14–16) or John the Baptist alive again in Jesus (6:16). The disciples repeat the popular estimations of Jesus, then Peter identifies him as the Messiah—the person specially chosen and entrusted by God with a culminating role in human history.

Now Jesus introduces a new element, using the phrase "Son of Man" to refer to himself. This new element is the reality of his rejection, murder, and rising from the dead.

We shall not enter into a discussion of what Jesus would probably have said (cf. 9:12 for a summary statement). He would only hade to have been normally sensitive to the build up of opposition and to remember the fate of John, and many prophets, to have foreseen the probability of murder.

However, the important details are Peter's rebuke to Jesus and the implied rejection of the possibility of murder and suffering and the sharpest reprimand in the gospel—"Get behind me, Satan" (8:33). The reason is given. Peter expresses a basic attitude inimical to God's vision. It is a narrow, worldly attitude that rules out genuine transcendent values and the possibility of transcending the self.

Jesus uses the following words: "For you are setting your mind not on divine things, but on human things." We all share Peter's attitude. Note that Mark says that Jesus, "turning and looking at his *disciples*," rebukes Peter. All disciples are in danger of a similar attitude. We are normally not conscious of the values and attitudes that make up "Peter's" way of looking at life and his failure to understand that God, his love, power, wisdom, and will are reflected in the crucified Jesus.

Jesus calls us along with the crowd and disciples (8:34) to hear his words, frightening yet liberating and life-giving. "Denying self," "taking us the cross," and "losing life" are really synonymous and are descriptions of "follow me," namely discipleship. Jesus refers to a way of life that is determined by our faith in God revealed in Jesus crucified. They refer to a counterculture way of life, a decisive affirmation of major values and not to sadistic pessimism or a joyless way of life. Out of love we are called to transcend the self, and follow Jesus crucified.

The reading from Isaiah (Is 50:5–9) portrays an ideal prophetic figure attentive to God and utterly faithful to his mission whatever be the price and humiliation, assured of God's fidelity and power. The psalmist confidently thanks God, who has saved him from terrible distress that brought him to the mouth of the grave. These readings prepare us to choose for Jesus, and be ready to pay the price of his prophetic mission.

TWENTY–FIFTH SUNDAY OF ORDINARY TIME: YEAR B Mk 9:30–37

Last of All, Servant of All

In today's liturgy all we need to do would be to allow Jesus to sit down, call us, and then listen to him as he says to each and all of us "whoever wants to be first must be *last* of *all* and *servant* of *all*" (9:35). The paradox is so evident. Attempts to explain it probably would dilute the stark stupidity of Jesus' words. From the moment most of us are born attitudes that are diametrically opposed to this wisdom are mingled in the very air we breath. The saying can be dangerous to a person with low self-esteem; it can be misunderstood, and you can find it in the "markets" of counterfeit forms and spurious imitations. Such an inner attitude is a gift of God. We are invited to *want* to travel the road that leads to such a basic attitude and to ask, in prayer, for such a disposition.

Like all of Jesus' teachings about basic inner dispositions, such an attitude is never fully attained. We journey and become. The absolute character of the saying expressed in the terms "last," "all," and "servant" indicates an ideal to which we journey. Maybe, if we were to go to a Vincent de Paul or Salvation Army center and see some of the women and men who come for meals, shelter, bath, bed, and speak to them, we might begin to sense what it is like to be "last of all." Our society does not have "servants." We would need to travel to other countries to appreciate what it means to be a servant.

Turning now to the full text (9:30–37), we find that some major texts have been omitted:

• the Father's affirmation of Jesus who has accepted the reality of his death (transfiguration 9:2–8);

• the disciples' inability to grasp the meaning of "rising from the dead";

• Jesus' reiteration of his coming death, relating it to John the Baptist's death (Elijah, 9:9–13);

- the colorful narrative of disciples unable to exorcise;
- a father desperate to help his epileptic son and yet aware of his fragile faith; and
- Jesus who exorcises the spirit (9:14–29).

Jesus withdraws with his disciples from the crowds and repeats again, clearly yet with less exact details, his teaching about his coming destiny: "they will kill him, and three days after being killed, he will rise again." This is God's beloved Son (9:7).

The reading from Wisdom (Wis 2:12, 17–20) creates a background for Jesus' prediction about his murder. Jesus shares the fate of many godly persons who are silent reproofs to evil people who plan not only to persecute them but plot their death. The whole passage in Wisdom (Wis 1:16—2:24) deserves to be read. The psalmist (Ps 54) is a religious person whose life is in danger. With confidence and gratefulness he prays to the God whom he trusts to save.

Two important aspects now follow:

- the disciples did not understand and were afraid to ask (9:32); and
- as they continued their journey to Capernaum they discussed "who was the greatest."

There is a certain humor in the narrative—Jesus' enquiry when they had settled in the house and their very embarrassed silence.

The manner in which Mark describes the way Jesus prepares to respond is important: "He sat down" (he will deliberately act as a teacher); "he called the Twelve" (the group, who represent the community created by Jesus, are taught).

There are two sayings that are related because of the link between "last" and "servant" and the child who has no status in contemporary society. The first saying is a radical reversal of values, and the second is equally shocking, since Jesus identifies himself, an adult religious teacher with prophetic consciousness, with a non-person, the child.

TWENTY–SIXTH SUNDAY OF ORDINARY TIME: YEAR B Mk 9:38–43, 45, 47–48

There Is Good Everywhere

The logic behind the stringing together of these sayings of Jesus and their interpretation in the early communities is not so obvious. Some communities may not find great inspiration in this gospel reading.

We can group the sayings in the following manner:

- the independent exorcist and an inclusive mentality (9:38–41);
- causes of sin: two aspects—of others and in one's own life (9:42–48);
- some sayings using the image of salt (9:49–50).

Ideas and similar words have played a role in the process of arranging the sayings.

The incident in the first reading recounts how the Spirit, which God has given to Moses for his leadership role, is shared with seventy others. This partially relieves his burden and is now used as a background to the account of the independent exorcist (Num 11:25–29). In the reading Joshua's over-anxious solicitude for Moses' honor, demands that Moses stop the two men who have prophesied within the camp area. Likewise, for the wrong reason John has attempted to prevent a person acting as an exorcist in Jesus' name. Moses' reply challenged Joshua to have a far broader mentality: "Would that all the Lord's people were prophets and then the Lord would put his Spirit on them" (11:29).

Jesus also affirms the value of an inclusive mentality. He comments on John's action in the context of attitudes to his and the early community's mission. The religious leaders condemned his ministry of exorcism, his action to free people from sickness, psychic and physical, which is attributed to evil spirits and which is a symbol of the absence of God's presence and power (3:22–29). On the contrary, this person accepts that God has endowed Jesus with power and uses Jesus' name for the good of others (cf. Acts 3:6; 16:4, 7, 10, 30). Such types of people are not only not against the coming of God's kingdom but positively promote and work for the kingdom of God, "Whoever is not against us is for us" (9:40).

The following saying reminds the early communities of the positive attitude they must have to all who seek the good, even in small ways. A gesture of this disposition in women and men who do not belong to the community that believes in Jesus Christ, is the giving a cup of water "because you bear the name of Christ"

(9:41). There could be many ways a community gathered in worship would profitably examine their openness to other Christian communities, to groups in a town or city working for human and civic development, to believers in other religions. The thought in 9:38–41 is triggered by Jesus' saying about the acceptance of the "child" (non-person), which is equivalent to accepting Jesus and therefore accepting "the one who sent me" (9:37). All goodness, big and small, reveals God.

The other group of sayings (9:42–48) are strongly worded cautions in which Jesus uses hyperbole, an exaggeration that shocks and underlines the utter seriousness of the teaching. To undermine the belief of "one of these little ones who believe in me" is a grave evil.

The series of sayings about hand, foot, and eye—the causes of major moral evil—are related to lust in Mt 5:27–32. The unspecified moral evil in Mark is paralleled in Mt 18:7–9. This type of saying is found in contemporary Hellenistic wisdom writings, and Jesus' audience would have understood the meaning. Jesus is concerned with major moral evil and its seriousness. The measures to be taken again are radical, expressed symbolically in amputation and gouging out of an eye. The consequence of major moral evil is unending punishment. The symbols are "unquenchable fire," "where their worm never dies and the fire is never quenched" [cf. Sir 7:17; Judith 16:17].

Examples of the type of things that can cause the loss of faith, or grave moral evil, are given in the explanation of the parable of the sower: trouble or persecution, cares of the world or wealth and *desire* for other things. (4:17–19). At what price shall we protect the gift of Christian faith and a Christian way of life?

TWENTY-SEVENTH SUNDAY OF ORDINARY TIME: YEAR B Mk 10:2–16

The Child

There is a certain quiet in the ministry of Jesus in the Twenty-Sixth, Twenty-Seventh, and Twenty-Eighth Sundays. In the narrative Jesus has been in Capernaum privately teaching his disciples (9:33–50). He moves south to the Judean region into the area east of the river Jordan, and there crowds gather. Mark says "as was his custom, he again taught them" (10:1b, cf. 1:21; 2:13; 4:1; 6:2, 34; 8:31; 12:35; 14:49). These texts describe Jesus as teaching:

- the quality of his teaching is praised with a view to entrapment (12:14);
- we are told the crowds are spellbound by his teaching (11:18);
- we are told that "the large crowd was listening to him with delight" (12:37);
- he taught with such ability that "no one dared to ask him any more questions" (12:34).

Mark has drawn the picture of a great teacher.

The narrative here falls into three distinct units marked by the action of three distinct groups:

- the *Pharisees* came and tested him... (10:2–9);
- in the house the *disciples* asked him... (10:10–12);
- *people* were bringing children...to have him touch them (10:13–16).

Next Sunday we shall meet another person who approaches Jesus (10:17–22).

The question about divorce is not an innocent question. Mark tells us that they ask to test him (10:2b). Probably in the narrative background is the divorce and remarriage of Herod and Herodias that provoked John's prophetic criticism, "It is not lawful for you to have your brother's wife" (6:17–18), for which he had been thrown into prison and eventually murdered.

When questioned about laxity in obeying ritual purity regulations, Jesus had contrasted God's commands and human tradition (7:7–9). Here he contrasts an exception granted by Moses (Dt 24:1–3; Sir 7:26, 25:25–26) and God's initial intention for marriage. However, Moses is not blamed. The cause of the concession to allow divorce was "your hardness of heart." In the purity discussion the hypocrisy of the religious leaders is underlined.

The reading of Genesis 2:18–24 and the praying of Ps 128 prepare us for Jesus' reflections on marriage. Commenting on Gn 2:18–24 we need to be aware of traditional anti-feminine interpretations in Scripture, church, and popular tradition. The text affirms equality, mutuality, and union.

Jesus combines Gn 1:27 and 2:24 and makes two comments:

- "So they are no longer two, but one flesh" ("one flesh" would signify a profound union. Behind the original Hebrew text are ideas related to the covenant of God and his people); and

- "What God has joined together let no one separate."

The very unusual nature of Jesus' teaching is underlined in the following scene where the disciples question Jesus (cf. other instances of this technique in Mark: 4:10–12; 7:17–23; 9:28). Jesus' explanation reflects not only the Jewish custom where normally only men initiate divorce but also the Greco-Roman custom that allows women to divorce. We pray about the sacred character of marriage and also pray that Christian communities and churches are able both to provide pastoral care and support to enrich married life, and have the wisdom to support and care for single parents, those who remarry after the breakdown of a marriage, and those who are divorced. The churches are challenged to give prophetic witness to the sacred and permanent character of the mutual personal self-giving in marriage and equally a prophetic witness in their care of those whose marriages have ended in divorce.

We move into another world when people bring little children to Jesus to touch them. First of all, children did not have the status and significance in ancient society that they have today. No Roman senator, consul, or general would receive any votes for kissing babies or promoting schemes for the welfare of children. The child was a non-person, had no status, was not valued, and belonged to the categories of leper, widow, orphan, foreigner. Second, the touch of a holy person was believed to ensure protection from evil powers and so was seen as a blessing.

The disciples acted in a way both intelligible and acceptable in their culture. What was highly unusual was both Jesus' indignation and his words. To assert that children had a special right to belong to the kingdom of God is like giving preferential membership to children in an exclusive club! Second, to allow the utterly insignificant child to model the way we have to be before God "to receive the kingdom of God" would make little sense in Jesus' world. Jesus does not refer to the innocence or frailty or dependency of the child. Rather it is the insignificance, the lack of status and power of this non-person—qualities that ought to be mirrored in the disposition of the disciple. We do not approach God with a golden credit card but with a simple look.

Earlier Jesus had taken a child, put him in front of his self-important disciples, taken him in his arms, and identified himself with the child saying "whoever welcomes one such child in my name welcomes me." To welcome a child and give a cup of water are alike. While being very insignificant gestures (9:36–37, 41) they are significant in the values of the kingdom.

Once again Jesus cuts the ground from under our feet. Pretensions, status, wealth, education, and race do not count. The Lord seeks a humble heart.

TWENTY-EIGHTH SUNDAY OF ORDINARY TIME: YEAR B Mk 10:17–30

The Ambiguity of Wealth

The teaching of Jesus today creates a strange problem for the churches that Jesus did not have to face. The churches, for various reasons, need "rich friends" who may have become wealthy in ethical, or unethical, ways. The churches need friends who, having wealth, have socioeconomic status and power. The massive institutional nature of the churches demands finance, with buildings to be built or renovated, schools and hospitals, clergy to be educated and supported, with associations and religious congregations involved in welfare work, famine relief, and developmental programs. At times the churches need the powerful to protect their interests in order that they may protect the vulnerable.

However, Jesus needed no "rich friends" and did not have anyone who could prevent his murder. After the good man, in shock, went away grieving because he had many possessions, Jesus' words do not mitigate his invitation to the man ("go, sell all you have, give to the poor...and come follow me") but reenforce a basic aspect of his teaching. "He looked around," Mark tells us, and said to his disciples, "How hard it will be for those who have wealth to enter the kingdom of heaven."

The initial question "what must I do to inherit eternal life?" is a major human question which is expressed by or lies hidden in every person—the search for that meaning of life that corresponds to the dignity, inner yearning, and deepest potentialities of the human person. (The issue in the contemporary debate about assisted suicide underscores these dimensions of the denial of the human spirit).

Jesus responds to the question of the rich young man. His invitation shocked the earnest and good man, and his subsequent words at first perplex his disciples and then astound them so that with exasperation they ask, "Then who can be saved?"

If we read the books of the religious tradition of Jesus' disciples we find a major thread affirming that wealth, prosperity, health, and children are the signs of God's blessing.

The reading from Wisdom (Wis 7:7-11), which is meant to form a background to Jesus' invitation, insists that the search for wisdom and its possession is the most exalted goal of human life (parallel to following Jesus, God's Wisdom). However another aspect of biblical thought intrudes: "*All good things* came to me along with her, and in her hands *uncounted wealth*" (Wis 7:11). In some cultures wealth is a sign of God's blessing (cf. Book of Job), yet in indigenous societies, who prize community and equality, wealth held by one family is a sign of greed and is evil. Probably, the near eastern patronage structure influenced the popular attitude to the wealthy, and the "limited available goods" nature of the economy meant that wealth led to widespread oppression and injustice.

Though Jesus assures an anxious Peter that their renunciation of all, and their following of him, will be abundantly rewarded, yet he adds the disconcerting phrase about "persecution." The Jesus we follow is the crucified Son of God.

Though we may want to discount, dilute, or explain away the radical nature of Jesus' teaching on wealth, yet we know we hear authentic words of Jesus when we are really shocked. Wealth and justice issues mean that some people's status and power are at stake, and Jesus' teaching is a scandal.

As we have not looked at a particular characteristic of Mark's portrait of Jesus, we draw attention to Jesus' initial question to the man: "Why do you call me good? No one is good but God alone" (10:18). If we pay attention to the way Jesus speaks and thinks, we will notice that he sees himself, and the people and reality around him, within a world where God is the center and is present and active everywhere. He is, in a very real sense, servant of God who alone is good.

Mark summarizes Jesus' life in terms of:

- "proclaiming the good news of God" and the kingdom of God (1:14-15);

- his disciple is the person who does the will of God (3:35) because the only concern of Jesus' life is to do his Father's will (14:36, 39);

- the Father shared his responsibilities with Jesus (1:9-11);

- at the center of human life and Jesus' life is the double commandment (12:29-31);

- when religious problems arise Jesus seeks the mind of God for human life within the Scriptures as God's word (2:25-26; 7:6-13; 10:4-9; 12:24-27). He rebukes Peter so harshly because he chose a human vision of life rather than God's purpose;

- Jesus' destiny is in the hands of God, so are the places at his right hand (10:40). The rejection of Jesus is so serious because it is the rejection of God and his Holy Spirit (3:29; 12:1-11);

- to welcome him is to welcome the one who sent him (9:37);

- to enter the kingdom is God's gift, a God whose power is not constricted or dependent on human possibilities (10:27).

There are other aspects as well.

Finally, we can profitably take note of the emotional content of the narrative: of the searching man and perplexed disciples. Jesus, we are told, "loved him," and the eager man left a disappointed person. The disciples are at sea, and Jesus speaks the truth, however painful.

TWENTY-NINTH SUNDAY OF ORDINARY TIME: YEAR B Mk 10:35-45

The Right Side

We are unable to understand today's gospel selection (10:35-45) unless we go back to understand its context (10:32-34) and see the pattern of events. As in 8:31-38 and in 9:30-37 we have three interlocked scenes:

- Jesus speaks explicitly of his sufferings, death, and resurrection (10:32–34);
- initially two disciples get it wrong, and the others also get trapped (10:35–41);
- Jesus spells out basic aspects of the life of disciples whose Lord is a crucified master (10:42–45).

With the reflection of the Christian experience the prediction of the passion is accurate in its detail:

- "handed over to the chief priests and scribes" (10:33 cf. 14:43, 53.15:1);
- "they will condemn him to death" (10:33; cf. 14:64);
- "they will hand him over to the Gentiles" (10:33, cf. 15:1);
- "they will mock him" (10:34; cf. 15:16–20);
- "spit upon him" (10:34; cf. 14:65; 15:19);
- "flog him" (10:34; cf. 15:15); and
- "kill him" (10:34; cf. 15:23–37).

We have not paused to ask how Jesus felt over these months, when he saw more and more clearly what would happen. However, our author tells us that as Jesus made his way inexorably towards Jerusalem the disciples grew more and more apprehensive. Jesus hides nothing from them.

The command of John and James, cloaked as a request: "do whatever we ask," does not sit well with Jesus' coming suffering. Were they just ambitious or giving expression to a misguided and naive generosity? The "cup" and "baptism" symbolize Jesus' death. Their unqualified readiness to share in this destiny (anything to get on the right and left!) does not agree with the fear expressed in 10:32. Later they will both share Jesus' suffering, James being the first to be killed (Acts 12:2). Jesus repeats his teaching that discipleship means real identity with him—surrender of the "self," sharing a "cross-bearing" way of life (8:34–35). As we saw above (10:40), names on the right and left chairs will be written by God alone.

The presumption of the brothers arouses jealous indignation in the other ten. Had they forgotten what Jesus said in 9:33–37? The need and desire for status, power, honor, influence, and recognition are so ingrained in us that we need to come back again and again to Jesus' example and words.

To get a feel for the problem we could go out into hotels, meetings, and celebrations to watch others and ourselves to see the desire and need for status, honor at work, even in the casualness of contemporary life. How we like a waiter, door person, a subordinate, or the general public to recognize us! How touchy we can be about status and power—photo in the paper, being with the right people, or on an invitation list.

Jesus draws three pictures for us. In the first are the "great" of this world. How subtly they can exercise power and dominate. The second is the community of his disciples, all competing to serve and take slave roles! The culture of this community is to be diametrically different from the club, board room, cabinet culture. The third picture is of Jesus himself, not only at complete odds with the great but also the example for the disciples—not only serving but even more, "giving his life as a ransom for many" (all).

The prophet servant described by Isaiah (Is 53:2,3,10–11; cf. 52:13—53:12) is insulted, rejected, and killed for the forgiveness of his people's iniquities. He is now proposed as forerunner of Jesus.

Mark does not actually relate "ransom for many" and sin. In our contemporary world stories of kidnapping, abduction, and demands for ransom enable us to see the possible meanings in the symbol of Jesus as a ransom. In the place of money he gives himself. We celebrate this, recalling his words "body given" and "blood shed for many."

THIRTIETH SUNDAY OF ORDINARY TIME: YEAR B Mk 10:46–52

The Disciple

The narrative of the blind Bartimaeus is very well written. With this incident we come to the end of Jesus' journey to Jerusalem. In 10:1 we find him on the southeastern side of the Jordan. In 10:32 he begins his journey up to Jerusalem, provoking deep apprehension among his disciples. Now having reached Jericho, he leaves the town accompanied by his disciples and a sizeable crowd. In a strategic spot for begging by the roadside, just outside the city, sits Bartimaeus, a blind beggar.

The narrative unfolds swiftly and with emotion. His initial shouts of "Jesus, Son of David, have mercy on me" are met with a concerted effort by many angry people in the crowd to shut him up. Rather than cow down he shouts louder and more insistently. In the midst of this commotion we notice Jesus who has stopped and stands still—a reaction so different to many in the crowd. The attitude of the people changes—hey! get up, he is calling you. The reaction of the blind man deserves to be noted. Off goes his cloak into the dust, he is on his feet in a second and standing before Jesus.

With Jesus' question we shall pause. He asks simply: "what do *you want* me to do for you?" We often do not know what we really want, or we are frightened to search our hearts to find out what we ought to want, and what we need to be more authentic as a Christian and a human person. We are also hesitant to ask God or Jesus Christ simply, and with trust, for what we want.

The blind man does not hesitate. With a type of devout reverence he addresses Jesus, "My teacher," and states *what he wants*: "Let me see again." Jesus acknowledges his faith, the fact that he reached out to Jesus as the special gift of God (Son of David) through whom God's creative mercy could give him sight. Bishop Geoffrey Robinson (*A Change of Mind and Heart*, 1994) described Jesus as "the window through whom we see God." We return again to the invitation to believe in Jesus Christ and the Father, no matter what may be our situation, reflected in Mark's gospel: the paralyzed man (2:4–5), disciples caught in a storm (4:35–41), incurable sickness (5:25–34), a dead child (5:35–36), and an epileptic boy (9:22–24).

The conclusion of the narrative has potential symbolic value. The cured blind man "followed him *on the road*" (10:52). In 10:32 we read: "They were *on the road* going up to Jerusalem, and Jesus was walking ahead...." They (disciples) were amazed, and those who followed were afraid." Bartimaeus follows Jesus on the road to Jerusalem without fear. The faith that enabled him to ask for what he wanted, enables him also to follow Jesus who is going to his death.

The reading from Jeremiah (Jer 31:7–9) describes God's promise to, and purpose for, the people living in exile. With joy they will return, the journey will be easy, God will be a Father to them. Special mention is made of the inclusion of frail and vulnerable groups. The psalm recalls this return with gratitude and prays for God's help in present dangers. These create a vague context for our gospel.

THIRTY-FIRST SUNDAY OF ORDINARY TIME: YEAR B Mk 12:28–34

Well Said

The focus of Mark's gospel now portrays two scenes taken from Jesus' ministry in Jerusalem and its Temple (chs 11–12; 12:28–34; and 12:38–44).

This week we jump over most of the ministry to the last of the interrogations of Jesus. Jesus has been in Jerusalem three days (11:11–12; 11:19–20).

The first day was taken up with a victorious entrance to the city and temple. The second day ended with a serious threat to his life caused by his cleansing the Temple and prophetic teaching (11:18). The third day passes in conflict. Jesus refuses to explain the source of his authority to obdurate and scheming leaders but, through the story of the tenants of the vineyard who murder the owner's son he condemns the leaders, and this arouses their anger ("they wanted to arrest him"), but the crowds shielded him (12:12).

This leads to an attempt to entrap him:

• first in a political crime (12:13–17 [Imperial colonial tax]), which is a failure ("They were utterly amazed at him."); and

• second to shame him in religious debate by a knotty question (12:18–27); and for his answer he gains the admiration of a scribe (12:28).

The same scribe questions Jesus (12:28–34). Probably his initial attitude is friendly. Questions about relative importance of commandments and the search for the core commandment were part of religious debate. There were 613 laws as well as the traditions of the ancestors.

The first significant point in the Marcan Jesus' response is the bond between the love commandments and the core credal statement: "Hear, O Israel, the Lord our God, the Lord is One." This is the famous "Shema Israel." This credo summarizes the long history of the experience of God who chose, created, liberated, forgave, saved, and protected his people time and again. He is their God, and they are his people. To this God they are to be totally loyal. They are to cling to him, worship and obey him, depend on him, and wait for him. This is what "love" means.

Coupled together with this single-minded loyalty, distinguished yet inseparable from it, is the commitment to the other (neighbor). This commitment also is to be total, as total as a person's instinctual and conscious concern for their own person ("as yourself"). To underline the primacy of this double commitment to transcend the self, and all types of autonomy, before God and selfishness before others, Jesus concludes "Greater than *these* there is no other commandment."

The scribe summarizes Jesus' authoritative interpretation of God's revelation with definite approval and adds a small remark that opens up for us a rich seam in the teaching of the prophets. To appreciate the comparison between the importance of the double commandment and "all whole burnt offerings and sacrifices" we could substitute the Eucharist. The sacrificial worship of God, especially the whole burnt offering, was of prime importance, a great value yet, in comparison with loyalty to God and commitment to neighbor, they are religious values of a different order. In a sense there is no "third."

This leads us into the way the prophets insisted upon the primacy of unswerving loyalty to God and care of the other. Reading the following texts enables us to place Jesus in the center of this rich tradition of the great prophets (Is 1:12–17; Jer 7:3–7; Hos 6:6; Micah 6:6–8; Hos 4:1–3; Amos 5:21–24; 1 Sam 15:22). The prophets also compare the core of faith life with sacrifice. Jesus uses the language of the Law codes (Dt 6:4–5; Lev 19:18) as he is asked about the Law. The prophets use other language.

The scribe is close to the kingdom. A clear commitment to Jesus, and Jesus as the crucified Son of God awaits him. The reading ends with the authority of Jesus and his "VICTORY" underlined: "No one dared to ask him any question."

THIRTY-SECOND SUNDAY OF ORDINARY TIME: YEAR B Mk 12:38–44

The Bothersome Widow

Our liturgy celebrates two widows. In the legendary story from the collection of stories about Elijah we meet a widow reduced to starvation because of drought and consequent famine (1 Kgs 17). Assured by Elijah, she expresses her faith in a simple yet extraordinary way. She shares with the prophet the meager food she has left. God promises to bless and protect her. The psalmist celebrates this God who in a clear and preferential way cares for the forgotten and discarded in human society (Ps 146).

The widow noticed by Jesus (10:41–44) has a basic characteristic by which Jesus described himself. Jesus spoke of himself as one who came "to give his life as a ransom for many" (10:45) and the widow is commended when "she put in *everything* she had, *all* she had to live on." "Her two small copper coins" dropped into the treasury as a gift to God are the symbol of her self giving, a total gift. Note, she could have kept one!

The narrative has some interesting features. Jesus, busy all day, sat and watched the crowd putting money in the treasury. The narrator allows us to watch with Jesus' eyes. His attention moved from the *many rich* people who were putting in large sums to the *poor* widow and *her two copper* coins (The contrast could not be greater). His words to his disciples, called to his side, first of all correct the obvious prevalent view, probably shared by the disciples (remember their remarks about the wealthy 10:23–27). This view would value the religiosity of people in proportion to the size of their contribution. Jesus emphasizes that the *poor widow* has put in far more than all, including the wealthy with their large gifts. He also compares not only their abundance and her poverty but the total gift. Therefore, he commends her.

Both widows are bothersome as they make us uncomfortable—our "all" is really just a portion, often quite small. Jesus invites and challenges us to a self giving that embraces more and more of ourselves. Love in marriage and friendship also matures, deepens, and grows the more we approach "the all we have."

Contrasted to this wonderful widow we have the sanctimonious and hypocritical scribes who devour widow's houses! Unfortunately, down the centuries the clergy have often been seen to be the successors of these scribes. The indictment is sharp and harsh. There is a sobering realism about both scenes. The Lord Jesus we are with in prayer and the Eucharist is no fool. He has seen life, seen through the masks we wear; and knows us too well. He cuts away with a surgeon's knife all the pretense in human life and asks us to look at truth.

Religion can mask so much hypocrisy, and so many apparently good attitudes and actions.

Finally Jesus emerges in both scenes more sharply as a prophet and an authoritative interpreter of true religion with chilling insight into human sinfulness and false values.

Let us allow the two widows to disturb us, and also remember the widows whose "houses" are plundered.

THIRTY-THIRD SUNDAY OF ORDINARY TIME: YEAR B MK 13:24-32

We Hope

Chapter 13 is a difficult part of the gospel to interpret. There is a fusion of future events, signs accompanying these, reassurances [13:11, 13, 27, 28-31] and warnings to the disciples about fidelity, watchfulness, and care not to be deceived [13:5, 9, 13, 23, 33, 35, 37].

It gives rise to wondering if Jesus was as confused about events in the future, after his death and resurrection as Mark's Jesus appears in chapter 13 (cf. Mt 24-25: Lk 17:20-37 and chapter 21).

The future events are:

• the destruction of Jerusalem (13:1-2,14-20);

• the desecration of the Temple (13:14);

• false prophets, messiahs, and persecution (13:6, 9-13, 21-23);

• the final event of history, namely the coming of the Son of Man as universal judge (13:24-27). There are also portents indicating the destruction of Jerusalem (13:7-8: 14), and

• the coming of the Son of Man (13:7-8; 24-25);

• and yet some signs, apparently pointing to these events, are deceptive (13:5, 8c). In the final analysis no one knows "that day and that hour," neither the angels, nor the Son, but only the Father (13:32).

A further problem with the chapter is the fusion of sayings from Jesus' ministry with interpretations of these sayings, in the light of the experience of the early believers, and probably some new sayings. Added to this, all talk about the end of saving history is very culturally conditioned and must use imagery. The early communities and perhaps Jesus himself thought that history would soon end.

Our reading is composed of three units:

• the coming of the Son of Man and the gathering of the elect (13:24-27);

• Jesus' teaching is reliable (13:28-31);

• only the Father knows that day and that hour (13:32).

This is followed by an exhortation to take heed, keep awake, and watch (13:33-37).

To create a backdrop for these sayings of Jesus a few verses from Daniel are chosen (Dan 12:1-3), which foresee both a final period of extreme anguish, and the deliverance of the elect (those whose names are written in the book). There shall be a limited resurrection—everlasting life for the wise and those who have guided others, and contempt for the wicked. The psalm is read as a hymn of praise and hope. The psalmist is sure that God will bless him with everlasting life.

There are major affirmations in our text and in chapter 13 that are part of our belief:

• in and through Jesus Christ, God will bring history to a close [judgment];

• all those who have been faithful to God and their conscience, be they dead or alive, will share in God's life forever;

• no one knows the day of judgment except God and there are no definitive signs when history will end;

• there will be many major upheavals within human history;

• believers will suffer and some will be deceived;

• Jesus' teaching about everlasting life as God's gift to believers is totally reliable.

At the end of the liturgical year, when the focus is on the last things, and when in popular devotion November is seen as the month of the dead, some of these elements, especially the first, second, and sixth, are relevant to this Sunday.

The difficulty in our text is to know to what do certain phrases refer:

• "After that suffering": this could be 13:5-8 or 9-17 or 14-23 or all bundled into one;

• the image of the fig tree is related to "these things," which is quite obscure;

• 13:30 refers to "this generation" and yet 13:5-8 and

9-13 imply a much longer period of history;

• "All these things" in 13:30 refers to what?;

• one of the points being made in 13:28-31 is clearly negated in 13:32 when knowledge of "that day and that hour" is the exclusive right of the Father (normally the phrase signifies the last judgment).

The community today needs to pray and reflect about that *hope* at the center of Christian faith, based on God's fidelity and Jesus Christ's death and resurrection. In the eucharistic prayers, in the prayer attached to the Our Father, and in the acclamations after the eucharistic narrative we have expressions of this hope. To reflect on this hope is the scope of this liturgy.

THIRTY-FOURTH SUNDAY OF ORDINARY TIME: YEAR B JN 18:33-37

Power for What Cause

The origin of the feast of Christ the King and its earlier celebrations were related to the ghetto and siege mentality of the Catholic church, when it was perceived as an alien and disregarded institution, in a secular and rationalistic world, yet proud of its achievements and independence. This feast was a public and civil assertion of the church's power with special processions, as it portrayed Jesus Christ as the triumphal and universal king.

The liturgy of the post-Vatican II era has not followed the earlier trend from the time when the feast was instituted by Pius XI in 1925 and celebrated with great pomp on the last Sunday of October. The Vatican II calendar transferred the feast to the last Sunday of the year, in the eschatological season that coincides with November.

As the three readings are intended to sketch various aspects of the person and role of Jesus Christ, we shall comment on all readings.

In a period when the Jewish people and nation were dominated by a particularly oppressive and irreligious colonial power, the author of Daniel both affirmed the dignity and superiority of a Jewish way of life (Daniel is an exemplary Jew) and foretold the end of colonial oppression in a particular style of writing, marked by visions, stories, and ascetic imagery usually called apocalyptic.

The short selection (Dan 7:13-14) describes the enthronement of "one like a son of man" (one like a human being). This person is given by God limitless and everlasting power and must be served by all. This vision influenced the picture of Jesus in some New Testament texts including the second reading (Rev 1:5-8).

In Revelation a series of descriptive titles are given to Jesus:

• loyal to his mission, he is "the faithful witness";

• He has precedence over all "as first born of the dead";

• He has been made supreme ruler, being "ruler of the kings of the earth";

• He shows he has loved us and "washed away our sins with his Blood";

• He makes us into a "a line of kings, priests" to serve his God and Father.

Up to here the writer looks back from the present situation (1:5-6); now he starts to look ahead (1:7):

• "He is coming on the clouds": and

• He offers words of comfort for communities suffering, at times gravely, because they believe (cf. 1:9).

He sketches the coming of Jesus Christ as universal judge.

• all will stand before him ("see him") even those who killed him (and those who persecute the believers):

• everybody will be filled with trepidation because he is both the ruler and judge of all. The believers, of course, will not fear.

The doxology (1:5-8) concludes as it began, referring to God, though Christian tradition has often described Jesus as the Alpha and Omega. The following text (1:9-16) has moving descriptions of Jesus Christ.

Our two texts and the celebration of God as king and creator with everlasting power and majesty (Ps 93) give us a picture of Jesus Christ as universal savior, ruler, hope, and judge. This is a part of our belief, a valuable aspect, but it may not appeal at times to us and can be misused.

The corrective, if one is needed, is given by John's Jesus. The gospel takes us into the world of religious and political power in the time of Jesus. John clearly and deliberately portrays Jesus as king in his passion, yet as a puzzling king (18:36-37, 39; 19:1-3, 14-15, 19, 21-22).

Jesus is handed over to Pilate (18:28—19:16). The narrative is broken into small scenes indicated by Jesus and Pilate being at Pilate's headquarters, whether outside (18:28-32, 38b—19:3; 19:12-16), or inside (18:33-38; 19:4-11). After the chief priests have stated that Jesus is a criminal who deserves death and therefore it is Pilate's responsibility to condemn and kill him, Pilate summons Jesus inside (18:28-32).

The dialogue evolves in a way typical of John. What Jesus says is misunderstood and he both clarifies who he is and leads Pilate to depths where he is lost. The interrogated becomes the interrogator! The whole interrogation centers around Jesus being king and the nature of his kingdom/kingship. Being a king has very different connotations for a political ruler and a man of God.

There is a negative aspect: "My kingship is not from *this* world" ("not from here") and a positive aspect: "For this was I born and for this I came into the world, to *testify* to the *truth*." There is the consequent challenge: "Everyone who belongs to the truth [believes in Jesus as sent by God and as the revealer of God] listens to my voice."

The term "world" is used by John to refer to the whole world in a neutral sense. Jesus is sent into the world, which is loved by God (3:16). However, it also has a definite negative sense. The world is dominated by the "prince of this world" (12:31; 14:30; 16:11) and is the place of darkness (3:19; 9:5; 12:46-47) needing salvation (3:16-19), a place dominated by evil and sin (8:23; 16:8) where people are closed to God, opponents to Jesus and his disciples (1:10: 7:7; 15:18-19; 17:6-9, 14-16). The world cannot know God (17:25), and Jesus is not of this world (8:23). As Jesus is from God so also his kingship is from God and is therefore so totally different from all other forms of kingship.

The second part of Jesus' confession (18:37) takes up in summary form major themes of the gospel. In the introduction to John we have commented upon Jesus' relationship to God the Father and his mission to testify to what he has heard and seen. Jesus is sent into the world as witness to the truth (3:31-36; 8:14-16, 42, 46; 14:6; 17:17) In Jesus' words we hear God's voice (5:42; 8:47; 12:49-50). His word is both life giving and a word of judgment for "those who do not belong to the truth" or "do the truth" (3:21; 8:47).

This term "truth" is also a special word for John. As the Word became flesh, Jesus has "the glory of the One and Only who came from the Father" (NIV) and is full of "grace and truth" (1:14). As God gifted and revealed himself through the Mosaic Law, so now he has gifted himself, his steadfast love and fidelity ("grace and truth"), through Jesus Christ (1:17). Jesus came to testify, to reveal, and make present the mystery of God (17:3). Jesus reveals God, who so loved the world that he gave his only Son (Jn 3:16). The majesty and power of Jesus Christ is that of love, God's love and his love (13:1). Those who belong to the truth will witness to the truth, namely the saving love of God, and they will witness to God the Father and Jesus Christ his Son, also in and through love (13:15, 34-35; 15:12-17). The measure of this love is his love (13:34-35).

Luke: Jesus Teaches "The Way" on his Way to Jerusalem

Jerome H. Neyrey, S.J.

Like Mark and Matthew, Luke collected many of the sayings of Jesus that pertain to discipleship and located them in the section of his narrative that is popularly called "On the Way." It begins with the notice: "When the days drew near for him to be received up, he set his face to go to Jerusalem" (9:51). Thereafter, Jesus is relentlessly "on his way" to Jerusalem, the cross, and the empty tomb. This journey ends with the parable of the talents in chapter 19, where we are told "he was near Jerusalem" (19:11). But "on the way," Jesus teaches his disciples the fundamentals of "his Way" of thinking, praying, and acting. Thus, Jesus both teaches and models the pattern of values and actions expected of his disciples.

The motif of a teacher teaching a "way of life" was quite common in Jesus' world. In fact, the Judean word for proper discipleship behavior is *halakah*, which comes from the Hebrew word "to walk." Hence, disciples "walk in the ways of the Lord." In many places we are told that there are "two ways": the way of God, which is righteousness and justice, and the way of the Evil One, which is iniquity and sin. Of all the New Testament writers, Luke is most explicit about calling Jesus' teaching and example "the Way." This is most clear in Luke's second volume, The Acts of the Apostles, where we find explicit mention of Jesus' new "Way" (see Acts 9:2, 18:25–26; 19:9, 23; 22:4; 24:14, 22). Thus we examine the gospel passages for the Sundays in ordinary time according to the special Lukan motif of "the Way of Jesus...."

This means that we will be presented with teachings and exhortations, not miracles. When studied in its totality, Jesus' "way" has a number of important themes running through it. It might prove helpful to sketch some of the general motifs and topics that are consistently presented in this compendium of Jesus' teaching, his "way."

BOUNDARY MAKING

We note that many times Jesus exhibits intense "boundary" concerns. How should his disciples think about themselves? How do they relate to non-disciples?

He presents contrasting figures, some of whom join him and many of whom turn away (9:57–62; 10:5–12; 12:1–3, 8–12; 15:1–32). Not all who hear the gospel are saved.

He often pronounces "blessings" on those who join him (10:17–24; 11:27–28).

He takes note of who is "with him" and who is not (11:14–26, 37–54; 14:16–24; 18–15–18, 19–30). And he has stern judgment for those who refuse his way (10:10–15; 11:29–32; 11:37–52).

Luke gathers many sayings of Jesus that have to deal with judgment of sinners, that is, those who do not walk in God's ways (12:8–12, 20–21; 13:33–35; 16:19–31) and with rewards for those who follow him (12:35–40, 41–48; 18:7–8, 14).

THE WAYS OF GOD

Christians maintain that Jesus' "way" is authorized by God, and so Luke is careful to show us "the ways of God" that Jesus himself followed. This includes both God's favor on Jesus and his way of the cross, in particular Jesus' radical obedience (9:22; 18:31–34).

God's chosen prophets were also rejected (11:14–23; 13:31–32, 33–34), which suggests that God's ways have always involved the just and the righteous in a struggle. Jesus lived God's pattern of prophetic behavior, as will his disciples (10:10–12; 12:4–7).

God is merciful and so delays judgment of sinners to give them time for repentance (9:52–56; 15:1–32; 13:1–5, 6–9).

Moreover, God surprises us by reversing worldly status and honor: low is high; poor is rich; despised is honored; out is in; humbled is exalted.

God's values are not those of this world, which is true for Jesus as well as his disciples (15:3-10; 16:19ff; 18:9-14; 19:1-10).

JESUS' OWN "WAY" OF DOING THINGS

The "way of Jesus" includes detailed instructions on reformed piety: Jesus' disciples relate to God in prayer, not Temple sacrifice (11:2-13; 18:1-14), just as Jesus himself models this prayer (9:28-29; 11:1).

Jesus teaches the right use of wealth: giving alms (12:33), "making friends" with alms (16:9, 19-22), prizing God above Mammon (18:18-30).

One of the more interesting aspects of Jesus' way is his table manners and the way he eats. Contrary to Jewish custom, Jesus eats with tax collectors and sinners, not with pious and observant people (15:1-2; 19:5-7). By this he signals that new and strange people are welcome at God's banquet.

Again contrary to custom, he neither keeps dietary laws nor enjoins them on his followers (10:7-8).

Once more, he criticizes the standard mealtime etiquette, which required special washings (14:1-6), celebrated places of honor (14:7-11), and limited hospitality to one's social peers (14:12-14).

In signalling a new way of eating, Jesus models the primary and basic form of association of his disciples: it is a new family that shares all of its possessions liberally with all members.

DISCIPLES' WAYS OF DOING THINGS

As a reformer, Jesus proposes new ways of living according to the Bible.

• He reforms the Sabbath as a time when creative healing should take place (14:1-6).

• He prunes away excess, so that the core of God's law, the Ten Commandments, are back in focus (18:18-20).

• Most important, he celebrates the core law, the law of love of God (10:38-42) and neighbor (10:29-37).

• His way is one of generosity, and so he has much to say on the proper use of wealth; and "use" is the operative term here: alms, benefaction, and sharing of wealth (12:13-34).

• He models this in his own generous bestowal of God's favor on the sick and needy (13:10-17; 18:35-42).

• He has specific injunctions on alms, prayer, and the keeping of traditional purity rules.

CHARACTERISTICS OF LUKE'S GOSPEL

"I hear where you are coming from." This modern refrain expresses our acute need to contextualize as sympathetically as possible the communication we receive. The same, of course, is true of the gospels. Luke wrote for a specific church in a unique context: he tried to articulate the good news about Jesus for a particular situation. Thus as we continue to study Luke's gospel for the liturgical year, we have two tasks: first, to understand "where Luke is coming from" and second, to craft how this gospel can speak to our particular context. This presentation of Luke, however, can only safely do the first part, namely, help us understand Luke in his own historical and social context.

Whenever we become familiar with the characteristic ways in which our relatives and friends express themselves, we notice their pet themes, their personal phraseology, their distinctive speech cadences, and their characteristic modes of expression. It may help us as we begin to grow familiar with Luke to be attentive to many of his particular and distinctive patterns. In fact, to study such at the beginning of our reading of Luke should make us that much more sensitive and alert to Luke's wonderful and clever way of articulating the gospel.

The following list itemizes the distinctive themes, terms, and modes of expression characteristic of Luke.

1) He loves to do things in "twos" and pairs. Both Zechariah and Mary receive angelic annunciations of the births of their sons: both sing a canticle to God. Jesus first heals a sick slave by his word, and then raises the widow of Naim's son by a powerful word. He tells a parable about searching for a lost sheep, followed by

one about seeking a lost coin. This sensitivity to "twos" in Luke's narrative will be important in how we read the gospels for the Twenty-Fifth and Twenty-Sixth Sundays: they are meant to be read as complementary. The same is true for practically all of the subsequent Sundays, and notice of this helps us in our prayerful understanding of Luke.

2) One scholar quipped that "Jesus was killed for the way he ate." Meals are very important in Luke: we note how Jesus is invited to supper and scrutinized while he eats, how he feeds others, how he commands that marginal folk be invited to Christian tables. Finally he eats his Last Supper with his disciples. His eating and table fellowship are often a conscious strategy to reform the prevailing sense of who counts in society: Jesus regularly upsets the comfortable and comforts the upset. We must read the story of Zacchaeus (thirty-first Sunday) in this light.

3) Along with this, Luke is known as the "gospel of the poor." The "poor" are not necessarily a financial category in Jesus' world: all peasants (of the ancient population) had little or nothing. But those who suffer misfortune (debt, illness, death, etc.) fall below even the subsistence level: they are the "poor" addressed by Jesus. The story of Lazarus lying hungry and abandoned at the gate of a rich man surely illustrates this (Twenty-Sixth Sunday).

4) One of Luke's strategies for dealing with the "social poor" is to urge a special kind of almsgiving and patronage that supplies the basic needs for them. Usually, "patrons" supplied food, clothing, and the like to their "clients" and in return received special honor, services, and the like. Luke urges that Christians with means should give and not look for a return—truly a countercultural idea at the time. This forms the subtext for a host of Sunday readings, such as the twenty-fifth, twenty-sixth, and thirty-first.

(5) Luke's gospel is one of the clearest messages about the God of Christians. In Mary's Magnificat and the Zechariah's Benedictus Luke introduces certain themes that he will articulate for the rest of the document. God regularly surprises us, doing something new and unexpected. Old couples become fertile (John the Baptizer) and virgins become pregnant (Jesus). God, moreover, reverses the status quo. The lowly are raised up and included: the least are made great. In short, God does not play by the social rules of society, simply because God is not protecting status but including the excluded, thus creating new rules for evaluating people. Three Sunday gospels in particular will develop this theme: the Twenty-Seventh, the Twenty-Ninth, and the Thirtieth.

6) This inclusivity is heralded from the very beginning: the gospel comes to the lowly, not the elite: shepherds (one of the most despised trades in ancient Israel) are chosen to hear the gospel first. Simeon prophetically proclaims that Jesus is the glory of Israel and the light to the Nations. Jesus' two models, Elijah and Elisha, both extended God's healing favor to non-Jews as well as the chosen people, thus indicating an ancient pattern of inclusion. If we read the miracle stories carefully, we will notice how God's healing power goes out to males and females, slaves and free, and Jews and Gentiles. We should read the gospel about the ten lepers in this light (Twenty-Eighth Sunday), as well as the contrast between the Pharisee and the Publican (Thirtieth Sunday).

7) In this vein, we note how frequently Jesus offers forgiveness and even fellowship to sinners, another mark of inclusivity (see the Thirtieth and Thirty-First Sundays). If the prevailing model of religion was located in the Temple, where only pure priests and unblemished persons were welcome, then Jesus is studiously creating an alternative system in which the unclean, the sinners, and the marginals can find access to God and God's blessings. Needless to say, this vision and strategy will surely lead to conflict with the established leaders of Jesus' day, since their special position is threatened by this.

(8) The novelty of Jesus' reforming gospel and ministry cry out for legitimation: how can a holy prophet systematically and consciously break the religious norms? Luke is very careful to present Jesus' legitimation in several ways. First, God twice appeared to Jesus in a commissioning vision, which both attests to Jesus' favor in God's eyes and indicates how he is now "anointed with the Holy Spirit" for new and unusual ministry. Second, Jesus fulfills the ancient prophecies of Scripture. Hence, it has always been God's plan and purpose that holy prophets, as far back as Elijah and

Elisha, act in ways that either criticize current injustice or herald inclusive strategies to bring non-Jews into God's covenant care. Third, even if Jesus is rejected by his own culture, this too is prophesied in the Scripture: hence, Jesus is no maverick, but lives a prophetic life fully in accord with the history of the classical prophets, who were all rejected and even killed by ancient Israel. God's plan and favor, then, explicitly legitimate Jesus when he fulfills the Scriptures.

9) In addition to Luke's distinctive presentation of God, he also has several particular and important things to say about Jesus. He begins with the angelic pronouncement that Jesus is the designated king, the shoot of David. Jesus is, then, the Royal Shepherd, for that is what David was. Shepherds feed, protect, and lead their flocks: Jesus in particular feeds the hungry, searches for lost sheep, leads and guides his flock. As king, he unites rich and poor, elite and non-elite in bonds of solidarity. As king, he issues a royal decree on the correct "way of life" in God's covenant community (i.e., Sermon on the Plain). As king, he welcomes the needy and the weak, even a dying thief, into God's kingdom (see Thirty-Fourth Sunday). As shepherd king, he goes in search of the lost, even on the day of his resurrection. Jesus is, moreover, a prophet, that is, a holy person authorized by God to judge sin and injustice, to reform the ways of religious life, to heal the needy, especially non-Jews, and even to suffer the fate of prophets, namely, rejection and martyrdom. He was a "prophet, mighty in word and deed," a phrase that interprets his whole ministry from his baptism though his death.

Jesus' strategy of inclusiveness and his behavior of reform cut two ways. He clearly articulates a new "way" of walking in God's service, comparable to the traditional Jewish "way of walking" (i.e., *halakah*). His way includes practical care of society's marginal people and mercy toward its outcasts (tax collectors and sinners); alms for the "poor"; table fellowship with "the poor, the blind, and the lame" as well as "tax collectors and sinners." In addition to inclusivity, he proclaims a reformed piety. No longer is the Temple and its system the locus of finding God through sacrifice; rather, "prayer" becomes the official vehicle, and prayer can be prayed by non-priests in non-consecrated space through nonsacrificial rituals (Thirtieth Sunday). Jesus himself regularly demonstrates his reformed piety by praying, and he teaches his disciples to do likewise. Furthermore, the core of the law of God is the law of Love, which extends to unfortunates who are utterly unrelated to us by birth or kinship or nation. Luke's gospel is far and away the most explicit teaching of Jesus on the right use of wealth: he warns against covetousness; he condemns the rich man who ignored the starving beggar at his gate; he urges those of means to be "rich toward God," which means being generous to God's needy "poor."

As much as we herald Jesus as "the Prince of Peace," Luke echoes the ancient tradition that Jesus came with a sword to divide and cause conflict. After all, he was a legitimate prophetic reformer who preached a word about God and God's kingdom that challenged the status quo. Hence, Simeon the prophet, who blessed Jesus in the Temple, saw the future of Jesus as one of bitter conflict: "This child is set for the rise and fall of many." Hence it is not surprising that at his inaugural visit home, his own townsfolk reject him. And frequently we read in Luke how the crowds were "divided" over him, some accepting him as God's prophet and shepherd and others condemning him. Almost all of Jesus' public appearances in Luke, moreover, tell of conflict and challenge. Jesus says something or does something, and invariably this is challenged by his rivals. Since Jesus is engaged in God's work, he necessary responds in a way to defend God's interests, which often entails very harsh words to those who challenge him. In the defense of God's gospel, Jesus never turns the other cheek, but exposes the folly and hypocrisy of those who do not think the thoughts of God. Conflict, of course, was part of the lives of prophets: it is the fate of prophets to "suffer and die in Jerusalem." And conflict remained a part of Jesus' career from start to finish. His passion and death are but the last instances of this.

Thus, as we continue "the Way of the Lord" according to the gospel of Luke, we have with us some important road signs that can help us locate ourselves. We have clear ideas about the God of Jesus Christ and what values and strategies this God espoused (inclusivity, surprise, reform). We expect to see Jesus both as king–shepherd and as prophet. We appreciate his authorization by God.

We expect him to proclaim a new kingdom of God in which those on the periphery or the outside are welcomed into the circle. We know that, like God, he too engages in an inclusive ministry. And the covenant community of disciples will itself be inclusive: males and females, slaves and free, Jews and Gentiles, and saints and sinners. In that group, the "poor" are the special objects of Christian assistance. And they gather in pious prayer, which situates them socially apart from the sometimes oppressive Temple system. God, Christ, and church.

LUKE IN YEAR C

With these themes in our heads, let us begin our liturgical reading of the selections of Luke for the lectionary. Most of the gospel selections in the Sundays of Ordinary Time in which Luke's gospel is featured come from this "Way of Jesus," which he delivers "on the way" to Jerusalem, to his death and resurrection.

Knowing these general themes and appreciating the overall structure of this part of the gospel story give readers, teachers, and preachers a rich context in which to appreciate the individual passages.

Knowing the large picture, moreover, aids us in discerning the shape and importance of the small vignettes that make up the vast canvas that is "The Way of Jesus."

TWELFTH SUNDAY IN ORDINARY TIME: YEAR C LK 9:18–24

Jesus begins the scene in prayer, the typical posture in which Luke regularly casts him. Thus seeking God's praise, Jesus is also privy to God's plans for himself. From the beginning of Luke's story, Jesus' history is a bipolar one. He is set for "the fall and rising of many in Israel" (2:34): and he will himself experience "suffering" so as to "enter into glory" (24:26). Thus, like the classical prophets (4:24), his own path will lead him through rejection into vindication. This dual nature of his career is highlighted in a new manner here. By his signs and wonders, people duly recognize him as a prophet "mighty in word and deed": and so he could be likened to "Elijah or one of the old prophets" (9:19). This is true enough: it reflects the logical conclusion of his miracles, which were seen by multitudes. Yet it is surface knowledge about him, it is what outsiders think, it is good, but incomplete information. Peter adds to this interpretation of Jesus by acclaiming him "the Christ of God" (9:20), echoing Jesus' own interpretation of Isaiah in the synagogue at Nazareth (4:18). There Jesus proclaimed that in fulfillment of Isaiah, he was the figure on whom God's Spirit rests because God has anointed him to a ministry of healing and saving signs and wonders (4:18). The name "Christ" simply means "the anointed one" (see Acts 10:38). And so, Peter does well to acknowledge what was already claimed on Jesus' behalf. Jesus is God's designated and consecrated prophet. His is a ministry of power, benefaction, and success.

Yet there is more to Jesus than miracles, success, and notoriety. After Peter's confession, Jesus reveals still more about himself and his career, which brings us to the second pole of his history, "suffering and rejection" followed by vindication (9:22). While God truly anointed Jesus as "the Christ," God also designated him as the suffering "Son of Man." This new label evokes a host of allusions to Ezekiel and Daniel. Ezekiel, despite all of his visions of God's throne, was reminded of his mortal nature and its unworthiness, when a revealing angel addressed him as "son of man."

Daniel described the Maccabaean martyrs who were rejected on earth and killed for their faith as the "son of man." This label basically speaks to our mortality, that is, our common human weakness and vulnerability. It also contains the added hint that despite rejection on earth, God's faithful ones will be vindicated in heaven. Thus when Jesus proclaims himself the "Son of man," he speaks about God's commission of him to "suffer and be rejected" on earth but also "on the third day be raised" (9:22). Both parts of Jesus' ministry are true: miracle/power/success and way of the cross/defeat/but vindication. Both are ordained by God.

When this story appears in its liturgical setting, it invites disciples to view once more the central mystery of our salvation, Christ's cross and empty tomb. Set in Ordinary Time, it reminds us that Jesus' career is a pattern of our own lives as disciples. We too, if we are "chips off the old block," will share this part of Jesus' life, both suffering and vindication. This is made clear by the way the gospel immediately continues with a demand that disciples imitate Jesus precisely in their taking up of their crosses daily. Our reason for doing this is simple: to save our lives.

Perhaps the point of this bipolar story lies in its simple insistence that God shepherds us in sun and rain, in good times and bad, on peaks and in valleys. Our sufferings are often proof of our discipleship. They certainly do not mean that God is ignoring us or punishing us. God's ways: the Christ rejected on earth was vindicated in heaven. The whole purpose of facing suffering and rejection is to "enter into glory" and to "find life." Jesus remains the perfect example of this paradox: as least, he became greatest: the last was made first. What is needed is trust in God's wisdom and power. When disciples embrace Jesus' teaching, they do so with the knowledge of faith in Jesus' vindicating resurrection. We know that God works all to good.

THIRTEENTH SUNDAY IN ORDINARY TIME: YEAR C LK 9:51–62

Jesus starts on his way and immediately is confronted with crises. First, one group, the Samaritans, firmly rejects him. His disciples wish to punish them and avenge Jesus' honor. But Jesus ignores both the Samaritans' rejection and his disciples' petition. His "way" is not that of saving face and gaining honor and satisfaction. Following this, three would-be disciples volunteer to join the group. Perhaps we are to see some balance here: one group refusing and the other volunteering"—two contrasting responses to Jesus.

We focus on the volunteers. The exchange between Jesus and them is scarcely cordial. Why? In Jesus' world people are generally invited to join or help, as we see in Jesus' calling of Peter, Andrew, James, and John (5:9–11). It is considered rash and even pushy to volunteer in that culture. Thus we are viewing a delicate, even a conflictual scene as three successive volunteers offer to follow Jesus. The master's remarks should sound crisp, even hard, for not all would-be disciples are worthy and can make the grade. A similar scene can be found in John 12, where would-be disciples seek Jesus, who lectures them on the costs of discipleship, namely, the grain of wheat dying.

But as we examine the pattern of exchanges in Luke 9:51–62, we note that all three have to do with relationship to one's family of origin. One man seems ready to leave his family, while the other two want to honor their family obligations before following Jesus. In each case, Jesus insists that discipleship with him will mean a radical change of allegiance. Disciples will not have homes and houses, fixed and secure sources of income, support, respect, and affection. One person is told to forgo the unthinkable, the universal and obligatory funeral rites for his father. Another cannot even return home to say goodbye. Here Jesus seems to take a strategic stand against "the family." Why? Families in antiquity were close-knit, tightly structured, and all-encompassing groups: they were the basic and sole social structure in the lives of peasants, who could not look to church or state or any other institution for support or assistance. The family gave identity, meaning, support, affection, and protection to its members. By the same token, families exerted great pressure on their members to conform to their traditions and interests. It was often the case that individuals feared to buck the family's choice of a spouse or the like. Loose or severed ties with the family were life-threatening, as one might lose housing, land, bride price, and the other social and economic resources for an honorable life.

Jesus seems to be asking just this: disciples should prize God's kingdom and Jesus' version of it over the interests of the group and institution that seems foundational to life. How much do disciples want to follow Jesus? What will they pay for this? How radical a break must they make? Are they fit: fit for the kingdom of God? We are constantly confronted in life with putting some sort of price on what we value, and the gospel story appeals to this crass sort of evaluation to ask us to clarify how much we value Jesus and the gospel of God's kingdom. Thus one of the things disciples do "on the way" is constantly to clarify their values and choices so as to hold on to the real prize.

FOURTEENTH SUNDAY IN ORDINARY TIME: YEAR C LK 10:1–12, 17–20

One of the first things Jesus does "on his way" is to share his labors with others. He sends 70 others in pairs to "every town and village where he himself was about to come." First he sends out the disciples (10:1–12) and afterwards he confirms their experience (10:17–21).

In the first part, if he is the sower, they are the reapers and harvesters. Again, they do not volunteer, but are sent and told to pray that God may send others. Jesus' exhortation then describes aspects of this labor and prescribes certain appropriate actions. First, the task is risky, just as it was for Jesus: they are "lambs" in the midst of "wolves." They are agents of God's peace ("peace" here is "shalom," a code word for justice, plenty, healing, etc.), but not all accept God's peace: they must be prepared for rejection. Then, disciples are told not to provide for themselves ("no purse, no bag, no sandals"), but to rely on a fair exchange for their labors. If they bring God's gospel and healing, then recipients owe them their sustenance (see 1 Cor 9:8–11). Third, their labors extend to Jews and non-Jews alike. We find this expressed in the double lack of concern for dietary restrictions: "eating and drinking what they provide…eat what is set before you" (10:7, 8). The ministry is not restricted to those who keep kosher diet, i.e., Jews, but extends to all people, just as God's impartial favor reaches to all. Finally, an elaborate ritual is described when the laborers are rejected, namely, "shake the dust off your feet." Hence, both the beginning and the ending of Jesus' remarks highlight hostility and failure. Disciples, of course, can expect no better treatment than their master.

No diocese or parish would ever structure its ministry in this way. We seek trained personnel and support them with just wages. We generally invest heavily where needs are greatest and do not tend to put as much effort into risky or hostile projects. So, in general, we do not follow the precise exhortations of Jesus. Yet, several things here remain constant in our labors. We, that is, all baptized disciples of Jesus, are the laborers whom previous generations prayed be sent to the harvest.

We are those who go ahead of Jesus and herald the arrival of God's kingdom of grace. All of us, then, understand ourselves as part of an ageless and ongoing concern of God for "the harvest." Anyone concerned with God's kingdom will surely meet with conflict and, alas, rejection at times. Both discipleship and service are costly endeavors, not glamour stints. Both call for faithfulness.

In their reunion with Jesus, the disciples are reminded of just how much providence and power surround their work, all of which belongs to God, not them. Excitement rests in being agents of both gospel and its power: we witness and facilitate God's generous favor flowing out into the world. "The way" of Jesus, then, is one of generous service of all peoples. Yet it is risky and will have its share of failure as well as success.

FIFTEENTH SUNDAY IN ORDINARY TIME: YEAR C LK 10:25–37

In Mark, the issue of the "greatest commandment" belongs to the extended challenges to Jesus during his "week of conflicts" in Jerusalem. But Luke transfers it to the "way of Jesus" because it fits so well in the instructions to disciples about the values and behaviors of those who walk in "the way" of Jesus. The context is one of challenge and controversy: a lawyer asks a hard question to put Jesus to the test (v. 25) and then asks another to avoid the shame of Jesus' superior knowledge (v. 29). Ironically, Jesus talks about love in the context of hate.

The topic, however, is about love: what does love mean? to whom does it extend? Love of God requires total dedication of one's whole self, "all your soul, all your strength, all your mind." This reflects the Judean equation of "wholeness" with perfection and purity. This much is not a matter of debate among Jesus or his adversaries: because of God's immense care for us, we should respond with "perfect" or total honor and respect.

But who is the neighbor, whom we should love as ourselves? In answer to the challenge, Jesus tells the parable of the Good Samaritan. The parable is teasingly complex, but of remarkable insight. If we hold in view the twofold aspects of love (God and neighbor) discussed in vv. 26–27, then the priest and the Levite who passed by the wounded man might be seen as "loving God," in that they maintained their states of ritual purity, so as to be able to worship God. Probably very few people in Jesus' audience would think that the priest and Levite did anything wrong: rather, they fulfilled the duties of their God-given status as cultic ministers and so honored God by keeping "wholly" pure for the worship of God. The Samaritan, then, represents the aspect of "love of neighbor" and illustrates, moreover, "who is my neighbor?" The details tell the story: the Samaritan is a non-Jew, a despised ethnic group, who owes Jews nothing. The wounded man technically has no claim on the Samaritan nor does the Samaritan in that culture owe the wounded Jew anything. No ties of blood or kinship bind them. So a most unlikely person, the Samaritan, acts, but in a surprising and unexpected way. It would be remarkable for a peasant to spend time and resources on a wounded stranger. But this Samaritan writes a blank check for health care: "Whatever you spend, I will repay you" (v. 35). In the poverty-stricken, subsistence world of the peasantry of Jesus' time, this is both unusual and foolish behavior: peasants should spend their extremely limited resources on their families and kin ("charity begins at home"). Hence, the Samaritan might be initially regarded as foolish and stupid by the audience. But this is Jesus' point, namely, to hold up surprising and even countercultural behavior as the new, but true "way of Jesus."

Thus the episode teaches us much about the "way of Jesus." His way is one that challenges cultural stereotypes of "neighbor." It reminds us of the gospel norm for wealth: use it to help others; give alms; share with the needy. Moreover, it confirms Jesus' radical reform of values—the last shall be first, the least shall be greatest, the meek and needy shall find favor. "Go, and do likewise." Of course, Jesus himself has modeled this behavior throughout the gospel of Luke. Jesus, as well as the "foolish" Samaritan, are our models for discipleship.

SIXTEENTH SUNDAY IN ORDINARY TIME: YEAR C LK 10:38–42

Today's episode balances that of last Sunday. Formerly, males contested with males in public and talked about male public behavior. Balancing that, females in private space are engaged in conflict where the issue of proper female behavior is highlighted. If males were exhorted to act counterculturally (i.e., radical generosity to any sort of person), then we should expect to hear Jesus exhort females to new forms of action that likewise upset cultural expectations for females in his world.

Jesus "went on his way," entering a domestic world in which two sisters received him into their house. Obviously this immediately clues Jesus' audience into expectations about how females in his world should act: since food preparation is one of the gender-specific tasks for females of that world, the audience expects all female hands to be busy preparing this impromptu feast. Moreover, females in that world generally did not sit with male guests or eat with them: in their gender-divided world, they would be in other space and doing female tasks. Native readers would immediately think that Martha is right: Mary, her sister, should be helping her with the food and not be sitting in male company.

But just as Jesus upset cultural expectations in the Samaritan parable, he does so again here. He praises the presence of females "sitting at the Lord's feet and listening to his teaching" (v. 39). He labels this "a good portion" and defends a female's participation both in the activity and in the space in which it takes place.

Clearly, this story has nothing originally to do with differences between consecrated and married life. But it has everything to do with two themes: (a) females in Jesus' circle and (b) the importance of Jesus' teaching. We should see the story as another instance of the inclusive strategy of Jesus whereby marginal people are welcomed into the center (e.g., the sick, sinners, strangers, females, etc.). The value of Jesus' teaching and being his close disciple may, and sometimes do, conflict with the demands of family and culture (see Luke 9:51–62). Just as Jesus praised the bizarre behavior of the Samaritan, so he lauds the unusual actions of Mary. Martha is not so much criticized—after all, hospitality is a wonderful Christian virtue—rather, Mary is welcomed into new relationship. It is less a question of "either/or" and more an issue of "both/and."

SEVENTEENTH SUNDAY IN ORDINARY TIME: YEAR C LK 11:1–13

Continuing on his "way," Jesus teaches his disciple

about prayer. First, we must appreciate how radical his remarks were. The temple was the cultural and political focus of relationship with God for Judeans: various sacrifices had been prescribed in the Scriptures to ritualize this or that petition to God. The temple was the authorized and official locus of praise and thanksgiving of God by them. It was moreover, an elaborate system that employed a special class of persons (priests), occupied an elegant space, and cost vast wealth to operate and maintain. Jesus' remarks about "prayer" utterly apart from the temple and its system are one more item in his countercultural reform of Judaism. Let us not underestimate the threat he posed to the system by his reforming piety.

The selection here contains three parts: the text of the ideal prayer (vv. 2–4), exhortation to constancy in petitionary prayer (vv. 5–10), and confirmation by familiar examples (vv. 11–13). The Our Father quickly became the defining prayer for Jesus' disciples, both because Jesus taught it and because he modeled it in his own behavior (see Luke 22:40–46). In substance, it addresses God as the head of the new household ("Father") who, in that culture, had the *right* to expect "honor" and "obedience" from his children and the duty to provide for their well-being. Thus the prayer begins by giving God honor and loyalty: respect due God's holy name and loyalty in following God's benevolent will. The second part of the prayer expresses the basic needs of Jesus and his peasant world: they ask their "Father" and patron for the necessities of a peasant farmer's life: daily bread in a subsistence-level world, debt relief in a tax-oppressive system, and deliverance from "temptation," which might simply be escape from the tax collector or the occupying Roman authorities. At any rate, the prayer asks God to meet the immediate and foundational needs of the people. What are "fathers" for, if not this?

In the subsequent parable, Jesus expands on the theme of "daily bread" and petition of a patron. One person comes at night and begs the loan of bread to feed a guest. Now, nocturnal movements were suspect and rare: baking might be done twice a week; in a subsistence world, there would be no extra loaves. But a petitioner badgers a neighbor until the loan is made. The point of the story unfolds in the direct commands which follow: ask ... seek ... knock. Clearly Jesus exhorts his disciples to be loyal petitioners of God, not on-again, off-again clients. Confidence, loyalty, and fidelity are the marks of Christian prayer.

The third piece of the gospel supports the above exhortation with an apt example from daily life. Parents are regularly petitioned for food (more "daily bread") by their children. And if parents, who might be negligent of their duties or cool to the requests of insistent children, give good gifts of nourishment in fulfillment of their duty as parents, how much more will the heavenly Parent, God, hear the cries for food on earth and grant them. Thus the gospel as a whole not only teaches us a basic formula for prayer, it discourses on God's goodness, generosity, and loyalty, even as it exhorts us to bold and faithful address to God. The very contact with our Parent God is as nourishing as the bread we beg for.

TRANSFIGURATION: YEAR C LK 9:28–36

The transfiguration story, which occurs also in Lent, is likewise celebrated in the joyful time of the year. It, too, has much to do with the "way of Jesus." The most salient feature of the transfiguration is its similarity to the baptism of Jesus: in both, God appears from heaven, addresses either Jesus or the crowds with him, and authorizes Jesus' subsequent ministry. In the baptism, God commissions Jesus as prophet or the gospel and agent of God's healing. He is the "beloved son" who enjoys God's favor and is authorized to speak and act with authority. As Jesus sets his face to Jerusalem, however, a new turn of events likewise needs comparable legitimation. How do Jesus, his disciples, and we know that the "way of the cross" works or leads to success or represents God's will? The transfiguration, which repeats God's theophany to Jesus, repeats the authorization for this part of the ministry.

The transfiguration, then, does not make sense unless we see it as the springboard for the journey to Jerusalem, the cross and the empty tomb. Indeed this is apparently the topic of conversation with Moses and Elijah who spoke with Jesus "of his departure, which he was to accomplish in Jerusalem" (9:31). Moses and

Elijah, moreover, represent to us figures both of whom enjoyed theophanies from God which authorized their ministry and became rejected prophets whom God vindicated. Jezebel and Ahab rejected the words of Elijah and sought his life, just as Pharaoh threatened Moses' leadership. Yet God rescued both prophets from distress, just as God will stand by Jesus through his passion and vindicate him in his resurrection.

When God's voice commands the disciples to "Listen to him," Jesus has not been speaking at the transfiguration: he is described as only listening, first to Elijah and Moses and then to God. But if God tells us to "Listen to Jesus," then we must back up to 9:22–27, the last words Jesus has spoken. There Jesus proclaimed how it was God's plan for him to experience rejection and death in Jerusalem, but also God's vindication. This word did not sit well in the disciples' ears: it was a hard saying, demanding, frightening, unpleasant, and off-putting. How can we know that Jesus is correct in this new teaching? The appearance of God at the transfiguration removes all doubt: the words of Jesus about his "way of the cross" are backed by God, as is the promise of vindication. After all, the point of Jesus' "glory" is to convince us that God's faithfulness may lead us through dark valleys, but it leads us to light, happiness, and peace, just as it did to Jesus in his resurrection. How important it is for us to know how the story MUST end for those who hear God and listen to Jesus. The transfiguration, then, is a necessary oasis for us "on the way": for our loyalty is confirmed and our faithfulness strengthened. We have God's own word backing up Jesus' words about "the way."

NINETEENTH SUNDAY IN ORDINARY TIME: YEAR C LK 12:32–48

On the way, Jesus continues his teaching on the duties of disciples in regard to wealth (12:32–34) and faithfulness (12:35–40, 41–48). Confident of God's generous support, disciples should use their wealth to help others. Fixation on wealth only leads to a ruined life, unless one thinks of God's kingdom as the repository of lasting wealth.

In the subsequent story, Jesus again upsets the cultural expectations of his audience. The tale sounds straightforward: servants are charged with the proper care of the master's household and his wealth. The honorable servants are only those who follow the master's instructions and are faithful to their jobs. But Jesus surprises the audience by saying in the story that the master will "gird himself and have them sit at table and come and serve them." No master in Jesus' world would do such a thing. Unthinkable! Impossible! So outrageous a reward for faithfulness, then, calls attention to the importance of the duties of the loyal servants. But what did they do? If we link vv. 35–40 to what went ahead (vv. 32–34), the servants would seem to be liberal with wealth, that is, "selling possessions and giving alms." This way they provided "purses that do not grow old." Thus, the master so values the proper use of wealth and resources, that he will turn the world upside down in approval of this virtue when he finds it. His "unreasonable" response underscores the importance of the command to be generous with wealth.

In the third part of the gospel, Peter asks the naive question whether Jesus' teaching applies to him (and presumably other leaders among the disciples). Jesus insists that the faithful and wise servants in his household are they who "give them their portion of food in due season." That is, they are generous in distributing the basic needs of life to those in their network or circle. Like the servants in 12:35–40, they too will be honored by Jesus and rewarded for their loyalty to the master's commands.

The whole gospel story, then, delivers a consistent exhortation to a wise and liberal use of wealth in support of others. "Every one to whom much is given, of him much will be required." This is reinforced by the constant reminder that faithful servants and stewards of God's good gifts will be surprisingly rewarded. This behavior is not optional, for the story also describes the fate of people who ignored the master's commands and abused the master's wealth. An important aspect of "the way" of Jesus, then, is our practical use of wealth and resources in support and care of others.

TWENTIETH SUNDAY IN ORDINARY TIME: YEAR C LK 12:49–53

On the way, Jesus has occasion to address a problem that plagued his early disciples, namely, loyalty to one's family. The Bible is quite clear and explicit that children, even adult males and females, should "honor your father and mother." The roles of father and mother were explicitly sketched both in popular proverbs and lore as well as in biblical texts. "Honor" in particular pointed to a complex overlapping of obedience to parental authority, respect for the elderly, concern for family well-being, acceptance of family traditions and ways, and countless other things. Since families were the major institution in which individual Judeans lived, they were the unique source of economic and emotional support, the locus of meaning and identity, and the provider of all the social services now offered by our state and federal governments. Families exerted a strong, coercive, and positive pressure on its members for near absolute loyalty: this meant survival and well-being for all in the family. Yet it might also become a negative pressure to conform to family ideas and structures at the expense of the teaching of a prophet like Jesus. When Jesus speaks about the family in this passage, he has in view a family pressuring its younger members to avoid this dangerous Jesus and to conform to local traditions and expectations.

Jesus proclaims that he brings "division" to the heart of the social fabric of his hearers. He sets a household in turmoil, fathers against sons and mothers against daughters. He also has in view married sons, as the daughters-in-law are in conflict with their mothers-in-law. On the face of it, Jesus' words are scandalous and shocking—unless we see him pleading for enough space and freedom for adult children to resist family pressures to conform and so to ally themselves with Jesus and his new family. Jesus speaks of a costly discipleship, and so this exhortation is found in the collection of his sayings on his "way to the cross." It ought to be read in combination with other remarks about family, such as the Four Beatitudes in Luke 6:20–23, which also envision a disciple who leaves family and thus becomes "poor" (disinherited), "mourning" (loss of kin), "hungry and thirsty" (no more family meals), and "persecuted" (ostracized by family and neighbors). Such loyalty brings Jesus' own approval and acclamation of respect: "Blessed!" which means "how honorable."

TWENTY-FIRST SUNDAY IN ORDINARY TIME: YEAR C LK 13:22–30

In the teeth of a gospel that proclaims God's impartiality and inclusivity, the question is eventually asked: "Will those who are saved be few?" Jesus does not answer this, and for good reason: such calculations are known only to God, and are not the business of mortals on earth. Rather, we are increasingly exhorted to the importance and value of discipleship with Jesus. Hence, "on the way," Jesus calls our attention to the goal of life: "Enter through the narrow door," which is the imitation of the Master.

Once "door" is mentioned, the imagery of the subsequent parable makes sense, for it too is about doors. In Jesus' world, a powerful person generally lived in a fortified villa in the countryside or in a comparably protected mansion in a city. With nightfall, the whole countryside and city settled down, and locked or barred whatever doors were available; for, night was the time of evil and those about at night were immediately suspect. Once doors, wall, gates, and the like were barred, one opened them at great peril; after all, one's friends were inside, but who knows who is outside seeking entrance?

In the parable a householder (Jesus?) locks the doors for the night. But some people come knocking and seeking entrance (men and women in his audience?). The householder speaks the most cutting of all social words: "I do not know you," that is, "I do not consider you on my side or part of my circle." They plead that indeed they are, for they ate and drank in his presence and he taught in their streets. But mere proximity does not make one a companion of Jesus or a member of his new family. Again, the householder dismisses these casual associates: "I do not know where you come from." These strong words remind us of the importance of Jesus' teachings on discipleship "on the way." We hear them regularly, but mere hearing does not mean discipleship. Mere proximity to Jesus' church does not a member make. And the issue is costly, to the point of being "left out in the cold and dark." Jesus, then, puts great value on his offer of discipleship: alas for those who do not.

The story ends with remarks that balance the question about "many? few?" that began the episode. God's kingdom is indeed inclusive: all peoples from north/south and east/west are welcome at God's table: God makes no distinction between male/female, slave/free or Jew/Gentile. Yet as much as all are welcome, not all will join this circle of intimacy. But God has not discriminated against any.

Thus Jesus' "way" is both inclusive and impartial in its openness to all peoples and so valuable that we need to be reminded of its worth. We would never treat our personal valued material possessions so lightly, lest they be stolen or lost. Pity so many disvalue the gospel.

TWENTY-SECOND SUNDAY IN ORDINARY TIME: YEAR C LK 14:1, 7–14

Many years ago, a film called "Guess Who's Coming to Dinner?" shocked us and provoked our attention. It forced us in a humorous way to confront cultural stereotypes and examine our attitudes to racism. A young girl is bringing home to dinner her steady boyfriend: she, a white female, introduces her black male friend to her parents with a view to their approval of a marriage. Who gets invited to dinner, then, is a long-standing and sensitive issue.

The gospel opens with Jesus being invited to dinner by a ruler of the Pharisees. Normally meals connote mutuality, honor, harmony, and similarity: after all, the ancients said: "Likes eat with likes." But this meal is not typical. Jesus is invited so as to be put on trial: "they watched him" to examine his words and gestures. As in the case with most of us, there are more or less fixed places at the table that indicate our role and status. Mother and father generally occupy the ends of table, mother close to the kitchen and father presiding over the meal. Guests are probably at the right hand of the hosts, and there might also be other "reserved" places. This was especially true in Jesus' world, which was based on honor and other hierarchial notions.

But Jesus typically articulates a new "way" of eating that forms part of his overall "way." Since Jesus' message and God's concern are focused on the poor and lowly, the old places of honor at table just will not do. As Mary said of God: "The rich he sends away empty, the poor he feeds with good things" (1:51–53). God's strategy of including the least, the marginal, the needy, and the stranger means that seating arrangements will have to change. Hence Jesus says that, although his Pharisee critics observe table seating as a sign of high status, among his circle of disciples you should choose the lowest place and let God or members of God's family include you and raise you up. "Friend, come up higher."

The gospel is a mixture, then, of social criticism and exhortation. The ways of the world that stigmatize and marginalize the poor and needy are simply wrong: God, for one, abhors them. It is less clear that Jesus exhorts his disciples to "humanity," but rather to strategies of inclusivity. After all, the welcome and invitation to "friendship" will come only within the circle of disciples, the new family of Jesus. Moreover, at God's table, all are welcome and God has no special seating arrangement.

TWENTY-THIRD SUNDAY IN ORDINARY TIME: YEAR C LK 14:25–33

This gospel continues the attack on smothering and controlling families seen earlier on the Twentieth Sunday (Luke 12:49–53). It too is about very important relationships that structure our lives. Moreover, it follows directly upon a parable, the proper interpretation of which will help us understand the present story. In 14:15–24, a rich man breaks faith with his social group. At the beginning of the story he typically does what people of his class do: a rich man invites his rich peers and neighbors to a great banquet. But the social relations are strained: the neighbors do not come. So the man progressively invites groups lower and lower on the social ladder to his house in the rich center of the city. In short, he breaks ties with his normal natural social network. In 14:25–27, the same thing is said in more direct language and with the family as its target. Breaking one's social network was not mandatory for disciples, unless the previous group acted in a smothering and controlling manner to prevent discipleship with Jesus. This is what is envisioned here. In the culturally typical manner of hyperbole, Jesus exaggeratedly states that his disciples must "hate" their closest kith and kin, even their own lives, honor, and reputation. When confronted with a dilemma, the wise and courageous disciple will choose Jesus.

This choice was bound to be highly risky and unpopular. And so, advice follows that urges would-be disciples to calculate the cost. This address seems to have males in view, for the two examples are of males doing typically male activity: building a tower in a field and going to war. The examples, moreover, work on a gut level for Jesus' culture: fear of shame or ridicule. The broad culture advocated the status quo: stay where you are: be content with what you have: beware ambition and hubris. Hence, any change of status, whether by building a tower to protect one's rich harvest or going to war to gain booty, is risky and only for the courageous and the steadfast. So, too, with discipleship. Changing status and allegiance to Jesus might well provoke the censure of family as a foolish or shameful thing to do. But Jesus praises this "deviant" behavior, although he warns us of the hardships of truly following him and imitating him ("bear his own cross and come after me," 14:27). Thus "the way" of Jesus can mean disruptive social relations, willingness to be labeled a deviant in the eyes of those closest to us, and even loss of status, possessions, and respect. This is what happened to Jesus himself.

TWENTY-FOURTH SUNDAY IN ORDINARY TIME: YEAR C LK 15:1–32

Jesus' ways were clearly not those of observant Jews in his time. Perhaps the most flagrant of his actions was eating with sinners. Since "likes eat with likes," it was shocking for the prophet Jesus to shun the table companionship of holy or observant Jews and to seek out the tables of "sinners." As Robert Karris once quipped: Jesus was killed for the way he ate! Today's gospel is all about being in the "wrong" company and about who is welcome at Jesus' table. Just as the rich man broke solidarity by inviting and compelling the lower social levels of his world to come to his banquet, so Jesus flagrantly upsets social and religious expectations by his commonality with sinners. Since the story opens with a savage attack, we read Jesus' parables as vigorous apologetic response to the charges.

Two parallel parables are told as apology to the criticisms about Jesus. One tells of a male shepherd who goes in search of one of his lost sheep, and the other of a female figure, presumably the wife, who searches for one of the coins of her dowry. Obviously we all labor to keep within our reach the things most valuable to us. Just so, Jesus says, the holy world of God's pure angels rejoice when just one sinner is rescued. We note two things: the balancing of male and female is hardly accidental, any more than it was in 10:29–42 with the stories about the good Samaritan and Martha and Mary. Jesus' concern for the "lost" is to be imitated by males, who have more public lives with other males, as well as by females within the female circles of their households. Second, the parables directly answer the criticisms of Jesus for "eating" with sinners: he is in search of the lost. This makes sense on earth and in heaven.

Another parable follows, which tells first about a profligate son and then about a loyal son. In the first part, a son greatly insults his father by asking for his inheritance, effectively telling his father to "drop dead!" He breaks faith with his family, but not for some virtuous reason such as following a prophet. He wastes and squanders his inheritance, which is also the honor and wealth of his family: not only he, but his whole family is thus disgraced and loses respect. All sin is social: it affects our whole network.

The point of the story lies in the prodigal father's generous and spontaneous actions. When the son "turns" and returns to his father, the prodigal father rushes to him, embraces him, clothes him in honorable robes, and fetes him. Most people in Jesus' cultural world would consider this father to be foolish: his son deserves reprimand and correction, for he has violated the great commandment, "Honor your father." But this father accepts the wayward and disgraceful son back. This shocking action is used by Jesus to legitimate his eating with sinners. Yes, what Jesus does goes against cultural customs! It is strange! Yet, what father would not welcome home a wayward child? This is what God does.

Balancing the disgraceful son is the dutiful son who has honored the father always and done what is expected of him. But he refuses to share in the "folly" of the father and sulks outside the house. If Jesus' own actions are mirrored in the "foolish" behavior of the prodigal father, then Jesus' critics' actions (15:2) seem to be reflected in the "honorable" reaction of the elder son. Feasting with shameful sinners is objectionable! But the "foolish" father reminds the complaining son of something more important than the earthly code of honor, namely, compassion and good will.

Once more "the way" of Jesus clashes with the ways of his world. He challenges again the most ingrained values of his world: honor and purity. He offers a different hierarchy of values: compassion over respect, love over purity. And so, in these stories Jesus justifies his actions in associating with non-observant Jews and silences his critics. In this push-and-shove game with the Pharisees, he articulates a new vision of social relations and proposes a reformed value system. This is his way, and the way of his disciples.

TWENTY-FIFTH SUNDAY IN ORDINARY TIME: YEAR C LK 16:1–13

Once more "on the way," Jesus addresses his disciples on an issue that was and is central to all who follow the Lord: What do we make of the wealth of this world? How do we value God and money? What priorities do disciples have? There is a subtext to the gospel: What provision are we making, not for retirement or old age, but for God's kingdom?

A shocking parable is told. The cast of characters is well-known to Jesus' peasant audience: an absentee landlord who lives in the city on the exorbitant income extracted from his many farms, his estate steward who hires the sharecroppers and collects the taxes, and the ubiquitous peasants who are always in debt. Since the landowner is generally absent and therefore out of sight, peasants focus their anger and frustration on the steward, who has apparently gotten quite wealthy defrauding his master and overtaxing the peasants. Yet praise is heaped on this dishonest steward who is about to be fired for a host of sins and crimes! What is in Jesus' mind?

The steward could be anyone in Jesus' audience who is confronted with wealth, be it much of it or very little. Whatever share one has of "mammon," all people seem to hold it very dear. The steward gets praise for doing two things.

First, when confronted with an audit, he acts promptly and decisively to ensure his future. As he calls in the master's peasant debtors and has them cut their IOUs to the absent landowner, he seems to be eliminating his own profit margin, the expected commission he charges for his services, which is his main source of income. He is not defrauding the master now, but giving away his own wealth to those in debt and need. He does this so that when he is homeless and jobless, they will take him in and assist him. Hardly the most noble of motives, but then, he is not praised for his motives but for his prompt and decisive action to save his neck. Part of the bite of the story is to see the least imaginable person, a known rascal, praised for finally acting to ensure his future, which is what the New Testament means by "conversion." One thinks of the sinners who ate with Jesus in last Sunday's gospel, and how they might have seized that one opportunity to repent and believe in the gospel.

Second, embedded in the shocking parable are hints of the proper use of wealth by followers of Jesus. The dishonest steward "made friends with his money" (v. 9), that is, he used his wealth for others: to relieve hunger, debt, and injustice. This reminds us of Jesus' frequent exhortation to "give alms" (12:32) and to invite to table those who cannot invite you in return (14:12–14). Luke echoes in various ways the exhortation in Mt 25:36ff. to feed the hungry and clothe the naked. The reason God called the rich man "Fool!" back in 12:20 was that he spent his wealth on himself, building bigger barns and making himself richer and "storing up treasure for himself," instead of sharing his extra harvest with the ubiquitous poor and needy.

The gospel always shocks us: a criminal is praised! the thief does the right thing! the man obsessed with wealth gives it away! the person most deserving of punishment acts in the nick of time to escape disaster! This parable, then, is another invitation by Jesus to assess the most important things in our lives ("God" and "Mammon") and to look beyond today toward the mysterious future. It touches the core of our lives in that it asks us to examine what we do with our wealth and to see that our choices and decisions have a direct relationship to our future: "Make friends with mammon, so that when it fails you may be received into eternal habitations."

TWENTY-SIXTH SUNDAY IN ORDINARY TIME: YEAR C LK 16:19–31

This gospel story illustrates the principle enunciated in

last Sunday's gospel, namely, the praise of the dishonest steward for "making friends with his wealth." Now Luke treats us to a profound parable that embodies and thus reinforces the point of the previous story. This, too, belongs in Jesus' teaching of "his way," since it highlights what all disciples, rich or poor, should do with their "wealth."

As the story opens, we are invited to view the honorable estate of a very rich man who is clothed in purple and feasts sumptuously every day. In contrast, a beggar covered with sores lies at his gate unattended by any family—truly a shameful state. Both die and instantly their fates are reversed. The rich man is tormented in hell, while the beggar is honored at the side of Abraham, the great patriarch. Why is the rich man in hell? The story does not say explicitly: but when we bring to bear the other teachings of Jesus on the right use of wealth, there is no doubt at all that the rich man is in hell because he did not "make friends with his mammon." The beggar was not fed even with the crumbs from the rich table, nor were his sores bandaged. The problem is not that the rich man was rich, rather that he was self-centered, haughty, and ostensibly stingy. He would not be in hell had he shown minimal justice to the poor man at his gate, as expected of rich patrons in that time.

Ironically, the rich man asks for a favor for his kinsmen. In view of the impending crisis, he wants to assist others to escape disaster, which certainly seems like a charitable thing to do. But Abraham refuses this, judging that with all the current wisdom and warnings available to them, they neither need this nor would they accept it, being so obtuse in the first place.

This story resembles the "way of God" that Luke heralded early in his gospel in Mary's Magnificat (1:51–53). God upsets the ways in which mortals think and act: God reverses the status of mighty and weak, rich and poor. It is not the case that God despises the rich and powerful, but that God favors those whom the rich and powerful ignore or reject. God includes them and gives them pride of place. This reversal reappears in the "beatitudes" and "woes" (6:20–26), where the "have-nots" are honored and the "haves" are shamed. Thus, together with last Sunday's parable, Luke gives us a very clear and dramatic treatment of "the way" in which disciples must use their wealth to "make friends" with it on behalf of the poor.

TWENTY-SEVENTH SUNDAY IN ORDINARY TIME: YEAR C LK 17:5–10

Today's gospel tells us about "duty" toward God, the "ought" which we learn when we study God's benefaction and transcendence. So much is left unsaid, but to get the flavor of Jesus' teaching "on the way," let us fill in the background. Jesus has in view a large estate typical of the agricultural countryside in which he lived and worked. The owner of the estate has hired servants to work it, with some plowing, others pasturing sheep, and still others tending his house and cooking his meals. The owner and presumably the servants consider the arrangement "fair": the master pays them wages and gives them support in return for their labors on his estate. As the story opens, we are well into the period when the owner supports his workers without seeing the harvest or the sheep-shearing. He is now their benefactor. Many oughts are pre-supposed in the story: the master ought to provide for them, and they ought to labor for him. This is nothing less than justice, and when each side satisfies its ought, there is no "thanks," but recognition of the just exchange. Only in our egalitarian world would we imagine that a master thanked his servants and expressed this by serving them at table. This modern idea is inconceivable in Jesus' world.

It is a cultural quirk that we tend not to think of our important relationships in terms of "duty" or "justice." So it is increasingly difficult to think of our just relationship and duty to God. God was and will be "other" than we, always transcendent, always our benefactor, always our redeemer. When we do God's will and fulfill our obligations to God, we have done a just thing: in no way have we begun to match God in faithfulness or generosity. No "thanks" are owed us, for we have only done our duty. What this gospel asks us to consider is God. In our worship we offer God "glory," "all honor and praise," and thanksgiving for God's faithful mercy. All life and all holiness come from God: our duty, then, is faithfulness and loyalty. Thus, Jesus teaches us "on the way" to take our eyes off of ourselves and put them on God.

TWENTY-EIGHTH SUNDAY IN ORDINARY TIME: YEAR C LK 17:11–19

Today's gospel continues the theme of last Sunday's story, namely, our "debt" to God in justice. Jesus is typically "on the way to Jerusalem" when he illustrates this aspect of "his way." As Jesus is about to the enter a village, ten lepers confront him: they must remain outside the warmth and sustenance of village life because of their contagion. They necessarily stand at a distance and shout to him for help. Typically, Jesus shows God's compassion and inclusivity. The lepers, by being sent to the priests according to Jesus' command, would get the obligatory public certification that their leprosy was ended: thus they could return and enter the village and resume their family lives. Thus Jesus' strategy is to heal the whole fabric of human relationships, not merely to master a specific disease. He is healing their whole lives and families, not merely their bodies. Up to a point, this story resembles other healings of lepers in the Scriptures (see Mark 1:40–45).

But the story takes a new twist when one, and only one, of the lepers realizes his cure and returns to Jesus. Ancient and modern readers might well ask what duty those healed had to the person who healed them. The healed man came back to Jesus, less to "thank" Jesus than to "praise God with a loud voice" (v. 15). And Jesus remarks how appropriately the man acted when he returned and "gave praise to God" (v. 18). In justice, those who receive God's favors and benefaction give God "glory and praise," the very words we use in our Sunday liturgy. This would seem to be one of the forms of prayer that Luke describes Jesus and others as praying throughout the narrative (see 2:14 and 28–32). Faithfulness and loyalty are other names for "justice" here: and when God has shown covenant faith and love, then God's people naturally respond in kind.

But the story tells more than the "way of Christian prayer." The healed man who returned to Jesus was a Samaritan. In Jewish history, Samaritans were at best degenerate and at worst idolaters. In the stereotypes of that time, Samaritans evoked from Jews emotions of repulsion and inferiority. And Jews had no dealings with them (John 4:9). Yet the upsetting of this ethnic stereotype by Jesus is conscious and heralds a new "way" of thinking about outsiders. They, too, are chosen and blessed by God. For truly in Christ, there is no Jew or Samaritan, slave or free, male or female. God's mercy and Jesus' ministry are inclusive—even of unclean lepers and Samaritans.

TWENTY-NINTH SUNDAY IN ORDINARY TIME: YEAR C LK 18:1–8

Once more Jesus teaches us about "the way" of Christian prayer as he proceeds on his way. Luke tells us the meaning of the parable right away, "to the effect that they ought always to pray and not lose heart" (v. 1). As with most parables, we expect shock and surprise: we will surely have our values and perceptions turned upside down. And this is no exception.

In the story a "wicked" judge neither "feared God" nor had any sense of shame for what people thought of him. In fact, Jesus labels him "the unrighteous judge" (v. 6). From this brief sketch of his character, there is no reason to think that this man judges justly and does what is right. On the contrary! In Jesus' world, he is a dishonorable man who fails in all the expectations of justice, a most serious sin. A woman comes to him for help. She is the weakest person imaginable: a widow without a husband or family to support and defend her. She apparently is in the right and demands that the judge give her justice: "Vindicate me against my adversary." Although he refuses for a while to do justice, eventually he does so, not out of principle ("I neither fear God nor regard man"), but out of convenience ("she will wear me out by her continual coming").

The fun begins when we are forced to remember that this is a story about relentless prayer. Hearers would readily identify with the widow and see their appropriation of the parable in constant petitioning of God. But if the widow models "prayerful" behavior, what of the judge? Is Jesus comparing our just God to the unjust judge? From the gloss at the end of the parable, the judge is clearly in view as Jesus remarks, "Will not God vindicate his elect, who cry to him day and night? Will he delay long?" No, God "will vindicate them speedily." Like the judge, God too is petitioned by needy people; unlike the judge, God will act "speedily" on our behalf; unlike the judge, God acts, not to quiet us, but to "vindicate" us.

Thus, we learn several things about "the way" of Christian prayer. Prayer that is insistent and relentless is indeed urged here: but perseverance counts. God, moreover, is hardly an unjust or heartless judge, but rather a generous and concerned patron who acts "speedily" on our behalf. Because we are God's own children, we should expect "vindication," that is, restoration of our rights as God's family. This type of prayer reminds us of our intimate relationship with a benevolent God, and so helps us to orient our lives that much more clearly.

THIRTIETH SUNDAY IN ORDINARY TIME: YEAR C LK 18:9–14

This gospel story is the companion piece to last Sunday's. Both are parables about prayer: they occur back-to-back on Jesus' "way to Jerusalem," and together they continue to fill out his "way of prayer." Like the previous parable, this one also begins with a clue to its proper interpretation: "He told this parable to some who trusted in themselves that they were righteous and despised others" (v. 9).

As most pious Judeans did, two men went up to the Temple to pray. And as most stories go, the two men are contrasted both in terms of their social status and the content of their prayer. Jesus picks quite representative figures as contrasts. A Pharisee, a member of a pious association generally praised for its piety and strict attention to holiness, stands close to the Temple center and boldly prays out loud. In contrast, a tax collector, blamed as the source of most social evils in Jesus' world, stands far off and does not raise his eyes from the ground. Jesus' original hearers would expect that the contrast would be between a praiseworthy pious man and a blameworthy scoundrel. Yet, the prayer that each prays jolts us awake. The seemingly pious Pharisee prays an arrogant prayer: he boasts that he is better than other men, especially the sinful tax collector over there; he prides himself on his fasting and tithes. Given Jesus' warning at the beginning of the parable, we are forced to hear this prayer critically. And curiously, we are thereby encouraged to listen sympathetically to the tax collector's prayer, which is very, very brief and simply begs God's mercy.

In Jesus' world, the rich are sent away empty and the poor are filled with good things (Luke 1:53); last is first and least is greatest; the humble are exalted and the exalted humbled. Likewise Jesus surprises us by praising a "sinner" and blaming a "saint." Ever the unconventional, Jesus sees in the tax collector's prayer the requisite lowliness of heart. And in prizing that kind of prayer, he offers a reform of popular piety, which can often canonize pious rituals that often mask impious hearts. Since God can read hearts, the only prayer must be one of utter dependence on God's faithfulness and forgiveness. Quite simply, Jesus was ever on the attack against piety that seemed to be mostly show. Whenever Pharisees were indeed fixated on rituals and externals, Jesus called for reform. Whenever he found true faith, humility, and simplicity, Jesus praised it, even when it was exemplified by those deemed "sinners" in their culture.

A gospel such as this is good news in that it warns us of a spiritual disease that can be fatal. It is good news in that it reminds us that even those deemed deviant by our culture may have a core of piety. It is good news because Jesus assures us that God pays far more attention to the truth of our heart than to the display of our hands. This gospel is never intended to be a stick with which to beat anyone. Rather it is as a call to repentance for those of us who acclaim God. It confirms our lowliness, praises our dependence, and exalts our trust in God.

THIRTY-FIRST SUNDAY IN ORDINARY TIME: YEAR C LK 19:1–10

Once more tax collectors appear on the scene (recall 15:1–2; 18:10), and we immediately share the bias of Jesus' audience about people who perpetrated terrible injustice on their fellow Judeans with ruinous collection of taxes. The tax collector in today's gospel is Zacchaeus, who was both a "chief tax collector, and rich." The gospel presumes that he could only be "rich" because he was remarkably efficient in gathering taxes from the poor, and so we are to imagine him as an unjust person. Jesus' peasant audience initially hopes that he will tell a story about how this shameful person gets his comeuppance.

At first the audience expectations seem to be fulfilled.

This "short" man makes a fool of himself first by running along the street for a place on the parade route, then by climbing a tree to get a good viewing position. But the foolishness ends when Jesus stops before him. For Jesus addresses by name this foolish and evil man, "Zacchaeus, come down," and invites himself to his table: "I must stay at your house today." No self-respecting prophet would associate with, much less dine with a public sinner such as Zacchaeus. And public disdain for so vile a man as Zacchaeus immediately becomes a reason to challenge Jesus: "He has gone to be the guest of a man who is a sinner." Not Zacchaeus, but Jesus now appears to be the fool.

Jesus, who can read hearts, knows the worth of the man he has called to repentance and possibly discipleship. That trust is vindicated by Zacchaeus' immediate public confession. He proclaims that he will give half of his goods in alms to the poor, an action that fully accords with Jesus' own insistence on sharing one's wealth with the needy (11:41; 14:12-14; 16:19-22). Moreover, given the recognized source of his ill-gotten wealth, Zacchaeus proclaims generous restitution: "If I have defrauded, I restore it fourfold."

Jesus never ceases to surprise us. He chooses to dine with society's most unlikely people, tax collectors and sinners. Why? because he was sent by God as physician to the sick and shepherd to the lost sheep. He chooses such people, moreover, to shame the self-righteous (see 18:9-14). He keeps widening the circle of God's mercy to include the Zacchaeuses of this world, when we would narrow it to include only those we consider "saints." Thank God that Jesus' vision and values are more "Christian" than ours. Thank God that we all find our place among his disciples because of our genetic resemblance to Zacchaeus.

THIRTY-SECOND SUNDAY IN ORDINARY TIME: YEAR C LK 20:27-38

Shortly after Jesus' entrance into Jerusalem and its Temple, opponents engage him in debate. It seems that whenever he is out in public, someone always challenges him to test his power or his wisdom.

One batch of opponents has just tried and failed (20:19-26), when some of the Jerusalem elite, the Sadducees, approach him. They ask him a question that ridicules the notion that God raises the dead (see Acts 23:6-8). The form of their question is part of the legendary sorts of questions that rabbis asked of other rabbis in a sort of "intelligence world cup."

The Sadducees build their argument on the Levirate law (Dt 25:5), which prescribes that if a man dies without a child, his brother must marry the woman and beget a child to carry on the family name and honor (*levirate* = raise up [a child]). One brother married and died childless, so his brother married the widow, but died childless, so five other brothers married her in turn. If there is a resurrection when the dead are raised and the world is restored, whose husband will the widow be? One can see the smirk on the faces of the Sadducees who think they have stumped the rabbi Jesus.

Jesus answers in two ways. First, he returns the challenge and makes light of the naive understanding his opponents have of the resurrection. The life to come is not a repeat of this life: it is life transformed and elevated above our mortal needs and wants. In part, Jesus' answer depends on an ancient understanding of "immortality" as coming from many children, a tradition which goes back as far as Abraham. Ancestors live on in the lives of descendants, and thus the patriarch is eternal as long as his offspring inhabit the earth. More important, Jesus shames the Sadducees who deny to God the power and the will to raise the dead. Our deity is God of the living, not the dead. And as God is life, so those in God's family share the divine life.

This gospel would be most appropriate in Lent, as we approach the paschal mystery of Jesus. But it is here at the end of church Ordinary Time, right before the beginning of Advent because it contributes to our full appreciation of the future that awaits us. There is a life after death: God has the power and the purpose to raise us up. That life is the life of a heavenly creature, "equal to angels and children of God." Let no one ridicule our hope, which is rooted in God and proved by Jesus' own resurrection. If this is so, what sort of godly lives should we live as people destined to share God's holiness?

THIRTY-THIRD SUNDAY IN ORDINARY TIME: YEAR C LK 21:5–19

There is a sort of symmetry in the return to the Mount of Olives. It was from there that Jesus viewed the city and its Temple and pronounced a lament upon it before he entered Jerusalem (19:29), and it is to that place that he returns and repeats his lament (21:6). Basically, Jesus warned that buildings such as the renowned Temple do not ensure well-being or confirm hope. In time, all such structures collapse, so trust belongs alone in God's hands.

The Temple was so important to ancient Judeans that its destruction could only herald some decisive world event, perhaps the arrival of the Messiah or the end of the world. From ageless time, mortals have always sought to know the events of the future and so have a hedge against disaster, as Noah did. But Israelites of old and Judeans of Jesus' time considered it sinful for mortals to try and get such knowledge, which belongs only to God. Hence, when asked, Jesus brushes aside the question of "when" to talk about the obvious and near events. His remarks are hardly very exact and could apply to any age; which is the point: they are non-temporal markers of crises that arise with great regularity. False prophets come and go: what age has not seen its share of wars and earthquakes or famines and pestilences? Even the saints will be occasionally persecuted and their faith tested.

But Jesus is not giving his disciples a calendar of events to come. His advice is more basic: "Take heed." If he mentions future events, albeit in a general sense, it is to exhort his disciples to faithfulness and constancy today, not to satisfy any sense of curiosity about tomorrow. "Do not be led astray…do not be terrified…do not meditate beforehand how to answer." The important part of Jesus' discourse resides in the list of his commands to loyalty and fidelity, especially in the face of adversity. The point of his words is the reassuring promise: "By your endurance you will gain your lives."

Hence, as the church concludes its Ordinary Time and yearns for the coming of Jesus to bring us full salvation, we know that the lives of all disciples contain many hardships, crises, and even disasters. We are nonetheless chosen by God and destined for salvation. Far better for us to show faithfulness, constancy, and loyalty in our lives than to know the future.

THIRTY-FOURTH SUNDAY IN ORDINARY TIME: YEAR C LK 23:35–43

This last Sunday in Ordinary Time is also the Feast of Christ the King. In other years, we read of great judgment scenes in which Jesus the Ruler gathers the nations at the end of time and separates the sheep from the goats. But today the church offers us a different but equally powerful view of Christ our Sovereign—the Crucified King.

The very choice of the crucifixion scene for the Feast of Christ the King conveys a powerful message. Jesus reigns, not in worldly power and with the trappings of honor, but as the one who poured out his blood in ransom for others. Not credal cries of honor, but mockery fills his ears: no confessions of power, but only proclamations of his mercy and forgiveness. Just as Luke's gospel began with a description of God's surprising reversal of status and power in the Magnificat (1:50–53), so the story ends with the Crucified Christ turning the world's notions of success and power upside down.

The action in the crucifixion narrative is plotted in two scenes.

First, Jesus is mocked. Although the pains of crucifixion must have been intense, all of the evangelists single out for comment the more bitter experience of mockery. The religious elite scoff at Jesus, mocking the very point that is being dramatized for them, namely, "salvation": "He saved others: let him save himself." How true it is that Jesus by his life and death "saved others"; how sad that those most in need reject this. Balancing this, Jesus' executioners likewise laugh at him, "If you are the King of the Jews, save yourself." Jesus' disciples are also pained with him to hear this dismissal of his great generosity and sacrifice. Nothing seems more tragic than to have wasted one's life in service of others, who reject the gift. But the gift is not wasted on us, surely.

The second scene begins with a repetition of the mockery in the first part, as a thief who was crucified with Jesus "railed at him: aren't you the Christ? Save yourself and us!" Immediately another voice is heard, which both silences this mockery and models for us genuine conversion. The other thief rebuked his comrade in crime and punishment by noting that both of them deserve what they suffer, whereas Jesus is utterly innocent and suffers unjustly—quite a confession of faith! Then, turning to Jesus, he asks, "Jesus, remember me when you come into your kingdom."

First, let us note that salvation is again the focus: "Jesus" means "savior" (Mt 1:21), a name that describes and sums up his role and identity.

Second, we all know Jesus' own teaching, "Ask and you shall receive." The prayer of the thief is immediately answered, but in ways that are astounding.

Third, Jesus continues his role as "Saving King" by promising "today you will be with me in Paradise," which is nothing less than God's kingdom of holiness and life. If the first scene portrays an utter waste of Jesus' saving power, the second scene positively sparkles with it.

What a fitting end to Ordinary Time! What a marvelous summary of our faith! What a remarkable image to lead our hearts! Most of us know of kings in terms of special privilege, often arrogance, but always wealth and status—all self-important markers. But Jesus is king both when he is weakest and when he gives away the most. King, Savior, and Benefactor. The emphasis here rests on one who has shared fully our human life with all its bitterness and pain, and redeemed it. Jesus is not a stranger to weakness, mockery, rejection, loneliness, and evil: but he is their conqueror. Hence, our faith is drawn to sing the song: "Worthy is the Lamb who was slain, to receive power and wealth and wisdom and might and honor and glory and blessing" (Rev 4:12). Who would not gladly follow a King who lays down his life for our salvation? And how clearly we should imitate the Good Thief and turn today, of all days, to "ask" so as to receive a share in Christ's kingdom.

The Structure of the Lukan Narrative of Jesus

Paddy Meagher S.J.

Initial Comments

The readings for the Sunday lectionary in Year C are taken from Luke, chs. 3 to 21. In this major part of his narrative Luke interacts with the Marcan tradition from 4:31—9:50 in a consistent manner except for some notable omissions and additional teaching and narratives. In the next large section of the narrative (9:51—19:27), often called the travel narrative, he interacts with that tradition found in a source common to Matthew and Luke as he had in the small teaching unit (6:20–49). However, throughout the narrative and teaching units, even when influenced by sources common to one or the other gospel, Luke authors the matter in his own characteristic ways and introduces many incidents that are found only in his gospel. We find the special Lukan characteristics of the life of disciples in the travel narrative and some insights into the person of Jesus.

When we study the texts chosen for the lectionary readings we note that there are *twenty texts* out of thirty-three that are totally or to a large extent *only* in Luke. Of the other texts, eight are shared in a Lukan way with Matthew and five are common to the three gospels. We also notice that the vast majority of the chosen texts present Jesus' teaching. There are relatively few healings or exorcisms.

Since there are so many narrative texts of Jesus' teaching, we need to pay attention to the literary patterns used. A common pattern is a *narrative setting*, which forms the context *for one or more major sayings* of Jesus. In these narratives, Jesus is either:

- *correcting* the attitudes or expectations of others,
- *responding to strong criticism* of or objection to his teaching or behavior (or his disciples' behavior),
- *commending* a particular action or attitude,
- or *responding* to *questions or inquiries*.

Another common pattern used by Jesus is the parable or exemplary story. As readers we need to pay close attention to the particular types of contrasting attitudes in the parables, the surprising point that Jesus made, and the challenge involved in the parables.

To read the gospel attentive only to the *literal* meaning would be to miss the evocative and symbolic nature of this type of faith catechesis. The gospel is a *literary communication* of God's word and needs to be interpreted as such. We also need to remind ourselves constantly of the cultural gap. Jesus' religiocultural world is very different from ours with its values, types of interpersonal relationships, expectations, and ways of structuring society and life.

Finally, throughout we are interacting and listening to a person, not studying ideas and a religion. We are listening to and watching Jesus of Nazareth, who lived in a real world. As we are listening we are being invited to respond to Jesus Christ who is our living Lord, addressing us in our real world.

There are so many ways to attempt to lead a reader into the heart of the gospel of Luke. We will approach this from various perspectives.

A Real World

We want to sketch some aspects of the world Jesus experienced to remind ourselves to fill in the gaps in the text so that we are aware that Jesus was in a real world of men and women. Obviously he lived in a world with the sick, lepers, people considered possessed, groups ostracized by the more religiously observant groups. The world had its "in" groups and its "out" groups and so plenty of discrimination on various grounds. There were plenty of people economically poor and vulnerable, no system of social assistance, and no nets to catch those who fell by the wayside because of sickness, unemployment, or other calamities.

We may not pay adequate attention to some aspects.

We have the very rich family with six wealthy brothers insensitive to the poor at their gate (16:19–31), the fraudulent manager, shrewd and smart (16:1–11); the self-righteous groups; the unprincipled judge who cared nothing for God or what others thought (18:1–8); the absentee landowner confronted with scheming and violent tenants (20:9–15); systems for banking and making money multiply without the stock exchange (19:11–27); the wasteful son tasting life overseas (15:11–20); the schemers who attempted to destroy with duplicity (20:20–26); the princelings scheming to get royal status and ruthless to all who opposed them (19:12–27); brothers fighting over inheritance (12:13–15); the banquets of the wealthy (14:12–13, 16); the hypocrisy of religious leaders (11:42–52; 20:45–47); the prostitutes and a society marked by immorality (like the time of Noah and Lot [17:26–30]); established power blocks ready to murder "legally" to protect their power; a commercialized temple. As we follow the gospel we can complete the picture. We are not strangers to this type of world.

Portraits of Jesus

Many people interacted with Jesus, normally once yet some more often. The first group whose reaction seems to remain fairly consistent is the "crowd." Though in the condemnation scene before Pilate the crowd is mentioned, and again "the people" are said to watch him dying, yet normally the "crowd" had a positive attitude. There are many references to them pressing upon him to hear or be healed, reacting with spontaneous admiration or praise to God. The multitude of disciples are always positive and their attitude came to a climax as Jesus entered Jerusalem: "…the whole multitude of disciples began to praise God joyfully with a loud voice for all the deeds of power they had seen, saying…" (19:37).

A number of people approached Jesus as an authoritative teacher asking him the crucial question on how to enter into life (scribe, 10:25; ruler, 18:18) and even whether many would be saved (13:23), and to be the divider of inheritance (12:13). Many saw him as mediating God's healing power and power to forgive sins. These and others would have seen him as a great prophet (7:17 [widow of Naim scene] and 7:39 [Simeon the Pharisee]). Popular opinion was that he was a great prophet (8:19).

Evil powers (Beelzebub)

Herod was puzzled and we are told he asked, "Who is this about whom I hear such things" (9:9). Later we are told he was attempting to kill him (13:31). Finally he made a mockery of Jesus (23:6–12). The religious leadership of the villages and towns (Pharisees and scribes) were normally antagonistic, yet they are said to warn Jesus about Herod (13:31). They were scandalized by his obvious disregard for those customs that identified a genuine religious Jew, the Sabbath, and laws of purity, like washing hands, careful avoidance of certain types of clearly impure people (sinners, toll collectors, prostitutes, lepers, and many ordinary types of people). His readiness to forgive sin in God's name was looked upon as dangerous religious presumption (blasphemy). His exorcisms were explained by some in the crowd as a proof of his close association with evil powers (Beelzebub). Another aspect of the smear campaign waged against Jesus of which we have some hints was the taunt: "Look, a glutton and a drunkard, a friend of tax collectors and sinners"(7:34). There were not just murmurs of disapproval (5:30; 15:1–2; 19:7) but a disinformation campaign.

The religious leadership in Jerusalem was aware of Jesus' religious self-understanding. They wanted him to clarify his authority, which he refused to do (20:1–8). Later they tried to force him to a clear statement of his identity (22:66–71). Each time he refused, because they were obstinately closed and intent on killing him (19:47; 20:19, 20; 22:2). During his trial before Pilate they accused him of political crimes. In the battle of wits Pilate consistently affirmed Jesus' total innocence until the end though he still condemned him. We learn a lot by paying attention to others' assessment of Jesus. They all took "faith" stances, either judging that he mediated God's saving presence or was a false prophet.

CHARACTERISTIC THEMES

There are a number of themes, common to all the gospels, which Luke develops and emphasizes in a special way.

Prayer

Jesus was not only the model for the disciples in prayer but stressed significant aspects of prayer. Major moments of his life took place in a context of prayer

(3:21; 6:12; 9:29; 11:1; 23:34; 23:46 [texts found only in Luke] 5:16; 22:39-46 [specific aspects in Luke]. The origin narratives (chs. 1-2) are punctuated with types of prayerful responses to God's extraordinary action. The small catechisms on prayer are worthy of note (11:1-13; 17:11-19; 18:1-8; and 18:9-14). The climax was Jesus in prayer before his death (22:49-46). Luke emphasizes the aspect of Jesus as Model and on the cross (23:34).

As the disciples were called to prayer, they were also meant to be outstanding as *"hearers of the Word"* (5:1; 8:11-15; 8:21; 10:39; 11:27). Luke does not highlight the frailty of the disciples as much as the other writers do. Yet his Jesus insisted on the total gift of oneself by genuine disciples (5:11, 28; 9:57-62; 14:25-33 [both texts related to Jesus' journey to his death]; 18:21). In Luke Jesus gave his instructions on service as the fundamental orientation in life in the context of the last meal (22:24-27). The child was the symbol of authentic greatness because the child in that culture was a "nobody" (9:48).

Women

Luke gives significant attention to women and to their place in Jesus' ministry. He uses gender pairs (Zachary / Mary; Zachary / Elizabeth; Simeon / Anna; the shepherd and woman who lost a coin; the woman with the blood disease and Jairus [faith theme]; two men in bed and two women grinding). Women are models of *faith* (Mary, Anna; the sinful woman; the woman with the blood disease) and *of hearing the Word* (Mary and Mary, sister of Martha); women fulfill the role of prophets (Elizabeth and Anna); women are associated with Jesus' ministry (8:1-3), with his death and burial (23:49, 55) and received the divine revelation of Jesus' resurrection with faith and became the first witnesses (24:1-11, 22-23). "The women who had followed him from Galilee" remain beside the crucified Jesus as a faithful and contemplative group (23:49). They remained with him until his burial and then went to prepare to come and show their deep devotion to him by anointing after the Sabbath (23:55-56). The wailing women accompanied Jesus on his way to his death. Three women played significant roles as examples of the marginalized in society—the widow of Naim bereft of her only son, the ostracized sinful woman, and the bent old woman, a daughter of Abraham (13:10-17). The poor widow with the contribution of her two "dollars" is the model of the disciple as she gave "all she had to live on" (21:1-4). To develop in an adequate way Jesus' teaching about woman in the faith community and society we need to pay careful attention to his consistent affirmation of the human person and the human dignity of all.

Wealth

This widow who shamed the rich could lead us to one of the more prominent and contentious themes in Luke. Zacchaeus was another model of those who had become disciples. However, it was costly—half his wealth to the poor and fourfold recompense to anyone he had cheated. The power, status, comfort, and security associated with wealth are contrasted with the powerlessness, pain, insecurity, and misery associated with poverty (6:20-26). The theme of reversal at the heart of Mary's Magnificat runs through the whole gospel with an insistence not to be found in the other gospels. The Lukan Jesus' beatitudes heighten the contrast. The story of the six brothers who are wealthy, with miserable Lazarus hanging around their home (16:19-31), the greedy brother concerned about his inheritance (12:13-21) are all special Lukan contributions. The God/wealth saying causes ridicule from "lovers of money" (13:11-14). The rich young man, earnest and seeking the way to life, confronted with Jesus' invitation to sell all and follow, "became sad." The narrator explained the reason: " for he was very rich." Only in Luke's gospel does the narrative continue: "Jesus looked at him and said, 'How hard it is for those who have wealth to enter the Kingdom of God. Indeed it is easier for a camel…." (19:23-25). Wealth is to be used for alms (11:41; 12:33) and for the good of the poor (14:12-14). Zacchaeus, a narrative only found in Luke, fulfills a special role in the gospel. His experience of Jesus, a gracious Jesus, led him to use his wealth for the good of the needy and to change his manner of life. He became an honest man. He did not leave his profession. He was not asked to leave all. Yet his wealth was not an obstacle but a means to be a disciple. A number of other well off people failed to become servants of their wealth (11:39-41; 12:13-21; 16:14-15,19- 31; 20:45-47). In Jesus' teaching wealth was a responsibility and to be used for others (12:21, 32-34; 16:9, 13-14).

Those on the Margin

Luke's Jesus also paid special attention to the poor. He

also was concerned for the ostracized—sinners (5:29-32; 7:36-50; chapter 15), lepers (5:12-13; 17:11-20), Samaritans (used in two parables as models of the love command [10:29-37] and gratitude and faith [17:11-20]), the bereft widow (7:11-17), the sick old woman (13:10-17). The classical summary in 7:18-23 states the deeds that authenticate that Jesus was "the One to Come." This summary is a summons to all Christian communities and to each believer. We need to recall that the majority of the "crowds" who gathered about Jesus were poor people living at hardly a subsistence level.

Holy Spirit

In Luke's gospel the whole era of Jesus' life was marked by the action of the Spirit. The series of prophetic figures in the infancy narrative were guided and empowered by the Spirit (Elizabeth and Zachary [1:41, 67] and Simeon [2:25-27]). John is gifted with the Spirit from his birth and therefore would be an extraordinary prophet. Jesus was conceived by the Spirit, who is God's power. At the outset of his ministry in those initial crucial moments he was gifted with the Spirit (3:22) and guided by it (4:1, 14). The Spirit was the gift par excellence given to Jesus (4:18). Though the Spirit is not mentioned again except at a moment of joyful prayer (10:21) yet the initial texts imply that the whole ministry was lived under the power and guidance of the Holy Spirit. This is the way Luke has Peter summarize Jesus' ministry (Acts 10:38). His ministry would bring the Spirit into our history in a very special way. This was indicated by John when questioned about his role (3:16), and stated by Jesus as he was about to leave his disciples, "And see, I am sending upon you what my Father promised; so stay in the city until you have been clothed with power from on high" (24:49). Already he had taught them that the gift of the Father is the Holy Spirit (11:13) and promised the persecuted disciples the supportive presence of the Spirit (12:12). The Acts is the story of this gift of the Father, poured out in abundance by the risen Lord on the communities of believers.

Indications to Readers of Responses

The disciples, many individual persons, and Jesus himself are models for the believing community. Luke also included short comments about the way individuals or groups reacted to Jesus and to the action of God. The great hymns attributed to Mary, Zachary, Simeon, and the angels are types of responsorial psalms. These guide us so that we understand what God is doing and respond with deep gratitude and wonder. They draw our attention to God's mercy, fidelity, power, and concern for the poor. The words of Elizabeth (1:42-45) and the reaction of Elizabeth's neighbors (1:65-66) and the amazed shepherds (2:20) guide us. Mary, treasuring and pondering in her heart (2:19, 51) is an invitation to the reader to follow the whole narrative of Jesus with this spirit.

Throughout the narrative there are a series of choral responses normally by the crowds or some individuals (4:15, 37; 5:15, 26; 7:16-17; 8:25, 37; 9:43; 11:14; 13:13, 17; 17:15; 18:43). We shall not comment on each text. At Jesus' approach to Jerusalem the final choral piece summarizes this aspect of the gospel: "...the whole multitude of the disciples began to praise God joyfully with a loud voice for all the deeds of power that they had seen. They said, 'Blessed is the King who comes in the name of the Lord! Peace in heaven and glory to the highest heaven'" (19:37-38). The tragedy of this text is that Jesus wept when he saw his city. The Centurion watching Jesus die made another model response. Luke says, "... he praised God and said, 'Certainly this man was innocent.'" The crowd returning home also indicates to us an appropriate response. "They returned home, beating their breasts" (23:47, 48). The crucified sinner, companion of Jesus on the cross, is also a model of the repentant and trusting sinner.

Jesus of Luke's Gospel

In one way there are no surprises in Luke's gospel because the fullest description of Jesus is given by the end of the "infancy" narrative. What is said in these chapters is most reliable since all those who speak about Jesus are in some way spokespersons of God. We need to remember that these chapters are written from the other side of the resurrection and express the rich faith of the community. First of all the whole life of Jesus and his person is placed within the great story of God with his people. This story began with his promises to Abraham and the ancestors. The divine oath to David about the everlasting dynasty and kingdom reiterated these promises in a specific way. In Jesus this whole history and all the promises are fulfilled. John the Baptist was a foil to Jesus. Jesus was holy and Son of God from his origin, the promised Messiah whose kingdom will never end. We are told that he is Savior, Christ the Lord by the Angel. Simeon spoke of his universal significance, and Anna of the culmination of the long history of God's liberative actions. Light entered into a world of darkness. Sin would be forgiven. God's fidelity and mercy were enfleshed in this man of Nazareth.

We are cautioned against false hopes. He will be the hope of the poor, the powerless, and lowly, and not the powerful of this world. He will also be a sign of contradiction. The shadow of the Passion already lay over his life. However he was the source of joy and hope for the world.

In the infancy narrative Jesus spoke only one sentence. This is highly significant. He must be about the work of his Father! He lived as Son through his obedience, total and unwavering to his Father in the pursuit of the goal of his life, the proclamation of the reign of God and his mission to the poor.

Throughout the gospel various people express their faith in Jesus as the prophet of God or reject him as blasphemer. We ought to pay attention to the stances taken by various people. For example, Simon, who invited Jesus to a meal judged him not to be a prophet. However, the sinful woman found God's mercy in him. Contrary attitudes are often placed side by side. The passion story illustrates this. The attitude of the leadership is sharply contrasted with the crowds who "would get up early in the morning to listen to him in the temple"(21:38).

As we listen to the gospel we see contrasting pictures of Jesus. We need to keep this diversity. The prophet who wept compassionately over his own sacred city also pronounced words of judgment (13:34-35; 19:41-44). Luke's Jesus was very sensitive, with eyes for those in need and at the same time asking all to strive to recover the image of God in the way they lived as disciples. Attention to diversity and contrast brings many insights in the listening to the gospel.

Jesus himself also allows us to see him through his own eyes. Each narrative in some way reveals him. In some, Luke has Jesus himself tell us about himself. We have the sayings about his mission. He says "I have come to call not the righteous but sinners to repentance" and "For the Son of Man came to seek and save the Lost"(5:32; 19:10). He spells out his program at Nazareth and reiterates this when questioned by John's disciples (7:18-23). Eating with sinners, offering God's forgiveness, healing and exorcising the spirits, and giving life to the widow's only son all reveal Jesus' self-awareness. His teaching with authority, the prophetic judgments he made, the total devotion he invited and demanded disciples to show to himself again revealed his own self-understanding. Jesus understood that facing the probability of death and moving relentlessly toward Jerusalem was the implication of his prophetic mission (13:32-33). There is a special term Luke's Jesus used in special contexts that underlined his decisive acceptance of the destiny his Father had willed. He used " it is necessary…" (2:49; 4:43; 9:22; 13:33; 17:25; 19:5; 22:37; 24:7, 26, 44). This is the "must" of God.

Therefore Jesus was aware of a very special relationship to his Father and his plan for the coming of the kingdom. He knew that God was present with power in a very particular way through his mission. The finger of God was active (11:29). He is able to interpret the immense mercy of his Father for sinners. This relationship to the Father is described in a prayer scene. Jesus said, "All things have been handed over to me by my Father; and no one knows who the Son is except the Father, or who the Father is except the Son and anyone to whom the Son chooses to reveal him" (10:22). We must not interpret this text to mean that Jesus had a type of "divine consciousness" during his earthly life. However, as we follow Jesus through the narrative of his few years of work we are aware that he had pushed to the limits the nature of the special responsibility he had received from God. Also his way of life spelled out his own special relationship to God whom he called Father, a relationship he shared with his disciples.

As we hear the gospel week after week we must remember that we are listening to Luke's faith interpretation of Jesus of Nazareth, Christ and Lord, the Son of God who speaks to us today through the gospel of yesterday.

The Gospel of Luke in Year C

Paddy Meagher

Second Sunday of Ordinary Time
Year C: Jn 2:1-11

The First Sign

We face some of the peculiarities of the Sunday lectionary today. Out of the blue we begin to read 1 Corinthians at chapter 12 (chs. 1-5 and 6-11 are read in Years A and B). The reading provides challenging reflections on the diversity of gifts within the Christian communities among Christ's faithful and the struggle to respect and nourish such diversity in order to enrich the unity of the community, parish, or diocese. Often the common good of the community is impoverished and the gifts of God are not recognized. This is an opportunity again to reflect on the role of the Holy Spirit. Three points are worthy of attention. The nature and variety of the gifts deserve attention. The list is not exhaustive. There will be gifts to be found in our communities that are not mentioned. Second, all the gifts of the Spirit are given for the common good. Each Christian, priests included, with their gifts are responsible to the community for the life of the community. Finally the one Spirit is the source of all the gifts. They are gifts because the Spirit takes the initiative and gives the gifts. To respect the community, to nourish and to use the gifts with a deep sense of wonder and gratitude would be one way for a Christian community to celebrate in the coming year.

John 2:1-12 also disrupts the reading of Luke (the same happens in years A and B). We could look at our gospel as another epiphany and a further presentation of major aspects of Jesus' ministry according to John's interpretation.

The brief narrative has a plausible literal character—an account of Jesus at a long wedding feast of presumably a relatively poor family. At the urging of his mother he saves them from great embarrassment by working a miracle. However, the writer clearly rules out such a literal reading by clear indications of the rich symbolic meaning of this account.

Jesus refuses his mother's request respectfully. He gives the reason "My hour is not yet come." The "hour" refers to that whole series of events through which Jesus in obedience to his Father revealed him and finally returned to him in glory. Through the events included in it Jesus manifested most distinctly and openly the saving fidelity and love, grace, and truth of his Father for the human family (7:30; 8:20; 12:23-27; 13:1; 17:1; see 17:1-5). Any act of Jesus that revealed Jesus as the Son who made present the saving presence and activity of his Father must be undertaken only in obedience to him; not even his mother has this right (4:34). Jesus' death and glorification are in a special way "his hour." As Mary was associated with Jesus at his death as the disciple (19:25-27), so she was also at the outset of his life.

This scene is also the climax of a series of earlier scenes linked by means of the time reference "on the third day" (2:1; cf. 1:29, 35, 43). Each scene reveals Jesus to the readers and is part of the journey to faith of the disciples. The extraordinary abundance of wine (and boutique wine at that!) and the comparison between the earlier wine and this wine evoke the sense of the new world order God would create in the last days, signs of the time of salvation.

Finally the real import of the scene—were we to miss the earlier indications of the symbolic significance—is underlined by the narrator. He refers to Jesus' act as "the first of his signs through which he revealed his glory." He concludes saying, "his disciples believed." The series scenes running from 2:1 to 12:43 are narratives of signs and a story of those who believed (4:53-54; 5:7; 6:67-68; 9:35-39; and 11:24) and especially of those who refused to believe (chapter 5; 6:60-66, chs. 7, 8; 9:40-41; chs. 10, 11; and 12:37-43). A summary of the gospel is expressed in these terms: "Now Jesus did many signs in the presence of his disciples.... These are written that you may continue to believe that Jesus is the Messiah, Son of God and that through believing you may have life in his name" (20:30-31).

Today we wish to celebrate a number of points. We note how Jesus began his ministry as the obedient son of the Father. With his ministry the new era of hope and life had also begun. Being the Son who came from the side of the Father (1:18) he revealed the depths of God's goodness. Finally he so reflected the glory of God in his human person and his obedient ministry. We are invited to deepen our faith. We share his risen Spirit to empower us to live in Christ.

THIRD SUNDAY IN ORDINARY TIME: YEAR C LUKE 1:1-4; 4:14-21

The Prophet

Many educators and priests could pause at the fine classical introduction to the gospel (1:3-4). This is a gentle reminder of our responsibilities as custodians of the Word. We are challenged by the conscientious devotion of the author as an interpreter of the Word and his concern to reassure Theophilus, a real or symbolic believer, about the reliability of the catechesis he had received. These words remind us to study both the nature of the gospel and to ensure that it speaks to our generation.

Today we read only the first part of a major scene in Luke's interpretation of Jesus' ministry. We need to recall the earlier scenes. The Son, chosen and empowered by the Father with the Spirit (3:21-22), bridged the gap between the world of God and the whole human race to whom he is sent, since he is presented as "son of Adam, Son of God" (3:23-38). He authenticated his right to be called "Son" who was entrusted with the uncompromising surrender to God and commitment to discern his will only in all he did and said (4:1-13, the Testing of Jesus).

As the final backdrop to our scene of Jesus at the threshold of his Galilean ministry, Luke gives a summary sketch. Jesus was full of the power of the Spirit. He began to teach in community centers and evoked universal admiration (4:14-15). We can recall that Jesus was full of the Spirit (4:1) and that the Spirit accompanied him throughout his period in the desert and his testing. He began his ministry in "the power of the Spirit" (4:14). Though the place of the Spirit in his life is unique, yet as the Spirit gave birth to the original communities of believers (Acts 2) so also the Spirit is the invisible power in all our lives as communities of believers and individuals.

Up to this point others have identified Jesus. Luke's Jesus now makes his own assessment of himself and his life's work. We are reminded in two phrases of the "hidden" years of his life at Nazareth "where he had been brought up" and that "as was his custom" he went to the community place of worship. In a few deft strokes Luke describes an aspect of synagogue worship. He stood up to read; the scroll of Isaiah was handed to him; he unrolled it and found the reading. Then having read the passage, he rolled it up, returned it to the attendant and sat to comment. Our first reading from Nehemiah reminds us of the public practice of reading the Word. The reading does not really help us to understand the gospel.

The text read is a combination of Is 61:1-2 and 58:6 —a sign that this scene is constructed by Luke. With these texts Jesus identified himself as the great prophet promised by God and empowered with the Spirit. He made this interpretation of his religious experience of God's call to him because of the specific way he understood the nature of the task entrusted to him. He was to bring good news to the poor. He was to bring to the poor that saving presence that God had promised so often in the past. The Spirit anointed and sent him for specific tasks. The nature of Jesus' mission reminds all of us Christians that a major aspect of the specific mission of the church as a whole and parishes in particular is to transform all types of poverty. We are reminded of the many saints of our history. As I write I see the old wrinkled face of Mother Teresa. She was the saint of those in the gutter. Jesus and the poor, God his Father and the poor and the Spirit and the poor are inseparable.

The other phrases in the text: "release to the captives, recovery of sight to the blind, let the oppressed go free" are symbolic expressions of ministry. The integral enhancement of the human person and human community, concern for human dignity and human rights, and the creation of an ever more humane and human society are at the heart of this ministry. However, we need to remind ourselves that the most needy are Jesus' specific concern. We also witness today the human destroyed by sin, despair, hatred, greed, oppressive laws and structures and economic systems, by media, drugs, war, racial conflict, gender oppression. We could re-express the final phrase, "a year acceptable to the Lord" in terms of a human society that God would not be ashamed to own.

During these three Sundays I suggest we look long and hard at Jesus Christ and hear how the Father, Peter, John the Baptist, the sacred authors John and Luke and Isaiah see him. He is our Lord.

The gospel provides ways of reflecting on the Holy Spirit in the life of the church and our lives as Christians. The second reading takes up this area of our faith life. The interplay between fundamental unity and rich diversity is a characteristic of a genuine Christian community (parish, diocese). Paul emphasizes that profound unity that is based on a shared union with Jesus and the Spirit. The Spirit, whom we all receive as a primary gift at baptism, breaks down barriers and incorporates into our faith community all types of diversity—be it of language, color, gender, or social status (12:12–13). He highlights the danger that some "individuals" (be they a group, or individuals) lack a sense of mutuality or fail to be responsible to the more needy groups or persons in the one community (12:14–26). Further dangers are that undue importance can be given to particular gifts and that the diversity of gifts is not appreciated (12:27–30).

FOURTH SUNDAY OF ORDINARY TIME: YEAR C Luke 4:21–30

Yet A Rejected Prophet

We begin our reflections with some comments on 1 Cor 12:31—13:13 in the context of Christian community life, including life in a Christian family. The gift of the Spirit is love. We could continue our meditation on the Holy Spirit as we spell out the meaning of this text. We could link this with the mission given by the Spirit of God to Jesus about which we reflected last week. Paul's concern is the interplay between diverse members or groups within the community, building or destroying the community. In parishes and dioceses we create structures and have diverse groups—consultative bodies, finance committees, parish and diocesan councils, school boards, ministers of the Eucharist, catechists, teachers, and so on. Paul makes three points. If love is lacking as the basic motivating force in our lives, we build sandcastles (13:1–3). Love is not promoted through the media, secularized culture, and consumerism. It is a gift of the Spirit. Therefore, love's self-portrait always catches us going the other way (13:4–7). Finally all the other gifts do pass away. Love abides and carries us into the mystery of God. The opening and closing phrases—"The still more excellent way" and "Pursue Love" (14:1) could be the guidelines for life. This poem is often seen as a portrait of Jesus of Nazareth. We could pray that we may be more aware of the nature of Christian love and what re-creation of our hearts signifies.

The lines selected from the description of Jeremiah's call (Jer 1:4–9, 17–19) provide a background to the continuation of the narrative of Jesus' ministry in Nazareth. Jeremiah is designated as a prophet to the nations whose ministry will be marked by intense conflict and rejection. He is, however, reassured by God's promise, "I will be with you."

Our text (Lk 4:21–30) combines two major themes of Luke-Acts. These are the acceptance and rejection of Jesus and his disciples. However the transition from 4:22 ("All acknowledged it and were surprised at the gracious words [eloquence]... Is not this Joseph's son?") to Jesus' comment on their cynicism (4:23–24) is awkward. Luke has not knit together his sources with elegance. However the Nazareth narrative (see Mk 6:1–6 for another way of presenting this event) is programmatic in purpose. Jesus was the prophet of God accepted by some and yet a cause of contradiction to many (2:34–35). His ministry and the ministry of the early church were first of all for his own people. However, he was rejected by so many of them as the early disciples so often were rejected. Luke's narrative will tell the story of those who believe that he is God's special prophet and those who reject him. There will be times when we shall be reluctant to accept what he says and asks of us as disciples. This was symbolized in the comparison with Elijah and the Sidonian widow and Elisha who cured the Syrian leper. Both prophets revealed God's mercy and fidelity to Gentiles. His ministry also brought judgment on those who reject him. Finally our test foreshadows Calvary in the abortive popular attempt to murder him. Luke does not explain in any way how Jesus escaped. The verses in the responsorial psalm (Ps 71) would be an apt prayer for Jesus after his escape.

The text can have a quite disturbing message for us. Jesus quoted a proverb: "Doctor, heal yourself." He explained it in terms of Nazareth's jealousy with regard to his ministry in Capernaum (4:23). Note that Luke has not given any data about this ministry so far (see 4:31–41). Jesus' words can be interpreted in relationship to our human tendency to define ourselves in terms of "we" and "they," "in" and "out," and all forms of exclusivism based on race, language, color, religion, gender, social status, and the like.

The universality of Jesus and his mission challenges Christian communities and persons not to allow any bigotry, narrowness, racial, and gender discrimination to enter either church or society. There are no horizons to genuine love. A trait of love is sincere hospitality in the richest and broadest connotation of this fascinating word. The universality of Jesus' mission is to be mirrored in Christian churches, schools, institutions, and groups.

FIFTH SUNDAY OF ORDINARY TIME: YEAR C Luke 5:1–11

Send Me

One stream of the catechesis for the next three Sundays concerns belief in the resurrection. Modern North American Christians will certainly not have the same difficulties and questions as the Corinthians. Ministers will need to identify these questions and see whether 1 Cor 15 throws light on their search to grasp this core aspect of our belief.

Paul initially recalls for his community the basic points of the gospel he preached to them and they had accepted (1 Cor 15:1–11). The statement of the basic creed—probably the earliest credal statement—is concise and carefully balanced (15:3–5). The core elements are: Christ died for our sins (according to the Scriptures), and he was raised on the third day (according to the Scriptures). These statements are supported by two confirming elements: he was buried and he appeared to Peter and then the Twelve. The reference to Scripture indicates that his redemptive death and being raised by God were essential elements in God's plan for human salvation. Paul was concerned with belief in the resurrection. Therefore he lined up a series of witnesses (15:8) including himself. There are no narratives in the gospels about these appearances. He commented on the amazing gift given to himself and his outstanding response. In this way he emphasized both his authority and the authority of the gospel he proclaimed to the Corinthians. At its center was that Christ was raised.

Two aspects of Isaiah's call (Is 6:1–8) enable us to understand Luke's narrative more clearly (Lk 5:1–11). Through his experience of divine holiness in the Temple vision, Isaiah was overwhelmed by the sense of his profound unworthiness. This was expressed in terms apt for the way his prophetic vocation was described. He says, "I am a man of unclean lips." Having experienced the divine cleansing, he responded with his famous "Here I am; Send me." Peter mirrors these two aspects, though fishing will be the symbolic world for his mission.

Luke's narrative is, as usual, very well crafted. There are two major contrasts: the listening crowd standing on the shore and Jesus in the boat teaching; and the fruitless and laborious night's fishing and the abundant catch with two overloaded and sinking boats. We have also the underlying major contrast between the divine and the human mediated by Jesus and Peter.

There are very close links between the initial and final scenes. At the beginning the crowds surrounded Jesus, eager to hear the Word of God. He taught them from Peter's boat. In the final scene Jesus commissioned Peter (and the others) with the words: "Do not be afraid; from now on you will catch alive people" (Lk 5,10b).

Peter and the others left all and followed him. They will continue his responsibility (see 4:43–44) of proclaiming the word of God, which is the gospel of the kingdom of God.

However the transition from "catching fish" to "catching people" is rooted in an overwhelming experience. The experience of God was mediated through Jesus the "Master" who became "the Lord" (5:4, 8). In exaggerated terms Luke described the utterly fruitless night of work and the superabundant catch effected by Jesus' word. This was an epiphany of the divine before whom Peter was utterly unnerved and aware of a proud unworthiness, the profane before the holy. This was also a creative moment. Jesus' words "do not be afraid" and "from now on..." enabled and empowered Peter to accept the responsibility entrusted to him. His leaving all, a typical description of discipleship in this gospel (5:28; 14:33) indicated not just material dispossession but also an inner disposition of surrender to Jesus Christ. This aspect of inner surrender, which has diverse concrete expressions in a disciple's life, finally concerns the search to discern and do God's will. We could ask the Spirit to lift us with the attitudes for which Tagore prays:

> Let only that little be left of me whereby I may name you my all.
> Let only that little be left of my will whereby I may feel you on every side,
> and come to you in everything, and offer you my Love every moment.
> Let only that little be left of me whereby I may never hide you.
> Let only that little of my fetters be left whereby I am bound with your will,
> and thy purpose is carried out in my life—
> and that is the fetter of your love.

SIXTH SUNDAY IN ORDINARY TIME: YEAR C Luke 6:17, 20–26

The Poor Are Blessed

The poem chosen from Jeremiah (Jer 17:5–8) and the responsorial psalm (Ps 1) are from the wisdom tradition. Jesus' succinct and blunt sayings belong to the prophetic tradition. Wisdom promised God's blessing upon those who trusted in the Lord and who took seriously the study of the Torah and a Torah way of life, avoiding association with the wicked. Wisdom gave dire threats to those who trusted primarily in other human beings and who had no regard for God's law.

A far more apt text from Jeremiah with an appropriate thematic content and not just some exterior formal similarities would be Jer 7:5–8. In this piece of his Temple sermon (chapter 7) the prophet underlined the conditions for God's continual presence among his people and consequently their continued existence as his people. This is the blessing of God. Jeremiah said, "if you truly amend your ways...if you truly act justly with another, if you do not oppress the alien, the orphan, and the widow...." It was this concern with the refuse of society and the most vulnerable groups that characterizes God in the finest threads of the religious traditions that Jesus inherited. The reason is not the "goodness" of the poor. However, in this way the inner being of God's immense graciousness and universal love find stark expression.

Jesus' promised blessings to the poor and the threatening woes to the rich are re-expressed in story form in the narrative of the rich person with five brothers and the poor man with his festering sores (Lk 16:19–31). We genuinely respect the scandalous import of Jesus' teaching, the way he turns upside down all normal ways of perceiving "the good life" and success, when we accept that such teaching contributed to his being "legally" murdered. The woes on the rich imply an irresponsible and selfish attitude and way of life.

We begin to grasp what Jesus is speaking about when from our middle class environment we regularly visit Vincent de Paul centers, refuges for alcoholics and discarded men and women, homes for street kids, centers for AIDS victims and drug addicts, slums. Our text is introduced by a scene of needy people crowding around Jesus who purposely has come among them. He speaks to all who wish to be his disciples. As Christians can we rejoice and be profoundly grateful for Jesus' teaching about the blessing for those who are poor, hungry, and weak? Do our security and desires, a sense of guilt or just puzzlement hamper us? There is a second message addressed to all those who make no attempts to dilute Jesus' gospel and strive to live in a prophetic way as disciples. They are not the most popular people. However, they are urged to rejoice in a foolish way (6:22–23). Yet Jesus noted that within his society, and in Luke's time in the Christian churches, there were the false voices (6:26).

By their consistent, humble, humane service, Mother Teresa and many others enable the poor, the hungry, and the broken to experience Jesus' promise of God's blessing. We are all invited to enable others in great need to experience the promise of blessing in our lives. What are the ways? Such service is the touchstone of the true service of God, the Father of Jesus Christ. This is beautifully expressed in a poem of Tagore:

> Here is thy footstool and there rest thy feet where lived
>   the poorest and lowliest, and the lost.
> When I try to bow to you, my obeisance cannot reach
>   down to the depths where your feet rest,
> among the poorest and lowliest, and the lost.
> Pride can never approach to where you walk in the
>   clothes of the humble
> among the poorest, and lowliest and the lost.
> My heart can never find its way to where you company
>   with the companionless
> among the poorest, the lowliest and the lost.

SEVENTH SUNDAY IN ORDINARY TIME: YEAR C Luke 6:27–38

A Variation on the Same Theme

Unfortunately Paul's extensive reflections on our resurrection are really mutilated by the few verses selected for the Sixth, Seventh, and Eighth Sundays. He affirms that the consequence of the denial of the resurrection of believers must be the denial of Christ's resurrection. The reason is the basic solidarity between believers and Jesus Christ and also Christ's universal role in God's plan for the human family (1 Cor 15:12, 16–20, and 21–28).

Paul knew that the dead would rise. He attempted to explain bodily resurrection in a way limited by his knowledge of science and biology (15:33–43). He ended this discussion with a contrast between the original human person (the first Adam) and the last human person (Christ, the last Adam) (15:45–49). He described how we all shared traits of Adam, being "living beings," "physical," and "from earth" ("of dust"). Because he understood that Jesus Christ was the archetype of the human and was in solidarity with all humans, he developed this argument. As we had borne the image of the man of dust, we would also bear the image of the man of heaven. The risen Jesus is not only a "living being" but now also a "life-giving Spirit": the resurrection is the powerful affirmation of human dignity, human solidarity, and the depths to which Jesus shared in our human nature. Jesus restored to us the fullness of the image and likeness of God through his resurrection. He also remains as the source of the Spirit who continually recreates us into his likeness and will be the source of our resurrection.

In a story from David's early life, the first reading creates a background for the gospel. The sick king, Saul, hunts David. David is presented as a model who breaks the spiral of violence and vengeance. He refuses to kill the king and rid himself of grave danger to his life. Luke's collection of Jesus' teaching is carefully ordered with repetitive patterns, terms, and themes. This emphasizes the importance of the teaching. Jesus speaks about occurrences that are part and parcel of our own lives and about choices we have to make. We cannot run away from enmity, hatred, and insults. People take advantage of us, dominate us, bludgeon us, and pressure us even with subtle forms of blackmail. Some of the expressions of oppressive domination or abuse used by Jesus, namely striking on the cheek, taking of a person's coat (outer garment), begging with threats, stealing belongings, are not normally part of our lives. However, violence, aggression, insult, slander, humiliating domination, and threats are still with us. They take many forms and create enmity and deep anger.

Also in normal life we set up patterns of social mutuality. We are able to understand Jesus when he spoke of loving those who are friendly, giving help to those who lend a helping hand to us. We lend with the assurance that we will not be worse off. Also we strongly believe in legal systems of redress and punishment. We are ready to judge and condemn others. So many relationships are structured around selfishness, calculation, status and racial or other types of affinity. Jesus places before us societal chaos. We must remember both that he was using paradoxical sayings and that we are in danger of diluting his teaching. He affirmed a forgiveness that was to be universal and limitless especially for the "enemy": He asked for the total repudiation of all forms of vindictiveness, retaliation, and "an eye for an eye." He spoke of utterly foolish generosity, "expecting nothing in return." He used an image from the grain market of his time. The grain in the measure is pressed down, shaken thoroughly, and overflows, like a really full glass of beer! What he taught is impossible unless we look at the God who had such a mastery over his life. He was not a word but the living God, the Father. The God whom Jesus knew from his tradition, his hours of silence, his journey of faith and whom he called Father was the measure of his life and is to be of our lives. Behind these sayings was his awareness that we are created in the image and likeness of God. In a simple phrase he motivated his disciples, "you will be children of the most High" who "is gracious to the ungrateful and evil." His challenge is simple and breathtaking, "be merciful (forgiving, giving, loving...) just as your Father is merciful (forgiving, non condemning, generous ...)." When our hearts have been through this crucible of purification, we can seek legal redress, justice, and our human rights, defend our name, separate from a dead and destructive marriage, seek maintenance... as disciples of Jesus. The measure of forgiveness and love is God, the Father's love and forgiveness enfleshed in Jesus of Nazareth. We could take away with us today the "Prayer of St. Francis":

> Lord, make me (us) a channel of your peace
> Where there is hatred, let me sow love.
> Where there is injury, pardon.
> Where there is discord, unity.
> Where there is doubt, faith.
> Where there is error, truth.
> Where there is despair, hope.
> Where there is sadness, joy.
> Where there is darkness, light.
> O Divine Master grant that I may not so much seek
> To be consoled as to console.
> To be understood as to understand
> To be loved as to love
> For it is in giving that we receive.
> It is in pardoning that we are pardoned.
> It is in dying that we are born to eternal life.

EIGHTH SUNDAY IN ORDINARY TIME: YEAR C Luke 6:39–45

Out of the Abundance of the Heart

We listen to human wisdom today. The proverbs of Ben Sirach about judging a person from their conversation resonate with our experience. The ancient wisdom teacher was a fine observer of human life when he wrote, "When a sieve is shaken, the refuse appears; so do a person's faults when he or she speaks" or "Its fruit discloses the cultivation of a tree; so a person's speech discloses the cultivation of the mind." The final observation would save us from much embarrassment, "Do not praise anyone before she or he speaks, for this is the way people are tested" (Sir 27: 4, 6, 7).

The reading forms a background to a wisdom saying from the Jesus tradition, "for it is out of the abundance of the heart that the mouth speaks" (Lk 6:45).

We could approach the gospel reading from the context of the responsibility so many have within the Christian community to teach, guide, and accompany others in the journey of life. To teach, guide, or accompany is part and parcel of all aspects of our life. Older people, people with experience, with education, with expertise, with roles and responsibilities fulfill these roles in society, church, and family. We shall pay attention to the Christian dimension of discharging these responsibilities. We think of the family, educational institutions, parishes, groups, and dioceses.

Jesus spells out some rather simple and basic principles. The blind cannot guide (6:39). People without self-awareness of their own vulnerability, ignorance, sinfulness, and needs cannot guide (6:41–42). A person who has not listened to the teachers of life is unable to teach, guide, or accompany others (6:40). Finally, we all, in whatever "teaching" role we assume, must look at our own hearts. Has our heart become a treasure chest of goodness, wisdom, and the gospel? If we are blind, have big "logs" in our eyes, have gathered plenty of rubbish in our hearts, and not allowed life and the teachers of life to mold us, then we are not able to fulfill roles in family, education, and human society. These require wisdom and a vision learned from Jesus Christ.

Jesus is not just being a wise person as he teaches. This group of sayings is to be related to what he taught in last Sunday's gospel. The eye that sees, the pupil who has learned from the teacher, the eye that can see clearly, being rid of "logs," and the heart that has become a treasury, refer to men and women who have listened to Jesus' teaching. This teaching includes his words on the boundaries of love, the depths of generosity, the foolishness of forgiveness, and the desire to become "children of the Father" who is merciful to the ungrateful and wicked.

There are other aspects of Jesus' teaching that can be found in Luke. These also are to mold our hearts. Parents and teachers, old and young, business people, men and women responsible for public life, priests and bishops…need to hear these warnings of Jesus. The blind cannot lead the blind. A priest who does not know how to interpret the Word, who does not read good theological literature, who does not learn about the human person and does not study the movements in modern life, is unable to guide the people to whom he is responsible. We can make similar reflections for parents, teachers. We must include the Christian dimension. Jesus' vision of life touches the most basic aspects of human life.

We conclude this week our readings about the resurrection. At the center of our Christian faith is the hope of eternal life, "to be with the Lord for ever." Death, with all its pain, mystery, and loneliness is not really an obstacle to hope.

What is an obstacle to hope is our own history of sin. However, Paul assured his community that we have no reasons for fear. He spelled out the basis of all hope writing, "thanks be to God, who gives us the victory through our Lord Jesus Christ" (1 Cor 15:57).

TENTH SUNDAY IN ORDINARY TIME: YEAR C Luke 7:11-17

The Authentic Mark of a Prophet

The actors who enter upon the stage during our worship today are God, prophets, and widows. These three groups will occupy our attention. Some among the worshiping community will surely be faced with great pain and distress. The vision of God in the hearts of some will be smudged and faded. Some will not really expect too much of God. Others will be living with God and Jesus Christ in those deep realms of the human spirit in faith, hope, and gratitude. There is something for all in our liturgy.

The reading from 1 Kg 17:17-24 and the gospel are well crafted and dramatic narratives. At times a celebrant or commentator ought to remind the community to pay attention also to the literary beauty of our Scripture. The narrative about Elijah and the widow, whose only son has died while the prophet is her guest, belongs to a series of popular religious stories ("legends"). God has determined that Israel will face drought (17:1-7), and Elijah becomes the guest of a widow who is totally impoverished because of the drought. She is about to prepare her last meal for herself and her son (17:8-23). Though the jar with the little flour and the cruet of enough oil to cook a meal remain the same, yet her son suddenly dies and she complains bitterly to Elijah. We witness his ritual of intercession and the recovery of the son. The woman's faith response is the climax: "Now I know that you are a man of God and that the word of the Lord in your mouth is truth." We face a God who has power over life and death and a God who remains close to us in prophetic figures. There is also the affirmation of the authenticity of the prophetic word. The woman's faith is contrasted to the king's lack of faith.

The psalm forms a bridge between this scene and our gospel. We can imagine the two widows praying the psalm. There is that interplay between anguished cries, gratitude, trust, and praise. The prayer gathers up the experience of suffering and comfort, finding meaning in life in the midst of pain.

Reading the gospel, it is important to follow the story line, or simple plot. Two crowds meet. At the center of one is Jesus. At the center of the other is a dead man being carried out for burial, and his mother. They meet at the two gates. We are told that the mother was a widow and the man her only son. Our attention is directed to Jesus. We watch Jesus and note his face and words to the widow, his deep compassion. He acts decisively and simply. He moves forward. He touches the stretcher. He says those simple words. The man sits up and speaks. We are inclined to stop here. However, Jesus directs our attention to the widow since we are told "Jesus gave him back to his mother."

The crowd helps us to understand the scene and

Luke's catechesis. They are aware that Jesus of Nazareth has brought them face to face with God. There is a sense of awe (fear as reverential awe), a spontaneous acknowledgment ("They glorified God"). This is put into simple words: "A great prophet has risen among us!" and "God has looked favorably [visited] on his people."

Often Christians conclude that the crowd spoke in this way because Jesus raised the dead man. However, the key to the narrative is Jesus' relationship to the widow. Widows are very vulnerable persons in traditional societies and often are reduced to scavenging and begging for their food. A widow whose only son has died is really vulnerable and on the very margin of society. This is the point of the narrative. Jesus has understood the mystery of God and has discerned and acted in such a way that he deserves to be call "a great prophet." If Elijah spoke the truth of God as a man of God, Jesus acted as a man of God and revealed God as the God of the vulnerable, the broken, those on the margin of society. Such a God is preeminently trustworthy. The compassion of God was tangible in Jesus.

We begin the reading of Galatians this Sunday (1:11–19). The letter is clearly polemical. There are two major issues. Both the authenticity of the gospel that Paul preached to the Gentiles and his own role and authority as an apostle are under attack. The issues are interrelated. In the opening verse Paul jumps into the fray, "Paul an apostle—sent neither by human commission nor human authorities, but through Jesus Christ and God the Father" (1:1). In the opening verse of our reading, he joins issue with the second aspect of the opposition to his ministry. He writes:"For I want you to know, brothers and sisters, that the gospel that was proclaimed by me is not of human origin; for I did not receive it from a human source, nor was I taught it, but received it through a revelation of Jesus Christ" (1:11).

With sarcastic astonishment, he has taunted his community, bewitched by the "gospel" of his opponents (1:6–10). Jewish Christians are insisting that Gentiles must be integrated within Judaism. Circumcision and those observances of Law, which identify the Jew, are essential. These include food laws and the many laws dealing with ritual purity.

Paul responds with an autobiographical account of his experience of Jesus Christ. God has enabled him to grasp that Jesus is the Son in and through whom God has revealed his saving purpose for all. He also includes as gifts from God his mission to the Gentiles and his independence from all those who were apostles before him. God's initiative is affirmed, an initiative similar to his initiative in the vocation of prophets like Jeremiah. The eternal purpose and utter graciousness of God have come to expression in that religious experience that is the core of Paul's life. God has revealed his Son to/in him. God has enabled Paul, who had judged that the crucified Jesus of Nazareth was a blasphemer, cursed by God and a false messiah, to understand that precisely the crucified Jesus is God's Son. Paul's devotion to Jesus Christ and gratitude to God are central to his spirituality. He is a great Christian.

ELEVENTH SUNDAY IN ORDINARY TIME: YEAR C Luke 7:36—8:3

A Surprising Model for Discipleship

We enter the "upside down" world of Jesus in today's gospel (Lk 7:36—8:3). There are a number of important contrasts in our readings. The first is between the sinful woman and the sinful king. The story of Nathan confronting David after his adultery and the consequent deceit and willful murder of Uriah has been chosen as a background (2 Sam 12:7–10, 13). David turns to God only when brought face to face with his gross sinfulness by Nathan. The meanness and callousness of his actions are thrown into his face through a simple story. David's actions are contrasted with God's graciousness and generosity toward him. Only then does David confess, "I have sinned against the Lord." The sinful prostitute is a much more noble person. She could pray the psalm chosen as a responsorial (Ps 29/30). She knows the journey from sinfulness via confession to peace and joy.

The second comparison is quite shocking. Though the image of priests and religious men has come in for some battering in recent years (no more than can be found in our long history), yet they are respected. In Jesus' world the Pharisee symbolized the religiously good person. They were held in high regard. Remember that that society was far more "religious" than modern western society. The Pharisee would be the guru, the mullah, the ascetic, the holy man in traditional societies. He is compared with a prostitute! What shame he must have experienced and what a shock and scandal for his friends.

Let us go back to the beginning of the narrative, again a literary masterpiece. A Pharisee has invited Jesus to a formal evening meal. We need to see a room with couches and the diners seated to the right of Simon in order of importance. The meal would consist probably of two parts, the actual meal and then a time for conversation, entertainment, and discussion over some cups of wine.

Luke describes the setting with a long description of the unabashed and endless display of devotion by the woman from the city, "a sinner." The critical moment arises when the narrator reveals Simon's inner thoughts. There was no need to mention his estimation of the woman. According to his judgment Jesus ought to have at least publicly disassociated himself from her and spoken harsh words of judgment upon her. If he was a prophet he would have assessed her life from God's perspective. Note how Luke highlights the point that the woman was touching Jesus. She was a source of pollution. Many of us have difficulty in grasping that mentality and culture where pollution and ritual impurity are major considerations.

Once the setting is set, our attention turns to Jesus and Simon. Polite and respectful as he ought to be as host, Simon is ready to hear Jesus, "Speak, teacher." Jesus is a good storyteller. The story is simple, with simple and stark contrasts. (A denarius is the daily wage of ordinary workers). The person with the greater debt would be more devoted to his creditor and hold him in greater esteem (love).

Simon did not expect the contrast between his behavior and the prostitute. He had broken all the expected norms of hospitality. Her lavish and continuous devotion is contrasted with the no water, no welcoming "kiss," and no perfumed oil. Such lavishness is indicative of a forgiveness of sin, many sins indeed, that she has experienced. We are not told how she experienced that she was forgiven. The contrast between Simon and the woman is indirect and so causes more embarrassment and is more pointed. Little sense of sinfulness, little forgiveness, and little devotion.

We need to remain with Simon. It is easier to identify with the woman. We can reenact her part. However, to see ourselves as contemporary Simons is more difficult. Jesus is concerned with "the Simon" in all of us.

The conclusion in some way forgets what has just happened. Jesus talks directly to the woman. He offers her the forgiveness of God. We get a glimpse of his own self-awareness according to Luke. He is able to mediate God's forgiveness to others. He recognizes and affirms her faith, that reaching out to God made present to her through Jesus, a genuine prophet. She has the same image of God, the compassionate and forgiving God as Jesus has. Jesus also extends to her the key blessing of God, peace, that inner wholeness and dignity God wishes we all possess. However, the narrator reminds us again that Jesus is the cause of scandal, and a question hangs in the air, "Who is this who even forgives sins?"

We do not want to load ourselves with guilt. Yet, we do not want to be Simons. We are all sinners. As we celebrate the Eucharist and look around us, as we walk in the streets, read the papers, comment on others we see on TV, we share in the sinfulness of our human family. We pray for that faith that leads us to Jesus Christ and to God. Those simple words, "Lord be merciful to me, a sinner" are meant to create and nourish the blessing of peace in our hearts as we search for truth in our confession of sinfulness.

The opening verses of the next chapter (8:1–3) preserve a precious memory of the women who were among the major disciples of Jesus. They accompanied him during his ministry, were present at Calvary until his death, and came to the tomb on the first day of the week. They became the first witnesses to the resurrection (23:49, 55; 24:1–11). None of these women are to be identified with the sinful women. Most of the women had experienced God's healing mercy and power through Jesus' ministry.

TWELFTH SUNDAY IN ORDINARY TIME: YEAR C Luke 9:18–24

"Who Am I?"

As we listen to today's gospel (Lk 9:18–24) we are like people who have missed about seven episodes of a carefully constructed drama or TV serial (not one of the endlessly repetitious soap operas!). We shall make a summary. The gospel itself is constructed around the "who" of Jesus of Nazareth. The crowds have come to some opinions—John the Baptist reappeared, Elijah, or one of the ancient prophets. The disciples estimate that Jesus is the anointed of God (Messiah of God). Jesus' self-awareness is contrasted with these two groups. He sees himself as the Son of Man who, in God's strong intention and purpose, must undergo great suffering, be rejected by those who hold real power among his people, and killed. Yet he will not be abandoned by God. He will live again.

Jesus agrees in a manner with his disciples and yet sees a grave danger in their perception. This grave danger will continue to dog them. At his actual death they will be so scandalized that their hopes will be shattered. The two on their journey away from Jerusalem to Emmaus will typify this scandal. His suffering and death are inexplicable and irreconcilable with all their hopes. Yet Jesus has grown to realize and to accept that to be the anointed of God within human history as it is he must be killed.

He also realized that the lives of his authentic followers must have a basic characteristic. Otherwise he cannot entrust to them the responsibility his Father has given to him. He had made and continued to live the basic choice between the self and God, or between mammon and God, or between the world and God, or between human cultural and religious traditions, prejudices and God. His disciples also had to make that basic choice: to live with open hands and hearts, ready to lose everything, however precious, to be authentic to the truth lived and taught by Jesus of Nazareth. This would entail "daily" choices and being "daily" out of tune with the values, attitudes, and ways of living of so many other people in their environment. By means of a paradox, Jesus places this choice before all his disciples: to save self is to lose the self but to lose the self is to save the self. He reformulates this basic attitude in the proverb about gaining/losing the world and the self. Leunig has expressed this basic choice in a forceful way in these words from one of his prayers:

> There are two feelings. Love and fear.
> There are two languages. Love and fear.
> There are only two activities. Love and fear.

In love we find ourselves and in fear we lose ourselves. Love is to follow him. Fear is to be lost in the cautious value of the closed, damaged, and small human heart. Jesus lived from love. His world attempted to frighten and control him by fear. We pray that we may move more and more away from fear into the highways and byways of the love lived by Jesus the Lord and so truly be his disciples.

The first reading (Zech 12:10–12) illustrates the weakness of the lectionary. A piece of a text, an uncertain and therefore problematic text, has been chosen to form some background to Jesus' future death. The citizens of Jerusalem will enter upon ritual mourning for a prophetic/Davidic or unknown figure, the victim of violent clashes between groups in their city around the 450s B.C.E. The victim will be recognized as a man of God. The psalm, expressing deep yearning for God accompanied by trust and praise, is a beautiful prayer. However, it is not too relevant to the theme of the reading.

The text from Galatians (3:26–29) is very rich. The prior argument has been omitted. To be "children of God," namely, to belong to the chosen people, demanded a bond with Abraham the primordial ancestor and recipient of the original promise. Paul has argued with a logic of his contemporaries that Christ is the key descendant of Abraham since he is the promised and genuine "seed" of Abraham. He alone is able to pass on the inheritance promised to Abraham. United to Christ in baptism, his disciples are the children of God and heirs. The key decision is to accept Jesus Christ as the person promised by God and in and through whom God acts. This is ritualized in baptism. Paul explores some of the implications of this decision.

Our surrender to Christ creates a new mode of existence, a Christ mode of existence. He uses the image taken from baptismal practice of "being clothed with." He wants to indicate that we are transformed. He spells this out. The basic divisions in human life, created by human society and experienced by all, are dissolved and transcended. Religious divisions (Jew/Gentile), socioeconomic divisions (slave/free) and gender divisions (male/female) continue to exist and yet in another sense are transcended and all become ONE in Christ. There are many implications from this simple and yet fundamental truth. There is so much discrimination, so many ways division is fostered, structured, nourished, and protected in society and by the churches at all levels of their life and policies.

THIRTEENTH SUNDAY IN ORDINARY TIME: YEAR C Luke 9:51–62

The Decisive Choice...Misguided Disciples

Again we have jumped ahead in our narrative. Let us fill in the missing episodes. Having accepted that suffering and death are on the path ahead if he is to be true to his mission, Jesus enters into prayer. As his mission began with an experience of God, who missioned and empowered him, so at this crucial juncture in that mission God affirms Jesus (the transfiguration, Lk 9:28–36). The scene underlines the future "exodus" of Jesus in Jerusalem (Moses and Elijah speak of his exodus) and the importance of his recent and future instructions on discipleship ("listen to him"). Jesus is found to be just Jesus, and he returns to his ministry with the exorcism of the epileptic boy (Lk 9:37–42). The crowd again intuited God's healing power mediated by Jesus and so "were astounded at the greatness of God" (9:43b). This created a dangerous situation. With characteristic simplicity and starkness, Jesus spoke again of his death. However, Luke notes that the disciples were really at sea. He writes: "they did not understand this saying; its meaning was concealed from them, so that they could not perceive it" (9:45). Therefore we are not surprised that they could have a heated argument about which one of them was the "greatest." The child is the symbol of greatest as Jesus says, "the least among all of you is the greatest."

We rejoin Jesus. A new milestone commences. We are told that "he set his face to go to Jerusalem" (9:51).

A short digression: at this point in the narrative Luke's Jesus begin his journey to Jerusalem. This journey is the frame for Luke to gather much of the teaching and some healing ministry, some common to Matthew and much peculiar to the Lukan tradition. The journey motif and its destiny in Jerusalem dominate the narrative (9:51; 13:22; 14:25; 17:11; 18:31; 19:11, 19, 28; see on Jerusalem 9:51; 13:22, 33–35; 17:11; 18:31; 19:11, 28). Jerusalem is the city of his destiny where as a prophet he must be killed (13:33–34) and the city that will be the end of his historical life and his exodus and the beginning of his presence with the believing community after his return to his Father. As we follow the long journey narrative we must remember that it is a construct of Luke, and Jesus seems to go in circles and not move ahead at all at places in the narrative.

Gradually Luke will draw a picture of the disciple of Jesus. Already last week we saw the type of commitment demanded (9:23–25) and the criteria to measure greatness (9:46–48). The shortest way to go to Jerusalem was through Samaria. However, since Jesus is making a pilgrimage to Jerusalem a Samaritan refuses to give him hospitality for the night. Ancient socioreligious antagonism explains this. For us it is good to see Jesus caught up in the human situation where memories of conflict, injustice, and discrimination have not been healed. How hard to heal memories that are embedded in racial and group conflicts and injustice.

John and James have concluded that Jesus is a prophet. To refuse a prophet of God ought to be punished. Imitating Elijah of old (2 Kgs 1:10) they would like to call down God's judgment. Jesus rebukes them. Very ancient manuscripts of the gospel add a saying that reflects the spirit and mind of Jesus. He says to them, "You do not know what spirit you are of, for the Son of Man did not come to destroy the lives of human beings but to save them." Church history, even recent history, tells us that the Christian communities have so often followed James and John and not Jesus. Jesus has given another lesson in discipleship. He has more to say on the subject.

To understand the three following sayings of Jesus on discipleship we need to pay attention to three points. Jesus is on the way to Jerusalem to his death, and his commitment to the kingdom of God entails his suffering and death. To follow Jesus, namely to be a disciple, means to have a vision of human life as God wants it to be lived and to be unconditionally committed to be involved in the realization of this vision of human society. Finally Jesus' sayings are paradoxical and symbolic. He compares two values. The human value chosen must be both a primary and obligatory human value. Contrasting following him and the commitment to the kingdom of God with this noble value, he does not deny the value. Rather he indicates that following himself and commitment to the kingdom are values all by themselves, and before them all other values must give place and are relativized and secondary. Jesus' values are in a category by themselves because they involve our fundamental response to God.

The enthusiastic person, ready to follow "wherever Jesus goes" is made to reflect. The Son of Man offers no security at all. The person called by Jesus is shocked by the apparent harshness of Jesus' remark, "Let the dead bury their own dead, but you go and proclaim the kingdom of God." Here we find that paradoxical contrast between two great realities drawn with a brutal harshness. The final example of inadequate grasp of discipleship is clarified by the first reading (1 Kgs 19:16, 19–21).

Elijah, having run away from his mission and God, is brought face to face with God in the "gentle breeze"(19:13). One of his future duties is to anoint Elisha as his successor. Meeting Elisha plowing, he transfers his prophetic role to him with the symbolic placing his mantle on him. However, Elisha is not resolute and want to go and and "kiss his father and his mother" and then come. Elijah is not interested in such a disciple. Elisha gets the message and makes an irrevocable break with his previous life, killing his animals and giving a royal party to the people. Jesus also wants such irrevocable decisiveness.

FOURTEENTH SUNDAY IN ORDINARY TIME: YEAR C Luke 10:1–12, 17–20

The Layperson in the Church

I have been puzzled how to write a commentary of this Sunday's readings. The opening reading (Is 66:10–14) with its accompanying psalm (Ps 65/66) are interrelated and yet provide little meaningful background to the gospel. I have decided to read the gospel from the perspective of Jesus instructing laypeople today to continue his mission.

The reading from Isaiah is full of beautiful imagery. Jerusalem as the central city of the Jewish people and the symbol of God's presence, his promises, and fidelity, is compared to a mother who comforts and nourishes her children who are in despair. The people are deeply disturbed by the miserable state of the city after their return from exile. Jerusalem is a petty city. God promises to make it prosperous and the center of the world. All the exiles will return. Mourning will be changed into rejoicing. The psalmist celebrates in a vibrant hymn of praise the great saving deed of God for his people. He mentions the momentous memory of the exodus from slavery and the continuous experience of God's actions in the cycles of oppression and misery they have experienced.

We turn to the gospel. The actual text is an instruction of Jesus Christ to seventy disciples. It repeats aspects of an earlier instruction given to the twelve (9:1–6, 10–11). The actual instruction combines sayings of Jesus with sayings of the risen Lord created by the prophets of the early Christian communities and adapted to the needs of their itinerant preachers. We are told that the seventy were sent to places "where he himself intended to go" (10:1). I shall not go through the whole interpretative process whereby we move from the situation of Jesus' life and the life of the early communities to our situation today.

We know that the layperson today goes into those areas of human life where "Jesus intends to go," and laypeople go in his name. We will read the instructions as a small handbook for lay ministry. The first saying about harvest being plentiful and laborers few is very relevant. We must pray and act in the church that more and more laypeople become aware of their vocation to be leaven within human society. There must be more and more conscious and enlightened Christian presence and action by all women and men who are disciples of Jesus.

We look at the world around us. There are many good people, great movements, outstanding figures with deep commitments to the quality of human life. However there are also ideologies, movements, structures, groups who promote in various ways a culture of death. Christians are in many ways like "lambs" in the midst of "wolves." There are great promoters of evil in our society.

It would be rather foolish to tell laypeople to go to work on a bicycle, with no wallet, no credit cards, no insurance (Jesus' no bag, no sandals) and to isolate themselves from others ("greet no one on the way"). However, the symbols indicate a sense of urgency. There are many spheres of modern life where there is a real sense of urgency to promote values worthy of the human person, to respond to crises, government policies, international issues, the state of life for marginal groups. In the life of each person and in the span of each generation there is that urgency of the present time. Each person and generation of Christians are responsible in the short span of time of their lives.

Jesus sends his disciples into houses and into towns. There is the area of family, neighborhood, school, and institutional life and there is the larger scene of town, city, state, and national life. God is concerned for all the scenes of human life. The true disciple is enabled to bring peace and to make the kingdom of God present. These two are related to each other. The more a human community, whatever be its size, moves toward truth, to the protection and promotion of human rights, has concrete commitment to the discards of society, to reconciliation and forgiveness, to equity and justice, to racial, social, and religious harmony, the more such a society is according to God's purpose. The disciple of Jesus is a person committed to the human. The gospel Jesus taught is the affirmation of all that is noble and genuine.

The commitment of Jesus to human society and history also includes an attitude of judgment, prophetic denunciation, and uncompromising confrontation with evil. We do not have to wipe off "the dust of your town that clings to our feet" but legitimate, clear, strong, consistent, organized public denunciation, opposition to all forms of evil is a part of the layperson's responsibility. The Christian community is to be leaven within society and a prophetic voice in the midst of evil, indifference, half truths, and corruption.

Many committed laypeople will know the experience of "your peace" returning to them. Rejection in various forms is an essential aspect of Christian presence and action in society. We also experience the ways human society and the lives of men and women, nature, and our natural resources are being destroyed because of evil. We witness to the reality of the destruction of Sodom being replayed in our days.

The gospel texts skip some verses (9:13–16), and we are told of the joy of the disciples who return to Jesus (9:17–20). What is important in the verses is that realization that the power of God is greater than the power of evil. We enter into the world as leaven with hope and with that reassurance that Jesus Christ and his Spirit are with us. We live our lives associated in the great venture of God in human history, and we share in the responsibilities entrusted to Jesus of Nazareth. Our "names are written in heaven," namely we belong at the heart of God's family because we are accepting and living out the responsibility he has given us for the quality of human life today in all spheres of human society.

FIFTEENTH SUNDAY IN ORDINARY TIME: YEAR C Luke 10:25–37

The Disciple—Being Neighbor

We have an open society, quite tolerant and allowing a lot of social mobility, yet there are social boundaries and racial boundaries. In the church we do make distinctions between good and bad Catholics, the married and the divorced and remarried, the one-parent families, the practicing and nonpracticing. In all our lives, we do have those who are "in" and those who are "out." The basis for social distinctions and discrimination differ. We could explore this area today.

The gospel challenges some of the social boundaries our culture upholds. The teaching of Jesus interacts with culture and customs, attitudes, behavior, and societal structures that, even if sanctioned by religion, are not according to his teaching.

We could read the narrative as if it were a TV interview. Jesus is being interviewed by someone trying to trap him on his views about the key to success in human life. What do you think a person must do to "inherit eternal life"? Instead of answering the question, he throws it back to the interviewer. "In our religious tradition what is said?" he inquires. The interviewer gives a great answer, combining Deut 6:2 and Lev 19:18. Jesus is a bit smart then. He simply says, "Do this and you will live" (you will find great meaning in life, great joy, and be really a genuine human person). Before we continue, note that the man combines two parts of the Jewish tradition into what is called the double commandment. This is not Jesus' contribution to religious history.

The interviewer is taken aback and wants to get the upper hand. Therefore, he asks a twister, "Who is my neighbor?" He would want to know within what social boundaries Jesus would operate. Will he choose occupation, gender, race, religion, socioeconomic status to define the boundaries of a person's neighbor? Jesus becomes again the storyteller. His choice of characters is masterly and so is the economy of his language. Priest and Levite belong to the respected group in society. What differentiates the characters is that two "see" and then "pass by on the other side." The third differs in two ways. He is a despised Samaritan. I am sure the interviewer would like an anti-clerical twist to the story and have the third a journalist or TV personality!! The Samaritan belongs to that human group who "see," "have compassion," and "go up to." With a few deft descriptive phrases, Jesus draws a picture of the practical expressions of compassion. Note there is nothing lavish or expensive in what he does. A little antiseptic, a band-aid and an inexpensive place with ordinary meals for a recovery.

There is another character. We know nothing about him. We may like to know what language he spoke, what he did, which political party he belonged to, where he worshiped and drank beer. We only know that he represents all those who "lie on the road half dead." He may be an AIDS victim, single mother, a parent who has not found in the church a God she can worship, an alcoholic, an irresponsible parent, a thief, a lonely old man, a refugee.

Jesus completes his story with the usual question. Note the interviewer is uncomfortable. He does not want to acknowledge that the indigenous person is a model for the true human person. However, his avoidance is precious. Instead of saying "the Samaritan," he says "the one who showed mercy." Jesus quietly ends the interview with a second " Go and do likewise."

Later the interviewer realizes that Jesus never answered his question, or did he? He wanted to know "who is my neighbor?" Jesus forced out of him the opinion of the bashed man about who had been neighbor to him. Jesus taught him three lessons for life. First, there are no boundaries with which we can define "neighbor." Anyone in need is our neighbor. To love the neighbor means we need to be willing "to see," to have hearts that can feel compassion, and be ready to express mercy in ordinary and practical ways.

This is at the core of human life. The reading from Dt 30:10–14 is chosen to remind us that the core demand on every human person is not something exotic, abstruse, and esoteric. We are reminded that if we journey within to our own interiority we will find this written in our being. The psalm, a fine example of an intense and urgent prayer of a needy person conscious of the fidelity, lovingkindness, and attentiveness of God, is not so apt for the themes of the readings.

We commence today reading Colossians. The passage chosen is a magnificent hymn of praise (Col 1:15–20). I am sure the writer of the letter would be quite annoyed at the few pieces chosen over the next four Sundays from his powerful letter. The opening prayer of thanksgiving and petition for the community is skipped. At the end of the prayer Paul wants the community to be deeply grateful to the Father who has rescued them from darkness. He has taken them into the community (kingdom) of the Son of his love who is the source of redemption and forgiveness for them. The writer is captivated by the relationship between the Father and "the Son of his love."

We make some comments on the hymn. God is always the beginning and end of all in each part of the New Testament when writers speak of Jesus Christ. Jesus Christ is the Son through and in whom God acts in history. In this text, the totality of God's saving power and love comes to expression in Jesus Christ. In the Son "all the fullness of God was pleased to dwell" (1:19; 2:9). Son has a unique relationship to God. He is the image of God, the firstborn of all creation and "from the dead." The writer considers two great theaters of God's action, creation and re-creation (redemption). God created everything, all the cosmic powers and all that exists, through and in the Son. He maintains the unity of all creation and is preeminent in all ways within creation. Here the author is using the reflections of wisdom writers about God as creator and wisdom.

The Son also is preeminent in the church as Head (symbol of sovereign authority). The Son has also primacy in God's redemptive work as in and though him in his death on the cross all is reconciled to God, and peace is created within the universe.

This profound reflection of Jesus Christ within the mystery of God the Father's action and sovereignty with the whole of human history needs silent pondering and quiet wonder. Such is the Lord of our lives, and we are his disciples. We are asked to help men and women experience within human society, the reconciliation and peace he has won today by our love for others, especially those "left dying by the roadside."

SIXTEENTH SUNDAY IN ORDINARY TIME: YEAR C Luke 10:38–42

The Disciple—To Hear The Word

Our liturgy of the Word opens with a great story of hospitality. We enter the world of a peasant or semi-nomadic extended family and the importance of welcoming guests who pass by your tent. Abraham is the model host. Offering to bring a "little" water to wash and a "little" bread, he rushes off and gets the whole family to work to produce a banquet with plenty of bread, a great tender roast, curds, and milk. He is rewarded when the guests promise that his barren wife will have a child. Note that Sarah keeps inside.

The psalm draws a broad picture of a noble and good person who can stand before God without any great reasons for shame. It is implied that Abraham is such a person, and his hospitality is just an expression of the nobility of his personality.

The gospel could create some problems if we do not see the main contrast and follow Luke's manner of presenting Jesus' teaching. We have to begin with a clear idea of the centrality of hospitality in the lives of Jewish people and the role a woman is expected to have in the society. The contrast is between the busy Martha and the quiet Mary. Martha is intent to welcome and entertain the guests in a fitting manner and ought to be praised for all her efforts. Mary deserves to be scolded. Martha's complaint to Jesus sets the stage for Jesus' saying. Again we are in his "upside down" world. Mary is sitting and listening to Jesus' word. In comparison to listening to the word of Jesus, hospitality can be described as "being worried and distracted about many things." Note that Abraham could also be described as being worried and busy about many things. We are again taken into another world of values.

Listening to the Word is a theme in Luke. Jesus is the one who has the Word of God. To listen to the Word of God taught by Jesus is a primary value. Jesus is pictured as responding to the crowd's eager desire "to hear the word of God" when he teaches from Peter's boat (5:1-3), and Peter and companions are called to carry on the speaking of the Word of God. All his teaching can be described as the "Word of God." People respond in various ways to the Word (8:11-15—Sower and Seed). The genuine family of Jesus are those "who hear the Word of God and keep it" (8: 21).

Our initial reflection could be about the obligations of pastoral assistants, catechists, and priests to be women and men of the Word of God. This would include reading and studying the Word and praying over the Word. This will also entail his or her being able to make the Word of "yesterday" a living Word for today and ensuring that the Word is well read in the liturgy. Attention needs to paid to the commentary that introduces the reading of the Word and is meant to prepare the community to hear the Word. There is so much good literature available now and yet many priests and others are really out of date in their understanding of the Scripture.

The Word must be part of the lives of all Jesus' disciples. It is hard to sit and read, sit and listen to the Word. To make "quiet time," to have personal time, to create "a sabbath" in the midst of our busy lives is not easy. Yet today this is the invitation of the gospel. Really it is more than an invitation. The disciple is one who "hears the Word" and "does the Word." We need to spend time with our Bible. We need to have a good Bible, one we can use. Often we need a small one we can carry around or use easily. One of the responsibilities of Christians is to nourish themselves with the Word of God. This will mean to take time to read or attend some courses so that we know how to read and interpret the Bible. Catholic Christians are not too good at this. We are better now, but still have a long way to go. The Word of God is the main source of knowledge of Jesus Christ and discipleship and of nourishment in prayer for us.

We also note that the narrative is about two women. To use the value of hospitality as a background to affirm the centrality of hearing the word Jesus needed a situation in which women are involved. We ought not to press the text too far in developing the theme of Jesus and women. However, the text does affirm that women are important to Jesus and his ministry. The Word of God is for all. He does not follow the normal custom of his time in this affirmation.

The second reading is from Colossians (Col 1:24–28). After indicating to the community how they have shared in the reconciliation gained by Christ (1:21–23), Paul turns to his own ministry. I judge that the author is a close associate of Paul and is writing in his name and about Paul who is in prison. Since Jesus suffered in his ministry, all who share his ministry must suffer. This suffering is effective for the faith life of the community. Paul stresses that he is a chosen servant of God's Word. This gospel of God is the mystery of his plan for salvation. The aspect he highlights here to this non-Jewish community is the universality of God's action in and through Jesus Christ. All that he has done in and through Jesus Christ is for all. The Gentile believers are united with Jesus Christ, who is their hope. One of the writer's concerns in the letter is that they remain faithful to their initial faith commitment to Jesus Christ. We do not share the shock of Paul who grew up in a very exclusive religious tradition. This erroneous sense of exclusivism is to be found still in Christianity and in Islam in some places and countries. That the non-Jew was loved by God and could belong to God's people was something that amazed Paul. The passion of his life was to proclaim such a God to all. He affirmed that before God, who was in no way partial, all were equal. There could be food for thought for us today since we may tend to see our Christian community as an exclusive club.

SEVENTEENTH SUNDAY IN ORDINARY TIME: YEAR C Luke 11:1–13

The Disciple—Living a life of Prayer

We move this Sunday from listening to the Word of God to our personal life of prayer. Abraham and his guests again form the background (Gn 18:16–32). The three guests leave accompanied by Abraham. We learn that one is the Lord and the others are "two men" who later become angels. Our reading is only interested in the dialogue between God and Abraham. God has heard of the evils of Sodom and Gomorrah. He intends to destroy the cities if the report is correct. The text itself is concerned with the role of just persons in the midst of evil. Even ten just citizens can save the whole city. In addition, the question of God's reputation is at stake. Is God a vindictive God, merciless and unmoved by human goodness? Finally, the text affirms the importance of the intercessory prayer of the righteous for the world. God is portrayed like a great king, and Abraham is a trusted and favorite courtier. He approaches the king with respect and with daring. The Judge of all the earth is proved to be just because even ten good people can protect a whole city from deserved judgment. (We may like to move from ten to one!)

The psalm is an appealing prayer of praise and trust by a poor person whose prayer has been heard (Ps 137/138). I do not find it so easy to identify Abraham with this psalmist. There is a great verse that moves me: "Your steadfast Love, O Lord, endures forever. Do not forsake the work of your hands."

As we consider prayer in our lives, we can pause and see the place of prayer in Jesus' life as described by Luke. The prayer to the Father that he gives to his disciples is the fruit of his own prayer. In addition, the great religious tradition in which he lived molded him. We shall develop the theme of Jesus at prayer.

We must remember that we are using a good measure of guesswork. We depend on the way Luke has interpreted Jesus. We also take seriously the true human life of Jesus. The mystery of his being divine remains incomprehensible to us. However, we must respect the integrity of his human life. Journeying in faith, discerning God's will in concrete circumstances, and making true and appropriate decisions are all part of human life.

We know really nothing about Jesus before his appearance at the Jordan. The movement of renewal begun by John for some reason attracted Jesus. He would have searched to know what this meant for his own life. We are told that in a context of prayer he becomes aware that God has called him to a task greater and more crucial than John's task (3:21–22). He experiences the special gift of the Spirit and an awareness that now he must begin a new phase in his life. This leads him to a period of solitude in which he has a sharpened awareness of the power of evil and his own uncompromising determination to be totally faithful to God, now in a public way (4:1–11).

We shall indicate how prayer is part of the texture of Jesus' ministry. The ministry creates great enthusiasm. In this situation, Jesus clarifies the contours of his ministry. The eager crowds of Capernaum want to restrict his movements and work. After prayer he asserts the scope of his ministry: "I must proclaim the good news of the Kingdom of God to the other cities also; for I was sent for this purpose" (4:42–43). Prayer is an integral part of his ministry and the very enthusiasm and popularity make this an imperative. We are told that "more than ever the word about Jesus spread abroad; many crowds would gather to hear him and to be cured of their diseases." Jesus' response to this recurring situation is stated: "But he would withdraw to deserted places and pray" (5:15–16). His ability to discern when and whom to heal and exorcise and what was the way to interpret his religious and cultural traditions in the light of God's vision for human society were the fruits of his regular solitude and his being with the Father.

Early in the ministry he had affirmed its scope. He had to clarify further the meaning of his life. The idea of the "church" was born in prayer on an unknown "mountain" in Galilee. After a night in prayer we are told he chooses from his disciples "the Twelve" (6:12). This implies that he intended his own ministry to lead to the creation of a community. This community was to continue the work God has entrusted to him. God was to be within human history in a special way through Jesus' community or Jesus' movement.

As his ministry unfolded and he faced opposition and conflict, he became aware of the consequence of his life's work. He would have to suffer and probably die. After prayer, he decided to share with his disciples both the consequences for his own life as the anointed of God and the cost of discipleship. He was aware that they would not grasp what he really was telling them (9:18 and 9:21–27; cf. 9:44–46).

This was a turning point in Jesus' own life. Therefore, we find him again alone with God on a mountain (9:28). He has to absorb for himself the implications of suffering and probably death. (The gospel writers make very explicit what Jesus would have realized gradually as the opposition became more organized and outright.)

During this prayer, his Father confirms him and the way he is proclaiming the kingdom in his deeds and teaching with their clear, prophetic character.

EIGHTEENTH SUNDAY IN ORDINARY TIME: YEAR C Luke 12:13–21

The Lure of Wealth

Our liturgy of the Word opens with a good dose of cynicism, a note of disillusion (Eccl 1:2; 2:21–23). There is a certain meaningless in life. The endeavors of life are like chasing the wind (2:11). "What do people gain from all the toil at which they toil under the sun?" (1:3). Our reading selects one example. A person, who has worked hard with wisdom and skill and amassed a fortune, dies, and the fortune is enjoyed by someone else who has not lifted a finger. He does not know whether it will be used wisely or foolishly (2:18). While Qoheleth reflects on the vanity of a life of toil, in the gospel God mocks a wealthy person on the eve of his death. Who will enjoy all he has amassed? The reading forms some type of background for the gospel.

The psalm (Ps 94/95), though not really connected to the opening reading, has one line we need to underline. The psalmist invites others gathered for worship to acknowledge with praise and gratitude God, the creator, the reliable protector and faithful shepherd. The priest admonishes the worshipers. To these words we need to pay attention: "O that today you would listen to his voice! Do not harden your hearts...." We could avoid listening to the gospel.

The perennial problems of, and conflicts about, inheritance are fought out in our courts. There is another way to handle the problem. The unknown man of the gospel narrative takes this path. He asks a recognized wise person, a man of God to use his persuasive power and authority to convince his brother. Jesus rejects this job description. However, the situation is an occasion for a classical saying: "Take care! Be on your guard against all kinds of greed; for one's life does not consist in the abundance of possessions." This is not the saying to put up in the corporate boardroom. We would not find it in big letters in a shopping mall or in the stock exchange or at cattle sales. It ought to be on each advertisement like the mandatory warning about the dangers of smoking on all packs of cigarettes.

Jesus illustrates the deceptive nature of "the abundance of possessions" by a good popular story. The story is interesting because of the soliloquies. The wealthy farmer decides on a program of expansion. New silos for all his grain. In his security he can enjoy life. The popular saying he uses has a further line "for tomorrow we die" (cf. 1 Cor 15:32). That is actually his fate in the story. God speaks the important line: "You fool...." Jesus comments upon his story. He contrasts two major orientations in life—to store up treasures for the self and to be rich toward God.

This is the point of Jesus' saying. The second saying also would not find a place on advertisements for clothes, cars, foods, wines, holiday houses. Some ideas expressed by Leunig in a prayer are apt for reflection. He appeals to God, "God help us. With great skill and energy we have ignored the state of the human heart. With politics and economies, we have denied the heart's needs. With eloquence, wit and reason we have belittled the heart's wisdom... We cannot hear our heart's truth...." The whole prayer is quite moving.

To be rich to God means giving great attention to our hearts, to our own inner selves, and to our deeper needs. Various forms of hedonism, the craving for more and the newest and the latest, and a materialism that practically excludes God from our lives, kill the heart. Life is not to be found in abundance, in the latest, in a share portfolio, in going up the ladder.

The reading from Colossians spells out for us what it means to be rich toward God. Last week the writer described who the Christian person has become. In 2:16–23 he evaluates and discards many spurious religious practices, customs, forms of piety, pseudo-asceticism, and celebrations of feasts. In contrast, he spells out the contours of a genuine Christian life. The Christian is united to Christ with the deepest bonds. Therefore he says, "Your life is hidden with Christ in God." The inner reality of the Christian person is invisible to the eye and to ordinary reflection and experience. However, the transformation effected from union with Christ who is the source of the inner life of the person will be totally visible and known when Christ is finally revealed. Therefore, they must live according to a very different value system. We need to note that the phrase, "things that are above" does not refer to a type of escape from the reality of life. He wants to describe a difference in quality and uses the contrast between realms of reality, the "heavenly/ above" and the "earthly/below."

He describes this transformation by means of various contrasting categories. He chooses ethnic, religious, social status categories, and two groups who represent the primitive and uneducated. Christ recreates the human family. This new community must live in an appropriate manner. He gives an attractive list of great human qualities at whose center are love and reconciliation.

NINETEENTH SUNDAY IN ORDINARY TIME YEAR C Luke 12:32–48

The Disciple—The Challenge to be Faithful
Today's gospel is not easy to comment upon. The world from which the images come is quite foreign: masters and slaves, slaves within a household, wedding customs, watchmen at gates/doors. There is also in the background the thought of the foreseeable return of "the son of Man" and judgment. Fidelity and watchfulness are linked to reward and punishment. Not only is the cultural background strange but the text is a combination of short stories (parables), allusions to such stories, sayings, and observations. We hear both the voice of Jesus and the early Christian teachers reinterpreted by Luke. Finally, the selection of text combines sayings linked back to Lk 12:13–31 and a series of sayings on a new theme beginning with 12:35. The theme of the early section is indicated by Jesus' saying, "Take care! Be on your guard against all greed" (12:15) while the saying, "Be dressed for action" ("Keep your aprons on" [Fitzmyer]) and have your lamps lit introduce the saying on the need for continual and attentive readiness.

We shall begin with the sayings linked to the theme of greed (12:32–34). We need to recall some of the previous sayings related to anxiety. Jesus says to his disciples: "Therefore I tell you, do not worry about your life, what you will eat, or about your body, what you will wear. For life is more than food and the body more than clothing" (12:22–23). We shall omit his illustrations of the birds and the wildflowers and God's care. He concludes: "And do not keep striving for what you are to eat and what you are to drink, and do not keep worrying." He continues: "For it is the nations of the world that strive after all these things, and your Father knows that you need them. Instead, strive for his kingdom and these things will be given to you as well" (12:29, 30–31). To live in anxiety is a sign of "lack of faith" in the Father (12:28). The tenor of this teaching reminds us of the sayings with which Luke's Jesus interprets the parable of the sower. Jesus explains the seed that fell among the thorns in this way: "As for what fell among the thorns, these are the ones who hear; but as they go on their way, they are choked by the cares and riches and pleasures of life, and their fruit does not mature" (8:14). The seed is the Word of God.

Jesus again sets up a paradoxical contrast between the basic needs of life, food, drink, and clothing and the kingdom of God. The values of two worlds are contrasted. Our commitment to the Father and his kingdom that is his will is so basic and primary that no other consideration may relativize it or become an obstacle to this commitment. The anxiety for these basic needs is linked to "greed" and not being rich toward God. Heavy stuff indeed.

Jesus proceeds to reassure his community ("little flock"). The Father can be trusted. As a way of life in contrast to anxiety Jesus proposes, "sell your possessions" and give away the money as alms to the poor. In this way they are assured of entering into the Father's kingdom. The poor are seen as intercessors for their benefactors. Also such dispossession will be rewarded with the gift of eternal life. He is promoting an insurance policy. This is symbolized by "purses" that don't wear out and "treasures in heaven" protected from both moth and thieves. There is a reason. Jesus is concerned about the "heart," which for the Jewish people was the center of a person, the place of decision and source of fundamental orientation in life. Luke does not teach that everyone must sell all. However, this disposition is needed to offset the power of greed and that type of anxiety that eats into the commitment to search for and follow God's will.

The following sayings (12:35–48) revolve around the theme of readiness with the promised rewards and threats of punishment. Such readiness must be a permanent feature of the disciple's life. In our lives the unknown time of death would be a motive. Note the extraordinary description of the reward. A master returning from a wedding (his own?) who finds his slaves awake and alert whatever be the hour turns around and puts on his apron and serves them!

Peter's question highlights a special feature of this exhortation. Those who have been entrusted with greater responsibilities will be more accountable and more richly rewarded. The manager of the household who is faithful will be given charge over all his master's possessions. The punishment is proportionately severe. There is a word of caution here for all within the Christian community who are given greater responsibilities for the sake of the community. The reward/punishment theme probably will not appeal to many or function as a genuine motivation. The great dignity that God has given us as humans, and the gifts that we receive through Christ, as well as the extraordinary character of God's love challenge us to live in a manner worthy of such gifts with responsibility. Luke's Jesus spells out many aspects of the responsibility in the readings of this year.

The first reading and the psalm create a vague background for Jesus' teachings. A wise teacher reflects on the night of the Exodus (Wis 18:6–9). He emphasizes how the Chosen People were ready and waiting for God's coming and saving acts. In contrast the Egyptians (= the wicked/enemies) were caught totally unprepared. The verses from the psalm (Ps 32/33) celebrate God's goodness to those who fear the Lord and hope in his steadfast love.

The reading from Hebrews (Heb 12:8–19) celebrates the ancestors as exemplary figures of belief, fidelity, and hope. We have a role of honor and fitting eulogies for each. These men and women were committed to God, to his goodness and his fidelity to his promises. In their own lives, they responded in appropriate ways in diverse circumstances. Special emphasis is given to the ways they lived and waited in hope. The preeminent ancestor and model is Abraham. His belief, fidelity, and hope are eulogized in a special way (11:8–19).

TWENTIETH SUNDAY IN ORDINARY TIME: YEAR C Luke 12:49–53

The Disciple—Unexpected Opposition

Many people who read the gospels would wonder how conscious Jesus was of his impending death. If we fuse together the human and divine then we have no problem. However, we must always protect the integrity of Jesus' human life. As his public life unfolded, he had to face not only popularity but also serious opposition. Luke records this fact in a graphic way. His Jesus has been interacting with the popular religious leaders over a meal (11:37–52). Obviously, Luke has used the meal setting to gather a series of prophetic challenges on authentic religion. At the end of the exchanges he writes: "When he went outside, the scribes and the Pharisees began to be very hostile toward him and to cross-examine him about many things, lying in wait for him to catch him in something he might say" (11:53–54). There are other similar passages (cf. 11:14—12:12 and 19:47–48; 20:1—21:4).

Luke describes the opposition's counter-propaganda to Jesus as an exorcist. (Exorcists were a feature of his world.) He writes: "Some of them (crowd) said, 'He casts out demons in the name of Beelzebub, the ruler of demons.' Others kept asking him for a sign" (11:15–16). Speaking of the dangers of wealth Jesus is ridiculed: "The Pharisees, who were lovers of money, heard all this, and they ridiculed him" (16:14). Herod is greatly disturbed by his work and teaching. Friendly Pharisees cautioned him, "Get away from here, for Herod wants to kill you." On each occasion of conflict, challenge, and danger, Jesus not only does not flinch but also in a prophetic way addresses the situation and the groups.

This forms a background for a series of sayings in today's gospel (12:49–53) in which Jesus reveals his awareness of impending danger. We need to listen again to a saying of John speaking about Jesus' ministry, "He will baptize you with the Holy Spirit and fire" (3:16). The enigmatic sayings about fire and a baptism refer to his mission and its prophetic character. The prophetic nature of his mission has built-in consequences. One of these is strong opposition and the possibility of death. There is a saying of Jesus that discloses his awareness: "Yet today, tomorrow and the next day I must be on my way, because it is impossible for a prophet to be killed outside of Jerusalem" (13:33).

His vocation is to proclaim the sovereignty of God within all realms of human society and to uncover all forms of sinfulness within religion and culture as well as government. His ministry is a ministry to bring fire. Fire purifies, discriminates between evil and good, and is a sign of God's judgment. Baptism refers to his ministry and to his destiny inseparable from his fidelity to this ministry. This vocation is like fire within him. He is gripped and mastered by his vocation. "Your kingdom come" are not just idle words in Jesus' mouth. They express his very identity.

In the light of the disturbing character of his prophetic mission, he disclaims that he wants to bring peace. No, his words and deeds and his very person sow discord at the very heart of human life, in the family. Possibly alluding to Micah 7:6 he speaks of the alignment of son, daughter, and daughter-in-law against their parents. As disciples of Jesus, we must pause with this very disconcerting aspect of discipleship. There is a peace with which Jesus gifts us. He also creates crises in individual lives and in the lives of groups.

As a background to this paradox of conflict at the heart of a family because of Jesus as the prophet of God, we read of Jeremiah. Jerusalem is under siege. The king and his officials have decided to resist to the last, hoping against hope that somehow God will save them. Jeremiah not only advises surrender, he publicly sows disaffection among the people and in the army. He urges all to surrender to the Babylonian army. Moreover, he assures them that they will be safe and live. His well-placed enemies among the courtiers force the powerless king to order his arrest and murder. Some of his friends engineer his release. He is placed as an example of two against three. The psalm (39/40) reports the grateful acknowledgment of a person face to face with death whom God has saved. The psalm could be read as Jeremiah's prayer.

Last week we heard about the exemplary faith of Abraham and other great Jewish saints. The author of Hebrews returns to his concern for his Christian community. Earlier he has referred to a period of contempt and severe persecution they have endured (10:32–34). He returns to this subject, because apostasy was a possibility due to the inimical environment of the small communities in the large urban world, probably of Rome. He begins with an image from athletics. Christian life is like a race and each is a runner. The stadium is full of spectators. As an athlete must strip down for the race, so the Christian must put aside all encumbrances. Sin in which we so easily get entangled is singled out. As athletes, we have a superb model in Jesus, who has run in the race of life.

The readers are exhorted to fix their gaze on Jesus of Nazareth. He is both the pioneer for the human family and he lived the perfect life of faith and fidelity. In his commitment to his Father's will, aware of the joy and glory, which would be in the future, he endured the horrible and shameful death on the cross. The community must keep in mind his endurance of intense opposition during his life and in his death. This will prevent them becoming disillusioned and faint-hearted. To cap off his exhortation he reminds them that however severe the earlier pain and public abuse have been and the enticement to give up their faith, yet they have not yet been asked to shed their blood. There are in this letter earlier reflections about Jesus of Nazareth's human life and its significance for us (Heb 2:9–18; 4:14–15; 10:5–7). Along with the points sketched in these verses we can see the importance for us of his faith journey with all its richness, humanness, vicissitude, and extreme pain. Throughout he was faithful to his Father and to us, his brothers and sisters. His was a life lived for us.

TWENTY-FIRST SUNDAY IN ORDINARY TIME: YEAR C Luke 13:22–30

The Disciple—Unexpected Winners

The prayer of the psalmist (Ps 116/117) could set the tone for one of the themes of this Sunday's liturgy. He invites all to pray: "Praise the Lord, all you nations! Extol him, all you people! For great is his steadfast love towards us, and the faithfulness of the Lord endures forever. Praise the Lord." The reading from Isaiah (66:18–21), taken from the conclusion of the book, announces the universal saving plan of God. God will gather all nations. He will send messengers to the most distant and unknown lands to proclaim his glory and deeds. Jewish people scattered among the nations will also return. Jesus affirms the universality of God's purpose. However, he will add some small print to the contract to which we need to pay attention.

The first part of Luke's journey narrative ends (9:51—13:2) and the second leg of the journey begins (13:22–17:10). He is asked a question touching on a basic concern of all people, "Lord, will only a few be saved?" Earlier a teacher had asked him, "What must I do to inherit eternal life?" and "Who is my neighbor?" (10:25, 29). An angry and troubled young man had demanded, "Teacher, tell my brother to divide the family inheritance with me" (12:13). Peter has asked, "Lord are you telling this parable for us or for everyone?" (12:41). A certain ruler will also be concerned and will ask, "Good teacher, what must I do to inherit eternal life?" (18:18). Jesus had a reputation as an important religious guide.

As on other occasions Jesus' answer is disconcerting. He does not really answer the question because this could absolve people of their responsibility. Entering "eternal life" is like entering a city through its narrow gate or a house through a narrow door. The gate/door is narrow as a protection in case of attack. Personal and continual endeavor is necessary. Jesus gives a reason. Many will try and not be able. Implied is that they did not endeavor in a proper way. This more general saying is followed by a small story. People must enter the door before the door is shut. The door is now the door to a house where a banquet is taking place. The banquet is an image used for "heaven" or eternal life (cf. Is 25:6–7). The door is shut. Disciples ("you") start to knock, wanting to enter, but they hear those frightening words, "I do not know where you come from." The outsiders insist that the owner of the house does know them. The owner has become Jesus Christ who lived in Galilee and Judea. With him they ate and heard him teaching in their neighborhood, the people insist. Jesus' second answer is more insistent. They are sent away with those condemnatory words echoing in their ears, "You evil-doers." There is no explanation of their evil. We have to fill in the accusation from Jesus' teaching. The initial instruction, "Strive to enter through the narrow door" is further underlined in this small story. Jesus tells the people that they have a serious responsibility to obey his teaching. Our future will depend on this effort.

This story about a banquet leads to another series of sayings. These sayings and the earlier sayings are found in other contexts in Matthew (cf. Mt 7:13-14, 22-23; 8:11-12; 19:30). Catchwords and similarity of theme link the series of sayings together. The initial question triggers off the series. The banquet becomes in a clear manner the final banquet of all the chosen. Those who have not striven and shouldered the responsibility of discipleship will find themselves looking in on the crowd, full of regret. The listing of those at the table leads to the theme of the universality of God's saving action. Our liturgy of the Word began with this theme. Maybe Christian communities need to pay attention to the universality of God's plan. Religious exclusivism is not part of the gospel. God is an impartial God. In a pluralist world and society we need to affirm our own religious identity and its responsibilities. We do not judge other religions or humanist movements that respect transcendence and the Transcendent. We respect and work with others for an ever more human and just society and world order.

The final saying is a free-floating proverb. Jesus hints that the upside-down nature of his teaching will also apply to those who finish the race of life and enter God's kingdom.

Parts of the passage are not easy to interpret. The major theme is the responsibility that we all have to live a sincere and committed Christian life.

The same theme is the content of the reading from Hebrews (12:5-7, 11-13). However, most people will be put off by the expressions used and the reference to good parents disciplining their child. The writer may find himself in court! The community is living in a difficult situation with various types of local persecution, discrimination, and slander. The writer is concerned about their fidelity to their faith in these trying circumstances. The sufferings are seen as God's discipline. He is testing their faith. The teacher exhorts them to get into the game of life, take the knocks, and be faithful whatever be the difficulties.

TWENTY-SECOND SUNDAY IN ORDINARY TIME: YEAR C Luke 14:1, 7-14

The Disciple—Status and the Poor

We shall begin our reflections on our readings by sitting at the feet of an ancient sage called Ben Sirach (Sirach 3:17-18, 20, 28-29). The verses chosen are taken from a long collection of sayings (3:17—4:10) Look up the verses from the longer collection. These will form a background to the sage advice of Jesus of Nazareth (Lk 14:1, 7-14). Ben Sirach's advice about humility and responsibilities to the "poor" are strangely contemporary. The first part of the collection of sayings concerns humility and pride. All our egos are fragile, and this seems to increase the more important we become in whatever field, sports, politics, business, profession. Sirach advises: "The greater you are, the more you must humble yourself, so you will find favor in the sight of the Lord." He describes pride as a noxious weed: "For the disease of the proud there is no cure, since an evil growth has taken root in them." His experience has taught him that only the humble are able to acknowledge God. He reflects: "For great is the might of the Lord; but by the humble he is glorified."

His advice about our obligations to the needy and the ways we may try to escape are insightful.

Praying the responsorial psalm (Ps 67/68), we commit ourselves to live according to the vision of Ben Sirach. The psalmist bestows titles of great honor on God, titles that many may claim, and yet few would have the right to such titles. The psalmist calls God "Father of the orphans" and "Protector of widows." What wonderful religious insight. God is the one who "gives the desolate a home to live in" and "leads prisoners to prosperity." The prisoners would be either prisoners of war, prisoners because of debt, or prisoners of conscience. Long experience leads the psalmist to state "in your goodness you provide for the needy." The exuberance of the praise of God with which the psalm begins is justified for such a God.

Jesus is presented as a wise teacher. The setting is a meal. Luke has gathered a series of instructions together in this setting (14:1-6, 7-14, 15-24). The lectionary omits the healing of the man with dropsy (14:2-6). As Jesus enters the house he is watched closely (14:1). Jesus himself is watching the guests (14:7) taking the honorable places, and the host (14:12). I have watched people agonizing over where to seat guests at meals or functions. Status, fame, and honor are at stake. Using this opportunity and aware of the sociocultural importance of public status and honor, Jesus turns the world upside down again. Earlier, addressing leaders of the community, he had criticized them because of their habit of choosing the "best seats" (11:43; cf. 20:46). There is a certain wry humor in his advice. Go to the least important place! The ruse may not work, as the host or hostess may leave you there! However, Jesus is not writing a page in a book of etiquette or of "How to Get on in Life." Even the floating proverbial saying can be misunderstood. He is undermining our sense of importance. He is speaking about genuine humility and a way of life that seeks "honor" only from God. The concluding saying (14:11) about "being exalted" refers to God's action. Real status in life is the status we have in the eyes of God now and forever. Jesus' teaching liberates a person from so much social stress and social consciousness and creates a genuine space for freedom and a rich and mutual interaction with all types of people.

He also has some advice for the host or hostess. This will not be in the handbooks or glossy magazines with tips for hosts and hostesses. Companies, government, churches, and other institutions have ritual ways to show care to the homeless, poor, and marginalized. Christmas and Easter or Thanksgiving are occasions to throw meals for such people. Jesus is not speaking of such rituals. He contrasts with two lists of guests: "your friends, your brothers and sisters or your relatives or rich neighbors" and "the poor, the crippled, the lame and the blind." He also contrasts the response of the two groups to the invitation and meal. The former may "invite you in return and you would be repaid" while the latter group "cannot repay you, for you will be rewarded at the resurrection of the righteous." We note that in the earlier illustrative story addressed to the guest they are promised that "they will be exalted." Jesus assures hosts who follow his vision of life that they "will be rewarded…." The hosts who are consistently concerned for the marginalized are those "who seek God's kingdom"(12:31). Jesus teaches an attitude to life by which we will grow to be like God. Meals are great investments to gain social acceptance, cement relationships, and gain status and entrance into the world of others. However, another value system must be the foundation of our lives. Jesus is like a good insurance agent. He offers the best life insurance policy and a great investment. It is rather expensive, because we have to be able to stand aside from sociocultural values and see life from a strange angle. He underlines again our responsibilities to the poor, sick, homeless…. This responsibility is not just occasional. It is to be an integral part of our lives.

TWENTY-THIRD SUNDAY IN ORDINARY TIME: YEAR C Luke 14:25–33

The Disciple—If you want to be…

Quite a number of the readings on various Sundays look at the reality of Christian discipleship from different perspectives. Most of us inherit our Christian faith and at various stages in our lives we personalize this faith and its accompanying belief system. Quite a number of Christians stop "practicing" at various stages in their lives. For some their Christian belief is more a social reality. Others pick and choose among the practices and beliefs and modes of worship. At times schools and parishes have a type of checklist to differentiate the "practicing" from the "non-practicing." Probably the criteria Jesus uses to differentiate between a disciple and non-disciple are not the same as that used by the "church."

In today's reading (Lk 14:25–33) Jesus addresses "the large crowd" and "all" who are following him. There are three typical sayings and two illustrative stories. The stories draw attention to the need to assess prudently financial or military resources before undertaking a building project or engaging in a war. Otherwise the person will face ridicule and shame or defeat. Discipleship is a major venture in anyone's life, and Jesus asks people to look at its implications.

The phrase that is repeated is "cannot be my disciple" (14, 26, 27, 33). There are conditions attached to genuine discipleship. There are decisions involved. These conditions are spelled out in an unambiguous and stark manner. Jesus speaks of "hate" in regard to our original family and our family after marriage. To make his point even more clear he adds "even his life itself." He pictures discipleship as "cross carrying." His last saying seems to be the most demanding: to "give up all your possessions." Justifiable people could have complained, and I am sure many did, and have, throughout history, "Who does he think he is?" "This is impossible." All of these invitations (or are they demands?) are related to "follow me." There is the heart of discipleship, a deep personal relationship to Jesus of Nazareth, who is Christ and Lord. If we read our gospel carefully we come to realize that Jesus himself was invited by his Father to live his discipleship as Son of the Father in this spirit. All bonds, all great and treasured values, all that is most precious in a person and in life are to God secondary in comparison with commitment. This commitment to God in Christian disciples is lived through a personal commitment and relationship with Jesus Christ.

One of the implications will be to share in a way of living that at times will mean being at odds with the value system and cultural and social expectations of contemporary society. If we look at Jesus' life we come to understand that throughout the gospel account he was "carrying his cross." His fidelity to his Father and to a way of looking at and living human life set him at odds with his own religious world and with his society. He was "out of place," an alien element, a subversive presence. Carrying the cross does not refer to the daily aches and pains of life, terminal illness, financial losses, problems with adolescent children, or marriage breakdown. "Carrying the cross" refers to what happens to a person or community that consistently strives to live according to the gospel of Jesus Christ.

There is a danger in this gospel passage and the comments made about radical discipleship. The impression can be given that there is a morbidity about Christian discipleship, if not a certain masochism. There is not much room for joy and delight in life. All the closest relationships are put into the category of "hate," all possessions have to go, and we are to be professional "cross carriers." However, all deep and prolonged commitments demand and yet give great meaning to life. We could look at the commitment to a football team even out there when it is raining and they are being trounced. Commitment—to family, to Vincent de Paul types of groups, to professional excellence, be it in education, medicine, business, or technical skills—place upon people so many obligations. All such deeply human and genuine commitments chip away at our selfishness, indifference, laziness, and ambiguous values. There is also another aspect. This commitment is another way of speaking of loving God with all our being and loving our neighbor. The commitment to Jesus Christ is a commitment to human life, human society, to a culture of life and dignity, human rights, and vibrant family and public life. Such commitments do entail struggle with a whole value system and movements that are anti-human, cultures of greed, oppression, and death.

Perhaps the small selection from the prayer of Solomon for wisdom in our first reading (Wisdom 9:13–18 [cf. 9:1–18]) can add something to our reflections. Aware of human limitations and yet human need, Solomon prays for wisdom to know the counsels of God. He wishes to shoulder his responsibilities as king in a worthy manner. I doubt if the historical Solomon would have been so conscientious to know God's will. The psalmist (Ps 89/90) wants the wisdom of the heart. He also is aware of human transience, insignificance, and sinfulness. He compares the human to the Divine and pleads for God to be merciful, and steadfast in his love. Graced by God he knows that his works will prosper. The only condition is that he is gifted with the wisdom of the heart. As disciples of Jesus Christ, we also need that wisdom of the heart, which marked his own life.

The selection from the short letter to Philemon allows us to see discipleship at work in the primitive church. Philemon owns a house. He is at least relatively wealthy. The local Christian community gathers at his home. One of his slaves, Onesimus, has run away. We do not know whether he worked in Philemon's house or in his business establishment. However, this was a serious offense. He may also have stolen from or injured Philemon in some other way. Philemon had the legal right to punish him. Onesimus had also tarnished his honor.

Paul writes to him about this matter. Paul is now an old man and imprisoned because of the gospel. He had converted Onesimus. He appeals to Philemon to act out of love. He has praised him because of the way he loves (vv 5, 7). Philemon is not only to forgive his runaway slave but also to receive him as a beloved brother! If we read the letter carefully, we shall be fascinated by all the ways Paul approaches the subject and motivates Philemon. He is asking him to demonstrate the radical nature of discipleship. Discipleship involves decisions that often go against social custom, legal rights, and cultural expectations. Paul urges him to be a disciple in his life at home and in business.

TWENTY-FOURTH SUNDAY IN ORDINARY TIME: YEAR C Luke 15:1–32

Jesus—Friend of Sinners

There are many rich themes in our readings. I suggest we begin by listening in an imaginative way to some of the apparently minor actors in the gospel's parables. Three "actors" are usually overlooked. The lost coin and lost sheep draw our attention. What about the 99 sheep and the 9 other coins? The younger, dissolute, wasteful and irresponsible son appeals to us as we identify with him. However, what about his elder brother, such a responsible son! The lost coin and the miserable lost sheep are given all the attention. The lost sheep gets privileged treatment and is the center of attention at a village party. The woman not only frantically searches for her coin in her poorly lit one-room home, but puts on quite a party for her women friends. Surely, the 99 sheep and the other 9 coins have good reason to be resentful. What about the elder son? He is faithful day and night on the large estate, working his guts out for his father. Yet, his father has never allowed him even once to have his friends over for a beer and barbecue.

We could also pay attention to the expected reaction of the audience listening to the stories of the sheep that strayed and the coin that was misplaced. At one point, the people would look at each other shaking their heads and smile. Who would put on a party for a lost sheep and a coin, even if it was a part of a dowry or a prized ornament? The audience would also be quite right, according to their culture, to side with the elder brother. The younger man had dishonored his father and family, wasting his inheritance, the fruit of years of hard work and good management by his father. What could be worse than wasting it with drink, prostitutes, and drugs? His father is irresponsible and shameless. Not only does he allow him enter the house again, but reinstates him and flings a party such as had never been seen before in the home. Each detail of the welcome given by the father is important. Some are very culturally conditioned. Sandals and a ring are the signs that he is not a slave in the house but a son. The young fellow had hoped that his father might accept him as a slave.

We need to look at the stories and see what shocks us. The shepherd, woman, and father all either break social customs or act in ways that are obviously exaggerated if not foolish and reprehensible. The opening verses will give us the clue to these three stories. We quote it: "Now all the tax collectors and sinners were coming near to listen to him." In this situation the Pharisees and the scribes were grumbling and saying, "This fellow welcomes sinners and eats with them." What they said is important. (Note the use of the disrespectful term "fellow"). When Jesus was with Levi's guests at a special meal, the leaders grumbled (5:29–32). Simon also grumbled and thought in a negative way about Jesus and the sinful woman (7:39). The same grumbling will recur when Jesus invites himself to Zacchaeus' home (19:1–10). Just to drive home his point Jesus will tell a story about a Pharisee and tax collector going to pray (18:9–14).

We are dealing with a rather common problem, which finds expression in different ways. Religious communities and persons set the agenda for God. We expect God and those who are his spokespersons to fit into patterns, which we determine. We define the behavior and attitudes proper for God and women and men who represent God. We define the boundaries and determine who are "in" and "out" of the community, who are "good" and "bad" and "religious" and "irreligious." We put limits on God's readiness to forgive and bless.

Many Christian groups, communities, and people would easily share in the elder brother's protests and anger. Many would feel let down like the 99 "good" sheep and 9 "safe" coins. Leaders of Christian communities and Christians have learned a lot about God from AIDS victims, from homosexual and lesbian groups, from the addicts and the drunkards, from divorced and remarried men and women, as they have also from the saints. We all struggle with the mystery of evil in our own depth and within groups and in the world around us. We can learn a lot about the mercy of God in this struggle.

We note that Jesus does not affirm sinfulness. However, he associates as closely as possible ("welcomes and eats with") with all who are broken by moral evil. Jesus drew sinners to himself. Are the Christian churches and groups able to draw us in our sinfulness? Are they able to speak of God in ways that are true to God and Jesus Christ? Do we have a distorted image of God and the inexpressible character of his mercy?

The first reading (Ex 32:7-11, 13-14) and the psalm (Ps 50/51) focus our attention more on human sinfulness and the prayer for forgiveness and the renewal of our hearts. In Exodus, the golden calf was the paradigm of Israel's sinfulness, a radical break with God. Moses pleads with God to put his anger aside and accept Israel, however sinful they may be. He twists God's arm. Finally God relents and both forgives them and commits himself again to journey with Israel throughout history whatever may happen. The psalmist expresses in classical terms a sinful person's repentance. The Exodus reading is wonderful provided we are aware that the author has pictured God in a very human way to make his point.

For the next five weeks, we shall read snippets from 1 and 2 Timothy. We begin with the reading about Paul, the prodigal who experienced the extraordinary mercy of Jesus Christ. I judge that the writer of these two letters is an unknown person who lived about a generation or more after Paul. This pretended "autobiographical" section will give weight to the instructions in the letter. It is a prayer of gratitude addressed to Christ Jesus, the Lord. "Paul" looks back over his life—persecutor, blasphemer, and man of violence (very unusual description!)—and pauses to consider his present situation. He has been chosen, appointed and strengthened for special ministry. He looks back again. The overwhelming experience of Christ's mercy and the gifts of faith and love given by him are the background for his reflections on his sinfulness. These lead him to a deep sense of gratitude. He is an extraordinary example of the boundlessness of Christ's patience and mercy. He stands as an assurance to all sinners who turn to Christ in faith. They will only experience mercy.

We could all share in the doxology as we all so often have received God's mercy in Christ Jesus: "To the King of the ages, immortal, invisible, the only God, be honor and glory forever and ever. Amen."

TWENTY-FIFTH SUNDAY IN ORDINARY TIME: YEAR C Luke 16:1–13

Jesus—Such a Jealous Master

A special aspect of the liturgical readings of this year is the emphasis on various aspects of the social responsibilities of the Christian community. Some may tire of the theme. There is a stark contrast between the lives of the business community in the Israel of Amos' time (Amos 8: 4-7; cf. 2:6-8; 5:10-11; 6:4-7, 12) and the way God is portrayed by the psalmist (Ps 112/113).

Amos describes the businessmen as those who "trample on the needy, and bring to ruin the poor of the land." He puts into words their silent thoughts. On the Sabbath and festival days, shops have to be closed. There was no "Sunday" shopping. On the Sabbath, they are impatiently waiting so that they can get back to business. The stable element of the people's diet was wheat. They have doctored their weighing machines. They sell debtors into bondage. The rubbish wheat is on sale. Perusing the other texts indicated above, we realize that Amos is the prophet of social justice. His famous critique of religious practice is in terms of the lack of justice in his society. He writes, "But let justice (social justice with its many implications in society) roll down like waters, and righteousness (the sense of social responsibility with its many ramifications) like an ever-flowing stream" (5:24). In our own day, we have to identify the areas of serious social injustice and irresponsible action by the business community, government, and other groups.

In contrast to the persistent behavior of the business class, the wealthy and those responsible for law and order, we are introduced to a picture of God. The psalmist is exuberant in his praise of the Lord whose uniqueness and majesty fascinate him. However, his God is the one "who raises the poor from the dust, and lifts the needy from the ash heap, to make them sit with princes, with the princes of his people." He is also the God who "gives the barren woman [a social misfit likely to be divorced and despised] a home, making her the joyous mother of children." He praises this God. The social critique of Amos and other prophets and of Jesus of Nazareth rises from their personal and communitarian experience of this God.

These readings create a background as we listen to the gospel. The gospel is problematic. We need to do some initial work on the text. We must distinguish the illustrative story (16:1-8a) from the wisdom sayings attached to it (16:8b, 9, 10-12, 13). The story is about a street-wise "manager of dishonesty" who rises to the occasion when faced with a real crisis. The sayings are attached to portions or an aspect of the story.

We have plenty of examples in recent years of dishonest and fraudulent managers and owners. Many salt away their wealth acquired in dishonest ways in bank accounts of others. Their future is assured. Jesus' manager worked for a wholesale company owned by some very rich person. The inner dialogue enables us to follow his dealings. Physical labor and begging are impossibilities. He acts very smartly. The owner praises the shrewd way he handles the crisis. By means of the original parable Jesus probably challenged his audience to respond appropriately to his ministry that had created a religious crisis.

The attached wisdom sayings take up different aspects of the story. The shrewd and decisive action of the manager, a worldly wise person ("children of this age"), ought to model for Jesus' disciples ("children of light") the way to respond to the responsibilities of discipleship (16:8b). The manager ensured a "welcome in the homes" of wealthy patrons (16:4). The Christians are to use the "wealth [mammon] of dishonesty" (which can lead to greed and dishonesty) in ways that will ensure that they inherit eternal life (16:9). Maybe readers would have seen a consistent practice of almsgiving as one suitable way to ensure that wealth does not rule the heart.

The next series of sayings (16:10-12) develops the theme of "responsible fidelity" in Christian life. The writer takes the manager as an example of infidelity. There are three contrasts: very little/much, dishonest wealth/genuine riches, and property of another/of one's own. In each case, what is at stake is an orientation in life. In our Christian lives we have to be immersed in so many normal realities of life, making decisions, taking responsibilities, using so many good things, building relationships. Interwoven into our lives there must be a fundamental commitment to God and Jesus Christ. We are to be disciples of Jesus in the world. We strive and search to live day to day as disciples of Jesus in all the varied circumstances of our journey.

The concluding saying focuses this commitment to discipleship around the opposition between "mammon"/ wealth and God. The image of a slave and two masters is used to draw attention to the fundamental "either/or" at the center of our human life. Wealth could be a valid symbol. We could also use career, social status, profession, or commitment to an ideology as symbols of values that can be the cancers of both a genuine human life and so the life of discipleship. Amos knew people who were enslaved to greed and power. Jesus also knew the human heart. We are called to pause. To whom are we devoted at the root of our being?

Were someone to continue to read this chapter of Luke they would find an example of a group whom Luke judges to belong to the club of mammon. He writes: "the Pharisees, who were lovers of money, heard all this and they ridiculed him. So Jesus said to them, 'You are those who justify yourselves in the sight of others; but God knows your hearts; for what is prized by human beings is an abomination in the sight of God'" (16:14-15). Hard hitting words indeed. We need to be careful of the polemic use of the term Pharisee. Normally, the type of persons to whom Jesus is referring is not found at worship. However, Jesus' teaching in this piece from the gospel is a challenge to all Christians. Again, we need to do "heart examination" and be ready for some "heart surgery."

We read another short selection from Timothy (1 Tim 2:1-8). The text ought to have been 2:1-7 as 2:8 belongs to a series of exhortations addressed to men and women in the community (2:8-15) prior to the instructions for the bishops and deacons (3:1-13). This is a great text. There is an emphatic statement of the universal desire of God for the salvation of all. The community did not participate in public prayers and sacrifice for the Emperor or public officials. However, the writer in an emphatic manner instructs the community to include in all its diverse types of prayer (supplications, intercessions, prayers of thanksgiving) prayer for all. He gives special mention to political leaders because of the impact they can have on public life and well-being. The community prays that they live and act peacefully and quietly and live in a dignified manner and with godliness.

What is the basis for such universal concern in a Christian community? Our God is committed to the salvation of all and that all come to know the truth. The truth is the universality of his saving will that God revealed in Jesus Christ. Using a small credal statement, he substantiates his affirmation. First there is only one God. Second, between this one God and the whole human race one mediator shared in that human life common to all. Finally, Jesus Christ gave himself in his death as a ransom for all. The focal point is the universal significance of his death. This death proves the universal desire of the one God for the salvation of all. The gospel is the attestation/witness of this universal plan and effective desire of God. Therefore, "Paul" again affirms his role as herald, apostle, and, above all, as teacher of the Gentiles. Often the aspect of Christ as the mediator is made the focal point. On this is built a theology of the universal and unique saving role of Jesus Christ for all who must come to know him. The text does not state this.

TWENTY-SIXTH SUNDAY IN ORDINARY TIME: YEAR C Luke 16:19–31

Jesus—No Friend of the Consumerist Society

Our liturgy today is again built around stark contrasts. We return to Amos (Amos 6:1, 4–7) and to a psalm akin to the psalm of last Sunday (Ps 145/146). Amos uncovers the gross and irresponsible self-indulgence of the economic and political leaders of the kingdoms of Judah and Samaria, especially Samaria. They are arrogant and self indulgent. The picture of luxury may not strike us at first. Ivory was a very expensive and rare object. They have beds and couches in the dining rooms inlaid with ivory. They use the most expensive toiletries (special oil), and they feast off an abundance of the choicest meat and most expensive wines. Their revelry can be heard for miles with music and song.

However, they have not the slightest concern for their country. ("They are not grieved over the ruin of Joseph" [Northern Kingdom]). As a consequence they will be the first to be taken as prisoners into exile (The exile took place in 721). Some of our self-indulgent and greedy figures spent time in jail.

The God of Israel however, does grieve over his people. The psalmist describes God. He "executes justice for the oppressed and gives food to the hungry. The Lord sets the prisoners free and opens the eyes of the blind." The lowly, stranger, orphan, widow, and broken are his major concern. However, "the way of the wicked he brings to ruin." This is the theme of Amos and of our gospel (Lk 16:19–31). A setting has been created for Jesus' teaching. Jesus belongs to and has been nourished on this prophetic tradition, and this rich experience of God to be found in his religious tradition.

His illustrative story belongs to a tradition of popular folktales in which we find a story of a rich man and a poor man, their deaths and the consequent reversal of positions. Our story is constructed around contrasts and the reversal of situations. We find the following contrasts: rich man/poor man, Hades/Abraham's bosom, torment/comfort, this life/next life, down/up, good things/evil things, agony/comfort, there/here. Death is the point of reversal. With a few deft strokes Jesus describes the situation of the rich man and Lazarus. How many artists have been inspired with his portrait? As we follow the story we have not much reason to have negative feelings toward the rich man. He seems to be very respectful to Abraham and Lazarus, deeply concerned about his five brothers and accepting of his own fate. There is no mention of violence, injustice, or oppression. However, the small phrase "at his gate" is pregnant with meaning. The contrast is emphasized, along with the insensitivity and irresponsibility of the rich man. He not only did not grieve but he also did not even see the poor man. Though we give much attention to the first part of the story and the conversation of the rich man and Abraham, the actual point of the story is in the second part.

The five brothers, living in the great villa and whose style of life is irresponsibly lavish, are the important characters. They represent the audience, we who listen to the story. How are obviously sinful men and women shocked out of their complacency, indifference, and irresponsible manner of life? There is a danger here. We may listen to the story as outsiders. We are still trying to pay off our mortgage, put the children through school, and attempt to save a little for old age. We do not fit into the shoes of any of the characters in the story. However, we all as Christians have social responsibilities. It may be that some families of different race, language, or religion are discriminated against in our neighborhood. There are the lonely widow, the broken family, the street kids, Vincent de Paul centers looking for a helping hand—and many other situations that we need to "see."

One of the frightening aspects of the story is Jesus' awareness that his contemporaries listen to the Word of God being read week after week in their synagogues and yet with what effect? He has seen his own age group come to and go from the synagogue week after week and remain on the level of social Judaism. What do we need to do so that we listen to the word of God with our inner heart and inner mind? What would enable us to listen to the word of God, our inner world of values and attitudes and the invitations and cries of the men and women around us?

In our reading from Timothy (1 Tim 6:11–16) we listen to an exhortation to Timothy, "a man of God," to be faithful to the ordained ministry entrusted to him (6:11–14). The short exhortation ends with a doxological prayer. This exhortation is sandwiched between a polemical attack on false and deceitful teachers who cause dissension and a few words about the dangers of wealth (6:3–10). The actual instruction to Timothy about his ministerial responsibilities spans the last section of the letter (4:6—6:16). Such small extracts are not very helpful because most Christians do not know the major lines of thought in the letter, most of which is omitted from the liturgical reading.

TWENTY-SEVENTH SUNDAY IN ORDINARY TIME: YEAR C, Luke 17:5–10

Jesus—The Unappreciative Master

All the liturgical readings of this Sunday are somewhat puzzling. The first reading is taken from Habakkuk (1:2–3 and 2:2–4). These two small excerpts are from the longer unit of complaints and woes (1:2—2:20). There are two complaints directed at God (1:2–4 and 1:12–17) and two "divine" responses (1:5–11 and 2:1–4). The remainder of the unit is made up of "woes" (2:5–20). The prophet complains to God (1:2–3). How long will violent turmoil afflict Jerusalem and Judah and why is there such turmoil? The city and kingdom are torn apart by civil unrest and oppression and are under attack from Babylonian armies. The response given by God (2:1–4) is related to a complaint not chosen for our reading (1:12–17)! The prophet is to record the visionary response of God on a public document. He is reassured that God will surely come though he tarries. Those who are faithful within Israel will be saved ("The righteous live by their faith"). It is this idea of fidelity that is taken up in the psalm (Ps 94/95) and is meant to provide some background to the gospel.

The psalm is part of the daily prayer of many Christians who pray the Liturgy of the Hours. There is an invitation to praise and thank God with gusto. The community enters God's presence with humble and grateful hearts. The psalmist pictures God as the shepherd of his people whom he describes as "sheep of his hand." This mood gives way to a stern warning to listen to his voice with open and receptive hearts. We can so easily harden our hearts, as so much of history proves. The theme of fidelity surfaces once more.

When we turn to the gospel we feel like someone who has walked in ten minutes after a class has begun and walks out after a few minutes. Jesus' few sayings seem to float in the air. We left Jesus last week at the end of his instructions about wealth. There is a small catechism in 17:1–10 directed at the disciples. Our sayings are preceded by a saying that underlines the gravity of causing a scandal that would lead persons of immature faith ("little ones") into sin (17:1–2). This leads to a saying about the necessity of a readiness both to rebuke anyone in the community who sins (and is a possible cause of scandal?) and also to forgive them when they repent (17:3). This saying attracts to itself another saying about the consequence of sin against a member of the community, repentance, and forgiveness. Disciples must be ready to forgive even seven times (17:4).

From among the disciples, Luke narrates that at this point the apostles ask their Lord, "Increase our faith."

This reaching out to God through their commitment to Jesus Christ is the basis for discipleship. Women and men of growing faith can follow Jesus' teachings, examples of which are given in 17:1–4. Jesus' response implies that the group lacks faith. Were their faith even as small as a mustard seed they could live as exemplary disciples. Faith has extraordinary power, illustrated by the grotesque image of a big mulberry tree being uprooted and then transplanted into the sea! Jesus is not referring to the ability to do miracles. The context indicates that faith is an essential condition of discipleship.

In Luke we have a rich catechesis on faith. We have a series of figures who exemplify how in crisis situations men and women reach out to the graciousness and power of God mediated to them through Jesus Christ. Jesus remarks about the faith of the the group who bring the paralytic (5:20), the non-Jewish centurion amazing even Jesus himself (7:20), and the sinful woman as an outstanding example of faith (7:50). Years of illness have made the sick woman sensitive and ready to recognize Jesus as a prophet of God (8:48). Jairus is challenged not to allow the grief of the death of his daughter to undermine his faith (8:49). Next Sunday we shall spend time with the lone leper who has the faith to grasp that this healing reveals God's power mediated through Jesus (17:19). There was a strange persistence and stubborness in the faith of the blind man outside Jericho (18:43). The crisis provoked by the storm at sea, symbolic of crises in discipleship, uncovered the weakness of the disciples' faith (8:25).

In Luke's gospel Jesus spells out many aspects of the life of a disciple. However, we are shocked by the small story he tells about the small farmer and his slave and the lesson drawn from it in 17:10. The story is about the master's attitude. Jesus asks his audience, "Who among you would say...?" Everyone would agree that it is unthinkable for a slave owner to ask the slave to eat before his master. No one would take objection to the implications of the final question, "Do you thank the slave for doing what was commanded?" The owner has every right to make the slave work and has no obligations of gratitude to him. The lesson drawn by the early church does puzzle us. Disciples however faithful and at whatever cost, can only say to the Lord, We are worthless slaves; we have done only what we ought to have done!

All "holy" arrogance and every boast is swept away. We have to acknowledge the mystery of God and his continued graciousness. Disciples we may be of Jesus Christ, and we are creatures. God is not obliged to us. Strange and bitter medicine for us. Again, we are in the upside-down world of Jesus Christ and discipleship.

We begin reading 2 Timothy (2 Tim 1:6–8, 13–14). The initial unit in the letter (1:3–14) is part of the longer exhortations to Timothy about his ministry (1:3–2:13). "Paul" recalls the fact that Timothy belongs to the third generation of a family of faith (1:5). He is grateful to God for this man. He then exhorts him. First, he must continually rekindle the gift of ministry given to him with its special gifts of power (God's power, 1:8), self-discipline, and love. Though gospel ministry entails suffering, yet he must not be ashamed of the gospel or of "Paul" imprisoned because of it. With Paul, he must share in the sufferings, trusting in God's power. The third point the writer makes is that Timothy must be faithful to the tradition he has received and rely on the indwelling Spirit. He will show his fidelity to the gospel in a life of faith and love. Three themes run through this letter. The second is the importance of sound tradition and fidelity to this tradition. Paul is a model of both themes. Running throughout is the disturbing presence in the community of false teachers and opponents. The readings from Timothy may be more relevant to people in ordained ministry and with leadership roles in the community.

TWENTY-EIGHTH SUNDAY IN ORDINARY TIME: YEAR C, Luke 17:11–19

Jesus—Does He Have a Racial Bias?

Being ungrateful and experiencing ingratitude from others is part and parcel of our lives. Being ready to acknowledge the thoughtfulness, kindness, and helpfulness of others is a fine human quality. There are the social rituals of gratitude, and there is that experience of gratitude that we carry with us in our memories and hearts for a long time. Jesus takes up this theme in today's liturgy.

As a background, we will provide some information about "leprosy" in that time. In a country like India, any traveler will often come across lepers with their damaged hands and feet and often faces. In the biblical world leprosy was a generic word used for various types of obvious skin diseases, often contagious, and also for fungal "infections" of clothes, leather, walls, and such. Concluding a rather long legislative section on the subject Leviticus says: "This is the ritual for leprous disease: for an itch, for leprous diseases of clothes and houses, and for a swelling or an eruption or a spot to determine when it is unclean and clean" (Lev 14:54). The leprous person was isolated from the community and there were regulations for his or her behavior. The law said: "The person who has a leprous disease shall wear torn clothes and let the hair of his head be disheveled; and he shall cover his upper lip and cry out, 'Unclean, Unclean.' He shall remain unclean as long as he has the disease; he is unclean. He shall live alone; his dwelling shall be outside the camp" (Lev 13:45–46). Since this type of disease was a source of ritual uncleanness, the priests were entrusted with the diagnosis of the disease and the right to declare that the affected person was healed. There was an accompanying ritual for the various types of "leprosy" and the various economic groups in the community. Leprosy brought with it a stigma, isolation, and ritual uncleanness.

One of the attractive stories about the prophet Elisha is his healing of Naaman the leper, the commander of the army of the king of Aram (2 Kgs 5:1–19). To provide a background to our gospel the first reading is a selection of a few verses from this prophetic legend. Persuaded by his servants to go and wash in the insignificant Jordan River, he is cured. Our texts draws our attention to his exuberant praise, "Now I know that there is no God in all the earth except in Israel" (5:15) and his desire to take soil from the sacred land of Israel's God so as to make an altar on it to the God of Israel. The reading omits the contrast between Elisha, who refuses any gift, and his servant Gehazi, who uses the opportunity to enrich himself to his own shame (2 Kgs 5:20–27). Naaman goes home cured and Gehazi goes home a leper! The theme of praise is taken up in the responsorial psalm (Ps 97/98). The hymn celebrates the salvation effected by God, who "has remembered his steadfast love and faithfulness." We are prepared to take up the gospel.

This Sunday we begin a series of texts that form a triptych on prayer over the next weeks. This initial panel depicts a scene that challenges us to reflect on the quality of praise, gratitude, and the acknowledgment of God's goodness in our prayer.

Jesus is moving relentlessly toward Jerusalem. The journey began at 9:51 when he turned his face to Jerusalem. He continued the journey, though under threat like his prophetic predecessors (13:22, 33). Now he is somewhere between Samaria and Galilee. He will arrive in Jerusalem in 19:28. To have some idea of a village at that time we would need to go today to the rural areas of Asia, Africa, or India. As he is entering a village ten men quickly move in his direction and yet are careful to keep the required distance. We hear their voices and the shout, "Jesus, master, have mercy on us." Jesus looks across and says simply, "Go show yourselves to the priests." The narrator informs us that "as they were going they were made clean." What will happen?

Luke draws our attention to one of them. He turned back praising God. Arriving in the village and finding Jesus he fell at his feet and thanked him. In our culture we do not fall at people's feet. In the East, this would have been a common way to show respect and gratitude. The narrator now highlights the jolt for the readers. The cleansed leper who returned was a Samaritan. We have two contrasts at play in our text, the one and nine, and Jesus' own people, the Jews, and the Samaritan, the heretic. Jesus underlines both contrasts in his comments on the scene. Note he is not speaking to the man but to us. He asks: "Where are the other nine?" and "Was none of them found to return to praise God except this foreigner?"

We note that Luke presents Jesus as a prophet gifted by God with healing power. He mediates to us God's healing power. Second, twice Luke underlines the idea of "praising God" since this is the theme. Obviously we all need to pause and be aware of how often and in how many ways we take God for granted. We pray the prayer to the Father and ask not only to do his will but also for daily bread, forgiveness, and protection. Do we say also each day "thank you" in some form or other?

We could look at the quality of gratitude in our lives. The other aspect of the text is the shame Jesus' audience must have felt to have the Samaritan portrayed as the model religious person. Again, we know from experience that so often the most unlikely people turn out to be the gems in our lives and lives of others. Jesus turns the world upside down in another way with his choice of the Samaritan as the model.

The reflections on ministry and suffering are continued in the second reading (2 Tim 2:8–13). All who are entrusted with the ministry of proclaiming the gospel and teaching the tradition will have to face sufferings. "Paul" is the model, imprisoned and yet still confident and active. Such suffering is an integral part of ministry and is profitable for the community. The writer urges Timothy to be faithful and endure suffering whatever may be the cost. He is promised the certain reward, which is eternal union with Jesus Christ. However, there is the danger of infidelity and apostasy and the consequent judgment. God, however, remains faithful to himself and will do all he can to prevent such a fate. We note that the essential elements of the gospel are the human life of Jesus and his resurrection. The causes of much of the suffering are within the community, coworkers ashamed of the gospel, faithful members of the community, and an unenthusiastic community. Next week we will also return to the same theme (2 Tim 3:14—4:2).

TWENTY-NINTH SUNDAY IN ORDINARY TIME: YEAR C, Luke 18:1–8

Jesus—A Corrupt Judge, an Image of God?

The court scene Jesus describes in his illustrative story would be strange to most readers. However, anyone who has been to local courts in many countries would appreciate the realism of the story. The two classical characters are the arrogant, unscrupulous, and venal judge, and the poor widow. The widow comes back day after day to seek justice against some type of oppression, possibly a case of stolen property or dispossession of her land. The judge pays no attention. Why should he, as she has no influence. After weeks of botheration by the insistent widow he yields because she is an utter nuisance. She will blacken his face, that is, besmirch his reputation, whatever reputation he had! Jesus describes him as a person who neither fears God nor has respect for anyone. He is proud of this as we see from his inner dialogue when he finally decides to rid himself of the troublesome widow. We are not told much about the persistent widow. We do not know whether she is old and poor, ugly and noisy.

The shock for the reader is that Jesus compares God with the ways of this wayward judge who normally does not dispense justice and delights to delay his cases. As the story closes Jesus asks two questions: "Will not God grant justice to his chosen ones who cry to him day and night?" and "Will he delay long in helping them?" He answers his own questions with the authoritative statement: "I tell you he will quickly grant justice to them." Persistence pulled down the walls of resistance and indifference in the callous judge. How much more will God respond to persistent prayer!

Possibly this illustrative story was a reassurance to marginalized groups and to the good who suffered at the hands of sinful people that God would vindicate them. The blessings pronounced on the poor and those who are hungry and weep serves a similar purpose (Lk 6:22–23). However, Luke has made this story an illustration of perseverance and persistence in prayer. This is the second panel in his triptych on prayer. The gospel text opens with an introductory interpretation, "...a parable about their need to pray always and not to lose heart" (18:1). The widow is the model for the community and individual believers. The rub in Jesus' teaching on prayer is his insistence on perseverance and persistence. This is what we find hard. Perhaps we also lack the genuine desire for change. Jesus is probably not speaking about a more "selfish" type of prayer. The prayer would be for gifts from God that would enable the believer or community to be genuine disciples of the Lord. All the petitions of the "Our Father" would come within the scope of the type of prayer about which Jesus teaches in this text.

The responsorial psalm (Ps 121/ 122) is a beautiful prayer of confidence with the repetitive insistence on God as the guard or protector of his people. God never sleeps or even slumbers. God can protect his people from all types of evil whatever they may be. His care and concern embraces the whole of our lives. The psalmist prays: "The Lord will guard your coming and your going both now and forever." The psalmist's understanding of God and his utter confidence enrich the theme of the gospel. Jesus knows his Father and that he is utterly faithful to us. Earlier he had drawn attention to the goodness and fidelity of the Father (11:1–13 cf. Seventeenth Sunday).

The theme of persistence in prayer is illustrated in the reading from Exodus (Ex 17:8-13). A marauding band of Bedouins attacks the people as Moses leads them through the Sinai desert. Moses goes up the top of the hill with two assistants and prays with outstretched hands. As long as his hands are outstretched, the small group of Israelites prevails. Growing tired he sits and his assistants hold up his hands. The writer vividly makes his point about the power of persistent prayer.

The text concludes with another interpretation of the illustrative story. The judge is a model of injustice and arrogance. His attitude to life leads to the interpretative question whether at the time of judgment God will find people faithful or evil. The widow would be an example of a just person.

We continue our reading of Timothy (2 Tim 3:14—4:2). The author draws a dismal picture of the sinfulness of some members of the community and the pernicious influence, especially on women, of some deceitful teachers (3:1-9; 4:3-4). In contrast he presents "Paul" as an outstanding model in all ways for all to whom God entrusts ministry and who have consequently to suffer persecution and opposition (3:10-12). In this context, he urges Timothy to be faithful to the tradition he has received from his youth and to the sacred writings (3:14-15). Timothy is solemnly warned and urged to be faithful also as a minister of God's Word found in the Scriptures whatever be the circumstances (4:1-2).

The mention of the sacred writings leads the writer to add a reflection on the key role of these God-given Scriptures in the life of the believing community. They are the primary source of sound saving knowledge, interpreted in the light of the Christ event (3:15-17).

THIRTIETH SUNDAY IN ORDINARY TIME: YEAR C, Luke 18:9-14

Jesus—His Strange Assessment of the Religious Person

I would suspect that Ben Sirach, the writer of the book of Sirach, would not have approved of Jesus' teaching in our gospel (Lk 18:11). The text chosen from his collection of wisdom teaching is a fine text, yet does not really turn the world upside down (Sir 35:15b-17, 20-22a [12-14, 16-18 in some translations]). His short instruction concerns God's justice for the oppressed and his judgment of oppressors (35:14-26). He singles out the poor, widow, and orphan, and the oppressed and wronged good person as figures for whom God has special concern. God hears their cries and anguished complaints. This does not destroy his impartiality. He insists that the prayer of these types of people "pierces the clouds and will not rest until it reaches its goal" and the most High has responded. He pictures God as the one "who does justice for the righteous and executes judgment." The judgment is described in blunt terms. I do not think that Ben Sirach would have included the sinful tax collector among his groups whom he reassures that God hears their prayers. However the reading does create an atmosphere and forms a background to our gospel.

The responsorial psalm (Ps 33/34) selects some verses from a psalm of confidence. The psalmist, who identifies himself with the suffering good members of the community of faith, would also have had trouble with Jesus' teaching. He echoes great themes of Jesus' religious tradition: "The eyes of the Lord are on the righteous and his ears are open to their cry. The face of the Lord is against the evildoers to cut the remembrance of them from the earth. When the righteous cry for help, the Lord hears and rescues them from all their troubles" (Ps 34:15-17). He identifies himself with the brokenhearted and affirms: "The Lord is near to the brokenhearted, and saves the crushed in spirit" (34:18). He concludes: "The Lord redeems the life of his servants, none of those who take refuge in him will be condemned" (34:22). The ordinary Jew and the religious teachers of Jesus' period would not have imagined that a tax collector could pray this psalm.

We now turn to the gospel, the final panel in the triptych in Jesus' teaching about prayer. In the first text, Jesus contrasts the nine insensitive men and the one attuned to God, and also the Jew to the heretical Samaritan. Last week before the callous judge stood the persistent and wronged widow. This week we again meet contrasting characters—the Pharisee and tax collector. The setting is the temple and prayer. The contrast is deftly drawn in a few words. The Pharisee expresses the intensity of his devotion to God in his bi-weekly fast and tithes. However, his heart is perverse. He regards others with contempt. All his religiosity is empty. We are reminded of a few words of Paul: "If... and lack love" then all is meaningless. We may judge that Jesus' story is a caricature of the Pharisee. However, we probably all know how easily it is to be judgmental toward others who are obvious and public sinners. We find it very difficult to own our sinfulness in an honest and transparent way before God and ourselves. The prayer of the Pharisee is a caricature, and yet Jesus touches the nerve. Many of us share the attitude of this man though we would rather identify ourselves with the tax collector.

The tax collector's prayer is not a caricature. His prayer is the genuine prayer of a person aware of true sinfulness. We note that he "stood far off" and "would not lift his eyes" and beat his breast. His prayer is a gem: "God be merciful to me, a sinner!" How many women and men over centuries have repeated this prayer and found deep peace. It is a prayer of each believer and of the community of believers. At times, we hesitate to own our sinfulness at the beginning of our liturgies or do so in a ritual manner. We need to be careful that we do not distort the image of God and turn him into a "forgiver of sins" and type of law enforcement agent. However, there is a very healthy type of prayer in which we acknowledge our sinfulness regularly and without an abiding sense of guilt.

We have included the three texts that teach aspects of prayer. In the first panel in the triptych, our teacher was the Samaritan leper, spontaneous and generous in his praise and gratitude. Our second teacher was the wronged widow, persistent in the face of great indifference. Finally we are asked in our prayer life to identify with the sinful tax collector and make his prayer, "God be merciful to me, a sinner" our own.

We complete our reading of Timothy. The writer returns to "Paul's" autobiographical narrative (2 Tim 4:6–8, 16–18). Paul's ministry and life are ending. He reviews this ministry with emphasis on his consistent fidelity and his hope of the reward of the "crown of righteousness," namely an Olympic gold medal. He has lived his whole life and exercised his ministry according to God's will. He is a righteous person and therefore God will reward him. He compares his life to a "fight" and a "race." He is sure he will win the prize. Often our writer links his exhortations to fidelity and constancy with the appearing of Jesus Christ as the Judge of the living and the dead and the reward to all who are faithful (1:12, 18; 2:10–12; 4:1–2, 8, 18). The writer adds some final comments about the painful aspects of the present court case and Paul's confidence in the Lord's goodness and power. In the gospel of the thirty-third Sunday, Jesus instructs his disciples not to be afraid when dragged into courts (Lk 21:13–15). "Paul" witnesses to the truth of this promise (4:17). The letters to Timothy have riches for pastors and catechists. There is also an atmosphere of fear and "conservatism" in the letters, which reflect difficult situations in some communities around the end of the first century. False and deceitful teachers created many tensions at that time.

THIRTY-FIRST SUNDAY IN ORDINARY TIME: YEAR C, Luke 19:1–10

Jesus—To Seek and Save the Lost

Our initial liturgical readings draw a particular picture of God. In the gospel, Jesus will act in a way that indicates that this God molds his whole attitude. The central verses in the responsorial psalm (Ps 144/145) gather a major experience of God that has matured over centuries. The psalmist praises God with an unaccustomed exuberance because "The Lord is gracious and merciful, slow to anger and abounding in steadfast love. The Lord is good to all, and his compassion is over all he made" (Ps 145:8–9; cf. Ex 34:6). This text gathers the great qualities of God, his graciousness and compassionate mercy, his steadfast love and his goodness. Human sinfulness has disastrous effects on communities and on individuals, and the Old Testament is one history of the destructive power of sin. There are any number of stories of the sinfulness of groups, nations, and individuals, and the consequences within human society and history. However, in the midst of all these terrible stories there is that story of God who is compassionate and merciful. This is the God whom we celebrate this Sunday.

A wisdom writer late in Israel's history retells the story of his people (Wis chs. 11–19) and includes various excurses into his retelling of the long story. One of these concerns that omnipotence of God, which is totally at the service of his love and mercy (Wis 11:23—12:2). Such mercy is meant to wean people from evil and lead them to a trusting commitment to God. He reflects: "You are merciful to all, for you can do all things and you overlook people's sins so that they may repent" (Wis 11:23). We turn now to the gospel.

By necessity, the lectionary jumps over many scenes. The scenes that follow the illustrative story of the two men at prayer focus attention on the conditions necessary to be part of God's people, namely to enter the kingdom of God. Jesus' disciples try to protect him from a group of mothers who wish to receive his blessing for their children. Reacting to the attitude of the disciples, Jesus teaches that anyone who enters the kingdom must have the dependent and humble disposition of a child (18:15-17). To the ruler who inquires about the conditions to share in eternal life he reiterates his teaching on the need to distance one's heart from wealth, and in his case this means "selling all" and giving the proceeds to the poor (18:18-30). Jesus again reminds his disciples unsuccessfully of their need to follow the crucified Jesus. They cannot understand his words about his death (18:31-34). However, the blind man, an example of living faith, once cured follows Jesus on his way to Jerusalem as a model for disciples (18:35-43). Our gospel introduces us to another surprising member of the people of God (Lk 19:1-10).

Zacchaeus was probably young (able to climb up the tree!) and a wealthy Jew. He had status among the colonial rulers and well-to-do groups in the locality. Jericho is quite near the capital, Jerusalem. He was a major tax collector and farmed out tax collection to others. He was also unpopular with many locals and of course with the religious authorities. There is quite a lot of humor in his straining to see Jesus, and his frustration because he was short. We watch him looking for a way to catch a glimpse of Jesus. Off he runs and climbs up a tree. He is quite an attractive person. He shows no antagonism to Jesus, probably more than curiosity, maybe a fascination with the young teacher about whom he has heard. This was the first time Jesus had come to Jericho.

The narrator heightens the humor as Jesus pauses beside the tree and looks up. Zacchaeus will never forget the words, "Zacchaeus, hurry and come down, for I must stay at your house today." We note the use of "I must" (*dei* in the Greek text). This small word indicates what is God's will for Jesus in his ministry. This adds a dimension to the whole account. Zacchaeus was so pleased to welcome Jesus into his home. We would like to know what he said to his wife when they were alone and what he asked her to prepare for Jesus.

However, not everyone was pleased. The crowd grumbled, "He has gone to be the guest of one who is a sinner" (19:7). This recalls the grumbling of the Pharisees earlier in Luke's narrative (5:30; 15:1-2). In this scene the crowd also shares in the attitude of Simon when the sinful woman spoiled his party (7:39) and of the Pharisee of Jesus' story of the two who went to the Temple to pray (17:10-12). Zacchaeus was more akin to the tax collector of that story (17:13).

The narrator has carefully set the stage and introduced all the elements needed for the central scene in which Jesus and Zacchaeus are inside and face to face. Jesus as a man of God was a challenge to him. He responded with realism and in a concrete way. Note he was not expected to "leave all" (5:11, 28; 14:33) or "sell all that he has" (18:12; 12:33). He was called to a radical change of attitude and behavior and he responded. We are reminded of John the Baptist's instructions to various groups in society (3:10-14). John challenges the ordinary people to share clothes and food with others. The tax collectors are told "Collect no more than the amount prescribed for you." No fraud is allowed! Soldiers (police) are told not to extort money by threats and false accusations and to be satisfied with their wages. John's teaching was both realistic and exigent.

Zacchaeus decided voluntarily to give half of his wealth to the poor and to follow the strictest provisions of the law for restitution. It is presumed that he has committed fraud in his social responsibilities.

Jesus did not make him a member of a religion. The term "son of Abraham," though linked to Judaism, is not denominational. It rather refers to Zacchaeus as an authentic Jew and as a genuine human person who deserves to be named a son of the God who is the Father of all good people. He is a repentant figure. Luke has included this account because his repentance is unusual. He is a paradigm of the person who does "hear" the Word of God and follows it. Normally we compromise. He makes no compromise.

Jesus gives us another glimpse of a major aspect of his own self-awareness. An aspect of his commitment and continued ambition in life is "to seek out and save the lost." Note the "seek out." The "lost" refers to the morally impoverished human person, the human person caught up in the sinfulness of his "profession." "The Lost" is the recurring thematic term in Jesus' parables of the lost sheep, lost coin, and lost son (15:6, 9, 24, 32). Jesus also reveals again the image of his Father as the God of mercy and the source of life who is the God of "the lost." Our liturgical year is ending. We have followed Jesus in Luke's gospel. Have we been affected in any way so that we can share in the joy of Zacchaeus and his experience of Jesus as a source of new and a more genuine human life?

We shall read selections from 2 Thessalonians for the following three Sundays. This is a difficult letter; a minor writing in the NT whose writer is probably unknown. The community was undergoing some type of suffering and persecution because they had accepted the gospel. There was confusion among them, caused by ideas spread in "Paul's" name about the "Day of the Lord" or the coming of the Lord Jesus (*Parousia*) and judgment.

In a prayer of gratitude to God, the writer praises the fidelity and love of the community and their steadfastness in spite of the severe afflictions (1:2–4). He reflects on the reality of suffering from the point of view of God's judgment, very positive in their case and yet terrible for those who persecute them (1:5–10). This leads him to pray that they may continue to be faithful to their call in practical ways. He wants them to glorify the Lord Jesus by their fidelity. He affirms that God will gift them with a share in the glory of Christ (1:11–12). He also addresses the problem of "the Day of the Lord." He cautions them against false reports of his prophetic words or teaching and forged letters attributed to him. The heightening of expectation and growing enthusiasm as if "the Day of the Lord" had come or was about to come was causing much confusion in the community (2:1–2). Even today, the "end of the world" is an "in-topic."

THIRTY-SECOND SUNDAY IN ORDINARY TIME: YEAR C, Luke 20:27–38

Jesus—Caught up in Religious Conflict

We approach the end of the liturgical year. The theme of this Sunday's liturgy is the last statement of the Apostles Creed: "We believe in the resurrection of the dead and life everlasting." Such a belief emerged into Jewish consciousness quite late in her history though it was a common tenet of the religion of Jesus of Nazareth. In the first reading we have one of the major texts from the inter-testamental period (2 Mac 7:1–2, 9–14). This book, written in Greek, was not included in the Jewish Canon, though it gives the narrative background for a major Jewish feast, Hanukkah. Antiochus Epiphanes (175–164 B.C.E.) carried out a major program of hellenization to make the Jewish people adapt to the religious and cultural world of the Seleucid Empire. There is a description of the process of Hellenization in 6:1–11. The second book of Maccabees narrates three major attempts to attack the Temple. Our reading is taken from the long narrative of the second attempt (2 Mac 4:1—10:9). There is a developed theology of martyrdom with the venerable Eleazar and the mother and her seven sons as the exemplary martyrs (6:18–31 and 7:1–42). In the middle of the gruesome details of their death the brief professions of faith by the second, third, and fourth sons include their belief in and hope of the resurrection of the just and their vindication.

The responsorial psalm (Ps 16/17) witnesses to the urgent cry of an innocent and just (17:5) person (17:1, 6) persecuted by others (17:9–12) yet buoyed up by his steadfast confidence in God (17:7–8). He concludes his prayer with these words: "As for me, I will behold your face in righteousness; when I awake I shall be satisfied, beholding your likeness" (17:15). Though the psalmist was not referring to the resurrection in this verse, it can be read in that sense. We could imagine the mother with her sons praying this psalm. These two readings form the background to Jesus' controversy about the resurrection.

We have jumped ahead in the Lukan narrative. Jesus has entered Jerusalem, wept over the city, and cleansed the Temple (19:28–48). The religious leaders have officially questioned his authority (20:1–8) and the initial part of his response was the story of the murder of the vineyard owner's son (20:9–18). At this point, the leadership had decided to arrest him but the fear of the crowds constrained them (20:19; cf. 19:47–48). Two more controversies follow the one about his authority to cleanse the temple. One concerns the payment of taxes to the hated colonial Roman government (20:20–26). The second is our reading about the resurrection (20:27–38).

There were many different factions or "denominations" within Judaism. The Pharisees believed in the resurrection but the Sadducees did not accept this later tenet of the belief system. Paul knew this very well, and he set the cat among the pigeons at his arraignment before the Jewish Council when he claimed that the case against him concerned the resurrection of the dead. The Pharisees and Sadducees in the Council immediately began to fight among themselves (Acts 23:6–10). The Sadducees, the priestly aristocratic group in Jerusalem, tried to trap Jesus in this controversy. They put an absurd case before him based on the custom enshrined in the Torah that a brother must ensure that his own brother's name lives on if he dies childless (Dt 25:5–6). The absurdity of the case (20:29–33) is meant to ridicule the belief in the resurrection. Jesus responded.

He used typical arguments from his own tradition. He compared "this age" and "the age to come." Procreation (= marriage) is necessary in this age but not in the age to come because no one dies. In the age to come, the status of all is different because humans are like angels and are children of God. To be children of God they must rise, that is, they are "children of the resurrection." This Hebrew phrase could be translated "those who are raised by God." To affirm the resurrection Jesus quoted from a biblical passage using his contemporaries' way to refer to passages in the Scripture. "in the story about the bush." There were no chapters and verses! If God is really the God of Abraham, Isaac, and Jacob, a major tenet of Torah belief that the Sadducees accepted, then they must be alive. God is the God of the living and not of the dead. To God they must be alive. The argument would not convince us today!

Our resurrection is one of the cornerstones of Christian belief. It is intimately linked to Christ's resurrection, which itself is inseparable from every aspect of our belief about God's saving work in and through Jesus of Nazareth, Christ and Lord. In the Creed and in a number of places in the eucharistic prayers we find this belief in our resurrection. We could reflect on the influence of this hope on our daily living. Can we face our own death or the death of a spouse, relations, or friends? Do we have the ability to accompany those suffering from incurable diseases, and those faced with tragedy? If I recall correctly, Malcolm Muggeridge was interviewing a nurse. He asked her about her belief in the resurrection. She dismissed it as a fairy tale. He just remarked something like, "I hope you are not near me when I have to die."

A further appropriate reflection would be about the resurrection of the body. We are body-persons, and our attitude to our body is an important aspect of our resurrection faith and Christian life. The sacred nature of the human body has many implications. We must be careful not to separate the human into two parts, body and soul, and to value the soul or the body to the detriment of the other aspect of the human. For Christians the "body-soul"person dies and lives forever with God. To speak of and to pray for and celebrate the Eucharist for someone's soul is an impoverishment of our Christian faith, if not erroneous. God created and loves the person, the "body-person." Christ as a "body-person" dies. He died for the human person. Jesus of Nazareth and not his "soul" is Christ and Lord. Therefore, God raises our "body-person" with all the rich and historical dimensions of the human person. We can reflect on the way we honor the dignity of ourselves as "body-persons." This will involve reflections on work, eating and drinking, rest and recreation, smoking and drugs, and health care. It also includes our attitude to aging, and to aged and disabled people. We believe in the "resurrection of the body," namely the "body–person" who belongs to the family of God.

The writer of Thessalonians has indicated to the community that there are certain apocalyptic signs that will accompany "the Day of the Lord." It has not come (2:3–12). He resumes his prayer of gratitude recalling the manner in which God has gifted them, beloved of the Lord whom he has chosen, with the Spirit and faith in the truth. They are destined to share in the glory of Christ. He also urges them to be faithful to their call and to the faith traditions they have been taught (2:13–15).

This again leads him to intercede for the community.

He prays that the Lord Jesus Christ and God, who loved them and gifted them with hope and assurance of eternal life, continue to strengthen and comfort their inner person so that they live meaningful faith lives (2:16–17). He also asks them to pray that his ministry be fruitful and that God may protect him from the enemies of the gospel (3:1–2). This awareness of the enemies of the gospel opens out into another prayer for them and an indirect exhortation that they remain faithful (3:3–4). There is a fine final wish. He writes "May the Lord direct your hearts (inner person) to the love of God (God's love for you) and to the steadfastness of Christ"(Christ's permanent relationship with them [3:5]). Pastors will note the way the writer takes his community and the concrete situations of their lives into his prayers of gratitude and intercession.

THIRTY-THIRD SUNDAY IN ORDINARY TIME: YEAR C, Luke 21:5–19

A Glance into the Future

The theme of the liturgy is not so clear. It is related to one of the statements of our Creed: "He will come again to judge the living and the dead." Judgment is not one of the more popular themes of Christian belief because many see it as a frightening element. However, for the Christian, and for all men and women of good will, the ultimate meeting with God/Jesus Christ is a joyful and wonderful aspect of our faith.

Malachi pictures the two aspects of the day of judgment (Mal 3:19–20 [4:1–2 in the Greek text and many translations]). For the arrogant and lawless it is a terrible day. He pictures them like stubble thrown into a burning oven, or swept away by a fierce bush fire that leaves nothing in its path. However, for those who revere the Lord it is a wonderful day. God is pictured like a winged solar disk, an image found in Egyptian and Babylonian religious iconography. God, who is the righteous judge, rises like the warm sun upon those who revere him to bring healing and give unspeakable joy.

The psalmist takes up his theme of joy (Ps 97/98). The whole orchestra is invited to celebrate God, the royal judge. All of nature is to rejoice. All are to sing "at the presence of the Lord, for he is coming to judge the earth; he will judge the world with righteousness and the people with equity."

There is an aspect of our piety that can be dangerous. It is symbolized in a prayer that was and is still very commonly said after each decade of the rosary. It runs "save us from the fires of hell and lead all souls to heaven especially those who most need your mercy." Our responsibility before God is a major theme in all biblical spirituality. We are able to sin in very grave ways. However, "hell" and punishment ought not to be major themes in our spirituality. The major reason is that the manner in which "hell" and "final damnation" are presented in some forms of popular piety damages the image of God and contradicts a major theme of the life of Jesus Christ. There is a danger that catechists and teachers do not give the necessary importance to sin, personal and social, personal responsibility, the ravages caused by human evil, and the gravity of sin. However, the Christian community is a community called to repentance by a God whose mercy we cannot conceive. Nothing ought to distort, corrupt, sow doubt, and call in question the core of Jesus' revelation that the Father is merciful.

The gospel is a difficult reading (Lk 21:5–19). This is a selection from Jesus' final instruction to his disciples in the precincts of the Jerusalem Temple (21:5–36). The texts include Jesus' teachings and their expansion by Christian teachers in the light of the actual destruction of Jerusalem and the Temple and the experience of persecution by the early communities.

His disciples were admiring the beauty of the Herodian Temple, one of the wonders of the ancient world. In a prophetic manner Jesus responds by speaking of the utter destruction of the Temple (21:5–6; cf. 19:42–44). This leads to two groups of sayings about the "when" of the destruction and the "signs" that will precede this judgment of God (21:7). Various sayings are strung together about false messiahs ("I am he"), about wars, earthquakes, famine and plagues, and astrological portents. The series of evils are typical of judgment oracles in the Old Testament. These sayings are more likely to be linked to a later saying in the text about the coming of the Son of Man (21:25–28), though some aspects would apply to the period of civil unrest and war prior to the destruction of the city and Temple in 70 C.E. (21:20–24).

Another series of sayings takes up a different theme, namely the persecution of the believing community (21:12-19). Persecution will arise from different groups: from local and state governments (21:12), from within the family and the circle of friends and relations (21:16), and from neighbors because of more popular and general antagonism (21:17). Persecution will take various forms: court cases, imprisonment, and even death. We know from Paul's letters the types of suffering he had to undergo and the trials of his communities (cf. 1 Cor 4:9-13; 2 Cor 6:4-10, 11:23-33). Acts also witnesses to the suffering of the early believing communities. Court cases and the like will enable the believers to testify to Jesus Christ and the gospel. They need not prepare a defense because Jesus himself will be with them and enable them to respond in appropriate ways. Jesus also reassures them that God will protect them, even each hair on their heads. We know that some were killed. God's protection does not rule out much suffering. The community is challenged to be faithful. What Jesus says in these sayings seems far away from modern American Christian life. There can be mockery, indifference, and discrimination yet not real persecution. Do men and women who seek to live according to the gospel not suffer? I suspect that many do suffer.

In an earlier letter to the Thessalonian community Paul had given them this brief warning: "We urge you... to aspire to live quietly, to mind your own affairs, and to work with your hands, as we directed you, so that you may behave properly towards outsiders and be dependent on no one" (1 Thes 4:11-12). The writer returns to this problem, which may have been caused because some were waiting so expectantly for the coming of the Lord (3:6-12). They were being busybodies, giving the community a bad name and imposing on others. The writer urges the community to isolate such members. He appeals to the example set for them by Paul who worked with his own hands to support himself when he had stayed among them (3:7-9, cf. 1 Thes 2:9). He again appeals to earlier teaching and warnings. No work no bread. It is not very easy to see the point of such a reading for most communities in today's world.

THIRTY-FOURTH SUNDAY IN ORDINARY TIME, SOLEMNITY OF CHRIST THE KING: YEAR C, Luke 23:35–43

The King Who Is Faithful to his Mission on the Cross

Traditional Christ the King feasts with large processions though parts of towns may not be at ease with a crucified king. The liturgy, however, draws our attention to the crucified king. The scene deserves attention, and Luke has crafted his narrative with care. He describes the crucifixion itself with an economy of detail (23:32–33). Jesus had already prayed for the men involved in this deed (23:34). Luke gives a careful account of what happened in the time that elapsed before Jesus' death. The narrator draws our attention to four groups. The people stood by watching the spectacle (23:35). The leaders sneered at him taunting him, "save yourself, if you are really the Christ of God, his chosen one" (23:35). Jesus remained silent. The soldiers mocked him, offering cheap wine to alleviate his painful agony and challenging him to prove that he was the King of the Jews by coming down (23:36–37). Jesus did nothing. Luke reminds us that the crime was scribbled above his head and it read, "The King of the Jews is this one" (23:38).

Next, we hear the repeated taunt of one of the criminals, "Aren't you the Christ? Save yourself and us" (23:39). The mood around the cross changes for the reader as the other criminal rebukes his companion. Stating clearly that Jesus is totally innocent and admitting his and his companion's guilt, he takes him to task because he has no fear of God, no conscience (23:40–41). We note that the innocence of Jesus is a major theme in Luke's passion. Pilate reiterates that Jesus is innocent (23:4, 14, 15, 22). The Centurion watching Jesus die summed up this attitude. Praising God he said, "Certainly, this man was innocent" (23:47). The women knew it, and the crowds admitted it, beating their breasts as they left Calvary (23:48).

The criminal turning to Jesus makes a simple and faith-filled request, "Jesus remember me when you come into your kingdom." Others have mocked Jesus because he cannot save himself, though they admit that he has helped ("saved") others during his lifetime. This criminal of Luke's gospel has understood that the new relationship between God and our human family is created by "body given" and "blood shed." Jesus answered the request of this person. The mission he had undertaken from his Father when he said "I must proclaim the Good News of the Kingdom of God to other cities also; for I was sent for this purpose"(4:43) he now completes. For the last time during his historical life Jesus brings the Good News to the poor (4:18, 7:22) in his brief and simple response (23:43) and shows himself to be the friend of sinners (7:34; 5:32; 15:1-2; 19:7). At the supper with his disciples when they began again to dispute about greatness, he had identified himself saying, "I am among you as one who serves" (22:27).

Throughout Luke's passion Jesus is deeply concerned for others. He prayed for Peter (22:32), encouraged his disciples to pray, and gave them an example (22:40-46). He healed the servant's ear (22:51). He turned and looked at Peter as he denied him (22:61). He spoke with deep feeling and concern to the distraught women of Jerusalem about their fate (23:27-31). He prayed for those who crucified him (23:34). He spoke words of hope to this dying man.

We dedicate ourselves to this king. Jesus is the king who brings God's forgiveness to sinners, no matter who they are or what they have done. All he asks is our readiness both to believe that God is merciful and to receive his mercy.

The reading from Samuel (2 Sam 5:1-3) does not provide a rich background for our gospel. David has been acclaimed king in his own province and among his own tribe, the Judah group. After much political maneuvering, he has forced the northern tribes to accept him as king. They save face by claiming that he is "our bone and our flesh." They accept him as their shepherd and prince. The text does place restraints on the king, who is forced to make a covenant with the people of Israel, spelling out his duties to them. The psalm (Ps 121/122) celebrates the greatness of Jerusalem, the royal city and place where God dwells.

The reading from Paul is a magnificent hymn celebrating Jesus Christ. We have commented upon this text (Col 1:12-20) on the Fifteenth Sunday. We add a few more reflections. The criminal at the cross could have shared in Paul's thanksgiving prayer to God the Father: "giving thanks to the Father.... He has rescued us from the power of darkness and transferred us into the kingdom of the Son of his love, in whom we have redemption and the forgiveness of sins" (Col 1:12-14). We learn a lot when we juxtapose the picture of Jesus crucified as narrated by Luke and the hymn to the Son. We have seen the mocked and powerless crucified king. The hymn portrays the Son in majesty gifted with power and with dominion over the whole universe. All depends on him. There are a series of expressions that underline the totality of Jesus' dominion over the creation and the recreated world (note the use of "all" and phrases like "earth and heaven" and "visible and invisible").

Through his death on the cross the Son is also the source of universal reconciliation, peace, and resurrection (1:18, 20). In Luke's narrative this is symbolized in Jesus' personal response to the repentant and believing criminal. All that can be described as "divine" is to be found in the Son (1:19; cf. 2:9). God created the universe in and through the Son. He reconciled the universe to himself through the crucified Son. As we move back and forth between the hymn and the narration of the crucified Jesus who is unable to save himself, we learn why he deserves the wonderful title "Son of his Love." We also learn about the type of king he was, is, and will always be. We can all approach him at any time and in any state.

THE PASCHAL MYSTERY
in the Order of Mass

The Paschal Mystery in the Eucharistic Prayer

Russell Hardiman

CELEBRATION AS ANAMNESIS

As regards the liturgical seasons and feasts, the paschal mystery has the most direct connection with the Solemnity of Easter and the total Easter season. This is not simply because of the chronological connection of Good Friday as the day of Christ's death or because of the connection of passover imagery with the passing over of Jesus from death to life. This connection is especially so because of the special characteristic of the notion of "anamnesis," of not-forgetting, of remembering, which is at the heart of the Judeo-Christian tradition of celebration.

In anamnesis, the church proclaims the death of Jesus, his resurrection from the dead, and his ascension into glory. As the memorial of these key events in the total paschal mystery, this action of the church in the power of Christ's risen Spirit proclaims the redemptive action of Christ, which is the essence of every eucharistic liturgy.

This sense of anamnesis is the key concept in the understanding of the eucharistic action. This is because of its unique fusion of past, present, and future into the one eternal time plane of God's salvific action. Most historical commemorations simply look back to the past to encourage those of the present to appreciate from where they have come.

In Judeo-Christian tradition the impact of anamnesis was, is, and will be twofold: while recalling or retelling the story of something done in the past, at the same time it makes the fruits of that memorialized action present now in anticipation that God's promise will always be fulfilled.

In the tradition of Jewish practice, remembering is linked always to action. This is the sense of anamnesis: not merely remembering something of the past but re-presenting that past action of God in such a way that the present generation become participants in it as well. This is the sense of the continued practice of the Jewish Passover, whereby everyone is to consider as if they had come out of Egypt and look to the continued reassurance of God's promise in the covenant.

In the Christian tradition it is through the Eucharist that the community of faith not only recalls Christ's death and resurrection but also makes present on earth Christ's sacrifice sacramentally, so as to share the fruits of his death in the power of his risen spirit.

This is succinctly expressed in the prayer over the gifts we pray on the Second Sunday of Ordinary Time: more than a happy coincidence so close to New Year's Day.

> Father,
> may we celebrate the Eucharist
> with reverence and love,
> for when we proclaim the death of the Lord
> You continue the work of his redemption,
> who is Lord for ever and ever.

Obviously this theme finds its origins in the phrase of St. Paul when he shared with the Corinthian Christian community, even its factions in that era, what he has learned about the Lord's Supper on the night before Jesus died. He challenged the divided community to examine themselves about the consequences of their shared action, for "When you eat this bread, then, and drink this cup you are proclaiming the Lord's death until he comes" (1 Cor 11:27; New Jerusalem Bible).

St. Paul was using his formal training in the rabbinic tradition when he expressly linked what he told the Corinthians with the very tradition he had received. This technical terminology used by the rabbis for the passing on of tradition was the language Paul used, not to claim a personal revelation, but the living tradition going back to the Lord.

That same living tradition has been expressed by the church with the introduction of a formal acclamation that paraphrases Paul's words. The church now encourages us to use this phrase (among others) to acclaim the mystery of faith.

> When we eat this bread and drink this cup,
> we proclaim your death, Lord Jesus,
> until you come in glory.

ANAMNESIS AS THE PATTERN OF CHRISTIAN PRAYER

A further example of the special characteristics of sacramental action in the Easter season is the theological thrust of the pattern of prayer in the Christian tradition. As Christians we give thanks to the Father, through the Son in the Holy Spirit. This is the by-product of the sense of anamnesis, of not forgetting, the unique time-frame of God's redemptive action that still continues until the time of its eternal fulfillment.

This focus of the eucharistic prayer is illustrated from start to finish, in fact from dialogue to doxology. When we respond to the invitation "lift up your hearts" and "give thanks to the Lord our God" we can truly affirm that it is right and fitting to do so, it is our duty and the source of our salvation everywhere and in all places to give thanks (to God the Father) through Christ the Lord. As climax, we return to that theme in acclaiming that it is through Christ, with Christ, and in Christ that all honor and glory are given to the Father in the unity of the Holy Spirit now and forever.

This pattern of prayer to the Father, through Christ in the unity of the Spirit was the primary form of early Christian prayer. We still use it as the formal conclusion—in the long form—of the opening prayer. It is intended in the abbreviated form of most orations when we conclude by simply saying "We make our prayer through Christ our Lord." Even in the most abbreviated form of "Through Christ our Lord" it is still projected to the Father, through Christ, in the power of the Holy Spirit.

Up until the fourth-fifth centuries, the traditional Christian doxology added to the Psalms was recited as "Glory be to the Father through the Son in the Holy Spirit," as in the eucharistic prayer. However, in the era of the Arian controversy about the divinity of Jesus, the pattern changed to emphasize the equality in unity of the persons of the Trinity and, as a result, we still say:

> Glory be to the Father
> and to the Son
> and to the Holy Spirit.

The unfortunate by-product of this historical precedent is that it becomes difficult to show a unified praying of all forms of doxologies, our formal genre of praise to God. The dual tracks point in the same direction without touching, which makes it difficult to see their common origin.

ANAMNESIS AND THE EUCHARISTIC PRAYER

Another strong Jewish connection is in the origins of the Christian eucharistic prayer. Recent generations of liturgical research have confirmed the obvious and the inevitable. Because the earliest Christian communities were composed largely of Jewish converts, their Jewish heritage meant that their worship patterns were based around home, temple, and synagogue. Scholars have traced the influence of particular Jewish traditions of prayers of thanksgiving (*Berakah*), of prayers of "sacrifice of praise" (*Todah*), and of prayers of blessing of God in the order of God's goodness in creation and salvation (*Birkhat ha-Mazon*).

The common denominator of the Jewish prayer forms is that there was a developing tradition in Jewish circles of acclaiming what God had done for the people of the past, what God is doing for the present generation, and what God will continue to do in fulfillment of his promise.

The unique time-frame of this tradition has opened up avenues of clarity amid the debates as to whether the Last Supper was a Passover meal or simply a Jewish religious fellowship meal (*Chaburah*). Regardless, the fact is, the Christian tradition soon developed Passover imagery to explain their interpretation of the way to fulfill Christ's command "Do this in memory of me." The unique pattern of prayer enabled Christian communities to develop a variety of ways of blessing God's name for the work of creation and redemption still continuing.

A special aspect of the Jewish connection is in the dimension of intercession. Most of the Jewish prayers expressed confidence in God's continuing benevolence by focusing their prayer of petition on Jerusalem. God's faithfulness to his promise would be revealed in the blessings showered on Jerusalem.

The early Christians transposed this focus from Jerusalem to the church. The earliest prayer, in the *Didache*, from the end of the first century, incorporates this for the church, whose scattered members are to be gathered together to share the promise of God's eternal banquet at the end of time.

The work of the liturgical movement, benefiting from the growth in biblical studies, ecclesiology, and the history of the early church, had led to a strong consensus as to the structure or pattern of the central prayer of Thanksgiving of the Christian Eucharist.

From those days when there was free composition within certain stylistic structure, scholarship has unearthed some hundreds of extant texts of eucharistic prayers. Even though the scholars divide them up into various groupings there are basic elements common to all.

The fruits of the research coming from the many facets of study associated with the liturgical movement can be illustrated by the consensus about the structure of the eucharistic prayer. Apart from the more scholarly works the consensus has been given to the church at large in the paragraphs of the *General Instruction of the Roman Missal* (1969) and reproduced in the *Catechism of the Catholic Church* (1994).

GENERAL INSTRUCTION OF THE ROMAN MISSAL no. 55

INVOCATION OF THE HOLY SPIRIT
Epiclesis: in special invocations
the Church calls on God's
power and asks that the gifts offered by human
hands be consecrated, that is, become Christ's
body and blood, and that the victim to be received
in communion be the source of salvation for those
who will partake.

THE LORD'S SUPPER
Institution narrative and consecration:
in the words and actions of Christ, that sacrifice is
celebrated which he himself instituted at the Last
Supper, when, under the appearances of bread and
wine, he offered his body and blood, gave them to
the Apostles to eat and drink, then commanded
that they carry on this mystery.

REMEMBERING
Anamnesis: in fulfillment of the command
received from Christ through the Apostles,
the Church keeps his memorial
by recalling especially his passion, resurrection, and
ascension.

MEMORIAL OFFERING
Offering: in this memorial, the Church—
and in particular the Church here and now assembled—
offers the spotless victim to the Father in the Holy Spirit.
The Church's intention is that the faithful
not only offer this victim but also learn
to offer themselves and surrender themselves,

CATECHISM OF THE CATHOLIC CHURCH no. 1352-no. 1355

INVOCATION OF THE HOLY SPIRIT
In the *Epiclesis*
the Church asks the Father to send his
Holy Spirit (or the power of his blessing)
on the bread and wine, so that by his
power they may become the Body and
Blood of Jesus Christ and so that those
who take part in the Eucharist may be one
body and one spirit (some liturgical
traditions put the epiclesis after the anamnesis).

THE LORD'S SUPPER
In the *Institution narrative*,
the power of the words and the action of
Christ, and the power of the Holy Spirit,
make sacramentally present under the
species of bread and wine Christ's body
and blood, his sacrifice offered on the
cross once for all.

REMEMBERING
In the *anamnesis*
the Church calls to mind the Passion,
resurrection, and glorious return of
Christ Jesus: she presents to the Father
the offering of his son which reconciles
us with him.

*through Christ the Mediator, to an even
more complete union with the Father and each other,
so that at last God may be all in all.*

PRAYING WITH THE CHURCH

Intercessions: *the intercessions make it clear
Eucharist is celebrated in communion
with the entire Church of heaven and earth
and that the offering is made for the Church
and all its members, living and dead,
who are called to share in the salvation and
redemption purchased by Christ's body and blood.*

COMPLETION OF THANKSGIVING

*Final doxology: the praise of God is expressed
in the doxology,
to which the people's acclamation is an assent and
a conclusion.*

PRAYING WITH THE CHURCH

*In the **intercessions**, the Church indicates that the
Eucharist is celebrated in communion with the
whole Church in heaven, and on earth, the
living and the dead, and in communion with the
pastors of the Church, the Pope, the
Diocesan Bishop, his presbyterium and
his deacons, and all the Bishops of the whole
world together with their Churches.*

ANAMNESIS WITH UNITY IN VARIETY

Because Vatican II was able to capitalize on the progress of insights through the liturgical movement, it re-expressed a theology of Eucharist based on a biblical theology, a theology of sacraments, and a biblical ecclesiology somewhat different from that of the Scholastic era. The council encouraged the opening up of our euchological tradition, similar to the pattern of prayer in the early centuries of the church. Since then we have been blessed with a much richer repertoire from the ancient treasury that has given us both new things and old.

The studies of the parallels between Jewish forms of prayer and its Christian extension have resulted in a consensus about the structure of the eucharistic prayer: a pattern of some variable parts in a literary form of consistent format.

The variables originate in the transformation of the Jewish pattern into a Christian pattern. In the format of the *Birkat-ha-mazon* the call to thanksgiving could be amplified and extended, to suit the feast (e.g., for Pentecost it could be illustrated in Yahweh's gift to the chosen people). Thus, extended further, the theme of thanksgiving is recounted in the focus on God's action in creation and in the history of salvation, especially in Christ the Lord and the continuing work of his Holy Spirit. This translates into numerous themes in the prefaces: in the continuation of that theme after the "Holy, Holy" known as the "post sanctus" (or Praise to the Father): in the themes of anamnesis as we list the main reasons for our memorial offering immediately after the institution narrative (also called the consecration): in the intercessions we pray that God be faithful to the promise of his Covenant in the mission of the church as witness to God's kingdom.

As well as these variables we have more fixed substructures, such as the opening dialogue, holy holy, Invocation of the Holy Spirit (epiclesis), institution narrative, memorial offering, intercessions for the living and the dead, and doxology.

With the multiplicity of variables and choices it can be confusing as to how best to use the available texts. The necessary choices can only come from a pastoral sensitivity to the appropriate needs of a local community informed by a profound theological awareness of the function, structure, and centrality of the eucharistic prayer. To encourage a reflection on personal practice a perusal of the elements in the accompanying box may help readers fine tune their attitudes in the choices they make and the practice they model in communal worship.

ANAMNESIS IN MULTIPLE FORMS

The historical evidence has been revealed by the studies of biblical scholars, liturgiologists, and the publication of critical editions of ancient texts from as far back as the

Apostolic Tradition of Hippolytus. This is the oldest (from c. 215 C.E.) extant written text of the unique genre of thanksgiving prayers proclaimed by a free style within the limits of the accustomed pattern. It is a significant indication of ecumenical convergence that what Catholics know as Eucharistic Prayer II is also used by many other Christian denominations today.

Guided by the insights from this scriptural and historical research, the church, through its formal Vatican and international language agencies, has consistently expanded the pool of euchological texts available for use.

The first significant change was the expansion beyond just the Roman Canon with the release in 1968 of three eucharistic prayers with the new Order of Mass (1969). Thus Eucharistic Prayer II was a remodeling of the ancient text of the *Apostolic Tradition* of Hippolytus from the early third century; Eucharistic Prayer III was a totally new composition, strongly resonant with the work of the Holy Spirit in the church and with Vatican II images of the church; Eucharistic Prayer IV was an adaptation of an Eastern rite prayer, based on the *Anaphora of St Mark*. The 1969 Missal also included about ninety prefaces, which roughly doubled the number from the previous Tridentine Missal.

In 1974, three eucharistic prayers for children and two eucharistic prayers for Masses of reconciliation were approved for experimental use and since then have been formally approved for permanent optional use.

For the Marian Year a larger pool of prefaces for Masses in Honor of Our Lady was created by further additions to the number of prefaces.

ANAMNESIS AND THE SWISS EUCHARISTIC PRAYER

In 1995 the so-called Swiss Eucharistic Prayer was finally approved for use in English speaking countries, thus making available to other language groups what was available to Switzerland with its three main languages since 1974 (when it was prepared for a Swiss Synod) and to countries who used those languages, like Italy, since 1983.

The process of approval for use elsewhere met the immovable object of Vatican protocol, because the text was originally prepared for trilingual Switzerland but had no official datum-base text in Latin. Many requests from episcopal conferences had been turned down, because of the lack of an official Latin text. Finally in 1991, an official Latin text, the *editio typica*, was prepared to serve as the point of reference from which all vernacular translations could be approved. This required translations to be from an official Latin text, then voted on by national episcopal conferences, re-editing by ICEL, formal approval from the national episcopal conferences, before submission to Rome for "confirmation" of the bishops' decision. The official procedures bore fruit in 1995 with the Roman confirmation of individual national bishops conferences' approval of the ICEL translations.

The formal name of this tenth eucharistic prayer is "For Masses for various needs and occasions." Such a title reflects the confusion about the number of eucharistic prayers and when a eucharistic prayer starts. Probably everybody has heard examples when, after the holy holy, the presider will give directions as to posture, when it may not be practicable to kneel, or the presider will announce which eucharistic prayer is to be used, as if the prayer starts after the preface. The preface is part of the eucharistic prayer and, seeing we have ninety prefaces and four variants in the Swiss prayer, one can say we have over 100 eucharistic prayers.

The distinguishing feature of the Swiss prayer is the way it has taken the original Jewish pattern of amplifying the themes of thanksgiving and the themes of intercession. Specifically, this means that the preface develops themes about the role of Christ and the role of the church as facets of the continuing mystery of the creative, redemptive, and salvific plan of God: the same themes are then reformulated as the opening of the intercessions when we pray that the church be faithful to God's plan in union with all around the world, and in union with the living and the dead.

The themes have formally assigned titles that give insights to their purpose and intent. It also means that each preface and each set of intercessions for the church makes a couplet, so the presider needs to choose consciously the one that amplifies its parallel theme. Just as the fourth eucharistic prayer is always to be read with its own preface, because the unique structure of that preface continues the thanksgiving theme immediately after the holy holy, now with these prayers presiders will need to be aware of the special structure and that it is not a case of mix and match.

The church is affirmed as

Our hope for the coming of Your kingdom
and is a sure sign of the lasting covenant
and we pray that
Your people may stand forth
in a world torn by conflict and strife,
as a sign of oneness and peace
(A: The Church on the way to unity):

As church we are encouraged:

You never abandon the creatures formed by your wisdom,
but remain with us and work for our good even now.
With mighty hand and outstretched arm
you guide your pilgrim Church today
as it journeys along the paths of time
as we unite with our fellow Christians
May we follow your paths in faith and hope, and radiate out your trust in all the world
(B: God guides the Church on the way to salvation)

When we affirm the role of Jesus with Christians of every generation we acclaim anew:

In the Word made flesh
You have given us a mediator
who has spoken your words to us
and called us to follow him.
He is the way that leads to you,
the truth that sets us free,
the life that makes our joy complete
For our part we are reminded
Keep your Church alert in faith
to the signs of the times
and eager to accept the challenge of the Gospel
(C: Jesus, way to the Father)

The model of Jesus is portrayed in the gospel images of the forgiving Father and the Good Samaritan:

He was moved with compassion
for the poor and the powerless,
for the sick and the sinner:
he made himself neighbor to the oppressed.

The mandate Jesus gives us is the call:

Open our eyes to the needs of all:
inspire us with words and deeds
to comfort those who labor and are burdened:
keep our service of others
faithful to the example and command of Christ.
(D: Jesus, the compassion of God)

Our prayers of intercession always link us to strengthen the bonds of our communion with the church that celebrates Eucharist "wherever two or three gather" in the Lord's name.

Sometimes these prayers sound excessively clerical when only pope, bishops, priests, and deacons seem to get a specific mention.

In fact, the focus is on the local church as the microcosm of the universal church, as we pray that the light of the gospel may renew the church of this diocese or place to strengthen the bonds of unity between the faithful and their pastors (Prayer A). This unity embraces the full sweep linking earth and heaven, because we are the communion of saints and share the one liturgy on this earth in anticipation of its fullness with all the saints.

To be in communion with "holy things" is the basis of the communion of the saints, whereby the church through its Eucharistic celebrations everywhere, unites with all living Christians, and those who have gone before us marked with a sign of faith.

The "communion of saints" should not take on a distorted meaning of who is unworthy compared to who is worthy. The evangelists all point out that at the Last Supper Christ was looking forward to celebrating this new Passover meal even when he knew them deeply, and knew one especially, to be "unworthy." Likewise, in the post-resurrection appearances, these same disciples—and others—seemed blocked in recognizing the risen Christ or the true nature of his mission and ministry until the coming of the Holy Spirit at Pentecost to initiate the era of the church.

It is no accident that, just before the intercessions, where we pray with all levels of the communion of saints, we invoke the Holy Spirit. We have already called down the Holy Spirit on our gifts that they become the body and blood of Christ (epiclesis on the gifts). At this point we pray that we who receive these gifts in the Body and Blood of Jesus may become one Body, one Spirit in Christ: that the church become the universal sacrament of the unity of God's people.

Celebrating the Eucharistic Prayer as Source and Summit of Eucharistic Action

Moving Away from Poor Practice	*Moving Toward Best Practice*
Avoid distortion as if the essence of Eucharist is in personal reception of Communion	Be conscious of the importance of the assembly being gathered as church in communion with Christ's risen Spirit

Avoid celebrating Mass as if it were merely a communion service or
    when the EP is poorly proclaimed
    where the fraction is minimal
    where customarily hosts are taken from the tabernacle rather than consecrated at that Mass
    where no option is given for drinking from the cup
	Plan to celebrate the EP as the central action and highlight of the Eucharist.
	    choose deliberately which EP
	    highlight fraction and decanting
	    where knowing the parish and numbers, bread and wine are prepared for each Mass
	    where the full sign of communion is set as a parish priority

Avoid contradicting the unity of the EP
    avoid announcing EP after Holy Holy
    avoid different postures during the EP
    avoid monotone recitation
    avoid using bells only at consecration
	Consciously emphasize the unity of EP
	    announce EP before the dialogue
	    choose kneeling or standing all through
	    emphasize key parts with tone of voice
	    use bells as auditory affirmation for all key parts: epiclesis, consecration, doxology

Don't always use the same EP
    avoid only using EP II
Avoid proper prefaces with EP IV
	Know the range of choices for EP
	    have priorities in making choices
	    proclaim EP IV as symbol of faith

Don't allow EP to be considered as "Father's part"
    avoid music as only a four-hymn sandwich
    avoid using only hymns
	Ensure levels of preparation include choice of EP
	    ensure planners include music in EP
	    Use acclamations, responses, hymns

Avoid mistaken enthusiasm for participation by common recitation of consecration/doxology
    avoid joining with presider
    avoid a spoken Amen
	Emphasize the experience of the mystery of God's presence in powerful ritual action
	    plan strong dialogue in song and word
	    plan a strong doxology with sung Amen

With "Sunday Worship in Absence of Priest"
    don't model communion from tabernacle as normal
    avoid "Prayers of Thanksgiving" that appear as substitute EP
    avoid pseudo-rituals to add solemnity or participation e.g., procession with finger bowl
	With "Sunday Worship in Absence of Priest"
	    affirm at the Eucharist the breads in tabernacle will be an extension of Mass
	    Affirm structure of EP and fraction rite as constituting Eucharist
	    let the symbol speak strongly in full ritual action in right priorities

Avoid contradictory rituals just to provide jobs or involvement for acolytes or servers
    e.g., extinguishing processional candles after use for each part of the Mass
	Train special ministers, acolytes, deacons, and servers to understand their proper role
	    e.g., appreciate the rhythm and flow of processions and active listening.

Rite of Blessing and Sprinkling of Holy Water

Jayne Newton Ahearn

Within the introductory rites of the Order of Mass the first option (A) following the sign of cross and greeting is the rite of blessing and sprinkling of holy water, known more familiarly as the sprinkling rite, or formerly the "Asperges." This option seems to be much less frequently used that its companion, the penitential rite (B). However, there are times and seasons—Feast of All Saints, Christmas, Easter—when this rite is the more appropriate one.

In the revised *Sacramentary*, and its companion *Order of Mass: Pastoral Introduction*, a significant change is that the opening rite is to be a single choice from among the six consecutive elements of the current rite. This will demand greater sensitivity to the season, to the occasion, and to the community, so as to make an appropriate choice.

THE DOCUMENTS

It is recommended that the reader take up a copy of the *Sacramentary/Pastoral Commentary* and read and study these portions. The foreword to the sacramentary was written for the purpose of drawing attention to, and clarifying, particular features, thereby facilitating its use. In the foreword is a section entitled "Sunday Renewal of Baptism."

> As an alternative to the penitential rite at all Sunday Masses, the blessing and sprinkling of the people with holy water may be substituted. This revised rite of sprinkling is no longer restricted to the principal Mass or to the parish churches but may be used "at all Sunday Masses, even those anticipated on Saturday evening, in all churches and oratories."

> To make this point clear, the rite is printed in the Order of Mass as an alternative to the penitential rite. The latter is simply omitted when holy water is blessed and sprinkled. The prayer of blessing of the water, which follows the priest's initial greeting, and the selection of songs to accompany the sprinkling indicate the purpose of the rite: to express the paschal character of Sunday and to be a memorial of baptism.

> The directions for this brief rite are given in the Order of Mass and in Appendix I of the Sacramentary. After the rite of sprinkling, the Order of Mass continues with the Gloria or the opening prayer. (*Foreword to Sacramentary*)

The rite is presented as an alternative to the penitential rite which is not restricted in use to place or celebration. In fact, it is presented as the first alternative, which might be interpreted as the preferred alternative. The intent of the rite is to recall our baptism into Christ's paschal mystery.

The reader is then referred to the directions for the rite within the Order of Mass and also in Appendix I. Paragraph I states that the rite may be celebrated in all churches and chapels at all Masses of Sunday including the Saturday Vigil Mass. The rite is located in the order in the place of the penitential rite and *Kyrie*.

Paragraph 2 provides a model introduction and three forms for the blessing of water. Paragraph 3 allows for the blessing and adding of salt, a cultural adaptation. Paragraph 4 directs that the priest move through the church sprinkling the people while a song is sung. Appropriate texts for this song are suggested in Appendix I. Paragraph 5 provides an absolution, which is used only if the opening prayer will not immediately follow. The *Gloria* is sung or said (No. 6) and the opening prayer follows.

HISTORICAL PERSPECTIVES

The blessing and sprinkling of holy water has its

beginnings probably in the eighth century in monastic ritual. The rooms and buildings of the monastery were sprinkled with holy water as a sign of sanctification. We see this continued in the current rite for dedicating a church in which not only the people, but also the walls of the new church are sprinkled with holy water. The parallel ritual that developed in the East for purification and sanctification was incensing of the worship space accompanied by chanting Psalm 51, the Miserere (*Have mercy on me, O God...*). Eventually in the West, the sprinkling was extended to include the people and took on a baptismal character. But this rite took place only before the principal parish Mass and was never considered to be part of the Order of Mass.

Medieval developments in the Western liturgy (interacting with the theology of those frightening times, which emphasized suffering and evil) included adding introductory rites for cleansing the soul in preparation for celebration of the Eucharist. The penitential rite eventually arose from the private penitential prayers for the priests such as the *Confiteor*. For the faithful the pre-Mass sprinkling took on a penitential emphasis as the *Asperges* or *Vidi aquam*. These names were taken from the chants associated with the rite:

> Have mercy on me, O God, in your goodness: in the greatness of your compassion wipe out my offense. Thoroughly wash me from my guilt and of my sin cleanse me...
>
> Cleanse me of sin with hyssop, that I may be purified: wash me, and I shall be whiter than snow. (Ps 51:3-4, 9)
>
> ...and I saw water flowing out from behind the threshold of the temple toward the east ... Wherever the river flows, every sort of living creature that can multiply shall live ... (Ez 47:1, 9)

This latter "living water" passage was used during the Easter season.

In sixteenth-century rural Germany the practice began of giving the concluding blessing of the Mass a physical reality by sprinkling the people with holy water. Again, holy water became a sanctification.

The Vatican II revision of the Order of Mass established the *Asperges*, now called the "Rite of Blessing and Sprinkling Holy Water," as an element within the liturgy. But it also returned the emphasis to baptism, which not only brings forgiveness of sin but also gives people an identity and calls them to mission.

PASTORAL APPLICATIONS

The shape of the rite is a brief introduction followed by blessing of the water, the actual sprinkling accompanied by song. According to the season the introductory rites are concluded with either an absolution and the *Gloria* followed by the opening prayer, or simply by the opening prayer.

The rubrics locate the priest at the chair and direct that a container of water be brought to him. But this seems to lead to a duplication of symbols. If we are to make the connection of this rite to baptism why not begin with the presider at the font where the water is blessed, if the font is accessible?

The text for the introduction and the blessing prayer bear the caveat *in these or similar words*. The introduction explains what the rite means and is an invitation to the community to pray. The first two blessing prayers are for use at any time. The third blessing text is for use during the Easter season and is reminiscent of the Easter Vigil blessing of water. But consider this: the water blessed at the Easter Vigil should remain throughout the Easter season. Thus, rather than a blessing, a thanksgiving over the blessed water is used. Additional texts for blessing water as well as thanksgiving over blessed water can be found in the *Rite of Christian Initiation of Adults* (no. 222b-e).

These texts invite active participation of the community in the blessing by sung acclamations. The rubrics specify that the presider prays the blessing with hands joined. But since we are invoking the Spirit to renew our baptism through use of this water, would it not be more appropriate to have hands outstretched over the water (i.e., the laying on of hands) coupled with touching the water after the sign of the cross?

The priest himself, the ministers, and the people are sprinkled with holy water while an appropriate song is sung. For this rite to speak, everyone has got to get wet. This means that the presider has to move about the entire worship space and not just make a brief pass through the main aisle. Those who prepare the liturgy have to map out the route to be followed. And those who choose the music must select something of appropriate duration, for example, in litany style or responsorial style. Pastoral musicians need to find good musical settings of the texts suggested in Appendix I of the Sacramentary. An alternative is to sing the *Gloria* which is the song of the baptized praising God through the Son.

The "sprinkler" (called the *aspergillum* by previous generations) most often seen is a metal wand that is hollow to contain the holy water. Consider this: the hyssop of Psalm 51 was a bush whose branches were just right for sprinkling water or blood in the Jewish rituals. What if we carried the water in a glass bowl (so it could be seen) and sprinkled it with the branch from a bush or tree (e.g., a local species)?

How might the sprinkling rite be celebrated throughout the Easter season? The font containing water blessed at the Easter Vigil remains in a central location along with the paschal candle and the cross. The liturgy begins with the presider going to the font, greeting the people (the sign of the cross is displaced to the time of sprinkling) and inviting them into the thanksgiving over blessed water For example,

> Dear friends, this water, consecrated at the Easter Vigil, will be used to remind us of our Baptism. Let us praise and thank God for the life and Spirit he has given us.

The acclamation for the thanksgiving prayer is the traditional Easter Vigil one, which will be used to remind us of our baptism.

> Let us praise and thank God for the life and spirit he had given us.

The acclamation for the thanksgiving prayer is the traditional Easter Alleluia (*O Filii et Filiae*) or, if the *Gloria* is the song for sprinkling, "Glory to God in the highest."

Water from the font is transferred to a portable container, and the presider circuits the entire worship space sprinkling everyone. The community sings: "Water of life, Jesus our light, journey from death to new life" (*Water of Life* by David Haas, GIA Publications, Chicago) or the *Gloria*. As people feel the holy water, they make the sign of the cross. The presider, after he has sprinkled everyone, ends up at the chair. From there he either says the opening prayer or, if the *Gloria* has not been sung, says the absolution and briefly introduces it (e.g., "Let us give glory to God.").

Throughout the entire 50 days, we continue what happened at the Easter Vigil: commemoration of the Lord's passion, death, and resurrection, the celebration of our passage through the waters of baptism to new life, and our participation in the paschal mystery of Christ.

The Penitential Rite

Jayne Newton Ahearn

Among the components that make up the introductory or gathering rites of the Mass is the penitential rite. To take advantage of the options offered, to express the penitential nature of certain seasons, and to make adaptations appropriate to the pastoral situation it seems appropriate to consider this often misunderstood rite.

THE DOCUMENTS

It is recommended that readers take up a copy of the sacramentary and read or study the pertinent portions for themselves.

In the sacramentary (revised according to the second typical edition of the *Missale Romanum*, 1975) the penitential rite is the second option (B) for what follows the sign of the cross and greeting. It consists of an introduction by the presiding priest followed by one of three options:

- a communal recitation of the *Confiteor*,
- dialogue of priest and people using psalmic phrases,
- invocations of Christ's mercy by the priest or deacon responded to by the people with the "Lord, have mercy" (*Kyrie eleison*) and "Christ, have mercy" (*Christe eleison*),

and a conclusion (named the absolution) by the priest, which invokes God's mercy and forgiveness.

The next item in the Order is the *Kyrie*. Functionally, this results in the use of the "Lord, have mercy: Christ, have mercy" responses regardless of which option was chosen as the penitential act.

The *General Instruction of the Roman Missal* (*GIRM*, found at the front of the sacramentary) devotes roughly two and a half paragraphs to the penitential rite and *Kyrie*.

...Then the priest invites them (the people) to take part in the penitential rite, which the entire community carries out through a communal confession and which the priest's absolution brings to an end.... (*GIRM* no.29)

....The Kyrie begins, unless it has already been included as part of the penitential rite. Since it is a song by which the faithful praise the Lord and implore his mercy, it is ordinarily prayed by all, that is, alternately by the congregation and the choir or cantor.

As a rule each of the acclamations is said twice, but because of the idiom of different languages, the music or other circumstance, it may be said more than twice or a short verse (trope) may be interpolated. If the Kyrie is not sung, it is to be recited. (*GIRM* no. 30)

HISTORICAL PERSPECTIVES

Probably the earliest church order that we have is the second part (chapters 7-16) of the *Didache*, which arose between 50 and 90-110 C.E. in Antioch of Syria. One of the directives for the celebration of the Eucharist says: "On every Lord's Day—his special day—come together and break bread and give thanks, first confessing your sins, so that your sacrifice may be pure" (*Didache* 14:1).

As this same community was the source of the gospel of Matthew, it is not surprising that this directive reflects Jesus' teaching that we should be reconciled with the one with whom we are at odds before offering our gift at the altar (Mt 5:23–24).

As the early Christian community came together on the Lord's Day and encountered the risen Christ in the breaking of the bread, their experience was of forgiveness, of unity with Christ and one another, and of peace (see for example Jn 20:19–23 and Lk 24:36–49). They also realized that this was totally a gift given even as they continued to struggle with sin. In the face of so great a gift the community could only and, in fact, had to, acknowledge its sinfulness and God's mercy and forgiveness.

For centuries there was no penitential rite in the order of Mass. The elements that are found in today's penitential rite evolved from two sources: the form of the general intercessions of the Eastern church, and the medieval prayers of the priest on the way to, and at the foot of, the altar.

Around 500 C.E. Pope Gelasius incorporated into the Roman liturgy the form for the general intercessions used in the East as well as in Gaul and Northern Italy. This consisted of petitions announced by the deacon, to which the people responded *Kyrie Eleison*. The form was brief and lively in contrast to the long and sober form that it replaced. At the same time, the position of the intercession was moved from after the homily to the beginning of the Mass.

Later, in about 600 C.E., when Pope Gregory the Great undertook a revision of the Mass to shorten and simplify, he dispensed with the deacon's portion—i.e., the petitions—and left only the *Kyrie* at the beginning of Mass.

During the Middle Ages, a time of great political, economic, and social upheaval, there was a general shift to a spirituality that focused on the sin and evil of the world and the suffering endured by Jesus to overcome this evil. The Mass was allegorized as a re-enactment of the Passion and all, including priests, were certainly unworthy to have part in it. Thus there developed prayers for confession of sin and petitions for mercy said *privately* by the priest on his way to the altar.

The length of these prayers increased while the distance to the altar decreased (most of the time there was no entrance procession) so these became prayers at the foot of the altar. Among them was a two-part prayer in which the priest announced his sinfulness and then begged for the intercession of Mary, the saints, and the whole church for his forgiveness by God. This prayer began *Confiteor*...I confess. Other such prayers were formulated using portions of psalms such as Psalm 85, verse 8: "Show us, O Lord, your kindness, and grant us your salvation." While these prayers were being offered silently by the priest, the people (or later just the choir) were singing *Kyrie eleison, Christe eleison* repeatedly.

PASTORAL APPLICATION

The penitential rite of our current Order of Mass was not intended to be "Confession" but rather an expression by the gathered church of its constant need for and its praise of God's mercy and forgiveness through Christ. The recalling of our sins makes the fact that we, as the baptized, have been called by God to gather around the Lord's Table and share the eucharistic meal, all the more wondrous and worthy of praise. While we have begun our journey toward perfection, we acknowledge before one another and the world that we still have a long way to go: that we are always undergoing conversion. A penitential act is an outward expression of the inward process.

That the penitential rite is one of two options for the beginning of Mass leads to the conclusion that it was not meant to be used all the time but probably seasonally. Certainly Lent is one season when the penitential rite is appropriate to use. And we must be careful to use it appropriately.

The introduction by the presider is simply an invitation to consider our situation and as church in relation to the gift of forgiveness and reconciliation given through Christ. It is not an exhortation to generate guilt or to list sins. Note that the examples provided in the Sacramentary are brief and clear: they or others similarly composed could well be used.

Posture is standing, but during Lent it would be appropriate to kneel. The directive: "Please kneel" or "Let us kneel" would be given by the deacon (or, in his absence, by the presider) at the end of the introduction. A pause for silent reflection is to follow. As with all times of sacred silence, the duration needs to be long enough for fruitful thought or prayer: at least 30 seconds.

The choice of which of the three forms for the penitential act to use would be made by the liturgy preparation group and certainly should be reviewed for each liturgical season. The *Confiteor* (which was once the private prayer of the priest) is probably the most often used, especially at daily Mass, because it does not require any preparation and everyone knows it.

In parishes where the *Confiteor* has been overworked, it might be good to use one of the other forms during key seasons, such as Lent, so that the season is not "just more of the same." The second (B) option is probably least well known but is powerful in its simplicity. Used after a significant length of silence by a kneeling community and followed by a well-sung Kyrie, option B sends the message that it is indeed Lent. This form also has its roots in the prayers at the foot of the altar, coming from the psalms.

Option C, that which has its origins in the early Eastern church's general intercessions, is also frequently used. However, the invocations sometimes become mini-confessions of sin. There are eight examples provided in the sacramentary, none of which is a list of sins. They demonstrate that the invocations are statements about Christ (Christocentric): who Christ is, and what Christ does. They are verbalizations of our praise of God's mercy and forgiveness through Christ. Invocations may be chosen from the eight sets provided, such as choosing i, iv, and v for the lenten season. Or they might be selected and rearranged into new combinations. It is also possible to compose invocations that are reflective of the gospel of the day or the feast itself.

The invocations are made by the deacon, or by the presider if there is no deacon. This form of penitential rite is often sung (see *GIRM* no. 30). A cantor sings the invocations and the people sing the response: Lord, have mercy. Some musical settings for the form C penitential rite include: Kyrie Eleison I-X in *Music from Taizé*, vol 1, Kyrie Eleison XI in *Music from Taizé*, vol II, Penitential Rite from the *Mass of Remembrance* by Marty Haugen (GIA), and *Penitential Rite C* by Bob Hurd and Barbara Bridge (OCP). These same settings may be used following the *Confiteor* or form B simply by omitting the invocations. It is important that people know, or are taught, that the *Kyrie* is to be sung.

The presider concludes the penitential rite with a prayer that God will have mercy, forgive sin, and grant everlasting life. Though called "absolution," this prayer is not the absolution of sin of the sacrament of reconciliation. Its origin is from the one of two traditional responses to the *Confiteor* or other confession of sin. The first form, the *Misereatur* (may almighty God have mercy…) is the invocative form, which laypersons can recite. This remains true today as well, for in the *Order for Holy Communion Outside Mass* it is the presiding minister—who may be a layperson—who says the "absolution prayer."

The other response, the "Indulgentiam," in its declarative forms, serves as the formula for sacramental absolution (I absolve you….).

OPTION A: RITE OF BLESSING AND SPRINKLING HOLY WATER

As was stated, the penitential rite was not intended to be used all the time but seasonally. The alternate rite, Blessing and Sprinkling Holy Water (also called the sprinkling rite), should be seriously considered as most appropriate during the Easter season since it calls to mind our incorporation into Christ and the paschal mystery through baptism. This rite is featured in the previous chapter.

The Word and the Lectionary

Russell Hardiman

THE WORD OF GOD AND OUR WORD

As the people of our contemporary world, we have been shaped for six centuries by the experience of the message of the printed word. We struggle to grasp the impact in more ancient oral cultures, where "to speak" was not to utter sounds or to say words, but rather to do something. Even today we have glimpses of this connection of the word and the person, when agreements are confirmed simply by saying, "I give you my word"; when promises are publicly effected through words, such as marriage vows; when people look for presence even in absence, when they say, "send us word when you get there."

The concept of "word," and especially the "Word of God," was not considered by the Israelites of old to be mere verbalization or articulation of thought. Rather, it was Godself communicating and revealing God's presence in self-communication. For Hebrews the term *Dabar*, was therefore the very manifestation of God. We notice, in many passages, the affirmation of this reality with the literary asides, "it is the Lord who speaks," as if it is a call to attention, a reminder of being in God's presence.

Another characteristic of the Hebrew term *dabar* was its sense of encounter or meeting. When God spoke, God was revealing Godself and being present to the chosen people. We have this as part of our common experience when we are conscious that our words reveal our thoughts and feelings, or make us present to others.

In this Jewish mentality, the word is always dynamic, it is always operative, for the power of the word is always equivalent to the power of the speaker, so that when God speaks, God externalizes the power that is God's life. For the Christian sense of this concept, we can glean further insight from the original sense of the word "dynamism": it is connected with the Greek word *dunamis*, which is the same word as the term for the Spirit. It is a pity that the Swedish inventor Dr. Nobel coined the word "dynamite," the source of his funds that endow the Nobel Prize, and thereby distorted a very positive insight into the power of God's continuing presence and activity wherever the Spirit blows where he will in our world.

The contrasts between the Judeo-Christian vision of the Word of God and our contemporary culture's preoccupation with words and their intellectual content is further illustrated in a difference in slogans. For those of an oral tradition it is "hearing is believing" not the "seeing is believing" of our contemporary worldview. This was the belief of St. Paul and other apostles who were convinced of their mission to proclaim the Good News, an oral kerygma. Some modern Scripture scholars have researched the gospels not merely as literary works but as recorders of an oral form of storytelling. The gospel of Mark is renowned as a narrative story, not only in its creation, but also in its performance, as shown by the success of the one-man play that consists solely of dramatizing Mark's gospel from the first verse to the last.

WHAT IS THE LECTIONARY

Put simply, a lectionary is a book of readings or a list of Scripture readings set for the seasons and feasts of the church year. The function of any lectionary selection is related to the statement of Jesus when reading in the synagogue at Nazareth: "today this passage is fulfilled in your hearing" (Lk 4:21).

The one continuing revelation of God's salvific redemption covers the "between times," between the resurrection of Jesus and the future coming in glory. Wherever two or three gather in the Lord's name his presence is continually revealed and the promise of life in its fullness is proclaimed, in the readings and in the rituals of acclamation, as well as in the preaching.

PRINCIPLES OF THE LECTIONARY

The starting point of the lectionary has its basis in the public proclamation of the paschal mystery. The lectionary and its formal use is at the service of the proclamation of the Word of God revealed in Jesus Christ and continuing through the presence of his risen Spirit. Even as a selection of texts, or a canon within the canon of Scriptures, its thematic unity is based on the paschal mystery already completed in Christ Jesus, and now in the process of being completed in us.

In the proclamation of the Good News of what God has done, and is doing, and will do, for his people, we seek to arouse a sense that for us too "our hearts are burning within us" as the Scriptures are being explained. This should preclude the perception that the readings are merely our favorite passages, or prevent the facile moralism that reduces all texts to simplistic exhortation to good works and renewed prayer.

Celebrating the many facets of the paschal mystery comes from a vision of the unity of revelation, redemption, and salvation in the single time frame of God, whose continuing presence we tend to divide into past-present-future and to become fixated with the present when we cannot appreciate the past stories of faithful or faithless response to God, nor anticipate the open-ended expectation of what we are called to be.

It may also be a challenge to personal attitudes and practice to highlight what the lectionary is not:

• it is bigger than pet viewpoints;

• it is not intended to be a systematic presentation of the theological teachings of the church;

• it is not an arrangement of the Bible to show the various literary genres in a collection of seventy-two books;

• it is simply not a history of the Jewish people, nor the Christian church, divided into two sections, because it has one author.

ORIGINS OF TODAY'S READINGS

As far back as 1963 the Vatican II Constitution on the Liturgy urged a deepening awareness of the Scriptures:

> The treasures of the Bible...be opened up more lavishly, so that richer fare may be provided for the faithful at the table of God's Word. In this way a more representative portion of Holy Scripture will be read to the people in the course of a prescribed number of years. (CSL no. 51)

This single paragraph of Vatican II has had the greatest ecumenical impact over more than thirty-five years to the extent that a generation of Christians have been sharing a common heritage in proclaiming and preaching the Word of God. The 1969 Roman lectionary *Ordo Lectionum Missae* (Vatican City: Polyglot Press) was adopted by the Episcopal Church in the USA in 1970, and the Presbyterian Church the same year. The Lutherans initially stuck with their one-year lectionary cycle but in 1974 they published a three-year lectionary.

The growing acceptance of the *Roman Lectionary's* principles and format culminated in the production in 1982, of the *Common Lectionary*. Nearly a decade of worship use and continued consultation resulted in the *Revised Common Lectionary* being published in 1992. This ecumenical acceptance was called by Raymond Brown "Catholicism's greatest gift to Protestantism."

The impact of the biblical movement over nearly one hundred years and the filtering down to all levels of the church give us hope that future years will continue to see further development of biblical theology that will have great pastoral benefits and enhanced ecumenical relations. The Swiss Eucharistic Prayer uses a phrase that sums up the connection of word and sacrament in our sacramental worship, which is the function of proclaiming the Word. "As once he did for his disciples Christ now opens the Scriptures for us and breaks the bread" (Eucharistic Prayer X).

SUMMARY OF LECTIONARY STRUCTURE

1. The readings are distributed over a three-year cycle. Years A, B, C for Sunday readings with a separate set of readings for weekdays.

2. The Liturgical Year keeps its traditional structure:
   a) Christmas Cycle:
      Advent, four Sundays before Christmas
      The Christmas Season
      Holy Family on the Sunday After Christmas
      Mary, Mother of God on January 1
      Epiphany, which according to local custom may be celebrated on January 6 or on the Sunday following January 1.
      Baptism of the Lord on the Sunday after January 6.

   b) Easter Cycle:
      Lent, six Sundays before the Holy Triduum, opening on Ash Wednesday with the celebration of the Ashes.
      The Easter Triduum, begins with Mass of the Last Supper, continues with the celebration of the Lord's death on Good Friday, and ends with the Solemn celebration of the Easter Vigil.
      The Easter Season, which continues to the Feast of Pentecost, the Sundays being called "Sundays of Easter" rather than "Sundays after Easter."

   c) Outside these "Privileged Seasons" there exists **"Ordinary Time"** (Tempus per Annum) which consists of thirty-four weeks beginning the day after the Feast of the Lord's Baptism, interrupted from Ash Wednesday until the day after Pentecost, and ending on the eve of Advent.

3. Each Sunday Mass text includes three readings and one psalm.

- The first reading is taken from the Old Testament, with the exception of the Easter Season, when the Acts of the Apostles are read.
- the Psalm highlights the message of the first reading for meditation in its antiphon.
- the second reading is taken from the New Testament Epistles or Revelation.
- the third reading is the gospel, which is preceded by an Alleluia with versicle, the latter often taken from the gospel which follows.

4. Great importance was accorded to the concept of "semi-continuous reading," especially with the gospels, with Matthew in Year A, Mark in Year B, Luke in Year C: semi-continuous readings of the Pauline epistles is also used but not the Old Testament books in the *Roman Lectionary*. The *Revised Common Lectionary* has some continuous reading from the Old Testament.

5. For pastoral reasons, a shorter version that retains only a part of the reading is allowed for certain readings that are lengthy or particularly difficult. One may omit either the first or the second reading. In children's Masses, this is particularly recommended, and someone other than the presider may break open the word for young children.

6. Usually the gospel passage determines the major thrust of the sets of readings, with the Old Testament passage chosen to connect with the gospel, and the Psalm chosen to extend or deepen those insights. In Advent, the readings from Isaiah help set the tone, while in the Sundays of Easter the Acts of the Apostles becomes the source of the first reading and describes the early Christian community.

The Two Principles of Lectionary Choices

LECTIO SELECTA
Thematic Reading: all texts chosen around one theme.

LECTIO CONTINUA
Semi-continuous reading from the main passages in sequence.

CHRISTMAS CYCLE
Advent (4 Sundays)
Christmas (3 Masses)
Holy Family
Mother of God (January 1)
Epiphany
Baptism of Christ

EASTER CYCLE
Lent (6 Sundays)
Sacred Triduum
   Holy Thursday
   Good Friday
   Easter Vigil
Eastertide (7 Sundays)
Pentecost

OCCASIONAL FEASTS
Trinity
Corpus Christi
Our Lady's and Saint's Feasts
All Souls Day and All Saints Day

YEAR A
Gospel of Matthew   OT   1 Cor 1–6
   Romans
   Philippians
   1 Thessalonians

YEAR B
Gospel of Mark   OT   1 Cor 6–11
John 6   2 Cor 1–12
   Ephesians
   James
   Hebrews

YEAR C
Gospel of Luke   OT   1 Cor 12–15
   Galatians
   Colossians
   Hebrews
   Philemon
   1 and 2 Timothy
   2 Thessalonians

Ongoing Formation of Lectors

Jayne Newton Ahearn

The Word of God was preexistent and is preeminent. In the beginning was chaos and darkness and God said,

> "Let there be light," and there was light (Gn 1:1–3).

> In the beginning was the Word…. all things came into being through him, and without him not one thing came into being (Jn 1:1–3).

God's Word spoken through the prophets and finally and fully, when the time at last was right, God's Word made flesh reveals to human beings the God who created them and calls all to redemption: eternal unity with God (*Dei Verbum* no.4).

To the church, those who have responded to God's call, has been given the work of making known the Word to every people and race in every time and place (Mt 28:18–20).

Paul wrote to the Romans:

> How are they to call on one in whom they have not believed? And how are they to believe in one of whom they have never heard? And how are they to hear without someone to proclaim him? And how are they to proclaim him unless they are sent?

> …So faith comes from what is heard and what is heard comes through the word of Christ (Rom 10:14–15, 17).

The Word of God in sacred Scripture is fundamental to the life of the church and to its mission.

FORMATION

Those who are entrusted with the role of proclaiming the readings from sacred Scripture to the church gathered for liturgy have an awesome responsibility. Lectors have the duty and the right to be prepared spiritually and technically for their ministry (*Lectionary for Mass: Introduction* no. 52, 55).

A one-evening session or even a series of three or four sessions at the beginning of their ministry is not enough. Lectors require ongoing formation in Scripture and the liturgy. They require continual practice of their proclamation skills. The ministry of the lector is just too important to be neglected. Monthly or even bi-weekly gatherings for the lectors should be a parish priority, and lectors who do not participate in such gatherings should be invited to find another ministry.

The Christian faithful have a right to hear God's word since, by their baptism and confirmation, they are to be witnesses to the gospel message (CCL no. 213 & 759). The People of God are first brought together by the Word of God, and in the hearing of God's Word the church is built up and grows. Effective proclamation of Scripture renews for the faithful the marvelous deeds of God for our salvation, not only as *past* events experienced by other people but as *present* action experienced by ourselves and as promise of what is *yet to come*. God's word is indeed a living word.

Effective proclamation of Scripture thus impels us to give thanks, leads us to the Eucharist. Effective proclamation of Scripture provides the living waters for the catechumens in our midst who are feasting on the Word. Effective proclamation of Scripture enhances the work of the Holy Spirit, who brings home to each individual what God has spoken for the good of the assembly, strengthens the unity of all, and fosters the diversity of gifts for the mission of the church. (*Lectionary for Mass* Introduction no. 4-10).

What will the lectors gain from having ongoing formation? By gathering regularly to share in preparation for their ministry the lectors will become a community, building up one another as well as building up the parish community. These gatherings are opportunities for communal prayer. Lectors will have a better understanding of sacred Scripture and of the relationship of Scripture to the liturgy. Lectors will have the opportunity to rehearse, to practice, and to improve their proclamation skills.

FORMAT OF TRAINING SESSIONS

What would be the format for a meeting of lectors? Once a month, or, if possible, once every two weeks, on a weeknight the lectors gather in the worship space for about two hours. The gathering must be in the worship space (the church) so that the ambo and microphones can be used for practice. Being in the church also enhances the prayer that is an integral part of the meeting. A weeknight is recommended over Saturday or Sunday since the weekend is usually taken up by domestic responsibilities for families and by liturgical activities for the church.

The meeting is led by the parish liturgy coordinator, the coordinator of the lectors, or the parish priest.

• The meeting begins with an informal gathering time. For about five minutes people exchange greetings, engage in conversation, and get settled in their places. At the same time the leader takes attendance and distributes schedules and/or informational materials.

• There should be communal prayer for about 15 minutes, for prayerful reflection is not a luxury or time wasted but is essential to illuminate the sense of the ministry. The prayer involves some of those in attendance in various roles such as presider, reader, cantor, announcer of intentions. The order for the prayer is: a song or instrumental music, a reading from Scripture, silent reflection, intercessions, Lord's Prayer, Sign of Peace. The reading may be taken from the Mass for the day, from the Liturgy of the Hours or from among those that will be proclaimed at Sunday Eucharist in the next month. In addition to prepared intercessions, intentions may be invited from the group.

• There is then an input section which is in two parts.

The first 20 minutes feature a liturgical season, a Scripture topic, or a proclamation skill.

The second 20-30 minutes are spent in exegesis of the readings for the coming month.

The goal is not only to understand the historical and cultural context and literary form of the individual readings but also to understand the relationship to one another of the three readings within each Sunday, as well as this Sunday's text to the previous week, or weeks, and even the subsequent week, or the structure of the gospel as a whole.

The readings for each Sunday are also related to the liturgical season as a whole. This is more than biblical exegesis: this is biblical-liturgical exegesis.

• The final 30-40 minutes of the meeting are devoted to the practicum. Each lector has the opportunity to proclaim for their peers a reading chosen from among those that will occur in the next month. Prior to each meeting they study and prepare at least those readings that they have been scheduled to proclaim at a Sunday Eucharist. Each lector is immediately evaluated by their peers and, if time allows, they may repeat the proclamation incorporating suggestions.

Criteria for evaluation include pronunciation and articulation, inflection (changes in pitch to suit the meaning of the passage), pacing (rate of speaking), pauses and emphasis, eye contact and facial expression, communication of the meaning of the passage, communication of the mood or feeling of the passage.

If the parish has the facilities, a few times each year lectors may be videotaped during the practicum so that they can review their own work.

The practicum is extremely important because proclamation is a skill that improves only with critical practice. The more a lector stands at the ambo, holds the book, works with the sound equipment, and relates to a community, the more comfortable they will become with all these aspects that might otherwise interfere with effective proclamation. Peer review is honest, constructive, fair, and offered lovingly. Peer review inspires lectors to work harder at their preparation, causes them to help and support one another in their ministry, and it builds community. In a parish where this writer worked, members of the assembly could discern after six months who among the lectors were going to the meetings and who were not.

• Several times in the year the meeting concludes with refreshments and opportunity for conversation: in other words, a party. Such occasions would be especially appropriate during the Christmas season and the Easter season.

TOPICS FOR TRAINING SESSIONS

What sorts of topics can be presented during the input sessions? It is good for lectors to know and understand the documents of the church that pertain to their ministry. Thus a study of *Dei Verbum* (the Dogmatic Constitution on Divine Revelation) and of the *Introduction to the Lectionary for Mass* can be undertaken.

Near the beginning of the liturgical year (October, November) the gospel for the coming year (A: Matthew; B: Mark; C: Luke) can be considered. John's gospel is featured each year during the Easter season as well as on the latter Sundays of Lent in Years A and B. During the middle of Year B the gospel shifts from Mark to John to present the Bread of Life discourse, the Johannine theology of the Eucharist.

A Pauline or other letter could be the focus of study when it will be featured in the Sunday readings for a period of time. For example, during Year A, Romans provides the text for the second reading beginning after the Easter season and continuing into mid-September, and during the Easter season the first letter of Peter is read. Preparation for Advent and Christmas may include a study of Isaiah.

To further enhance their understanding of sacred Scripture, lectors should be encouraged to participate in Bible studies offered by the parish.

The liturgical seasons as well as the Sacred Triduum and the celebration of Sunday may be examined for their historical origins and theological meanings as well as pastoral practice in which the lector is involved.

Since lectors are often the ones who announce the petitions of the prayer of the faithful, a study could be made of this prayer's origins, form, and function.

The other rites and prayers in which lectors may exercise their ministry might be studied: for example, the Order of Christian Funerals and the Liturgy of the Hours.

There are any number of proclamation skills that may be the subject of consideration. These include storytelling, paraphrasing, sensory recall and emotional recall, text gathering, inflection, and deliberation or pacing.

PERSONAL PREPARATION

How should lectors prepare? In the course of the meetings lectors are trained in and encouraged to practice a preparation method that allows the word to become their own.

To prepare to proclaim at a Sunday liturgy the lector begins the previous Monday by reading through the text and using a good commentary. The text is read again and again until it is understood. Then the question for reflection is: How does this reading speak in my life? The word must have power within the life of the lector or they cannot convey it to others. On Tuesday the task is to express the reading in the lector's own words by paraphrasing. Then beginning on Wednesday and continuing through the rest of the week the lector begins to practice proclaiming the reading aloud.

The task becomes how to say words, phrases, and sentences effectively so that the meaning is most clearly expressed. This is the time to check on the pronunciation of words. Practicing in front of a mirror and listening to tape recordings of oneself are very helpful.

In the end it is important to remember that the lector alone cannot effectively proclaim God's word. The lector becomes an instrument through whom God speaks. The Holy Spirit was the inspiration of the writing down of sacred Scripture, and the Holy Spirit makes the Word proclaimed in the liturgy a living, active word so that what is heard outwardly has an effect inwardly.

Always recall what God told Jeremiah when the prophet said he did not know how to speak.

> But the Lord said to me......you shall go to all to whom I send you, and you shall speak whatever I command you, Do not be afraid of them for I am with you to deliver you
>
> …Now I have put my words in your mouth (Jer 1:7–9).

Perhaps the prayer a priest or deacon says before proclaiming the gospel can be an inspiration for all lectors in their ministry:

> May the Lord be in our hearts
> and on our lips
> that we may worthily proclaim
> the good news of salvation.

REFERENCES AND RESOURCES FOR LECTORS

The Church Documents

Dei Verbum (Dogmatic Constitution on Divine Revelation) 18 November 1965 (available in a number of collections of the Vatican II documents, eg., edited by Austin Flannery or by Walter M. Abbott: sometimes found in the front of the Bible).

Lectionary for Mass Introduction, 1982 (available with overview comments in *The Liturgy Documents: A Parish Resource*, Third Edition published by Liturgy Training Publications of Chicago, 1991).

Proclaim the Word: The Lectionary for Mass, 1982. Liturgy Study Text Series No.8. United States Catholic Conference, Washington, D.C.

To Hear and Proclaim, 1983. Introduction to the Lectionary for Mass with commentary by Ralph A. Keifer. National Association of Pastoral Musicians, Washington, D.C.

Ministry of Lectors

Bartow, Charles L., 1988. *Effective Speech Communication in Leading Worship*. Abingdon Press, Nashville, TN.

Champlin, Joseph M. 1982. *Messengers of God's Word: A Handbook for Lectors*. Paulist Press, Mahwah, NJ.

Gallaghan, Molly, 1982. *Readers at Liturgy* (New Parish Ministries) Winston Press, Minneapolis, MN.

Harrison, G.B. and John McCabe, 1976. *Proclaiming the Word: A Handbook for Church Speaking*. Pueblo Publishing Company, New York.

Lonergan, Ray, 1982. *A Well-Trained Tongue: A Workbook for Lectors*. Liturgy Training Publications, Chicago, IL

Sparough, Michael, S.J., 1988. *Lector Training Program* (This is the Word of the Lord). Liturgy Training Publications, Chicago, IL.

Staudacher, Joseph M., 1975. *Lector's Guide to Biblical Pronunciations*. Our Sunday Visitor, Inc., Huntington, IN.

Tate, Judith, 1975. *Manual for Lectors*. Pflaum Press, Dayton, OH.

Wallace, James A., C. SS. R., 1981. *The Ministry of Lectors*. Liturgical Press, Collegeville, MN.

The Readings

This Is The Word Of The Lord (Readings for Holy Week, major feasts and selected Sundays arranged in dialogue form) Ave Maria Press, Notre Dame, IN.

The Passion of Our Lord Jesus Christ (The four Passion narratives arranged for several readers) Catholic Book Publishing Co., New York.

Brown, Raymond E., 1981. *The Critical Meaning of the Bible*. Paulist Press, Mahwah, NJ.

Brown, Raymond E., 1979. *The Community of the Beloved Disciple*. Paulist Press, Mahwah, NJ (on John's gospel).

The Collegeville Bible Commentary, 1988-9. Dianne Bergant, C.S.A. and Robert J. Karris, O.F.M., general editors. The Liturgical Press, Collegeville, MN (available as a series of booklets or in one volume).

Ellis, Peter F., 1963. *The Men and the Message of the Old Testament*. The Liturgical Press, Collegeville, MN.

The New Jerome Biblical Commentary, 1990. Edited by Raymond E. Brown, S.S., Joseph A. Fitzmeyer, S.J. and Roland E. Murphy, O.Carm. Prentice-Hall, Englewood Cliffs, NJ.

Soggin, J. Alberto, 1980 (translated by John Bowden) *Introduction to the Old Testament*, revised edition. The Westminster Press, Philadelphia, PA.

Senior, Donald (General Editor), 1990. *The Catholic Study Bible*, Oxford University Press, New York.

The Lectionary

Barnecut, Edith, 1992. *Journeys with the Fathers: commentaries on the Sunday Gospels Year A*. New City Press, New York.

Crotty, Robert, C.P. and Gregory Manly, C.P., 1975. *Commentaries on the Readings of the Lectionary*. Pueblo Press (now a subsidiary of The Liturgical Press, Collegeville, MN).

Fuller, Reginald H., 1971-74. *Preaching the New Lectionary*: The Word of God for the Church Today. The Liturgical Press, Collegeville, MN.

Nocent, Adrian, O.S.B., 1977. (translated by Matthew J. O'Connell) *The Liturgical Year*. Vol. 1: Advent/Christmas/Epiphany, Vol. 2 Lent/ Holy Week, Vol. 3: The Easter Season, Vol 4: Sundays in Ordinary Time. The Liturgical Press, Collegeville, MN.

Rotelle, John E. (editor) 1995 *Meditations on the Sunday Gospels Year A*. New City Press, New York.

Sanchez, Patricia Datchuck, 1989. *The Word We Celebrate: Commentary on the Sunday Lectionary, Years A, B, and C*. Sheed and Ward, Kansas City, MO.

Van Olst, E.H., 1991. (translated by John Vriend) *The Bible and Liturgy*. William B. Eerdmans Publishing Company, Grand Rapids, MI.

The Prayer of the Faithful: What For and How To...

Jayne Newton Ahearn

Although a part of the tradition even in the earliest descriptions of Christian liturgy, the prayer of the faithful in the revised Mass was still a rather new component of the liturgy revised according to the vision of Vatican II's Constitution on the Sacred Liturgy.

Overnight (it seemed) parishes went from a liturgy celebrated in Latin to the use of the vernacular with sensitivity to culture and mandated participation by all the faithful. No one had much experience preparing the prayer of the faithful. There were no texts given in the sacramentary under that heading in the *Order of Mass*. The sacramentary itself did offer "Sample Formulas for the General Intercessions" in an appendix (Appendix I).

There were a plethora of new publications like *Scripture in Church, Celebration, Pastoral Liturgy*, and any number of others in the intervening years, that sought to aid those responsible for preparing their community's liturgy by offering examples or models for the prayer of the faithful.

Some subscribers to these publications have commented that they wish the full text was not provided, so that the local group would be forced to write their own, while others have said they could not do without a prepared text. A transitional process from set texts to local texts can be encouraged by providing suggestions based on the readings of the day within each of five general categories, and teaching the locals how to prepare the text for the prayer of the faithful and the structure and function it has.

Currently, in many parishes it is the practice for members of the community, such as liturgy preparation teams, lectors, or deacons, to write the prayer of the faithful for Sunday liturgy. But in many other parishes the priest still has a corner on that endeavor, or on Sunday morning the lector just reads from some liturgy service publication or collection of prayers of the faithful published as a book.

Published texts for the general intercessions, because they are prepared for many local communities, are at best expressive of human news in broad categories. While it is always appropriate to pray for concerns in general categories, needs arising out of current world and local events can never be voiced by published texts.

The sacramentary provides texts for the eucharistic prayers, opening prayers, prayers over the gifts, prayers after communion, and blessings to be used by every Roman Catholic community. That texts for the prayer of the faithful are not provided indicates that this prayer should be distinctive of each local community. The prayer of the faithful or general intercessions addresses the needs of all humanity but in a way specific to each local community.

THE DOCUMENTS

The restoration of the prayer of the faithful came about with the mandate of Vatican II to recapture the intercessory spirit of earlier ritual prayer forms.

> Especially on Sundays and holy days of obligation there is to be restored, after the gospel and the homily, "the universal prayer" or "the prayer of the faithful." By this prayer, in which the people are to take part, intercession shall be made for holy Church, for the civil authorities, for those oppressed by various needs, for all people, and for the salvation of the entire world. (*SC* no. 53)

The article immediately following gave suitable place for the use of the vernacular, first for the readings and the universal prayer. Ultimately, the reason for restoring the universal prayer in the vernacular was the very nature of the liturgy itself.

> Christ always truly associates the Church with himself in this great work wherein God is perfectly glorified and the recipients made holy ...

Rightly, then, the liturgy is considered as an exercise of the priestly office of Jesus Christ. In the liturgy, by means of signs perceptible to the senses, human sanctification is signified and brought about in ways proper to each of these signs: in the liturgy the whole public worship is performed by the Mystical Body of Jesus Christ, that is, by the head and his members. (*SC* no. 7)

The Church earnestly desires that all the faithful be led to that full, conscious, and active participation in liturgical celebrations called for by the very nature of the liturgy. Such participation by the Christian people as "a chosen race, a royal priesthood, a holy nation, God's own people" (1 Pt 2:9) is their right and duty by reason of their baptism.

In the reform and promotion of the liturgy, this full and active participation by all the people is the aim to be considered before all else. (*SC* no. 14)

The church, composed of all the baptized when it gathers, participates in the one priesthood of Christ, mediator between humanity and God. It is the right and duty of the gathered church to intercede in Christ for the life of the world. In its public exercise of, and participation in, the one priesthood of Christ, the church identifies itself and furthermore, makes real that identification. By praying or interceding for the needs of humanity, the church models how to pray for the needs of the world and becomes the pray-er for the needs of humanity.

HISTORICAL PERSPECTIVES

General intercession made by the baptized (the faithful) was a part of early Christian worship. Writings from the second half of the first century to the early third century witness to this.

> First of all, then, I ask that supplications, prayers, petitions, and thanksgivings be offered for everyone, for Kings and for all in authority, that we may lead a quiet and tranquil life in all devotion and dignity. This is good and pleasing to God our savior, who wills everyone to be saved and to come to knowledge of the truth. (1 Tim 2:1–4; 55-150 C.E.)

> We, however, after thus washing (baptizing) the one who has been convinced and signified his assent, lead him to those who are called brethren, where they are assembled. They then earnestly offer common prayers for themselves and the one who has been illuminated [baptized] and all others everywhere, that we may be made worthy, having learned the truth, to be found in deed good citizens and keepers of what is commanded, so that we may be saved with eternal salvation. (*First Apology of Justin Martyr*, 65; 150 C.E.)

> Then [after the readings and homily] we all stand up together and offer prayers. (*First Apology of Justin Martyr*, 67)

> Each time the teacher finishes his instructions, the catechumens are to pray by themselves apart from the faithful. (*Apostolic Tradition of Hippolytus*, 18; 215 C.E.)

> Now [after baptism] they are to pray together with all the people, since they did not pray with the faithful before their baptism. (*Apostolic Tradition of Hippolytus*, 20)

That for which the early Christians prayed (for all people, for kings and those in authority, for the church, for local needs, for the salvation of the world) is not very different from that for which the church prays today. The prayers, because they were exclusive to the baptized, followed the readings and homily when the catechumens were dismissed for their own prayers. However, as the catechumenate declined there were fewer and fewer unbaptized in attendance at the liturgy of the word.

Around the early sixth century the position of the prayer was moved to the beginning of the liturgy. And at the beginning of the seventh century, Pope Gregory the Great effectively dropped it from the liturgy as part of his reform by abbreviating the Mass. For over one thousand years the only witness to the previous tradition of public intercessory prayers was in the Solemn Bidding prayers in the Liturgy of Good Friday. The prayer was restored in 1963 and placed in its original position of response in faith after the proclamation of the Word (*CSL* no. 53).

DOCUMENTS

The general intercessions are described in both the *General Instruction of the Roman Missal* (*GIRM* no. 45-47) and the *Introduction to the Lectionary for Mass* (*ILM* no. 30-31).

> In the general intercessions or prayer of the faithful, the people, exercising their priestly function, intercede for

all humanity. It is appropriate that this prayer be included in all Masses celebrated with a congregation, so that petitions will be offered for the Church, for civil authorities, for those oppressed by various needs, for all people, and for the salvation of the world. (*GIRM* no. 45)

As a rule, the sequence of intentions is to be:
a. for the needs of the Church:
b. for public authorities and the salvation of the world:
c. for those oppressed by any need:
d. for the local community.

In particular celebrations, such as confirmation, marriages, funerals, etc., the series of intercessions may refer more specifically to the occasion. (*GIRM* no. 46)

It belongs to the priest (presider) to direct the general intercessions, by means of a brief introduction to invite the congregation to pray, and after the intercessions to say the concluding prayer. It is desirable that a deacon, cantor, or other person announce the intentions. The whole assembly gives expression to its supplication either by a response said together after each intention or by silent prayer. (*GIRM* no. 47)

Enlightened by God's word and in a sense responding to it, the assembly of the faithful prays in the general intercessions as a rule for the needs of the universal Church and the local community, for the salvation of the world and those oppressed by any burden, and for special categories of people.

The (priest/presider) introduces the prayer: the deacon, another minister, or some of the faithful may propose intentions that are short and phrased with a measure of flexibility. In these petitions "the people, exercising their priestly function, make intercession for all" with the result that, as the liturgy of the word has its full effects in them, they are better prepared to proceed to the liturgy of the Eucharist. (*ILM* no. 30)

For the general intercessions the (priest/presider) presides at the chair and the intentions are announced at the lectern.

The congregation takes part in the general intercessions while standing and by saying or singing a common response after each intention or by silent prayer. (*ILM* no. 31)

These paragraphs present the theology of the prayer (discussed above) and the form of the prayer. The most ancient form for the general intercessions in the Roman liturgy is still found today in the liturgy of Good Friday. The deacon invites or bids the people to pray for a particular intention, the people kneel and pray silently, and finally all stand and the one who presides sums up all the prayers in a collect.

The form of the prayer of the faithful with which we are more familiar was incorporated into the Roman liturgy from the East by Pope Gelasius at the end of the fifth century. This is the litany form in which the deacon addresses the people proposing for what to pray and the people pray silently and say or sing a prayer response.

It is important to realize that the petition or intention spoken by the deacon or lector or sung by the cantor is addressed to the people and tells them for what to pray. The people, in turn, pray to God in silence or through the sung or spoken response. The prayer is made by all the people together.

Paragraphs 45 and 46 of the *GIRM* define categories for which, and in what sequence, prayer is to be made. Because this prayer is a response to the Word (*ILM* no. 30), the readings for the day help to bring specificity to the broad categories. However, the church is realized or enfleshed in the gathered local community of the baptized. And the local community exists in a particular time and place and within a cultural context. Each of these parameters defines the needs for which the local community must pray.

Events in the life of the local community as well as in the world are the real subject matter for prayer. Thus, the local community really should prepare the petitions for the prayer of the faithful for each Sunday or holy day with the Scriptures in one hand and the newspaper and parish intention book in the other. The petitions are the community's response to the needs of humanity in this time and place in light of God's Word. Input for the petitions might come from the liturgy team, the deacon, the lectors, and those involved in parish social justice or outreach ministries.

The petitions are not prayers directed to God. Rather, each petition is an invitation for the people to pray for a certain intention after the intention is named. It can be announced in the form "for N. that ..." or simply "for ..." or "that ..." and is concluded with a verbal cue familiar to people such as "we pray to the Lord" or "let us pray to the Lord" or, after a time for silent prayer, "Lord, hear us." The response of the people so addressed is to pray for that intention, so the reader needs to give them time to pray.

The people are more drawn into the prayer and make it their own if the petition is brief and if silence is given for their prayer before the verbal prayer response is made.

The prayer of the faithful is not for instruction, or for information, or to advance causes. Neither is it the place for thanksgiving—for that we have the eucharistic prayer. A good indicator for well-composed petitions is that they can be sung.

The sung or spoken prayer response of the people is just that: prayer addressed to God. It is not acclamation. The most frequently used response is: "Lord, hear our prayer." When the general intercessions were originally assimilated from the Eastern liturgy the response was "Kyrie eleison / Lord, have mercy." This response is quite appropriate especially during the season of Lent. Other possible responses, which can be used seasonally, include "Lord, you are our hope" during Advent and "Lord, hear us" or "Hear us, O Lord" used in Ordinary Time. It is wise to use a response for an entire season rather than to change the response every Sunday.

It is also wise to use a brief response rather than a long one that is difficult to remember. (If the response to the prayer of the faithful has to be read from the bulletin, it probably should not be used). The thoughts of the faithful should be on praying the intention, not on remembering the response. Remember the response is not the prayer: it only sums up the silent prayer preceding it.

The people are called or invited to the general intercessions by the one presiding. This invitation is addressed to the people and is not a prayer itself. It reminds us that we pray for the needs of humanity in response to the Word of God, which we have heard this day (*ILM* 30). Thus, this introduction briefly recalls the readings or uses imagery from the Scriptures of the day.

Following the final petition, the presider sums up the prayers of all in a concluding prayer or collect. This prayer is addressed to God the Father through Jesus Christ (and perhaps here is the place to remember that all prayer is made in the Holy Spirit: "for we do not know how to pray as we ought, but the Spirit itself intercedes with inexpressible groanings" (Rom 8:26).

This summing up may be with a published text or spontaneously composed but in each instance the presumption must be that the author knows the structure and function of the prayer. As a mnemonic to remember the sequence of thought in the collect form of prayer the components are: address (You), thanksgiving/praise (who), intercession (do), and theology (through). This structure is illustrated in the phrasing of a classic text such as:

Faithful God,
you have called us to be your people, and given us a
share in the priesthood of Christ.
Open our eyes to the needs of others and teach us how
to pray.
We ask this through Jesus the Lord.

REFERENCES

General Instruction of the Roman Missal, 1969 (available with overview comments in *The Liturgy Documents: A Parish Resource,* Third Edition published by Liturgy Training Publications of Chicago, 1991).

Lectionary for Mass Introduction, 1982. (available with overview comments in *The Liturgy Documents: A Parish Resource,* Third Edition published by Liturgy Training Publications, Chicago, 1991).

Proclaim the Word: The Lectionary for Mass, 1982. Liturgy Study Text Series No.8. United States Catholic Conference, Washington, D.C.

Fitzgerald, Timothy, 1990. "General Intercessions." *Liturgy '90* 21(4): 9-12, 15.

Fitzgerald, Timothy, 1990. "General Intercessions—Continued." *Liturgy '90* 21(5):4-7, 15.

Melloh, John A., 1987. "The General Intercessions—Revisited." *Worship* 61(2):152-163.

Singing the Liturgy: What Are the Priorities?

Jayne Newton Ahearn

What is often parodied as the "four-hymn sandwich" highlights the comparatively late development of the use of vernacular hymns to replace the use of psalms that accompany the four processions at Mass. As recently as this practice arose, with the practice of dialogue Masses after the 1958 *Papal Instruction on Sacred Music,* it has now become a case of "the last shall be first." For many people this is presumed to be the only model for sung liturgy. The "four-hymn Low Mass" with gathering song, song at the preparation of the table and gifts, song during communion, and closing song is still the common experience of many communities as they gather for Sunday liturgy.

Apart from the four processions there are other ritual functions whose meaning is contradicted by the way they are celebrated. For example the responsorial psalm is treated as another reading, the Alleluia gospel acclamation is spoken, the litanies Lamb of God, Kyrie eleison and prayer of the faithful are recited, and the acclamations of the eucharistic prayer are said.

These contradictions lead us to ask some key questions.

What should we be singing in the liturgy?

What is the role of music?

Is music just decoration?

Is music just solemnity?

Is music used at liturgy just because it sounds pleasant?

Do we sing hymns so that the people can have a part in the liturgy?

Is music the means by which the people get to participate?

The underlying issue as regards these questions about the function of music is primarily one of ritual language whereby words and all the gestural actions (embracing the aural, verbal, visual and body language elements) simultaneously become the vehicle for the belief of the community.

One of the major shifts that occurred in the celebration of the liturgy as a result of Vatican II was from an emphasis on the priest as celebrant to the entire assembly of the faithful as celebrant. The *Constitution of the Sacred Liturgy* (*SC*) states that Christ is present in the gathered faithful as they pray and sing, and that it is the entire church in its public worship that participates in the one priesthood of Christ (*SC* no. 7). Therefore, the liturgy constitution called for the "full, conscious, and active participation in liturgical celebrations" by all the faithful because that is what liturgy is (*SC* no. 7). The early response to this call for active participation by the people was to add vocal participation and hymn singing to the liturgy where previously the priest said everything.

This pattern developed in the context of the Latin Mass, which could accommodate song in the vernacular only at certain points. These hymns were borrowed from other Christian traditions with a history of singing in the vernacular, and from Catholic popular devotions with the special language of the era in which they were written. Hymns in the vernacular based on Scripture and written for liturgical use were not yet available. Musical settings of the ordinary parts of the liturgy and settings of the responsorial psalms, all in the vernacular, also awaited composition.

Now there is a lot of music written for the liturgy. There has been a concentration on songs and hymns. The quality of composition and text varies but discerning music ministers can find good to excellent music for their community's liturgy. Yet is it enough that the assembly sings some songs of good quality, and does that define really active participation?

The liturgy constitution also has a chapter on sacred music which begins by ascribing to sacred music the purpose of giving glory to God and sanctifying the faithful (*SC* no.112). These are the same purposes which the document gives earlier to the liturgy itself (*SC* no.7). Furthermore this section on music establishes music as constitutive of the liturgy when it says of music: "as sacred song closely bound to the text, it forms a necessary or integral part of the solemn liturgy" (*SC* no. 112).

As Michael Joncas has written: "fundamentally, the purpose of liturgical music is to accomplish the rite itself, to 'do' the liturgy" (*Worship* 66).

How music functions in doing the liturgy has been explored by Edward Foley in *Music in Ritual: a Pre-Theological Investigation* published by the Liturgical Press. He examines the psychological power of music, music as a means of communication, and music as language.

Ultimately in the liturgy music is symbol. To quote philosopher Paul Ricoeur:

> symbol gives rise to thought. Contrary to perfectly transparent signs, which say what they want to say in positing what they signify, symbolic signs are opaque because the first, literal, obvious meaning itself points analogically to a second meaning which is not given otherwise than in it.... This opacity constitutes the depth of the symbol which, it will be said, is inexhaustible. (*Symbolism of Evil*, p. 15)

Foley summarizes his discussion of music as symbol:

> ...we come to see that music is well understood in symbolic term as a presentational (wordless) non-discursive (not having permanent units of meaning that are combinable into larger units) form of communication. Such an understanding begins to explain the power and potential of music, since symbols are potent by their very inexhaustible nature. Furthermore, as music employs the medium of sound, it is thus specially suited to 1) exist in the present, 2) to be a special key to interiority, 3) unite groups of living beings as nothing else can, and 4) situate people in the midst of actuality and simultaneity. (*Music in Ritual*, p. 17)

As do the other symbols we use in our liturgy—water, light oil, bread, wine—music has an ambivalence of content and multiplicity of meaning. It serves as a bridge to carry us from where we are to where we could not go without it: to an encounter with God who is hidden and *Presence*. This is what Michael Joncas has termed the "transcendental" function of music.

It we understand music as symbol without which we cannot do the rite, and if we understand that through the liturgy we are transformed by grace and thus come to participate in the very Presence of God, then we must conclude that participation of the people is more than a few added hymns but is by singing and doing the parts of the rite which properly belong to them.

What are those parts that properly belong to the assembly? What should be our list of priorities for music/song in doing the liturgy? There are three documents that contribute to these questions: *Musicam Sacram* (Congregation of Rites, 1967), *Music in Catholic Worship* (U.S. Bishops' Committee on the Liturgy, 1972, rev. 1983) and *Liturgical Music Today* (U.S. Bishops' Committee on the Liturgy, 1982)

Musicam Sacram (no. 29) proposes three degrees for sung participation, stating that the degrees must be so employed that the first may always be used without the others but that the second and third may never be used without the first.

Of greatest importance are acclamations, dialogical responses, and litanies. These should have the first priority for being sung. *The acclamations* include those for the eucharistic prayer, the holy holy, the memorial acclamation, the great amen, the gospel acclamation, the Alleluia or lenten gospel acclamation. *Dialogical responses* are the "And also with you" in response to "The Lord be with you" and the three responses in the preface dialogue. The *litanies* are the Lamb of God of the fraction rite, the Kyrie eleison of the penitential rite when it is used, and the general intercessions.

A middle level includes antiphons and psalmody. Primary in this group is the *responsorial psalm*. The Lectionary for Mass specifies a psalm for each Sunday and holy day. For communities just beginning to sing the psalm there is the option to use a seasonal psalm: these are found in the lectionary at the end of Sunday readings under the title "Common Texts for Sung Responsorial Psalms." The antiphon sung during the sprinkling rite would come in this group.

And the third level is hymnody. Among hymns, precedence is given to major processions; hence, the gathering song and the song during communion. But note that neither of these should be sung if the parts in levels one and two have not been sung. This represents a real reversal from practice in many parishes.

It is noteworthy that a closing song is not found in the Order of Mass but has come through the "four-hymn" usage. A closing song should be sung only if all of the above have been sung.

The song at the preparation of the table similarly has a very low priority. The transition time between liturgies of Word and Eucharist should not receive undue emphasis through song but rather can be made with instrumental music or silence.

There is a worthy place for corporate silence.

> Silence should be observed at the designated times as part of the celebration. Its function depends on the time it occurs in each part of the celebration. Thus at the penitential rite and again after the invitation to prayer, all recollect themselves: at the conclusion of a reading or the homily, all mediate briefly on what has been heard: after communion, all praise God in silent prayer. (*General Instruction of the Roman Missal* no. 23)

Filling up these silence with commentary, song, or instrumental interludes is contrary to the needs of the rite.

Communities that have been using music as constitutive of their liturgy are encouraged to continue and to share their experience with those who have yet to make that step toward the fullness of worship. Communities that have been challenged by this article are encouraged to redirect their musical energies from the four hymns to the acclamation, dialogical responses and litanies, and the responsorial psalm.

> … If liturgy is what we baptized do, week by week, what we do because we need to, and if liturgy so done is what forms us into what the baptismal plunge proclaimed, the liturgy is sung because that's all we have. There is a place for silence and a place for plain speaking, but singing is all we have when it comes time to acclaim, to intercede, to process. Oosterhuis would say that singing is the only way to make a sound at such a moment. Bonhoeffer would say that singing is the only way to act together, to be the church and not so many individuals. What should be sung but is left unsung will not be simply stifled, kept inside, frustrated. What is unsung will not be. (Gabe Huck, *How Can I Keep From Singing,* p. 40-41)

REFERENCES

Bishops' Committee on the Liturgy 1972/1983. *Music in Catholic Worship* (available with overview comments in *The Liturgy Documents: A Parish Resource,* Third Edition published by Liturgy Training Publications of Chicago, 1991).

Bishops' Committee on the Liturgy 1982. *Liturgical Music Today.* (available with overview comments in *The Liturgy Documents: A Parish Resource,* Third Edition published by Liturgy Training Publications, Chicago, 1991).

Foley, Edward *Music in Ritual: a Pre-Theological Investigation,* The Liturgical Press, Collegeville, MN.

Huck, Gabe 1989. *How Can I Keep From Singing?* Liturgy Training Publications. Chicago.

Joncas, J. Michael 1992. "Re-reading Musicam Sacram: Twenty-five years of development in Roman Rite Liturgical Music," *Worship* 66:212-231.

Language and Liturgy: Why Be Inclusive?

Jayne Newton Ahearn

INTRODUCTION

Much has been said and written about work in progress by ICEL (International Committee on English in the Liturgy) to revise the sacramentary including giving attention to inclusiveness in language. In the meantime, some parishes have gone ahead and implemented some language usage changes aimed at inclusiveness. Among both parishioners and those who prepare the parish liturgy there is confusion, misunderstanding, and apprehension about inclusive language. The questions being asked are: Why be concerned about inclusive language? What is inclusive language? What are the priorities for implementing inclusive language? This article briefly addresses each of these questions.

HUMANITY MADE ONE IN CHRIST

We celebrate the Easter season from Ash Wednesday to Pentecost as the great 90 days, in which we intensely reflect upon and actualize in our lives here and now the mystery of Jesus' passion, death, and resurrection. Through this mystery humanity has been reconciled with God and restored to unity with one another.

Saint Paul wrote to the faithful in Galatia: "As many of you as were baptized into Christ have clothed yourselves in Christ. There is no longer Jew or Greek, there is no longer slave or free, there is no longer male or female, for all of you are one in Christ Jesus" (Gal 3:27–28).

Baptism transforms us by the power of the Holy Spirit from individuals who are identified and valued because of what we are into a community who care and love one another because of who we are—the Body of Christ.

LITURGY MAKES MEANING IN THE DOING

The letter in which Paul develops the theology of the community as the Body of Christ (the first letter to the Corinthians) was written because that community was divided in several ways. There were factions who followed various charismatic leaders (1 Cor 1:10–13) and there was division between the haves and the have nots, the wealthy people with free time and the working people (1 Cor 1:17–21). When the Corinthians gathered to celebrate Eucharist, the sacrament of the death on the cross and resurrection of Christ, which reconciles humanity with God and makes us one, they did so in their various factions. The rich who could come at any time did not wait to begin until the working people could arrive. What was being done at their liturgy clearly was not what the sacrament was to signify. Paul admonished them saying that celebrating the ritual always has an effect, and if they were not signifying God's presence then they were partners with demons (see 1 Cor 10:14–22).

When we gather to celebrate the liturgy, what we do and say tells us who we are. In the liturgy we identify ourselves as a people called together and formed by God's Word who participate in the death and resurrection of Christ and so share together in the very life of God. The eucharistic assembly is the sign or sacrament of God's presence among humanity: it is the sign of the reign of God.

We hear Sunday after Sunday in Advent in those beautiful readings of Isaiah what the reign of God is like. All people, yes, all people, are called to be part of God's reign. There is justice and peace, all manner of affliction and disability is healed, even creation is refreshed and made new.

Jesus' description of the reign of God is the Sermon on the Mount. The blessed include those who are persecuted, hungering for justice, seeking peace, mourning, have an emptiness in their lives. In order for our Eucharist to be authentic we must in both deed and word not exclude anyone whom God has called.

CULTURAL ADAPTATION OF THE LITURGY

The reform of the liturgy mandated by Vatican II, opened the way for the liturgy to be inculturated or to assimilate the local cultural patterns such as language, thought, art, ritual, and symbol (*Sacrosanctum Concilium* no. 36-38).

The first step was the celebration of the liturgy in the vernacular, which for us is English. Unlike Latin, which is a static language because it is no longer spoken by any cultural group, words do not have the same meaning from one century to the next or even from one generation to the next. For example, in the sixteenth and seventeenth centuries the words man, mankind, or men were usually generic terms meaning men and women, human beings, humanity. But today our meanings are more precise so that *man* or *men* usually means the male and not female. The same is true for the third person singular pronouns: *he, him, his* refer to the male but not the female. Since English has become a more precise language we must be more precise in the way we use its words.

FORMATIVE POWER OF LANGUAGE

The human sciences, especially linguistics and psychology, teach us that the way we use words and language both identify us and shape our behavior. The words we choose to say both identify us and shape what we shall say, what we really think, and who we really are. Likewise, the words we hear being used by others about us tell us who we really are and how we should think about ourselves.

For example, men and women who for years have recited the Creed that says "for us men and for our salvation he came down from heaven" may wonder whether women are included among the saved and, if so, why the church does not acknowledge them. This is an issue for those who have become sensitized to it, yet it is not perceived as a problem by some others.

The formative power of language is precisely why changing words in a text, when it is done, is such an emotional issue for some. It is because it strikes deeply at our identity and challenges who we are. Yet, the gospel call to the baptized is to examine constantly and reform our identity with the help of the Holy Spirit so that we might become more and more like Christ. Therefore, for us as individuals to become more Christlike and for us as a community to become a more authentic sign of God's reign, we accept that our liturgical language must be inclusive.

DEFINING INCLUSIVE LANGUAGE

In 1990 the Canadian Conference of Catholic Bishops defined inclusive language as "using words which affirm the equality and dignity of each person regardless of race, gender, creed, age or ability."

Our Western culture and specifically our Judeo-Christian tradition is patriarchal and therefore androcentric. Women had to achieve identity and status through their relationships to men. But this is not the way it is supposed to be in God's reign. It has taken us 2,000 years to make a beginning at change, and we do it through how we talk about ourselves and how we talk about God.

LANGUAGE ABOUT PEOPLE

When speaking of ourselves as a community of believers, nouns and pronouns must include both genders. A more subtle form of androcentric bias and thus of exclusion is the stereotyping of qualities and roles as male or female. A good example of this is one of the nuptial blessings of the marriage rite which places the woman in the home rearing children while the man's locus of activity is left unspecified. If the texts of the Feast of the Holy Family are examined, one sees that they have been selected or written to inform and thus form men and women in stereotypical roles: Joseph is the active head of the Holy Family, wives are to be submissive to their husbands, the son is to care for and honor his father, and God is praised for crowning creation with the family of man.

LANGUAGE ABOUT GOD

Our God language is an even more difficult and

complex issue. This is because all of our language about God is metaphorical. The nature of God is always more than we could imagine, and our language is not adequate to express the fullness of the mystery of God. Certainly God does not have gender: yet, in our efforts to describe and relate to God, we have presented God as male (again the androcentric bias). We need to widen the metaphors and images through which we pray and relate to God, conscious that God is all qualities and virtues. The Scriptures themselves present a variety of images and metaphors for God.

The naming of God is done by God. To the Jews, God revealed through Moses the name I AM WHO I AM. God is the one who is: God exists. The new covenant in Jesus Christ is a new revelation of God's name. Jesus called God Abba, Father. Those who are baptized into Christ share in that same organic relationship. For Christians God not only is, God is in intimate relationship with Godself and with us.

We express this relationship with God, who comes through baptism and confirmation, by calling upon God as Father. We express the mystery of God in Godself by naming the Trinity as Father, Son, and Holy Spirit. To cease calling upon God as Father is to deny our very life in God. To name the Trinity according to functions such as creator and redeemer and sanctifier is to relate to God according to what God does rather than who God is. Such division according to function is called Modalism and was condemned as heresy in the early third century.

IMPLEMENTING THE USE OF INCLUSIVE LANGUAGE

As early as 1975 the International Commission on English in the Liturgy (ICEL), the body responsible for translating Latin texts into English, made the commitment to using inclusive language. Thus texts translated after 1974, such as the *Pastoral Care of the Sick*, *Order of Christian Funerals*, *Rite of Christian Initiation of Adults* and *Book of Blessings* use inclusive language.

The problem lies with texts revised and translated prior to 1975, which most notably include the sacramentary. In 1980, an interim revision of the eucharistic prayers by ICEL included a change in the language of the institution narrative, saying the cup of Christ's blood, the blood of the new and everlasting covenant, was shed "for all" instead of "for all men." (This change was made not for reasons of inclusivity but because it better reflects the Latin text. Thus the first translation can be said to have had an androcentric bias).

The Vatican Congregation for Divine Worship, which oversees the Roman liturgy, set up a committee on inclusive language in 1985. The sacramentary is currently under revision, which will make the texts inclusive in language and new editions will be available soon, once issues about authorized biblical translations for liturgical proclamation are resolved.

The following are categories of liturgical use in which words and language express and form our identity. They are presented in order of their possibility to be submitted to inclusive language criteria and thus in order of priority for implementation by a parish.

1. The Homily and The Prayer of the Faithful (General Intercessions)

We have great freedom here because there are no official texts given for either of these parts of the liturgy. Those who write the prayer of the faithful must be careful that their language neither excludes nor denies the dignity of anyone in the liturgical assembly. At the same time we can pray for conversion of heart and mind to become a more authentic sign of God's reign. Those who prepare and deliver the homily need to be careful and sensitive in their use of words. Those who preach also have the responsibilities of explaining texts, especially of Scripture, that reflect exclusive thought and behavior, and of challenging the community with the gospel call to be a sign of God's reign where people of every race, language, and way of life are gathered.

2. Readings from Sacred Scripture

It is God's Word that calls us together and forms us. The Word is addressed to all peoples. The Word is primary, and by canon law (can. 213) the faithful have a right to hear the Word proclaimed in the liturgical assembly. Yet they also have the right to hear the Word proclaimed in language they can understand according to their culture, for the gospel does not stand outside of culture but is enfleshed in it (e.g., *Ad Gentes* no.11).

The lectionary is simply the list of readings from sacred Scripture specified for each Sunday, feast, and weekday. The readings themselves are also provided based upon a translation of Scripture that has been approved for liturgical use by the National Conference of Bishops.

The various bishops' conferences are revising the lectionary by basing it on a recent translation of Scripture that uses inclusive language. In late 1992 the Canadian Conference of Catholic Bishops published the new Canadian Lectionary, which uses the New Revised Standard Version translation of the Bible. In the United States, after long delays and much debate and discussion with Rome, a revised lectionary for Sunday Mass was issued with the understanding that it would be reviewed after five years of use. Its New Testament readings are based on the Revised New American Bible (at the time the lectionary was issued, the Old Testament of the RNAB had not yet been completed).

The way in which these readings are then presented during the liturgy should follow the directives of the *Introduction to the Lectionary* (no. 35-37) and the *Environment and Art in Catholic Worship* (no. 91). The book in liturgical celebration is a symbol of the sacred and thus should be worthy and beautiful. The book is not to be replaced by other pastoral aids such as leaflets for preparation or meditation.

3. Presidential Prayers

The current sacramentary is being revised. In the meantime we have to make wise and sensitive use of the prayer texts given to us. There is always a choice given between alternatives for the opening prayer. There is also a choice among eucharistic prayers. Selection can be made with the criterion of inclusiveness in mind. No one should undertake to change the prayer texts spontaneously, for they are not the prayer of the individual but the prayer of the community and evoke the response "Amen."

4. Hymn Texts and Psalm Texts

This is the most problematic of all the categories. Psalms are sacred Scripture, and the translations used are subject to the same discipline as the readings. Many of the traditional hymn texts are from the centuries where words, which now refer to males, were generic in meaning. Even some contemporary hymns and songs do not show a sensitivity in use of language about people or about God.

Unless the hymn text is in the public domain, words cannot be changed because they are protected by copyright law. Where it may be lawful, changing words in hymn texts must be done with caution and care not to destroy the hymn's poetic flow or ability to be sung. Discernment in the selection of hymns and psalm settings we use in our liturgy and in applying the criteria of careful language is the best approach.

The subject here has been about language in the liturgy, about the use of words. As a final thought, consider who prepares those words, who speaks the words, and who enacts the words at liturgy. The teams that prepare the liturgy should be inclusive. Liturgical ministries should be inclusive.

(The author is grateful to Dr. Tom Elich, Executive Secretary of the National Liturgical Commission [Australia] for his helpful comments and criticisms.)

REFERENCES

Collins, Mary, OSB 1987. "The Words of Worship" in *Worship: Renewal to Practice* Pastoral Press, Washington, DC, pp. 136-229.

Cooney-Hathaway, Patrica 1990. "Women in Worship: the issue of inclusivity." *Assembly* 17 (1) 500-502

Groome, Thomas H. 1991. *Language for a "Catholic" Church: A Program of Study.* Sheed & Ward, Kansas City, MO.

Hughes, Kathleen RSCJ and Ronald Lewinski 1987. "Inclusive language in the liturgy." *Liturgy '80* 18 (5) 14-15.

Notre Dame Center for Pastoral Liturgy Staff 1990. "Inclusive language references and resources" *Assembly* 17 (1) 504-506.

Wainwright, Elaine 1992. "Let the words of my mouth be acceptable: inclusiveness and the language of liturgy." *Liturgy News* 22 (3) 8-10

Wren, Brian 1989. *What Language Shall I Borrow?* Crossroad Publishing, New York.

THE PASCHAL MYSTERY
in Bereavement

The Funeral: Meaning, Value, and Function

Gerry Smith

INTRODUCTION

When someone dies, one of the first things we have to consider is the type of funeral arrangements. In the confusion and numbness that may accompany the news of a death, grieving survivors may have difficulty in making decisions about funeral arrangements. Caregivers are sometimes called upon to give advice and assistance at such a time as this. It is therefore important to understand the sequence the funeral process follows after a death, and to be aware of some of the alternatives that are available today. Why do we do things the way we do? Is there meaning and value in what we do?

In addition to the caregiver's assistance at the actual time of the funeral, many people today are giving consideration to funeral arrangements before death occurs. Such pre-planning and forethought mean that people are more able to consider the options available and to make wise decisions without being under the added stress of a newly experienced loss. In this chapter we address ourselves to the matter of appropriate funeral processes.

When we use the word funeral most have in mind the actual service and committal of the deceased person to burial or cremation. The words "funeral arrangements" can also be used to describe all the processes between the moment of death and the final act of disposition. It is with the second concept in mind that we approach the subject of the funeral.

DEFINITION AND PURPOSE OF THE FUNERAL

It is difficult to come up with an all-inclusive definition of the word *funeral* because of the variety of traditions involved.

In the Macquarrie Dictionary, we find the following definition:

Funeral 1. the ceremonies connected with the disposition of the body of a dead person: obsequies. 2. a funeral procession (...)

Dr. William M. Larmers Jr., who is a psychiatrist in the United States, has developed a definition of a funeral that is widely used and quoted. He says that "a funeral is an organized, purposeful, time-limited, flexible, group-centered response to death."

Many psychologists and pastoral counselors tend to define the funeral on the basis of the needs that a family in bereavement is experiencing.

A combination of some of these definitions would indicate that a funeral becomes that experience in which a person can face the reality of what has happened, let memory become a part of the process of grieving, express honest feelings, accept the community support that is offered; and attempt to place the death in a context of meaning acceptable to the individual and to the group experiencing the trauma of the separation.

We could say that the purpose of the funeral is generally threefold:

1. To dispose of the body of the dead person.

It is normal to see that such disposition is carried out with dignity—though of course different cultures and individuals will interpret "dignity" differently.

2. Publicly to acknowledge the life that has been lived by the person now deceased and to pay tribute to that life. The funeral provides us with one opportunity to reflect on the value and meaning of the person's life and what its worth to us has been.

3. To help those who survive the death to begin the process of grief.

This can be achieved by encouraging them as they consider the task of moving forward to rebuild and re-establish their own life experience without the living presence of the now deceased person.

In this chapter we cannot go into a lot of detail about the history of the funeral. In general it appears to be accepted that throughout history, all cultures have had some ceremonial traditions and rituals associated with such life passage events as birth, puberty, marriage, and death.

Robert Fulton writing in his chapter on "Death and the Funeral in Contemporary Society" in the book *Dying: Facing the Facts* edited by Hannelore Wass (McGraw-Hill 1979) states: "Burial of the dead is an ancient practice among humans. From Paleolithic times to the present, human beings have responded to their fellow humans with solemnity and ceremony" (p. 236).

The funeral is as old as recorded history, as recent archaeological discoveries at Shanidar in Iraq illustrate. The way people buried their dead was presumably for specific ideological or religious reasons. Entombment is not universal in history, but it has been practiced in many societies far back into archaeological time, and has served to express the idea of immortality. All the great civilizations of the past have left evidence of this. The earliest records of humankind reveal rituals and ceremonies associated with disposal of the dead.

THE MEANING AND VALUE OF THE FUNERAL

We ought to recognize that the funeral can be one of the most important facilitators for the process of grieving. It does not always achieve this role for a number of reasons.

Funeral and mourning rites are justified because they offer a healthy way of meeting genuine need. But there are more needs than one—and not all are immediately obvious.

Death can both *separate* and *unite* people simultaneously. Funeral ritual can assist this process as it both recognizes life, and acknowledges the death of the deceased and unifies family and friends. Death has two basic directions—those who die *leave us*—those who mourn *lose someone*. These are two different actions and will draw forth different responses. They witness both our belief in where the dead go, and also our sense of loss. This is not always understood, or acknowledged, by some of our religious rituals. It is this opposite "pull" of death that many of us have most difficulty in coming to terms with. As death separates, it also unites. Because the death of another reminds me of my own mortality, I may well take comfort in the presence of others (living) around me when I attend a funeral. Funerals can reinforce this need.

> The Church through its funeral rites commends the dead to God's merciful love and pleads for their forgiveness of their sins. At the funeral rites, especially at the celebration of the eucharistic sacrifice, the Christian community affirms and expresses the union of the Church on earth with the Church in heaven in the one great communion of saints. Though separated from the living, the dead are still at one with the community of believers on earth and benefit from their prayers and intercession.
>
> At the rite of final commendation and farewell, the community acknowledges the reality of separation and commends the deceased to God. In this way it recognizes the spiritual bond that still exists between the living and the dead and proclaims its belief that all the faithful will be raised up and re-united in the new heavens and a new earth, where death will be no more. (*Order of Christian Funerals* [*OCF*] no. 6).

Funerals the world over have certain things in common despite all the variations and alternatives that exist. They usually center around public ceremony, mostly religious in context, which seeks to honor the life of the deceased and to acknowledge that this life, as far as this world is concerned, is now terminated.

They usually allow for some visual confrontation with the body, through a viewing, or visitation, or through the preparation of the body for burial or cremation. It is true that in Australia such visual confrontation is less common than in other countries. Yet even here, a survey suggested 40% of Australians may view a deceased person at a funeral parlor. Even where the body itself is not seen, there will normally be visual confrontation of the coffin or casket containing the body.

There is usually a funeral procession, from the place of final service to the point of committal or disposition, where further ceremony, rituals, or prayers focus on the leavetaking experience, and the final moment of separation from the physical remains of the deceased.

Such funeral procedures can serve a variety of therapeutic and practical purposes. They give some comfort and support to the survivors, causing them to be aware that many share with them in their loss. They help us to dispose of the body with dignity, mark the end of a person's life, and help us to establish the significance of that life. The funeral processes can also make a significant contribution to the healing process just beginning for those who grieve.

Yet unhappily, we have to say that funerals in our society do not always achieve such ends. When funeral rituals are allowed to lose all realism and appropriateness, or deteriorate into a set of seemingly meaningless repetition of trite phrases and unhelpful liturgies and prayers, or where the process is so depersonalized as to be irrelevant to the needs of the mourners, the funeral rituals have failed to realize their therapeutic and practical purposes.

In general, we would have to say that not enough attention is given to the planning and implementing of funerals that recognize in real and honest terms the life of the deceased in such a way that it has meaning for those who survive. However, when this is well done, we see funeral services that celebrate a person's life and assist the mourners to grieve positively and healthily. Helpful funerals better enable those who grieve to work through their grief and cope with their losses.

The challenge to assist mourners to create meaningful funeral services at a time of a relative's or friend's death is one of the most significant challenges facing funeral directors, clergy, civil celebrants, social workers, and other caregivers today.

What are some of the needs that funerals help to meet and what are funerals meant to achieve? We would have to say for many people, and where it is appropriate, the funeral service meets certain religious or spiritual needs. In other words, when a person has died, it is usually necessary for those who survive to affirm something of their belief, something of their faith and trust in a divine being or spiritual values. So where the person who has died, or his or her survivors, hold to a religious faith, the intervention of death normally has a religious significance and this needs to be recognized in a religious service. It is normal, for instance, in the Christian church for the theme of resurrection to be proclaimed at such a time. Such a proclamation will normally be helpful to the survivors, especially if it is given with due regard for the fact that suffering, pain, loss, and sorrow also belong to the world of the dying and the bereaved.

It must be noted that in most Christian traditions the value of the funeral service is particularly for the living and not the dead, although that is not to deny that in some traditions the rituals have significance for the future of the soul of the deceased. There needs to be balance in such services, however, so that the emotional and psychological needs of the mourners are not ignored.

> The celebration of the Christian funeral brings hope and consolation to the living. While proclaiming the Gospel of Jesus Christ and witnessing to Christian hope in the resurrection, the funeral rites also recall to all who take part in them God's mercy and judgement and meet the human need to turn always to God in times of crisis. (*Order of Christian Funerals* no. 7)

Apart from the religious needs, which of course are not always appropriate, there are other needs that exist. There are probably a range of needs on the part of the survivors, and we could place them together under three main headings.

The first needs are **Personal Needs,** and these needs are such that they will reflect the degree of attachment that the survivors have had to the deceased person. For those who are survivors there are personal needs as they have experienced a personal loss. The loss will vary from person to person depending on how they have been attached to the person who has died.

Consider the death of a man. His wife will respond and react in certain ways and have certain needs because of his death. His children, or his grandchildren, will have other needs to be met, and they respond and react in other ways. The same goes for his parents, if they are still alive, or his workmates, business associates, his friends and neighbors. There's a wide circle of people who will have a variety of personal needs as a result of the death of someone they have known.

The closeness to the deceased person will determine the type of personal needs. However, it is a little difficult to define closeness because sometimes we can be closer to people with whom we do not have a blood relationship than we are to our family. Sometimes the closeness may depend on the time we've known a person or it may depend on the depth of appreciation we have of the person's life. It may depend on the sense in which we depend on the person for all manner of things, or the depth of love for that person, or what that person's death means for us as the survivors.

Other factors that will affect our personal needs will include such things as the circumstances of the death, the context in which the death took place, the age of the person who has died, and the effect that their death will have on our living.

The second group of needs are **Familial Needs.** We often hear the comment: "The only times we seem to get together as a family today are at weddings and funerals." Sadly that is true for many families. At a time of death we may suddenly rediscover our sense of family. Death may prompt us to reflect upon the value of family ties and remind us of the worth of being part of a family. At the time of the death some members of the family may develop a new appreciation of the value of family relationships, something that they often overlook in day-to-day living. There may also be an awareness of the fragmentation that has been taking place in the family circle. Perhaps death is just one of those examples of fragmentation. There are others, as people move from one community to another, or as relationships break down, or as we lose our sense of dependence on other members of the family.

Death in a family may stimulate members toward restoring damaged relationships. These needs may often be well served by a funeral service and whatever may follow a funeral service, as a family comes together and celebrates and reflects upon the life of a person who has died. Often families have a sense of one generation passing on and another moving up, and that is particularly the case when an old person dies. And perhaps, as the family comes together at the time of the funeral, they are able to understand that concept afresh, now that the older person has died and moved *out of* the context of family life. Often families have a very real sense of their ongoing life through coming together at a funeral service.

> Christians celebrate the funeral rites to offer worship, praise, and thanksgiving to God for the gift of life which has now been returned to God, the author of life and the hope of the just. The Mass, the memorial of Christ's death and resurrection, is the principal celebration of the Christian funeral. (*Order of Christian Funerals*, no. 5)

The third set of needs that may be met through a funeral are **Social Needs**, the group needs. This is particularly relevant where the death is of someone significant to the whole community, or a large part of a community.

At the time of a person's death the community needs to affirm the fact that life goes on. Yes, a life has ended, but at the same time other lives have begun, and our own life continues, and it is important for the community to identify those truths. The community also needs to affirm a sense of meaning in the life now ended—that it was a life well lived—and to reflect upon what this life has meant to the community. The community however, also needs to affirm a sense of meaning in the lives of those who live on, and so, at the time of a person's death the individuals may be reflecting on what it has meant for them to be alive. How have *I* lived my life? What has *my* life achieved? Who have *I* touched through *my* living? What will *I* do with the life *I* have yet to live?

In his book *Funeral: Vestige or Value*, one of the most helpful available on the subject of the funeral, Paul Irion lists a number of criteria concerning funerals. One of the criteria is that the funeral manifest opportunities for expressions of shared loss and be the means by which support from the group of mourners is conveyed to the bereaved.

Too many funerals do not allow for this to occur. Too often the mourners are spectators who arrive at a funeral service, watch what happens, and then take their leave and return to their normal duties, often with undue haste. Although it is not suggested that clergy, funeral directors, and cemetery staff fulfill their obligations with undue haste, the busyness of such people does produce a situation of pressure. This happens when funerals are conducted to a controlled timetable, even going so far as telling the bereaved that "the service must not go longer than a certain period of time or we will be late arriving at the crematorium. After the service at the crematorium please leave quickly and quietly as the next funeral procession is about to arrive." Such things are facts of life, but they do restrict the ways in which people can support the bereaved and express their own grief.

> so too when a member of Christ's Body dies, the faithful are called to a ministry of consolation to those who have suffered the loss of one whom they love. Christian consolation is rooted in that hope that comes from faith in the saving death and resurrection of the Lord Jesus Christ. Christian hope faces the reality of death and anguish of grief but trust confidently that the power of sin and death has been vanquished by the risen Lord.... (*Order of Christian Funerals* no. 8)

This means that the support given to the bereaved in physical and verbal interaction usually takes place away from the location of the funeral, such as in the home of the bereaved. This is not necessarily a bad thing but it does probably preclude other mourners from being involved.

In country towns there is much more of this involvement and support on the part of the mourners than there is in the city, and often the time involved in the funeral and the service and going out to the cemetery is longer than in the city. Then the folk gather afterward and spend time together.

It could be argued that merely by their own attendance at a funeral the mourners are supporting the bereaved. This is acknowledged but still in a sense is seen to be inadequate. The bereaved need time to be alone before, during, and after a funeral service, but they also need to feel the support and care of their fellow mourners. It is interesting to note that some funeral companies are at present developing alternative styles that may help to overcome some of there problems.

> Members of the community should console the mourners with words of faith and support and with acts of kindness, for example, assisting them with some of the routine tasks of daily living..... The community's principal involvement in the ministry of consolation is expressed in its active participation in the celebration of the funeral rites, particularly the vigil for the deceased, the funeral liturgy, and the rite of committal. For this reason these rites should be scheduled at times that permit as many of the community as possible to be present. (*Order of Christian Funerals* no. 10-11)

There should be more opportunities for people to participate in services and funeral activities, when that is appropriate to the needs of the bereaved and the mourners who are supporting the bereaved. Support can better be given through the sharing of personal feelings rather than through the more commonly used gifts of flowers or submission of printed notices to the daily papers, or sending cards. While not always inappropriate, they can be, if they represent an attempt to replace personal contact and involvement. A recent trend has developed of the family asking that sympathy be expressed by making a memorial offering to a selected charity relevant to the deceased. This donation usually is requested in lieu of flowers and other memorials.

Care should be taken so that a memorial service does not become a means of avoiding the reality of death. Similarly, private funerals, while often appropriate can, in some cases, reduce the opportunity to share the loss. Some of these alternatives may suit people's emotional need more than others.

Regardless of the alternatives selected, the funeral ceremony ought to be designed in such a way that it provides opportunities for:

• the recognition of the life of the person now deceased;

• the strengthening of family ties and responsibilities;

• the reenforcement of beliefs about life and death;

• the support of the bereaved family and friends, assisting them to accept the reality of the death and express their emotion, and encouraging them as they prepare for living in the future.

While funerals are usually sad occasions, meaningful funerals can and do assist the bereaved to cope with the loss they have experienced. Such funerals can be sources of strength, hope, and peace.

There are many different types of funeral services that can be conducted. Most churches or religious groups have specific services that are relevant to their beliefs and which minister to the needs of their members. Whether a funeral service is religious or non-religious, there are various factors that affect the appropriateness and helpfulness of the service.

Acknowledgments
Tricia Warwick (NZ)
Australian Funeral Directors Association
Death and Bereavement Educational Services, Melbourne Vic.

A Funeral Service at the Crematorium

Russell Hardiman

GATHERING RITES

When the funeral procession arrives at the Crematorium Chapel and all have gathered, the Presider greets and welcomes them in these or similar words.

P: In the name of the Father and of the Son and of the Holy Spirit.
R: **Amen.**

P: May the grace of our Lord Jesus Christ, the source of all consolation, be with you.
R: **And also with you.**
P: And with our dearly beloved departed N.

INVITATION

The Presider invites the mourners to reflect on why they are gathered and calls them to trust in God's promise of eternal life.

P: Our brother/sister N. has gone to his/her rest in the peace of Christ.
May the Lord now welcome him/her to the table of God's children in heaven.
With faith and hope in eternal life, let us assist him/her with our prayers.

Let us pray to the Lord also for ourselves.
May we who mourn be reunited one day with our brother/sister:
together may we meet Christ Jesus when he who is our life appears in glory.

SCRIPTURE VERSE

One of the following verses or another brief Scripture verse is read. A fuller Scripture reading may be used. The Presider first says:

P: We read in sacred Scripture:
Matthew 25:34
Come, you whom my Father has blessed, says the Lord: inherit the kingdom prepared for you since the foundation of the world.

John 6:39
This is the will of my Father, says the Lord, that I should lose nothing of all that he has given to me, and that I should raise it up on the last day.

P: In the presence of the Risen Lord Jesus those who die still live and the human person does not perish in death but is transformed by the power of God's grace.

P: Since Almighty God has called N. from this life to himself, we commend him/her to the Lord. May the Lord receive him/her into his eternal peace and raise him/her up on the last day.

P: Let us pray.
(*Pause for silent prayer*)
P: O God, our ever-loving Father, we gather today to remember and pray for N.
For us he/she has been and will always be our earthly father/mother.
May his/her love and care for his/her own family always be a sign of your eternal love and care for all of us.
In that love lead him/her to eternal life through Jesus Christ your Son who was raised from the dead to be with you and the Holy Spirit as our God for ever and ever.
R: **Amen.**

LITURGY OF THE WORD

A brief service of the Word with reading, homily and intercession may help to prepare people for the committal and final farewell.

GOSPEL READING (John 14:1–6)
At that time Jesus said to his disciples "Do not let your hearts be troubled. Have faith in God and faith in me. There are many dwelling places in my Father's home. Otherwise I would have warned you. I am going to prepare a place for you, and when I do go and prepare a place for you, I am coming back to take you along with me so that where I am, you may also be. And you know the way to the place where I am going." "Lord," Thomas said, "we don't know where you are going. How then can we know the way?" Jesus told him, "I am the way, the truth, and the life: no one comes to the Father except through me."

HOMILY OR RECALLING THE LIFE OF THE DEAD
The minister may introduce this reflection in these or similar words:

P: And now, O Lord, we remember (Name) your servant recalling times spent together and giving thanks for his/her life, for joys and trials shared, for work accomplished, for leisure, for family life, and friendship.
The Presider may expand on the life of the deceased. And then conclude:
P: In silence we share the memories of our hearts.

PRAYER OF THE FAITHFUL
P: We have heard the words of Jesus that encourage us to have faith in him.
In the faith we share, whether strong or struggling, let us turn to him in confidence because he IS the Way, the Truth, and the Life.
Let us ask together in prayer that he lead N. to eternal life.
N. was first given the promise of eternal life in baptism. Give him/her now the fullness of life eternal.
(*Pause*)

P: Lord, hear us.
R: **Lord, hear our prayer.**

P: N. received the Spirit of God in Confirmation and ate the bread of eternal life, the Body of Christ. May the Lord raise him/her up on the last day.
(*Pause*)

P: Lord, hear us.
R: **Lord, hear our prayer.**

P: Let us pray for the family left behind. May the Lord who turns the darkness of death into the dawn of new life lead this family through their present grief and sadness to the peace and light of God's presence.
(*Pause*)

P: Lord, hear us.
R: **Lord, hear our prayer.**

P. Let us pray for all of us gathered here in fellowship and faith. May we always remember that we too are most certain to meet death. May the Lord make us all one in his kingdom of eternal peace. (*Pause*)
P: Lord hear us.
R: **Lord, hear our prayer.**

P. Let us pray in confidence the prayer that Jesus himself taught us.
Our Father ...

COMMITTAL

P: Since Almighty God has called N. from this life to himself,
we commend him/her to the Lord.
May the Lord receive him/her into his eternal peace and raise him/her up on the last day.

ASPERSION OF CASKET
P: I bless you, N., with the holy water that recalls the day of baptism.
When you were baptized you were christened or made like Christ through grace and brought into the community of believers in the Church.

May this sprinkling of the waters of baptism lead you to the hope we share that, if in union with Christ we have imitated his death, we shall also imitate him in his resurrection.

PRAYER OF LIGHT

P: O Lord by whose word the heavens were made, whose love made us from dust, receive now the mortal remains of this your servant, who has died and departed this earthly life. Dutifully we give his/her body for cremation, as ashes to ashes and dust to dust, eternal life is our trust,

During these last words the coffin is removed and the Presider continues with minimum pause

P: that as the flames of earth end our mortality so in the fullness of time, the flame of your love may remake us eternally in the glory and stature of Christ. He alone is the Light of the world, the light no darkness can end, who with you and the Holy Spirit, is God for ever and ever,

R: Amen.

PRAYER OVER THE PEOPLE

After the Consignment of the Casket the Presider continues:

P: N. has gone to eternal life in the grace and peace of Christ.
With faith and hope in eternal life let us commend him/her to the mercy of God and assist him/her by our prayers.
May the Lord lead him/her to inherit the promise of eternal life.

A hymn, e.g., "Amazing Grace," may be sung by the congregation.

P: The amazing Grace we share in Christ is the pledge of eternal life, our hope of eternal peace.
P: Let us pray.
Father of heaven,
into your merciful hands we commend N.
We thank you for all the blessings you gave him/her in this life and pray that his/her memory may inspire us to love and honor you.
We ask you that he/she may go on
living in our hearts and minds
and that all who were associated with him/her in life,
now because of his/her death,
may be even more closely associated with one another.
We are encouraged by the sure hope
that he/she will rise again on the last day
with all those who have lived and died in Christ.

Accept our prayer through Christ Our Lord.
R: Amen.

CONCLUSION

P: Eternal rest grant to him/her, O Lord,
R: And let perpetual light shine upon him/her.

P: May his/her soul
and the souls of all the faithful departed.
R: Through the mercy of God rest in peace.
R. Amen.

Ceremony of Interment of Ashes

Russell Hardiman

GATHERING RITES

P: In the name of the Father and of the Son and of the Holy Spirit.
R: Amen.

P: May the grace of the Risen Lord Jesus, the source of our consolation in death be with you.
R: And also with you.

Invitation

P: There are times in life when words alone are inadequate to express what we would want to say. Then, we express ourselves in gesture and symbol, the language of ritual. Your very presence here now is one such gesture, a sign of wanting to pay your last respects for N., an expression of solidarity with N. & N., and all those who mourn N.'s passing. We come to this special place as a sign of wanting to commemorate the life and death of N.

This place is the final resting place for the mortal remains/the ashes of N. It is called a COLUMBARIUM. This is a Latin word that is connected to the word for "a dove" and so has the connotation of being a symbol of peace. It is the final resting place of those whose ashes lie here. It is, we trust, the visible reminder and sign to us, who are left behind, that our loved ones now share eternal peace.

Let us ask the Lord Almighty to bless this niche and grant eternal peace to N. and to all those who rest here.

Blessing of Niche

P: Let us pray.
(*Pause for silent prayer*)
Lord Jesus Christ,
by the three days you lay in the tomb
you made holy the resting place of all who trust in you.
Bless this columbarium and give our brother/sister N. peaceful rest here until that day when you,
the resurrection and the life, will raise him/her up
in eternal glory. We ask this through you, Christ Our Lord.
R: Amen.
(The niche may be sprinkled with baptismal water in silence or using these or similar words.)
P: May this sprinkling of the waters of baptism remind us of our first sharing in the life of Christ, that day of which St. Paul wrote, "When we were baptized with Christ, we were baptized in his death. If we have imitated him in his death we shall also imitate him in his resurrection." By the power of the Lord Jesus may he/she who rests here rise to eternal life in him.

INTERNMENT

The urn of ashes is placed in the niche
P: With faith in Jesus Christ we reverently bring the ashes of our brother/sister N. to be sealed in this place of rest. As Christ was the first to rise from the dead, we know that he will raise us up to share his glory.
May the Lord Jesus receive our brother/sister N. into his peace and raise him/her on the last day.
Since Almighty God has called our brother/sister N. from this life to himself we commend him/her to the Lord.

GESTURE OF FAREWELL

P: Before we part, let us take leave of our brother/sister N.
May this last farewell express the depth of our love for him/her. May it ease our pain and sadness. May it strengthen us with hope.
Family members and mourners are invited to make a gesture of farewell e.g. placing flowers or some memorabilia near the

niche.

Sign of the Cross
Make a large sign of the cross
P: Lord God, Almighty Father, You have made the cross for us a sign of strength and marked us as yours in the sacrament of the resurrection. Now you have freed our brother/sister from this mortal life, make her/him one with your saints in heaven. We ask this through Christ Our Lord.
R: Amen.

Prayer of Thanksgiving for the Life of the Deceased

P: Father of heaven,
into your merciful hands we commend N.
We thank you for all the blessings you gave him/her
in this life and pray that his/her memory may
inspire us to love and honor you.
We ask that he/she may go on living in our hearts and minds
and that all who were associated with him/her in life,
now because of his/her death,
may be even more closely associated with one another.
We are encouraged by the sure hope
that he/she will rise again on the last day with
all those who have lived and died in Christ.
Accept our prayers through Christ Our Lord.
R: Amen

P: Eternal rest grant unto him/her, O Lord,
R: and may perpetual light shine upon (him/her).

P: May his/her soul, and the souls of all the faithful departed,

THE PASCHAL MYSTERY
and Popular Devotions

Popular Devotions of the Christian People

Russell Hardiman

INTRODUCTION

> The spiritual life is not confined to participation in the liturgy.... popular devotions of the Christian people are warmly commended, provided they accord with the laws and norms of the Church... these devotions should be so drawn up that they harmonize with liturgical seasons, accord with the sacred liturgy, are in some fashion derived from it, and lead the people to it, since the liturgy by its very nature far surpasses any of them. (*CSL* no. 12,13)

Like many of the statements in the Vatican II documents this affirmation of an ideal is scarcely verified in practice, for quite often the popular perception of, and enthusiasm for, devotional practices is in a different direction that makes them quite remote from the mainstream sacramental worship of the church. The affirmation that shines through at the grass-roots level of parish life and in personal prayer is the appeal on the human level for what people can understand and relate to, which is often quite indifferent to theological subtleties.

The root cause of this dichotomy is perhaps, the movement away from the communitarian theology that dominated in the early centuries of the church to the private sense of devotion that emerged in the Middle Ages and has become increasingly strong right up to our day.

What history shows is that the appeal to the emotions, the engagement with the imagination, and even the guarantee of spiritual rewards are likely to be the attraction that inspires individuals to express their relationship with God, or their expectation from their image of God. In practical terms this shows itself in the blossoming of a myriad of devotions to Jesus, to Mary, and to the Saints, where the common denominator is an easy bridge to cross the gap and so meet the divine in and through human activity. The current plethora of revelations and the fervent response they engender serve to underline the perennial appeal of a guaranteed way to God that offers security to people.

Over the centuries there have been particular devotional practices associated with certain seasons that powerfully illustrate this tension between the popular practice and a more nuanced theological reflection. In this context, intense popularity shows forth with the Christmas crib, the Stations of the Cross, and the rosary, while other seasonal customs such as the Advent Wreath, Advent Calendar, and Jesse Tree may be more likely to be found in certain cultures. These very valid customs offer us possibilities that may help us bridge the gap between popular devotion and liturgical spirituality.

The theme of the following chapters is to trace the origins and variations through history of some of these customs as a step to affirming what is perennial, and opening up possible ways to reinforce the natural human propensity for visual, tangible, direct ways of finding meaning in the cultural and religious traditions that lead to our experience of God. In today's terms, most recently in the *Catholic Catechism* (no. 1066f.) this is celebrating the paschal mystery, of finding God in the human and raising the human to the divine.

BRIDGING THE GAP

Pius Parsch was a prominent pioneer in promoting popular involvement in the church's liturgy. He never let the monastic connections of his life at Klosterneuburg clash with his vision for the people's involvement in the liturgy, even when he was pastor of the parish church in that town in Austria.

Parsch had spent the years of World War I as chaplain with the Austrian army and had been shocked by the passivity of the soldiers when he celebrated Mass with them. This led him to promote formation through his "Popular Liturgical Apostolate" using these publications to continue his mission of popularizing the work of the liturgical movement of the previous century. Parsch published his famous five-volume work *The Church's Year of Grace* in 1929 (first published by Liturgical Press in English in 1957), but that followed a journal for parish liturgies, which was his way of linking the biblical renewal with the insights from the history of liturgy.

Coincidentally, a similar monastic and religious formation underpinned the pastoral vision that enabled Joseph Jungmann, SJ, to prepare his monumental work *Missarum Solemnia* (1948), published in English as *The Mass of the Roman Rite* (1951). From an Anglican monastic background Dom Gregory Dix, OSB, prepared during World War II his book *The Shape of the Liturgy* published in 1945.

Parsch foresaw the pastoral potential of active participation in the liturgy when it was celebrated as the culmination of the parish's communal prayer and the source for family and personal prayer.

Parsch wrote that the celebration of the Christmas season is the time of exaltation of the King of Peace. At first sight, he said, it may be difficult to see this in the stable of Bethlehem, but he puts the birth in the stable as the beginning of the human life that is the source of blessing for us all.

> …in Bethlehem's stable he humbled himself even to the point of being born an infant, coming from the womb in a stable…. Referring to his death, Jesus once said "The hour is come for the son of man to be *glorified*." His gaze was directly beyond Calvary and death, for these served only as a passage or as a means to transfigured life, to exaltation. The kernel of wheat dies and decays in order to produce the plant. Liturgy raises our sights above the stable, above the manger, for these are only the dying grain of wheat: the final flower and fruit is the Church. Stable and manger formed the cradle for the Church: stable and manger were the seed from which the mighty tree of God's kingdom grows, the Church with all her saints, all her virtues, all her good works—and this is Christ's exaltation. (Parsch, Pius. *The Year of Grace*. Vol 1 Liturgical Press, 1957. pp. 200-201)

Another illustration of the gap between grass-roots perceptions and the wishful thinking of official or formal statements could be in the example of the Liturgy of the Hours or the Divine Office. Another liturgist shaped by his experiences at the parish level, the notable British scholar Monsignor J. D. Crichton, notes that: "The Church holds a high doctrine of the Divine Office yet its practice must be said to be low."

What he acutely applies to the prayer of the church is applicable also to the areas of seasonal celebrations of the church year, where the praxis of the people is often at a different level than the formal teaching of the church.

THE PASCHAL MYSTERY IN POPULAR DEVOTIONS

One of the common misconceptions about our celebrations of the paschal mystery shows itself in the danger of a form of historicism, which makes the liturgical year a tableau series of Christ's life through the individual feasts. This has the effect of turning the calendar into a chronology of Christ's life, as if at Christmas we celebrate his birth only and the events of the Triduum celebrations become perceived as times for a piecemeal remembrance of the single events. This is even further enhanced with the trend to have Palm Sunday processions or Last Supper footwashings reduced to the "passion play" model by dressing up in period costume, with a "cast of thousands" in the style of Cecil B. DeMille.

This misconception comes about because people fail to grasp the basic sacramental principle of celebrating the mystery of Christ through sacramental signs and symbols. They find it easier to participate as spectators of something to watch, rather than embrace the reality of Christ's new mode of presence through his Spirit lived in and through them. This is an age-old problem—even the disciples failed to grasp the reality of Jesus' presence after the resurrection, but the disciples at Emmaus recognized him in the "breaking of bread."

The danger of this historical and theological distortion is in confusing paschal mystery as if it were a strict parallel with Passover and Exodus imagery. In other words, it almost presumes paschal mystery refers only to the death and resurrection of Jesus: as if paschal mystery is celebrated only at Easter; as if paschal mystery does not include Christmas, Epiphany, and Baptism of the Lord; as if paschal mystery does not include the Ascension and the sending of the promised Spirit. This distortion comes from an isolation of the elements into discrete feasts, feastdays, and seasons as if each was self-contained with no interconnection.

However, in a more profound liturgical theology we can gain insights from the traditional practice of the church. This is expressed in a pattern of prayer we call *celebration*, whereby the linking of past, present, and future in the one conceptual time-frame is the key to unlocking our patterns of prayer and worship. This sequence in a unified understanding of past, present, and future means "death and resurrection" always go together when "sufferings" or "passion" are used. In fact, "death, resurrection, and ascension" are a trilogy of key moments in the one story. Even more so, "death, resurrection, and ascension and the expectation of future coming in glory" open up the future final chapter in our vision of salvation history.

The key element hinges on this unified vision of salvation history: the theology of events of the life of Christ and the life of the risen Body of Christ the church, leading from the present era to the future (eschatology). This theological sense is lived out in the unified vision expressed in the patterns and structures of worship:

- in the different eucharistic prayers with their unique formulations of the story of salvation;

- in the prefaces used for the single feasts of any particular season, and their own proper motifs;

- in the church calendar with its cycle of feastdays, seasons, vigils, and octaves, breaking open into manageable facets the mystery of Christ.

Unfortunately this unified vision is hard to instill at the level of popular faith and devotion, and leads to some obvious pastoral tension. This is illustrated with the problem of communicating the theological priorities of Easter over Christmas; of explaining the sense of sharing the fruits of the death, resurrection, and ascension of Jesus, compared to the emotional pull of the image of a mother and newborn baby; of the ease of explaining a birth as a promise of hope, over considering death as a source of life.

The liturgy presumes this unified vision but communicating it is an ongoing challenge.

The Paschal Mystery in the Christmas Crib

Russell Hardiman

Readers of this book may have noticed that it is dedicated to the first Bishop of Bunbury, Launcelot C. Goody, my mentor as a liturgist.

One of my most enduring memories, when I first arrived in Rome as a seminarian in October 1962, the week before Vatican II was formally inaugurated, was when Bishop Goody took the Western Australian seminarians on a "gita." Usually a gita is a trip, an excursion, even a picnic, but under the aegis of Bishop Goody it was a cultural heritage tour. He even hired a car and a driver. He had a plan to take us first to the Fafa monastery, where St. Benedict established his second monastery, after Subiaco, to Lake Bracciano for lunch, where he expounded on the subtleties of "Saltimbocca alla Romana," and finally to Greccio monastery, where St. Francis created the first Christmas crib. What remains vivid in my memory has been mirrored a billion times over in the way the crib scene has appealed to people's imaginations and still is a substantial part of people's memory banks regarding the Christmas story.

This phenomenon immediately opens up the issue of the role of emotion, memory, feelings, and the power of the imagination in religious experience compared to the function of doctrine, teaching, and orthodoxy in words. The universal appeal of the cuddly child at the center of the Christmas story reflects the natural intuition to relate to and understand this scene, which is far more easily accessible as a human experience than the notion, or any image, of resurrection and being raised from the dead.

This is connected with the predilection for many people to relate to Good Friday, changing the focus from the suffering servant of Yahweh to a scene of death on a cross on Calvary. This is the ready understanding in the ever-present human experience of death, even—or especially—in a dramatic episode like the crucifixion of an innocent man. The ready understanding of experience becomes the memory bank that is the source for the imagination always to draw from, to relive and renew, that experience.

It typifies the continual tension in liturgical celebration, when the ever-present tendency may be to reduce the profoundest Judeo-Christian expression of the linkage of the past-present-future dimensions of God's presence with God's people to a single plane of attraction, of emotional pull, or of nostalgic warming.

To counter this tension is where the full meaning of the paschal mystery becomes all-important. Then, the issue moves beyond the representation of a biblical tableau or a pictorial scene in a passion play, to the *re-presentation* of the mystery of God's presence in the human events and people that are the mediums of God's continuing revelation and redemption.

This emphasis on the paschal mystery in the Crib or Manger was well expressed by Pius Parsch over forty year ago.

> Referring to His death, Jesus once said: "The hour is come for the Son of Man to be glorified." His gaze was directed beyond Calvary and death, for these served only as a passage or as a means to transfigured life, to exaltation. The kernel of wheat dies and decays in order to produce the plant. Liturgy raises our sights above the stable, above the manger, for these are only the dying grain of wheat: the final flower and fruit is the Church. Stable and manger formed the cradle for the Church: stable and manger were the seed from which the mighty tree of God's kingdom grows, the Church with all her saints, all her virtues, all her good works — and this is Christ's exaltation. Therefore the liturgy, in spite of the Infant's poverty and lowliness, sings jubilantly: "The King of peace is exalted!" For the birth of Christ is beginning and the ultimate cause of the all blessings upon earth. (*Church's Year of Grace* pp. 200-201)

His words are a continual reminder that the goal of

liturgical renewal and formation is the full sense of Christian celebration so that even Christmas, not just Easter, becomes a season for celebrating the fullness of the paschal mystery. A good use of the crib can help achieve this.

VENERATION OF THE CRIB THROUGH THE CENTURIES

First we should clarify what is meant by the word "crib." Strictly speaking, the crib was the eating place for the animals in a stable, hence the word "manger," connected with romance language words like "mangiare" ("to eat" in Italian). Possibly the manger was hewn out of the rock or the very material of the grotto, or cave, itself and was simply a hollowed out area where the food was strewn, though St. Jerome in one of his Christmas homilies refers to it as molded in clay.

More often, the crib is taken to signify the entire nativity scene and may be expressed in a variety of mediums, whether as painting, fresco, bas relief, stained glass, or, more frequently nowadays, as individual figures, carved or shaped in any material or texture available. For most people now, the crib is understood in this applied sense, referring to the scene set by the figures arranged in a multitude of ways to highlight the Christmas season.

Before we come to the representation of the Nativity scene as we know it since the time of St. Francis of Assisi there are several references to the esteem shown by early Christians for the veneration of the site of Christ's birth.

From earliest times, there have been references to the events of Christ's birth as illustrated by differing styles of witness in his historical details and theological reflection in the gospels according to Matthew, Luke, and John. Ancient traditions also assert that an ox and an ass were in the stable when Christ was born. The first reference to this tradition, drawing on Isaiah 1:3 and Habakkuk 3:2, was developed in the Gospel of Pseudo-Matthew:

> On the third day after the birth of our Lord Jesus Christ holy Mary went out from the cave, and went into the stable and put her child in a manger, and an ox and an ass worshiped him. Then was fulfilled that which was said through the prophet Isaiah: "the ox knows his owner and the ass his master's crib." Thus the beasts, ox, and ass, with him between them, unceasingly worshiped him. Then was fulfilled that which was said through the prophet Habakkuk: "Between two beasts are you known." And Joseph remained in the same place with Mary for three days. (*New Testament Apocrypha*, p. 462)

Authors such as Justin Martyr in the second century (died 165) and Origen in the third century testify that, in accordance with the gospel narratives, at Bethlehem is shown the grotto of Christ's birth.

In the fourth century with the era of Christian freedom, the mother of Emperor Constantine, St. Helena, was able to draw on the devotion and drive of her son who saw it as his responsibility to endow significant sites with magnificent basilicas. St. Helena erected over the site of the grotto at Bethlehem the first basilica, which over the centuries has been rebuilt and remodeled to the extent that today the traditional site of Christ's birth is below the floor level of the Basilica of the Nativity. The exact spot is marked with a star surrounded by the words:

Hic de virgine Maria Jesus Christus natus est

(Here, of the Virgin Mary, Jesus Christ was born)

Like so many of the early Christian beliefs, the funerary practices show how the Christians adapted the Roman customs for their burials. Thus, the oldest datable bas relief as a Christian sarcophagal sculpture (343 C.E.) already pictures the ox and the ass, which the Pseudo-Matthew had popularized. A well-known picture of a Nativity scene is a wall decoration in the burial chamber of a Christian family, discovered in the Catacombs of St. Sebastian in 1877 and subsequently dated to about 380 C.E. Another representation is the fresco of The Three Magi worshiping before the infant Jesus and his mother in St. Priscilla's Catacombs.

Similarly, with the trend to reproduce, outside the Holy Land, the memories of the shrines and customs practiced there, Rome was endowed with connections with Jerusalem and Bethlehem. Thus, when Pope Sixtus III renamed the former Liberian Basilica as the Basilica of St. Mary Major in the fifth century, he set out to express the newly confirmed orthodox doctrine after the Council of Ephesus (431 C.E.) declaring Mary to be the Mother of God. Against the Nestorians he emphasized the role of Mary as Mother of God by having a small oratory built like the cave of Bethlehem. This gave rise to the Basilica's secondary title "S. Maria ad Praesepe or ad Praesepem" (St. Mary Major at the Crib) which began to be used at least by the mid-sixth century. This gave rise to the custom, still observed, of the second Papal Mass of Christmas being celebrated at dawn at St. Mary Major.

The connection with Bethlehem of St. Mary Major in Rome was further amplified, supposedly since the seventh century, with the veneration of what was claimed to be the original crib of Christ from Bethlehem. The five small boards of sycamore tree from the Middle East were first mentioned by John the Deacon the Younger writing in the twelfth century, about the year 1169.

In general, we can affirm that the gradual process of the Christianization of Europe had reached something of its zenith by the high Middle Ages. This is due to the conversion of the pagan tribes by the great missioners, such as St. Patrick in Ireland, St. Augustine of Canterbury in England, the Irish monks like St. Columban and St. Gall in Switzerland and Western Austria, St. Boniface in Germany, St. Ansgar in Scandinavia, the brothers Sts. Cyril and Methodius in the Slavic tribal areas, and St. Adalbert in Hungary. Their work over five centuries transformed the Europe of the original Roman empire, so devastated by the invasions that gave rise to the "Dark Ages," into Christian Europe. This transformation had powerful influences at all levels of social, family, civil, and church life both as regards the calendar of events that were celebrated and the emphasis that developed through popular interpretation of events. Thus, in 813 C.E. a synod in Mainz officially regulated the observance of Christmas festivities. Subsequent centuries saw the peak of the development of customs in celebrating the general Christmas period of the nativity, not only in churches and monasteries but in every home as well.

From this era carols were sung as popular participation, Christmas mystery plays were written, legends and superstitions were developed, dances were performed, special foods prepared and eaten, ceremonies of light were expressed, and customs with trees and lights developed. In short, Christmas as we have come to know it began. The last shall be first is expressed with the emergence of the crib.

The origin of the crib is sometimes attributed to the initiative begun by Marie de Oignies (1177-1213). She was one of the first of the Beguines, a twelfth-century spiritual movement for laywomen in the Netherlands and Belgium. This movement gave women and men the capacity for religious and communal life without vows, which left them free to hold private property and leave the community and marry.

The real popularization of the crib is attributed to St. Francis of Assisi who launched the crib devotion by painting on the wall of his cell at Greccio monastery a fresco of the crib scene. His biographer, Thomas of Celano, writes in graphic detail of the living crib, complete with live ox and ass around a manger with straw, prepared at Greccio three years before Francis's death, hence in 1223.

> Blessed Francis often saw this man [John, Messer Giovanni Velitta]. He now called him about two weeks before Christmas and said to him "If you desire that we should celebrate this year's Christmas at Greccio, go quickly and prepare what I tell you: for I want to enact the memory of the Infant who was born at Bethlehem, and how he was deprived of all the comforts babies enjoy: how He was bedded in a manger between an ass and an ox. For once I want to see all this with my own eyes." When that good and faithful man had heard this, he departed quickly and prepared in the above mentioned place everything that the Saint had told him.
>
> The joyful day approached. The brethren [Franciscan friars] were called from many communities. The men and women of the neighborhood, as best they could, prepared candles and torches to brighten the night. Finally the Saint of God arrived, found everything prepared and rejoiced. The crib was made ready, hay was brought, the ox and ass were led to the spot .... Greccio became a new Bethlehem. The night was made radiant like the day, filling men and women with joy. The crowds drew near and rejoiced in the novelty of the celebration. Their voices resounded from the woods, the rocky cliff echoed the jubilant outburst. As they sang in praise of God the whole night rang with exultation. The Saint of God stood before the crib, overcome with devotion and wondrous joy. A solemn Mass was sung at the crib.
>
> The Saint dressed in deacon's vestments, for a deacon he was [out of humility, St. Francis never became a priest, remaining a deacon all his life], sang the gospel. Then he preached a delightful sermon to the people who stood around him, speaking about the nativity of the poor King and the humble town of Bethlehem .... And whenever he mentioned the Child of Bethlehem or the name of Jesus, he seemed to lick his lips as if he

would happily taste and swallow the sweetness of that word." (*The Christmas Book*, pp. 106-107)

The popularity aroused by the crib reflects something of the genius of St. Francis in his ability to offer the ordinary people imaginative, visual, and sensual ways of entering into the divine mystery. As we have seen elsewhere in this book, this was the era in which the major popular devotions had their origins, and the perpetual appeal of the rosary, the Stations, and the crib still continues.

The tradition popularized by St. Francis moved from the street and village level to the most formal levels of the church. This is exemplified in the oldest devotional crib being the marble crib carved by Arnolfo di Cambio (1232-1302), when he remodeled the oratory of the crib in St. Mary Major. The members of the Franciscan Order, and other religious in this era of mendicant friars evangelizing the common people, promoted the custom of the crib that spread widely through all of Europe.

Pre-Reformation England had its own crib custom, with the baking of a Christmas mince pie in an oblong manger shape that could cradle an image of the Christ child. In the excesses of the Reformation era, with the phobia about idolatry of images, the British Puritans were particularly strong in outlawing the Christmas mince pie as "idolatrie in crust." The popularity of home cribs in Catholic Europe, and especially in the north, meant that some of the German sects, notably the Moravians, kept the custom of Christmas cribs. These Moravians carried the tradition to America and founded the town of Bethlehem, Pennsylvania, on Christmas Eve, 1741, and ever since have continued their customs.

By the Baroque era in the seventeenth century the crib scene had developed to become an intricate landscape with a multitude of gospel and secular figures with biblical and domestic farm animals included. Crib making also developed as a folk art in particular cultures, especially in Portugal, the Tyrol, and Kingdom of the Two Sicilies.

In the era of expansion to the new world, especially in the eighteenth and nineteenth centuries, immigrants from the European countries and their conationals, who followed them as missionaries, perpetuated their native customs in the new colonies or lands, and local color was gradually added to the practice of crib making by particular forms of indigenization.

In our own time the home crib has become increasingly common with the availability of commercially produced popular images of crib scenes, replacing the tradition of folk art that was actually hand produced or carved within the family circle.

One of the ironies about the popularization of the crib as synonymous with the nativity scene has been the objection, in an age of multiculturalism and many faiths, that public parks, buildings, schools, and commercial venues should not have images of the Christian tradition. The classic example of this is the ubiquitous Christmas pageant, promoted by the commercial television stations in self-glorifying style, which can have thirty or forty floats featuring every image from Disney creations, and secular images like Rudolph, but not a nativity scene. It seems the claim to be a Christian country that has public holidays for Christian events cannot be expressed with Christian symbols. The challenge is for our liturgical environment and celebration to be truly countercultural, along the lines of the success of St. Francis' gesture, and yet invite all groups to encounter the "Emmanuel—The God Among Us" at their own level.

REFERENCES

Cross, F. L. (ed) (1983) "Crib, Christmas," in *The New Oxford Dictionary of the Christian Church,* Oxford University Press, Oxford.

Donovan, Stephen (1908) "Crib" in *The Catholic Encylopedia,* Robert Appleton Co., New York.

McNamara, R.F. (1967) "Crib" in *New Catholic Encyclopedia* vol 4. McGraw-Hill, Washington, DC.

Parsch, Pius (1962) *The Church's Year of Grace: Vol 1.* The Liturgical Press, Collegeville, MN.

Schneemeleher, William (1991) Extracts from the Gospel of Pseudo-Matthew in *New Testament Apocrypha vol I: Gospels and Related Writings.* James Clark & Co, Cambridge; Westminster/John Knox, Louisville, KY.

Walsh, Michael (1993) "Crib" in *Dictionary of Catholic Devotions*: HarperSanFrancisco, San Francisco.

Weisser, Francis X. (1952) *The Christmas Book.* Harcourt, Bruce and Company, New York.

Cross or Crucifix: The Tradition Continues

Russell Hardiman

This chapter will outline the historical and theological paradigms related to the use of crosses and crucifixes in church worship. It will show the progression of the use of the cross as a fundamental symbol of Christianity throughout church history with a view to highlighting the issues with relation to the type of cross that could be integrated into worship or which could be judged most appropriate in a particular worship center.

HISTORY OF THE CROSS

In the first generation the Christians had to struggle with the fact that their founder was crucified on a cross as a common criminal. In the season of Easter the readings of the lectionary give us examples from the sermons of Peter, Paul, and the early church in confronting the dilemma of explaining Christ's death as interpreted by the Christian experience of Christ's risen presence among them. The testimony of the early church is strong in the classic claims and phrases about the power of Christ's resurrection and the faith of the believers in the reality of his presence after his death. The illegal nature of the church in the era of persecutions meant that the practices and customs were revealed only to those who were initiated into the church and accepted Christ as Lord. In that earliest period there were few external, visual expressions of Christian belief because the concentration was in the experience of the life of the community. Only with funerary practices and the belief in life beyond death are there testimonies, which are frequently oblique expressions of the Christian belief—the use of such symbols as the fish, the anchor, the tree of life, Daniel in the lion's den, and the CHI RHO sign, whose hidden meaning was positively interpreted.

The era of Christian freedom after Constantine's Edict of Milan (313 C.E.) represented a new epoch in more ways than one. Now, the possibility of crucifixion as one form of capital punishment was no longer a likelihood for Christians. Constantine's vision of a cross in the sky had inspired him to inscribe the cross on the shields of his troops. His conviction that the cross led him to victory now inspired him to order new policies about the use of the cross. It was now the major Christian symbol and became particularly prominent in the internal decoration of the Christian churches, the converted basilica of the Roman law courts. The apsidal shape enabled the Christians to adapt the use of the triumphant arch by the Romans in turning the curved apsidal roof and the supporting structure into a scenario for portraying the glory of Christ the Risen Lord.

Among the many forms the cross has taken during the course of history is that of the crucifix, with the figure of Christ on it. The first known figure of Christ is from the early fifth century. There is a sarcophagus with a figure of Christ on the cross. Also, there is a figure of the cross on the door of the Church of St. Sabina in Rome, which became the stational church for the papal liturgy on Ash Wednesday. These images show Christ in rather a stylized form, in triumph rather than suffering.

The cross without any human form continued to be the dominant form, and in the fifth and sixth centuries, a period described as "the high time of the glorified cross," crosses were sometimes made of gold and decorated with jewels; sometimes they were inscribed with the Greek letters alpha and omega. This kind of cross continued to be used for many centuries, and an example exists that was made as late as the seventeenth century.

The Christological debates of the fifth and sixth centuries had "trickle down" effects, which permeated to the grass-roots of Christian practice in emphasizing the equality of all persons of the Trinity. Thus, the original pattern of Christian prayers: "to the Father, though the Son in the Holy Spirit," was lost, except in the doxology of the eucharistic prayer, in an attempt to counter the Arian denial of the divinity of Jesus. Hence, the common doxology prayer changed to "Glory be to the Father and to the Son and to the Holy Spirit...." Even so, the doxological practice and the calls of provincial synods to honor Jesus as true God did not lead immediately to a total and universal adoption of the body of Jesus on the cross.

The new trend, in the sixth century, was the depiction of the crucifixion of the human nature of Jesus. This depiction was to counteract the dissident groups, Gnostics, Docetists, and Monophysites, who tended to exalt the divinity of Jesus as if there could be no real suffering endured by a human Jesus.

At this time, even when a body was represented on the cross, the figure of Christ on the Cross was not realistic. Christ was vested in solemn long robes emphasizing his kingship and royal priesthood in his humanity. Usually, on his head there was no crown of thorns but, in some cases, a royal diadem. He was portrayed as Christ in glory, the Christ of victory, the universal ruler ("pantocrator"), as illustrated by the great mosaics of the Ravenna Basilicas and similar ones of the era. They united crucifixion, resurrection, ascension to heaven, and crowning in glory in one image.

The debates about the humanity of Christ were again significant in the trend toward more realistic forms over symbolic ones. Even the depiction of Jesus in glory as a lamb, evocative of the images of the Book of Revelation, was forbidden by the seventh-century council. With yet no strong sense of universal authority or discipline in the Christian church it often took centuries for the groundswell of support to accept totally a different interpretation. From this era the figure of Christ changed to be a more dramatic image of the humanity of Jesus, who in his dual nature suffered as man but was glorified as God.

In the eleventh century came the emergence of a new theology of Christ's redemption according to the theology of "atonement," formulated by Saint Anselm. This provided a stimulus that was expressed in a variety of devotional forms leading to understanding the death of Christ as being the atonement for our sins. The focus on the sufferings of Christ connected with the Suffering Servant of Yahweh, as in the "fifth gospel," the book of the prophet Isaiah. From this time Byzantine art began to show an anguished Christ.

Another style developed during the medieval period where all aspects of divinity had been stripped away to expose the human Jesus at the moment of a painful and tortured death. Clearly the physical suffering of the victims of the Black Death played a critical role in the artistic depictions of the dying and dead Jesus during this period, as a message of hope in a suffering world. This led to a form of realism to portray the scene of Calvary at roughly the same era as the use of the crib scene began to be popularized.

From the fourteenth century, the use of the crucifix over the cross began to dominate, which continues to be reflected in the popular perception by some that this is the only practice in the church's tradition over the centuries. It is not the full tradition. The shift in devotion from the cross to a realistic representation of the crucified Christ as an object of devotion came about at the time in the Middle Ages when the Augustinian vision of a total symbolic universe had broken down. Augustine believed that anything created could be used as a symbol for Christ's transcendent life. Now, the secular, humanistic thought of the Renaissance began to take over.

This shift also marks a low point in sacramental life and practice in the church, when laws had to be passed to force sacramental reception, as in the Easter obligation of Lateran IV, 1215. Now came the emergence of opportunities for laypeople, not merely clerics or monks, to take part in the liturgical life of the church, which resulted in a piety and spirituality that had foundations less in the traditional sacramental practice of the church, than in devotion. This was the era of new devotions such as the Christmas crib, Stations of the Cross, and the rosary, which also appeared at that time and were popularly promoted by the new religious orders, such as the Franciscans and Dominicans. Elsewhere in this volume there are articles about the origins of these individual devotions.

LITURGICAL USE OF THE CROSS

The fundamental origin of the use the cross in liturgical functions is connected with the adaptation of Roman Empire customs by the newly liberated Christian church. This freedom was granted by Constantine in 313 C.E. as the expression of his personal conviction about his divine calling, first in the vision he had and its promise that "in this sign you will conquer," and then in his marvelous victory aided by the Christian symbol painted on his soldiers' shields. Constantine was so enamored of the cross that he even forbade its image in mosaics on the floors, so that no one could walk on it.

In the era of adaptation Christians now assembled under the authority of the cross, and Christians processed to their place of gathering with all of the ceremonial the Romans used to express honor due to the source of the authority. Where Romans used incense, lights, or candles to accompany the mace of the official's status, Christians now used the same ritual forms as they assembled under the power of the Christ crucified and risen. The processional cross thus became the primary symbol when Christians met for worship.

There is some indication that at the end of the fourth century Christians were encouraged by St. John Chrysostom to carry a silver cross in processions to counteract the hymn-singing processions of the Arians. There is evidence from the sixth century that the processional cross was in general use.

Originally these crosses were placed beside, or near, the altar, but from the twelfth century it became customary to place them on the altar. In the thirteenth century Pope Innocent II prescribed that the cross be placed on the altar. This effectively ended the ancient custom of having nothing on the altar except what was needed for the Eucharist.

The visual focus traces its origin to the manuscript tradition of the sacramentaries, whereby the opening letter of the *Te igitur* prayer after the holy holy was elaborately decorated to be like a cross. Finally in printed missals, a painting of the Calvary scene was placed on the facing page to replicate the manuscript tribute to the tree of life, as the formal beginning of the Canon of the Mass, in an era when there was little appreciation of the full structure of the eucharistic prayer as beginning with the dialogue, preface, and holy holy.

Many of the crosses used in processions and on the altar, being the formal *vexillum* or Christian standard, did not have a figure of Christ on them up to, and including, the Renaissance. After the fourteenth century crucifixes became the norm and replaced the crosses more and more. It was not until the middle of the eighteenth century that a specific requirement came into force that the altar crosses must have a figure of Christ on them. With the priest's back to the people, and facing the tabernacle in the reredos in front of him, the cross became an integral part of altar superstructure, as still can be seen in some sanctuaries.

The consolidation of the practice of daily Mass after the eighth century and the growing tendency to celebrations by a sole priest celebrant, without the many ministries of the assisting community, led to a pattern of many "low Masses," as distinct from sung community Masses. Where the communal forms prevailed or where they were especially prepared for particular occasions, then the ritual practices showed equal importance given to particular objects of cultic veneration.

The cross had originally been the sign of the Christian community's authority to gather together. Like the Emperor's *vexillum*, it was honored with the customary Roman honors of incense and lights (candles) and was formally given the place of honor in leading a procession, preceded in veneration by the smoking censer. The traditional signs and gestures of reverence were accorded to relics and to the gospel book in its special procession.

The growing cult of the worship of the eucharistic bread outside of Mass meant that, from the eleventh century, the cross was now used to show reverence for the eucharistic bread primarily. As the new style of procession grew, and as the Feast of Corpus Christi developed after 1246, the focus in procession was now solely on the eucharistic presence in the host, and thus the cross became an accessory element in the veneration rituals.

Earlier in the Middle Ages the cross or crucifix came to be incensed after the gifts and before the altar, presider, and people were incensed. In this context, veneration of the cross was given a new form.

The visual impact of the cross came to be given new

impetus. As crosses and crucifixes became common in church buildings, a special medieval form of this was the "Rood Cross." This referred to a large cross or crucifix being placed on the beam at the top of the choir or screen (from whence its name), which had become a feature of late medieval churches. Thus it was the large crucifix, above the altar, that caught the eye of anyone entering the building. This was the cross that came to be veiled during Lent, but was not usually appropriate in size, or easy to maneuver, to be used for the veneration of the cross on Good Friday.

There was also the custom of painting twelve "consecration crosses" on the walls when a church was formally consecrated, as rare as that subsequently became. The symbols of the "consecration crosses" on the walls, and the crosses associated with the Stations of the Cross, both shed light on the issue at hand, whether a cross or crucifix. Originally, in both instances, the primary symbol was the cross at the particular place. However, in popular devotion the primary symbol is confused, when the candle of anointing is mistakenly judged to be more important than the cross at that site. Likewise with Stations, the image, whether pictorial or sculptural, of the event portrayed in that meditation is understood as the main focus. Visually the candle, or the picture, is usually far more prominent than the cross, which should be the primary focus of the reflection at that point.

The pattern of realistic crosses or even ultra-realistic crosses in the Hispanic tradition does not emerge until the cult of the passion of Christ became dominant in the fifteenth century. The Protestant Reformation of the sixteenth century saw a movement away from was what was perceived as excessive realism. In reaction, the Counter-Reformation in the Baroque era especially, saw the practice of towering crucifixes as part of the reredos behind the main altar. It is this heritage that shapes the expectation of many Catholics even today, who presume that the most prominent image they see on entering a church is a large realistic crucifix.

When considering the issue in any worship space, we have an opportunity to correlate sound theology with devotional practices, so as to achieve the goal of Vatican II:

> devotions should be drawn up [so] that they harmonize with the liturgical seasons, accord with the sacred liturgy, are in some fashion derived from it, and lead the people to it, since the liturgy by its very nature far surpasses any of them. (*CSL* no. 13)

THE LITURGICAL ENVIRONMENT

The formal church documents presume the presence of a cross in the area of the sanctuary, but presume that it may be on or beside the altar or behind it.

> there is also to be a cross, clearly visible to the congregation, either on the altar or near it. (*General Instruction of the Roman Missal* nos. 236, 270)

The *Appendix to the General Instruction for the Dioceses of the United States of America* emphasizes:

> Only a single cross should be carried in a procession in order to give greater dignity and reverence to the cross. It is desirable to place the cross that has been carried in the procession near the altar so that it may serve as the cross of the altar. Otherwise it should be put away during the service. (no. 270)

Thus the cross carried in procession is placed near the altar. Otherwise it should be put away during the service, to focus on the altar, the primary symbol of Christ in the worship place.

Environment and Art in Catholic Worship further explains the reason for using only one cross.

> A cross is a basic symbol in any Christian liturgical celebration. The advantage of a processional cross with a floor standard, in contrast to one that is permanently hung or affixed to a wall, is that it can be placed differently according to the celebration and other environmental factors. While it is permissible for the cross to rest on the altar, it is preferable that it be elsewhere, not only for non-Eucharistic liturgies but also so that in Eucharistic celebrations the altar is used only for bread and wine and book. (no. 118)

The documents cited thus far all use the word cross and do not mention the word crucifix. It is likely "the cross" means the cross without corpus, since the word does not seem to be used in the generic sense.

However, in another document, there is what would seem to be a conflicting statement in the sense that the word cross does include a crucifix. In the introduction to the *Order for the Blessing of a New Cross for Public Veneration* one finds the following:

> The image of the cross should preferably be a crucifix, that is, have a corpus attached, especially in the case of a cross that is erected in a place of honor inside a church. (*Book of Blessings*, no. 1235)

It is to be noted that the word used is "preferably," certainly not mandating prescription. The text of the ritual itself, especially in the Blessing, uses many of the images that are traditionally associated with the cross:

> The tree, once the source of shame and death for humankind, has become the cross of our redemption and life.
>
> ...the Lord Jesus, our King, our Priest, and our Teacher, freely mounted the scaffold of the cross
>
> and made it his royal throne, his altar of sacrifice,
>
> his pulpit of truth.
>
> On the cross, lifted above the earth, he triumphed over our age-old enemy. (*Book of Blessings* no. 1250)

These images show the variety used in connection with the cross and, as a symbol, it is the cross that can bear this multitude of images, rather that the crucifix.

The seeming contradiction can be enlightened further by looking at the context of the passage. It is in the "Order for the Blessing of a New Cross for Public Veneration," whose introduction reads:

> Of all the sacred images the "figure of the precious, life-giving cross of Christ" [Council of Nicea II, Act 7] is preeminent, because it is the symbol of the entire paschal mystery. The cross is the image most cherished by the Christian people and the most ancient: it represents Christ's suffering and victory and at the same time, as the Fathers of the Church have taught, it points to his Second Coming. (*Book of Blessings* no. 1233)

The quote included from the Second Council of Nicea (787 C.E.) still leaves ambiguous how the "cross" is to be interpreted. For some, the phrase "cross" conjures up literal images of Calvary, but it is questionable whether the interpretation is always understood as "the symbol of the entire paschal mystery."

CROSS OR CRUCIFIX?

It is clear from the historical perspective, from the liturgical texts used in the veneration of the cross, and from the nature of symbols, that the cross, not the crucifix, is the more appropriate symbol of the paschal mystery. The celebration of the liturgy today requires a symbol that authentically expresses the whole of that paschal mystery, the suffering, death, and resurrection of Jesus and the presence of Christ in the community, here and now, where his work of salvation continues. That symbol is the cross, significant in size and in relationship to the assembly place, and capable of expressing the many dimensions of the mystery.

One still cannot say definitely that only the cross and not the crucifix should be seen—it is not a black and white issue. There are still many who are emotionally attached to the crucifix, and at a pastoral level both the devotional needs of the people and the needs of the liturgy should be respected. This can be done by keeping the two needs separate.

The processional cross, which is not an object of devotion, moves through the assembly and has its place in the assembly. An empty cross invites people to pass through that open center to be transformed. It is important for the community that the multilayered meaning of the cross not be limited.

For the devotional life of those who want it, a crucifix can be "enshrined" in its own place, away from the focal points of the assembly during the liturgy. A crucifix that can be moved would allow for a variety of pastoral applications including vigil prayers at, or before, a funeral Mass, or to enable the people to gather at the foot of the cross during reconciliation. Gathering in this way has a far greater impact on people than keeping the crucifix, or the cross, up on the wall, as if there is only one possible position.

CONCLUSION

In the consideration of cross or crucifix it is important that the whole paschal message be considered. There are those who see a need to have a realistic corpus clearly visible in the sanctuary because they think that the sanctuary is "another Calvary," and that the passion is the central mystery memorialized in the eucharistic liturgy. Such thinking would require a crucifix and seems contrary to the theology of the resurrection. It seems that those who aspire to such pieties may in some way be seeing only Good Friday, rather than both the death and resurrection celebrated in Easter, and every Eucharist.

A cross allows for a greater understanding of the risen Christ. The suffering is now within the body of the church, the Body of Christ in its mystical understanding, not the human body of a historical Jesus. A cross without a body allows the people to reflect more thoroughly on the mystery of the resurrection and to ask "Where is the body?" The body is not on the cross because it is here with us every day, living, breathing, suffering, as the Body of Christ, as the church of God.

REFERENCES

Constitution on the Sacred Liturgy, 1963.

Congregation of Divine Worship 1969. *General Instruction on the Roman Missal.* Rome.

Congregation of Divine Worship 1989. *Book of Blessings.* Catholic Book Publishing Co, New York.

Canadian Conference of Catholic Bishops 1981 *A Book of Blessings.*

United States Bishops' Committee on the Liturgy 1978. *Environment and Art in Catholic Worship.* United States Catholic Conference. Washington, DC.

Boyer, M. G. 1990. *The Liturgical Environment: What the Documents Say* The Liturgical Press, Collegeville, MN.

Maier, Z. 1996. "Symbol for the Church: cross or crucifix" in *National Bulletin on Liturgy* Vol 28 (140) pp 22-36.

Neyrey, J. H. 1995. *Texts on the theology of the cross* unpublished manuscript.

The Stations of the Cross through the Centuries

Russell Hardiman

INTRODUCTION

In the days of my doctoral studies there was a requirement to have two modern languages besides our native tongue and the two ancient languages of Greek and Latin. On a bursary from the German Embassy to the Vatican, I studied at the Goethe Institut at Boppard-Am Rhein, a delightful venue on the Rhine, just near the confluence with the Mosel at Koblenz where we all could ensure our studies did not interfere with our education.

The street up the hill to the Goethe Institut was called Stationenweg, literally the "Street of the Stations" or the "Way of the Stations" (of the Cross). It became a fascination for non-Catholic students to study the sequence of A-frame shrine-chapels marking the pathway up the hill, with their carved scenes of Christ's journey to Calvary. For many it was their first introduction to this enduring focus of devotion in the church.

Most Catholics who grew up in the pre-Vatican II era would have vivid memories of the regular pattern of the Stations in parish and school life. Wednesdays and Fridays during Lent were highlighted by the Stations. Most parishes had the Stations every Friday. For many, the Stations were such an integral part of their faith heritage that they may have difficulty in accepting that the Stations have only been such a prominent feature of devotional life of parishes for less than three centuries. What is more, there has never been an official text for the Stations, nor has the number been fixed during that time. Even today, many would be unaware that there has been a different set of titles for the Stations for over twenty years, as well as a different set used by the pope at the Colosseum on each Good Friday.

What these reflections show is that the more things change, the more they remain the same. Over the centuries the constant has been the invitation to take up the cross and follow Jesus, whether in Jerusalem itself at the actual holy places, or in other places, wherever the opportunity is available.

In today's language, which emphasizes the priority of the paschal mystery as the key concept for sharing the humanity of Jesus to share his divinity, we renew the invitation by reflecting on the terrible suffering of Jesus and enter into his passion by being conscious of our struggles, and our failures to be fully and divinely human.

HISTORICAL ORIGINS

The devotion has its origins in Jerusalem itself with the early Christian practice of retracing the path of Jesus in his suffering and death: from the Garden of Gethsemane, through the Kidron Valley, down into the palace of Pilate, out into the streets of Jerusalem, back outside the walls and onto Calvary. In essence this path was inclusive of the entire passion, death, and resurrection of Jesus. It is no coincidence that this is the timeframe now included in the contemporary stations since 1975.

As a general principle in tracing liturgical customs and practices, it is commonplace that many rites were exported back to Europe from the Holy Land, and copied for Christian worship outside Jerusalem. The pilgrims visited the various sites in Jerusalem and recounted their experiences to others who could not go there, as witnessed by the fourth-century Spanish nun Egeria, whose diary of her travels are our best source and witness to fourth-century practices in Jerusalem.

In the era of freedom for the Christian church the emperor's patronage now enabled a time of building assembly places at the major Christian shrines. In particular, the finding of the true cross by the mother of Constantine, St. Helena, provided inspiration that became a pious goal for pilgrims to follow the path Jesus trod and to worship at the very scenes of Jesus' suffering and glory.

The similar connection with Jerusalem was the motivation for Saint Petronius, in the fifth century, at the monastery of Santo Stefano in Bologna, who built a group of seven interconnected churches to represent the most sacred shrines in Jerusalem. This desire to reproduce the holy places elsewhere for those unable to go to Jerusalem enabled them still to make a pilgrimage.

Beyond the erection of shrines at the actual biblical sites there was another phenomenon operating as well. This reflects the trend to export the traditions of Jerusalem to centers beyond Jerusalem itself, where they could continue to be observed in a new context. Thus, the Good Friday service is the classic example of this, with the ceremony of the Veneration of the Cross, originally built around a relic of the true Cross in Jerusalem, now being carried out as well.

With the fall of Jerusalem to Moslem domination, the way of the Cross in Jerusalem became all but impossible, and the practices of the pilgrims could be performed more devoutly elsewhere than in the Holy City.

In the high Middle Ages, following the rise of the various orders of mendicant friars and their preaching and apostolates of missionary efforts to the uneducated and rural poor, there was a systematic attempt to link the piety of the ordinary believer with the badges of honor of the educated and the upper classes. If unable to read the chant of 150 psalms, the simple faithful could say the 150 Ave Marias of the rosary. If unable to join in the formal liturgy of the monastic office at morning, noon, and night, devout Christians could bow their heads and pray the "Angelus," whenever the bells' tolling was heard. If unable to visit the places of the Holy Land, whether as a knight to join the Crusades, or as a pilgrim to visit the places of the gospels, the peasant in the village could still imagine what the events of Jesus life meant by visiting the crib, studying the stained glass windows, or following the last events of Jesus' human life by doing the Stations. The village missions and preaching of the Franciscans offered indulgences to those who could not go to the Holy Land personally, encouraging the objective of sharing Christ's suffering even if not physically in the Holy City.

In this period the numbers in the Stations varied from place to place, and different biblical and non-biblical scenes were remembered. For example:

the house of Dives (the rich man),

the City gate,

the Probatic pool,

the "Ecce Homo" Arch, and

the Blessed Virgin Mary's School

was one set of five stations. These were included in a set of seven together with the House of Herod, and the House of Simon the Pharisee.

Numbers varied to as many as thirty-one or even thirty-seven.

This fostered the capacity for local traditions to develop as well as the scriptural scenes. For example, the three falls of Christ (3rd, 7th, and 9th Stations in the former series) are seemingly remains of the Seven Falls, a set of Stations that was depicted by Kraft at Nuremberg and further copied elsewhere. The other falls coincided with Jesus' meetings with Mary, with Simon of Cyrene, with Veronica, and with the women of Jerusalem. In these latter four, the mention of the fall has dropped out but it has survived in the three falls because they had no other distinguishing feature.

In the Middle Ages the focus on the suffering of Jesus for the sin of the world encouraged the pious pilgrims to follow the sorrowful Way of Jesus, specifically from the condemnation at the "Ecce Homo" Arch in the Praetorium by Pilate to the place of burial. The medieval reconstruction of the sacred city in the time of the Crusades enabled the pilgrims to keep within the walls of the new city.

The era of the Crusades saw a special focus on the liberation of the Holy Land. Even the very word in some of the emerging vernacular languages made the connection of "crux, cruce, and croix." The crusaders recaptured Jerusalem in 1099 thus initiating an era of intense interest in keeping safe the places of the Holy Land for the Christians of Europe. Soon after in the twelfth century, the influence of the atonement doctrine of Saint Anselm led to a growth in devotion to the humanity of Jesus, Mary, and the saints. This coincided with the era of the Crusades and the call to knighthood and chivalry as the epitome of Christian service.

In the fourteenth century, after the fall of Jerusalem and the demise of the crusader movement, the Franciscans took over the custody of the Holy Land shrines in 1342. They saw it as their Order's mission to popularize these shrines. A major strategy to encourage this was the offer of indulgences attached to various devotions associated with biblical themes, such as the Stations, the crib, the Angelus, and the rosary. Even the rhythm of time was marked for the whole Christian world by the village church bells calling people to prayer, morning, noon, and night.

Around the fifteenth century is the first use of the word "station," in the narratives of the English pilgrim William Wey in 1458. Now came the era of erection of copies of the stations in churches all around Europe. Some examples were:

- 1420: Blessed Alvares of Cordoba (Spain) built a series of chapels in the Dominican friary;
- 1468: Martin Ketzel at Nuremberg (Germany) highlighted the seven falls of Jesus;
- 1491: Blessed Eustochia in Messina (Sicily) erected Stations at the Poor Clare Convent;
- 1505: Peter Sterkx erected Stations in the University town of Louvain (Belgium);
- 1507: The chapels of the Knights of Rhodes in Fribourg (Switzerland) and the Island of Rhodes were endowed with Stations.

After 1515 there were attempts to duplicate not merely the places in Jerusalem, but also the exact intervals and distances between them. This led to firming up the *Sanctus circulus* to describe the *via crucis* through Jerusalem with more fervid and pious imagination. In 1530 is the first use of the phrase *via dolorosa* used to describe the Jerusalem site.

The popularity of the Stations became more widespread in Europe from the end of the sixteenth century onwards. The original *Catholic Encyclopedia* (1912) concludes:

> It therefore may be conjectured, with extreme probability that our present series of Stations, together with the accustomed prayers for them, comes to us, not from Jerusalem, but from some of the imitation Ways of the Cross in different parts of Europe, and that we owe the propagation of the devotion, as well as the number and selection of our Stations, much more to the pious ingenuity of certain sixteenth century devotional writers that to the actual practice of pilgrims to the holy places (vol II p. 570)

The manuals of popular piety of the era shaped the practice of the Stations in various places, which gave rise to additions and omissions that were not always part of the Jerusalem tradition. In 1584 Adrichomius published a book *Jerusalem sicut Christi tempore floruit* (*Jerusalem as it was in the time of Christ*), which was subsequently published and translated into many European languages. Previous pious manuals had given the numbers of stations in various configurations such as thirty-one, nineteen, twenty-five, thirty-seven. Adrichomius' book gives twelve stations, up to Jesus' death on the cross, which corresponded exactly to what subsequently became the formal set.

The Reformation era saw a challenge to many traditional practices but in the Catholic Counter-Reformation era came a renewed encouragement of the Stations. In 1585 Christian Cruys established the number of stations to be fourteen, and this number was standardized by Pope Clement XII in 1726. Now came the era of almost universal erection of the Stations with public use in nearly every church.

Pope Innocent XI in 1686 granted all indulgences, which were tenable for doing the Stations in Jerusalem, to be available wherever the Franciscan Way of the Cross was prayed. The papal encouragement of the Stations continued through the eighteenth century. In 1726 Pope Benedict XIII extended the indulgences of Franciscan privilege to all the faithful. These papal indulgences to encourage the Stations led the *Catholic Encyclopedia* to conclude that "the popularity of the practice seems to have been chiefly due to the indulgences attached" (vol III p. 571).

In 1731 Pope Clement XII established as standard the series of fourteen stations that most people knew. Under Clement's provisions the erection of the Stations was to be by the Franciscans with the sanction of the ordinary of the Diocese. This sanction of the Franciscans was connected with their custody of the Holy Land.

The Franciscan friars have taken a corporate responsibility for the promotion of the devotions of the Stations. In their official position as Custodians of the Holy Land, they have presided over, and led, devotions in Jerusalem and encouraged pilgrimages to the sacred sites. In addition, the Franciscans have held the faculty to erect Stations in any place, and the local bishop even had to act in conjunction with the local Franciscans or apply to the Holy See for extraordinary faculties to delegate parish priests or superiors to erect the Stations.

In 1742 Pope Benedict XIV exhorted all priests to enrich their churches with Stations. Such an invitation was amply followed by the Franciscan Saint Leonardo of Port Maurice (+1751), who set up over 500 sets around the world.

The papal promotion of the Stations was continued, when, in 1750, Pope Benedict XIV inaugurated the Stations of the Cross at the Colosseum. Recent popes since Pope Paul VI have reestablished the practice of the Good Friday Stations at the Colosseum.

For centuries the number of Stations has varied from as few as five to as many as thirty-seven: the titles have varied accordingly: the texts of the personal or communal meditations have also varied considerably. Officially there has never been a formal, single, definitive text for the Stations, though the text of St. Alphonsus Liguori (the founder of the Redemptorists, who died in 1789) may be perceived by many people as the "official" text because that is the single text they had heard. Many people will remember from their childhood phrases like "allowed him to die with anguish on this infamous gibbet"—though they never thought to ask what a gibbet was.

In the general reform after Vatican II, as sacramental and liturgical forms were revised in light of the theological emphasis of the Council, the Stations were also reviewed. In 1975 the Congregation of Rites from Rome released a new set of fourteen Stations, omitting those not in Scripture and including others from Scripture, events not previously in common use, and concluding with the resurrection. With the modern practice of the Stations on Good Friday, in 1991 Pope John Paul II, at the Colosseum, publicly prayed a slightly different set of Stations, which has been used quite extensively.

The principal emphasis was to underline the paschal mystery of Christ's death and resurrection by beginning with the last supper and concluding with the resurrection. The secondary principle was fidelity to the scriptural accounts, which led to the omission of the Stations that are not found in the gospels (such as the falls and the scene with Veronica) and included others that are found in the Scriptures, such as the crowning with thorns, the dialogue with Peter, the dialogue with Mary and John at the foot of the cross, and the dialogue with the Good Thief.

Following this essay are the full sequences of various groupings of Stations that confirm how they have varied through the centuries and still do today, yet have a common characteristic of inviting reflection on our own lives and the call to carry the cross with Jesus.

CELEBRATING THE PASCHAL MYSTERY

We are all accustomed to the greetings at Mass, when the presider addresses the gathered faithful and summarizes why we gather after the sign of the cross. There are three alternate texts, and a bishop says "peace be with you." The common denominator of these formulas for the greeting is the translation for the great sacramental mystery: the divine life of the Trinity is shared with humans.

In the ceremony for the blessing of the Stations another variant is offered for this particular ritual: "May the Lord Jesus, who suffered for us and by his paschal mystery redeemed us, be with you all"(*Book of Blessings* no. 1405).

This text synthesizes the aim of the devotions of the Stations, that by meditating on the mystery of Christ's passion and death we may be raised to the glory of his resurrection. This goal is spelled out in more detail in the formal prayers of blessings, where both the optional texts link together the action of Christ's being raised from the dead and our being raised in glory, while devoutly recalling these mysteries of Christ's passion.

> O God, your son was delivered up to death
> and raised from the dead,
> in order that we might die to sin
> and live lives of holiness.
> By the favor of your blessing
> draw near with mercy to your faithful people,

who devoutly recall the mysteries of Christ's passion.
Grant that those who follow his footsteps
in bearing the cross patiently
may receive as their reward
the vision of Christ in his glory,
for he reigns with you for ever and ever. (no. 1412)

Lord and Father all holy,
you will that your Son's Cross
should become the source of all blessings,
and the cause of all graces.
Grant that we who on earth
hold fast to the mysteries of His sacred passion
may enter into the joys of his resurrection. (no. 1413)

Further, the rubrics for the conclusion of the blessing of the Stations suggest there be some reminder of the resurrection before the final prayer of blessing the people. Again, this is an extension of the concept that meditating devoutly on Christ's passion may lead us to follow the crucified Christ to come to the glory of his resurrection.

Through the death and resurrection of his own Son, the Father has given the human race the great gift of redemption. May he give you the grace to meditate devoutly on Christ's passion and to follow the crucified Lord, so that you may come to the glory of his resurrection. (no. 1416)

The thrust of these prayers is the thrust of the *Catholic Catechism* where it is so strong in developing the celebration of the paschal mystery in the liturgy of the church.

The thrust of these prayers is the thrust of the famous hymn St. Paul incorporated into the Letter of the Philippians (2:5–11). The hymn Paul quotes is often used to encourage a moralistic acceptance of the need to accept obedience and suffering, but the point is made that it is not merely the historical Jesus that is our ideal to follow but the entire Christ-event, that we too be raised to the glory of God the Father.

REFERENCES

Alston, G. C. (1912) "The Way of the Cross," in *The Catholic Encyclopedia* vol III. Robert Appleton Co., New York.

O'Loughlin, F. (1997) "Stations of the Cross" in *Summit* February, pp. 19-20.

Smith, Peter E. (1997) "Stations of the Cross" in *Environment and Art Newsletter* February, pp. 136-138, 143.

Walsh, M. (1993) "Stations of the Cross" in *Dictionary of Catholic Devotions.* HarperCollins, New York, pp. 250-252.

TEXTS OF THE VARIOUS FORMATS OF THE STATIONS

Clementine Order and Titles

(1978). *The Way of the Cross.* Liturgical Press, Collegeville, MN.

Breuer, F. (1956). *Crucis via cum Jesu et Maria.* [Italian text] Siegbrug, F. Schmitt.

Cenci, F. (1964). *Via crucis.* [Italian text] Editrice Alma Mater, Roma.

Enzler, C. (1970) *Everyman's Way of the Cross.* Ave Maria Press, Notre Dame, IN.

Enzler, C. (1986). *Everyone's Way of the Cross.* Ave Maria Press, Notre Dame, IN.

Enzler, C. (undated). *Everyone's Way of the Cross.* Modern Cassette Library.

Garofalo, S. (1964). *La via crucis.* [Italian] Editrice cor unum figlie della chiesa, Roma.

Kenneally, C. (1979). *Stations of the Cross.* Dublin, Veritas Publications.

Liguori, St Alphonsus (1969). *The Fourteen Stations to the Way of the Cross with the Meditations.* Catholic Book Publishing, New York.

McKenna, M. (undated). *Stations of the Cross.* National Catholic Reporter Publishing Co, Kansas City, MO.

Newman, J. H. (1978). *The Gate of Heaven: Two Ways of the Cross.* Dimension Books, Denville: NJ.

Nolli, G. and A. delGiudice (1965). *Via crucis.* Edizioni Paoline, Roma.

Quenon, P. (1979). *Carved in Stone: the Peter Watts Way of the Cross.* Ave Maria Press, Notre Dame, IN.

Wintz, J. (1988). *Way of the Cross: The Catholic Update.* St Anthony Messenger Press, Cincinnati, OH.

Stations from the Congregation of Rites 1975.

Schumacher, M. A. (1987). *The Way of the Cross.* Tan Books, Rockford: IL.

Tokarz, R. (1993). *The Way of the Cross for Caregivers to the Sick.* Liturgical Press, Collegeville, MN.

1975 adapted

Bonetti, A. (1980). *[La nuova via crucis. English] The Way of the Cross*. Pueblo Publishing Company, New York.

Stations prayed by John Paul II at the Colosseum on Good Friday since 1991

Huebsch, B. (1993). *The New Scripture Way of the Cross: Based on the Stations led by Pope John Paul II*. Twenty-Third Publications, Mystic: CT.

John Paul II adapted

Dubruiel, M. A. (1991). *The Biblical Way of the Cross*. Ave Maria Press, Notre Dame, IN.

Stations of the Resurrection

Gibbins, R. C (1988) *The Stations of the Resurrection: Devotions for Use at Easter*. Liturgical Press, Collegeville, MN.

Jerusalem Stations

Jabusch, W. F. (1986). *Walk Where Jesus Walked: A Pilgrim's Guide with Prayer and Song*. Ave Maria Press, Notre Dame, IN.

Madden, T. (1966). *The Jerusalem Way of the Cross: Specially Written for Use on the Via Dolorosa Jerusalem*. Inter-Church Travel Ltd, London.

Madden, T. (1967). *The Jerusalem Maundy Thursday Walk*. Inter-Church Travel, London.

Wenig, L. J. (1993). *Walking the Way of the Cross in Jerusalem*. Hi-Time Publishing Co, Milwaukee: WI.

STATIONS OF THE CROSS - DIFFERENCES IN RITES

CLEMENTINE ORDER & TITLES (1726)
1. Jesus is condemned to death
2. Jesus carries his cross
3. Jesus falls the first time
4. Jesus meets his sorrowful mother
5. Simon helps Jesus carry the cross
6. Veronica wipes the face of Jesus
7. Jesus falls the second time
8. The women of Jerusalem weep over Jesus
9. Jesus falls the third time
10. Jesus is stripped of his garments
11. Jesus is nailed to the cross
12. Jesus is raised upon the cross, and dies
13. Jesus is taken down from the cross
14. Jesus is laid in the sepulcher

CONGREGATION OF RITES (1975)
1. The Last Supper
2. The Garden of Gethsemane
3. Jesus before the Sanhedrin
4. Jesus before Pilate
5. Jesus is whipped and crowned with thorns
6. Jesus carries his cross
7. Jesus is helped by the Cyrenean
8. Jesus speaks to the women of Jerusalem
9. Jesus is stripped and nailed to the cross
10. Jesus and the good thief
11. Jesus speaks to Mary and John
12. Jesus dies on the cross
13. Jesus is buried
14. Jesus rises from the dead

JOHN PAUL II, GOOD FRIDAY AT THE COLOSSEUM 1991
1. Jesus prays in the Garden of Olives
2. Jesus is betrayed by Judas
3. Jesus is condemned to death by the Sanhedrin
4. Jesus is denied by Peter
5. Jesus is judged by Pilate
6. Jesus is flogged and crowned with thorns
7. Jesus carries his cross
8. Jesus is helped by Simon
9. Jesus encounters the women of Jerusalem
10. Jesus is crucified
11. Jesus promises paradise to the good thief
12. Jesus speaks with his mother and John
13. Jesus dies on the cross
14. Jesus is placed in the tomb

STATIONS OF THE RESURRECTION
1. The empty tomb
2. The Emmaus walk
3. The upper room
4. The doubting disciple
5. The sea of Tiberias
6. The Damascus Road
7. The Ascension
8. Come Lord Jesus

The Rosary through the Ages

Russell Hardiman

At almost every level of Catholic life the rosary has become the principal badge of identity in linking the common practice of vocal prayer, regardless of any variation in educational background. From the highest levels of office in the church, especially in the encouragement by the popes of the last century fostering the devotion, to the simplest of family or parish settings, the rosary has been, and still is, a common unifying pattern of personal and communal prayer.

In many situations of persecution, of lack of access to sacramental worship, and in myriad ways of personal need the rosary has provided comfort. For example, to provide some local illustrations, in the early days in Sydney, Australia, when there was no priest in the colony, faithful Catholics gathered in the home of the Davis family where the Blessed Sacrament had been left. Likewise, in early Western Australia, Lawrence Mooney, the only Catholic at King George Sound, climbed Mt. Clarence each Sunday and prayed the rosary in the hope of a priest being sent to the settlement. His prayer was answered when Archbishop Polding of Sydney sent Father Brady in 1843 as the first missioner in the territory and who was to return in 1846, as bishop of the Swan River Colony, with 27 other missionaries.

The universal appeal of the rosary can be expressed in the multi-layered levels of prayer and reflection it encourages and the way each individual develops a pattern that resonates for them. Perhaps this is so because, over the seven centuries of its prominent use, it has been virtually the only remaining vestige of the contemplative and meditative traditions in common practice in Christian life. Recently, a glance through a dictionary of symbols revealed the claim that the use of the rosary was a Christianization of the Middle Eastern practice of "worry beads." Regardless of the accuracy of this claim, while agreeing that many Christian customs have been adaptations of preexisting secular or religious cultural practices, the attraction of the rosary can be based on the linkage of meditative and intercessory prayer being grasped by people at the level they can handle.

This linkage is often very important for people who either feel excluded from the sacramental life of the official church or feel that their circumstances of life are such that they do not feel comfortable in joining with the community in its regular worship or devotions. In these instances, the very capacity for private prayer reinforces the individual's sense of belonging, even in exclusion, and enables them to express a sense of control over the affairs of their life by the private practice of silent solitary prayer. The very repetitive nature of the pattern of prayer is, then, its strength, for it provides a method that even the unlettered can remember, and the familiarity of its pattern provides a reassuring sense of contact with God. At a further level of identity, in some instances the mere possession of beads, or placing the beads in a public place, or even a very private place, is the reassurance of belonging.

The Vatican II statement about the relationship of liturgy and popular devotions is a mandate:

> Popular devotions of the Christian people are warmly commended….
>
> Nevertheless these devotions should be so drawn up that they harmonize with the liturgical seasons, accord with the sacred liturgy, and are in some fashion derived from it, and lead people to it, since the liturgy by its very nature surpasses any of them. (SC no. 13)

The mutuality of this relationship can be illustrated by the value and pastoral appropriateness of the tradition of the rosary before a funeral. In many instances people may not be able to attend the funeral Mass or the internment itself and consequently there is a strong attraction to expressing their solidarity with the bereaved by attending the rosary. The revised Vatican II rites, The Order of Christian Funerals, presumes vigil prayers the night before the funeral. Instead of just advertising that the rosary will be recited, and instead of confusing people who may not know what a vigil is, best practice would be to advertise the "Vigil Prayers and Rosary." This is combining the best of both worlds, by creating the entry point into liturgical practice for those who may feel excluded, or who may choose to exclude themselves, while still expressing the mainstream of Catholic practice. It is no accident that the vigil is very well attended.

HISTORICAL PERSPECTIVES

This pastoral blending of what are the strengths of popular devotion and the insights of the theological vision of contemporary worship can lead us to consider the factors that gave rise to the development of the rosary. Such historical insights may also encourage us to reflect on the ways we can learn from the adaptability of the church in other epochs.

FROM PSALTER TO "OUR LADY'S PSALTER"

Texts of the fifth and sixth centuries that survive represent the practices in churches and monasteries that are the forebears of the rosary. To give a New Testament flavor, when reciting the 150 psalms of the Hebrew Scriptures, the psalms could be introduced by an "antiphon" or followed by a prayer with Christian themes.

The original aim was to give the illiterate laity a simple form of common prayer similar to the monastic pattern of praying the 150 psalms. This was extended to the practice of suffrage for the dead, so that while priest-monks said Masses and psalms for the dead, the lay brothers could say simpler patterns of Our Fathers instead of psalms.

The popularization was extended by the Carthusian order, eventually by the Dominicans and Franciscans, who involved laypeople to share the spiritual benefits of their orders by obligations of prayers as members of a confraternity associated with the religious orders.

The "mysteries" evolved by adding a phrase, that by referring to either Jesus or Mary, created Psalters dedicated to them. Eventually the individual psalms were omitted leaving just the phrases which provide a biography of Jesus and Mary from the angel's annunciation to the vision of heavenly glory.

The "Hail Mary" as a formula of devotion emerged in the middle of the twelfth century at a time of increasing devotion to Mary. The visitation greeting, added to the angelic salutation, enabled the prayers to be recited in dialogue form, leading to the insertion of the variable mystery as referring to Jesus or Mary, e.g., "…thy womb, who nurtured Jesus born for us."

As Latin ceased to be the people's language and vernacular languages developed after the twelfth century laypeople began a recitation of the Psalms by repeating the "Our Father" or, when devotion to the Virgin Mary became central to Christian life, by replacing the angelic salutation, the "Hail Mary."

Around the thirteenth century came the emergence of the major devotional practices we recognize still in use today: devotion to the Blessed Sacrament, Benediction, procession: Stations of the Cross, the Christmas crib, and the rosary. The common denominator in this era was the outreach to the lay Catholics in an evangelistic mode that provided them with means of sharing in the prayer of the church, which was now largely done by the professional clerics and monastics. The dichotomy in prayer, associated with the transition from the so-called "Cathedral Office," which sought to embrace all levels of the church, to the "Monastic Office," was now fixed with the preoccupation on texts and the multiplication of psalms and prayers. Quality in meditation and reflection was now subsumed in quantity; for example many monasteries chanted daily all one hundred and fifty psalms, the "Office of the Dead," and the "Office of the Blessed Virgin Mary." The genius of the new devotions was in their capacity to appeal to the imagination and so be grasped at a personal level by anyone in the church as we have observed above.

FROM PSALTER TO DECADES

Early in the fifteenth century, standardization became prominent whereby matching sets of alternative "Our

Fathers" and "Hail Marys," in numbers 5, 10, 15 or 20, 50, 100 or 150 were simplified into patterns of 50 "Hail Marys" separated into decades by inserting five "Our Fathers."

Toward the end of the fifteenth century the mysteries were reduced from as many as 50 to 15, and the new forms of the mysteries were especially promoted by the Dominicans.

This order, and other new mendicant orders like the Franciscans, promoted these new mysteries especially through the *Manuals of Prayers* created for the Confraternities promoted by each order. These *Manuals* through their illustrations (woodcuts) frequently portrayed Jesus or Mary handing the rosary to particular individuals. The Breton Dominican Alan de la Roche (c. 1428-75) is a major protagonist in spreading the devotion associating its origins (doubtfully) with St. Dominic himself.

Around 1465 Alan de la Roche made the saying of the *Psalter of the Virgin Mary* one of the obligations of membership of the Dominican Confraternity at Douai. The Dominican Prior of Cologne, Jacobs Sprenger, imposed the rosary as an obligation of membership of his confraternity at Cologne and set up negotiating indulgences for it. A year later he had 5,000 members. The Master General of the Dominicans granted licenses to friars to establish confraternities in Florence and elsewhere.

In the same era (1480), the use of the word "mysteries" was first used in the statutes of the confraternity established in Venice, which divided them up into joyful, sorrowful, and glorious. The present division appeared whereby rosaries of 50 mysteries were reduced to five, one for each decade. In 1483 the rosary book *Our Dear Lady's Psalter* reduced the mysteries from fifty to fifteen, identical to the present mysteries, except that the assumption was combined with the coronation, and the last judgment was included.

By the early sixteenth century the vocal prayers of the rosary were standardized with the addition of the doxology (Glory Be To The Father…) and the second half of the Hail Mary.

A NEW FEAST

In the period of the Catholic Counter-Reformation many new styles of feasts now came to be added. These were not just the feasts of saints or martyrs: now feasts could celebrate an idea as well as a devotion. Originally the Confraternities had especially celebrated the First Sunday of the Month.

On 7 October 1571, the combined fleets of the Christian powers defeated the Turkish navy in the Battle of Lepanto. The date was the first Sunday of the month, traditionally a day of celebration for the rosary confraternities and the victory was attributed to Our Lady of the Rosary. In March 1572 Pius V granted a feast of Our Lady of Victory to a Barcelona confraternity. In April 1573 Pope Gregory XIII allowed the Feast of our Lady of Victory to be celebrated in any church that had a rosary confraternity. Only in 1716 did the Feast of Our Lady of Victory become a feast for the whole church, in thanksgiving for another victory over the Turks at Peterwardein in Hungary. In 1913, the date of Our Lady of Victory returned to the date of the Battle of Lepanto (7 October) with the new title of the Feast of the Holy Rosary.

In this Counter-Reformation period the rosary confraternities developed under the aegis of the Dominicans. The Master General of the Dominicans issued a summary of indulgences surrounding the rosary in 1671.

In Dominican churches, beginning in Rome and spreading around the world, ways of praying the rosary spread and gradually became standardized. Thus, a para-liturgical method of saying the rosary developed at the Dominican church of Santa Maria sopra Minerva in Rome, with the people either alternating with the priest, or reciting the Hail Mary with half the congregation saying the first part and the other half reciting the remainder. The "Hail Holy Queen" and the "Litany of Loreto" were added to the recitation of the rosary "Hail Marys" at Santa Maria sopra Minerva. All churches of the Dominican order were instructed to organize the saying of the rosary three times a week according to the manner it was said in Rome.

In 1629 Timoteo Ricci established the Perpetual Rosary, when he persuaded the Dominican house at Bologna to allocate every hour in the year to one of its members, who undertook to say the rosary during that period, as special intercession during a time of plague.

In 1826 Pauline Jaricot established the Living Rosary which linked the saying of the Rosary with missionary activity of the church. This association came under the auspices of the Dominicans 40 years after its foundation.

MARIAN APPARITIONS AND PAPAL ENCOURAGEMENT

In modern, almost contemporary times, there have been several emphases coming together that have served to propagate and popularize the devotion of the rosary. First, the apparitions of Our Lady, particularly at Lourdes (1854), Knock in Ireland (1877), and Fatima (1917), all added impetus to the growing devotion, which has been further reinforced in the multitude of contemporary Marian apparitions.

Second, the strong consistent encouragement by modern popes has nurtured the prominence given to the rosary in public church life. Pope Leo XIII published 12 encyclicals on the rosary encouraging its frequent use and added to the Litany of Loreto the invocation "Queen of the Most Holy Rosary."

The attribution of May as the month of Our Lady, and October as the month of the rosary have made the rosary a prominent part of the extra-liturgical life of the church, so deeply ingrained in the popular psyche that many people still observe those months with their unique devotions.

The most recent addition to the sequence of prayers in the public recitation of the rosary is associated with Fatima. In 1917 an apparition who revealed herself as "the Lady of the Rosary" appeared to three children at Fatima in Portugal. The prayer taught by Mary to the children has been added to each decade: "O my Jesus, forgive us our sins, and save us from the fires of hell, lead all souls to heaven, especially those who most need your mercy."

In 1931 a shrine was built at Fatima, and permission was given for devotion to Our Lady of Fatima, which continues strongly today, especially with the visit of Pope John Paul II to Fatima in 1979 and the fall the Communist empire after 1989, which has introduced issues of interpretation about the Fatima message of prayer for the conversion of Russia.

The 1950 declaration of the Assumption of Our Lady is a further expression of the strong place given to Marian devotions in the life of the church. A good example of the popular devotion in modern times was the Rosary Crusade of Fr. Patrick Peyton, CSC, in the 1950s, under papal approbation, with his famous slogan "The family that prays together stays together." This gave a strong experience for that generation reaffirming the impetus of the historic Irish Catholic heritage, where the family rosary, made famous in John Hartigan's "The Trimmins on the Rosary," provided a reinforcement to the traditional devotional piety in the last era before Vatican II. For example, in Kojonup, Western Australia, the Jeffs family initiated in 1956 the practice of a rosary pilgrimage on their farm "Marylands," which still continues today in the parish.

CATHOLIC IDENTITY

The Irish Catholic heritage is probably the memory of most practicing Catholics in Australia. It was nurtured in a combination of daily, weekly, monthly, annual, and occasional pastoral strategies that provided the discipline that supported Catholic identity. Included in these strategies were such things as:

• parish missions, led by Redemptorists or other preachers;

• sodalities encouraging monthly confession and communion;

• the weekly or monthly prayers of the lay and apostolic groups;

• the daily schedule of religious communities, seminaries;

• the evening devotions in parishes, especially for Sundays or Novena nights;

• processions in honor of Corpus Christi, Our Lady, or St. Joseph;

• family, parish, and school devotions in May and October;

• crowning of Our Lady ceremonies in May;

• novenas and parish rosary and benediction devotions.

Almost all forms of parish and school life strongly reinforced the rosary as part of "the" Catholic practice.

The emphasis of Vatican II embraced the biblical movement and reinforced the value of the Scripture-based themes and forms of prayer. It also integrated insights from ritual studies on the validity of repetition and familiarity in vocal communal prayer, providing the counterpoint for private meditative and contemplative reflection. These modern insights reaffirmed the values of the traditional practice of the rosary.

Vatican II's Constitution on the Church *(Lumen Gentium)* incorporated the place of Mary in the economy of salvation and her relationship to the church by specifically creating chapter VIII: "The Role of the Blessed Virgin Mary, Mother of God, in the Mystery of Christ and the Church." This was further expressed in the declaration of Vatican II of Mary as Mother of the Church.

In the years since Vatican II, and in the plethora of liturgical changes, it can be readily affirmed that there is a serious lack in opportunities for devotional prayer, meditative experience, and the familiar practices, by the tendency to celebrate all public worship as if the eucharistic tradition is the only one in the life of the church. It is not solely a case of having to catch up, or regain the past, but contemporary pastoral pressures raise the question of what other forms of prayer leadership and pastoral outreach are the role of the local church without presuming that priestly ministry and leadership is the only one available. We have much to learn from the fullest tradition of our church.

REFERENCES

Hinnebusch, W. A. (1967) "Rosary" in *New Catholic Encyclopedia* McGraw-Hill, New York.

O'Carroll, Michael, editor (1982) "Rosary" in *Theotokos : A Theological Encyclopedia of the Blessed Virgin Mary.* Dominican Publications, Dublin.

Thurston, H. (1912) "Rosary" in *Catholic Encyclopedia* University Press, New York.

Walsh, Michael (1993) "Rosary" in *Dictionary of Catholic Devotions.* HarperSanFrancisco, San Francisco.

Liturgy/Theology
ISBN: 0-89622-977-7

$29.95

At the Heart of Liturgy
An Essential Guide for Celebrating the Paschal Mystery, Years A, B, C
RUSSELL H. HARDIMAN, *Editor*

This comprehensive resource for all liturgical ministers covers the liturgical seasons, the Order of the Mass, popular devotions, and more. It also offers helpful information and practical suggestions to enhance parish liturgies.

At the Heart of Liturgy is divided into five parts.

- *The Paschal Mystery in the Liturgical Seasons* covers historical background, suggestions for celebration (e.g., environment and music), special seasonal considerations (e.g., Advent wreath and the scrutinies), and the major themes of the Sunday readings.

- *The Paschal Mystery in Ordinary Time* treats Sunday as a special liturgical day and gives homily suggestions for the Sunday readings for all three cycles.

- *The Paschal Mystery in the Order of the Mass* gives suggestions for proclaiming the eucharistic prayer, gathering rites, readings, and prayers of the faithful; and it outlines music priorities in liturgy.

- *The Paschal Mystery in Bereavement* covers funerals and cremations.

- *The Paschal Mystery and Popular Devotions* treats the stations of the cross, the rosary, and more.

Rooted in solid liturgical practice and extensive pastoral experience, **At the Heart of Liturgy** is an indispensable guide to parish worship.

Russell H. Hardiman, a priest of the Bunbury Diocese in Western Australia, is Senior Lecturer at the University of Notre Dame Australia and editor of **Pastoral Liturgy** *magazine.*

XXIII **Twenty-Third Publications**
P.O. Box 180 • Mystic, CT 06355 • 1-800-321-0411

9 780896 229778